Princeton
April 10, 1989

For
Andrew J. Goodpaster,
With
appreciation
and
Highest Regards,

Kent E. Calder

Crisis and Compensation

Written under the auspices of the
Center of International Studies,
Princeton University

CRISIS AND COMPENSATION

Public Policy and Political Stability in Japan, 1949–1986

KENT E. CALDER

PRINCETON UNIVERSITY PRESS

Published by Princeton University Press, 41 William Street,
Princeton, New Jersey 08540
In the United Kingdom: Princeton University Press, Guildford, Surrey

Library of Congress Cataloging-in-Publication Data

Calder, Kent E.
Crisis and compensation: public policy and political stability in Japan, 1949–1986 / Kent E. Calder.
p. cm.
Bibliography: p. Includes index.
ISBN 0–691–05650–1 (alk. paper)
1. Japan—Politics and government—1945– I. Title.
DS889.C28 1988 320—dc19 88–9730

Publication of this book has been aided by the Whitney Darrow Fund of Princeton University Press

This book has been composed in Linotron Trump

Clothbound editions of Princeton University Press books are printed on acid-free paper, and binding materials are chosen for strength and durability. Paperbacks, although satisfactory for personal collections, are not usually suitable for library rebinding

Printed in the United States of America by Princeton University Press, Princeton, New Jersey

Designed by Laury A. Egan

To
Rose E. Calder
and to the memory of
Grant H. Calder

A state without the means of change
is without the means
of its conservation.

—EDMUND BURKE

Contents

List of Illustrations

List of Tables

Preface

EPOCHAL ECONOMIC and social change have been a central reality of the twentieth century, and coping with such change a constant preoccupation of its politics. Rural nations have moved into the Industrial Revolution and some beyond, to manufacturing decline and its adjustment dilemmas; urban anomie has replaced the cohesive communities of the countryside as the basic unit of modern society. Uncertainty has often plagued this uneven and discontinuous process of transition, with growth rates, exchange rates, unemployment rates, and commodity prices oscillating sharply over time.

Japan has encountered the turbulence of twentieth-century transformation in special measure. To be sure, Japan has had a powerful and technically proficient economic bureaucracy in place since the 1930s, to guide and fine-tune the process of industrial and trade policy formation. It has also had an unusually rich network of private sector organization, which has enhanced underlying social stability. But economic growth since the early 1950s, at double the average for the industrialized world as a whole in the context of sociopolitical fluidities brought by urbanization and occupation reform, also generated unusual and often unrecognized uncertainties of its own.

The research embodied in this book began nearly ten years ago, in an attempt to understand the seeming efficiencies of the Japanese technocratic state in the allocation of scarce and valued resources. But my initial empirical work on Japanese credit and fiscal policies generated a paradox. Although the objectives of the Japanese bureaucracy I examined seemed highly strategic and its central role in the policy process virtually unassailed, the output of Japanese credit and fiscal policies often flowed to inefficient firms and redistributive policies central to the program of leftist opposition parties far from the corridors of political power. Why one of the world's most apparently successful strategic states would make such allocation decisions was a question which motivated my doctoral research at Harvard and my research beyond.

Although the issues with which this book deals were provoked by my doctoral research with Edwin O. Reischauer and Raymond Vernon, that research, on the transformation of modern Japan's control-oriented financial system under political and market pressures is a separate story, to be published shortly under different auspices. Entirely different policy areas and case studies are explored here. But a common interest in the processes by which strategic states generate public policy and the relationship of their strategic and nonstrategic dimensions animates both works. This book investigates why and how the requirements of macropolitical stability intrude on and compromise the strategic state; its sequel considers the capacities of the Japanese state more generally, in the face of market and political pressures on its ability to devise coherent fiscal and credit policies.

Over the three years that I have been writing this book in earnest, my debts for assistance and intellectual stimulation are legion. At the top of the list stands my gratitude to a small group of researchers who have given an extraordinary measure of commitment to a project which has turned out to be far more complex and tangled than any of us at first anticipated. Scott Callon has been with this project throughout, from the time he walked into my first Japanese Politics course at Princeton in 1983, right down to the bitter end. Scott's contribution in research assistance and commentary has been invaluable; the dialogue with him has been one of the genuine pleasures of writing this book. Sakurai Rie and Ijiri Mayumi have both spent months of full-time research work on this project, and they enriched it greatly through their efforts, with Rie also producing original versions of all charts and figures. Kojō Yoshiko's scholarly precision contributed much to the chronology of policy change presented in Appendix 1, as well as to several other sections of the manuscript. Zenda Kuo helped with basic research part-time across a full year and more in Princeton, as did Yoshizaki Kimio in Tokyo. Richard Larach, Emily Thornton, John Ozeki, and Xiao-wei Yu all devoted summers to this project.

Undertaking a project ranging broadly across history, nations, and policy sectors, I was particularly grateful for the advice and criticism of other scholars and commentators. John Campbell, Funabashi Yōichi, Terry MacDougall, and Amy Porges read the full manuscript, as did Scott Callon and Toshiko Calder. I am grateful for the useful criticism which all of these people provided. Aoki Masahiko, Hirose Michisada, Chalmers Johnson, Kojima Akira, Kunihiro Masao, Matsuda Taiko, Murakawa Ichirō, Nukazawa Kazuo, Noguchi Yukio, Daniel Okimoto, Richard Rose, and Satō Seizaburō, among others, made suggestions to help make this a better book.

The production side of this volume would not have proceeded far without Edna Lloyd. Her patient typing of countless drafts and unrivaled skills at putting complex pieces of an eight-hundred-page manuscript together contributed greatly to the completion of this book. Gwen Hatcher and Betty Pizzarello also assisted Edna with the manuscript. Sally Coyle typed the bibliography, and Ellen Kemp formatted it for publication. Sandy Thatcher and the staff at the Princeton University Press also did a superlative job of handling the production process itself. Lisa Jerry handled copyediting, Jenna Dolan coordinated production, Richard Boscarino produced the illustrations, and Diana Witt prepared the index.

Beyond the details of the research and production process itself, the role of Richard Missner stands out for the inspiration and generous support which he gave to this project from its very early stages. With an unusual combination of practical business and public affairs experience on the one hand, and Princeton, Harvard, and MIT academic training on the other, Richard patiently critiqued the ideas of this volume as they were emerging and continually encouraged all those engaged in direct research. His contribution was invaluable. The Japan Foundation, Japan-United States Educational Commission, Fulbright Program, and the Sumitomo Bank, together with the Woodrow Wilson School and the Center for International Studies of Princeton University, also provided much appreciated financial support.

Special thanks must go to the International House of Japan, an institution which has rendered selfless, invaluable service to the scholars of many nations since its inception in the early 1950s. International House has been second home to me in Japan on the innumerable research trips which provided the basis for this book, with much of the manuscript having been written during a 1985–1986 Fulbright fellowship year spent in residence there. Katō Mikio and his staff, particularly Togasaki Tamio, Koide Izumi, Kurita Junko, and others of the library staff have provided a wide range of assistance for which I am most grateful.

Toshiko Calder has played a crucial role in the inception and development of *Crisis and Compensation*, by no means limited to moral backing. A professional journalist herself, who experienced many of the events detailed in these pages, Toshiko provided basic data, incisive commentary, expert editing, and in its latter phases, justified intolerance of this project, which made it a much better work and one completed sooner than it otherwise would have been. Mari and Ryan Calder also contributed meaningfully to this project. They have my gratitude for helping with calculations and graphs, for supplying me with cold drinks on hot summer days, and for helping me keep a sense of perspective.

None of the people mentioned here should be held responsible for details of fact or interpretation, which I assume as mine alone.

For ten years and more my parents, academicians both, have been stressing to me the importance of getting this book done. Unfortunately my father Grant H. Calder did not live to see this day. But it is to him, and to my mother Rose Calder, whose Eyring heritage has deep roots at Princeton, that I dedicate this book.

Princeton, New Jersey
October 1987

A Note on Conventions

Japanese personal names throughout the text are presented in Japanese form—that is, with the surname followed by the given name, in reversal of standard Western practice. Exceptions to this convention are made only in the case of Japanese scholars long resident outside Japan, whose names are conventionally presented in Western fashion in the English-language literature. In such cases Western conventions are observed here. Macron marks have been used where relevant in all cases except where the word in question appears so commonly in English discourse without macrons that such usage has become relatively standard. Tōkyō and Kyōto are the two major cases in which macrons would be relevant where this convention is employed. Most figures are given in yen, but when currency translations are undertaken, they are made at contemporaneous exchange rates for the item in question, unless otherwise indicated.

Crisis and Compensation

Introduction

WHEN WESTERNERS today ponder what is distinctive about Japan, the first thing that often comes to mind is industrial strength. With global trade and financial surpluses spiraling relentlessly, Japan as it approaches the twenty-first century appears the quintessence of a strong, vital power on the ascent. Its industrial productivity, financial power, political stability, and skills at organizational coordination seem to contrast sharply with the rising social conflict and apparent economic stagnation of Western Europe and even much of the United States.

When Japanese ask themselves what is distinctive about their country, they often answer "weakness." Many cite first Japan's lack of natural resources and isolation on the global diplomatic stage, as the only non-Western member of the advanced industrial world. But pressed further, the discussion of weaknesses frequently moves to deeper Japanese domestic traits, particularly the distinctive dual structure of Japan's economy. It moves to the proliferation of inefficient sectors, such as agriculture, distribution, and labor-intensive industry, which coexist with the industrial juggernauts so well known abroad.

Much has been written recently about the economic miracle of Japan's major traded sectors, such as steel, electronics, and automobiles. The institutional configurations behind global competitive success in those areas are also increasingly well known. There has been a proliferation of corporate studies, looking at firms such as SONY and Honda and recounting their dramatic rise to global competitiveness. There has also been Chalmers Johnson's classic study of the Ministry of International Trade and Industry (MITI), together with a rash of recent Japanese-language analyses of industrial policy.[1] Big business federations are also receiving increased attention.

Yet the inefficient, largely nontraded side of Japan's political economy, to which Japanese observers themselves so often allude in their general discussions of Japanese weakness, remains remarkably unexplored. Few book-length studies, in either Japa-

[1] Chalmers Johnson, *MITI and the Japanese Miracle.* See also Komiya Ryūtarō, Okuno Masahiro, and Suzumura Kotarō, eds., *Nihon no Sangyō Seisaku* (*Japanese Industrial Policy*); and Takenaka Heizō, *Kenkyū Kaihatsu to Setsubi Tōshi* (*Research, Development and Capital Investment*).

nese or English, have appeared concerning Japanese policies toward distribution, small-scale manufacturing, or agriculture. Little discussion of the political economy of land use has flowed into print, despite urban housing conditions which lag sharply behind those of even densely populated nations elsewhere in the industrialized world. Little research traces Japanese policies toward these weaker sectors back to their historical origins, the way Johnson's work has so provocatively done for industrial policy.

This study began as a search for a parsimonious understanding of Japanese public policy profiles in comparative context and their relationship to domestic political processes within Japan. From a background in industrial and foreign economic policy, the author's initial impulse was to look to Japan's decisive, efficient foreign face, together with the powerful bureaucratic and business institutions which have shaped it, as the primary object of study. But upon closer inspection, it became clear that much of Japanese public policy—and most of Japanese politics—cannot be understood simply by observing such elite institutions in their contemporary global setting. A more profound and parsimonious explanation lies deeper in Japanese history, in the interaction among domestic forces for whom global competitiveness and economic efficiency were often either irrelevant or secondary concerns.

The Problem for Analysis

As one looks beyond the efficient foreign face of Japan and begins to probe the course of domestic policies and their political origins, one often encounters apparent paradox. One finds sudden shifts from quietude to frenetic change, followed by paradoxical return to quietude in Japanese policymaking. One finds powerful, strategically oriented bureaucracies, well-organized big business, and a long tradition of hierarchically ordered, intensely personalistic decision making behind closed doors. One finds the long-term predominance of a government closely identified with higher-income groups, in a nation without a major independent agrarian party, where labor-affiliated parties have almost never participated in government.[2]

[2] The only exceptions are the Katayama and Ashida coalition cabinets of 1947–

Yet despite a seemingly pervasive structural and cultural bias toward elitism and technocratic policymaking, one also finds patterns of income distribution currently among the most equitable in the advanced industrialized nations. Income equality has become significantly more pronounced since the 1950s in Japan, in apparent contrast to patterns in the United States, Britain, France, or West Germany.[3] Japanese income distribution patterns are even more strikingly equitable when seen in global time series comparisons which include the developing nations.[4]

While Japanese income distribution patterns appear surprisingly equitable, distribution of land assets appears sharply more inegalitarian.[5] Inequality in this area seems to have grown increasingly more pronounced since the occupation land reform of the late 1940s, with little public policy intervention to alter the situation. Equality patterns with respect to both income and land undoubtedly result from multiple factors, including many outside the realm of public policy. Yet Japanese government policies throughout most of the postwar period have generally promoted income equality through higher agricultural supports and a broader range of small business policies than common in most industrialized nations. At the same time, Japanese public policy has condoned inequalities to an unusual degree with respect to the accumulation and taxation of land assets. One cannot call conservative postwar Japan's land use policies either equitable or creative.

The pronounced oscillations in Japanese domestic policymaking—between quietism and change, between efficiency and welfare, between creativity and markedly more rigid approaches to policy—make it hard to parsimoniously characterize postwar Japanese public policy in terms of any clear, undeviating pattern of policy outputs. But these variations over time suggest deeper is-

---

1948: the first led by the Japan Socialist Party, with the Democratic Party as coalition partner, and the second with the reverse situation.

[3] See Martin Schnitzer, *Income Distribution: A Comparative Study of the United States, Sweden, West Germany, East Germany, the United Kingdom, and Japan*, for a more general study.

[4] See Shail Jain, *Size Distribution of Income*; Mizoguchi Toshiyuki, "Sengo Nihon no Shotoku Bunpu to Shisan Bumpu" ("The Distribution of Income and Wealth in Postwar Japan"), *Keizai Kenkyū* 25 (October 1974), p. 360; and Kabashima Ikuo, "Supportive Participation with Economic Growth: The Case of Japan," *World Politics* (April 1984), pp. 309–38.

[5] Mizoguchi Toshiyuki, "Sengo Nihon no Shotoku Bunpu to Shisan Bumpu," p. 360.

sues for analysis. Why have Japan's own policy approaches to efficiency and equity apparently been so internally inconsistent? Why has the Japanese state alternatively expanded its redistributive activities, despite a technocratic structure, and then periodically retrenched? What do these anomalies have to do with Japan's unusual high-speed economic growth and social transformation? How are they related to institutional structure? Why do surges of policy innovation in Japan tend to occur in close proximity across numerous policy areas in such compressed time spans? Most fundamentally, what is the relationship between Japan's recurring periods of political flux amidst general stability over the past two generations and the distinctive profile of policy change which has periodically surged across the Japanese political landscape?

States change, or fail to do so, as Skowronek points out, through political struggles which are rooted in and mediated by preexisting institutional arrangements.[6] The problem for analysis here—understanding why Japanese domestic policies exhibit the broad range of distinctive anomalies described above—is thus a dual one. It is necessary to understand both the institutional context within which Japanese public policy since 1949 has been made and also the nature of the political struggles which have swirled around and within those institutions, to give policy its distinctive flavor.

Set within the context of Japanese political and economic history, both analytical tasks—understanding the institutional context within which policy has been made and also grasping the political struggles which have animated it—must begin with an examination of the early Allied occupation of Japan (1945–1948) and the pluralistic forces it unleashed in both the cities and in the countryside of Japan. What institutional changes in state structure and corporatist semigovernmental bodies such as the agricultural associations (*nōkai*) did the occupation mandate, with what political consequences? How did the Japanese conservatives, when allowed to do so, attempt to reverse these early liberalization moves, or to neutralize their implications for stable conservative preeminence? Where occupation reforms remained in effect, what long-run implications did they have for how Japan was to be governed?

Less than two years after Japan's conservatives began in 1949 to cope with the crisis of pluralism inherited from two years of

[6] Stephen Skowronek, *Building a New American State*, p. ix.

Socialist-Democratic coalitions and three years of occupation reforms, the conservatives faced an onset of economic growth which was to continue at close to double-digit levels for two decades and more. This growth, the high financial leverage which sustained it, and the social transformation which accompanied it likewise profoundly affected the profiles of Japanese public policy. How did growth and its consequences for corporate strategy relate to political fluidity and social change to influence the profile of public policy in key domestic sectors? This issue, and the others outlined above, are rarely considered in the analysis of Japanese politics, yet they are basic to understanding Japanese public policy and its relationship to political processes.

Gaps in Current Models and Theories

Comparative political analysts have found a significant bias toward high-unemployment, low-inflation policies in West European and North American political systems regularly governed by center and rightist parties and a converse bias in nations dominated by the Left.[7] Japan presents a perplexingly complex picture. For some periods, such as the early 1960s and early 1970s, its macroeconomic mix was highly expansionist and resembled the policy tradeoffs typical of the European Left. Yet during the mid-1950s and the mid-1980s determined retrenchment was the order of the day, even with inflation low and the specter of unemployment rising. Transitions from left- to right-oriented administrations, or vice versa, cannot explain these policy nuances over time in the case of Japan, since there have been no such transitions since late 1948.

Japanese policy profiles often defy not only standard comparative paradigms but the conventional wisdom of Japanese political analysis as well. Analysts have frequently stressed the central role of big business in Japanese policymaking.[8] Yet government financial institutions in the mid-1980s lent substantially more to small business than they did to large, while government taxation policies offered a range of special benefits to small firms which they did not provide to their larger counterparts. Big business protested the alleged inequity of these patterns throughout the

[7] Douglas A. Hibbs, Jr., "Political Parties and Macroeconomic Policy," *American Political Science Review* 71 (1975), pp. 1467–87.

[8] The classic source, of course, is Chitoshi Yanaga, *Big Business in Japanese Politics*.

early 1980s, with little immediate result. In policy areas such as distribution-sector rationalization, small firms have frequently bested their large-scale competitors in direct political confrontations.[9] The Federation of Economic Organizations (Keidanren), chief representative of big business in Japan, in 1986 called for total liberalization of restrictions on agricultural imports. Yet Japan's producer rice price in 1988 remained more than eight times world levels, with no immediate indications of a shift to imports in sight.

Careful analysis of the late 1940s, the 1950s, the early 1960s, and even the early 1970s suggests a pattern of frequent political turbulence and policy fluidity in Japanese politics. This picture forces qualification of some longstanding generalizations about Japanese decision-making processes. First, it calls into question conventional notions that Japanese policymaking is harmonious and consensus-oriented. To the contrary, it tends to confirm recent revisionist arguments stressing conflict as a dominant theme in Japanese social history.[10]

The policy fluidity of the first two post–World War II decades also forces qualification of longstanding notions stressing balance and stability in Japanese policymaking.[11] As Campbell's research clearly shows, general account budgetary shares in several policy sectors were quite stable during the late 1960s and early 1970s. But the research of Noguchi and others indicates that "balance," "fair shares," and "stability" have not been pervasive across the postwar period.[12] Campbell himself, in work subsequent to his volume on budgeting, shows how suddenly budgeting equilibrium and symmetry can at times be broken.[13]

[9] On the politics of distribution sector policy formation, see Ōyama Kōsuke, "Ōgata-Ten Funsō ni okeru Tsūsanshō Shōkō Kaigisho no Chōsei Kōdō" ("The Mediation Activities of *MITI* and the Chamber of Commerce in the Large Stores Dispute"), in Nakano Minoru, ed., *Nihongata Seisaku Kettei no Henyō* (*The Japanese-Style Policy Process*), pp. 50–78.

[10] See, for example, Ellis Krauss, Thomas Rohlen, and Patricia Steinhoff, eds., *Conflict in Japan*; Tetsuo Najita and J. Victor Koschmann, ed., *Conflict in Modern Japanese History: The Neglected Tradition*; and Andrew Gordon, *The Evolution of Labor Relations in Japan.*

[11] See, for example, John C. Campbell, *Contemporary Japanese Budget Politics.*

[12] See, for example, Noguchi Yukio, "Yosan ni okeru Ishi Kettei Rūru no Bunseki" ("Decision Rules in the Japanese Budgetary Process"), *Keizai Kenkyū* (January 1978), pp. 23–32.

[13] John Campbell, "The Old People Boom and Japanese Policy Making," *Journal of Japanese Studies* (Summer 1979), pp. 329–50.

If balance and stability are not pervasive in Japanese policymaking, when do they apply, and why? How have policy sectors varied in their degree of stability in public resource allocation patterns? Why the variations? Campbell's analysis provides important insights into why cross-sector budgetary changes often co-vary in magnitude but does not explain why some sectors co-vary and others do not, or why, indeed, abrupt change occurs at all. Noguchi suggests some sophisticated decision rules drawn from economic theory, but even he admits that some budgetary outputs, such as public works spending, cannot be accurately modeled on the basis of economic indicators alone.[14] Discontinuities in budget allocation patterns exist which appear to require political explanations as yet undeveloped.

Static characterizations of the Japanese political system cannot account for the substantial and generally sudden change which has distinguished Japanese policymaking during the past thirty years. The elite-oriented "ruling triumvirate" view (often known in its less sophisticated formulations as the "Japan Incorporated" argument) has difficulty accounting for the salience of redistributive welfare and small business policies during the 1970s since these policies did not directly benefit big business or bureaucracy. The so-called "patterned pluralism" perspectives, while useful in accounting for interest group compensation during the 1970s, have difficulty explaining the budgetary retrenchment of the early and mid-1980s, which ran counter to the interests of many established pressure groups.

An understanding of political structure must be the point of departure for understanding Japanese politics and policymaking in comparative perspective, since preexisting institutions shape and mediate the pressures which ultimately generate public policy. In this respect, Kyōgoku Junichi, Chalmers Johnson, Inoguchi Takashi, Ellis Krauss, Muramatsu Michio, and T. J. Pempel, among others, have all made important recent contributions to understanding Japanese conservative policymaking. Kyōgoku has produced a classic synthetic study of Japanese political structure, processes, and psychology, presenting the deeply personalistic and indulgent dimensions of Japanese nonadministrative politics which distinguish it from common patterns in the West.[15] John-

[14] Noguchi Yukio, "Decision Rules in the Japanese Budgetary Process," *Japanese Economic Studies* 7 (1979), p. 60.

[15] Kyōgoku Junichi, *Nihon no Seiji.*

son has complemented this with a narrower, but also classic, study of the Japanese administrative state in its industrial policy role, as noted earlier. In stressing the pluralistic character of Japanese policymaking, Inoguchi, Krauss, and Muramatsu[16] make more comprehensible the sudden, often unplanned shifts which distinguish Japanese policymaking, together with its manifest sensitivity to interest group pressure. Pempel's characterization of Japanese politics as "corporatism without labor" may be overstated, particularly with respect to the post-1975 period which witnessed the rise of a pragmatic economic unionism engaged in steadily intensifying contact with the ruling conservatives.[17] But Pempel points insightfully and parsimoniously to labor's traditionally precarious role in Japanese policymaking and to the policy biases, such as late introduction of comprehensive welfare measures, which have thus accrued.

Despite their manifold insights, these analyses of Japanese political structure cannot in themselves provide a sufficient understanding of policy dynamics, including contrasts in the evolution of postwar Japanese and Western European policy patterns in nonwelfare related sectors. Analyses stressing the central role of bureaucracy are compromised by the rise of political party influence over individual bureaucratic promotions, by the emergence of integrated political bureaucratic networks,[18] by jurisdictional conflict among bureaucratic agencies which pushes major issues into the hands of the political world for decision, and by developments in sudden periods of political turmoil. In such circumstances, the bureaucracy has trouble reacting with dispatch, and the interest of politicians in shaping outcomes is often, although not universally, high.

Chalmers Johnson has provided important insights into Japanese policymaking in comparative perspective in his characterization of Japan as a "developmental state," in which the state assumes specific responsibilities for industrial development and

[16] See Inoguchi Takashi, *Nihon Seiji Keizai no Kōzu* (*Contemporary Japanese Political Economy*), and Muramatsu Michio and Ellis Krauss, "Bureaucrats and Politicians in Policymaking: The Case of Japan," *American Political Science Review* (March 1984), pp. 126–46.

[17] See, for example, Kōsaka Masataka, ed., *Kōdo Sangyō Kokka no Rieki Seiji Katei to Seisaku: Nippon* (*Interest Group Politics and Public Policy in Industrialized States: The Case of Japan*).

[18] On the emergence of these integrated bureaucratic-political networks, known as *zoku* (policy tribes), see Nihon Keizai Shimbun Sha, ed., *Jimintō Seicho Kai*, especially pp. 70–130.

national economic security.[19] Johnson also presents a classical historical-institutional analysis of how the role of the state in Japanese economic development evolved from the mid-1920s until after the oil shock of 1973. But parsimony did not permit him a detailed exploration of the political correlates of the Japanese development state. We do not have, as yet, studies of politicians, such as Tanaka Kakuei, or political institutions such as the Liberal Democratic party or the Ministry of Construction, to parallel Johnson's study of MITI. Political, social, and economic turbulence outside the bureaucracy had an impact on the mode and substance of its decisions and sometimes on its position of institutional preeminence in policymaking, beyond the scope of Johnson's framework of analysis in *MITI and the Japanese Miracle.*

Kyōgoku, to be sure, provides deep insight into the psychic origins of Japan's strong support for the weak and the small, in his discussion of "parent-hearted politics" (*oyagokoro no seiji*).[20] But he provokes no detailed framework for understanding either when that sort of politics prevails over bureaucratic rationalism or what the functional relationship is between the realms of the technocratic and the indulgently political. Due perhaps inevitably to its sweeping level of generality, Kyōgoku's analysis provides few tools for understanding the timing of policy change or how specific structural changes influence the evolution of politics over time.

The concept of patterned pluralism and its implied emphasis on the power of interests from below are useful in the analysis of routinized distributive policymaking—on questions such as the evolution of small business policy in the late 1970s. But in its structural emphasis it fails to capture broad, complex cross-issue tradeoffs which emerge out of unique historical circumstances, such as the United States-Japan Security Treaty crisis of 1960 and Prime Minister Ikeda Hayato's announcement of the Income Doubling Plan. Pluralist perspectives on Japanese politics also have trouble explaining tendencies toward government retrenchment during the 1980s which seemed to defy interest group pressure, such as stagnation of rice price increases and the surprising successes of administrative reform.

The "corporatism without labor" perspective is likewise incomplete. It provides important theoretical insights into the

[19] Johnson, pp. 17–28.

[20] Kyōgoku Junichi, pp. 244–91.

structural biases of Japanese politics, particularly the bias away from high labor costs and high welfare benefits. But this approach cannot explain why policy in fact diverged sharply from its predictions during the 1970s through the sudden emergence of major welfare programs benefiting labor, for example. It is also often overpredictive, ignoring as it does both the frequent role of crisis and the grassroots bias of Japanese party politics in driving policy innovation.

Murakami Yasusuke, in his "middle-mass politics" approach[21] provides a persuasive explanation for the basic trends of Japanese politics in the mid-1980s and the social structure which underlies these. It provides an insightful, comparatively oriented analysis of the relationship between nationalism and conservative revival in Japan, together with some suggestions about why Japanese politics might well exhibit more stable, conservatively oriented tendencies in the short term future than the politics of France or Italy. Murakami's work can generate plausible explanations for the increasingly nationalistic cast of Japanese foreign and defense policies in the mid-1980s. But his analysis is not structured to provide parsimonious general explanations for political patterns before the 1980s, or to account for nuances of timing and sequence in domestic policy formation. It is, in a word, underpredictive as a tool for explaining policy change. And understanding sudden policy change in the midst of crisis lies at the heart of perceiving why Japanese public policy patterns diverge from those of the industrialized West in the ways they do.

Nonstatic, "structural evolution" perspectives add importantly to understanding the unusual priorities, comparatively speaking, of Japanese public policy. The "trans-war studies" approach, pioneered in unconnected studies by Chalmers Johnson concerning MITI and John Dower regarding Yoshida Shigeru,[22] implicitly recognizes the need for periodization in understanding Japanese politics and public policy. Johnson's evidence also points to the role of crisis, especially war, in driving change, as he outlines the dramatic changes in Japanese public institutions and policies toward industry spurred by the two decades of

[21] See Murakami Yasusuke, "Shin Chūkan Taishū Seiji no Jidai" ("The Age of New Middle Mass Politics"), *Chūō Kōron* (December 1980); also Murakami Yasusuke, "The Age of New Middle Mass Politics: The Case of Japan," *Journal of Japanese Studies* (Winter 1982), pp. 29–72.

[22] See Johnson, *MITI and the Japanese Miracle*, and John Dower, *Empire and Aftermath.*

depression and war which rocked Japan after 1925.[23] But neither transwar formulations nor the cyclical approaches to policy evolution, appearing intermittently in U.S. historical studies, render this notion of crisis-related policy change explicit.[24]

The work of Peter Gourevitch and Stephen Skowronek casts important light on the problem of crisis-related policy change in both Skowronek's examination of the expansion of American state capacities during 1877–1920[25] and Gourevitch's broad-ranging comparative analysis of American, French, British, Swedish, and West German policy responses to international economic crisis during the late nineteenth and the twentieth centuries.[26] Gourevitch makes the important point that crisis years put systems under stress, leading to the collapse of old relationships and the emergence of critical periods of flux during which new relationships and institutions have to be constructed.[27] There seems little question that this has been true in postwar Japan, and that this reality is crucially important in understanding Japanese public policy in comparative perspective. But an understanding of Japan's post-1949 public policies and the unique politico-economic character of crisis in postwar Japan lies deep in distinctive features of the 1945–1948 Japanese experience with reform under Allied occupation, juxtaposed to the rapid economic growth which soon followed. Class conflict does not figure as centrally as in Europe and America, and adverse developments in the international economic system have not had a strong impact on domestic Japanese postwar politics. In some respects the Japanese political economy of the postwar period has seemed remarkably stable by Western standards. But the stability requirements of that political economy, as noted above, have been extremely high, due to Japan's unusual, risky growth strategies, producing a different, more restrictive conception of what constitutes unwanted and dangerous political change (i.e., political crisis)

[23] Emphasis on the catalytic role of war and international crisis is also, of course, an influential argument for the emergence of strong "developmental states" in Western Europe. See, for example, Charles Tilly, *State Formation in Western Europe*; and Alexander Gerschenkron, *Economic Backwardness in Historical Perspective*.

[24] See, for example, Arthur Schlesinger, Jr., *The Cycles of American History*; and Samuel Huntington, *American Politics: The Promise of Disharmony*.

[25] Skowronek, *Building a New American State*.

[26] Peter Gourevitch, *Politics in Hard Times: Comparative Responses to International Economic Crisis*.

[27] Gourevitch, *Politics in Hard Times*, p. 9.

among Japanese policymakers than has prevailed elsewhere in the industrialized world. These differences in the nature of Japanese and Western political development make it difficult to directly apply the notions of crisis and political response developed by Gourevitch and Skowronek to the Japanese case.

The general failure to appreciate political crisis as a central force shaping patterns of Japanese public policy is closely related to major gaps in the empirical examination of postwar Japanese politics and public policy, by both Japanese and Western scholars. Despite substantial attention to the occupation in general,[28] there has been surprisingly little detailed examination of major changes in Japanese administrative and interest group structure during the 1945–1948 period, such as the abolition of the Home Ministry and of the agricultural associations (*nōkai*). These changes undermined traditional conservative mechanisms of social control and significantly increased uncertainty for the conservatives in the Japanese political process.

Japanese conservative politicians themselves have suggested both the trauma, from a conservative perspective, of this early postwar flux and turbulence and the importance of this trauma in bringing to birth the characteristic distributive grassroots-oriented policies of the 1950s, and 1960s, and 1970s.[29] In many respects the very essence of conservative struggle throughout the three decades covered by this volume was to reestablish the predictability in political relationships which occupation reforms had undermined, within the context of a volatile, high-growth economy and a changing society which made reestablishing such predictability very difficult. It is thus critical to know just what those destabilizing early postwar administrative changes were, what sort of crises they provoked, and how the uncertainties created thereby generated policy changes by the conservatives after 1948. All this requires a much more detailed understanding of Japanese politics and policymaking during the first postwar decade—particularly with regard to the agricultural, regional, and

[28] See, for example, Hans Baerwald, *The Purge of Japanese Leaders under the Occupation*; Ronald Dore, *Land Reform in Japan*; Chalmers Johnson, *Conspiracy at Matsukawa*; Masumi Junnosuke, *Gendai Seiji* (*Contemporary Politics*); and Robert E. Ward and Sakamoto Yoshikazu, *Democratizing Japan*.

[29] See, for example, Yoshida Shigeru, *The Yoshida Memoirs*, pp. 287–88; Tanaka Kakuei, *Building a New Japan*, pp. 13–17; and Hayasaka Shigezō, *Hayasaka Shigezō no Tanaka Kakuei Kaisōroku* (*Hayasaka Shigezō's Memoirs of Tanaka Kakuei*), pp. 8–59.

small business policies that neutralized the effects on political stability of early postwar reforms—than has thus far been available.

An understanding of Japanese policy outputs over the past three decades must rest not only on an understanding of history, but also on an appreciation of the structural dimensions of the Japanese policy process, especially of mechanisms employed in Japan for resolving policy conflict. Understanding that process means paying attention to factions, interrelationships within the business world, and the media. It also requires looking at systems of local government and center-periphery relations. In all these respects Japan is highly distinctive structurally, with its unusual structural traits helping to generate differences with the other industrialized nations in policy process and ultimately of policy output.

Over the past decade, knowledge regarding the details of both Japanese politics and Japanese policy formation has accumulated rapidly. There have also been useful suggestions that the two are related and that policy studies may be an important vehicle for understanding Japanese politics.[30] Yet few have systematically tried either to clarify the dynamic relationship between Japanese politics and policymaking or to show how, in fact, politics in Japan actually drives the policy process.

The conventional wisdom on this matter is Marxist or neo-Marxist. Policy, in this view, is driven deterministically by both economic transformation and the resultant needs of the social groups created in that transformation process. Crises, arising naturally from the contradictions of capitalism, cannot be conclusively resolved without revolution, although they can be papered over.

Marxists and neo-Marxists have offered some highly sophisticated and detailed analyses of Japanese state structure, especially for the pre–World War II period.[31] Indeed, intense, extended debate over the nature of Japanese capitalism as it evolved after the Meiji Restoration was a central intellectual concern of Japanese

[30] See especially T. J. Pempel, *Policy and Politics in Japan*.

[31] See, for example, *Nihon Shihon-shugi Hattatsu Shi Kōza* (*Symposium on the history of the development of Japanese capitalism*); and Tsuchiya Takao, *Nihon Shihon-Shugi Shi Ronshū* (*Collected Essays on the History of Japanese Capitalism*). In English, see John W. Dower, ed., *Origins of the Modern Japanese State: Selected Writings of E. H. Norman*.

Marxists.[32] Yet such analyses fail to anticipate or explain the thrust of Japanese small business policy. Instead of discriminating consistently in favor of big business, as Marxist analysis might hypothesize, Japanese policies have been much more nuanced. At times, as in the case of Japanese agriculture, distribution, antitrust, and corporate taxation policies, government appears to have discriminated significantly against big business, often provoking apparently bitter and sincere protest from Keidanren.[33] Yet at other times, policies have been substantially more supportive of capitalists. Marxist arguments do not on their premises provide a basis for explaining such distinctions. Yet as the following pages suggest, these shifts in the orientation of public policy toward big business appear to significantly influence both Japanese political stability and the functioning of the Japanese economy. Over time they also shape the balance of political and economic power within Japan.

It has been suggested that "conflictual outbursts in the midst of consensus" and "egregious failures submerged in conspicuous success" are two major anomalies of Japanese politics.[34] These are both important empirical observations, raising the crucial related questions of why such patterns prevail and how they are functionally related to one another. Conflict and consensus lie in a dialectic relationship to one another, so their connection needs to be spelled out through detailed, theoretically guided historical analysis. Although some specifics of this relationship between conflict and coopertion have been investigated in individual case studies, powerful cross-sectoral synergisms remain to be explored.

Japanese conservative public policy is not consistently creative. There are sectors, like land use policy, where Japanese policies have not only been consistently less creative than those of major Western European nations, such as West Germany, but have been strikingly rigid and uninspired. Even in sectors where Japanese policies exhibit unusual flexibility and pragmatism, intervals of stasis, rigidity, and retrenchment also occur. Japanese

[32] On the details of the debate and its broader historical and intellectual context, see Germaine A. Hoston, *Marxism and the Crisis of Development in Prewar Japan*.

[33] Keidanren, the Federation of Economic Organizations, is Japan's major business organization, counting as members about 110 industry-wide groups, together with over 800 of Japan's largest corporations.

[34] Pempel, *Policy and Politics in Japan*, p. 3.

welfare, environmental, and small business policies, for example, once considered primitive by international standards, were relatively static during the early 1980s, despite their striking innovativeness a decade previously. Even the creativity of Japanese agricultural policies has fluctuated markedly over time.

It is thus necessary to move beyond the concept of "creative conservatism,"[35] without denying its utility in some circumstances, to ask when and why Japanese conservative policies are either creative, as in welfare policy during 1972–1974, or noncreative, as in the case of land use policy across most of the postwar period. Previous research gives the analyst no clear means for distinguishing among such cases, and explaining why a given pattern prevails. Pempel's characterization of Japanese political and social structure (conservative social support base of government, combined with a strong, cohesive state apparatus),[36] for example, provides little basis for supposing that Japanese conservatism would be creative, particularly not in a redistributive direction. It does not, in other words, explain the engine of policy innovation—why policy innovation in Japan occurs and takes the form that it does. To the contrary, the emphasis on elite, particularly bureaucratic, dominance and cohesion would seem to imply stable, routinized, even rigid policies, frequently oriented toward the narrow concerns of big business. Pempel presents evidence concerning the creativity of Japanese public policy, without resolving the seeming tension between his findings regarding political structure and the policy output which he observes, and leaves the question of *why* largely unresolved.

Comparative political analysis suggests some possible explanations for the seemingly contradictory profiles of public innovation in Japan. Putnam, Heclo, Kingdon, and Polsby present relevant hypotheses, yet their arguments in turn raise further questions. Nelson Polsby and John Kingdon, for example, draw attention to the relationship between political crisis and policy innovation,[37] noting how crisis calls forth a range of earlier developed policy proposals ("incubated innovations") and supplies politicians with the will and the ability to implement those proposals. This analysis raises several questions: Which proposals

[35] On the underlying notion, see ibid., pp. 296–313.

[36] Ibid., p. 11.

[37] Nelson W. Polsby, *Political Innovation in America: The Politics of Policy Initiation*, pp. 167–72, and John W. Kingdon, *Agendas, Alternatives, and Public Policies*.

are selected? And why are these particular items chosen? At the same time, it also provokes hypotheses regarding the dynamics of Japanese policy innovation.

Hugh Heclo reminds one of the crucial role of administrators in both defining the fine print of policy options[38] and orchestrating policy implementation. But he also notes the periodically crucial role of political parties in organizing general predispositions toward policy choices[39] and even in creating policy choices themselves.[40] Heclo also draws attention to the role of interest groups in vetoing policy change.[41] The variations he describes raise the question of the relative distribution of policy patterns, both across issue area and nationality.

Aberbach, Putnam, and Rockman suggest some additional important refinements regarding the sort of policy process which generates Japan's seemingly contradictory mix of rapid, creative policy innovation and policy rigidity.[42] They note the sharply contrasting functional roles of politicians and bureaucrats in Western political systems, with politicians more sensitive to broad social forces and bureaucrats more involved in the smaller world of interest group mediation and problem solving. Their analysis suggests that an alternation in the relative involvement of bureaucrats and politicians at various periods may help explain the oscillations of Japanese policymaking. But what drives these alternations is beyond the scope of their analysis.

Richard Rose provides a final important clue from the comparative literature to Japan's uneven patterns of policy change in his examination of what political parties do to influence government policy. The most important role of parties in policymaking, he notes, is often simply taking initiatives. By breaking the ring of silence surrounding a policy, parties effectively "de-routinize" that policy and hence open the way for active debate regarding alternatives.[43] A party can thus create movement on a given issue, even though it cannot guarantee the direction in which in-

[38] Hugh Heclo, *Modern Social Politics in Britain and Sweden*, p. 301.

[39] *Ibid.*, p. 295.

[40] Politicians, for example, generated the new Swedish "crisis" policy of the early 1930s, as well as the Socialists' superannuation plan in Britain during the late 1950s. See ibid., pp. 295–96.

[41] *Ibid.*, p. 298 and pp. 310–11.

[42] Joel D. Aberbach, Robert D. Putnam, and Bert A. Rockman, *Bureaucrats and Politicians in Western Democracies.*

[43] Richard Rose, *Do Parties Make a Difference?*, p. 152.

tensifying debate will lead. Rose's observations raise, of course, the questions of what sort of movement political parties, including both Japanese conservatives and their opposition, generate on policy issues and why they generate the sort of movement that they in fact do.

Beyond the sphere of political analysis itself, the unusual profile of Japanese economic growth in the postwar period provides some important insights into patterns of policymaking in Japan since late 1948. Books have been written which skirted tantalizingly on the edges of this important relationship,[44] but none have treated it systematically. Between 1955 and 1973, Japanese real economic growth averaged 10 percent and soared as high as 14 percent annually in real terms during the late 1960s. Rapid growth created both unusual opportunities and unusual problems for the Japanese state politically, which in turn profoundly shaped its relationship with the broader Japanese society.

The problems flowed from the infrastructural and capital shortages, rapid urbanization, and shift in the relative power and status of key social groups produced by the process of rapid growth. The enormous financial leverage required by rapid heavy industrialization—producing debt: equity ratios of over 6:1 in many basic industrial sectors on the eve of the 1973 oil shock—intensified the intimate political interdependence of the Japanese state and Japanese industrial society on one another. This interdependence made the big business community and the conservative political world hypersensitive to threats of political change, as did the aggressive, risky, export-oriented competitive strategies of many Japanese corporations.

The opportunities for the Japanese state, as opposed to its problems, came in the rapidly rising stream of public resources generated by the growth process. Even though the Japanese government routinely enacted annual tax cuts for more than twenty years from the early 1950s, national government revenues rose over fifteenfold between 1955 and 1973.[45] Local government revenues also rose substantially, giving prefectural and municipal authorities unaccustomed freedom to develop and implement innovative policies.

[44] Arthur Stockwin wrote ably in the early 1970s, for example, of *Divided Politics in a Growth Economy* without directly addressing the question of how high-speed economic growth shaped Japanese political institutions and policy outputs.

[45] (Ōkurashō Shukei Kyoku Chōsa Ka), ed., *Zaisei Tōkei* (*Financial Statistics*), 1986 ed., p. 60.

High growth, in short, forced the Japanese state and industrial society into increasingly intimate interdependence on one another, without assuring the stability of that relationship. This intimacy profoundly affected patterns of both politics and policymaking in Japan, with consequences that may be of conceptual relevance in the study of both high-growth political economies and of state-society relations more generally.[46] But the dynamics of the Japanese growth process alone provide one with little means of understanding either the content or the timing of public policies to assure that stability.

The fact of economic growth suggests that resources will be available to the state for allocation. But it does not predetermine whether those resources will be devoted to industrial subsidies, to defense, or to welfare concerns. Similarly, the reality of growth does not determine whether nations will address problems continuously and piecemeal, systematically in a specific sectoral sequence, or simultaneously in broad waves of cross-sectoral policy innovation. We must turn to the politics of policy formation for a fuller explanation of policy transformation in postwar Japan.

An Explanation for Policy Profiles in Japan

This volume presents a parsimonious explanation for both major policy change and for political stability in postwar Japan. It argues that the principal engine of domestic, non-industrial policy innovation in Japan, particularly in its redistributive dimensions, is crisis, rather than the routine lobbying of corporatist interest groups (either business federations or labor unions) or even the strategic planning of the state.

First and foremost conservative politicians, businessmen, and even bureaucrats have been preoccupied with creating a stable political framework, both to assure their own personal preeminence and to facilitate Japan's distinctive, highly leveraged growth. Japanese conservative policies have been creative, first and foremost, because Japanese conservative politicians have been insecure and hence preoccupied with stabilizing their own positions. Despite the long persistence of conservative rule, in-

[46] In particular, the Japanese high-growth political economy presents a case of unusual social pressures upon a developmental state, in ways which may well force qualification of statist arguments developed in the analysis of lower-growth political economies.

dividual politicians have been turned out of elective office in Japan with unusual frequency, relative to patterns in the West, often due to grassroots intraparty competition. Cabinets have also frequently fallen due to factional competition within the ranks of the dominant conservatives. Even when conservative politicians have not been turned out, they have been continually apprehensive about the prospect, undifferentiated from their major competitors by ideology or any other distinctions save the ability to garner material compensation for constituents. The complex character of the Japanese legislative process also compounds the insecurity of politicians, especially since their futures are often predicated on success within a legislative process over which, despite the nominal conservative majority, they have relatively little control.

Politicians have generally *not* been dominant in Japanese policy processes, and have frequently had difficulty imposing their preferences on bureaucracy and big business, as Johnson, Pempel, and others have pointed out. But the Japanese political economy of the post-1948 period has given politicians more leverage in achieving their demands than an analysis of party and bureaucratic structure alone might initially suggest. The aggressive, highly leveraged growth strategy of the Japanese business world gave business strong incentives to acquiesce in conservative political demands, even when those demands were economically irrational. Only with the coming of low growth and increased political stability in the early 1980s did business opposition to economically inefficient support policies for agriculture, small business, and other such groups begin to harden.

Japanese conservative politicians hence have aggressively bestowed benefits on pivotal prospective supporters in an effort to stabilize their perennially precarious personal political situations, while big business and often bureaucracy tacitly condone this uneconomic behavior in the interest of broader stability. Counterclaims to defense spending in such areas as agricultural and small business support have made major increases in the defense budget difficult, even in the face of rising external pressure on Japan to expand its regional and global security commitments. Such counterclaims can be intensified by external economic shocks and by demands within Japan for countermeasures, as was true following the two oil shocks and three major yen revaluations of the past two decades. Conversely, the waning of domestic political vulnerability for the conservatives, such as Japan witnessed during the early 1980s, reduces counterdemands from civilian constituents within Japan, decreases the incentives of big business to acquiesce in redistributive policies to aid small business and agriculture, and increases governmental leeway to expand defense spending. The implications of crisis and compensation for Japanese national defense are a major concern of this volume, discussed at length in chapter 10.

This volume begins by examining Japanese policy outputs as they have evolved since World War II, with particular emphasis on five major concerns of the domestic political economy: agriculture, small business, welfare, land use, and regional policy. Defense policy is also considered to show the indirect effects on Japan's international commitments of its strong domestic political preoccupations. I chose these six sectors because through their evolution they show in their aggregate how and why the bias of Japanese public policy shifted from a nationalistic and technocratic cast to a much more decidedly distributive orientation over the first three post–World War II decades, with some marginal return to the nationalistic and technocratic after the mid-1970s. Since policy outputs in all these sectors have been influenced heavily by Japanese domestic political processes, such outputs provide especially good insights into how politics itself affects policymaking in Japan.

The current prevailing conception of Japan, in both academic literature and the popular view, is of Japan as technocracy, ruled by a select group of bureaucrats motivated primarily by efficiency and by economic, rather than political, concerns.[47] This volume strives to redress that bias by pointing out the strong materialist orientation of Japanese policymaking in broad sectors of the non-traded Japanese political economy. It denies neither a persistent, technocratic orientation in industrial and trade policy, the general contours of which I consider in chapter 3, nor does it deny a central role in routine decisionmaking to the bureaucracy in many other sectors.[48] But this research stresses the contrasts be-

[47] Johnson's *MITI and the Japanese Miracle*, for example, is a classic exposition of the technocratic dominance perspective, although it focuses closely on the institutional history of MITI, and does not make detailed claims regarding the technocratic role outside industrial policy.

[48] This research does not, for example, contest the empirical findings of Steven Reed that routine distribution processes for grant money or approval of local borrowings may be conducted through bureaucratic channels, although it stresses (1) the relationship of even routine distribution to politics through political-bureau-

tween (1) policy patterns in the industrial and trade policy areas where the bureaucracy has been relatively cohesive and political pressures diffuse, and (2) patterns in domestic sectors where the bureaucracy, thrown into serious disarray by postwar reforms, was forced to accommodate the political world, thus intensifying the importance of distributive politics and political-party intervention in these sectors. In the aggregate, dominant policy profiles in most sectors of Japanese domestic policymaking appear driven by the crises and compensation dynamic, whomever the principal formal government liaison with the broader society on a routine basis may be. The efficiency-oriented patterns so seemingly common in the industrial and foreign economic policy areas appear to have been intermittently compromised elsewhere in the Japanese political economy.

Even where technocracy clearly dominates Japanese policymaking, as in defining the optimal content of future Japanese industrial structure, there are elements of materialist politics, as in the regionalist bias of Japan's high-technology policies in the late 1980s and in the small business orientation of government credit policies. As the strength of the ruling Liberal Democratic Party in Japanese policymaking has risen since the early 1970s, such areas where technocratic concerns merge with those of the conservative political world become increasingly important linchpins of industrial and trade policy as a whole. They are considered in detail in their regional and small business dimensions in this manuscript.

In this volume I place particular emphasis on understanding policy and political developments during the period from 1949 to 1986. I chose 1949 as the point of departure because early that year the postwar Japanese conservative strategy of seeking political stability through systematic compensation of strategic interest groups began clearly to emerge in public policy. For the previous three years of the Allied occupation, policy emphasis had been on encouraging pluralism, with only lesser concern for stability. July 1986 is taken as the point of conclusion, due to the dramatic fashion in which persistent conservative aspirations toward political stability were realized in both the massive conservative landslide of that year and the dissolution of the principal

---

cratic ties, and (2) the role of politicians as initiators with respect to large-new programs. Reed does not appear to disagree with this view. See Steven R. Reed, *Japanese Prefecture and Policymaking*, pp. 38–40 and 152–55.

conservative splinter group, the New Liberal Club, which followed soon thereafter.

Japan's postwar political history is first addressed, laying out in some detail the crises Japan's conservatives have faced, the options available to them in response, and the choices made. National budgetary shares are also examined, comparatively insofar as relevant and possible, to determine succinctly both Japan's current policy profile and also how that profile has changed over time. Compared with patterns in other major industrialized nations, Japanese budget allocations appear heavily skewed toward the inefficient, largely untraded sectors, such as agriculture, distribution, and labor-intensive manufacturing, although there has been some limited rationalization since 1980. These patterns are somewhat paradoxical since Japan's political structure appears to have an elite, technocratic bias, with its strong bureaucracy and weak labor movement. Yet the seemingly redistributive aspects appear more pronounced—and also more divergent from general Western conservative policy patterns outside social welfare—than was broadly true twenty-five years ago.[49] Unusual political dynamics in Japan, in interaction with unusual patterns of economic development, appear to have generated increased Japanese divergence from policy patterns typical in most Western industrialized nations.

After looking at the theoretical framework, the analysis also considers in detail the history of policy evolution within the six key policy sectors designated, noting the periods of particularly active innovation as well as the policy initiatives taken. Concerning both budgetary shares and new policy initiatives, the argument is that Japanese policy change is rapid and seemingly discontinuous when it occurs, with abrupt changes of direction and short feverish periods of policy innovation following long intervals of stability. Most programmatic and redistributive policy innovations occurred during such periods of sudden flux.

Structural features of postwar Japanese politics, especially the electoral system and the factional competition within large national parties which it stimulates, are important in explaining why Japanese policy outputs have their strongly compensation-oriented cast. But the real key to understanding Japanese policy

[49] Welfare policy and, since the early 1980s, defense policy are a partial exception to this pattern of divergence from Western patterns, as will be seen in chapters 8 and 10, for reasons consistent with the argument of this volume.

profiles seems to be grasping the intense interactions on domestic policy questions which develop during periods of political instability between conservative governments and the populations they rule. The key to understanding both domestic policy patterns on the one hand and Japan's unprecedented span of stable one-party political dominance on the other is that central characteristic of postwar Japanese domestic policymaking—what I call the "crisis and compensation" dynamic.

Central to this dynamic is the notion of "circles of compensation." Japanese politics, like Japanese administration and Japanese government-business relations, operates largely in terms of institutionalized networks of players engaged in special reciprocal relationships of obligation and reward with public authority. Expectations on both sides are relatively pragmatic and accommodating, analogous to what Tilly calls the "politics of the polity member."[50] Government provides benefits to private sector participants, in return for their consistent political support. Outside "circles of compensation" such reciprocal relationships of obligation and reward do not apply. Decisions are much more ad hoc and often fraught with conflict. Uncertainty, that most uncomfortable of circumstances in political and bureaucratic Japan, prevails.[51]

The essence of crisis and compensation, this volume maintains, is the complex process of accommodation between government and its opponents—both intraparty and interparty opponents. It is, to put it differently, the process of creating circles of compensation among opponents. That accommodation occurs at crucial junctures when either the continuance of a given administration's tenure in office is perceived to be severely threatened or internal political unrest seriously impairs its international credibility.

Three significant domestic political crises since 1949 have induced major policy change in Japan: the 1949–54 economic and political turbulence induced by both the early postwar occupation reforms and the so-called Dodge Line and reverse course which followed;[52] the 1960 United States-Japan Security Treaty

[50] Charles Tilly, *From Mobilization to Revolution.*

[51] Conditions outside the "circles of compensation" are somewhat analogous to what Tilly calls the "politics of the challenger." See ibid.

[52] The Dodge Line was a complex of austerity measures centering particularly on a balanced budget and work-force reationalization in public corporations; the measures were pressed on the Japanese government by U.S. occupation forces

crisis, together with related events preceding and following; and the 1971–1976 political crisis for the conservatives, induced by sharp urban political gains by the Left in the April 1971, unified local elections, and the December 1972 general elections. Five international "shocks"—abrupt yen revaluations in 1971, 1977–1978, and 1985–1986, together with the oil shocks of 1973 and 1979—have also spurred important, although less fundamental, transformations of Japanese public policy. In each of these periods, the Liberal Democratic party and its bureaucratic allies tried to maintain political stability through a range of policies directed at maintaining and expanding the LDP's circle of compensation.

Generally speaking, the LDP expanded its circle through a process of competitive rivalry with the opposition for swing constituencies, particularly those that were organized. Thus, the opposition often determined the agenda of LDP policymaking and the way in which the conservative circle of compensation would expand. Together these domestic and international crises produced the policy initiatives giving recent Japanese conservative policies their unusual distributive cast, despite a technocratic political structure. Among these distributive policies have been high rice prices, with complex quality differentials, no-collateral small business loans, and extensive public works programs in remote parts of Japan. As the circle of compensation concept would imply, these resources have been distributed broadly to conservative political allies of the ruling conservative party but not universally to all the people of Japan.

The Approach to the Problem

To achieve an explanation for policy change sufficiently predictive to suggest the *direction* of change, one needs to combine structural and historical approaches. The approach of this volume is first to clarify the structural biases of the Japanese political system, concentrating on configurations in the late 1940s as

economic advisor Joseph Dodge early in 1949. The objectives of these policies were to increase efficiency in the utilization of public resources and thus to lay the basis for long-term economic self-sufficiency in Japan. On the details of the Dodge Line policies and their relationship to the broader Japanese domestic politics of the period, see Soong Hoom Kil, *The Dodge Line and the Japanese Conservative Party*.

the Japanese policy patterns analyzed here began to unfold. Then I attempt to catalogue the crises which have confronted the political system, with particular emphasis on defining the specific political challenges these crises have posed for existing authority. This study explains Japanese policy profiles, the ultimate concern of the analysis, in terms of the interaction between crisis stimuli and preexisting structure.[53]

Comparative studies in the politics of public policy formation increasingly show that the distinctive policy orientations of nations typically form through an interaction of preexisting institutions and external stimuli during relatively short, climactic periods when these systems are under unusual economic or political stress.[54] In years of turbulence, periods when old relationships crumble and new ones are formulated, circles of compensation are recast. The new institutions and policy patterns forged during these short periods of flux often persist long after the original pressures that forged them have died away. Comparative policy analysis, in the sense of understanding why the policies of nations differ or converge, hence becomes in substantial measure a form of political archaeology, in which detailed historical examination of both preexisting social structure and newly arising pressures for change during periods of crisis is crucial.

Structural and cultural peculiarities of the Japanese case make short periods of political flux especially important in determining profiles of Japanese public policy over relatively long periods of time. First, the Japanese policy process in general is quite bureaucratized. This does not necessarily preclude policy creativity; indeed, Japanese public policies often have been creative in the midst of crisis. But as students of organization have found in other cultural contexts, bureaucratization tends to generate biases toward continuity, consistency, and routine solutions in

[53] The analysis of Japanese public policy presented is in this sense mainly a series of interpretive case studies using theory to deepen understanding of the Japanese case, although some aspects involve deviant case analyses with broader implications for theory. On purposes and methods of comparative analysis see Arend Lijphart, "Comparative Politics and the Comparative Method," *American Political Science Review* (1971), pp. 682–93.

[54] See for example, Margaret Weir and Theda Skocpol, "State Structures and the Possibilities for 'Keynesian' Responses to the Great Depression in Sweden, Britain, and the United States," in Peter B. Evans, Dietrich Ruechemeyer, and Theda Skocpol, *Bringing the State Back In*, pp. 107–68. Also Peter Gourevitch, *Politics in Hard Times: Comparative Responses to International Economic Crises*.

the absence of crisis.[55] This institutionally rooted conservatism in normal times is reinforced by the consensus orientation of Japanese political culture, also making major policy change difficult under normal circumstances. Moreover, the complex structure of Japan's powerful big business federations and the intense factionalism of the ruling conservative party reinforce this bias toward inaction.

Japanese institutional structure, while producing resistance to change in normal times, also accelerates the pace of change in periods of crisis. The unusual power of the Japanese media, factionalism within the ruling Liberal Democratic party, cross-party networks linking conservative and progressive political actors, and subtle pluralism within the big business community all work to accelerate the pace of change once it seems inevitable. Even the bureaucracy, once given unequivocal guidance, often plays a role at the operational level in bringing change to fruition. This was true in welfare and environmental policy formation during the early 1970s, for example.

One final, crucially important factor in making crisis and compensation highly salient in Japanese policymaking has been the broader economic and financial context, all too often ignored in political analysis. During the 1950s Japanese industry rapidly became the most highly leveraged in the world, while pursuing aggressive, long-term corporate strategies based on heavy industrialization that involved a high degree of risk. Both big business and the bureaucracy were thus hypersensitive to any suggestions of political risk that might imply changing the stable growth-oriented public policy parameters that made aggressive corporate strategies possible.

A parsimonious explanation of Japanese domestic policy profiles in comparative context thus inevitably focuses on climactic periods of political crisis, when long-established patterns are suddenly called into question, and new, unusually enduring relationships forged. These institutional and political changes in turn influence the range of future policies seriously entertained by the political process, as Verba's branching tree model of sequential

[55] This dynamic, of course, is also pervasive in other highly bureaucratized political systems, such as France and China, where institutional conservatism also inhibits change in the absence of crisis. On the organizational dynamics making for continuity of policy in bureaucratized systems, see, for example, Anthony Downs, *Inside Bureaucracy*, pp. 261–80.

development would suggest.[56] Since the primary analytical concern in this volume is the relationship between politics and Japanese public policy, the principal research concern becomes how Japanese government authority has confronted and dealt with the periodic challenges to political stability in times of crisis. Since government authority throughout the 1949–1986 period lay continuously in the hands of self-proclaimed conservatives, this sort of analysis also casts light on the unusual adaptive capacity of Japanese conservatives and their use of policy tools which their Anglo-Saxon counterparts might eschew.[57] No attempt is made to systematically generalize concerning the particular characteristics of Japanese conservatism or its relationship to self-styled "isms" elsewhere in the world. The profound methodological complexities implicit in cross-national comparisons of situationally specific national patterns of conservatism take such comparative examination beyond the feasible scope of this analysis.

Studying Japanese public policies in historical perspective also generates important new insights into the character of Japanese politics, as does the cross-national comparative perspective outlined above. The historical perspective is especially important in drawing attention to the often neglected details of political and policy developments from the late 1940s through the early 1960s and to the picture of political uncertainty combined with rapid policy change which emerges therefrom. Historical analysis also reaffirms the crucial importance of the late 1940s, 1950s, and early 1960s in creating the internationally distinctive profile of Japanese public policies which prevails today.

Chalmers Johnson, John Dower, and others have already shown the important continuities across the transwar period in industrial policy and diplomatic history. It does not, however, follow from the analysis of these scholars that the policy and political profiles of the current Japan were established primarily before and during World War II. Indeed, the 1946–1963 period, especially 1949–1954 and 1958–1963, were years of remarkable policy innovations; 1971–1976 was also important.

[56] Sidney Verba, "Sequences and Development," in Leonard Binder et al., *Crises and Sequences in Political Development*, p. 308.

[57] Japanese conservatives, for example, have backed far-reaching, welfare-oriented government support for agriculture, public works, and depressed regions where contemporary Western conservatives have often opposed it. Sunbelt American conservatives have consistently backed guns over butter while their Japanese counterparts have often done exactly the opposite.

During the early postwar period, elective Japanese local government was established, the Home Ministry dissolved, large numbers of administrators purged, the military disbanded, land reform undertaken, and the traditional agricultural associations (*nōkai*) dissolved. These changes created, for a short period at least, fundamental uncertainties for the Japanese conservatives, particularly since they lacked a unified political vehicle until formation of the Liberal Democratic party in 1955. One major theme of postwar Japanese politics is the protracted struggle of the conservatives to perpetuate their rule on terms necessarily less coercive than in prewar Japan, due to democratization and pluralization imposed by the Allied occupation. During the three postwar crisis intervals of the early 1950s, 1960s, and 1970s, the distinctive distributive bias of Japanese domestic policy was shaped, under the pressure of crisis for the ruling conservative leadership, which lacked non-distributive tools of response. Historical analysis, with the sensitivity to the turbulence of Japan's early postwar years it generates, is crucial to establishing the plausibility of the crisis and compensation policy dynamic. It also provides new insights regarding Japanese policy formation processes.

This volume strives to understand policy outputs by examining policymaking structures and the process through which they are transformed, by probing what Krasner calls the process of "punctuated equilibrium."[58] Policy change occurs, in this view, mainly in a succession of short, creative intervals, followed by placidity. Data requirements under this approach are in the main qualitative, and concentrated in the areas of historical and structural-functional analysis. Quantitative measures are invoked where appropriate to support the argument as a whole.

A purely quantitative approach would have been undone by inadequate data. Establishing composite cross-national indicators of crisis and compensation would be methodologically difficult because some important policy outputs are intrinsically difficult to compare cross-nationally in quantitative fashion. Some of these outputs, such as regulatory and tax dispensations regarding land use, are potentially important means of compensating interest groups in the event of political crisis.

With respect to budgetary and public employment outputs,

[58] Stephen D. Krasner, "Approaches to the State: Alternative Conceptions and Historical Dynamics," *Comparative Politics* (January 1984), p. 242.

quantitative cross-national comparison should in principle be somewhat easier. Some limited cross-national comparisons of budgetary allocation patterns will in fact be made throughout the book to roughly substantiate generalizations about patterns of emphasis in Japanese public policy. But precise comparison, even of budgetary profiles at any given time, is difficult. Definitional complications and accounting differences, such as use of capital budgets in many nations, as well as different national-local divisions of responsibility from country to country, make this so. Only for the post-1972 period is even fragmentary standardized cross-national data available on national government budgetary appropriations by sector;[59] otherwise one is forced to examine infrequent studies of budget allocation patterns at specific points.[60] In such studies, as in the underlying budgets themselves, definitions and accounting practices frequently vary from case to case, making comparison over time through time-series data—potentially a powerful means of testing the crisis and compensation argument quantitatively—virtually impossible. United Nations data provide extended budgetary time series from the early postwar period to the present, but the budgetary categories provided are not specific enough to be useful in this analysis.

Where budgetary analysis is undertaken, primary attention is directed to the shares of national general account budgets devoted to specific items of expenditure and to changes in these budgetary shares over time. Principal attention is given to budget shares and their transformation, rather than to changes in the absolute level of budgetary expenditures, or relationships to GNP, because the object of analysis is understanding the conscious tradeoffs among alternate prospective uses of public funds which governments make. Budget shares are also used as central units of analysis in much of the literature related to the theoretical concerns of this book.[61] Although there are inevitable methodological shortcomings in any quantitative budgetary data, shortcomings enumerated in part above, changes in budgetary shares

[59] International Monetary Fund, *Government Finance Yearbook*.

[60] See, for example, Organization for Economic Cooperation and Development, *Public Expenditure Trends*.

[61] See, for example, John Creighton Campbell, *Contemporary Japanese Budget Politics*; and Noguchi Yukio, "Yosan ni okeru Ishi Kettei Rūru no Bunseki" (Decision Rules in the Japanese Budgetary Process), *Keizai Kenkyū* (January 1978), pp. 23–32.

over time provide as useful an indicator, albeit a rough one, of changing government priorities as is readily available.

Since precise cross-national quantitative comparison, especially on an extended time-series basis, is so difficult, cross-national propositions presented in this volume are probabilistic, middle-level generalizations. A range of climactic political episodes have been examined, drawn from Japanese as well as United States, French, German and British history since the advent of mass political participation. Through such international comparison the analysis seeks possible Western parallels both to the crises which post-World War II Japanese authorities have confronted and to Japan's compensation-oriented mode of policy response to crisis. Tentative evidence from these cases suggests some limited Western parallels to Japanese patterns, though definitive comparative conclusions await more comprehensive research on the European and North American cases.

Implications of the Analysis

The assessment offered here is intended primarily as a parsimonious academic exposition of the politics of domestic, non-industrial policy change in postwar Japan, but it has considerably broader implications; the most important, from a global perspective are, related to defense, trade, and finance.

Defense

The crisis and compensation dynamic in domestic policymaking, combined with the bias toward "compensation politics" which it has generated over time, hold major implications for a broad range of domestic policy sectors like agricultural, small business, and welfare, as well as for Japanese defense policy. Political crises within Japan, and the institutions created thereby, have generated strong claims on resources that would otherwise go to defense. These counterclaims, in such areas as agricultural and small business support, make major increases in Japanese defense spending difficult, even in the face of rising external pressure on Japan to expand its regional and global security commitments. Such counterclaims can be intensified by external economic shocks and demands within Japan for countermeasures, as was true following the two oil shocks and three major yen revaluations of the past two decades. Conversely, the waning of domestic political vulnerability for the conservatives, such as Japan witnessed during the early 1980s, reduces LDP vulnerability to demands from civilian constituents within Japan and thus increases governmental leeway to expand defense spending. The implications of crisis and compensation for Japanese national defense are a major concern of this volume, discussed at length in chapter 10.

Trade

The analysis presented here also has substantial implications for Japanese trade policy and for non-Japanese policymakers concerned about how to influence it. Some important market access prospects in Japan may well exist for foreigners in traditionally traded, relatively nonpoliticized sectors of the economy, such as electronics and precision machinery. But this analysis suggests the likelihood of more substantial political resistance within Japan to the liberalization of the labor-intensive manufacturing and distribution sectors, coupled with extensive compensation of domestic interests for losses suffered through such liberalization as actually occurs. Small business insecurity, and the sensitivity of conservative politicians to it, severely complicates foreign efforts to gain expanded market access in Japan's less competitive sectors. This was dramatically evident in the resistance of the ruling Liberal Democratic Party to American demands for tariff reductions on plywood imports into Japan during 1985–1986. Many observers also saw a similar dynamic in the massive 1986 "yen-revaluation countermeasures" support program for small business, despite MITI protestations that this program was not trade-related.

As noted earlier, Japanese conservative politicians have concerned themselves primarily with the untraded sectors of the political economy, leaving export industries such as steel, autos, and microelectronics to a combination of technocratic and market guidance. But generic support policies for small business, agriculture, and depressed regions have also had some indirect bearing on Japanese competitiveness abroad. Indeed, the case can be made that the bulk of the policy incentives for Japanese industry in the 1980s lies in these areas, and that regional and small business policies, in particular, are consciously integrated with broader industrial policy. The concerted operation of these policies since the 1950s has created a Japanese political economy whose periphery has become nearly as industrial as its metropolitan centers. For example, 60 percent of Japan's integrated circuits are produced in semirural areas, where regional incentives often aid both employers and their workforce. Direct small business supports may also aid export competitiveness, either in the forms of ongoing programs or of special efforts, such as the $1.5 billion yen revaluation countermeasures program of 1986.

Finance

Among the most important international implications of Japanese conservative policymaking relate to its impact on Japanese public finance. When domestic political crisis reigns and compensation policies prevail, strong pressures exist to expand government spending and hence frequently the government deficit.[62] Not surprisingly, the budget deficit as a share of total government expenditures rose more rapidly in Japan during the often politically precarious 1971–1981 period[63] than in any other major industrialized nation except Britain, despite strong Ministry of Finance and big business opposition during the late 1970s. Conversely, when crisis does not prevail, Japanese budgeters are relatively tightfisted. Between 1981 and 1986, the Japanese budget deficit fell from 26.4 to 21.4 percent of expenditures, while the analogous, deficit figure was rising sharply in the United States and France.[64]

The years of sharp and rising Japanese national budget deficits, driven by government sensitivity to grassroots pressure, spawned a massive government bond market and strong pressures during the early 1980s toward liberalization of Japanese domestic interest rates. Those deficits also absorbed substantial and rising shares of Japan's consistently high domestic savings within the country itself. The waning of crisis and the ensuing government

[62] During the 1949–1954 period of political turbulence, most such expansion was in "off-budget" government credit programs, but during the 1970s it was in the general account budget. Following the 1960 Security Treaty crisis, both the general account and the Fiscal Investment and Loan Program budgets expanded rapidly, but did not generate a deficit due to rapid economic growth.

[63] As a share of total expenditures, Japanese deficits during 1971–1981 rose 18.3 percent (from 8.1 to 26.4 percent) compared to 15.6 percent in West Germany, 21.4 percent in Britain, and -0.8 percent in the United States. See Bank of Japan Research and Statistics Department (Nihon Ginkō Chōsa Tōkei Kyoku), *Kokusai Hikaku Tōkei* (*Comparative Economic Statistics*) *1982*, p. 78.

[64] Ibid., 1985 ed., pp. 83–84.

retrenchment after 1981, however, had the reverse effect. Deprived by budget cutbacks of an investment haven within Japan and allowed by foreign exchange liberalization to move freely abroad, excess Japanese savings in the billions of dollars surged into global markets. The weak yen of 1981–1985 and the pace of massive Japanese foreign investments (both then and later) have had, of course, multiple origins. But they appear to have been significantly influenced by the dynamic of crisis and compensation. This dynamic created pressures for fiscal expansion during the early 1970s but facilitated retrenchment after 1980, as political pressures for fiscal expansion grew weaker. Future policy planning for Japanese involvement in global finance can usefully take account for this crisis and compensation dynamic. It significantly affects Japanese government spending patterns; they, together with savings rates and domestic investment levels, shape Japanese capital outflows, with their substantial impact on global interest and exchange rate patterns.

• • •

BEYOND any particular utility it might have, the analysis of Japanese conservative policymaking is also intellectually attractive for the important incongruities it presents. For radical or socialist politicians in the modern industrial world, supporting low income groups and the dispossessed of remote regions is not unusual. It was through such identification, in fact, that the modern Left itself was born in Europe during the nineteenth century. But for conservatives, intent on stability, identification with the restless underprivileged in industrial society has always been a more complex proposition. Even where tactics for both sides have demanded such identification, cultural differences and economic interests have often militated against it, both in Japan and elsewhere. The profile of the challenge to governance which Japanese policymakers have faced is the central concern of the next two chapters, with the first chapter outlining features of Japanese economic, social, and political structure enhancing a propensity toward crisis, and the second providing an historical account of the major post-1949 political crises themselves.

1

The Specter of Crisis

> The so-called democratic form of government is still in its infancy in my country. And though its outlines may now seem to have been determined, so far we see little indication that its spirit has come to live amongst us. The state of our political world has probably never been more unsettled; public opinion fluctuates constantly; laws are enacted and later abolished, without much regard from the first as to whether they can be observed.
>
> YOSHIDA SHIGERU
> *The Yoshida Memoirs* (1961)

ANALYSTS of the Japanese political system today often stress the stable preeminence of the ruling Liberal Democrats—"the party that will rule half an eternity." Indeed, the LDP and its conservative predecessors have provided Japan's prime ministers continuously since World War II with only one exception four decades ago.[1] Even in the Fifth Republic France of De Gaulle, Pompidou, and Giscard d'Estaing, conservative dominance lasted only twenty-three years. In Italy, Christian Democratic rule was compromised during the 1980s by the advent of Socialist Prime Minister Bettino Craxi. But in Japan, conservative dominance has continued unbroken for well over three decades, a record unparalleled elsewhere in the democratic world. Following their massive election triumph in July 1986 and the subsequent collapse of the New Liberal Club, the LDP held just over three-fifths of all Diet seats—over three times the share of any single opposition party.

Stability also appeared by the late 1980s to be a central reality of the Japanese economy. In the fifteen years following the Nixon shocks of 1971, Japan weathered two severe oil price increases and three periods of yen revaluation which saw the value of Ja-

[1] Japan Socialist party leader Katayama Tetsu served briefly as prime minister during 1947–1948, at the head of a coalition cabinet including several members, such as prime minister-to-be Miki Takeo, who ultimately joined the Liberal Democratic party when it was founded in 1955.

pan's currency more than double against the U.S. dollar. Yet major firms survived, and most prospered. Unemployment rose only slightly from levels by far the lowest in the industrialized world. From the late 1970s on, a pervasive sense of awe began to arise, in both the West and increasingly within Japan itself, concerning the strength of the Japanese economy in the face of adversity. Its problems, such as they were, seemed to flow only from its strength—and centered on trade and capital surpluses among the largest in modern history.[2]

In the alternate celebration and condemnation of Japan's current stability and prosperity, the perceptions of pervasive weakness which created and long sustained the policy framework for rapid growth and were paradoxically intensified by that growth are easily forgotten. Yet in understanding the internationally distinctive patterns of Japanese public policy, what is important is not the secure current preeminence of Japanese conservative politicians, but their intense, self-perceived *vulnerability*, from World War II to the recent past, and the intense concern with which the business world has long viewed that vulnerability. Indeed, it was preeminently the state of intermittent *crisis* that Japanese conservatives often believed themselves to be facing—both collectively and often individually as politicians—which drove the patterns of *compensation* that are the hallmark of postwar politics and policymaking, as I will show in later chapters. The powerful big business world acquiesced in such measures, which often ran counter to its narrow economic interests, out of overwhelming, economically rooted desire for political stability. Conversely, when crisis did not portend, as during the early 1980s, retrenchment in policymaking became more likely. Then the underlying technocratic structural bias of the Japanese state, outlined in chapter 3, began to assert itself, and big business felt less need to acquiesce in economically unproductive policies, such as rural public works spending and rice price supports.

Crisis, defined as a prospect of major loss or unwanted change that threatens the established order,[3] operationally refers in the

[2] In 1985, for example, Japan's current account surplus exceeded the combined total for the OPEC nations at the height of their influence and increased further in 1986 to $85.8 billion.

[3] For further elaboration of the concept, see Robert S. Billings, "A Model of Crisis Perception: A Theoretical and Empirical Analysis," *Administrative Science Quarterly* 25, no. 2 (June 1980), pp. 300–16; Michael Brecher, "A Theoretical Approach to International Crisis Behavior" in *Studies in Crisis Behavior*, pp. 1–21;

Japanese case considered here to the prospects as perceived by conservative politicians and businessmen for continued preeminence of the ruling conservative party. The big business world in particular had a rather low risk-tolerance threshold and corresponding adversity to political change, as will be seen, due to the unusual high-leverage, high-growth strategy pursued in industrial development. Crisis has in practice had two major dimensions for Japan's postwar conservative politicians. First, there have been crises "within"—major disputes internal to conservative ranks; examples included the bitter Yoshida-Hatoyama struggle during the early 1950s for control of the Liberal Party; rivalries between Kishi and Kōno for preeminence within the LDP during 1959–1960; and the so-called *"Kaku–Fuku Sensō* (Tanaka–Fukuda War) for control of the LDP, which continued for a decade from 1972.[4] Grassroots rivalries among Dietmen representing various LDP factions can also be considered an ongoing, low-level manifestation of "crisis within." While loose informal factions are a reality of political life everywhere, few democracies experience the sort of intensely organized factional conflict which routinely prevails among the Japanese conservatives.[5]

A second variety of crisis for Japan's conservatives has been crisis from "without." There have been confrontations between the ruling conservatives and their opposition, as opposed to those strictly within conservative ranks. The wave of left-right confrontation which followed initiation of the Dodge Line in 1949, together with the Security Treaty crisis of 1958–1960, are the two best-known examples of this sort of political crisis. In addition, foreign pressures on Japan, both political and economic, have also at times sharply exacerbated the domestic political

---

James A. Robinson, "Crisis: An Appraisal of Concepts and Theories," in *International Crisis*; ed., Charles F. Hermann, pp. 20–35; and Stephen Skowronek, *Building a New American State*, p. 10. Gourevitch also employs the concept of crisis in a theoretically important work in international political economy, but uses it in an economic sense beyond the scope of this research. See Peter Gourevitch, *Politics in Hard Times*, pp. 20–21.

[4] For perceptive insights into the "Kaku-Fuku Sensō," see Itō Masaya, *Jimintō Sengoku Shi* (*A History of the Liberal Democratic Party's Wars*).

[5] Among the advanced industrial nations, only Italy shares Japan's pattern of highly institutionalized factions. And rivalry among Italy's factions does not appear to be as strongly intensified by the electoral system as is true in Japan. On factionalism and party politics in a variety of political systems, see Frank P. Belloni and Dennis C. Beller, eds., *Faction Politics*.

problems of individual conservative leaders, such as Satō Eisaku during late 1971 and early 1972.

Seen in comparative context, the crises from without faced by Japanese conservative governments also appear to have been unusually severe, particularly in comparison with the United States and the Northern European democracies. Formal left-right opposition has been open and unremitting. Japan has no analogue to the grand coalition between Socialist and Christian Democrats that defused left-right conflict in West Germany during 1967–1969, or to the minimal policy differences often typical of American politics. Japan has never outlawed its Communist party, which routinely runs candidates against the LDP in every constituency across Japan.

Crises from within and crises without, it is important to note, have often been *interactive* in Japan, as they were in 1949–1954, 1958–1960, and 1971–1974. This third variety of crisis and its consequences are the central analytical concern of this book. It is this sort of broad political turbulence in which intraconservative, left-right, and often foreign policy concerns interrelate, and this turbulence generates maximum political uncertainty for the business world, exerts maximum pressure on conservative political leadership, and tends to generate the most clear-cut compensation-oriented policy innovation. Indeed, the three interactive political crises of the early 1950s, 1960s, and 1970s have together shaped the profile of Japanese public policy more profoundly than any other developments in post-1949 political history.

Crisis: The Point of Departure

Since Japanese conservatives are preoccupied with stability, they see political crisis, not surprisingly, as an elemental threat and a stimulus to counteraction. Political crisis has, as a consequence, had an exceedingly powerful impact on Japanese conservative public policy, particularly in shaping its unusual redistributive qualities and the distinctive volatility of policy innovation in Japan. In the high sensitivity of Japanese conservative politics to major threats to conservative preeminence—in the high premium placed on stability, continuity, and organic cohesion in political life—Japanese conservative policymaking's commonality with the classic Western conservative tradition is most convincingly affirmed. Japanese conservatives clearly agree with Edmund

Burke that the ability to adapt is crucial to a state's survival capabilities, and they have developed mechanisms to assure that such change is possible when necessary.

Crises have drawn considerable attention over the past fifteen years as an explanatory variable shaping the pattern of a society's political evolution and the profile of its public policies.[6] As a tool for explaining the distinctive profiles of conservative politics and policymaking, particularly in Japan, emphasis on crisis has several strengths. This mode of analysis is neither teleological nor deterministic; it postulates no overall metaphysical end toward which a political system is evolving, with all the requisite complexities of proof.

As an analytical vehicle for explaining conservative politics and policymaking, the concept of crisis is useful because it focuses on stability, order, and their absence—precisely the central preoccupations of conservative policymakers themselves. As a tool for explaining cross-national *variations* in public policy outputs, crisis is particularly valuable because it focuses on the periods when policies are most open to change. Particularly in highly bureaucratized systems, such as France, China, and Japan in the postwar period, institutional conservatism often inhibits major innovation in the absence of crisis.[7] This pronounced tendency toward policy rigidity in periods of stability makes patterns of innovation when crisis emerges especially important to an understanding of why policy assumes the configurations it does in bureaucratized societies. And as societies generally become more bureaucratized, the crisis and compensation dynamic becomes increasingly the central mechanism through which policy innovation occurs.

Both cultural and structural considerations specific to Japan enhance still further the importance of crisis to an understanding

[6] See, for example, Binder et al., *Crises and Sequences in Political Development*; Raymond Grew, ed., *Crises of Political Development in Europe and the United States*; and Gabriel A. Almond and Scott C. Flanagan, eds., *Crisis, Choice and Change*. Also, see Polsby, *Political Innovation in America*; pp. 167–72; Gourevitch, *Politics in Hard Times*; and Stephen Skowronek, *Building a New American State*.

[7] As Downs, Aberbach, Rockman, and Putnam, and others have observed, bureaucrats tend to be preoccupied with system maintenance. The politicians are principally concerned about initiating major policy departures, even when bureaucrats supply the details. See, for example, Downs, *Inside Bureaucracy*; Aberbach, Putnam, and Rockman, *Bureaucrats and Politicians in Western Democracies*, pp. 238–62; and Rose, *Do Parties Make a Difference?*, pp. 151–57.

of Japanese policy profiles. Japanese political culture is highly consensus-oriented; the importance of achieving consensus makes major change enormously difficult under normal circumstances. Crisis is the one occasion when the rules are suspended and leaders have more latitude in acting decisively. Japanese conservative policymakers, with their deep preference for order, understand in a crisis the need for change *in* a system to prevent change *of* the system itself.

Bureaucratic dominance of policy, as noted above, appears to introduce a conservative hesitance regarding policy innovation outside the industrial and trade policy sectors where Japanese national economic survival necessitates bureaucratic innovation. But political structure heightens the unusual flexibility of Japanese policymaking in times of crisis, helping to make the concentration of policy innovation during crisis periods especially pronounced in Japan. The huge and influential mass media are one reason this is so, as is the complexity of a legislative process which forces even large majorities into pragmatic concessions when timely resolution of issues is required. The electoral system, as always, forces unusual sensitivity to grassroots interests. This sensitivity has in turn helped promote agricultural and small business policy innovation in periods of political crisis.

The factionalism of the ruling Liberal Democratic party, within which leaders compete furiously to present new policy solutions when the need for them is clear, is another reason for the flexibility of Japanese policymaking during crisis periods, as is subtle pluralism within the big business community. Also important are the close personal ties between some conservative leaders and the opposition; these create the frequent danger, in time of political crisis, that conservative ranks themselves might split and force right-wing LDP leaders to become sensitive to more progressive views.

Crisis often figured importantly in driving policy innovations such as those that took place in the heavily technocratic prewar Japan. As Chalmers Johnson points out, for example, the sharp post–World War I economic crisis experienced by Japanese small business led to Japan's first, rather experimental steps toward industrial policy, through the Exporters' Association Law of 1925.[8] The Financial Crisis of 1927 similarly played a major role in propelling the transformation of Japan's banking system that fol-

[8] Johnson, *MITI and the Japanese Miracle*, pp. 98–99.

lowed.[9] Mobilization for war inspired extensive industrial policy innovation during the 1930s and early 1940s.

Yet the postwar Japanese policy process has been much more clearly and extensively responsive to political crisis than that of the prewar period had been, especially in the agricultural, small business, and regional policy areas. Postwar changes in state and social structure, especially in political party, media and legislative structure and their relationships to policymaking, are partly responsible. These changes, together with the return of the multimember district electoral system in 1947, stimulated much more strongly interactive links between politician and voter, especially in conservative ranks, than in the prewar years.

The lack of resource constraints has also been important. Japanese economic growth has been rapid, foreign debt-service burdens and defense commitments have been small, and domestic savings rates have been high. Even when the LDP has seen fit to create enormous deficits, such as the massive 6 percent of GNP deficit during 1979, these actions have not generated serious inflationary pressures. Japanese savings rates have averaged 19 percent of national income since the oil shock of 1973, or over three times the scale of the national fiscal deficit at its highest point. Important fragments of explanation for the responsiveness of Japanese conservative policymaking to crisis also lie in the intimate linkages between state and economy in Japan.

The Fragile Economic Base and Its Political Imperative

Many Japanese conservatives, particularly businessmen and bureaucrats, have traditionally viewed Japanese politics in terms of its implications for the economy. Ever since the coming of Perry's black ships in 1853, a competitive economy has been seen as the guarantee of isolated Japan's autonomy in an uncertain and often hostile world. The Japanese nation's ability to tolerate pluralism and political change, in this view, profoundly depends upon the ability of the economy to operate smoothly in the presence of such internal political division and uncertainty. For a nation whose economic existence is in peril, in this interpretation,

[9] See Chō Yukio "Exposing the Incompetence of the Bourgeoisie: The Financial Panic of 1927"; and Kent E. Calder, *Politics and the Market,* chapter 1.

an unusually strong, overriding political stability imperative exists.

The logic of this integrated political economy perspective is clear in the writings of Yoshida Shigeru, Japan's longtime early postwar prime minister. Yoshida argued, for example, that the Communist party "had for its design . . . the obstruction of the economic recovery of Japan. It was this fact that placed the Liberal Party diametrically in opposition to the Communists throughout the years following the termination of the war."[10] Geopolitics or notions of right, in short, did not drive Yoshida's interpretation in this matter; rather, economic circumstances were generating a political stability imperative.

Japanese perceptions of their nation's economy as strong and successful are clearly of recent vintage. Chalmers Johnson argues that "the 'miracle' first appeared to the Japanese people during 1962," when the *Economist* of London published a long two-part essay entitled "Consider Japan," subsequently destined to become a Tokyo best seller as *Odorokubeki Nihon* (Amazing Japan).[11] Even after that date substantial skepticism remained, until the late 1970s, as to how durable Japanese economic success would actuallly be. Pessimistic, critical analyses of the Japanese economy's prospects, such as those of Ryū Shintarō, Kiuchi Nobutane, Shimomura Osamu (after 1973), and, at the popular level, Sakaiya Taichi, were given substantially more credibility in Japan than the optimistic pronouncements of Western authors such as Herman Kahn and Norman Macrae, even though the works of the optimistic foreign authors occasionally sold well. For the conservative business and political worlds, this sense of economic fragility continually intensified the desire for political stability, enabling the Japanese people to face the turbulent outside world in unified, coherent fashion.

The long-standing and deeply ingrained pessimism about economic prospects expressed by the conservatives—indeed, by virtually all Japanese—flowed from Japan's basic economic circumstances. Fuji Steel president Nagano Shigeo succinctly expressed that pessimism in 1955: "Shigen ga tarinai; tomi mo tarinai; shigoto ga tarinai." (Not enough resources; not enough wealth; not

[10] Yoshida Shigeru, *Yoshida Memoirs*; p. 232.

[11] See, "Consider Japan," *The Economist*, September 1 and 8, 1962, as well as Johnson, *MITI and the Japanese Miracle*, p. 5.

enough work.)[12] During the early Meiji Period Japan, broadly regarded as rich in raw materials, ran an export surplus in that area until 1890.[13] But raw material and foodstuff deficits increased sharply with industrialization—to 40 percent of exports in 1900, to 52 percent in 1914, and to 79 percent by 1950.[14] Throughout the first post–World War II generation and beyond, Japan was continually preoccupied with the grim prospect of being unable to feed itself and supply its factories with raw materials.

Resource shortages and uncertainties frequently translated into the currency of political unease through their potential relationship to food shortages, unemployment, and labor unrest. These persistent themes of prewar Japan continued to preoccupy postwar conservative political leadership through the Security Treaty crisis of 1960 and beyond. Japan's population had grown explosively during the early twentieth century, often under troubled economic circumstances which raised the specter of rising unemployment;[15] not surprisingly, a repetition of this pernicious dynamic was keenly feared by both Japanese and Western analysts after World War II as well. Repatriation of over six million Japanese from the former colonies during 1946–1949[16] sharply

[12] Tsuchiya Kiyoshi, "Zaikai Interview: Nagano Shigeo," p. 215. This duplicated virtually verbatim the assessment of long-time SCAP adviser Joseph Dodge shortly after his return from Japan: "The fundamental problem of the Japanese nation can be expressed in the simple terms of too many people, too little land, and too few natural resources. These combine to press heavily on every circumstance of national life." See Joseph Dodge, "Japan—Its Problems, Progress, and Possibilities" (Address delivered at the 48th Annual Banquet of the American Institute of Banking, New York, February 2, 1952), p. 5.

[13] In 1890 Japan exported ¥8.3 million in raw materials and imported ¥6.8 million. This favorable balance shifted sharply thereafter, to ¥52.5 million deficit in 1900, and ¥75.3 milllion deficit by 1918. See Bank of Japan Research and Statistics Department (Nihon Ginkō Chōsa Tōkei Kyoku), *Meiji Ikō Hondo Shuyō Keizai Tōkei* (*Fundamental Economic Statistics for Japan since Meiji*), pp. 280–81.

[14] *Ibid.*

[15] Between 1920 and 1935, for example, Japan's average annual rate of population increase per thousand was 14.4, leading to a 23.7 percent increase in Japan's total population during that time. This high rate of growth continued more or less unabated through the mid-1950s, and then fell steadily to 7.25 per thousand in 1985. See Tōyō Keizai Shinpō Sha, ed., *Shōwa Kokusei Sōran*, 1980, vol. 1, p. 23; and Bank of Japan Research and Statistics Department (Nihon Ginkō Chōsa Tōkei Kyoku), *Keizai Tōkei Nenpō* (*Economic Statistics Annual*) 1985 ed., p. 302.

[16] 5.1 million Japanese (civilian and military combined) were repatriated to Japan during 1946; 744,000 during 1947; 303,000 during 1948; and just over 17,800 during 1949. See Ministry of Welfare Support Bureau (Kōseishō Engo Kyoku), *Hi-*

compounded this population problem. Raw material and food shortages, low growth, and rising unemployment had explosive potential for generating political unrest, especially when combined with elite-level factionalism in the military and the bureaucracy. The potential, feared by Konoe Fumimaro, Yoshida Shigeru, and other conservative leaders at war's end,[17] was etched still deeper in the minds of conservatives by events such as the massive Food May Day (*Shokuryō May Day*)—demonstrations of famished thousands before the Imperial Palace on May 19, 1946.

Broadly held fears that the nation's population would continue to increase as it had before World War II, without a commensurate acceleration of economic growth, made Japan's food and raw material dependencies on the outside world look especially ominous in the early postwar period. In 1950 Japan had twelve times as many people to feed for each square mile of farm land as did the United States. In slightly different terms, Japan had a population density of 3,596 persons per cultivated square mile, versus 1,639 for China, 509 for France, and 213 for the United States.[18] One demographer expressed his professional pessimism regarding the Japanese demographic situation as follows:

> I believe the rate of population growth will probably fall from the 2.2 percent of 1948 to 1.0 to 1.2 percent in the next ten years. But I do not believe this is fast enough or will occur soon enough to permit a substantial increase in per capita production under the conditions prevailing today and likely to prevail in the next few years. . . . Hence, I find myself highly skeptical regarding the outlook for the future of Japan. . . . A real catastrophe involving millions of persons may be in the making, and it may very well be precipitated by the rather sudden withdrawal of American support from the economy of Japan, before the Japanese have been able to make any workable adjustment of population to resources.[19]

---

kiage nado Engo San jyū Nen no Ayumi (*The Thirty Year Course of Evacuation and other Support*).

[17] Konoe expressed many of these sentiments to Emperor Hirohito in the Konoe Memorial of February 1945, in which Yoshida also had a hand drafting. See Dower, *Empire and Aftermath*, pp. 255–65.

[18] Jerome B. Cohen, *Economic Problems of Free Japan*, pp. 6, 8.

[19] Warren S. Thompson, "Future Adjustments of Population to Resources in Japan" (Paper delivered at Milbank Memorial Fund Annual Conference, "Modernization Programs in Relation to Human Resources and Population Problems," New York, 1950), p. 152, cited in Cohen, *Economic Problems of Free Japan*, p. 6.

Following the onset of a Korean War economic boom induced by a sudden surge of American military procurements (¥14.4 billion in the first two months of the war alone),[20] concern over the so-called "population problem" (*jinkō mondai*) and its relationship to resource shortages became temporarily muted. But it reappeared once again after war's end in another guise. As Hitotsubashi University professor and government economic adviser Nakayama Ichirō pointed out in late 1955, the Japanese economy of the 1950s was absorbing the rising number of new entrants into the work force, but was doing so long at the cost of mounting underemployment, especially in agriculture and small business.[21] Work forces in these areas were rising much faster than productive outputs, due to extensive "work-sharing" encouraged by public policy. This development was creating an "economy devouring itself" (*tomogui keizai*), which faced acute long-run danger of both unemployment and declining international competitiveness due to its growing inefficiencies in some labor-intensive sectors.[22] The specter of crisis had not passed, it had only been transformed.

Business leader Nagano Shigeo forecast gravely that the unemployment problem would become more serious, rendered more volatile by the "excess supply" of college graduates generated by the educational policies of the recent Allied occupation.[23] As late as the protracted Miike coal strike of 1960, the specter of the "population problem," especially in its unemployment dimension, hung heavy over the Japanese political economy. It inflamed left-right conflict, while also encouraging rival conservative politicians to outbid each other in the creation of labor reservoirs in agriculture and small-scale industry which were by definition grossly inefficient in economic terms. In a major press conference at the prime minister's residence on September 5, 1960, Ikeda Hayato gravely invoked the specter of prospective unemployment—the problem of finding jobs for the over 1.7 mil-

[20] Tōyama Shigeki, ed., *Shiryō: Sengo Ni Jyū Nen Shi* (*Data: A History of the Twenty Postwar Years*), Vol. 6 (Tokyo: Nihon Hyōron Sha, 1967), p. 102. Over the period June 1950 through June 1954, U.S. war-related expenditures in Japan came to $4 billion.

[21] In agriculture alone, Nakayama observed, employment increased by three million between 1951 and 1954, without a substantial increase in farm production. See Nakayama Ichirō, "Hoshu Seiken no Shin Kadai" ("New Topics of the Conservative Administration"), pp. 64–65.

[22] *Ibid.*, p. 66.

[23] Tsuchiya Kiyoshi, "Zaikai Interview: Nagano Shigeo," p. 215.

lion new workers expected to join the labor force by 1962–1963—in support of his fledgling Income Doubling Plan.[24]

To be sure, Japan by the mid-1950s was in the early stages of what would later appear as a miraculous, sustained economic boom, but day-to-day developments appeared by no means miraculous at the time. Indeed, Japan's double-digit economic growth rarely evoked a clear sense of euphoria and confidence within Japan while it was actually occurring. Aside from the "population problem" and its unemployment correlate, gradually receding as the 1960s progressed, there was persistent concern about massive resource shortages. In 1955, for example, raw material, mineral, fuel, and food imports together came to $2.17 billion or $160 million more than Japan's entire export income in that year.[25] In 1960 such imports still consumed 86 percent of export income,[26] leaving precious little leeway for the capital goods imports necessary to build Japan's massive new steel, shipbuilding, and petrochemical plants. All this meant a continually precarious balance of payments situation and greater reliance on foreign capital at critical stages in the postwar developmental process than is often realized. Japan's imports exceeded exports *every year from 1946 through 1964,* as indicated in table 1.1, if U.S. military special procurements in Japan (mainly to support forces in Korea) are excluded from the calculation. Even with the benefit of income from these and other miscellaneous sources, Japan's current account balance was in the red quite regularly from 1952 until the late 1960s. On five occasions—three times during late 1953 and twice again in the summer of 1957—Japan was forced to draw major loans from the International Monetary Fund to finance basic imports, and to avoid serious foreign exchange crises.[27]

As Japan in the 1950s resumed the process of heavy industrialization which it had begun before World War II, huge sums of capital became increasingly necessary, both from domestic and foreign sources. Moving away from traditional patterns in both

[24] *Asahi Shimbun*, September 6, 1960. Also Itō Masaya, *Ikeda Hayato to Sono Jidai* (*Ikeda Hayato and His Era*), p. 108.

[25] Bank of Japan Research and Statistics Department, *Keizai Tōkei Nenpō* (*Economic Statistics Annual*), 1985 edition (Nihon Ginkō Tōkei Kyoku), p. 281.

[26] *Ibid.*

[27] Uchino Tatsurō, *Japan's Postwar Economy: An Insider's View of Its History*, pp. 77–78, 99–100. In 1953 Japan borrowed £22.3 million from the IMF to cover a swap arrangement in that amount with the British Treasury, necessitated by a shortage of sterling to cover imports from the United Kingdom. In 1957 Japan borrowed $125 million from the IMF.

TABLE 1.1
Japan's Precarious International Balance of Payments, 1946–1970
(in U.S. $ million)

	Exports	Imports	Trade Balance	Special Procurements[a] (U.S. Military)	Current Account
1946	103	306	−202	—	−78
1947	174	526	−353	—	46
1948	258	684	−426	19	75
1949	510	905	−395	49	207
1950	820	974	−154	63	476
1951	1,355	1,995	−640	624	329
1952	1,273	2,028	−755	788	225
1953	1,275	2,410	−1,135	803	−205
1954	1,629	2,399	−770	602	−51
1955	2,011	2,471	−461	505	227
1956	2,501	3,230	−729	498	−34
1957	2,858	4,284	−1,426	449	−620
1958	2,877	3,033	−157	404	264
1959	3,456	3,599	−143	378	361
1960	4,055	4,491	−437	413	143
1961	4,236	5,810	−1,575	389	−982
1962	4,916	5,637	−720	377	−49
1963	5,452	6,736	−1,284	356	−779
1964	6,673	7,938	−1,264	329	−480
1965	8,452	8,169	283	326	932
1966	9,776	9,523	253	466	1,254
1967	10,442	11,663	−1,222	509	−190
1968	12,972	12,987	−16	587	1,048
1969	15,990	15,024	966	641	2,119
1970	19,318	18,881	437	660	1,970

[a] (1) Special procurement figures are for military related government to government transactions. (2) Trade balance figures are for trade excluding military transactions. (3) All figures are Ministry of Finance statistics.

Source: Tōyō Keizai Shinpō Sha, *Shōwa Kokusei Sōran*, Vol. 1. (Tokyo: Tōyō Keizai Shinpō Sha, 1980), pp. 613, 649, 652.

Western and Japanese industry, major Japanese enterprises became heavily reliant on debt, particularly bank debt. Equity capital as a proportion of gross capital for manufacturing industries in Japan fell from 67 percent in 1935 to 34 percent in 1955, and to less than 28 percent in 1960, as indicated in table 1.2. During the five years from 1956 to 1961 the total amount of outstanding bank loans more than tripled.[28] At the time of the 1960 Security Treaty crisis the steel industry alone had around ¥1 trillion ($2.8 billion at prevailing exchange rates) in current and fixed liabilities—more than double the level of 1954.[29]

Under the impact of Ikeda Hayato's Income Doubling Plan (1960), low interest rate policies and rising land prices that raised the value of loan collateral, debt-equity ratios increased further still during the 1960s, breeding a deep sense of unease among analysts of this period. Ryū Shintarō, chief of the *Asahi Shimbun* editorial board, in 1962 termed Japan a "sake-drinking, cherry-blossom viewing economy" (*hanamizake keizai*) in which assets were being traded back and forth at steadily rising prices, fueled by dangerous expansion of credit, with only minimal creation of real value.[30] Kiuchi Nobutane, president of the Institute of World Economy, argued three years later that the Japanese economy was like a wild horse, galloping ever more swiftly in response to artificial goading by such allegedly reckless expansionists as Ikeda Hayato. The financial structures of Japanese corporations, Kiuchi noted, were a shambles by Western standards, with inter-enterprise credit (*kigyōkan shinyō*) standing at 92 percent of GNP, beyond the huge bank debt which Japanese firms had already incurred. Such realities made a mockery of the optimistic London *Economist* forecasts of the day and could only lead to national disaster, he contended, echoing Ryū's earlier warnings.[31] Yet

[28] From 1956 to August 1961, Ryū noted, the total amount of outstanding bank loans tripled—from ¥2 trillion to ¥6 trillion. See Ryū Shintarō, "Some Doubts about Economic Growth," *Japan Quarterly* (July–September 1962), p. 279.

[29] Combined current and fixed liabilities for the Japanese steel industry in 1960 were ¥1.115 trillion, compared with ¥412 billion for primary metal products (almost the same category at that time) in 1954. See Prime Minister's Office Statistical Bureau, ed., *Nihon Tōkei Nenkan* (*Japan Statistical Yearbook*), 1955 and 1961 eds., various pages.

[30] Ryū Shintarō, "Some Doubts about Economic Growth," pp. 275–84.

[31] Kiuchi Nobutane, "A Japanese Viewpoint on 'Reconsider Japan,' " *The Oriental Economist*, May 1965, pp. 257–61. See also Kiuchi's essays in *Sekai Shūhō*, October 23, 1962; and in *Tōyō Keizai*, January 23, 1965, which took violent ex-

Table 1.2

The Heavy Debt Burden of Japanese Industry, 1952–1986 (equity/total capitalization, expressed in percent)

Year	Manufacturing	Steel	Electric Power	Shipping	Electric Machinery	All Industry
1952	35.2	35.2	64.1	16.1	37.0	36.7
1953	36.1					28.4
1954	34.5					29.4
1955	34.0*					29.0*
1956	39.1*					27.3*
1957	28.2*					25.3*
1958	28.9*					25.5*
1959	27.7*					23.8*
1960	27.6*					22.6*
1961	27.3*					22.3*
1962	27.1*					22.0*
1963	24.7*					20.5*
1964	24.2					19.7
1965	23.1					19.0
1966	22.7					18.4
1967	21.4					17.5
1968	23.8					21.4
1969	23.0					20.3
1970	22.1					19.3
1971	20.7					18.0
1972	20.4					17.5
1973	18.2					14.4
1974	17.9					14.3
1975	17.0					13.9
1976	13.7					13.7
1977	17.4					14.1
1978	18.3					14.3
1979	19.3					14.3
1980	20.6					15.3
1981	20.9					15.6
1982	22.6					16.0
1983	23.6					16.0
1984	24.4					16.9
1985	25.7	16.0	16.1	10.8	33.8	17.7
1986(p)	28.1	16.5	16.8	11.8	33.9	19.6

Notes: (1) Figures are for the April accounting period unless otherwise noted. Those for October are marked with asterisks. (2) Figures for 1986 are provisional.

Source: Ōkurashō Shōken Kyoku, *Hōjin Kigyō Tōkei Nenpō (Yearbook of Corporate Statistics)* (Tokyo: Ōkurashō Insatsu Kyoku, 1952–1986).

debt-equity ratios continued to rise even higher thereafter, propelled by Japan's double-digit growth based on a capital-intensive heavy-industrialization emphasis unequalled elsewhere in the world.

As table 1.2 indicates, own-capital ratios for Japanese industry as a whole had fallen by 1976 to only 13.7 percent of total financing—less than one part equity to six parts debt. Japanese corporations had over ¥300 trillion in liabilities in 1976, about fourteen times the level of 1960 and forty-seven times that of 1954.[32] Although differences in asset valuation practices make cross-national comparisons in this area difficult, it seems safe to say that average Japanese firms by the early 1970s were twice as heavily leveraged as their counterparts in the West and more than twice as leveraged as they themselves were in the early 1950s. This heavy leverage and the potential risk implicit in it made Japanese industry, particularly the heavy industrial firms at its core, such as those in steel and shipbuilding, highly sensitive to prospective changes in their political and regulatory environment.

In addition to substantial domestic debt, large firms in a number of key sectors, particularly steel and electric power, also began to borrow heavily from abroad.[33] This dependence of Japanese firms on foreign loans was highest in the six years before introduction of the U.S. interest-equalization tax of 1963, as I will show later in more detail. Like its domestic counterpart, the rise of foreign borrowing also generated complex emotions within Japan, heightening the sense of economic vulnerability among many.

A strongly leveraged industrial structure, heavily in debt to both domestic and foreign banks, naturally increased the priority that both big business and the conservative political world placed on stability; it also compounded the corresponding sense of unease felt at economic and political uncertainty. Yet on the economic side, at least, uncertainty was often unavoidable. Apart from perennial balance of payments uncertainties, heavy debt burdens, and the early postwar fears of unemployment and the population problem, there was also the highly volatile and in

---

ception to the London *Economist's* optimistic assessment of Japanese economic trends.

[32] Prime Minister's Office Statistical Bureau, ed. *Nihon Tōkei Nenkan* (*Japan Statistical Yearbook*), 1976, 1961, and 1955 eds., various pages.

[33] For details, see Masaki Hisashi, *Nihon no Kabushiki Kaisha Kinyū* (*Japanese Corporate Finance*), pp. 235–87.

many ways unpredictable character of Japanese growth to unsettle the conservative political world and the big business community.

Japanese growth of the postwar period, particularly the 1950s and 1960s, typically came in surges. Many of these volatile surges were totally unanticipated, arising as they did from sudden overseas stimulus. Japanese industrial production, for example, rose 86 percent between 1950 and 1953 and 165 percent between 1965 and 1973. But in both instances growth was strongly stimulated by American offshore procurements to support wars in Korea and Vietnam whose scale and substantial economic benefits for Japan were previously unanticipated.

In both 1950 and 1965 pessimism was deep in Japan regarding the economic future, with neither of the major postwar American wars in Asia clearly foreseen.[34] The so-called Jimmu boom of 1956–1958 was also largely unforeseen, precipitated as it was by the 1956 Arab-Israeli War, closing of the Suez Canal, and the consequent surge of new contracts for one of Japan's few competitive sectors of the period—shipbuilding. Japanese growth was also stimulated significantly during the 1981–1985 period by a dollar overvalued in trade terms, due to currency misalignments rooted in an expanded American budget deficit. Once again, the sudden weakening of the yen and the export-driven buoyancy of the early 1980s seems to have been largely unanticipated in Japan.

To be sure, postwar Japan has experienced major growth surges driven largely by domestic demand, most notably the so-called Iwato Boom of the early 1960s, sustained by massive capital spending following announcement of Ikeda Hayato's Income Doubling Plan. But, like the other major economic surges, that of the early 1960s was largely unanticipated. And the euphoria it instilled was tempered with severe anxiety concerning the impending "opening of the Japanese economy" to foreign imports. Japan's trading partners insisted that Japan's pending assumption of the IMF and OECD membership obligations necessarily implied such an opening, which promised to be painful.

From a political point of view, Japan's rapid economic growth of the 1950s, 1960s, and 1970s was clearly beneficial to the conservatives in the public resources which it generated for allocation. High growth in Japan spawned a pattern of "compensation

[34] See Arisawa Hiromi, ed., *Shōwa Keizai Shi* (*An Economic History of the Shōwa Era*), pp. 465–67.

politics," this was both rather distinctive in comparative context and rather far from the conceptions of many early postwar conservative political leaders as to how politics ought to operate.[35] The pattern of compensation politics also clearly helped keep the ruling conservatives in power. But Japan's explosive, albeit volatile and often unpredictable, growth just as clearly generated persistent political demands against the conservatives: it stimulated urbanization, which increased demand for social services, and it led to tighter labor, land, and capital markets, which often led to small business protest.

Growth also widened income differentials between town and countryside, leading to rural demands for redress. Demands against the conservative politicians were often heaviest in periods of highest growth, just as the political stability imperative confronting the increasingly leveraged big businesses of Japan was also rising to its zenith. These persistent demands against the LDP contributed to a pervasive sense of unease in political ranks that only began to decisively abate in the late 1970s and early 1980s. Political dominance seemed rarely assured for the Japanese conservatives, even though the intensity of their unease clearly waxed and waned over time.

Growth generated political uncertainties for many individual conservative politicians through its impact on their major nonelite political constituencies, especially farmers and small businesses. Farmers saw their relative income level deteriorate, while industry expanded and both workers and executives grew increasingly prosperous. Small business, to the extent that it was not structurally integrated with big business through the subcontracting system, found itself competing for perennially short supplies of capital and labor. As Japan's double-digit growth economy overheated, it was always small business—and its numerous political collaborators in the LDP and rival parties—which first felt the impact of policy restraint. Yet heavily leveraged, risk-

35 This disjunction was most apparent during the 1970s and 1980s in the continual appeals of the 40-year veteran antimainstream conservative Miki Takeo against "money-power politics." But it was also clear in the political style of many of Miki's political contemporaries during the late 1940s, such as Yoshida Shigeru, Ashida Hitoshi, and Hatoyama Ichirō. One careful political observer of the period even went so far as to characterize Hatoyama's distinctly nineteenth-century position on economic and social problems, which eschewed compensation politics, as "Gladstonian liberalism." See Kenneth E. Colton, "Pre-War Political Influences in Post-War Conservative Parties," *American Political Science Review* (October 1948), p. 942.

averse big business trembled at any serious political manifestation of small business distress.

The meteoric course of postwar Japanese economic development, in short, did not generate the sense of ease in Japanese conservative business and political ranks which hindsight might now suggest. Deep raw material and food supply dependencies on the outside world were a concern for politicians, as they were for all Japanese. The population problem and the related specter of unemployment generated anxiety across Japan for most of the first two postwar decades. The volatile, episodic character of the major economic growth surges seems to have dampened conservative confidence regarding long-run future growth prospects for a surprisingly extended period. There was also the inexorably rising mountain of corporate debt, so strikingly large in comparative context. Despite high growth, Japanese conservatives thus lived in a world of persistent, underlying political tension, with unusually strong stability requirements. In this world catalytic events could readily invoke a "threat to the established order of things," seemingly minor were it to occur in a Western political system, which might clearly be termed "crisis" under the definition adopted here.

It is important to reemphasize that there have been both periods of deep turmoil and islands of relative calm amidst the underlying economic and social tension outlined above. Tensions have increased and decreased through a complex interaction of social, political, and economic factors. Economic business cycles, foreign pressure, and the fate of both individuals and their interpersonal networks have all shaped the pulse of Japan's cycles of crisis, as we will see in subsequent pages. But in the complexity of these events one can also discern systematic patterns amenable to social science research.

A Heritage of Political Division

Japan, it is often said, is a homogeneous land, oriented toward consensus; certainly class and ethnic cleavages are not as salient in Japanese politics as in those of many nations of the world. But postwar Japan has nevertheless had important political divisions which cannot be neglected. And a highly geared, rapidly changing, and potentially vulnerable postwar economic structure has made its conservative politicians and businessmen unusually averse to political risk and prone to magnify the consequences of political fluidity that would be commonplace elsewhere. The economic uncertainties outlined above gave Japanese conservative politicians strong incentives to defuse such crises and they urged the business and bureaucratic world to support them in such endeavors.

Two generations have now passed since the bitter divisions of 1945 and earlier years. But in the first two postwar decades, when many of the basic policy profiles which distinguish Japanese conservatism today were determined, World War II and the bitter struggles within Japan which preceded it were a living memory. Bitter thoughts of those earlier turbulent times deeply divided the conservatives themselves and estranged many of them from the long-repressed opposition. All this contributed to an overall atmosphere of tension in which full-fledged crises, fraught with emotion and symbolic meaning, could readily erupt.

Central to the historically rooted tensions of the early postwar years were the small group of figures purged by the Allied occupation who made it back to the political stage. Preeminent among them, of course, was Kishi Nobusuke, minister of commerce and ultimately minister of munitions in the Tōjō war cabinet, who moved in five years from the status of depurged war criminal to prime minister of Japan. But there were others, such as Hatoyama Ichirō, chief cabinet secretary in the prewar cabinet of General Tanaka Giichi (1927–1929) and also a future prime minister (1954–1956).[36] There were major nuances and complexities in the backgrounds and world views of these people, which made many of them more ambivalent about the militarist interlude than either the Left or the Allied occupation generally recognized.[37] But after years of prison and/or political eclipse at the hands of the Allied occupation, these people by the early 1950s were consumed with righting what they conceived as deep personal and in many cases national injustices. Constitutional revision, rearmament, and compensation for landlords were not just abstractions; they were rectification of what the purgees and their allies conceived as grievous wrongs. Securing these changes was a matter of honor.

Arrayed against former collaborators with the prewar military

[36] Hatoyama was also minister of education in the Inukai and Saitō cabinets of 1931–1934.

[37] See Hans H. Baerwald, *The Purge of Japanese Leaders under the Occupation.*

were men who had suffered directly at its hands. Japan Communist party chief Nosaka Sanzō had served years in the caves of Yenan with Mao; many of his colleagues, such as JCP Secretary General-to-be Miyamoto Kenji, had been imprisoned by the *Kempeitai*. Even such conservatives as Miki Takeo and Yoshida Shigeru had had brushes with the police in wartime days which may have complicated their later dealings with the Right.[38] Others, such as maverick LDP Dietman Utsunomiya Tokuma, whose father was a prominent general in the Imperial Army, had reacted against the wartime experience vicariously, generating intense emotions which shaped their later political behavior.

Within conservative ranks division was intensified not only by contrasting reactions to the militarist interlude but also by differences in prewar political background. Contrasting affiliation with Seiyūkai or Minseitō, the major prewar parties, had lingering influence; indeed, such prewar party allegiances prevented Hatoyama Ichirō from creating an all-embracing conservative party just after the end of World War II.[39] Such divisions also helped generate the pronounced factional structure that has characterized Japanese conservative politics ever since. The prewar tradition of multiple conservative parties also undermined the legitimacy of the 1955 conservative merger in many eyes and enhanced the continuing outside prospects of a subsequent conservative split. Veteran antimainstream LDP leader Matsumura Kenzō, for example, had come of age in prewar Minseitō politics, and throughout a political career stretching well into the 1970s he believed firmly in the ideal of two conservative parties. He opposed the conservative merger of 1955 (as did other major figures, including Yoshida Shigeru and Satō Eisaku), refused to vote on the U.S.-Japan Security Treaty of 1960, and several times made common cause with other mavericks threatening to split the LDP once it had been established.[40]

Prewar divisions and wartime experiences, in short, combined to create deep fractiousness in conservative ranks. It is crucially important to remember that for the first ten years after World

[38] Miki strongly opposed the restoration of civil rights to purges in the early 1950s, perhaps partially on these grounds. See Ashida Hitoshi, *Ashida Nikki* (*The Ashida Diaries*), Vol. 4, p. 6.

[39] Colton, "Pre-War Political Influences."

[40] On Matsumura's political career and his strong belief in political pluralism, see Matsumura Masanao, *Hakō Getsuen: Matsumura Kenzō Ibunsho* (*The Legacy of Matsumura Kenzō*).

War II, there was no unified conservative party in Japan, and strong opposition in some conservative quarters to such a concept. Indeed, throughout the 1945–1955 decade there were generally two to four broadly conservative parties in Japan, as indicated in figure 1.1. The LDP was only the *fifty-first* party founded in Japanese postwar political history.[41] And all but six of those fifty earlier parties included Dietmen who were ultimately to join the LDP after 1955.

Before 1955 the Japanese conservatives were less unified and politically dominant in many respects than their counterparts in West Germany or Italy. Despite his "One Man Yoshida" appellation, for example, Yoshida Shigeru could manage only four years of absolute parliamentary majority for his conservative party (1949–1953) as opposed to five years of absolute majorities (1948–1953) for Alcide de Gasperi in Italy and eight for Konrad Adenauer (1953–1961) in Germany.[42] There is no analogue in early postwar German history to the Katayama-Ashida conservative-socialist coalitions of 1947–1948, while in Italy and France the cross-party ties generated under early postwar coalitions were sharply compromised by severe and rapid subsequent polarization. Japan's first postwar decade—and particularly its coalitions of 1947–48—left an internationally distinctive heritage of cross-party communications—particularly between antimainstream conservatives and the moderate Left—that had major implications for the Japanese policy process of subsequent decades. Disturbing to both big business and the conservative mainstream, these cross-party ties intensified the unease with which the Right viewed the political scene, even after the conservative merger of 1955.

The conservatives tried several times, beginning with Hatoyama at war's end, to unite as a single party during the decade before the birth of the LDP in 1955. Yet each time (as in the Yoshida-Hatoyama dealings of 1951–1954) they ran afoul of complex personal rivalries with deep historical roots. Even when the unified conservative party was finally inaugurated in November 1955, divisions remained deep; Yoshida himself and his protege Satō Eisaku, the longtime Liberal party secretary general, refused to join the fledgling LDP until February 1957. Miki Bukichi, one

[41] Satō Seizaburō and Matsuzaki Tetsuhisa, *Jimintō Seiken* (*The LDP Administration*), p. 178.

[42] On the political fortunes of Adenauer and De Gasperi, see R.E.M. Irving, *The Christian Democratic Parties of Western Europe*, pp. 127–32, 64–67.

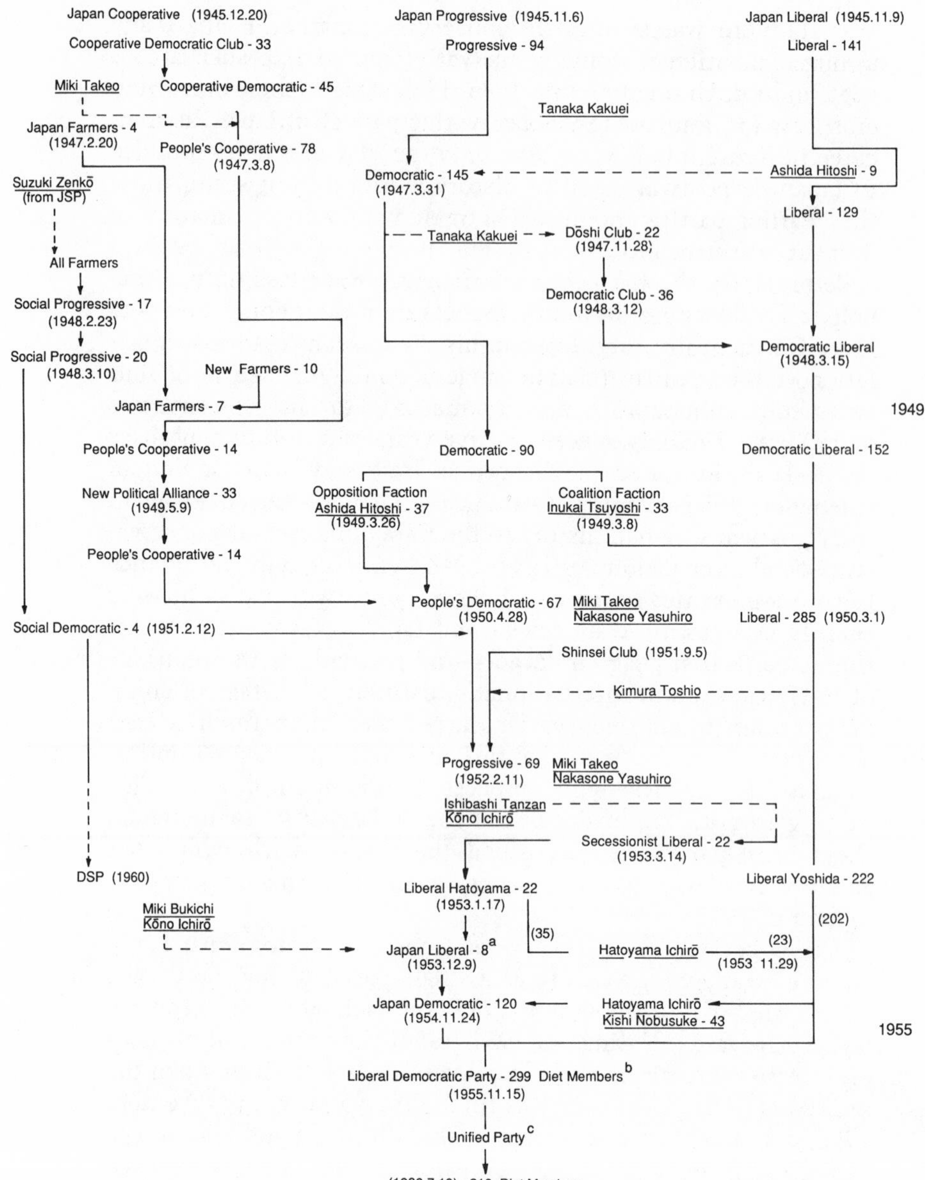

Figure 1.1. Divided Within: Japan's Fragmented Conservative Political World, 1945–1955.

[a] The Japan Liberal party (Nihon Jiyūtō), founded in December 1953 and disbanded in November 1954, was distinct from the Liberal party of Yoshida Shigeru and included many of Yoshida's chief opponents.

of the key architects of the 1955 merger, predicted at its inception that the merger would be lucky to last two or three years (*ni san nen moteba ii yo*). In this context, the skepticism concerning prospects for a united conservative party which the 1955 data in table 1.3 present was symptomatic of the times.[43] These results reflect early postwar Japan's turbulent postwar heritage of political division, so often forgotten in light of subsequent events.[44]

While substantially exacerbating the latent tensions in early postwar Japan, the prewar and wartime heritage of division also helped create complex interpersonal networks. These informal linkages, generally based on common formative experiences before post-1955 political divisions clearly emerged, helped behind the scenes in generating policy solutions that could defuse the periodically explosive political crisis. Such networks, in short, provided the communications infrastructure which allowed Japanese conservative policy makers both to respond flexibly to such crises and devise consensus solutions incorporating a broad range of majority and minority views.

Among the most important such networks were those flowing from the Economic Stabilization Board (*Keizai Antei Honbu*) of the early postwar period. This group included figures ranging from Wada Hiroo, longtime director of the Japan Socialist Party's International Bureau, to Ōkita Saburō, foreign minister under the

---

FIGURE 1.1. (*cont.*)

[b] Lower and Upper House members of the Diet combined.

[c] Six LDP Dietmen, led by Kōno Yōhei, left the party on June 25, 1976, to form the New Liberal Club (NLC). This, however, was disbanded in July 1986, when virtually all members returned to the LDP.

Sources: Satō Seizaburō and Matsuzaki Tetsuhisa, *Jimintō Seiken (The LDP Administration)* (Tokyo: Chūō Kōrōn Sha, 1986), pp. 180–81; *Asahi Shimbun Shukusatsu Ban*, Aug. and Sept. 1986. Asahi Shimbun Sha, ed., *Sengo Nihon no Seitō to Naikaku (Postwar Japanese Parties and Cabinets)* (Tokyo: Jiji Tsūshin Sha, 1981), pp. 134–36.

[43] Two respected American academic analysts of the period pointed to the inability of the fledgling LDP to even agree upon a president to head the organization and concluded: "The fact . . . that the merger was an entente of expediency, concealing rather than dissolving factional rivalries, imperils the existence of the party as a permanent fixture in Japanese politics." See Harold S. Quigley and John E. Turner, *The New Japan: Government and Politics*, p. 302.

[44] *Asahi Shimbun*, December 28, 1955, p. 1. Most respondents to the poll felt that a dissolution of the Diet was also imminent, due to instability in the new two-party political order. This dissolution did not in fact occur, however, until May 1958, in part because both conservative politicians and zaikai feared the stress on the fragile new conservative party of an early election campaign.

TABLE 1.3
Skepticism concerning the Prognosis for Conservative Unity, 1955

Question: Are you optimistic regarding the future prospects of:[a]

	The Recent Conservative Merger (Liberal Democratic Party)	The Recent Socialist Merger (Japan Socialist Party)
Yes	18 percent	22 percent
No	40 percent	30 percent
No opinion	42 percent	48 percent

Source: Asahi Shimbun, December 28, 1955, p. 1.
Note: Results of *Asahi Shimbun* stratified sample opinion poll of 3,000 persons, randomly chosen from the electoral rolls in 338 locations across Japan, undertaken two months after foundation of the Liberal Democratic Party.
[a] "Korekara saki matomatte umaku iku darō to omoimasu ka?"

Ōhira government in the late 1970s. Among other major networks were the *Dōkō Kai*, an anti-Tōjō group in the Diet from November 1941–May 1942, including both LDP Prime Minister Hatoyama Ichirō and JSP Prime Minister Katayama Tetsu; various labor relations groups that included both *zaikai* figures and labor leaders such as longtime Democratic Socialist party leader Nishio Suehiro; the Katayama coalition cabinet of 1947–1948, including both right-wing Socialists like Nishio and conservative mavericks like LDP Prime Minister to-be Miki Takeo; and study groups at Keizai Dōyūkai in the early postwar period, which likewise lined Socialists with conservative politicians.

Thus, the complex mosaic of transwar Japanese history produced a seeming contradiction. It intensified the formal, mass-level conflict between Left and Right in early postwar Japan; this was also true in Germany and Italy. These nations had had experiences of dictatorship, war, defeat, and occupation which closely paralleled Japan's. Yet history also generated a maze of elite back channels for negotiations that could partially defuse this mass-level conflict. These back channels, which appear to have been stronger and more durable than in the other former Axis nations due to the late conservative merger and moderate Left-Right polarization, have significantly affected strategies of both Left and Right in the Japanese policy process throughout the postwar period.[45] Enduring cross-party ties both intensified the specter of crisis confronting mainstream conservatives, for whom a recreation of the 1947 cross-party coalition was anathema, and opened the prospect of policy change to defuse such crisis when it flared to intolerable levels.

Institutionalized Insecurity: Japanese Conservative Politicians and Their Electorate

Central to classic Western conservative thought has been the notion of legislator as representative not of constituent opinion but of a broader, deeper, historically rooted vision of what society is and can become. As Edmund Burke argued to the electors of Bristol: "Your representative owes you not his industry only, but his judgment; and he betrays, instead of serving you, if he sacrifices it to your opinion."

Contemporary Japanese conservative Dietmen, in contrast to aristocratic British Old Tories of Burke's day, could never openly express the sentiments of Burke at Bristol, even should they entertain them. For they find themselves, as individual legislators, to a degree highly unusual in the industrialized world, intensely vulnerable. Despite the enduring strength of their party at the national level, they are vulnerable to defeat as individuals, due to pronounced intraparty competition induced by Japan's unusual electoral system.

Despite their rising influence in the policy process, Japanese conservative politicians are vulnerable in the public estimation. They are not, as a general rule, broadly respected the way bureaucrats or key executives of established firms are; for a century and

[45] Satō and Matsuzaki note, for example, that Japan's LDP has been unusually flexible and pragmatic, while the Japan Socialist party was pragmatic in the early postwar period; later it became more ideological, in contrast to the transition to moderation its counterparts in Italy and Germany undertook around the end of the 1950s. See Satō Seizaburō and Matsuzaki Tetsuhisa, *Jimintō Seiken* (*The LDP Administration*), pp. 19–21. These differences between Japan on the one hand and its former Axis counterparts on the other may well have had their origins in the unusually strong cross-party interpersonal networks in Japan, which underlay the crisis and compensation policy dynamic, as suggested in later pages. The growing JSP rigidity after 1963 flowed mainly from the growing strength within the party of its militant left wing, a phenomenon largely unrelated to cross-party personal networks.

more they have been seen to represent particularistic interests in a nation philosophically at odds with the *Federalist Paper #10* and its esteem for pluralism. In contrast to patterns across most of Europe, Japanese conservative politicians have no roots in a religious or class base which might confer legitimacy. Thus, politicians, unlike bureaucrats, are marginals, forced to use materialist appeals to bolster their standing at home.

Perhaps the single most important source of personal political vulnerability for Japanese conservative politicians today—an ongoing, institutionalized insecurity forcing them into solicitous concern for their constituencies unmatched in the industrialized world—is the unusual Japanese electoral system. Virtually all the candidates for the powerful Lower House of the Diet,[46] together with a substantial fraction for the less powerful Upper House[47] are elected from multimember districts. This means, of course, that multiple candidates of a single party frequently run against one another for election from any given district. It is consequently possible to win with substantially less than a majority, or even a plurality, of the total vote in one's constituency.

The current electoral system has not prevailed throughout modern Japanese history. From 1889 to 1925 the electoral system alternated between small, one- to three-seat districts (1890–1900 and 1919–1925) and large districts with four to thirteen seats each. The franchise was also highly restricted, expanding only gradually from 1.24 percent of the population in 1889 to around 5.5 percent in 1924. Although a rough approximation to the current system prevailed from 1925–1945 (minus female suffrage), the large electoral districts of the Taishō Period were reintroduced for one election in 1946. Only in March 1947 was the medium-size electoral district system restored.

The most important implication of the current Japanese electoral system for policy is that it puts representatives of relatively large parties in direct competition with one another.[48] Practically

[46] The only exception is the representative for the Amami Ōshima Islands off southern Kyūshū, who is elected from a single-member district.

[47] In the Upper House (House of Counsellors) 74 of 252 members are elected from multimember constituencies electing from two to four members each per election. From single-member local districts 52 members are elected, and 126 from the so-called national constituency under a list system similar to those commonly used in Western Europe.

[48] Arthur Stockwin emphasizes that Japan's unusual multimember constituency electoral system "reinforces cultural conservatism, fragmenting the Opposition and fostering personal factionalism." It may well be true that the Japanese

speaking, this once meant both the Liberal Democratic Party (LDP) and the Japan Socialist Party (JSP); but since the late 1950s, it has increasingly come to mean the LDP alone, as the JSP has splintered and declined in strength.[49] Of the 259 LDP members of the Lower House in 1984, 229, or 91.5 percent, represented districts in which there was more than one LDP Dietman with whom they were forced to compete for a finite number of conservative votes; 248, or 95.8 percent of these LDP Dietmen, were elected in December 1983 from districts where more than one LDP affiliated candidate ran. In addition, there were several independent conservative candidates in the 1983 elections, most of them rivals of the official party candidates who simply failed to obtain formal party endorsement. Ideological differentiation among conservative candidates was minimal, forcing them to compete strongly in terms of constituency service.

This fierce intraparty competition which LDP Dietmen must undergo contrasts sharply, it should be noted, to the quasimonopoly situation which individual opposition parties confront. While nearly 96 percent of LDP candidates in 1983 ran from districts where they had intraparty competition, this situation prevailed for only 31.2 percent of JSP candidates and for virtually none of the other opposition party candidates. This sharply contrasting competitive situation has intensified the strong incentives of LDP Dietmen to satisfy their local electorates, while it has made opposition party politicians secure in their local monopoly situations, even should their party not take power.[50] Political insecurity prevails perennially for conservatives as individuals; this encourages them to preempt crisis as a group.

---

electoral system helps to fragment the prospective unity of the middle of the road opposition parties and hence to ensure LDP political preeminence. But as the following pages will demonstrate, it does not follow that the Japanese electoral system fosters rigid public policies. Indeed, the reverse may more frequently be the case. On Stockwin's views, see Arthur Stockwin, "Japan," in Vernon Bogdanor and David Butler, eds., *Democracy and Elections*, pp. 209–27.

[49] In 1958 there were 166 JSP Dietmen competing in 118 districts. This number fell to 128 with formation of the DSP in January 1960, recovered somewhat in the 1960 election, and fell below the one member–one district level in December 1969, from which it has never recovered.

[50] Hokkaidō, Akita, and Yamagata prefectures in northern Japan, which each elected more than one JSP Dietman per district in 1983, are the exceptions that prove the rule. In these areas, where monopoly situations do not prevail for JSP Dietmen, responsiveness to the grassroots appears greater than in the case of other Socialist Dietmen, and JSP strength has been more resistant to decline.

The insecurity of Japanese conservative Dietmen is graphically illustrated by looking at the electoral fate over time of a single cohort of Dietmen. Of the class of forty-three Dietmen elected in 1969, only twenty-six, or 54.2 percent, remained by 1983.[51] One-third of the original cohort had retired or been defeated within seven years, or two elections, of first entering the Diet. And this survival rate was better than that of five of the seven cohorts since 1958 with whom comparison is possible.[52]

Those conservative Dietmen who survive the competitive selection process within their constituencies have developed sensitive institutionalized modes of interaction with constituents which render them unusually responsive to grassroots pressure. Most successful LDP Dietmen, particularly those in the small- and medium-size towns where LDP political strength has come increasingly to be concentrated, rely heavily on personal support organizations, or *kōenkai*.[53] Although precise calculations are difficult, roughly one-third of all LDP voters are associated actually with such groups.[54] Conservative Dietmen typically leave Tokyo on Friday and return early the following week, frequently spending the weekend meeting with organized constituents.[55] This so-called *kinki karai* system[56] of intense and frequent aired grassroots consultation has analogues in the machine politics of the U.S. Northeast,[57] although there is no strong evidence of its being highly pervasive in the Western industrialized world.

Virtually no electoral systems in the Western industrial world

[51] Satō and Matsuzaki, *Jimintō Seiken*, p. 46.

[52] *Ibid.*, p. 47

[53] For detailed, highly readable introductions to kōenkai, see Nathaniel B. Thayer, *How the Conservatives Rule Japan*, pp. 88–110; and Gerald L. Curtis, *Election Campaigning Japanese Style*, pp. 126–51. On an intriguing cross-national parallel in Senator Robert Byrd's political operation in West Virginia, see David Mayhew, *The Electoral Connection*, p. 40.

[54] Watanuki estimated in 1967 that around 10 million voters were members of LDP kōenkai, while Curtis in 1971 suggested a membership of 12 million for kōenkai of all parties. See Watanuki Jōji, *Nihon no Seiji Shakai* (*Japan's Political Society*), p. 67, and Curtis, *Election Campaigning*, p. 136.

[55] This practice of intensive interaction with highly organized constituents contrasts sharply with much less structured representative–constituent relations in the United States. See, for example, Richard F. Fenno, Jr., *Home Style*.

[56] Literally "coming Friday, returning Tuesday."

[57] Congressman William A. Barrett of Philadelphia, for example, prided himself on having spent only three nights in Washington, D.C., in six years and in consulting his constituents incessantly. See Mayhew, *Electoral Connection*, p. 74.

stir the sort of routinely fierce grassroots intraparty rivalries, rendering legislators vulnerable to constituent pressure. Of twenty-eight functioning democratic systems in 1981, nineteen, including Japan, employed a multimember constituency system.[58] Yet sixteen of these nineteen employed proportional representation party list systems, in which national parties, rather than voters, determined the ordering of party candidates within individual constituencies.[59] Only Ireland, Finland, and Japan use electoral systems that elect more than one member per district and simultaneously leave intraparty ranking among a given party's candidates entirely to the voter.

There are many important differences among the electoral systems of these three nations.[60] But the impact of multimember district electoral systems in forcing legislative responsiveness to the grassroots in Japan also appears to prevail to some extent in Ireland and in Finland. In both Ireland and Finland, politicians frequently complain that they are continually forced to cater to constituency whims and lack the time or political ability to think more strategically about the nation's future. In the Irish Dail, a deputy is frequently referred to as a "constituency messenger,"[61] an expression that could be aptly applied in Japan as well.

Despite limited parallels with Western European systems in general, the Japanese electoral system nevertheless appears to exert significantly greater pressures on *conservatives* per se than is the case in Finland, Ireland, or anywhere else in the Western industrialized world. The major reason for this, of course is that the conservative party in Japan, the LDP, is much larger relative to other parties than its conservative analogues elsewhere[62] and has

[58] David Butler, Howard R. Penniman, and Austin Ranney, eds., *Democracy at the Polls*, pp. 12–18.

[59] *Ibid.*, p. 230. Among these sixteen nations, it should be noted, several allow the voter some latitude for altering the list ordering established by the national party headquarters. But such systems provide voters at the grassroots with only marginal practical influence over the ultimate relative standing of candidates for any given party.

[60] Sarlvik and McKee argue, for example, that politicians in both Ireland and Finland tend to be markedly responsive to local interests. See Bogdanor and Butler, eds., *Democracy and Elections*, pp. 134–35, 183–87.

[61] *Ibid.*, p. 187.

[62] In Ireland, for example, the ruling Fianna Fail obtained 49.1 percent of the seats in the February 1982 election and has never been in power for a protracted

been in power continuously for thirty years. The LDP's size creates greater pressures for internal competition than would be true of smaller parties. At the same time, its long tenure as a dominant ruling party facilitates access to state resources and encourages routinized ties between legislator and constituents (the so-called *kōenkai* described above) to exploit this access.

Electoral uncertainties for individual conservative politicians—institutionalized insecurity, to put it succinctly—drive a continual competition within conservative ranks to provide roads, cultural halls, and other amenities to local constituencies in return for support. This pressure on politicians for distributive political benefits is intensified by the highly organized character of both Japanese politics and Japanese society; thus, the mobilization of voters in support of specific interest group objectives is relatively easy. It is also fostered by the preoccupation of politically active interest groups in Japan with material compensation for their support. Demands against rank-and-file conservative Dietmen for compensation generally come from a relatively small number of indispensable supporters; given their long ties to the legislator in question, those demands are especially difficult to resist. When intraparty competition increases the value to party leadership of a rank-and-file Dietman's support or when such Dietmen's political survival is threatened by opposition challenge, both the demands against Dietmen and the level of support available to them tend to increase, generating the cyclical fluctuations in distributive policy outputs outlined in chapter 4.

Electoral Vulnerability of Japanese Conservative Dietmen: Comparative Perspectives

The vulnerability of Japanese conservatives to grassroots pressures is once again underlined by cross-national comparisons. As is indicated in table 1.4 the margin of victory for individual LDP Diet candidates in Japan is dramatically lower than it has been in recent American congressional elections, despite the LDP's long tenure in power. This becomes strikingly clear from cross-national analysis of 1986 general elections in Japan and the United

period. In Finland, the National Coalition Party (Conservatives), obtained 23.5 percent of the seats in a system characterized by four major parties any one of which almost never obtain a majority of the vote. See *ibid.*, pp. 186, 136.

TABLE 1.4
Margins of Victory for Japanese Diet and American Congressional Candidates, 1986 (in percentages)

Party	Share of Candidates Winning/Losing by Under 1,000 Votes	1,000–5,000	5,000–10,000	Over 10,000
Liberal Democrats	0.6	7.4	12.0	80.0
Republicans	2.3	2.8	4.5	92.6
Democrats	0.4	1.9	1.6	93.1

Sources: Miyakawa Takayoshi, ed., *Seiji Handbook (Politics Handbook)*, September 1986 ed. (Tokyo: Seiji Kōhō Center, 1986), *U.S. Congressional Quarterly*, November 8, 1986.

Notes: (1) U.S. figures are for November 1986 House of Representatives elections, while Japanese figures are for July 1986 Lower House Diet elections. (2) Margins of victory presented in numerical rather than percentage terms to show clearly the importance of individual voters in the personalistic Japanese political system. (3) Investigation on a percentage basis, also undertaken, produces comparable cross-national results. (4) LDP margins calculated as difference between last candidate of any party not elected (*jiten*) and LDP candidate in question. (5) Exploratory time series analysis suggests that these patterns, if anything, overstate typical win/loss margins of LDP candidates, thus strengthening the analytical point in question. In the 1983 Lower House general election, for example, 3.3 percent of LDP candidates won or lost by less than 1,000 votes, 19.3 percent by 1,000 to 5,000, 19.0 percent by 5,000 to 10,000, and only 58.4 percent by more than 10,000 votes.

States. Twenty-seven lower house Dietmen, in fact, were elected in 1986 by less than 5,000 votes—a "cliffhanger" margin in the United States.[63] Yet this was the product of the greatest Japanese electoral landslide in over a generation for the ruling LDP.[64] Only eighteen American congressmen were elected in 1986 by such a slim margin—that is, less than one House member out of twenty; and forty-eight U.S. congressmen were elected without

[63] Of the LDP Lower House candidates in 1986 nineteen, or about 6 percent, won or lost by less than 1 percent of the popular vote, in comparison with the nearest nonelected (jiten) candidate. See Miyakawa Takayoshi, ed., *Seiji Handbook* (*Politics Handbook*), September 1986 ed.

[64] In 1983, by contrast 65 LDP Dietmen were elected by less than 5,000 votes. See Miyakawa Takayoshi, ed., *Seiji Handbook* (*Politics Handbook*), February 1985.

TABLE 1.5
Reelection Ratios for Parliamentary Incumbents: A Cross-National Comparison

Country	Competition Ratio (Candidates/Seats)	Share of MPS Standing for Reelection (percent)	Incumbent Reelection Ratio (percent)
West Germany	5.8	76	85
France	4.6	92	73
Britain	2.7	92	91
Japan	1.9	92	81

Sources: Nishihira Shigeyoshi, *Senkyo no Kokusai Hikaku (International Comparison of Elections)* (Tokyo: Nihon Hyōron Sha, 1969), p. 125; also, Satō Seizaburō and Matsuzaki Tetsuhisa, *Jimintō Seiken (The LDP Administration)* (Tokyo: Chūō Kōron Sha, 1986), p. 47.

Note: Comparative data drawn from the 1960–1968 period. For 1969–1983, the incumbent reelection ratio in Japan averaged 78 percent and fell to only 66 percent in 1983. Thus, insecurity for Japanese incumbents continued to persist into the 1980s.

even nominal opposition from the other major party—a situation without parallel in any Japanese electoral district.[65]

Not surprisingly, given the relatively thin margins by which many Japanese elections are decided, a larger proportion of Japanese conservative incumbents customarily lose in any given election than is common in the United States, although their constituent-service "support organizations," or kōenkai, frequently continue. Almost invariably these support assocations move on to another LDP candidate, often of the same faction, rather than shifting parties when their sponsor loses or voluntarily withdraws from politics. As is indicated in table 1.5, higher proportions of incumbents typically lose in Japan than is true in either Britain or West Germany, even though fewer candidates nor-

[65] Although the multimember district system affords many incumbent Dietmen, especially rural JSP legislators, relative security, in no constituency in the 1986 general elections was the total number of major party candidates (including the LDP JSP, DSP, Kōmeitō, and JSP) as small as the number of seats up for election. See Miyakawa, ed., *Seiji Handbook*, September 1986 ed.

TABLE 1.6

Volatility of Representation at the Electoral District Level (in percentages)

Country	Proportion of Districts Awarding Single Party a Majority of Seats	Proportion of Districts Awarding Same Party/Faction Majority for Three Elections
Britain	3	80
West Germany	68	58
France	15	49
Japan	58	44

Source: Nishihira Shigeyoshi, *Senkyo no Kokusai Hikaku (International Comparison of Elections)* (Tokyo: Nihon Hyōron Sha, 1969), p. 219.
Note: Data drawn from the 1960–1968 period.

mally run against those incumbents in Japan. Although the figures here are for all Dietmen, turnover is more pronounced in the case of conservative than opposition Dietmen in Japan because competition is substantially more intense in conservative ranks.

Within individual electoral districts as well as nationwide, the stability of LDP rule contrasts sharply with the insecurity of individual Dietmen and the electoral turbulence at the grassroots. As is indicated in table 1.6, at the electoral district level one political party consistently takes a majority of electoral districts in both West Germany and Japan, although in the West German case it is not always the same party. But the Japanese and West German patterns diverge sharply in the stability of configurations in any given district over time. There has been far more volatility over time in the individual and party membership of the Japanese Diet delegations from specific electoral districts than in either Britain or West Germany. There has been nearly as much turnover as in France, where a complex and polarized political history, combined with the two-ballot voting system, has introduced unusual uncertainty into the electoral process.

Throughout the postwar period, Japan's conservative politicians and businessmen have confronted deep uncertainties, economic, factional, and electoral, in their bid to bring Japan into the community of advanced industrialized nations. In the retrospective view of the prosperous and politically stable Japan of the late

1980s, a pervasive sense of unease at future economic and political prospects prevalent during the early postwar period may seem to have been unjustified, but that unease was nonetheless a reality, intensified by Japan's debt-oriented development strategy. The uncertainties that Japanese conservatives experienced have tended to converge in distinct periods of perceived danger to continued conservative rule, a subject to which we now turn.

2

A Chronology of Crisis

NAGGING UNCERTAINTY about both the economic and the political future was endemic in Japan across the long decades which shaped the current bias of Japanese public policy. But this uncertainty, almost subliminal at times, translated only periodically after 1949 into major threats to the conservative political preeminence seen as necessary for continued economic growth. This chapter chronicles the process and dynamics of that periodic transition.

If the concept of crisis is to be useful as an analytical variable, one must be able to clearly delimit crisis periods, when tensions escalated above the general levels already discussed, and to distinguish them from noncrisis periods in terms of a clear set of indicators. Although such a process of definition is inevitably subjective, the following indicators would appear to demonstrate the "prospect of major loss or unwanted change which threatens the established order"—in this case the prospect of major threat to continued stable rule by the Japanese conservatives:

(1) The relative strength of the principal conservative party (the Liberals[1] from 1945 to 1954; the Democrats from 1954 to late 1955, and the Liberal Democrats since the conservative merger of November 1955) and its major nonconservative opposition. This relative strength can be presented in two forms: (a) opinion poll data indicating conservative support at any given time and (b) electoral data, both from national and local elections.

(2) Turbulence within conservative ranks, such as sudden, controversial resignations of major cabinet officials, strongly contested and narrowly decided party presidential elections, and overt, active criticism of the incumbent conservative government by other major conservative leaders.

(3) Legislative turmoil, as in low success rates for Cabinet

[1] The Liberals were known as the Democratic Liberals from March 1948 through March 1950, but it was essentially the same group throughout, with the additional Inukai faction of the Democratic Party after March 1949.

bills, due to opposition and intra-party conservative delaying tactics.

(4) Economic dislocation, including levels of economic stagnation, inflation, and unemployment.

Where these various political indices of instability co-vary with one another at a high level, it would seem legitimate to speak of major "prospects of unwanted change" or crisis, under the definition adopted here. This would seem appropriate especially when contemporary statements of conservative leadership and other analysts confirm that the conservative political world in Japan in fact perceived the prevailing state of affairs as suggesting a dangerous possibility of unwanted change.

A review of the unusual, integrated political-economic character of political crisis in postwar Japan is important here. Compared to much of Western Europe and the developing world, the Japanese have historically had rather weak social class consciousness, broad cultural acceptance of hierarchy, and strong cross-societal interpersonal networks reducing the prospect of sudden, cataclysmic, revolutionary social change. In these respects Japanese society would seem presumptively stable and the prospects for wrenching political crisis remote. But it is crucial to remember the extraordinary social and political fluidity created in Japan during the early years of occupation (1945–1948), the formidable task of reconstruction that confronted the Japanese, and the high-leverage, high-risk growth strategy pursued by the Japanese developmental state in pulling Japan out of its precarious economic straits. Japan's risky economic growth strategy, in short, gave its postwar business and political leadership an *extremely low level of tolerance* for political risk and uncertainty. Political developments which might have seemed innocuous in less highly geared political economies presented a "prospect of major loss or unwanted change" in highly leveraged and risk averse postwar conservative Japan.

The unusual character of Japan's early postwar conservative political world compounded the fears of big businesses and mainstream conservative politicians. The conservatives did not form a unified political party until 1955; many of those who did join the LDP in 1955 had been either aligned with socialists in a coalition government only seven years before or had, like Prime Minister to-be Suzuki Zenkō, been socialists themselves.[2] Such

[2] Suzuki Zenkō, LDP prime minister during 1980–1982, had, for example, begun his postwar political career as a Socialist Dietman during 1946–47.

politicians were no strangers to the process of party secession and partisan realignment. Conservative political ranks were rent throughout by deeply personalized factional rivalries, to a much greater degree than in any other institutionalized democracy except Italy. Although the conservative antimainstream—including mavericks such as Miki Takeo, Ishibashi Tanzan, and Kōno Ichirō, with long-standing personal ties to the Left—could not readily control conservative politics, they could always threaten defection or forge issue-specific cross-party coalitions. The stronger the opposition and the more turbulent the conflict within conservative ranks, the more credible this implicit threat of defection became, abhorrent as it was to the risk-averse, growth-oriented big business and mainstream conservative political worlds.

As indicated in figure 2.1, empirical analysis appears to clearly support the notion of three distinct intervals of major domestic crisis in the postwar period. To be sure, there are differences in the profile of crisis during each period. In the early postwar crisis, for example, economic circumstance aggravated political uncertainties more than was generally true later, while political pressures from progressive-controlled local governments were less acute than in the 1970s. But, during all these periods, uncertainty regarding the preeminence of conservative governments over the major left-oriented opposition parties (as expressed in public opinion polls and recent electoral results) coincided with turbulence inside conservative ranks, generating interactive crises with the potential for inducing major departures from the status quo in a broad range of policy areas. Although economic difficulties (recession, inflation, or both together) seem to have exacerbated politically induced crises in both 1949–1954 and 1971–1976, it is important to note that economic factors alone were insufficient to provoke domestic political crisis, as was demonstrated during the noncrisis recession of 1965.

Years of Fluidity: 1945–1948

The years of unbroken conservative dominance in Japan which are the primary concern of this volume began with the fall of the Ashida coalition cabinet in October 1948 and the Yoshida general election victory of January, 1949. But the incoming Yoshida government of 1948–1949 confronted social demands and political

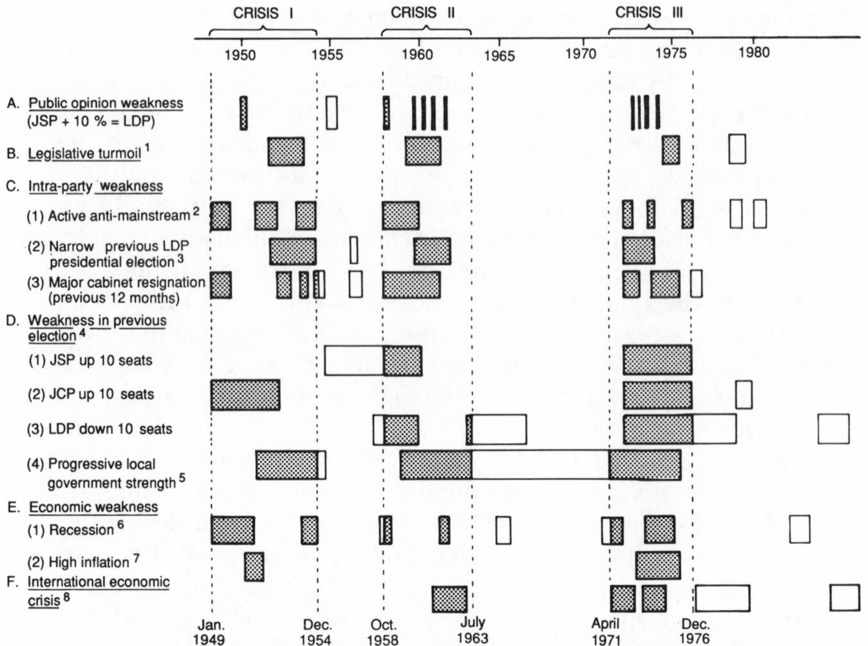

Figure 2.1. Profiles of Domestic Crisis for Japan's Conservatives, 1949–1986.

Notes:[1] Success rate of cabinet bills less than 80 percent.[2] Major faction leaders actively challenge prime minister.[3] Most recent election of LDP president determined by runoff between top two candidates.[4] For pre-1955 period, holds clear majority support within conservative ranks. Figures before 1955 are for largest conservative party.[5] Progressives hold at least two of five largest urban governorships.[6] Annual growth rate declines one third, or real economic growth drops below 3 percent, whichever is lower.[7] Consumer price index rises above 10 percent annually. International economic crises include: (a) OECD liberalization crisis (preceding Japan's entry into OECD (9/61–7/63). (b) Nixon Shock/yen revaluation crisis (8/71–6/72). (c) Oil Shock crisis (9/73–6/75). (d) Yen revaluation II crisis (3/77–12/78). (e) Oil Shock II crisis (following Iranian Revolution) (1/79–6/80). (f) G-5 yen revaluation III crisis (9/85–12/87).

Sources: Jiji Tsūshin Sha, ed., *Sengo Nihon no Seitō to Naikaku (Postwar Japan's Parties and Cabinets)* (Tokyo: Jiji Tsūshin Sha, 1981); and supplementary recent Jiji Tsūshin public opinion data; Satō Seizaburō and Matsuzaki Tetsuhisa, *Jimintō Seiken (The LDP Administration)* (Tokyo: Kōdansha, 1986); (Nihon Ginkō Tōkei Chōsa Kyoku), *Keizai Tōkei Nenpō (Economic Statistics Annual)*, various issues; Tsuji Kiyoaki, ed., *Shiryō: Sengo Ni Jyū Nen Shi (Documents: A History of the Twenty Years After the War)*, Vol. 1. (Tokyo: Nihon Hyoron Sha, 1966), pp. 346–51; *Asahi Shimbun*, evening edition, Dec. 1, 1966, p. 1; Tōyō Keizai Shinpō Sha, *Shōwa Kokusei Sōran (Shōwa National Almanac)*, 2 vols. (Tokyo: Tōyō Keizai Shinpō Sha, 1980); and Tanaka Zenichirō, *Jimintō no Doramatsurugii (The Dramaturgy of the LDP)* (Tokyo: Tokyo Daigaku Shuppan Kai, 1986), pp. 68–69.

fluidity intensified profoundly by developments of the previous two years of occupation reform.

Thus, the seeds of crisis were sown, in terms of challenge for the conservatives, during 1946–48. At that point reformists within the Allied Occupation headquarters SCAP[3] began dismantling many of the social control mechanisms through which conservatives had dominated pre-1945 Japanese society and politics. These mechanisms combined to form an elaborate system of indirect rule through private bodies controlled by government, sharply amplifying the control capabilities of the state.

SCAP reforms began with a major challenge to the conservative power structure in the countryside. Conservative control over the five million farm households of Japan was undermined with the beginnings of land reform in December 1946 and rising rural frustration at the slowness with which the reform effort at first proceeded.[4] Membership in the left-oriented peasant unions spiraled within a year, exceeding one million members—one for every five farm households in Japan—on the eve of the critical April 1947 elections.[5]

A week before the 1947 elections, SCAP abolished the neighborhood unit system, which had allowed 240,000 conservative city, town, and hamlet bosses to monitor and influence the political behavior of urban households through such mechanisms as their responsibility for the distribution of rationed goods. In the elections themselves, massive Socialist gains displaced the conservative Liberal party government of Yoshida Shigeru from power and inaugurated eighteen months of Socialist-Democratic coalition cabinets.[6] Most local governments remained in the hands of the Right, due to the lingering power of prewar grassroots conser-

[3] Literally "Supreme Commander Allied Powers," this term referred collectively to the headquarters staff of the Allied occupation armies in Japan, who oversaw the administration of Japan from September 1945 until April 28, 1952.

[4] Only 14 percent of the transfers scheduled to take place were actually accomplished in the fifteen months to March 2, 1948. See T. A. Bisson, *Prospects for Democracy in Japan*, p. 92. As Ronald Dore points out, "The land-reform programme was not an easy one to carry out. It involved changes in the property rights of some six million families, of whom over two million had every motive for trying to obstruct its purposes." R. P. Dore, *Land Reform in Japan*, p. 149. The technical and political complexity of the reform provided little comfort to the millions of farmers and their families waiting for it to occur.

[5] T. A. Bisson, *Prospects for Democracy*, p. 50.

[6] The Socialists gained fifty-one seats in the April 1947 Lower House elections, an increase of 55 percent in their overall strength.

vative organizations. Socialist governors were returned only in Nagano, Fukuoka, and Tokushima.[7] But basic damage had been done to the conservative structure of grassroots control—damage which loomed as a threat for future years.

The new Socialist-Democratic government promptly moved to compound the damage. On December 15, 1947, it succeeded in passing a major revision of the old Agricultural Cooperative Association Law. This revision decreed abolition of the conservative agricultural associations, or nōkai, which had dominated the Japanese countryside on behalf of landlords and the state since the mid-Meiji period. This action led to a steadily escalating struggle during 1948 over both forms of agricultural organization in the countryside and their control.

The Katayama cabinet, despite its political fragility, combined with reformist forces within SCAP to dismantle major elements of the conservative control structure in other areas as well. It passed legislation to abolish the Home Ministry, decentralize the police system, reform the public service, enact measures providing for unemployment insurance, establish a Labor Ministry, and deconcentrate industry.[8] Socialists within the cabinet also tried gingerly to nationalize the coal industry, under pressure from their left wing, provoking a political crisis which helped bring down the government. Nationalization failed, but remained a major goal of the Left late into the high-growth period,[9] thus intensifying fears in the highly leveraged business world of political changes which might bring the Socialists back to power.

The precedent of the Katayama coalition cabinet and its short-lived successor under Ashida Hitoshi continued to trouble conservative politicians and businessmen over the years, particularly as economic growth and rising corporate leverage intensified the need for political stability during the 1950s and 1960s. One fear was the prospect of socialist gains should the corporatist bonds underlying conservative political dominance in Japan be loos-

[7] At the mayoral level, the Japan Socialist party elected candidates only in Yokohama, Moriguchi, Maizuru, Izumo, and Ueno City. See Soma Masao, ed., *Kokusei Senkyo to Seitō Seiji* (*National Elections and Party Politics*), p. 16.

[8] On the history of the Katayama cabinet, see Katayama Naikaku Kiroku Kankōkai, ed., *Katayama Naikaku* (*The Katayama Cabinet*); and Kinoshita Takeshi, *Katayama Naikaku Shi Ron* (*A Theory of the History of the Katayama Cabinet*).

[9] On March 15, 1968, for example, the JSP formally introduced legislation to nationalize the coal industry and to establish a public corporation (*Nihon Sekitan Kōsha*) to administer it, although this was easily resisted by the LDP. For details see *Asahi Shimbun*, March 16, 1968; March 2, 1968; and February 21, 1968.

ened, as they were with the abolition of *nōkai* during 1947–1948. A second specter was the prospect of a conservative split. Only once in postwar Japanese history have Socialists been strong enough electorally to head a cabinet and entice politicians further right to break ranks and align with them. But the prospects of leftward realignment of antimainstream conservatives, a reincarnation in some guise of the coalition of 1947, stirred concern in business and mainstream conservative political circles three decades after Katayama, as they warily contemplated the maneuverings of mavericks such as Kōno Ichirō, Miki Takeo, and Matsumura Kenzō in periods of broader political crisis.

Crisis and the Struggle for Conservative Order: 1949–1954

After the Shōwa Denkō scandal, in which Prime Minister Ashida and sixty-three others were indicted for bribery,[10] the Democratic-Socialist coalition government that had succeeded Katayama was forced to resign in late 1948. Following the brief second Yoshida cabinet and a whirlwind election campaign, Yoshida Shigeru returned to office during January 1949 in a seemingly decisive position to govern. The election sharply repudiated the middle-of-the-road Socialists and Democrats; their joint strength fell from 242 seats to 138 in the 466-seat Diet, and then to 105 when 33 Democrats joined Yoshida's Democratic Liberals. Even Socialist leader and former Prime Minister Katayama Tetsu was defeated in the Yoshida landslide.

Yet as the conservatives prepared to govern once again, with the first absolute majority of the postwar period, the political atmosphere was tense and foreboding. Union strength, whose prewar peak had been 425,000, soared sixteenfold to 6.85 million by the end of 1948. Farmer union membership had also spiraled from the 240,000 of April 1946 to more than a million in June 1947 and to more than two million by early 1949.[11]

The newly confirmed Yoshida administration faced an equally

[10] Ashida, JSP leader Nishio Suehiro, MOF Budget Bureau Director Fukuda Takeo, and sixty-one others were accused of accepting bribes from Shōwa Denkō, Japan's largest fertilizer producer, in return for special consideration in arranging a low-interest loan from the Reconstruction Finance Bank. Only two of sixty-four indicted were found guilty in the final judgment, handed down in 1962.

[11] Ronald Dore, *Land Reform*, p. 168.

emboldened communist party, whose strength had soared from four seats to thirty-five in 1949.[12] With only 50,000 members, the JCP had polled a popular vote of almost three million to become in the eyes of many the "moral leaders" of the opposition. Deepening the sense of crisis from the Left which confronted Yoshida early in 1949 were dramatic developments on the Chinese mainland, where Beijing had fallen to the Peoples' Liberation Army just five weeks earlier and Tientsin less than ten days before Yoshida's election victory.[13]

A sense of the deep disquiet Japanese conservatives felt at the occupation-induced reforms and the fluidity those reforms had induced in Japanese society and politics of the postwar period is clear in Yoshida Shigeru's own retrospective on the occupation:

> a purge was enforced which deprived our nation of a trained body of men at a crucial moment, . . . the financial concerns were disintegrated through the complete breakup of Zaibatsu and by the institution of severe anti-monopoly measures, gravely retarding our economic recovery, . . . notorious Communist leaders were released from prison and praised for their fanatical agitation, causing untold injury to our body politic, . . . organized labor was encouraged in radical action, thus endangering law and order, . . . education was reformed, sapping the moral fibre of our bewildered youth. Besides, our politics were so disorganized that militant unions, heavily infiltrated by Communism, ran amok in defying the authority of the Government.[14]

Within conservative ranks, as in society more generally, the political situation in early 1949 was delicate, despite Yoshida's substantial new majority in the lower house. Yoshida's decision to include two members of the renegade Inukai faction of the Democratic party in his new cabinet stirred sharp internal struggle within his newly preponderant Democratic Liberal party,[15]

[12] This level was not even remotely approached again until 1972. In the eight Lower House general elections between 1949 and 1972, an average of less than five JCP members were elected each time. JCP Lower House representation increased to thirty-eight seats in December 1972.

[13] Beijing fell to the Peoples' Liberation Army on December 15, 1948, and Tientsin on January 15, 1949.

[14] Yoshida Shigeru, *Yoshida Memoirs*, p. 288.

[15] See Kuroki Hisatoki's detailed analysis of internal factionalism in the new cabinet, in *Nippon Times*, February 20, 1949.

exacerbated by internal struggles over selection of a lower house speaker and vice-speaker. Yoshida's position was also constrained by weakness in the House of Councillors, where his party held only 52 of the 250 seats and depended heavily on support from the 75 members of the *Ryokufū Kai* (Green Breeze Society, a group of independent members of the house) to secure passage of legislation.

More importantly, Yoshida's position was delicate because of the nine-point economic stabilization plan—the essence of the so-called "Dodge Line,"[16] transmitted to the Japanese government on December 19, 1948, by Douglas MacArthur for implementation. The plan—calling for a balanced budget, strengthened tax collections, and stringent curbs on Reconstruction Finance Bank loans—was designed to break the back of Japanese inflation and provide the basis for stable economic growth. The political problem for Yoshida was the plan's strong tension with the campaign pledges in the 1949 elections of Yoshida's Democratic Liberal party. It also required sharp deflationary policies, including a tight budget that ultimately required firing 30 percent of all government employees. And these employees were represented by increasingly powerful unions generally sympathetic to the Left.

Pronounced economic weakness and the magnitude of the policy demands placed on an already weak economy by the draconian Dodge Line rationalization measures, intensified a political crisis that, as suggested in figure 2.1, was relatively mild in terms of purely political indicators. By 1949 Japan had only returned to 53 percent of its 1937 level of mining and manufacturing production, compared to 78 percent in West Germany.[17] Japan was being squeezed out of prewar markets in textiles and hemmed in severely by the currency and trade barriers of other nations. The average Japanese still consumed only 2,100 calories daily—closer to Burmese levels (1,990) than Brazilian (2,440) and just two-thirds of those in the United States (3,170).[18] Japan's trade balance was very deeply in deficit, with imports nearly twice the

[16] The economic stabilization program was known as the "Dodge Line" because Joseph Dodge, president of the Bank of Detroit, was appointed by Washington to monitor the progress of the Japanese government in implementing the program.

[17] "Recent Changes in Production," Supplement to *World Economic Report, 1950–1951*, United Nations, April, 1952, pp. 2 and 4, cited in Cohen, *Economic Problems of Free Japan*, p. 18.

[18] *Statistical Yearbook of the United Nations for 1951*, pp. 292–93, cited in Cohen, *Economic Problems of Free Japan*, p. 16.

level of exports.[19] That balance threatened to deteriorate even further due to the 30.5 percent devaluation of the British pound against the U.S. dollar in September 1949.[20]

Virtually all observers agree that the period between the onset of the Dodge Line in February 1949 and the outbreak of the Korean War, the heart of the *butsujō sōzen no jidai* (period of confused feelings), was one of the most tense in postwar Japanese political history. Inflation was rampant, the cities were jammed with people due to immigration and demobilization, wages were low, and wildcat strikes were common.[21] During the summer and fall of 1949, more than 100,000 workers were dismissed from the Japan National Railways alone, and many more were released nationwide, leading to a sharp wave of labor unrest. On July 6, 1949, the dismembered body of Shimoyama Sadanori, president of the Japan National Railways, was found beside a railroad track in suburban Tokyo, two days after he had handed out dismissal notices to 37,000 railroad employees. Ten days later a driverless train rammed at full throttle into Mitaka station, also in suburban Tokyo, killing six bystanders. On August 17, another train was derailed, apparently due to sabotage, at Matsukawa in Fukushima Prefecture, deepening further the specter of labor violence looming over Japan.[22]

Tensions rose further early in 1950. During January, the Cominform in Moscow sharply criticized Japan Communist party (JCP) leader Nosaka Sanzō's peaceful parliamentary tactics, stimulating a process of further radicalization within the Left. On May 30 several U.S. officers who had come to witness a left-oriented "National Meeting of the People" in the outer grounds of Tokyo's Imperial Palace and had taken some pictures were badly mauled by demonstrators. Meanwhile, *Akahata*, the JCP party newspaper, was keeping up a steady stream of sharp and often provocative criticism of the occupation; this culminated with a

[19] Supreme Commander for the Allied Powers, "International Transactions of Japan," August 8, 1950, cited in Jerome B. Cohen, *Economic Problems of Free Japan*, p. 62.

[20] The British devaluation on September 18, 1949, caused thirty other nations to devalue, just after Japan had pegged its currency at ¥360 to the dollar. Sterling devaluation thus rendered the yen overvalued in major export markets. See Chalmers Johnson, *MITI and the Japanese Miracle*, pp. 199–200.

[21] Chalmers Johnson, *Conspiracy at Matsukawa*, p. 48.

[22] For a detailed, trenchant analysis of the Matsukawa incident, its turbulent political background, and the legal-political process of assessing guilt, see *ibid.*, pp. 108–395.

large picture of Kim Il-Sung and laudatory treatment of North Korea on its front page the day after the invasion of South Korea in June 1950, in retaliation for which SCAP decreed suspension of publication for thirty days.[23]

Shaken by both political unrest and the dismal state of the Japanese economy, the Tokyo Stock Exchange index declined from 150 to 101 in the first quarter of 1950 alone. Stock sales for the whole of 1950 were only slightly over half of their relatively meager levels in 1949. Amidst this crisis of economic confidence, Japan's population was soaring at a rate of 4,500 people a day, or 1.6 million a year.

Had matters continued as they were in the spring of 1950, the Yoshida administration might well have left office as a discredited Japanese "Hoover" administration, despite its strong initial electoral mandate.[24] But the Korean War intervened. Within six weeks of war's outbreak on June 25, 1950, the U.S. military had placed $40 million in special procurement orders with Japanese firms, an amount that grew to a total of $4 billion by June 1954. By fall 1950, the Japanese economy had begun to recover, labor unrest had diminished, and the overall sense of economic crisis that had hung heavily over the nation only six months before had begun to abate. Despite temporary economic recovery with the Korean War boom, economic fluctuations continued to buffet Japan during the 1950–1954 period.[25] The protracted Korean truce negotiations during 1951–1953 created considerable uncertainty, as did perennial balance of payments difficulties. Moreover, the recessions of 1951 and 1954 triggered a large number of bankruptcies.

Political tensions also continued, and even intensified, leading to a new phase of the early postwar crisis. This phase, stretching from the onset of war in June 1950 through the resignation of Yoshida Shigeru as prime minister in December 1954, juxtaposed for most of its duration deep and complex political divisions and rapid economic growth. Following the end of the Korean War in June 1953, Japan fell into temporary recession, but the political tensions continued until "One Man" Yoshida, who had taken leadership of the Liberal party from Hatoyama Ichirō following the latter's purge in 1946, was finally deposed.

[23] Yoshida Shigeru, *Yoshida Memoirs*, p. 239.

[24] Chalmers Johnson, *Conspiracy*, p. 24.

[25] Chalmers Johnson, *MITI and the Japanese Miracle*, pp. 218–19.

Activities of the Left throughout 1950–1954 continually stimulated a sense of disquiet among conservative politicians and businessmen. The Japan Communist party, as noted above, had moved sharply left. In April 1950 the Left elected Ninagawa Torazō, former economics professor and first head of the Small Business Agency, as governor of Kyoto, where he was able to declaim sharply against conservative policies. The looming presence of Communist-controlled mainland China, the shadowy Mecca to which JCP leader Tokuda Kyūichi had fled during the Red Purge and whose egalitarian welfare and employment policies held such attraction for Japanese intellectuals, also disconcerted the conservatives.

The end of the occupation in April 1952 introduced the prospect of further challenge for the conservatives from the Left. As Yoshida Shigeru points out, it meant the end of a range of major control measures, such as the Organizational Control Law, which had been introduced under SCAP directives to restrain the Communists and other allegedly radical groups.[26] On May Day, 1952, just three days after the end of the occupation, there was a major, violent confrontation before the Imperial Palace in Tokyo, in which two demonstrators were killed.

The end of the occupation also meant the removal of military censorship and a new barrage of criticism for the conservatives and their American allies. For example, previously suppressed pictures and accounts of the Hiroshima and Nagasaki atomic bombings were suddenly widely circulated in the mass media. This inevitably stimulated new feelings of revulsion against war and political polarization within Japan.

Gradually, the conservatives recovered many of their major powers to control the Left, although they failed to introduce a Japanese analogue to the U.S. House of Representatives Un-American Activities Committee, as Yoshida had initially desired.[27] In July 1952 a Subversive Activities Prevention Law was passed in Japan; it provided many of the control powers of its occupation period analogue. But the onus for such measures shifted after 1952 from the Allied occupation to the Japanese conservatives themselves, with many on the Left fighting Yoshida's proposed measures as a new version of the repressive Peace Pres-

[26] Yoshida Shigeru, *Yoshida Memoirs*, p. 234.

[27] *Ibid.*

ervation Law of 1925. These developments polarized Japanese politics and raised overall political tensions.

One final major source of unease from the Left for Japanese conservatives during the early 1950s was the labor movement. By French or Italian standards, of course, the Japanese labor movement was miniscule and somewhat divided politically. But it was nevertheless a formidable presence in a still poor and turbulent land relatively unaccustomed to intense, class-oriented confrontation. In 1953 the Labor Ministry reported the existence of 30,129 unions with 5.842 million members, constituting 40.9 percent of all workers. These totals showed a decline from the apex of March 1949, when 56 percent of all Japanese workers were organized. But these still represented spectacular growth from 973 unions and 420,589 members (6 percent of the work force) in the prewar peak year of 1936.[28] The recession at the end of the Korean War was punctuated by two major strikes that caught national attention and galvanized the Left, much as the Miike strike in the coal mines of Kyūshū was to do in 1960: first, in 1954, a major dispute erupted between Mitsui Mining and its work force; also in 1954, the six-month strike at the Japan Steel Works in Muroran, Hokkaidō began.

Sharp rivalries within conservative ranks paralleled the activism of the opposition during 1950–1954 to create the prospects of interactive crisis, typically such a powerful stimulus to policy innovation in postwar Japan. Rivalries between Prime Minister Yoshida Shigeru and his predecessor Ashida Hitoshi, leader of the Democratic party, were sharpened with the gradual return to public life of nearly 100,000 politicians, bureaucrats, and businessmen who had been purged for wartime activities. Between October 1950 and August 1951, Hatoyama Ichirō, Kishi Nobusuke, Ishibashi Tanzan, Kōno Ichirō, and several other prominent, charismatic public figures of the prewar and wartime period were depurged, and several immediately began planning entry or reentry into political life.[29] Hatoyama, purged on the eve of be-

[28] Allan B. Cole, *Japanese Society and Politics*, p. 95.

[29] The lifting of the purge came in four major waves. On October 13, 1950, 10,090 members of the bureaucratic, financial, and political worlds were depurged, including Ōkubo Tomejirō, Andō Masazumi, and Makino Ryōzō, all followers of Hatoyama. On June 20, 1951, 2,958 people, including Ishibashi Tanzan, Miki Bukichi, and Kōno Ichirō, were depurged, followed by 66,425 more on July 2, 1951. Finally, on August 6, 1951, 13,904 people were depurged, including Ha-

coming prime minister in 1946, directly challenged Yoshida, and many of the other purgees sided with Hatoyama as well.

The Hatoyama faction of the Liberal party began political activities in January 1952. The next month, another essentially conservative group, the Reform party (*Kaishintō*), was founded with Miki Takeo as secretary general. In April the Japan Reconstruction League (*Nihon Saiken Renmei*) was established, with Kishi Nobusuke as chairman. All of these groups vigorously challenged the preeminence of Yoshida, just as the Allied occupation was ending, and intensified the political turbulence of the period.

The Liberal party, led by Yoshida, narrowly retained its Diet majority in the October 1952 general elections. While all thirty-five JCP Dietmen lost their seats, both the Left and the Right Socialists remained viable political forces, and opponents of Yoshida on the Right were significantly strengthened. On the right, both ex-Colonel Tsuji Masanobu, the strategist behind the conquest of Singapore, and Kuhara Fusanosuke, the former Manchurian industrialist, were elected to the Diet by heavy majorities, in what Robert Scalapino then saw as "an ominous sign of the times."[30]

The newly formed fourth Yoshida cabinet lasted only six months. The Opposition was continually attacking the Yoshida government for its restrictions on trade with China and its plan to scrap occupation reforms by centralizing the police and educational systems. Meanwhile, the Hatoyama backers periodically withheld support from Yoshida, embarrassing him and weakening his political position. Ultimately twenty-two of the Hatoyama rebels and other conservative dissidents voted for a no-confidence motion introduced by the Opposition, bringing down the government. In the subsequent elections, held on April 19, 1953, Yoshida's Liberals, losing their majority in the Diet, were forced into a precarious and unstable alliance with the right-oriented Kaishintō.

Throughout the rest of 1953 the turmoil in conservative ranks continued, intensified early in 1954 by the shipbuilding scandal, in which Yoshida had to intervene personally to prevent the arrest of the Liberal party's secretary general, Satō Eisaku. On April

---

toyama himself. For details, see Masumi Junnosuke, *Postwar Politics in Japan*, pp. 279–81.

[30] Robert Scalapino, "Japan and the General Elections," *Far Eastern Survey* 21, no. 15 (October 29, 1952), p. 154. On the intensifying activities of the right during this period, see Robert Guillain, "The Resurgence of Military Elements in Japan."

24, 1954, a no-confidence vote against Yoshida presented jointly by the Right and the Left Socialists failed by twenty votes. Within a month, the Kashintō had proposed a new conservative party to be established following the ouster of Yoshida; by October this proposal had received major support within the business world.[31] When Yoshida returned from a two month round-the-world diplomatic trip, he was deposed by a broad coalition of forces within both the Liberal party and the opposition, with Hatoyama and the Socialist Party, despite their ideological differences, threatening a joint resolution of no-confidence if Yoshida did not leave.

Some might view the conservative merger of October 1955 as a watershed ending Japan's early postwar political crisis. But the fall of the fifth Yoshida cabinet on December 7, 1954, and the formation of the Hatoyama cabinet three days later, seem more fundamental in terms of my analytical framework for three reasons. First, Yoshida's fall in late 1954, rather than the formal conservative merger that followed, more significantly reduced tensions within conservative ranks. If anything, the merger intensified rivalries within the ranks of the Right, as conservative politicians realized within two years of the merger. The unusual character of the Japanese electoral system, as conservatives soon learned, produced this rather surprising result.[32]

Second, the merger of 1955 did not produce much more de facto unity within conservative ranks than had existed at the end of 1954, since both the *zaikai* and most of the conservative political world had already agreed on a conservative merger by that point. However, the departure of Yoshida led to a major reduction of tensions within conservative ranks; it removed the smoldering, highly personalized conflict between Hatoyama, the original Liberal party leader in 1946, and Yoshida, who had refused to concede the chairmanship of the Liberal party back to Hatoyama when Hatoyama was depurged in 1951.

And third, December 1954 also proved a watershed in relations between the conservatives and the Left, mainly due to Hatoyama's policy of rapproachment with the Soviet Union and main-

[31] On October 7, 1954, for example, five major business leaders agreed publically on the importance of Yoshida's ouster and a conservative merger. See Tōyama Shigeki, *Shiryō: Sengo Ni Jyū Nen Shi*, Vol. 6, p. 136.

[32] This, of course, was a major reason why the conservatives tried to modify the multimember district electoral system in 1956. See Kishi Nobusuke, *Kishi Nobusuke Kaikoroku* (*The Kishi Nobusuke Memoirs*), pp. 230–36.

land China. On February 4, 1955, after receiving expressions of Soviet interest, the Hatoyama cabinet formally voted to enter negotiations with the USSR for normalization of relations.[33] These negotiations were on-going for virtually all of Hatoyama's tenure as prime minister.[34] Thus, although Hatoyama also made proposals which sharply alienated him from the Left, including those for constitutional revision and accelerated military spending, there were always important elements of parallelism between his positions and those of the opposition regarding detente with the Soviet Union and China. This parallelism helped to dampen left-right political conflict more generally.

With the coming of Hatoyama, the deep turbulence which characterized the Japanese political process from 1949–1954 was thus temporarily at an end. Stability was further reinforced in late January 1956 by the sudden death, amidst the twenty-fourth Diet special session just weeks before the first LDP presidential election, of Ogata Taketora, Hatoyama's arch-rival, and leader of the former Liberal Party Dietmen, who were the least enthusiastic supporters of the conservative merger and the fledgling LDP.[35] Yoshida Shigeru, Liberal prime minister until December 1954 and long Ogata's superior, continued to harbor deep antagonism against Hatoyama, and he himself did not join the LDP until February 1957, after Hatoyama's prime ministership had ended. Ogata's death threw the former Liberals into disarray, paved the way for a succession of three former Democrats (Hatoyama, Ishibashi, and Kishi) as prime ministers, and muted internal tensions enough within the LDP to assure its survival, widely considered problematic in late 1955.

Economic Development and Political Turmoil: 1958–1960

The second major period of crisis for the Japanese conservatives, as figure 2.1 suggests, began in fall 1958. In this case, economic

[33] On the details of these negotiations, see Donald Hellman, *Japanese Domestic Politics and Foreign Policy*.

[34] The decision to begin them came within two months of Hatoyama's becoming prime minister, and he resigned within two months of their conclusion.

[35] Journalists recognized at the time the importance of Ogata's death for inter-factional balance within the fledgling LDP, but that it could be a major event in the long-run survival of one-party conservative dominance in Japan they could not, of course, know. See *Asahi Shimbun*, January 29, 1956.

circumstances were far less threatening than during 1949–1950, and imminent social disorder, which so unsettled Japan in the earlier period, was not a threat. But the shadow of economic uncertainty was nevertheless quite real. Under the impact of Bank of Japan deflationary policies to control an emerging balance of payments crisis, industrial production and wholesale prices fell 10 percent between the second quarter of 1957 and the first quarter of 1958. In its 1958 Economic White Paper, the Economic Planning Agency was extremely pessimistic about the prospects of early recovery.[36] Indeed, this recession, which actually reached its nadir in June 1958, was known as the "bottom of the pot" recession (*nabezoko fukyō*), with a prospectively flat, slow recovery path rather than the V-shaped trajectory of rapid recovery which had occurred during 1954–1955.[37]

Memories of recession as Japan was just returning to high growth coincided in late 1958 with a highly combustible mixture of political developments. These developments called into question both the continued preeminence of conservative governments over the major left-oriented opposition parties, and the internal unity of the fledgling conservative party itself. This second period of domestic crisis for the conservatives began amidst reports of an 18 percent fall in public support for the ruling Liberal Democrats following their qualified general election triumph of May 1958.[38] Amidst an intensifying international crisis over Quemoy and Matsu,[39] controversial within Japan given the confrontation involved with mainland China, the Kishi administration declared its clear intention of strengthening the Self-Defense Forces on August 28 and renewing (albeit renegotiating) the United States-Japan Security Treaty on September 11. Kishi also

[36] See Economic Planning Agency (Keizai Kikaku Chō), ed., *Keizai Hakusho 1958* (*1958 Economic White Paper*).

[37] See Uchino Tatsurō, *Japan's Postwar Economy*, p. 103.

[38] In the May 22 Lower House elections, the first following LDP and JSP unification in 1955, the LDP polled 287 seats, or 61.5 percent of the total. But the Socialists gained 166, ten more than they had held before the elections, to deny the LDP the two-thirds majority the conservatives needed to achieve constitutional revision. Following the election, popular support for the LDP fell sharply, from 46.3 percent in June 1958, immediately after the elections, to only 27.3 percent by December 1958. See Jiji Tsūshin Sha, ed. *Sengo Nihon no Seitō to Naikaku* (*Postwar Japanese Parties and Cabinets*), p. 21.

[39] On August 24, 1958, the Chinese Air Force made its first attack on Nationalist-held Quemoy, with the United States immediately responding by ordering a Seventh Fleet alert in the Formosa Straits. See *Asahi Shimbun*, August 25, 1958.

introduced a highly controversial police bill on October 8, proposing, in the view of opponents, to revive important features of the prewar police system. It was presented to the Diet just four days after the formal opening of the MacArthur-Fujiyama talks on Security Treaty revision.

To a much greater extent than previous conservative administrations, the Kishi cabinet was often purposely confrontational in its relationship to the opposition, particularly to the Left. This showed up clearly, for example, in the Diet. Between 1955 and 1958, the LDP had split committee chairmanships with the opposition in some rough proportion to overall Diet strength. This arrangement gave those out of government leverage over the legislative process, disproportionate to their actual numerical strength, especially in such areas as labor relations and welfare. Kishi reversed this.[40]

In the police bill controversy, the Kishi government was provocative with respect to substance as well as procedure.[41] This bill, had it been passed, would have substantially enlarged the powers of the police in preventive action, including interrogation, search, and arrest. The Left violently opposed the bill on the grounds it would violate basic human rights and return Japan to a police state. In protest the Socialists boycotted the Diet and barricaded committee rooms to prevent deliberations. To circumvent this obstructionism, the Kishi government extended the Diet session three days before its scheduled end in a surprise maneuver; this move in turn led to strikes and workshop rallies by four million people as well as severe condemnation by the press.

After weeks of turmoil, Kishi on November 22 finally agreed to shelve the bill, leaving a residue of both ill will and political vulnerability that complicated many of his subsequent policy initiatives. In the wake of his police bill defeat, Kishi confronted an "interactive" crisis. On December 27, 1958, three of the most prominent members of Kishi's cabinet—Ikeda Hayato, Miki Takeo, and Nadao Hirokichi—suddenly resigned and demanded

[40] From 1955 to 1958, for example, Japan Socialist party members had chaired the finance, education, local administration, telecommunications, and accounting committees in the Lower House, despite the JSP's minority party status. Kishi rescinded these concessions to the JSP. See Satō and Matsuzaki, *Jimintō Seiken*, pp. 346–47.

[41] For details on the points at issue and the course of events, see George R. Packard, III, *Protest in Tokyo*, pp. 101–5. Formally this was a bill to revise the Police Duties Performance Law.

sweeping personnel changes in the Kishi administration. Although this group was repudiated in the LDP presidential election called a month later, intraparty strife continued and intensified. On June 12, 1959, longtime Kishi supporter Kōno Ichirō, annoyed at not being selected LDP secretary general as he had anticipated, abruptly broke with Kishi and declared heatedly that he would henceforth accept no cabinet or party post under Kishi.[42] Only a hasty deal with Ikeda Hayato, naming Ikeda MITI minister, allowed Kishi to continue in power at all. And he faced rising domestic opposition, as he headed into crucial negotiations over the United States-Japan Security Treaty.

Relations with the United States during 1958–1960 had crucial importance for Japanese conservatives in government and big business. The United States provided a security umbrella for Japan in an increasingly turbulent world. The United States also provided crucial markets for the Japanese exports that seemed in political danger during this period, following U.S. protectionist moves in cotton textiles.[43] Together with multinational financial institutions which the United States dominated, such as the World Bank, American bankers were cautiously beginning to play a major role as capital supplier in the development of Japanese utilities and heavy industry, particularly steel.

Balance of payments constraints were continually the major cap on Japanese growth during this period, as had been demonstrated painfully to Japanese planners during the Jimmu boom of 1956–1957. As the economy became overheated, demand for imported raw materials and capital goods expanded sharply, resulting in a balance of payments crisis. Foreign currency reserves fell from $910 million at the end of 1956 to $455 million in Septem-

[42] Kōno remained bitterly hostile to Kishi throughout the ensuing year of crisis, and he was one of the few LDP Dietmen to purposely absent themselves from the midnight snap vote in May 1960 at which Kishi's valued United States-Japan Security Treaty was passed.

[43] In December 1955, in the midst of rising congressional agitation for quotas, the Japanese government imposed "voluntary" limitations on textile exports to the United States. In January 1957, the two nations imposed further limitations in a five-year bilateral agreement, once again in the midst of interest group pressure. See John Lynch, *Toward an Orderly Market*, pp. 67–125; and I. M. Destler, Haruhiro Fukui, and Hideo Satō, *The Textile Wrangle*, pp. 29–30. In response to these incipient protectionist moves in the United States, Keidanren set up a U.S. Trade Committee (*Taibei Bōeki Iinkai*) on January 30, 1958. This committee cautiously monitored United States-Japan trade developments throughout the turbulent 1958–1960 period and in the years of stability which followed.

ber 1957. The government was forced to apply for IMF loans of $87 million in July 1957 and of $50 million in August, simultaneously submitting to the IMF administrative guidance it considered onerous. [44] Foreign investment, which Japan since Meiji had traditionally spurned as compromising national sovereignty, was attractive as a partial solution to the growth and foreign exchange dilemma posed so acutely by the Jimmu boom and the foreign exchange crisis that followed. This was especially true of loans and bonds that did not involve foreign equity participation in Japanese firms. Japanese interest in loans from American banks was stimulated still further by efforts of the World Bank and other multilateral aid institutions to disengage from lending in Japan as the Japanese economy "graduated" from the ranks of the developing world to advanced nation status.

Japan moved on several fronts during the late 1950s to encourage American investment and loans. On February 13, 1958, Finance Minister Ichimada Naoto proposed creation of an Asian Development Bank to senior visiting American ICA (International Cooperation Administration) officials.[45] And on October 2 his successor as finance minister, Satō Eisaku,[46] formally announced preparations for the first Japanese corporate issues of dollar-denominated bonds.[47] As indicated in table 2.1, $30 million in such bonds were issued overseas in 1958—the first stage of what was to become a major source of capital for Japanese firms during the 1961–1964 period.[48] In addition, foreign loans to Japanese firms nearly doubled during fiscal 1958,[49] as table 2.1 suggests, and restrictions on capital participation in Japanese firms were also relaxed in late July 1959 to permit expanded foreign stock purchases. Yet American capital seemed clearly wary of aggressive commitments in Japan, especially in the midst of po-

[44] See Uchino, *Postwar Economy*, pp. 98–102.

[45] *Nihon Keizai Shimbun*, February 14, 1958.

[46] Prime Minister during 1964–1972, Satō was also, of course, the brother of Prime Minister Kishi, although they had different surnames, since Kishi had been adopted into another family.

[47] *Nihon Keizai Shimbun*, October 3, 1958.

[48] *Nihon Keizai Shimbun*, July 22, 1959.

[49] Among the major new foreign loans to Japanese firms during 1958 were an $80 million World Bank loan to Kawasaki Steel; a $15.8 million U.S. Export-Import Bank loan to Tokyo Power and to Kansai Power; a $29.2 million World Bank loan to Chūbu Power; and a $22 million World Bank loan to Nippon Kōkan. See Tōyama Shigeki, ed., *Shiryō: Sengo Ni Jyū Nen Shi* (*Data: A History of the Twenty Postwar Years*), Vol. 6, pp. 162–68.

TABLE 2.1

The Volatile History of Foreign Lending to Japan, 1950–1970 (in U.S. $ million)

	Stock Transactions	Bank Loans	Foreign Bonds	Total
1950	3	—		3
1951	13	4		17
1952	10	34		45
1953	5	49		55
1954	4	15		19
1955	5	47		52
1956	10	94		103
1957	11	124		136
1958	11	231	30	273
1959	27	128		155
1960	74	127	10	212
1961	116	388	72	578
1962	165	358	155	679
1963	185	504	194	884
1964	84	651	175	913
1965	83	380	63	529
1966	127	330		457
1967	160	638	50	848
1968	670	947	219	1,837
1969	2,463	740	235	3,488
1970	1,556	846	122	2,624

Source: Masaki Hisashi, *Nihon no Kabushiki Kaisha Kinyū (Japanese Corporate Finance)* (Kyoto: Minerva Shobō, 1973), p. 237.

Note:[1] Figures are for Japanese fiscal year (April 1–March 31).[2] Results are not perfectly additive, due to rounding.

litical turbulence. As indicated in table 2.1, the sharp increase in American lending to Japan during 1958 was reversed in 1959, as domestic political tensions in Tokyo continued to build.

It is within this context of deepening United States-Japan economic relationships, particularly in a financial sector uniquely sensitive to political risk, that the United States-Japan Security Treaty negotiations, and the accompanying turbulence, must be seen. The importance of foreign trade and foreign capital to stable

Japanese economic growth—sensed particularly strongly by the big business world and such bureaucrats-turned politicians as Ikeda Hayato[50]—intensified an already strong stability bias in the Japanese political world. These economic developments increased both the apprehension of Japanese conservatives at the turbulence which steadily deepened during 1958–1960 and simultaneously their willingness to countenance a broad range of welfare and redistributive policies, largely originating with the opposition, as the price for stability.

Another important backdrop to the security treaty crisis, heightening its drama and intensifying the fervor of the Left, was the bitter, at times bloody, Miike strike, the longest in Japanese history. Taking place at Ōmuta, in the aging coal mines of northern Kyūshū, this year-long struggle broke out to protest what labor considered to be management's arbitrary efforts to rationalize the coal industry in the face of rising imports of cheaper oil. The heart of the confrontation began January 25, 1960, with a lockout of 15,000 miners by Mitsui Mining, following the breakdown of discussions on rationalization. Throughout the spring and summer of 1960, as the security treaty crisis began to build in Tokyo, the Miike mines and plants of Mitsui Mining were continually besieged by over ten thousand strikers and their supporters. Massive demonstrations and rallies occurred almost daily, and Sōhyō is said to have mobilized at least 350,000 outside supporters at various points to mount a vigil at Miike.[51] In response, the government mobilized 530,000 policemen, in addition to local constabularies, company guards, and others, to more than equal the opposition. The combined forces of government and opposition who massed at Miike, as Labor Minister Ishida Hirohide pointed out, came to more than the total that fought in the great Satsuma Rebellion (*Seinan Sensō*) early in the Meiji period.[52]

Paralleling the highly visible drama at Miike, reported incessantly and sensationally by the Japanese media, was a related, but

[50] Ikeda served as minister without portfolio in the second Kishi cabinet (June–December 1958), as MITI minister in the third Kishi cabinet (June 1959–July 1960), and subsequently as prime minister (1960–1964).

[51] John G. Roberts, *Mitsui*, p. 459. All Miike figures are cumulative totals of successive mobilizations.

[52] Ishida Hirohide, *Watakushi no Seikai Shōwa Shi* (*My History of the Shōwa Political World*), p. 109. The Satsuma Rebellion (Jan. 29–Sept. 24, 1877) was the last major armed uprising to protest the reforms of the Meiji government.

less well-known train of events in the political world. The Diet and the major political parties all took up the Miike struggle as a major object of inquiry. Both houses of the Diet sent study missions to Miike, and three committees within the ruling LDP took up the problem, slowing legislative progress on other matters and heightening tensions within the Diet as it prepared to consider the United States-Japan Security Treaty.[53]

The already well-known political story of the 1960 United States-Japan Security Treaty crisis need not be recapitulated in detail here.[54] Negotiations on a new pact began in November 1958 to replace what was broadly conceived in Japan as an "unequal treaty" negotiated under the duress of occupation, giving U.S. forces broad rights to intervene in Japanese domestic affairs. The completed treaty revision was signed by Prime Minister Kishi, U.S. Secretary of State Christian Herter, and others on January 19, 1960, in the East Room of the White House, with President Dwight D. Eisenhower looking on, and appeared initially as a major political achievement for Kishi. Both before and after the apparently successful signing, major American investment missions visited Japan, exploring prospects for expanded business cooperation.[55]

The Eisenhower state visit, which held substantial symbolic and practical significance for the Japanese conservatives, was

[53] On political investigations into the Miike controversy, focusing particularly on Liberal Democratic party investigations and findings, see Mitsui Kōzan Kabushiki Kaisha, ed., *Miike Sōgi* (*The Miike Dispute*). Tokyo: Nihon Keieisha Dantai Renmei, 1963, pp. 885–87.

[54] For a detailed, scholarly, and highly readable account, see Packard, *Protest in Tokyo*, especially pp. 125–331.

[55] Between October 23 and October 28, 1959, for example, a major investment mission visited Tokyo to attend a Business International conference and undertake plant tours and commercial discussions. A U.S. steel industry delegation headed by U.S. Steel Corporation Vice President Young arrived in Tokyo on January 23, just two days after the ratification, while a large U.S. securities industry mission arrived on May 8, 1960. Japanese executives who dealt with American securities industry delegation described them as impressed with the growth potential of the Japanese economy and Japanese firms, but they were worried about Japanese debt-equity ratios, particularly in view of declining World Bank support for Japan. They were also apparently concerned about the prospect of nationalization in the electric power and steel industries, the major candidates for American loans. This concern was not lessened by the political turmoil of the period. See "Doru Chōtasu no Kanōsei to Genkai" ("The Prospects for and Limitations on Raising Dollar Funds"), *Ekonomisuto* (May 31, 1960), pp. 6–18, especially p. 9.

scheduled to begin June 20, 1960. As John Roberts points out, this milestone in Japan's postwar resurgence was anticipated by the business world as heralding a new era of cooperation, expanded trade, and increased foreign investment.[56] Pending at the time of the visit were World Bank loans on the order of $100 million for the development of basic industry, transportation, and communications; an Arabian Oil Company $100 million loan for oil-well development in Kuwait; and final resolution of repayment terms for Japan's $2-billion debt to the United States for early postwar assistance.[57] Many other industrial firms were still negotiating for loans or for the floatation of bonds on Wall Street.

But the treaty ratification process within Japan proved stormy and violent, shaking Japanese conservatism to its roots, and casting fleeting shadows over the rapidly intensifying United States-Japan economic relationship. The treaty was ultimately ratified in an abruptly called midnight Diet session involving forcible removal of protesting Socialist Dietmen by the police from the Diet Chamber.[58] But several LDP Dietmen, including leaders of two powerful factions, refused to participate, thus dramatically underlining deep intraparty tensions.[59] The forceful way in which the treaty was passed triggered massive demonstrations. On three separate occasions in June fifty industrial unions, with 800,000 members in all, staged the biggest political strikes in Japanese history. On the climactic day, June 15, 1960, these demonstrations left hundreds of students and police injured, 18 police trucks totally destroyed, 196 students arrested, and a Tokyo University student activist crushed to death in turbulence which swirled through the streets of Tokyo until 4:30 A.M. the next

[56] John Roberts, *Mitsui*, p. 461.

[57] *Ibid.*

[58] This was only the second time in postwar history that the police had entered the National Diet chamber. The first time was on June 2, 1956, in a House of Councillors dispute over educational bills. On June 3, 1954, police had entered the Diet Building, ironically in connection with passage of legislation establishing the National Police Agency. But they did not at that time enter the Diet Chamber. See Packard, *Protest in Tokyo*, p. 241.

[59] Among the LDP Dietmen who refused to participate in the snap midnight vote through which the United States-Japan Security Treaty was passed were former Prime Minister Ishibashi Tanzan, Prime Minister-to-be Miki Takeo, and senior faction leaders Kōno Ichirō and Matsumura Kenzō. Kishi Nobusuke makes a special point of listing every one of them in his memoirs. See Kishi Nobusuke. *Kishi Nobusuke Kaikoroku*, p. 548.

morning.[60] Troops of the Self Defense Forces were being readied to move into the streets of Tokyo should violence continue to escalate.[61]

Both Japanese bonds on Wall Street and the Tokyo Dow Jones stock market average plunged.[62] The turmoil forced the cancellation of President Eisenhower's Tokyo visit just three days before it was to begin, and it also induced the resignation of Prime Minister Kishi, announced on the very day that instruments of treaty ratification were exchanged. In the midst of the political turmoil, Japan's four major business federations issued a dramatic joint plea for political stability and then participated actively in the search for a new prime minister to replace Kishi.

The Tensions of Reassessment: 1960–1963

The man they found, whom some had not predicted as the immediate prime minister to be,[63] was Ikeda Hayato, longtime finance and MITI minister. The consummate technocrat, in the early 1950s Ikeda had been famous for anti-egalitarian pronouncements.[64] But in 1960, when the requirements of rapid growth so strongly dictated stability, his actions were different. Ikeda's first major step, taken the very evening of his formal installation as prime minister on July 17, was a move to solve the increasingly violent Miike strike;[65] the strike combined with the turbulence of the security treaty crisis threatened the prospect, albeit remote, of a slide toward political chaos. Since the Mitsui Mining management was at first intractable, Ikeda and his Labor Minister Ishida Hirohide mobilized key figures in the big busi-

[60] Packard, *Protest in Tokyo*, p. 297.

[61] Interview with senior U.S. Embassy staff member posted to Tokyo in 1960, Washington, D.C., April 1987.

[62] Between May 2 and June 17, 1960, the Tokyo Dow Jones average fell from ¥1101 to below ¥1000.

[63] Ishii Mitsujirō had seniority over Ikeda as Ogata Taketora's direct successor. U.S. Ambassador Douglas MacArthur cabled Washington on June 15, 1960, that he anticipated either Ikeda or Ishii as Kishi's successor, "while Yoshida could make a strong bid if he is so inclined." See MacArthur to DOS, Classified Memo, No. 4229, June 15, 1960.

[64] Among Ikeda's early technocratic, unpolitic statements were "A few small business bankruptcies cannot be prevented (1950), and "The poor should eat barley" (*Bimbōnin wa Mugi o Kue*), in 1952.

[65] Ishida Hirohide, *Watakushi no Seikai Shōwa Shi*, pp. 108–12.

ness world—Nagano Shigeo, vice president of the Japan Chamber of Commerce; Sakurada Takeshi, executive director of Nikkeiren; and Uemura Kōgorō, vice chairman of Keidanren—to help mediate with Mitsui and its bankers.[66] Within a few days movement was evident. On August 1, 1960, the Coal Mining Facilities Corporation was reorganized, with increased price subsidies and government funds for reemploying dismissed miners, buying up mining rights, and so on.[67] By November 1, 1960, the long strike was over. During the two years following the strike a major rationalization program followed in coal; it combined employment cutbacks with a sharp expansion of regional assistance for affected areas and job retraining programs, even beyond the levels of late 1960.[68] The strike also spurred broader political debates which increased pressures for policy innovation in areas of welfare policy not directly related to coal, as I will discuss in chapter 8.[69]

Apart from specific policy steps, Ikeda tried hard to defuse the tense political atmosphere of the post-treaty crisis period with his strong efforts to identify with the masses and establish some pragmatic rapport with the opposition. He appointed Japan's first female cabinet minister, denounced gold and geisha parties, and ate curried rice in small restaurants. He also cultivated the mass media, particularly the traditionally Left-oriented *Asahi Shimbun*. Ikeda's unassuming "low profile" (*teishisei*), combined with strong underlying LDP strength in rural areas and a sudden outpouring of zaikai political funds for the LDP, helped the conservatives break the political momentum which the Left had generated during the Security Treaty crisis. On July 27 the LDP handily won a major gubernatorial election in Gunma Prefecture, where antitreaty demonstrators had been quite active, by 401,000 to 214,000—virtually the same margin as in the previous elec-

[66] *Ibid.*, pp. 110–11.

[67] Chalmers Johnson, *Japan's Public Policy Companies*, p. 129.

[68] For details, see *Ibid.*, pp. 129–31; and Vogel, *Comeback*, pp. 103–13.

[69] Much of this debate was waged in the pages of *Chūō Kōron*, involving an unusually broad range of academics, union leaders, Nikkeiren executives, and LDP politicians. See, for example, Ishida Hirohide, Ōta Kaoru, and Hayakawa Masaru, "Miike Igo no Rōdō Mondai" (*Labor Problems after Miike*), *Chūō Kōron* 75, no. 9 (1960), pp. 110–36; Horie Masanori, "Miike Sōgi no Kyōkun" ("Lessons of the Miike Dispute"), *Chūō Koron* 75, no. 6 (1960), pp. 140–52; and Shimazaki Yuzuru, "Miike Sōgi Sōkatsu no tame no Hōkoku" (A Report Summarizing the Miike Dispute), *Chūō Kōron* 76, no. 6 (1961), pp. 122–36.

tions.[70] In November 1960, the voters returned the LDP to power with 296 seats, 13 more than in 1958.[71]

But the turbulence of 1958–1960 left uncertainties and tensions in both the conservative political world and in the left-right relationship which reverberated throughout the first three years of Ikeda Hayato's tenure as prime minister. These "echo effects" of crisis had a major effect on policymaking during the early 1960s, as I will show in chapter 4. First of all, Kōno Ichirō, Kishi's antagonist during 1959–1960, tried to create a new conservative party in August 1960, and he had to be continually placated by the Ikeda government even after he abandoned his separatist plans.[72]

Developments on the Left were even more dramatic and prospectively important. On October 12, 1960, Asanuma Inejirō, chairman of the JSP, was assassinated in the midst of a nationally televised preelection debate by seventeen-year-old Yamaguchi Otoya, whose father was an officer in the Self-Defense Forces. Following the nonfatal stabbings of JSP faction leader Kawakami Jōtarō (June 17) and Prime Minister Kishi (July 15) the polarization between Left and Right intensified. At a more prosaic level, seeming success with direct grassroots action during the treaty debates encouraged the Socialists to intensify local organizing with the formation of support organizations (*kōenkai*) in rural areas during the early 1960s; this, too, intensified left-right rivalries at the grassroots.[73] Communist Party grassroots membership also expanded sharply, from 40,000 in 1958 to 90,000 by 1961, after years of stagnation during the mid-1950s.[74]

Furthermore, the treaty crisis and its echo effects introduced new tensions into Japan's legislative process. The first post-treaty regular Diet session, convened in late October 1960 was dominated by denunciations of "rightist violence," epitomized by the assassination of Japan Socialist Party Chairman Asanuma Inejirō

[70] Packard, *Protest in Tokyo*, p. 324.

[71] For details on the election, see Douglas H. Mendel, Jr., "Behind the 1960 Japanese Diet Election," *Asian Survey* (March 1961), pp. 3–12.

[72] Kōno served under Ikeda as minister of agriculture (July 1961–July 1962), minister of construction (July 1962–July 1964), and as special minister without portfolio responsible for the Tokyo Olympics (July–November 1964).

[73] Some Socialists opposed the existence of Kōenkai within the JSP. See for example, Taguchi Fukuji, "Nihon Shakaitō Ron" ("A Theory of the Japan Socialist Party"), *Chūō Kōron* 76 (1961), p. 41.

[74] See Nihon Seiji Keizai Kenkyū Jo, *Nikkyō no Tebiki* (*An Introduction to the Japan Communist Party*), various issues. Also Packard, *Protest in Tokyo*, p. 314.

only five days before the sessions began.[75] Despite an eloquent, carefully prepared tribute to Asanuma by the new conservative Prime Minister Ikeda,[76] Diet proceedings remained turbulent and slow. The issue of arbitrary violence continued to dominate proceedings throughout the session, impeding the progress of regular legislation.

The legacy of arbitrary LDP Diet management left by the crisis encouraged the conservatives to make institutional changes enhancing the ability of opposition parties to affect policymaking. Chairmanships of six upper house committees, for example, were newly awarded to the Socialists, despite their minority party status.[77] The heritage of 1960 also rendered opposition obstructionist efforts within the Diet more legitimate in the eyes of the public. This combination of circumstances effectively gave the opposition more of a veto on government legislation than it previously held. The Ikeda Cabinet only got 71 percent of the bills it proposed through the 1961 regular Diet session, the lowest proportion in many years,[78] at a time when rapid economic change created pressures for legislative decisiveness from the business world. The bills that in fact passed reflected opposition views much more clearly than had been the case for several years.

Most importantly, perhaps, the security treaty crisis set the Socialists to thinking more creatively about means of actually appealing for political power, while also stimulating conservatives to sense their political frailty. The crisis, as Reischauer pointed out in its aftermath, had "left a curious sense of excitement, even euphoria, among intellectuals. Since they feel that the greatest weakness of democracy in Japan is the apathy and political inexperience of the people, they view the mass response of the city crowds, and particularly of themselves, to the political crisis as symbolizing the beginning of true democracy in Japan."[79] Yet

[75] See Dai San Jyū Rokkai Kokkai, *Shūgiin Kaigi Roku* (*Record of Lower House Proceedings*), October 17, 1960.

[76] Ikeda apparently accorded this address considerable priority, and Itō Masaya, Ikeda's secretary at the time, spent considerable time on its preparation. See Itō Masaya, *Ikeda Hayato to Sono Jidai*, pp. 117–29.

[77] Upper House Telecommunications, Construction, Audit, and Punishment Committee chairmanships were awarded to the Socialists during 1962, in a classic parliamentary case of "crisis and compensation." See Satō and Matsuzaki, *Jiminto Seiken*, p. 351.

[78] *Ibid.*

[79] Edwin O. Reischauer, "The Broken Dialogue with Japan," *Foreign Affairs* (October 1960), p. 23.

these intellectuals and their political compatriots in the opposition were also painfully aware of how unresponsive the periphery of Japan had been to progressive appeals in 1960, as evidenced by the string of overwhelming defeats in prefectural and national elections they suffered only weeks after the massive demonstrations in Tokyo and the cancellation of Eisenhower's visit.

Among the earliest and most influential steps in the Socialist reassessment which followed the security treaty crisis was JSP Secretary General Eda Saburō's piece in the October 1960 issue of *Sekai*, in which he stressed that the Left had been led by the masses, rather than leading them.[80] For Eda the implications of the 1960 struggle were that the JSP needed a clearer and more pragmatic strategy for confronting conservatives all across Japan. But, in his view, Diet activism, so successful in dramatizing and giving visibility to the issues the opposition wanted to stress, should certainly continue. Better Socialist organization at the grassroots also seemed to Eda imperative.

Many progressive analysts felt that the failure to create a "worker-farmer alliance" (*rōnō dōmei*) lay at the heart of the Left's failures in 1960, and they urged redoubled efforts to appeal to farmers.[81] Others, such as Asukata Ichio, stressed not class alliance but more generalized grassroots participation, particularly at the local government level.[82] Through successes at the local level, confronting conservative power through mass grassroots actions, and through progressive local governments where they existed, Japan as a whole could be changed, such progressive analysts argued.[83]

The outlines of a pragmatic, welfare-oriented Socialist strategy were prefigured at the October 1960 JSP national convention. There the party stressed the importance of redistributive policies

[80] See Eda Saburō and Shinohara Hajime, "Kakushin Seitō to shite no Hansei" ("Reflections of a Progressive Party"), *Sekai* 10, no. 178 (1960), pp. 79–86.

[81] Nakano Yoshihiko, Horikoshi Hisasuke, and Hidaka Rokurō, "Nōson o Dō Kaeruka?" ("How do we Change the Agricultural Villages?"), *Sekai* 8, no. 179 (1960), pp. 64–88. Also, Matsushita Keiichi, "Chiiki Minshushugi no Kadai to Tenbō" ("Prospects for Regional Democracy"). *Shisō* 5, no. 443 (1961).

[82] See Asukata Ichio, "Kuni no Seiji kara Chihō no Seiji e" ("From National to Local Politics"), *Sekai* 7, no. 223 (1964), pp. 142–52; Asukata Ichio, "Shakaitō e no Teigen" ("A Proposal to the Socialist Party"), *Sekai* 16, no. 263 (1967); and Asukata Ichio, "Kakushin Jichitai no San Jyū Nen" ("Thirty Years of the Progressive Local Governments"), in Ozaki Hideki, ed., *Shōwa no Sengo Shi* (*The Postwar History of Shōwa*), pp. 10–41.

[83] See Nagasu Katsuji, Narita Tomomi, and Shimizu Shinzō, "Nihon no Kōzō Kaikaku" ("Japan's Structural Reform"), *Sekai* 3, no. 183 (1961), pp. 98–114.

oriented toward peasants, small- and medium-scale businessmen, and low-income laborers.[84] The JSP's seven slogans for the general election campaign that followed included four with a strong welfare orientation, appealing for programs to aid farmers, small businessmen, the poor and aged, and the working class.[85]

JSP Secretary General Eda Saburō unveiled an expanded version of his Socialist pragmatism in his so-called "Eda Vision" (*Nikkō Danwa*) address to a JSP regional party congress in the resort city of Nikkō, July 27, 1962.[86] In many ways the program he advocated, of moderate, welfare-oriented socialism which did not imply radical social transformation, closely paralleled that which the West German Social Democrats began to evolve after the Bad Godesberg conference of 1959 and which ultimately led the German SPD to political power within a decade. But Eda faced contrasting assessments of both the problems confronting Japanese socialism and the appropriate responses.[87] Ultimately these led both to his personal political eclipse and to the demise of his pragmatic policy line.

In the wake of *Ampo*, as the security treaty crisis was known, conservatives were also more conscious of the ultimate vulnerability of conservative rule, especially in the cities.[88] As Ishida Hirohide, labor minister in the Ikeda cabinet, pointed out in *Chūō Kōron*, Japanese society was steadily changing in directions unfavorable to continued conservative preeminence.[89] With the

[84] Nihon Shakaitō, *Nihon Shakaitō no San Jyū Nen* (*Thirty Years of the Japan Socialist Party*), pp. 338–60.

[85] The other three appeals were for normalization of Japan–China relations, withdrawal of U.S. forces from Japan, and strict defense of the constitution implying the dismantling of the Self-Defense Forces. See Nihon Shakaitō Hensankai, *Nihon Shakaitō Shi* (*A History of the Japan Socialist Party*). Tokyo: Nihon Shakaitō Hensankai, 1963, p. 63.

[86] See *Asahi Shimbun*, July 28, 1962; and Tamura Yūzō, *Sengo Shakaitō no Ninaitetachi* (*The People Assuming Responsibility for the Postwar Socialist Party*), pp. 426–29.

[87] Among Eda's prominent critics was Ōta Kaoru, chairman of the huge Sōhyō labor federation. For Ōta's views on the challenge facing the JSP in the early 1960s, see Ōta Kaoru, "Shakaitō no Kōzō Kaikaku Ron ni taisuru Nanatsu no Gimon" ("Seven Questions about the Theory of Structurally Transforming the Socialist Party"), *Chūō Kōron* 3, no. 76 (1961), pp. 136–45.

[88] Astute analysts outside Japan were also sensitive to this and its broader foreign-policy implications. See, for example, Reischauer, "The Broken Dialogue with Japan," *Foreign Affairs* (October 1960), pp. 9–26.

[89] Ishida Hirohide, "Hoshu Seitō no Vision" ("Vision of a Conservative Party"). *Chūō Kōron* (January 1963), pp. 88–97.

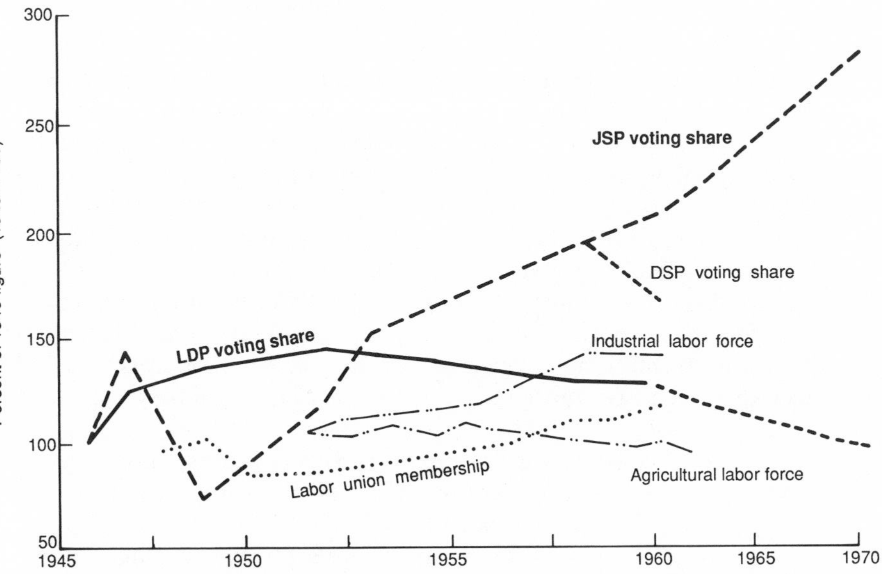

Figure 2.2. The Ishida Vision: Premonitions of Crisis for Japanese Conservatism (January 1963).

Note: Ishida did not project future support levels for the Democratic Socialist party (DSP), so no extrapolations are presented on this graph.

Source: Ishida Hirohide, "Hoshu Seitō no Vision" ("Vision of a Conservative Party"), *Chūō Kōron* (Jan. 1963), pp. 88–97.

share of manufacturing workers and union members in the Japanese electorate steadily rising and that of farmers falling, as indicated in figure 2.2, the Socialist vote would almost inevitably pass that of the LDP by 1970, Ishida forecast.

The interaction of JSP pragmatism and assertiveness with LDP defensiveness perpetuated a sense of crisis in conservative ranks which persisted throughout most of Ikeda Hayato's tenure as prime minister. Ultimately, the formal censure of Eda Saburō's pragmatic vision for Japanese socialism at the JSP national convention on November 27, 1962, coupled with a muting of intraconservative rivalries during 1964–1965 through generational change in leadership,[90] brought the extraordinary second period of crisis to a distinct end.

[90] Ōno Bamboku died on May 29, 1964; Kōno Ichirō on July 8, 1965; and Ikeda Hayato on August 13, 1965.

Interlude of Stability: 1964–1971

The eight years of Satō Eisaku's tenure as Japan's prime minister were, to be sure, turbulent and dramatic years for Japan in foreign affairs. They began with Tonkin Gulf and the deepening, bitterly controversial American involvement in Vietnam; they ended with two dramatic Nixon shocks during 1971 and return of Okinawa to Japan in May 1972. But in domestic politics these years were striking for their stability, epitomized by Satō's own record-breaking tenure in office. Only during Satō's last year in office, following massive victories by the Left in local elections (March 1971) and escalation of internal conflict within the LDP over succession to Satō from the fall of 1971, did this stability begin to seriously erode.

The Left, to be sure, was vehement in its fury against Satō, and its protests were accorded seeming force by the course of war in Southeast Asia.[91] Students occupied Tokyo University in 1969 and demonstrated militantly against Satō's policies throughout much of his tenure. The LDP majority was slowly eroding from 54.7 percent of the popular vote in 1963 to 47.6 percent in 1969. Tokyo elected a progressive governor, Minobe Ryōkichi, in a 1967 election which Satō pronounced a catastrophic loss for the LDP. This loss was compounded by the victory of new progressive candidates in Ōsaka and Kōbe, together with Minobe's reelection in Tokyo and Ninagawa's in Kyoto, during the spring of 1971.

Yet the prevailing domestic political environment until near the end of Satō's tenure was fundamentally stable, despite the superficial symbols of "camp conflict." First, erosion of LDP strength during the middle and late 1960s was largely at the hands of the middle of the road Kōmeitō; it was not coupled with a strong resurgence of the Left at the national level. As appendix 2 suggests, the LDP decline during the late 1960s almost precisely mirrored a parallel decline in support for the JSP, with the Communists not yet strong enough to cause the LDP major concern. Most importantly, these were years of generational change in conservative factional leadership. Satō was well supported by powerful party elders: Kishi was his brother, and Yoshida his longtime confidante who had brought him into politics. And the successors to leadership of the Kōno, Ōno, and Ikeda factions, all

[91] On the relationship between the Vietnam War and Japanese political developments, see Thomas Havens, *Fire across the Sea*.

prospective rivals to Satō, were still too young to effectively challenge him. This situation left the maverick Miki Takeo and the elderly Matsumura Kenzō as the sole alternatives to an LDP mainstream strongly backed by the United States and by the business world. As the new leaders of the 1970s gradually emerged, all but Nakasone Yasuhiro, successor to Kōno, were much more sharply circumscribed by intrafactional considerations than their predecessors had been ten to fifteen years before.[92]

Satō was also fortunate to enjoy extraordinarily rapid national economic growth throughout most of his tenure. After a recession in 1965, Japan's real GNP rose sharply, at annual rates averaging 12.3 percent from 1966 through 1970. Even in 1971, another recession year by the Japanese standards of the period, real GNP grew by 5.2 percent. While rapid growth inspired short-run national satisfaction and confidence, it also generated important long-run transformations in the political economy. These intensified the ultimate threat to LDP preeminence posed by urbanization and an economic structure shifting from agriculture to industry.

The Crisis of the Early 1970s

Both left-right and intraconservative political dynamics began to shift sharply during the early 1970s, as suggested in figure 2.3, bringing on the third of postwar Japanese conservatism's great interactive crises. Political change was driven by a sharp intensification of both domestic and international pressures on the Satō government, resulting from Japan's five consecutive years of double-digit economic growth (1966–1970) and the economic affluence and social transformation this produced. In 1965 Japanese GNP passed that of France, and in 1969 that of West Germany; by 1972 only the Soviet Union and the United States remained economically larger than Japan. By 1969 both MITI and the Organization for Economic Co-operation and Development (OECD) had officially recognized that Japan had a structural surplus in its bal-

[92] For a more detailed analysis of why Satō survived so long as prime minister, also stressing the leadership vacuum within the LDP and strong business support for Satō, see Takagi Sanae, Enoki Akira, and Seki Masahiko, "Satō Naikaku Chōmei no Uchimaku" ("The Inside Story of the Satō Cabinet's Long Life"), *Chūō Kōron* 85, no. 1 (1973), pp. 112–23.

ance of payments,[93] inducing growing criticism of Japan's highly reactive trading policies. These rising tensions culminated in the increasingly acrimonious United States-Japan textile negotiations and in the so-called Nixon shock of August 1971.

Domestically the explosive pace of economic growth in a crowded land was leading to rapidly intensifying urban problems—pollution, inadequate transportation infrastructure, social welfare, and rising land prices. Rapid urbanization was also spawning a mass of uprooted rural voters—now urban newcomers. As city dwellers these people were much more poorly integrated into the corporatist social structures through which the LDP perpetuated its rule than they had been in the countryside.[94] Despite important differences of economic context, there were striking parallels to the pervasive social fluidity of the late 1940s. That fluidity had also spawned deep unease among conservatives, followed by the incorporation and compensation policies of the third Yoshida cabinet after January 1949.

As figure 2.1 suggests, diffuse social anxieties and tensions were translated rather sharply during 1971–1972 into a clearly definable and relatively severe interactive crisis for Japanese conservatism. Local elections helped provoke the deepening crisis. In April 1971 Minobe Ryōkichi, the opposition coalition candidate, was reelected Tokyo governor with two-thirds of the vote; at the same time LDP incumbent governor Satō Gizen lost in Ōsaka to Kuroda Ryōichi, a JSP-JCP backed professor of constitutional law.[95] In the wake of these developments, Tokyo, Ōsaka, and Kyoto—the political, economic, commercial, educational, and cultural "capitals" of Japan—were all governed by JSP-JCP supported governors. Other progressive governors were elected in Okinawa, Saitama, and Okayama prefectures during 1972.[96]

[93] See Organization for Economic Cooperation and Development, OECD *Economic Surveys, Japan* (1969 Annual Report). Paris: OECD, 1969, p. 39; and *Ministry of International Trade and Industry* (Tsūshō Sangyō Shō), *Tsūshō Hakusho* (*White Paper on International Trade*) (Tokyo: Ōkurashō Insatsu Kyoku, 1969).

[94] In many instances, of course, this first led to political apathy rather than active political opposition. See Bradley M. Richardson, "Urbanization and Political Participation," *American Political Science Review* 67 (1973), pp. 433–52, especially pp. 447–48.

[95] On the rising strength of the Left at the local level, see Terry E. MacDougall, "Political Opposition and Local Government in Japan: The Significance of Emerging Progressive Local Leadership" (Ph.D. diss., Yale University, 1975), pp. 216–78.

[96] *Ibid.*, p. 223.

A steady stream of setbacks in foreign affairs, which undermined the credibility of the Satō government and intensified factional maneuvering within the LDP concerning the succession to Satō, closely followed local election defeats for the LDP. In July 1971 Richard Nixon suddenly announced plans for a major trip to China, giving the Satō government only an hour's notice.[97] The U.S. Ambassador to Tokyo heard about the overture on Armed Forces Radio while having a haircut.[98] A month later the United States suspended the convertibility of dollars into gold and imposed a unilateral surcharge on American imports, with U.S. Secretary of State William Rogers once again informing Prime Minister Satō on very short notice. In October the Nixon administration achieved a controversial restriction on Japanese textile exports to the United States, which many Japanese felt unjustified, and in December it successfully pressed Japan at the Smithsonian Conference for a 16.88 percent yen revaluation that many felt would severely damage the Japanese economy.

Crucial to the emergence of interactive crisis, in 1971–1972 as in 1958, was the sharp intensification of factional conflict within the ruling LDP. Supporters of MITI Minister Tanaka Kakuei, using the Nixon shocks as a point of departure, began to vigorously criticize Foreign Minister Fukuda Takeo, another prime ministerial aspirant. This rivalry, soon known as the *kaku-fuku sensō* (Tanaka–Fukuda War) for its bitterness, intensified sharply during the spring of 1972, as Satō formally announced his decision to retire. In July 1972 Tanaka, energetic parvenu from Niigata Prefecture with a fifth-grade education, defeated Fukuda—an elite graduate of Tokyo University fourteen years Tanaka's senior and Satō's heir apparent—for the prime ministership. This struggle opened wounds which remained painful for a decade and more.[99]

Full-scale interactive crisis was intensified by the crucial Lower House elections of December 1972, where LDP seats slipped sharply and alarmingly from 288 to 271. The LDP share of the popular vote also declined, as indicated in figure 2.3, contin-

[97] On the details of the disclosure process, see Henry Kissinger, *White House Years*, p. 758.

[98] Armin H. Meyer, *Assignment Tokyo*, pp. 133–37.

[99] For details on the contrasting careers of Fukuda and Tanaka, which culminated in this epic conflict, see Kent E. Calder, "Kanryō vs. Shomin: Contrasting Dynamics of Conservative Leadership in Postwar Japan," in Terry E. MacDougall, ed., *Political Leadership in Contemporary Japan*, pp. 1–31.

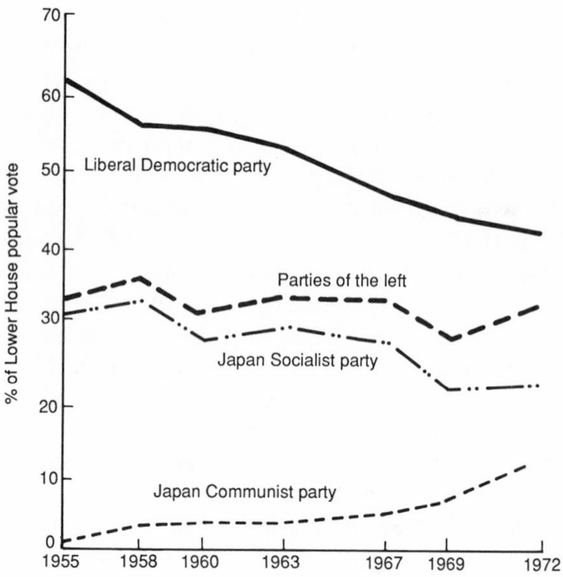

Figure 2.3. The Narrowing Left-Right Gap in National Elections, 1955–1972.
Source: Soma Masao, ed., *Kokusei Senkyo to Seitō Seiji (National Elections and Party Politics)* (Tokyo: Seiji Koho Center, 1977).

uing a steady process of decline which had given the conservatives a smaller share of the vote in every national election since 1952. Even more importantly in the eyes of conservatives, communist support soared, with JCP seat totals in the Lower House nearly tripling from fourteen to thirty-eight. Overall, the gap between conservatives and progressives as a share of the national vote had narrowed to less than half the margin of 1955, with the Communists taking a third of the progressives' total.

In some urban centers, such as Kyoto, Communists garnered well over 20 percent of the total vote in 1972, with especially heavy margins among small businessmen.[100] Tokyo, Ōsaka, and Kyoto all were witnessing a doubling of communist strength in only five years. This trend, reinforced by earlier progressive vic-

[100] Communist support in the 1972 election reached a high of 30 percent in the Kyoto I district, where it exceeded the LDP's 27.1 percent. For Kyoto as a whole the JCP vote was 24.6 percent; it was also 27.5 percent in Ōsaka, 19.7 percent in Tokyo, and 16 percent in Kanagawa Prefecture. See Soma Masao, *Kokusei Senkyo to Seitō Seiji*, pp. 570–72.

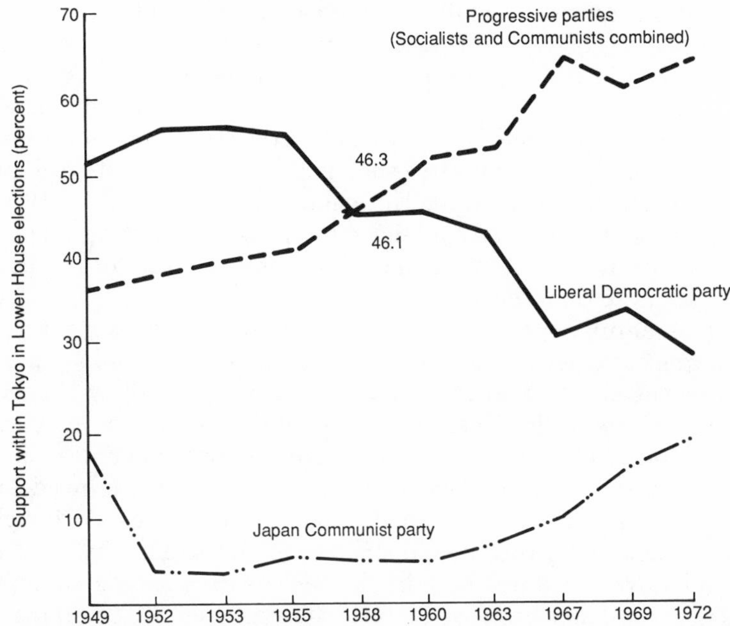

Figure 2.4. Crisis for Conservatives in the Nation's Capital: Socialist and Communist Support in Tokyo, 1949–1972.

Source: Soma Masao, ed., *Kokusei Senkyo to Seitō Seiji (National Election and Party Politics)* (Tokyo: Seiji Kōhō Center, 1977), p. 362.

tories at the local level, had allowed the Left to begin building a political infrastructure.[101]

As is evident from figure 2.4, Communist support in Tokyo by the 1972 election was approaching that for the LDP itself, coming much closer even than during the JCP's previous period of strength in the late 1940s. The JCP showed prospects of replacing the Socialists as the major opposition party in Japan's national capital just as the debt burden of Japanese industry was rising to its zenith under the stimulation of double-digit growth. At slightly over 30 percent, LDP support in Tokyo was little more than half that of the progressive parties.

[101] In Kyoto, where Ninagawa Torazō had served continuously as governor since 1950, the Left's tactics for systematically building political strength through "compensation politics" strikingly paralleled those of the conservatives at the national level. See Ellis S. Krauss, "Opposition in Power: The Development and Maintenance of Leftist Government in Kyoto Prefecture," in *Political Opposition and Local Politics in Japan*, eds. Kurt Steiner, Ellis S. Krauss, and Scott C. Flanagan, 383–426.

Also confronting the Liberal Democrats at the end of 1972 was the prospect of Upper House elections only eighteen months hence. In the 1971 House of Councillors election, the LDP had garnered only 44 percent of the vote. Many analysts predicted that 1974 might well be the year the conservatives would lose their Upper House majority, spurring a possible major realignment of the political world. Throughout most of 1973 and 1974, as indicated in figure 2.1, public opinion polls showed JSP support levels within 10 percent of the ruling conservatives for the first time in more than ten years.

The seemingly precarious prevailing political situation spurred a chorus of criticism against the LDP from business ranks, intensifying the sense of ferment and the prospects of policy change. *Keizai Dōyūkai*, the most progressive of the four major business federations, held dialogues with a range of opposition politicians, including the Communists. It vigorously stressed the need for policy change, particularly in the social welfare area. Although *zaikai* backing for the LDP remained generally strong, many businessmen were irritated both by the conservative party's vulnerability to pressures from agriculture, construction, and small manufacturing and LDP's "egotism" intensifying the polarization of Japanese politics. Members of the business world went so far as to stress flatly, if anonymously, in national publications that the LDP did not represent the interests of the majority of the Japanese people, that an LDP split and major party realignment was likely, and that the likely outcome would be a regime similar to the social democratic parties of Western Europe.[102]

Within the LDP itself, criticism of prevailing policies was also increasingly lively during the 1973–1974 period, with much of it centering on the economic management of Prime Minister Tanaka Kakuei. Tanaka's policies produced first soaring inflation and then recession, causing economic hardships to actually intensify political crisis for the first time since the beginning of the Korean War. Former MITI Minister and Economic Planning Agency Director General Miyazawa Kiichi,[103] for example, described growing imbalances in the distribution of wealth and in-

[102] Kikuiri Ryūsuke, "Jimintō ga Yatō ni naru Hi" ("The Day the LDP Becomes an Opposition Party"), *Bungei Shunjū*, April 1973, pp. 162–74, especially pp. 165–66.

[103] Miyazawa served as EPA director general for five years under prime ministers Ikeda and Satō, followed by a year as MITI minister in the third Satō cabinet (1970–1971).

come arising out of rampant land-price speculation, arguing that they exacerbated social cleavages, intensified cynicism, and contributed to the expanding influence of revolutionary political parties in Japan.[104]

Ishida Hirohide and other maverick members of the LDP with strong and long-standing ties to the opposition kept up a steady stream of criticism of the LDP mainstream in the pages of *Sekai, Asahi Jyānaru, Chūō Kōron*, and other progressive journals. After abruptly resigning as vice president of the LDP in mid-1974, Miki Takeo, with strong opposition ties dating from the Katayama cabinet of the 1940s, reportedly used those ties to seriously explore the prospects of a cross-party coalition government splitting the LDP. At the same time, the Ōhira-Fukuda rivalry for succession to Tanaka was also placing severe strains on party unity. Given the heavy debt burden and precarious high-growth strategies of the Japanese private sector, which had reached their most expansionary by 1973, any serious prospect of political turmoil was of course anathema to big business as well as mainstream conservatives. Miki gave up his covert separatist bid only after being offered presidency of the whole LDP, and hence the prime ministership, through Shiina Etsusaburō's mediation in late 1974.

The Reemergence of Stability

The late 1970s are a complex, transitional period in the history of the Japanese political world, with important contrasting strands of both turbulence and stability. To be sure, the Liberal Democrats held only a precarious Diet majority until the Double Election of 1980, and they suffered from protracted internal conflict and proliferating scandal.[105] On the Left, the heady memories of progressive local governments dominating a Tōkaidō urban belt of fifty million people were still fresh, and expectations

[104] See Miyazawa Kiichi, "Seiji no Genba kara no Shiron: Kisoteki Jūyō no Settei ni Tsuite" ("A Sketch from the Real World of Politics: About Establishing the Fundamentally Important"), *Chūō Kōron*, July 1974, pp. 72–89; and Miyazawa Kiichi, "Shakai Seigi no tame ni" ("Toward Social Justice"), *Jiyū Shinpō*, July 1973. Miyazawa proposed that city land be considered "public property" (*kōkyōzai*), with substantially greater public regulation that was common at the time.

[105] On the details of internal conflict, see Itō Masaya, *Jimintō Sengoku Shi* (*The Civil War in the LDP*).

for the future high. But a crisis dynamic that had produced such broad waves of policy change in the early part of the decade was unmistakably broken.

The unraveling of the crisis configuration of the early 1970s had several dimensions. One of the most important was the sharp erosion in the Diet position of the Japan Communist Party in the general elections of December 1976. After steady, continuous gains for a decade, to thirty-eight seats and 10.5 percent of the total national vote in the December 1972 Lower House elections, the JCP suffered an abrupt setback in 1976, falling to less than half its previous Diet strength; this defeat was sharply contrary to general expectations and helped neutralize the deep-seated fear among business and the ruling conservative party of the one group in Japan with which they could not make some sort of accommodation.

Also important in muting conservative crisis consciousness and pressures for policy change were political developments at the local level. During the early 1970s, as noted earlier, all five of Japan's largest cities had progressive mayors. These mayors controlled expanding budgets generated from the process of economic growth which could support either expanded distributive compensation, on the LDP pattern, or new policies.[106] The oil shock of 1973 broke the ability of these progressive local politicians to compensate strategically by sharply straining the fiscal resources at their command; most of the progressive governors and mayors had fallen from office within seven years of the oil shock. In 1978 another conservative, Hayashida Yukio, replaced governor Ninagawa Torazō, a major innovator in small business policy, in Kyoto, ending a twenty-eight-year career that had profoundly shaped Japanese public policy, despite Ninagawa's opposition status. The following year the Left suffered another major defeat in the 1979 unified local elections, with retiring Tokyo Governor Minobe Ryōkichi being succeeded by the conservative Suzuki Shunichi.

The late 1970s also witnessed complex developments within the LDP which, while confrontational and often bitter at the personal level, ultimately led to greater stability within conserva-

[106] The political strategies of some progressive local politicians were remarkably close to those of the LDP. For details on one such case, see Ellis Kraus, "The Urban Strategy and Policy of the Japanese Communist Party: *Kyoto*," Studies in *Comparative Communism* 12 no. 4 (Winter 1979), pp. 322–50; and Krauss, "Opposition in Power."

tive ranks than had prevailed during the early 1970s. In mid-1976 Kōno Yōhei, son of the persistent maverick Kōno Ichirō, emulated his father's abortive attempt to form a second conservative party and actually seceded from the LDP with five other conservative Dietmen. Even more importantly, in 1976 the complex story of the Lockheed Scandal and its relationship to former Prime Minister Tanaka Kakuei began to unfold.

"Lockheed" began as a phenomenon in Japanese politics as a result of testimony given in 1976 before a subcommittee of the U.S. Senate Foreign Relations Committee. The testimony indicated that certain senior Japanese business and government officials had received bribes to promote sales of Lockheed L1011 wide-body passenger planes to Japan's major domestic carrier, All-Nippon Airways.[107] After months of preliminary maneuvering, former Prime Minister Tanaka Kakuei was indicted in August 1976 for having accepted ¥500 million ($1.6 million at then prevailing exchange rates) from Lockheed agents. Former Minister of Transportation Hashimoto Tomisaburō, a senior leader in the Tanaka faction, and Parliamentary Vice Minister of Transportation Satō Takayuki were also alleged to have received payments.

Ultimately Tanaka went on trial and was convicted in October 1983 on the bribery charges. But more striking than the outcome, which many had foreseen, was the major centralization of power within the Japanese political system achieved by a Tanaka Kakuei preoccupied by the Lockheed Scandal, and intent on rendering himself politically invulnerable to an adverse verdict. Tanaka expanded the strength of his own faction from around 75 at the time of his indictment to around 118 when he was convicted six years later. He also forged strong, self-dominated alliances with first the Ōhira faction and later the Nakasone faction as well.

Although the Fukuda and Miki factions were consistently and often bitterly opposed to Tanaka, they represented a vocal but steadily declining minority within the party as a whole. Fukuda was defeated by Ōhira in the 1978 LDP presidential primary with the assistance of Tanaka, while several Miki-affiliated Diet and

107 For details on the scandal, see, among others, Larry Warren Fisher, "The Lockheed Affair: A Phenomenon of Japanese Politics" (Ph.D. diss., University of Colorado, Boulder, 1980); and Hans H. Baerwald, "Lockheed and Japanese Politics," *Asian Survey* (December 1976), pp. 817–29. On its deeper structural origins, see Tachibana Takashi, *Tanaka Kakuei Kenkyū: Zenkiroku* (*Research on Tanaka Kakuei: The Complete Record*).

gubernatorial candidates were also defeated in the late 1970s through Tanaka's support. The Fukuda and Miki factions retaliated by cooperating with a successful socialist no-confidence vote against Ōhira Masayoshi in 1980. But that only paved the way for the double election of 1980, in which centralization of power in the hands of Tanaka Kakuei proceeded still further.

In addition to assembling a large faction and an impressive range of political party allies, Tanaka also forged unprecedented ties with the bureaucracy to enhance his power. Most importantly, he actively supported high-level bureaucrats from a broad range of ministries who were interested in postretirement political careers. Both Hatoyama Iichirō and Aizawa Hideyuki, vice ministers of finance in the early 1970s, subsequently entered the Diet with the assistance of Tanaka, followed by former head of the National Police Agency Gotōda Masaharu and vice ministers of Construction, Agriculture, Labor, Posts and Telecommunications, and even MITI. Through developing an unprecedented political-bureaucratic network, Tanaka achieved a centralization of political power which went by the early 1980s beyond party politics to the very heart of policymaking in the major government agencies of Japan. His influence was reportedly especially strong at ministries such as Construction and Posts and Telecommunications, which dealt heavily in such distributive allocations to the private sector as public works and broadcasting-license authorizations.

What is striking about the Lockheed scandal and its aftermath, seen in the broader context of postwar Japanese politics, is not the drama and animosity it generated, given the appearance of a deep national political crisis in its presentation by the Japanese media. Whatever the moral and personal crisis dimensions of Lockheed might have been, the Lockheed drama in the end helped temporarily ameliorate the endemic structural crisis of conservative politics in Japan in order to neutralize the personal political crisis of Tanaka Kakuei. Lockheed did so by stimulating the important concentration of political power which occurred between Tanaka's indictment in 1976 and his conviction seven years later. This was lessened only slightly during the succession of Takeshita Noboru to leadership of the overwhelming majority of the faction during 1985–1987.

Overlapping and reinforcing the concentration of political power within conservative ranks effected by Tanaka Kakuei were major shifts after 1976 in the relative political balance of government and opposition. Conservative gains at the local level, the only level at which the Left has ever held power in Japan since late 1948, were important. From their high-water mark in the early 1970s, the Left lost rapidly after 1975. By 1980 only four governorships out of forty-seven prefectures remained clearly in opposition hands,[108] a figure which remained constant through 1986, [109] and contributed to growing opposition weakness at the national level. Although both France and Italy experienced an erosion in the strength of the Left at the local government level in the early 1980s, it was neither as pronounced as in Japan nor as early.[110] Although the Left held its own in Japan's unified local elections of April 1987, there were few signs of a strong comeback for progressive local governments.

Concentration of power in conservative hands also proceeded steadily within the Diet, although more slowly than in local government. In the 1976 general elections the momentum of the Japan Communist Party, the LDP's most implacable foe, was dramatically stopped, although the LDP itself also suffered reverses. After a 1979 election influenced by the LDP's abortive and half-hearted attempt to introduce a value-added tax, the LDP gained decisively in the double election of 1980, gaining 56 percent of seats in the Lower House. After a setback in the 1983 elections, dominated by the Lockheed issue, the LDP in the July 1986 double elections exceeded even its 1980 record, garnering 300 seats of 512 at stake and electing 94 percent of its officially endorsed candidates. The LDP gain in 1986 came largely at the expense of the largest opposition party, the JSP, which dropped from 112 to 85 seats, sharply less than one-third of LDP strength. Within the conservative party, concentration proceeded, with 70 percent of the total 1986 party increase in seats going either to the dominant Tanaka or Nakasone factions.

Following the LDP double election victory of June 1980 Japan's

[108] In 1980 opposition parties in coalition held the governorships of Saitama, Shiga, and Kagawa prefectures, together with a curious coalition governorship (JSP plus the Kanemaru faction of the local LDP) in Yamanashi. Left-oriented governors also held sway in a few other prefectures such as Kanagawa, where they were supported by all parties, including the LDP.

[109] In 1986, the clear opposition governorships were Hokkaidō, Tokushima, Fukuoka, and Saitama.

[110] See Stephen Gundle, "Urban Dreams and Metropolitan Nightmares: Models and Crises of Communist Local Government in Italy," and Andrew F. Knapp, "A Receding Tide: France's Communist Municipalities," in Bogdan Szajkowski, ed., *Marxist Local Governments in Western Europe and Japan*, pp. 66–95, 119–49.

domestic political scene seemed to have become more stable than at virtually any other point in the postwar period. The Lockheed scandal, to be sure, continued to stir political waves up to the conviction of Tanaka Kakuei in October 1983, and indeed even thereafter. The LDP, it is true, secured only a bare majority in the November 1983 general election that followed and ruled until the July 1986 election in coalition with the New Liberal Club. But within the LDP the concentration of political power during the 1980s continued rising to levels rarely seen in the postwar period. The strength of the Left continued to atrophy, accelerated by the privatization of Nippon Telephone and Telegraph in 1985, the Japan National Railways in 1987 and the accompanying decimation of public-sector labor as a political force.[111] The massive conservative electoral triumph of July 1986, in which the LDP emerged with nearly 60 percent of total Diet seats and the numerical strength of the dominant Nakasone and Takeshita affiliates within the party grew sharply, likewise suggested intensified short-run stability. This tendency toward stability was also reinforced by deepening ties between key members of the ruling LDP and the mass media, as well as intensifying cross-party legislative cooperation in the Diet Management Committee.

Despite the appearance of unusual short-run stability during the 1980s in the prevailing factional and party alignments of Japanese politics, important ingredients remained to suggest the possible longer-run reemergence of political fluidity, albeit fluidity turning on different issues and possibly requiring different policy solutions than the domestically driven crises since the 1940s. The gradually waning influence of the major business federations, with the decentralization of political finance following the Election Finance Law of 1976, created some prospects for greater fluidity in Japanese politics. Zaikai had, after all, been a consistent and central force for conservative unity before the conservative merger of 1955, and had reportedly been crucial in

[111] Kokurō, the JNR workers union, was long one of the principal political supporters of the Japan Socialist Party. But as the deliberations on the future of the JNR proceeded this militant union found itself with dramatically declining membership. From 245,000 members in October 1982, Kokurō's membership fell to only 85,000 as of January 1987. See *Japan Labor Bulletin* (October 1982), p. 3; and *Nihon Rōdō Kyōkai Zasshi* (*Journal of the Japan Labor Association*), May 1987, p. 18.

both inspiring the merger and deterring attempts to split the LDP, such as that of Kōno Ichirō in 1960. The gradual decline in corporate debt, in the zaitech-oriented world of the late 1980s, gave big business marginally more freedom to condone political fluidity; leverage remained extraordinarily high by international standards for firms in basic sectors like steel and other heavy industries, which remained politically influential.

The most fundamental reasons for possible fluidity and realignment in Japanese politics in the long run, however, flowed from the changing character of the electorate and the growing divergence of interest among supporters of the catch-all Liberal Democratic Party. Since the late 1960s a rising proportion of the Japanese electorate has consisted of fundamentally nonaligned, but largely nonpolitical voters, many of them urban white-collar, who are moderately conservative and nationalistic but primarily concerned about the quality of urban life and public policy insofar as it bears on that. This is the so-called "new middle mass," about which Murakami Yasusuke has written.[112] Prime Minister Nakasone Yasuhiro argued, in a landmark August 1986 speech at the LDP Karuizawa Seminar, which accepted important aspects of this analysis, that 40 percent of the Japanese electorate was essentially nonpolitical and potentially fluid in its allegiances; thus, the secret of the LDP success in the 1986 double election was its ability to capture 60 percent of this nonpolitical segment of the electorate.[113] Yet this increasingly important group has been demonstrably volatile and unpredictable in its political participation, leading to the fluctuations in voter turnout in Japan since the late 1970s, from 67.9 percent in 1979 to 74.5 percent in 1980, to 67.9 percent again, in 1983, and back to 71.4 percent in 1986.[114] These fluctuations have translated primarily into large fluctuations in support for the LDP, with the absolute number of

[112] See, in particular, Murakami Yasusuke, "The Age of New Middle Mass Politics," *Journal of Japanese Studies* (Winter 1982), pp. 29–72; and Murakami Yasusuke, *Shin Chūkan Taishū no Jidai* (*The Age of the New Middle Mass*).

[113] For an analytical account of and reaction to the speech, see Hirose Michisada, "Jiyū Ha to Minshu Ha to Jimintō Seiji ni ima Kiretsu ga Hashiru" ("A Crack Now Runs through LDP Politics between the Liberal Faction and the Democratic Faction"), in Ishii Shinji, ed., *Jimintō to iu Chie* (*The Wisdom called the LDP*), especially pp. 245–48.

[114] Murakami Yasusuke, "The Japanese Model of Political Economy," in Yamamura Kōzō and Yasuba Yasukichi, eds., *The Political Economy of Japan*, vol. 1, pp. 81–82.

LDP voters varying by an average of over 13 percent per election between 1979 and 1986, compared to 5 percent for the Socialists and only 4 percent for the Communists.[115] This sort of volatility in actual votes for the LDP, magnified by the middle-size district electoral system, may well continue or intensify with the growth of the new middle mass in Japanese society, creating the possibility of future crisis, despite the prevailing short-run stability of 1986–1987.

Another related force for future turbulence or realignment in Japanese politics could be the growing divergence of economic interest between what Hirose Michisada has termed the "Liberal" and the "Democratic" elements of the catch-all Liberal Democratic Party.[116] The liberal elements are the expanding group of LDP supporters, including big business and elements of organized labor, as well as the emerging new middle mass, who favor cutbacks in subsidy programs, privatization, expansion of agricultural imports, and a generally more market-oriented approach to public policy where it does not adversely affect basic economic interests of the coalition. Seen in historical perspective, there are striking parallels between this increasingly salient configuration in Japanese politics and the coalition in British politics which secured repeal of the Corn Laws in 1848. The democratic elements of the LDP, including residents of more remote, disadvantaged areas, and others who have benefited from the long cycle of crisis and compensation over the past four decades, are more supportive of continuation in the welfare-oriented status quo, both domestically and internationally.

Despite intensifying divergence of interest within the catch-all LDP support coalition, it is by no means certain that domestic forces alone can generate interactive crisis and major policy change within Japan, as they have previously done three times since 1949. Following the LDP's overwhelming 1986 election victory and the long atrophy of antimainstream factions in the LDP, dating back to the 1970s, the classical combination for the emergence of change-inducing domestic crisis—opposition strength and intense, evenly balanced factional struggle within conservative ranks—was lacking. Some other catalyst was necessary.

[115] Miyakawa Takayoshi, ed., *Seiji Handbook* (Politics Handbook), 1987 ed., p. 210.

[116] Hirose Michisada, "Jiyū Ha to Minshu Ha," in Ishii Shinji, ed., *Jimintō to iu Chie*, pp. 239–52.

IMPORTED CRISIS?

With many of the traditional agents of major policy change, especially redistributive policy change, increasingly ineffective by the 1980s in playing their accustomed roles, attention was increasingly focused on international pressure (*gaiatsu*) as an agent of domestic transformation in Japan. This section explores the prospects for such internationally induced domestic change and concludes that it is a prospectively powerful supplement to market forces when focused strategically and applied in sectors where substantial consensus for change within Japan already exists. Foreign pressure can also piggyback on preexisting domestic crisis, as it did in 1971–1972, to influence the timing and dynamics of domestic leadership change within the LDP.

Foreign pressure as the primary tool for inducing sweeping political or policy change within Japan, however, is much more problematic. The nationalist backlash inside Japan, which such pressure often evokes, and its generally diffuse, unfocused quality, limits its prospective utility in provoking interactive crises that might generate major policy change. Where strong market forces and multilateral Japanese interests beyond the country do not give Japanese domestic interest groups reasons of their own for supporting change, foreign pressure can actually be counterproductive. Whatever changes occur within Japan due to foreign pressure will likely benefit domestic actors, including subsidiaries of foreign multinationals, and the United States. Concessions to such pressure are only reluctantly generalized beyond individual cases, in part due to the pervasive sense of international vulnerability that food and fuel insufficiences, together with diplomatic isolation, continue to generate in Japan. But the farther Japan's integration into the global economy proceeds and the sharper the exchange-rate realignments that occur, the stronger the economic pressures toward overcoming the autarkic impulses of the past become.

As the Japanese domestic political environment became progressively more stable during the late 1970s and early 1980s, Japan's international environment became more turbulent; international developments were also becoming more important to key Japanese domestic political actors. As suggested in figure 2.5, many of the key international parameters within which Japan operated during the high-growth period, such as exchange rates and energy prices, were remarkably stable: the yen remained fixed at

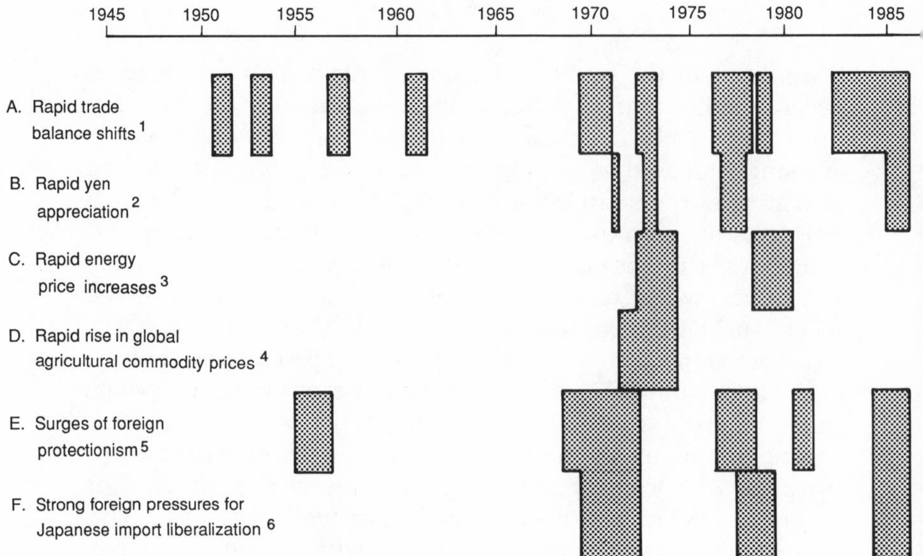

Figure 2.5. Growing International Pressures on Japanese Conservative Policymaking, 1971–1986.

Notes: [1]Rapid trade balance shifts are year-to-year changes over 20 percent in annual Japanese multilateral trade balance figures.[2] Rapid yen appreciation defined as increases of over 15 percent in yen value on a year-to-year basis, as reported in year-end statistics.[3] Defined as shifts over 30 percent in market price of crude oil, on a year-to-year basis.[4] International soybean market prices increase over 30 percent on a year-to-year basis.[5] Major orderly marketing agreement concluded with Japan's largest trading partner within previous twelve months.[6] United States–Japan trade deficit mounting rapidly and U.S. trade negotiators making insistent import liberalization demands of Japan.

Sources: IBRD, *Commodity Trade and Price Trends, International Commodity Statistics*; Tōyō Keizai Shinpō Sha, *Shōwa Kokusei Sōran (Shōwa National Almanac)*; IMF, *Direction of Trade Statistics*; Bank of Japan Research and Statistics Department *(Nihon Ginkō Chōsa Tōkei Kyoku)*, *Kokusai Hikaku Tōkei (International Comparative Statistics)*; and Economic Planning Agency (Keizai Kikaku Chō), *Keizai Yōran (Economic Almanac)*.

¥360 = $1.00 from 1949 until August 1971; and the price of crude oil actually declined during much of this period.

Yet beginning in the early 1970s these parameters became progressively more uncertain. Two energy shocks of 1973 and 1979, together with erosion of the Bretton Woods monetary system and three sharp revaluations of the yen within the space of fifteen years (1971, 1977–1978, and 1985–1987), destroyed old parameters that a risk-averse, raw material dependent Japan had used to calculate national economic security and well-being. A $6.5 billion current account surplus in 1978, for example, turned suddenly to a $8.7 billion deficit the following year, in the wake of the Iranian Revolution and a doubling of the world price of crude oil. The United States introduced a further note of insecurity into Japanese calculations with an ill-considered, albeit brief, soybean export embargo during mid-1973 still remembered in Tokyo today.[117]

Japan's global political environment was also becoming progressively less predictable. The so-called Nixon shocks of 1971, in which Richard Nixon within one month announced a presidential visit to Beijing and suspended convertibility of the dollar into gold, sharply inaugurated the new era of uncertainty for Japan, which also involved unilateral European protectionist measures against Japan and periodic spasms of anti-Japanese protectionist sentiment on Capitol Hill. Rising American trade deficits and declining American political hegemony caused de facto exceptions to the General Agreement on Tariffs and Trade (GATT) free-trading rules to proliferate in a nonsystematic fashion. Following "voluntary" Japanese restraints on exports of cotton textiles (1956), crude steel (1968), specialty steel (1974), color televisions (1977), automobiles (1981), semiconductors (1986), and machine tools (1987) to the United States, to cite a few examples, more than 30 percent of United States-Japan trade was effectively cartelized by the late 1980s. Ad hoc, politically negotiated arrangements, whose outlines could not be precisely foreseen beforehand within Japan, were even more salient in Japan's foreign economic dealings with other nations.

Always looming over the horizon during the 1970s and 1980s was the ominous possibility of worse to come on the political front, partly because economic circumstances were so volatile. During the early 1970s a bitter United States-Japan textile trade wrangle was papered over, but only after the Nixon administration had threatened to invoke the Trading with the Enemy Act and had imposed two Nixon shocks on Japan.[118] During 1977–1978, an acrimonious "beef and orange war" erupted, as Japanese

[117] On the details of the soybean embargo, see I. M. Destler, *Making Foreign Economic Policy*, pp. 50–64.

[118] For details, see I. M. Destler, Hideo Satō, and Haruhiro Fukui, *The Textile Wrangle*.

global trade surpluses soared over $24 billion in 1978,[119] only to subside following the oil shock of 1979. During 1986–1987, a sudden collapse in global oil prices and a related consumer spending boom in the United States caused the Japanese global current account surplus to soar over $80 billion and the U.S. global deficit over $160 billion, with more than $59 billion of it attributable to a massive trade deficit with Japan. Despite the disequilibriums and a 40 percent revaluation of the yen, U.S. exports to Japan in 1986 expanded only 5.5 percent, compared to a 21 percent expansion of Japanese exports to the United States. The sudden strains of rapidly rising U.S. trade deficits on long-standing global trading relationships ignited Western protectionist sentiment once again, a course both Japanese and Western observers found hard to predict.

Japan has, of course, confronted an uncertain and turbulent world before, as a dependent, vulnerable participant in international markets. Ever since 1890 it has been a net importer of food, fuels, and raw materials in increasing quantity. From the late 1950s through the 1960s, it faced periodic pressure from both the United States and multilateral institutions such as the International Monetary Fund (IMF), GATT, and the OECD to liberalize international trade and capital flows into Japan. For most of the past century Japan has depended on the American market alone to absorb one-fifth to one-third of the exports it must generate to cover an unusually heavy raw materials import bill.

But, in their implications for Japanese domestic policymaking, the combination of unusual instability in the economic and political *parameters* surrounding Japanese interaction with the international economy, on the one hand, and the unprecedented degree of *mutual interdependence* with other advanced industrial nations that has emerged in the trade, monetary, technological, and personal exchange areas, on the other, has been new and important about the past two decades. Japan has added, as Keohane and Nye might put it, substantially increased "sensitivity interdependence" with its major trading partners to the underlying "vulnerability interdependence" it has long experienced.[120] Increasing uncertainty in commodity prices, exchange rates, and

[119] See Kusano Atsushi, *Nichibei Orange Kōshō* (*The United States-Japan Orange Negotiations*); and I. M. Destler, ed., *Coping with U.S.–Japan Economic Conflict*.

[120] Robert O. Keohane and Joseph S. Nye, *Power and Interdependence*, pp. 11–19.

international trading rules have made the transition to deepening interdependence even more difficult for Japan.

The rising interdependence shows itself most graphically in international trade and capital flows, particularly with the United States.[121] In 1970 total Japanese foreign trade was approximately $35 billion, or roughly 16 percent of the gross national product; by 1985 this trade had risen to over $292 billion, or 22 percent of GNP.[122] In 1970 Japanese overseas direct investment was negligible; by end of 1986 cumulative overseas investment was $108 billion and rising sharply.[123]

Mutual Japanese interdependencies with the broader world were intensifying even more rapidly in finance than in trade. In 1980, for example, Japanese overseas portfolio investment was negligible; Japan was a net debtor on current account. By the end of 1986, however, Japan had $130 billion in external foreign assets, substantially more than the total for all of OPEC at the height of its financial power in the mid-1970s. Major Japanese securities houses had become primary dealers in U.S. Treasury securities, and Western investment bankers were flocking to Tokyo in unprecedented droves. The stakes of trans-Pacific interaction were rising rapidly for Wall Street, Kabutochō, and the city of London as well, as global finance moved toward a trilateral twenty-four-hour trading structure in which Tokyo played a pivotal role.

During the 1970s and the 1980s, in short, the consequences of international developments for the Japanese economy became at once both more important and more uncertain. Accompanying this evolution has been rising structural integration of foreign pressures into the Japanese policy process, as Japanese officials become increasingly capable of using international uncertainties to achieve policy objectives at home. More and more Japanese bureaucrats and politicians have extended study and work experience abroad, with the transnational personal networks which naturally flow from this. Improved telecommunications and more frequent travel, together with proliferating ties to lobbyists

[121] For an examination of the underlying transformations in economic and political structure underway, see Kent E. Calder, "The Emerging Politics of the Trans-Pacific Economy."

[122] Bank of Japan Research and Statistics Department (Nihon Ginkō Chōsa Tōkei Kyoku) *Keizai Tōkei Nenpō*, 1986 ed., pp. 241–42.

[123] Japan Institute for Social and Economic Affairs, *Japan 1988: An International Comparison*, p. 56.

in the United States, make it even easier to maintain such transnational networks. Growing integration of the Japanese press and the conservative political world, combined with the rising dependence of LDP politicians on input from the media as a basis for their own decisions, make it easier for bureaucrats and politicians to use these networks to generate internationally orchestrated but domestically initiated pressure for policy change.

Substituting Imported Crisis for Domestic

With this waning of domestic crisis since the late 1970s, a major engine of Japanese policy innovation—historically *the* engine of policy innovation regarding large, new redistributive programs and major realignments of budgetary shares—has stalled. For those intent on "opening the policy window," in Kingdon's terminology,[124] a functional equivalent of domestic crisis is needed to stimulate change. In the Japan of the 1980s, the U.S. Congress and U.S. trade negotiators have been forced, often unwittingly, toward the role of catalyst for change within Japan, a role played more consciously and subtly a generation earlier by progressive local government and LDP policy entrepreneurs.

By the late 1980s the LDP had a stable Diet majority and was evolving corporatist, intraparty policymaking mechanisms, such as the subcommittees of the Policy Affairs Research Council, which were less structurally sensitive to broad social pressures than was the Diet during the three domestic crisis periods examined in this volume.[125] The bureaucracy was often impeded by interministerial disputes in taking decisive policy initiatives, throwing ultimate decisionmaking powers back into the hands of the LDP.[126] While these developments facilitated policy retrenchment in such matters as administrative reform and privatization of major public corporations, they left few alternatives to foreign pressure as means of decisively generating new governmental programs. The functional need for crisis as an engine for major policy change remained substantial, despite changes in the locus of pressures for change.

Throughout the examination of domestic crisis in chapters 1

[124] Kingdon, *Agendas, Alternatives, and Public Policies*, p. 175.

[125] On the details of this transformation, see Satō and Matsuzaki, *Jimintō Seiken*; and Nihon Keizai Shimbun Sha, ed., *Jimintō Seichō Kai*.

[126] Johnson, *MITI, MPT, and the Telecom Wars: How Japan Makes Policy for High Technology*.

and 2, crisis has been defined as a "prospect of major loss or unwanted change that threatens the established order," meaning operationally the continued political preeminence of the ruling party. The definition also seems relevant with respect to the impact of international events, although their political effect is, of course, mediated through domestic political developments. Imported crisis, then, is domestic political crisis precipitated by international developments. By this definition, international developments could be considered to have seriously exacerbated the domestic crisis of the early 1970s and indeed advanced its advent to the time of the second Nixon shock (forcing the end of fixed exchange rates) in August 1971. The international crisis, coupled with the related textile crisis, influenced both the timing and the pattern of succession to Prime Minister Satō Eisaku, by implying the inability of Satō and his Foreign Minister Fukuda Takeo to deal effectively with the United States and offering the nationalistic and entrepreneurial MITI Minister Tanaka Kakuei the opportunity to demonstrate his skills in dealing with a fluid, turbulent, and threatening situation. The international turbulence of 1971 also stimulated a range of new policies in the small business and regional policy areas, suggesting that international crisis can broaden the scope and policy implications of preexisting domestic political crisis in Japan.

International developments once again exacerbated domestic political crisis in late 1973, when Japan was hit suddenly by the oil shock with major adverse consequences for a range of domestic groups. The adjustment process involving limited new policies for depressed sectors, continued from late 1973 to mid-1975, following the trough of the post-oil shock business recession in March 1975. International economic developments generated limited pressures for policy change in three specific periods: from mid-1977 through 1978, during and just after the sharp yen revaluation; 1979–1980, in the wake of the Iranian oil crisis; and 1986–1987, following another sharp yen revaluation. During the latter period, yen revaluation and escalating trade frictions with the United States weakened Prime Minister Nakasone Yasuhiro and intensified the internal LDP struggle for succession, just as they had in the case of Satō Eisaku fifteen years before. But in sharp contrast to the early 1970s, the opposition parties of the late 1980s were extremely weak, dampening the prospects of an interactive political crisis and large-scale policy change such as that which occurred during the early 1970s.

The most pronounced compensation-oriented policy effects have clearly occurred when external pressures have overlapped with domestic crisis, as was true between the Nixon shocks of mid-1971 and Tanaka Kakuei's ascent to the prime ministership a year later. Both the shipbuilding and the textile industries, for example, were compensated heavily for the losses they suffered due to foreign actions at that time. Foreign pressures, it must be emphasized, have typically had somewhat more limited policy consequences than domestically generated crisis when domestic crisis and external pressures do not occur together. This more limited impact of foreign pressures has been due both to the nature of the issues involved and because the "prospect of major political loss or unwanted change" which these foreign pressures pose is typically less fundamental than that presented by domestic crisis. For example, the politically adverse implications of international developments for individual politicians tend to be neutralized to some degree by the national solidarity which international confrontation typically generates. Emergence of full-fledged imported crisis thus would seem to require relatively powerful interparty and intraparty opposition to an incumbent government and strong outside pressure.

To the extent that the underlying policies of Japan's major allies are perceived stable, and not fundamentally challenging to Japanese economic well-being, international developments harming major groups in Japan necessitate only piecemeal compensatory responses toward LDP constituencies directly affected, rather than broad structural change. Such developments during the 1970s and 1980s generated extensive compensatory changes in small business and depressed industry policies. But, as of 1987, they had not triggered the spillover effects and broad, cross-sectoral waves of policy innovation typical in 1971–1976, 1958–1963, and 1949–1954, when many saw the continuing preeminence of the ruling conservatives jeopardized.

Due to the difficulties in the 1980s of generating policy change from within Japan, many groups interested in policy change have sought to invoke foreign pressure strategically in an effort to generate such change. Among these groups have been the supporters of domestic reflation in 1978 and 1986–1987, as well as the backers of expanded agricultural imports and landuse and housing policy reform during the late 1980s.[127] In limited cases where re-

[127] On the politics of domestic reflation in 1978, see I. M. Destler and Mitsuyu

form efforts were narrowly focused and well-coordinated, these attempts have succeeded, but they have not provoked the sort of major transformations in the Japanese political economy which occurred during the major domestic crisis periods of the past.

The Prospects for Change

Some analysts suggest that institutional rigidities make deeper responsiveness to broader global pressures problematic no matter what configuration of political forces develops within Japan.[128] Such arguments often neglect sophisticated mechanisms for limited change under pressure which the Japanese political economy clearly possesses. To understand the prospects for future change, one must look first at the circumstances that have stimulated major policy transformation within Japan in the past. Fundamental in each case was an interaction between a relatively powerful opposition and a dominant conservative party rent by severe internal division. Crucial in determining the lines of prospective policy, once the prospects for some change were opened by crisis, was the underlying configuration of interest groups to be compensated. As Japan confronts the future, that would suggest the importance to policy transformation of organized consumer groups, both industrial and individual, with political influence in ruling conservative ranks, as well as a revitalized opposition willing to appeal to consumer rather than purely producer interests, and an electorate which strongly desires change.

By the late 1980s a stronger consumer orientation was beginning to emerge in the Japanese political economy, especially with regard to agricultural imports. Keidanren and the Democratic Socialist Party had expressed support for major changes in agricultural import policy, while even Zennō, the national agricultural-cooperative federation, had expressed acceptance of some change. Dietmen were increasingly taking up consumer issues as a major concern. The nascent tensions between Liberals and Democrats within the LDP intensified during 1985–1987 by continuing fiscal restraint, and steady yen revaluation increased the prospect of major policy reorientation on trade and related domestic demand

---

Hisao, "Locomotives on Different Tracks: Macroeconomic Diplomacy, 1977–1979," in *Coping with U.S.–Japan Economic Conflict*, eds. I. M. Destler and Hideo Satō, pp. 243–70.

[128] See, for example, Karel van Wolferen, "The Japan Problem," *Foreign Affairs* (Winter 1986–1987), pp. 288–303.

stimulation issues. But any Japanese government would be constrained by Japan's basic vulnerabilities in food and fuel supplies, as it contemplated more decisive promotion of manufactured imports.

In the final analysis one is left with a nuanced picture affirming the importance of foreign pressure in generating policy change in the Japan of the late 1980s but simultaneously stressing its limitations and dangers. Due to the rising threat of nationalist backlash, external pressures on Japan must be in the short run ever more clearly focused on sectors within Japan where established consumer interests, market forces, and corporate concern about reciprocal access in foreign markets converge to reinforce the efficacy of such foreign pressure on Japan. The prospect of triggering from abroad an "inter-active crisis" stirring broad and fundamental waves of policy change within Japan must probably await a longer-range reordering of the Japanese domestic political world, and the clearer emergence of powerful groups inside Japan with a strong consumerist orientation. The history of previous post-1949 policy change suggests that support from the mass media, pressure from a resurgent opposition, and some acceptance within conservative ranks would all be crucial. But when change comes, the precedents of the past suggest, it could be rapid and fundamental, although subject to the requisites of Japan's underlying international economic vulnerability and the realities of its small business dominated employment structure.

Domestic crisis may have temporarily waned, as Japan confronts the turbulent world of the 1990s and beyond. But the very turbulence of that broader world, to which Japan is ever more tightly linked, inevitably reverberates within Japan. The specter of crisis has not disappeared from Japanese politics and policymaking, despite new constraints on policy change. But the character of crisis over the past generation has indeed undergone basic transformation.

3

The Technocratic Possibility

To put it bluntly, as far as the Japanese are concerned, there is no state, it has such a scant existence . . .

NAKASONE YASUHIRO (1978)

The Japanese state's awesome ability to extract unlimited compliance from its subjects and to mobilize all of the economy's resources for specific goals of the state indicates a perfect synchronization of polity, society, and economy.

SUMIYA MIKIO AND TAIRA KŌJI (1979)

ANALYSTS have differed sharply in their assessments of Japan's administrative state and its historical role in broader policymaking processes. For some, the technocracy is or has been powerful and autonomous; for others, the striking dimension is its incapacity. There is truth in both generalizations, if the empirical reference points are carefully specified. Their reconciliation distinguishes the important context of state structure within which the crisis and compensation dynamic of Japanese policymaking has taken place over the past two generations.

Increasing attention has been given in recent years to the implications of state structuring, and state-society relations more generally, for patterns of economic growth in the advanced industrial world.[1] Much of this has focused on state administrative structures promoting growth, generating useful analytical constructs, such as that of the "developmental state."[2] Other analyses have focused on private sector organizations and interpersonal networks supporting the developmental state.[3] But the political correlates of the developmental state—particularly the

[1] See, for example, Johnson, *MITI*; John Zysman, *Governments, Markets, and Growth*; and Peter Hall, *Governing the Economy*.

[2] For the classic formulation, see Johnson, *MITI*.

[3] See, for example, Richard Samuels, *The Business of the Japanese State: Energy Markets in Comparative and Historical Perspective* (Ithaca: Cornell University Press, 1987).

party-political structures and interest-articulation processes that allow the state to successfully reconcile political stability and growth—remain relatively unexplored, as do the broader relationships between politics and state structure itself.

Governments have differed sharply in strategies for maintaining legitimacy in the midst of economic transformation and the emergence of mass politics which often accompanies that transformation. The most common approach has been *martial*: to finesse the redistributive issues often raised from below through state-generated appeals, stressing the primacy of patriotic over material goals in the face of external challenge. The perceived challenge can be either political, as in the confrontation with foreign foes, or spiritual, as in the case of religious appeals to national unity. A second strategy, less often successfully employed, has been to stress the *technocratic* credentials of incumbent leadership and its superior ability to understand and respond to problems of economic and social transformation. A final approach, which blurs at some indefinite point with welfare-state liberalism, attempts to sustain elite legitimacy *materially* through strategic compensation of nonelite groups in return for mass support.

This chapter begins with a taxonomy of the approaches available to governments to maintain legitimacy during periods of change. It then proceeds to a discussion of the Japanese state's structural disposition toward technocratic solutions to societal and political problems. This disposition is presented in the dual context of Japan's prevailing international situation, on the one hand, and domestic economic and social circumstances on the other. The chapter concludes with an examination of crucial changes in Japanese state and political structure during the 1945–1948 period, opening the way for the pronounced patterns of crisis and compensation discussed at length later in the volume.

Government Approaches to Maintaining Legitimacy

Underlying all approaches to administration and policymaking is the prior problem for government of maintaining public order and legitimacy. Doing so can be particularly difficult in periods of fundamental social and economic change, when anomie and problems of status incongruity are often especially pronounced.

In maintaining legitimacy during periods of change, three basic approaches are available to governments: the martial, the technocratic, and the material.

The Martial Response

Until after 1870, European traditionalists generally saw nationalism as a radical force, rather than as a vehicle for promoting elite legitimacy, and broadly opposed it. But nationalist appeals emerged after 1870 as an increasingly important conservative tactic for generating mass support, and hence political stability, during the turbulent industrialization and social mobilization process.[4] Disraeli's belligerent imperialism after 1875 and Bismarck's militant drive for unification of Germany and subsequent confrontation with France were two typical patterns, paralleled by the assertive nationalism of Yamagata Aritomo in Japan and Teddy Roosevelt in the United States.[5] Even after the turbulence of modernization waned, nationalism persisted as a frequent means of assuring stability, as was true in Nasser's Egypt and Sukarno's Indonesia during the 1950s.

The strong attraction of the martial response as a conservative political strategy has been the way it bridges the gap industrial society creates between elites and ruled, recreating a sense of national unity on noneconomic grounds. When such a sense of unity is achieved, there is no need for redistributive policies to generate national consensus. Hence nationalism can be employed in a wide range of national economic settings, including low-growth zero-sum environments where redistribution or other policies of assistance to the emerging working class would trigger severe domestic social tensions. In addition, nationalism is attractive for politicians because it preserves their legitimacy in competition with technocrats, who often decry the legitimacy of politics altogether in their emphasis on technical expertise.

The problem with nationalism as a means of sustaining polit-

[4] Aristotle and Machiavelli both noted this proclivity of governments to channel mounting conflicts into external tensions or war. See Ernest Barker, ed., *The Politics of Aristotle*, book 5; Nicolo Machiavelli, *The Prince and the Discourses*, p. 79; On the nineteenth-century European phenomenon, see John Weiss, *Conservatism in Europe*, especially pp. 71–173.

[5] The strong emphasis on a unifying national church in multi-ethnic empires such as Austro-Hungary and Tsarist Russia might also be seen in this light. See Weiss, *Conservatism in Europe*, pp. 115–30.

ical legitimacy and stability has been the bias toward war and crisis—themselves destabilizing forces that it creates in a political system. The human and material costs of this approach, not to speak of the long-run threat to national consensus, are often high. Sometimes, invoking nationalist, militarist symbols may be politically counterproductive, particularly in the aftermath of a costly defeat such as Japan and Germany suffered in 1945. Such circumstances, particularly, require different strategies for assuring legitimacy and political order.

Conceptually parallel to nationalism, and sometimes operationally unified with it, are spiritual variations. Conservative elites may strive to forge social bonds with lower classes by creating or appealing to a common religious heritage. State Shintō in prewar Japan, together with established religion in Imperial Russia, were two salient examples of this pattern. Transcendent spiritual appeals for unity have often been less economically costly, of course, than militarily oriented appeals, but their efficacy has steadily waned over the past generation in the industrial world with the progress of secularization.

The Technocratic Response

In establishing a basis other than nationalism for elite legitimacy, conservative political leadership since the Industrial Revolution has continued to employ a version of the classic elitist argument: the intelligent and rigorously trained know best. In its modern incarnation, this argument has normally dictated the dominance in policymaking of highly trained career civil servants.

Technocrats, as Aberbach, Putnam, and Rockman have noted, often tend toward an equilibrating bias.[6] Their bias is generally toward harmony within existing parameters rather than toward fundamental innovation. Under the turbulent conditions marking the emergence of mass social involvement, the denial of pluralist politics, often implying either civilian or military bureaucratic rule, has generally been the preferred course of technocratic elites, although they have varied in their strategies for neutralizing new mass influences.[7] Distributive politics im-

[6] Aberbach, Putnam, and Rockman, *Bureaucrats and Politicians in Western Democracies*, p. 257.

[7] It is out of crises, where elements of discontinuity are salient, that corporatist

poses major financial burdens on the state in societies where the counterclaims of economic development are also large; technocrats have generally tried to avoid or minimize reliance upon this approach. Distributive politics offers at best an uncertain stability dividend, particularly in nations with minimal political party organization and rapidly rising expectations, giving technocrats further reasons to avoid such an approach. When clear national economic imperatives exist and bureaucracy has a strong voice within state decisionmaking, such a technocratic response to the dual challenges of Industrial Revolution and mass politics is especially likely to prevail.[8]

Successful technocrats can occasionally be highly pragmatic, even in highly centralized, bureaucratically dominated societies. This is especially likely when their position of preeminence within the broader political economy is at stake.[9] But their general tendency is to avoid politics for its own sake, for reasons suggested above. The depoliticization often prominent in the technocratic response (attractive to new military governments that have just replaced civilian politicians) fits well with corporatism's organic view of the state. This view seeks to replace interest group–oriented mass politics with harmonious, integrative interest articulation under the auspices of a technocratic elite. Private groups are "chartered" by the state to assume representational and often administrative functions in place of central authority. Such a decentralization of decisionmaking often reduces the political pressures that would otherwise build against the state itself.[10]

Government officials, effectively denying the legitimacy of pluralist political decision, seek solutions through improved bureaucratic or market functioning to such social problems as rise

institutional experiments in which technocrats are typically preeminent have normally emerged. See Alfred Stepan, *The State and Society*, p. 55.

[8] There have been major elements of the technocratic response to social mobilization in a broad range of recent cases in the newly industrializing countries (NICs), including the *Estado Novo* of Brazil, the postrevolutionary regime of Mexico, the Lee Kwan Yew government in Singapore, and the Chyun Do Hwan regime in South Korea.

[9] This appears true, for example, of the French Grands Corps since World War II. See Ezra Suleiman, *Elites in French Society*, pp. 193–222.

[10] As Stepan points out, this procedure is posited under Roman law, which forms the basis of most Latin American legal codes. It is also common practice in East Asian political systems. See Alfred Stepan, *The State and Society*, p. 37; and Roy Hofheinz, Jr., and Kent E. Calder, *The Eastasia Edge*, pp. 68–86.

to the level of public issues. Often they engage in extensive formal consultation with social groups, using corporatist advisory mechanisms, but they strive to keep the policy process closed to spontaneous political inputs. They argue, often on the basis of economic theory, that, if only efficiency and productivity can be improved, in the long run all will be better off.

Substantively, the technocratic response normally involves predominant, although not exclusive, reliance on "regulative" rather than "distributive" policies.[11] In other words, intervention through policymakers is limited largely to stimulating growth by selective development incentives and regulating the market by administrative means. There is little effort at achieving welfare goals or in responding to other political demands from below.[12]

Where a technocratic approach is employed by a regime not dependent upon popular assent for its continuation in office, as in the cases of the Brazilian or South Korean regimes of the high-growth 1970s[13] or of the early Meiji government in nineteenth-century Japan, such an approach may successfully generate economic growth. It may also create new social and economic power centers and so alter the center of political gravity that stable conservative rule allowing a central role for established elites may continue for some time. This is especially true when such a regime succeeds in retaining the loyalty of the countryside, as the major East Asian modernizers have done.[14]

But where the authoritarian regime is weak, as in Count Witte's Imperial Russia, success is more problematic for the technocratic response.[15] Where parliamentary democracy prevails and mass influences are strong, technocratic approaches may experience problems assuring *political* continuity or responding to mass social demands.[16] Raymond Barre succeeded

[11] This distinction is developed more fully in Theodore J. Lowi, "Four Systems of Policy, Politics, and Choice," pp. 298–310.

[12] The technocratic response embodies many of the policy correlates associated with Tarrow's "productive coalition." See Sidney Tarrow, *Between Center and Periphery*, p. 38.

[13] On technocratic approaches to issues of economic development in the Third World, see Samuel P. Huntington and Joan M. Nelson, *No Easy Choice.*

[14] Hofheinz and Calder, *The Eastasia Edge*, pp. 41–52, 87–101.

[15] On Imperial Russia's abortive version of the technocratic response, see Theodore H. Von Laue, *Sergei Witte and the Industrialization of Russia.*

[16] Technocrats may, of course, be able to perpetuate their own preeminence *despite* political change, as the case of France under a Socialist administration during 1981–1986 demonstrated. But how common this ability to maintain preemi-

admirably in restraining government deficits during the late 1970s, while also beginning the painful rationalization of noncompetitive French basic industry. Indeed, he curbed the rise of government spending more effectively during his tenure as French prime minister than any other head of government in the industrialized world.[17] Yet Barre's stern fiscal discipline, which involved denying subsidies to fishermen in Brittany and steelworkers in Lorraine who had been crucial lower-income members of the French conservative constituency, also appears to have contributed to Valéry Giscard d'Estaing's presidential defeat in 1981 and the massive National Assembly defeat of the Right which followed soon thereafter.[18] The purer forms of technocratic regimes, to which the Barre government was remarkably close for a parliamentary democracy, have had the common political problem of limited sensitivity to grassroots circumstances and interests, whatever their virtues in various other aspects of economic management might be.

The Material Response

Technocratic strategies generally appear superficially simpler and safer for conservative modernizers than does explicit involvement in mass politics, with all its turbulence and uncertainty. Detached representation of broadly held national goals, such as economic growth, has generally seemed a firmer basis of legitimacy for conservatives than direct competitive appeals to citizen self-interest, especially given the frequent divergence of elite and mass interests outlined above. But sometimes there is no alternative. Weakness in intraelite factional competition may dictate an appeal to competitive political decision in a broader based forum, as it did for Disraeli. Encouraging nonelite political

---

nence is, despite political turbulence and change, remains questionable since unique historical experiences have created an unusually powerful and centralized administrative state in France. In any event, party political continuity and persistence of technocratic elites are clearly separate issues.

[17] Between 1975 and 1981, the ratio of government spending to GNP in France actually declined from 22.9 to 21.9 percent of GNP, while it remained constant at 23.6 percent in the United States, and rose from 13.7 to 18.9 percent in Japan. See Bank of Japan Research and Statistics Department (Nihon Ginkō Chōsa Tōkei Kyoku), *Kokusai Hikaku Tōkei (International Comparative Statistics)*, 1982 ed., p. 78.

[18] See Howard Machin and Vincent Wright, "Why Mitterand Won: The French Presidential Elections of April–May, 1981."

participation may appear as a safety valve or mode of incorporation, as it seems to have done at times for Bismarck and Itō Hirobumi. Broad based distributive political appeals offering roads, schools, and other public works may be necessary in forging a viable ruling coalition, as employed in Italy since 1945.[19] Or conservative modernizers may be simply forced into more grassroots-oriented political strategies by occupation induced changes in political structure, as they were in Japan, Italy, and Germany after World War II.

The most distinctive substantive feature of the material response is its nonmarket orientation. Forms of compensation politics—the explicitly distributive, election-oriented aspect of the materialist response—include subsidies, public works, and low-interest credit for areas and social groups of political importance in maintaining continued ruling party preeminence. They can also, however, include nondistributive entitlement policies, such as social welfare programs, which materially benefit large numbers of people and help to secure the support of such people for the prevailing political order. The key elements distinguishing material from technocratic response are the former's specifically distributive political character and its central involvement of party politicians, as opposed to the central role of bureaucrats in the latter instance.

Nonmilitary, explicitly distributive political strategies for perpetuating political stability were by no means invented in postwar Japan, although they have certainly been quite pronounced there.[20] Despite its turbulence in the 1860s and 1870s, even the Imperial Germany of the Blood and Iron Chancellor Bismarck could not rely exclusively upon patriotic appeals to stem the prospective tide of socialist advance stirred by the Industrial Revolution and the increasing cohesiveness of the German working class in the 1880s. Faced with the rapid migration to the industrial centers of the Midlands, deepening poverty and disease in urban Britain, and an increasingly cohesive and politically insistent working class, Disraeli could not confidently calculate that stirring nationalist passion would be sufficient to maintain Tory political preeminence. Preserving or recreating the organic fabric upon which conservative political primacy rested required

[19] See Tarrow, *Between Center and Periphery*, pp. 35–38.

[20] On some of the possible political strategies in the developing world, see Ellen Kay Trimberger, *Revolution from Above*.

"preemptive conservative reform"—strikingly similar to the political forms subsequently to emerge in Japan a century later. In all these cases political stability, the unifying concern of conservatives across the ages, appears to have been the guiding intent.

Once the choice of an explicitly political, yet nonmartial strategy toward lower income groups was made, it almost inevitably had to be a material response, since material benefits were consistently the central demand of lower-income groups against the conservative state. For Bismarck, preemptive conservative reform was an explicit "carrot and the stick" policy, conceived largely in material terms. It involved systematically adopting popular elements of the opposition socialist program in an attempt to undercut the socialist political movement itself and to generate popular support for political measures aimed ultimately at repressing the socialists themselves.[21] After attempting to severely circumscribe the Social Democrats in 1875 and 1878, Bismarck suddenly proposed a comprehensive state welfare program, the first of its kind in the world. In April 1881 he proposed establishing an Imperial Insurance Office to insure against accidents all workers in mines and factories with incomes under 2,000 marks a year. The Sickness Insurance Law of 1883, the Accident Insurance Law of 1884, and the Old Age and Invalidity Law of 1887 were all enacted during Bismarck's chancellorship. Later, in 1911, these acts were unified into a great social insurance code which set a standard for the world.

Disraeli as well adopted "preemptive conservative reform," with his prescription for "Tory men and Whig measures." It appears that Disraeli was by no means committed philosophically to principles of either a broad popular franchise or of welfare policy, as we know them today.[22] But rising working-class consciousness, together with a desire to undercut both Gladstone's Liberals and rivals within Tory ranks led Disraeli to support sweeping reform of the franchise. Disraeli spurred the Reform Bill of 1867, which enfranchised nearly a million new voters, including much of the urban working class. During 1874–1876, following the first clear-cut conservative electoral victory in over thirty years, the Disraeli conservative cabinet introduced and passed eleven major acts in the fields of education, housing, pub-

[21] For an explanation of the rationale for these programs in Bismarck's words, see Louis Snyder, *The Blood and Iron Chancellor*, pp. 280–83. See also A. J. P. Taylor, *Bismarck*, pp. 202–7.

[22] Paul Smith, *Disraelian Conservatism and Social Reform*, p. 3.

lic health, and labor legislation. Due to complications which domestic reform posed within Tory ranks, Disraeli turned after 1876 from domestic reform back to nationalistic gestures—purchase of the Suez Canal shares and confrontation abroad in Afghanistan and South Africa—to sustain his political base. But in both the Reform Act of 1867 and the social reforms of the mid-1870s, he demonstrated dramatic pragmatism and flexibility, a sharp contrast with the rigid praxis of the gentry-oriented Tory politicians who had dominated conservative ranks for the previous several generations.[23]

Conservative politicians have not, of course, universally preempted progressive opposition proposals, as this case of British Toryism suggests. To the contrary, preemptive conservative reform has been the exception rather than the rule throughout the industrialized West. Nineteenth-century French conservatives, for example, were much more rigid than their German, British, or even Swedish counterparts in introducing social insurance or pension schemes.[24] Indeed, as Ashford points out, conservatively-oriented France did not have a full-fledged social security system until 1946.[25] Similarly, patronage politics has been limited to a relatively small range of cases in the Western industrialized world.[26] But preemptive reform and a strong emphasis on distributive politics have been extremely common in post–World War II Japan; indeed, they have been the defining hallmarks of Japanese conservative policymaking in practice, particularly during and shortly after periods of political crisis.

A crucial issue for comparative analysis of stability-oriented policymaking is thus *why* some policymakers depart so abruptly from established patterns of policy, even in opposition to their established constituencies, when most do not do so. Earlier Western examples of preemptive reform suggest for verification in the postwar Japanese case the hypothesis that three conditions are crucial to preemptive reform. First, pressing mass demands exist for change. In both the Germany of Bismarck and the Britain of Disraeli, the Industrial Revolution and the rapid urbanization it fostered created rapid deterioration in working conditions, which

[23] For more details on the evolution of British Conservative attitudes on social issues during the mid-nineteenth Century, see Samuel Beer, *Modern British Politics*, pp. 245–76.

[24] On the contrasting forces driving the development of the British and Swedish welfare systems, see Heclo, *Modern Social Politics.*

[25] See Douglas Ashford, *Policy and Politics in France.*

[26] Martin Shefter, *Patronage and its Opponents.*

naturally stimulated demands for change. Industrialization also, as Marx noted, led to changes in the social basis of production, particularly the concentration of workers in larger production units, where they were more susceptible to radical organization than otherwise. Not surprisingly, social demands for state action in late nineteenth-century Germany rose rapidly, much more so than in France, where industrialization itself had not proceeded as rapidly.

A second background social factor facilitating conservative reform in both Britain and Germany was a rapid expansion of resources available to the state for allocation. The insurance schemes with which social reform began were not nearly as expensive as the entitlement programs of the mid-twentieth century have been, but they did presuppose a solid, growing revenue basis. The rapidly expanding economies of Germany and Britain provided this base much more readily than did the more stagnant economy of France.

The third and final precondition for preemptive reform suggested by European experience is a strong perception by conservative leadership, ironically, of its own political weakness. Prior to the Reform Act of 1867, for example, Disraeli was not only the leader of a minority government, but he even failed to fully control his own party, deeply rent by factional divisions.[27] The prospect of developing new constituencies to which he could appeal, thus solidifying his position within the party system, may well have driven Disraeli to reform.[28] Bismarck, while chancellor of a more autocratic system, also was vulnerable to both the parties, especially the Social Democrats and the Kaiser himself. His unusual vulnerability may have given reform greater attraction for him than it would otherwise have possessed.

The Technocratic Structural Bias of the Japanese State

In no nation have political elites exclusively pursued one of the three approaches to legitimacy and stability outlined above. Everywhere in the industrialized world policy responses have

[27] Paul Adelman, *Gladstone, Disraeli and Later Victorian Politics*, p. 15.

[28] The drive toward reform seems to have dissipated in the latter part of Disraeli's career as his intraparty position stabilized, supporting the notion that intraparty vulnerability helped drive the original reform orientation. See James Cornford, "The Transformation of Conservatism in the Late Nineteenth Century."

been hybrid, but there have been central tendencies, relatively constant over time and shaped heavily by political structure and culture. The French state, for example, has long been martially and technocratically oriented, with a relatively weak material orientation. American government, by contrast, has less frequently pursued technocratic strategies, although it has oscillated between distributive compensation politics, preeminent in the 1920s and 1930s, and nationalistic approaches to problems of political unity and stability.

Historical and cultural factors long predisposed Japanese conservative policymaking toward nationalism and technocracy. Perhaps most importantly, late industrializer status, coupled with the war and economic confrontation that Meiji, Taishō, and early Shōwa Japan perennially experienced, stimulated creation of a strong bureaucracy before many of the other major institutional actors in the modern Japanese political economy began to emerge. Historical forces also created strong and cohesive private sector Japanese industrial groups, without allowing labor to gain nearly the prominence it attained in Western Europe.

Some aspects of Japan's technocratic bias preceded economic confrontation with the West. Japan's powerful bureaucracy began to emerge during the mid-Tokugawa Period, as warriors moved from the countryside into the regional castle towns (*jōkamachi*) to become administrative officials; however, they were not bureaucrats in the Weberian sense of officials whose power is vested in their office since these warriors retained hereditary samurai status. The shogunate in *Edo* also established a protobureaucratic administrative office (*goyōbeya*). Moreover, the strong Confucian influences that pervaded Tokugawa Japan further reinforced the institutional position of the emerging samurai-bureaucratic class. Following the coming of Perry's black ships in 1853, new requirements of defense and foreign affairs produced additional bureaucratic offices, although these at first were rather unsystematically appended to existing structures.[29] The first two decades following the Meiji Restoration of 1868, however, produced thoroughgoing administrative centralization and rationalization,[30] creating a strong technocracy formally responsible directly to the emperor. This technocracy emerged as the central force in both policymaking and implementation.

[29] Marius B. Jansen and Gilbert Rozman, eds. *Japan in Transition*, p. 16.
[30] *Ibid.*, pp. 17–18.

Like France and Germany, Japan in the late nineteenth century was a follower nation in the process of global industrialization, facing all the pressures such nations typically confront, as Gerschenkron has pointed out so well.[31] As in continental Europe, Japan's follower nation status reinforced the role of the bureaucracy in policy formation and implementation. It also intensified Japan's strong orientation toward economic efficiency in traded sectors of the economy. But in Japan there was special urgency, since Japan was much more severely handicapped in international economic and political competition than the major continental states. Japan was a non-Western nation in a world of predatory imperialist European powers, forced suddenly to open itself after two centuries of self-imposed isolation which had left it technologically backward. Its unusually large population was rapidly growing in the late nineteenth century, and its relatively narrow resource base generated rising deficits in food and raw materials after 1890.

Unequal treaties prevented Japan from exercising full control over its tariffs from the 1850s until 1911. Furthermore, Japan lacked the extensive protected colonial markets that insulated Britain and France from global market forces. Overwhelming economic pressures from the West on Japan, exploiting its vulnerable circumstances, brought into question Japan's very survival as an independent nation. The bureaucratic structures Japan set up to respond ultimately became vital to national economic survival, although at the time of their inception they were often not clearly designed to do so.

There was also a powerful domestic rationale in Meiji Japan for the emergence of a strong nationally oriented bureaucracy, as Chalmers Johnson points out.[32] The Meiji leadership, sensitive to the criticism that the two major feudal domains that had overthrown the Tokugawa shogunate (Satsuma and Chōshū) were monopolizing power, wanted both to establish a broader basis of legitimacy and neutralize rampant corruption. Furthermore, the Meiji leaders needed a vehicle for maintaining authoritarian control after 1890, when the National Diet opened and the political parties began pressing for an expanded role in policymaking.

The essence of the modern bureaucratic structure was estab-

[31] Alexander Gerschenkron, *Economic Backwardness in Historical Perspective.* Cambridge, Mass.: Harvard University Press, 1960.

[32] Johnson, *MITI and the Japanese Miracle,* p. 37.

lished during the first fifteen years after the Meiji Restoration, with the foundation of the ministries of Finance and Foreign Affairs in 1869, the Home Ministry in 1873, the Ministry of Agriculture and Commerce in 1881, and the Bank of Japan in 1882. The key ministries were thus set up significantly before the emergence of full-fledged political parties during the 1880s and 1890s—a reality with profound significance for evolution of the Japanese political system. This historical precedence of the bureaucracy strongly reinforced the institutional preeminence of technocrats in prewar policymaking.[33]

The birth of Japanese industrial policy and the emergence of a systematically strategic Japanese state was a long, incremental process,[34] despite the strong external pressures operating on Japan to adopt a "plan-rational" approach to economic management.[35] During the 1870s the Meiji government had tried to blunt the force of foreign economic inroads and stimulate industrialization by encouraging public enterprise, but it largely abandoned this approach after 1880.

Although the Ministry of Agriculture and Commerce, established in 1881, sponsored and operated the large Yawata steelworks opened in 1901, agriculture was a greater concern of the Japanese bureaucracy than industry until 1925.[36] Only following a major change in state structure during that year—the formation of an independent Ministry of Commerce and Industry giving industrial bureaucrats more autonomy—did industrial policy begin to take shape. Industrial policy began to emerge in reaction to economic crises, initially concentrated in the small business area. The sense of the economic bureaucracy's national security importance to Japan as a whole emerged more clearly after 1931, during the mobilization for war first with China and ultimately against the Anglo-Saxon powers of the West as well. World War II immeasurably strengthened the institutional position of the

[33] Bureaucrats were, as Silberman points out, at times sensitive to political pressures. But the institutional context in which they operated pushed them continually in the direction of technocratic, efficiency-oriented approaches to public policy. See Bernard Silberman, "The Bureaucratic Role in Japan, 1900–1945: The Bureaucrat as Politician," in *Japan in Crisis*, eds. Bernard Silberman and Harry D. Harootunian.

[34] Johnson, *MITI and the Japanese Miracle*, pp. 83–115.

[35] Under a "plan-rational" approach, the state, in Johnson's conception, will give greatest precedence to promoting the structure of domestic industry that enhances the nation's international competitiveness. See *ibid.*, p. 19.

[36] *Ibid.*, p. 88.

economic bureaucracy within Japanese policymaking,[37] as did selective postwar U.S. occupation reforms. Leaving the economic bureaucracy virtually untouched, these reforms decimated major political rivals.

Parallel to the national economic security bureaucracy and overshadowing it in size, prestige, and policy importance throughout the prewar period was a strong domestic administrative apparatus.[38] At the center of this bureaucratic complex was the powerful Home Ministry (*Naimushō*), supervising the police forces and the highly centralized local government structure (including subunits named prefectures after the French pattern) created in 1871 to replace the feudal *han* system of local governance prevalent before the Meiji Restoration. The Naimushō also handled a broad range of other administrative functions, from election management to fire control.

Reinforcing the substantial power of the Meiji administrative state were deeply rooted traditions in Japanese political culture. For centuries there had been great respect for scholarly men of affairs, reinforced by the neo-Confucian traditions that pervaded Japan during the Tokugawa period. Japan also had a traditionally strong hierarchical consciousness, which even today appears to give particular legitimacy to nonelected, technocratic leadership and the corporatist modes of administration it often employs.[39] Reinforcing the underlying "subject-participant" cultural orientation of the Japanese people,[40] the Meiji government placed strong emphasis on loyalty to the emperor. This reinforced the position of bureaucracy in Japan because bureaucrats, in contrast to politicians, were regarded as servants of the emperor, and hence selfless representatives of the general will. Although nominally servants, bureaucrats were in fact able to make policy by ruling through imperial ordinances which they themselves

[37] *Ibid.*, pp. 116–97.

[38] The centralization of the military bureaucracy through dissolution of the han (1871) and the introduction of military conscription (1873) was another major parallel development, although tangential to the analysis presented here.

[39] Verba, Miyake, and Watanuki have found in recent research that this strong hierarchical consciousness and willingness to defer to administrative authority continues to pervade Japan to a much greater extent than it influences most nations of the world.

[40] This is an orientation highly sensitive to policy outputs, but not insistent on active participation in policymaking. It appears to prevade both German and Japanese political culture. See Sidney Verba, *The Civic Culture*, pp. 24–26.

drafted. These ordinances became an extralegal means of exerting direct bureaucratic control over wide areas of policy.

To be sure, the Meiji bureaucracy and its immediate successors were not in positions to rule autonomously. After 1878 local elective assemblies determined local budgets under the authority of appointive prefectural governors[41]—a more democratic situation than typically prevailed in the nations of continental Europe. Anti-Meiji political pressures combined with a Japanese desire for international legitimacy to spur the opening of an Imperial Diet in 1889. Like the German parliament, however, the new Diet was severely circumscribed in its formal powers; it was only able to expand its influence very slowly through crucial leverage it possessed over government budget expansion proposals.

In international economic affairs, the influence of politicians was sharply circumscribed by the overriding national economic threat posed by Western imperialist competition and the need for a strategic, technocratic response.[42] Until 1945 and even after, bureaucratic influence over politicians was substantially greater than the reverse. An 1899 amendment to the Civil Service Appointment Ordinance sharply limited political appointments to bureaucratic posts, preserving the technocratic character of the government ministries, even as the power of the political parties slowly increased. Yet 36 percent of all Japanese cabinet members over the 1900–1945 period were former career government officials, and local government officials were also predominantly active members of the career civil service. In few major nations, other perhaps than France and Germany, was the power of the technocratic administrative state greater than it was in Meiji and Taishō Japan (1868–1925).

A central element of the pre–World War II Japanese technocratic state was, of course, the military, since the strong consciousness of external siege most Japanese experienced had both military-political and economic dimensions. In the early twentieth century, as urbanization and industrialization proceeded, encouraging patriotism was clearly a central element of the Japanese conservative strategy for preserving the position of dominant elites. But the military dimension was largely swept away,

[41] Jansen and Rozman, eds., *Japan in Transition*, pp. 34–35.

[42] Japan's relative lack of colonies (in contrast to Britain and France), coupled with unequal treaties which limited tariff autonomy until 1911, made the Japanese economy considerably more open during the Meiji period than major economies of the West.

institutionally speaking, with the dissolution of Japan's armed forces and military industry, together with the purge of wartime leadership after 1945; a powerful, preeminent civilian administrative state remained. Economic necessity and the mandate of foreign occupiers encouraged Japanese conservative policymakers to formulate a technocratic response to the problems confronting them and to strengthen the bureaucratic institutions capable of implementing this.

Over time, the big business community assumed a major role in the Japanese political economy, and by the Taishō Period (1912–1925) it even challenged the bureaucracy for preeminent influence over policymaking in certain sectors. Prior to the Meiji Restoration there were, of course, some major commercial houses that played central roles in economic life, including Mitsui and Sumitomo. But the sharp concentration of Japanese business activity in a few firms was preeminently a phenomenon of the period after 1880. An attempt to create an indigenous industrial base capable of competing with the Western imperialists[43] began with extensive government contracts after 1868 and the sale of a wide range of government enterprises to the private sector after 1880.[44] Government holdings were sold primarily to the "political merchants"—in the main, the leaders of the four major *zaibatsu*[45]—on highly preferential terms, greatly augmenting their asset base and potential profitability.

These zaibatsu received powerful stimuli from the government military and naval programs, especially during and after the Sino-Japanese War of 1894-1895.[46] During the 1890–1910 period, spanning both the Sino-Japanese and the Russo-Japanese wars, heavy industry and marine transportation also began to grow rapidly in Japan, stimulating the economic development of the zaibatsu still further. During this period the zaibatsu rose to a decisively powerful position in the Japanese political economy,[47] becoming

[43] For details, see Thomas C. Smith, *Political Change and Industrial Development in Japan*, pp. 86–100. On the case of the strategically important shipping industry, see William Wray, *NYK*.

[44] This effort to create "national champions" has strong parallels in the French and, to a lesser extent, the Japanese industrial policy of the 1960s. Government financial crisis was, however, a more important factor for the Meiji leadership than in the post–World War II French and Japanese cases.

[45] These included Mitsui, Mitsubishi, Sumitomo, and Yasuda.

[46] Tsuchiya Takao, *Nihon Keizaishi* (*An Economic History of Japan*), p. 142.

[47] See G. C. Allen, *A Short Economic History of Japan*, chapter 8, on this topic.

increasingly large and diversified shipbuilding, engineering, commercial, and financial combines.

In the decades following, between 1910 and 1930, zaibatsu political influence also rose steadily, a consequence of the increasing economic power of these large industrial and commercial groups and their willingness to support the emerging political parties financially. Influence over the parties aided the largest of the zaibatsu in restraining the growth of competitors. Mitsui for example, used the Diet effectively to break the power of the parvenu Suzuki zaibatsu after World War I.[48]

Big business political influence with the parties also allowed regressive policies, often inimical to social welfare, to proceed, giving the Japanese state of the period an antiprogressive bias. But this business influence could not seriously undermine the Japanese technocratic state, however much it influenced the fledgling political parties, for the parties remained strongly subordinate to the bureaucracy in the policy process as a whole. Despite Hara Kei's persistent efforts to expand the flow of distributive political benefits, the cohesiveness of major ministries and the opposition of the oligarchs made this difficult. Hara himself was assassinated in 1921, and the attempt to systematically develop political parties as a counterforce to bureaucracy in the policy process stagnated soon thereafter.

As Henry Rosovsky points out, throughout the entire 1887–1940 period government was the largest and most important investor in the Japanese economy. Its share of domestic capital formation never averaged less than 40 percent and very rarely dropped that low.[49] And the disposition of this massive investment—devoted largely to infrastructure with military and heavy industry—was almost totally at the discretion of the bureaucracy, despite some intermittent intervention from politicians in the first three decades of the twentieth century. This massive flow of resources through the public sector, together with cultural esteem for career government officials and the formidable structural advantages of the technocratic state, prolonged bureaucratic preeminence over big business into the postwar period. The demise of the parties, the populist orientation of the military in the 1930s, and the mobilization for World War II all enhanced the power of bureaucrats versus the big business world

[48] John G. Roberts, *Mitsui*, pp. 242–45.

[49] Henry Rosovsky, *Capital Formation in Japan*, p. 23.

in Japan, even though the weight within the business community of the largest firms was itself steadily rising.[50]

The technocratic bias of the prewar Japanese conservative state, then, included a prominent advisory although not politically dominant role for big business. At least until 1931, the distinctly marginal role of organized labor sharply contrasted to the substantial and steadily rising influence of big business in the policy process. This was partly due to the distinctive character of Japan's industrial revolution, which did not stimulate the rise of a vigorous organized labor movement; political repression and preemption by the technocratic state also inhibited the emergence of a powerful labor movement.

Among the most crucial implications of Japanese industrialization patterns for political development was the fact that in contrast to most Western experience, industrialization occurred predominantly in small organizations. "Socialization of the mode of production," in Marx's phrase, did not occur to nearly the degree that it did in most Western nations, forestalling the emergence of large, potentially radical groups of factory workers, and enhancing the prospective short-run political viability of Japan's technocratic state. In 1930, some 30 percent of all Japanese workers were engaged in manufacturing, with 70 percent of these in plants of less than fifty people; however, Russia by 1910 *already* had over one half of its workers in factories of over five-hundred, while Japan *even in 1940*—thirty years later—was well below this figure.[51] The more rapid progress of heavy industrialization in Russia, coupled with subcontracting, distribution, and handicraft sector complexities in Japan, account for most of the difference. The small group character of Japanese manufacturing encouraged intimate, face-to-face management-labor relations in a society where cultural factors made such personal relationships

[50] The share in terms of paid-in capital of the "Big Four" zaibatsu in some key sectors of the Japanese national ecoomy changed as follows between 1937 and 1945:

Sector	*1937*	*1945*
Banking	21.0	48.0
Insurance	49.0	51.2
Machine Tools	18.6	46.2
Marine Transportation	16.2	60.8
Total	10.4	24.5

Source: Eleanor M. Hadley, *Antitrust in Japan*, pp. 48–49, 54–55.

[51] Cyril Black et al., *The Modernization of Japan and Russia*, p. 188.

enduring. The net effect helped give workplace relations a highly conservative, paternalistic cast; this, in turn, reduced prospects for the sort of militant worker political action in Japan that helped subvert Witte's technocratic state in tsarist Russia.

While living in the city, most Japanese workers had an integrated workplace and residence. In 1930, 60 percent of male manufacturing workers and 80 percent of female workers lived in company dormitories. After 1930, the lifetime employment system began, further undercutting the rise of class consciousness in the classic European sense. In addition, there was much more movement back and forth between village and factory in Japan than in Russia and elsewhere, partly because factories were frequently located either in the countryside or in small towns close to rural areas.[52]

As a consequence of the foregoing, an industrial working class which could challenge the technocratic state was late to develop in Japan. It finally arose in an era when both management and the state were more inclined to concede social benefits to labor than had been true when Britain was modernizing.[53] Pragmatic conservative impulses were already emerging, as evidenced by introduction of health insurance in 1922, although flexibility in the face of demands from below was much less widespread than after World War II. The combination of labor weakness and conservative pragmatism meant there was little basis in Japan for either development of a strident political Left bent on using the state to expropriate capitalists or for the emergence of a well-defined working-class consciousness.

To be sure, an energetic working-class movement was beginning to develop in the growing industrial centers of Ōsaka, Kōbe, Tokyo, and Yokohama during the first two decades of the twentieth century, threatening the industrial paternalism Japanese management was just beginning to espouse.[54] At this point political action by the Japanese technocratic state became crucial in preventing the emergence of labor as a major political actor.

Three fundamentally political conditions worked against labor.[55] First, the Japanese state frequently used coercion to inhibit

[52] See *ibid.*, p. 190.

[53] See Ronald Dore, *British Factory-Japanese Factory*, 338–71.

[54] On these developments, see Gordon, *The Evolution of Labor Relations in Japan*, pp. 107–21, 421.

[55] See T. J. Pempel and Keiichi Tsunekawa, "Corporatism without Labor? The

and suppress the labor movement and the leftist parties to which that movement was affiliated. In 1900 the government passed the Public Peace Police Law, prohibiting anyone from forcing strikes upon workers or forcing employers to concede demands regarding labor conditions and wages; this law made the development of the labor movement extremely difficult. In 1925 this legislation was augmented by passage of the infamous Peace Preservation Law and the creation of the Special Police Force to act against any "radical organizations." Under the revised version of the law passed in 1928, the penalty for labor activities deemed subversive was death.

Second, electoral-parliamentary considerations also worked against the emergence of labor as a political force in prewar Japan. When universal manhood suffrage was finally introduced in 1925, it was accompanied by a Peace Preservation Law aimed directly at labor-related political movements. Very strict electoral laws impeded effective campaigning by labor. In the face of harassment and the rather mild character of Japan's industrial revolution, which encouraged acceptance of paternalistic solutions to labor problems, the parties of the Left failed to gain over 10 percent of the total vote, even at their high point in 1937.[56]

Third, the preemptive actions of both employers and government bureaucrats, intent on heading off the development of a powerful labor movement, contributed to the political weakness of labor in prewar Japan. Enterprise unionism, as opposed to industrial unionism, was one major manifestation of this; it was introduced on the National Railways in 1906 and spread rapidly to the private sector, especially to larger corporations. Moderate factory legislation, job security, and seniority wages were also introduced in an attempt to prevent a militant labor movement from emerging.

Nonlabor interest group politics were not, of course entirely dormant in prewar Japan. Landlords, small businessmen, and other regional notables (*meibōka*) played significant roles in national politics through their mobilizing support for the political parties. This political role did generate some impact on policy-making—stimulating the creation of the *Nōrin Chūkin* Bank in 1923, while encouraging railways, schools, and promoting agri-

---

Japanese Anomaly," in *Trends toward Corporatist Intermediation*, eds. Philippe Schmitter and Gerhard Lehmbruch, pp. 253–54.

[56] *Ibid.*, p. 254.

cultural public works construction during the first third of the twentieth century. But the magnitude of distributive benefits spread across Japan, both in absolute terms and in comparison with expenditures on military and industrial development, was minor by postwar standards,[57] and the major institutions allocating these distributive benefits were likewise mostly postwar creations.

The agricultural and small business sectors had clearly needed and strongly desired distributive benefits from government. But the bureaucracy, clearly controlling most agricultural and small business pressure groups, was generally able to resist their demands. The relative institutional weakness of the political parties, their domination by big business, and the panoply of corporatist mechanisms for coopting nonelite pressure groups all worked to minimize the leverage of such groups with the bureaucracy.

Despite occasional ad hoc concessions to conservative parties, particularly the Seiyūkai, the prewar Japanese technocratic state was relatively insulated from mass interest group pressure for four reasons. First, bureaucrats under the Meiji constitution were formally servants of the emperor, with no direct public accountability. Second, local governments, a major venue for mass interest articulation in the postwar period, did not elect their executive leadership. Third, national level parties, relatively receptive to meibōka demands, had marginal influence on policymaking. Finally, the bureaucracy was able to incorporate mass interests and thereby neutralize their political influence through the use of nōkai (prewar agricultural associations) and other such corporatist organizations, heavily regulated by the bureaucracy. Government officials, in short, largely insulated from broader social demands, were able to maintain their institutional preeminence even when response to such demands became politically necessary.

The structural heritage, then, which prewar Japanese politics bequeathed to political evolution after 1945 was the very antithesis of a populist one. To be sure, a history of experience with

[57] Agricultural public works surged during 1910 and then increased steadily from 1920–1934 to 23.5 billion for the 1930–1934 period. But this later figure was only one-fifth the level, adjusted for inflation, of such public works during the first post–World War II agricultural public works spending surge of 1950–1954. See Sawamoto Moriyuki, *Kōkyō Tōshi Hyaku Nen no Ayumi* (*A Hundred Year History of Public Investment*), p. 80.

democratic institutions left a residue of abstract familiarity with notions such as popular sovereignty.[58] But in terms of enduring political structure and culture, bureaucracy was dominant, backed by an oligarchic coalition of landlords and big business reminiscent of Germany's alliance between iron and rye.[59] Such redistributive impulses as one discerns in prewar and wartime Japanese politics, especially during and after the 1930s had been centered in the Home Ministry, abolished at the end of 1947, and in the military, disbanded in the wake of Japan's defeat in 1945.

The prevailing Japanese conservative political coalition, in a word, was biased strongly toward the technocratic response, with a martial tinge. Fiscal resources were directed toward economic and military development at all costs, often drawn from the impoverished countryside. Rice imports were encouraged to facilitate lower wages. Industrial concentration was promoted where efficient—even if the cost was rising inequities between the emerging zaibatsu conglomerates and small traditional firms. There was little structural impetus for welfare programs, while a strong bias dominated in state spending for nationalistic ends, both economic and military. Above all, Japan's technocratic state was rigid in the face of pressures from below, when efficiency criteria failed to dictate a response.

Postwar Reforms and the Technocratic Possibility: 1945–1948

This volume, as noted in the introduction, is a search for a parsimonious explanation of the relationship between Japanese politics and public policy for the years from 1949 to 1986, as Japanese conservative politicians and businessmen strove to create and maintain political order amidst intermittent political crisis. But the three early postwar years, between the coming of MacArthur to Atsugi in late August 1945 and the return of Yoshida to power following the Shōwa Denkō scandal of late 1948, are crucially important as background to the following conservative struggle for stability. During the early postwar years complex transformations occurred in both state structure and the balance

[58] As Edwin O. Reischauer and others point out, this residue of familiarity was a major element in facilitating the rapid revival of Japanese democracy after World War II.

[59] See Alexander Gerschenkron, *Bread and Democracy in Germany.*

of broader social forces. Early postwar changes undermined the technocratic possibility in nontraded sectors such as agriculture and construction, permitting the emergence of the crisis and compensation cycle so central to Japanese domestic policymaking after 1949. But those changes simultaneously enhanced technocratic preeminence still further in industrial policy and other related areas. They thus intensified the bifurcated, uneven overall profile of bureaucratic preeminence in Japan, reflected in the sharply contrasting yet valid observations of Nakasone Yasuhiro and other observers with which this chapter began.

In the fields of trade and industrial policy, the first three years of Allied occupation consolidated the dominance of technocrats in areas where they had never previously been able to exercise full dominance. Throughout the prewar and wartime periods, for example, the Ministry of Commerce and Industry, predecessor of MITI, had waged a constant struggle with the zaibatsu and the industrial control associations regarding pricing, output, and resource allocation decisions. But SCAP, declaring the zaibatsu responsible for the war economy, banned private cartels and insisted that government officials—that is, technocrats—exercise the powers previously accrued to the control associations.[60] It thus helped reinforce the bureaucratic preeminence in industrial matters, the basis for frequent assertions about bureaucratic primacy by students of industrial policy.

SCAP also approved foreign exchange budgeting controls for the bureaucracy and ordered dissolution of the zaibatsu.[61] Only the holding companies of the zaibatsu, together with two large general trading companies (Mitsui and Mitsubishi), were thoroughly dismembered,[62] and the traders had largely recovered by the late 1950s. But SCAP's deconcentration and antimonopoly program threw a degree of uncertainty into intercorporate relations in Japan, allowing the bureaucracy to dominate by manipulating tensions within the disunited private sector.

The postwar purge of officials implicated in the war effort also helped strengthen the economic bureaucracy and the prospects for a technocratic response to policy problems in its sectors of responsibility by undermining rival power centers and leaving

[60] Johnson, *MITI and the Japanese Miracle*, p. 73.

[61] On the details of the deconcentration and antimonopoly measures undertaken, see Hadley, *Antitrust in Japan*, pp. 107–24.

[62] Both Mitsui and Mitsubishi were split into around 200 successor companies each.

the economic bureaucracy almost untouched. Of the 1,800 civilian bureaucrats purged, only 9 were from the Ministry of Finance (MOF), and around 42 officials (bureau chiefs and above) were from the Ministry of Commerce and Industry, known during wartime as the Ministry of Munitions.[63] Around 1,300 of the officials purged, by contrast, were from the Home Ministry, representing 70 percent of those purged in the entire civilian sector of the government. Disbanding the armed forces also strengthened the relative position of economic technocrats in Japan. When the Self-Defense Forces were reconstituted during and after the Korean War, MITI and MOF gained positions of preeminence within the postwar military that would have been inconceivable had there been no occupation interlude.[64]

Reinforcing SCAP willingness to accept the preeminence of the economic bureaucrats in their spheres of policymaking was the precarious state of the Japanese economy at the point that fundamental deconcentration decisions were made. Growth was stagnant, inflation high, and until the Korean War began, Japan was incapable of generating the foreign exchange to pay for foreign imports. The great danger seemed to be of Japan remaining an indefinite ward of the United States. Thus, allowing the economic bureaucracy to remain intact and guide the traded sectors toward optimal efficiency in technocratic fashion seemed a wise, self-interested course for the occupation authorities.

Occupation-period reforms had sharply different implications for the nontraded sectors of the Japanese economy, providing the empirical basis for Nakasone Yasuhiro's scepticism about Japanese state capacity and the Japanese consciousness of the state, noted at the beginning of this chapter. Most importantly, SCAP insisted, as a key element in its democratization reforms, on the abolition of the Home Ministry (Naimushō) at the end of 1947, of which Nakasone himself had once been a member. Of the Home Ministry's former officials 1,300 were also purged. At the same time, provisions were made for the election of governors, mayors, and a wide range of other appointed government officials.

At the same time that it dismantled many principal organs of

[63] Johnson, *MITI and the Japanese Miracle*, pp. 41–42. Of the officials purged 70 percent were police and other officials of the Home Ministry.

[64] MITI, for example, gained control of the Procurement Bureau (*Sōbi Kyoku*) within the Defense Agency, while MOF captured control of accounting functions within the agency.

TABLE 3.1
The Explosion of Political Organization in the First Postwar Decade, 1946–1955

	Founding Period of Organizations, by Type					
Organization	1868–1924	1925–1945	1946–1955	1956–1965	Post–1966	N
Agricultural	4.3	4.3	73.9	13.0	4.3	23
Welfare	—	3.3	40.0	33.3	23.3	30
Economic (business and financial)	3.4	4.5	44.3	34.1	13.6	88
Labor	—	3.8	51.9	28.8	15.4	52
Administrative	33.4	6.7	40.0	13.3	6.7	15
Educational	—	8.3	83.3	8.3	—	12
Professional	22.2	—	55.6	22.2	—	9
Citizen/political	—	5.3	26.3	36.8	31.6	19
Other	—	25.0	50.0	25.0	—	4
TOTAL	4.4	4.8	48.8	28.2	13.9	252

Source: Muramatsu Michio and Ellis S. Krauss, "The Conservative Policy Line and the Development of Patterned Pluralism," in Kōzō Yamamura and Yasuba Yasukichi, eds., *The Political Economy of Japan*, Vol. 1 (Stanford: Stanford University Press, 1987), p. 522.

Note: Based on a 1978 survey by Muramatsu Michio of 252 of the most influential interest groups in Japan.

state control in the domestic policy sphere, the occupation also encouraged the formation and expansion of a broad range of interest groups, particularly in the labor, educational, and agricultural areas, suppressed or strongly incorporated by the Japanese state prior to 1945. The number of interest groups was augmented after 1952 by a proliferation of conservative religious and right-wing political groups, similarly suppressed by the Occupation. The overall result, indicated in table 3.1, was the most forceful explosion of political organization in Japan during the first postwar decade that has occurred since the Meiji Restoration in 1868. The proliferation of new organizations during 1946–1955 was especially intense relative to other periods in policy areas, such as labor and agriculture, where redistributive demands were strong. Coupled with the changes in state administrative structure noted above, and the dissolution of the corporatist agricultural associations (nōkai) in 1947, this proliferation in private-sector interest group formation severely circumscribed the technocratic autonomy of the prewar period in many areas of domestic policymaking. It paved the way, especially following the coming of high growth after 1950, for a compensation politics largely oblivious, in its pursuit of material advantage, as Nakasone Yasuhiro had complained, of broad state concerns.

Allied reforms in the domestic policy area were more sweeping in Japan, in the main, than in the other occupied nations. The contrast to Italy is especially instructive. In Italy, from which all Allied forces had departed by January 1, 1946 (more than six years earlier than from Japan) there was no Allied purge of local governors, no Allied imposed administrative decentralization,[65] no dissolution of the Interior Ministry, no devolution of control over police forces to local authority, and no basic change in the prevailing status or structure of labor unions or agricultural cooperatives.[66] SCAP undertook fundamental reforms in all these areas in Japan.

The contrasts to Germany are also important. In both Germany and Japan the collapse of militarist regimes ultimately led to fundamental occupation-inspired changes in many areas. But Allied authorities in Japan undertook several of the most basic reform measures, such as the abolition of the Home Ministry and the dissolution of the nōkai both relatively abruptly and a significant length of time after war's end, in a society where political parties had begun once again to actively function. In Germany, by contrast, many of the reforms were in effect accomplished de facto by the violence which rolled across Germany at war's end, destroying virtually all social and political institutions with it. No functioning parties or individual political entrepreneurs could move in to systematically exploit the political vacuum created by administrative decentralization, as ultimately became possible in Japan.

With the Home Ministry abruptly disbanded and Japanese domestic party politics increasingly organized, strategic opportunities existed during the 1948–1949 period for party politicians to

[65] The Italians themselves provided in their constitution for regional governments but ignored this provision until 1970.

[66] On details of the Allied occupation of Italy, see David W. Ellwood, *Italy*; Ekkhart Krippendorf, *The Role of the United States in the Reconstruction of Italy and West Germany*, and Robert Wolfe, ed. *Americans as Proconsuls*.

assert influence over the successor ministries—construction, labor, and local autonomy among others—in ways not possible while the powerful Home Ministry existed. Not surprisingly, enterprising party politicians rapidly seized these opportunities as Hayasaká Shigezō points out.[67] The chance to link newly autonomous but financially pressed local governments systematically with funding sources presented politicians with additional prospective dividends from Home Ministry dissolution, which tended to intensify the distributive bias of Japanese domestic policymaking even further and offer incentives to politicians to intrude into policymaking.

None of these early postwar changes in Japanese governmental structure, it should be emphasized, directly dictated any particular bias to Japanese public policy or dominance of policymaking by any particular set of actors. In this sense, state structure arguments alone cannot provide sufficient explanations of either policy or policymaking processes in the Japanese case. Continuity and change in the Japanese state structure of the early postwar period tell us much about the ultimate biases of public policy—toward continuity and technocratic responses in economic policymaking and toward change and broader public policy in the more domestic sectors. But state structure alone cannot explain the surges and ebb tides of Japanese domestic policy—the principal concerns of this book.

During 1949 and thereafter, as the story of this volume begins, large numbers of former bureaucrats began entering the conservative political world to assume many of its most prominent positions.[68] Ikeda Hayato became Minister of Finance less than a month after election to the Diet in January 1949, while Transport Vice Minister Satō Eisaku became chief secretary of Yoshida's Liberal Party soon thereafter. At times during the post-1949 period as many as two-thirds of cabinet ministers have been former bureaucrats.[69] But these former bureaucrats could not consis-

[67] Tanaka Kakuei, as was so often true in postwar Japanese politics, was one of the first among them. For details, see Hayasaka Shigezō, "Tanaka Kakuei Mumei no Jyū Nen" ("Tanaka Kakuei's Ten Years without a Name"), pp. 381–82.

[68] In 1946 only 2.7 percent of all Diet members were Liberal party (i.e., conservative) ex-bureaucrats. That proportion rose to 18.2 percent in 1949, and this ratio has roughly continued since, with a slight decline during the 1980s in favor of former local politicians and Dietmen's private secretaries. See Johnson *MITI and the Japanese Miracle*, p. 46, on the 1946–1949 transition.

[69] This was, for example, true during the second Kishi cabinet of 1958. See ibid.

tently impose technocratic policy solutions in the domestic realm, where occupation reforms created maximum turbulence and international competitiveness imperatives exerted few constraints on interest group demands. As the political world became better organized to represent these demands, with the formalization of factions and with strengthened kōenkai, politics pressed in on the bureaucracy selectively but with increasing force. The state may set parameters and predispositions; it may erect barriers to political advance in sectors of recognized common concern. But it is ultimately back to society that we must turn for answers to how the turbulence of democratic pluralism and the stability imperative of a risky, debt-laden dash for economic growth ultimately reconciled themselves to produce domestic policy in postwar Japan.

4

From Crisis to Compensation

An American standard of living, Soviet levels of social welfare, a British parliamentary system, and Japan's peace constitution . . . these are our aspirations for Japan.
EDA SABURŌ
JSP Secretary General (1962)

Tory language and Whig measures . . .
EDMUND BURKE (1782)

DESPITE RECURRENT CRISIS, documented at length in the preceding pages, Japanese conservative political hegemony has been remarkably persistent over the past two generations. By the late 1980s the conservatives had not only recovered their dominant electoral share of the 1950s, but had increased it. Paralleling this unusual political stability amidst crisis have been five equally distinctive features of Japanese public policy, in many ways sharply at variance with the technocratic, elite-dominated political structure of Japan as it first confronted the turbulence of postwar politics.

First, Japanese policies, seen in comparative context, have had a strong distributive orientation. Japan's emphasis on public works and agricultural spending has rarely been matched internationally since the New Deal. This distributive emphasis has waxed and waned in intensity in Japan over the past forty years. But it has been sufficiently persistent to constitute one of the central traits of Japanese public policy since 1949, when seen in comparative context.

Second, distributive benefits in Japan have been skewed heavily toward both the peripheral and relatively low-income segments of the population. For example, the primary beneficiary of Japan's low defense spending of the past two decades, in terms of increased budgetary shares as defense declined, appears to have been public works spending, especially on the long-depressed Japan Sea coast, together with welfare and agriculture. Loans for small business have also risen substantially, while direct assistance for export-oriented big business has actually declined. The areas of strongest policy emphasis have been those where all major segments of the surprisingly populist conservative political coalition—agriculture, small business and large firms—actually benefit.

A third striking reality of postwar Japanese public policy, as noted in chapter 3, has been a broad, seemingly cyclical oscillation from martial responses to materialist responses and then back again. The years 1949–1954, 1958–1963, and 1971–1976 were periods of increasingly salient distributive bias and policy orientation toward equity rather than efficiency. But the 1980s, and to lesser degrees the mid-1950s, late 1960s, and late 1970s, were periods of retrenchment, coupled with greater conservative reliance on nonmaterial sorts of political appeals, both nationalistic and technocratic.

Fourth, postwar Japanese public policy has been characterized by a volatile, discontinuous process of transformation. When fundamental change has occurred in public resource allocation patterns or policy profiles, it has tended to occur in sudden, sharp jumps or surges. Most commonly, policy change has occurred almost simultaneously in several sectors. These surges have been especially important, it appears, in initiating redistributive changes in Japanese policy, such as its pro-small business and pro-agriculture cast. Indeed, virtually all major redistributive shifts in Japanese policy have been made rather abruptly. Fiscal retrenchment on distributive issues, often coupled with policy departures toward the Right such as the gradual defense buildup after 1981, have, by contrast, often occurred in more gradual, more ambiguous fashion. But this latter pattern of rightward policy shifts has been more the exception than the rule for the postwar period as a whole.

Most striking of all, perhaps, is the anomaly that can be found in the epigraph to this chapter: the broad thrust of conservative public policies in postwar Japan strongly reflects the most visionary, creative aspirations of the socialist opposition. There have, it must be stressed, been twists and turns in the road, and noncrisis periods typically bring conservative insensitivity and policy retrenchment. Yet the general thrust of Japanese conservative policymaking for most of the postwar period has, ironically, been toward realization of the Socialists' Eda Vision for Japan; by the late 1970s the conservatives had achieved it to an uncanny degree. By pragmatically coopting the proposals of their opponents, the Japanese conservatives had not built a coherent legislative record of their own. But they had successfully diffused dissent and improbably succeeded in maintaining political power longer than any other democratic regime in the modern history of the industrialized world other than the Swedish Social Democrats, who left office briefly in the late 1970s.

Given the frequency with which the Liberal Democratic party and its predecessors have adopted policies initially proposed by the Left, one might wonder how they can actually be considered conservative. The important commonality with forms of conservatism elsewhere in the world is the continuing, overriding emphasis of the Japanese Right on political stability, which has, indeed, animated the intense pragmatism of Japanese conservative policymaking. Given its risky, debt-ridden strategies for capital intensive industrialization, the big business community felt a continuing—indeed, intensifying—need for political stability across the socially turbulent and changing years of the high-growth period. It expressed its concern for stability both in dramatic joint declarations of the major business federations and in intense personal lobbying with LDP political leaders.

Conservative politicians similarly stressed the importance of political stability in their appeals to the general public. In a content analysis of political speeches during the 1955 Japanese general election campaign, for example, "stability" or "stabilization" (*antei*) was clearly and consistently used more by the Right than by the Left; this was the only one of twenty-one political terms to show such a clear pattern.[1] This consistent emphasis on stability has continued to the present day. It marks the Liberal Democrats and occasionally some of the middle-of-the-road opposition politicians as clearly conservative, despite their frequent adoption of left-oriented policies.

This chapter explores the connecting mechanism between the political crisis which has recurrently shaken the Japanese political economy across the postwar period and the policy outputs which crisis has generated. With force and nationalism constrained as means for neutralizing dissent and assuring stability, materialist policy options became of particular importance. This

[1] See Ronald P. Dore, "Japanese Election Candidates in 1955," *Pacific Affairs*, June, 1956, pp. 174–81. The Dore data is drawn from Kokkai Shiryō Kyōkai, ed. *Zenkoku Sōsenkyo Kōhō Shūroku* (*Collected Official Reports of the National General Elections*).

chapter shows how complex, distinctive structural features of the postwar Japanese political system have combined with the dividends of economic growth to generate an alternating cycle of policy rigidity and often retrenchment, followed by broad waves of policy change oriented toward prospective support groups.

Compensation as a Conceptual Variable

In this volume "compensation" is juxtaposed to crisis as a major element in the explanation of postwar Japanese politics and policymaking. Unlike crisis, compensation is not used broadly as a concept of political analysis. Yet it has particular richness in describing the relationship of policy outputs to interest group behavior, which lends itself particularly well to research on the political processes by which long-dominant parties maintain their preeminence. The notion of compensation also speaks to the personalistic dimensions of politics in a nation like Japan where, as Kyōgoku Junichi observes, politics is deeply rooted in human relations.[2]

Compensation here refers to "material benefits, usually distributive in character, extended to support groups exerting strategic political efforts on behalf of the grantor." These benefits can take a wide variety of forms, including public works expenditures, small business loans, incremental adjustments in agricultural price supports, and specialized corporate-tax dispensations. Compensation can also involve institutional or policy changes that benefit specific interest groups that have aided the grantor, such as the establishment of new government financial institutions for small business. Political transactions of this variety between grantor and recipient can have, as Kyōgoku suggests, a certain commercial form (*Shōtorihiki no Katachi*) about them and are often extended on an *ad hoc* basis.[3] What is crucial is the existence of some perceived sense of mutual obligation—a "politics of reciprocity," as Muramatsu puts it.[4] This need not be within a patron-client context, although it is often so.[5]

[2] On the heavily personalistic character of Japanese politics, see Kyōgoku Junichi. *Nihon no Seiji* (*Japanese Politics*).

[3] *Ibid.*, p. 261.

[4] Muramatsu Michio, "Center-Local Political Relations in Japan," *The Journal of Japanese Studies*, Summer, 1986, p. 316.

[5] For a sensitive examination of the connections between patron-client rela-

Politics directed primarily toward advertising and satisfying demands for material satisfaction between grantors and supporters, as opposed to those politics oriented toward attaining nonmaterial goals, is known as "compensation politics." Such interactions take place, of course, in a broader social context. The networks of regular participants among which such interactions take place, in which members have reciprocal benefits and obligations, are known here as "circles of compensation"; these contrast to patterns of interpersonal behavior among strangers, where such regularized norms of mutual obligation tend not to prevail.[6]

The Materialist Bias of Postwar Public Policy

Contrasts between recent Japanese government budgetary allocation patterns and those of the prewar period bring the strikingly materialist orientation of postwar Japanese conservative policies sharply into focus. As is indicated in table 4.1, expenditures for foodstuff subsidies, small business assistance, and foreign economic aid were nil in 1935; social welfare expenditures and local government support were next to nothing, and even civilian public works were a relatively minor concern. Welfare aspects of the budget, broadly conceived, were all subordinated to defense.

The mid-1980s present a strikingly different picture. The largest individual Japanese national budget item in 1986, aside from interest on the mounting national debt, was support for local government, followed by social welfare (see table 4.1). One out of every nine yen was spent directly on public works, with most of these projects constructed in outlying areas of Japan;[7] a large

tionships and the functioning of modern Japanese politics, see Ike Nobutaka, *A Theory of Japanese Democracy*, pp. 13–24.

[6] The distinction between in-group and out-group developed here and the implication that behavioral norms vary critically with the distinction corresponds to those of Ishida Takeshi between "uchi" and "soto" and that of Max Weber between "Binnenmoral" and "Aussenmoral." See Ishida Takeshi, "Conflict and its Accommodation: Omote-Ura and Uchi-Soto Relations," in *Conflict in Japan*, eds. Krauss, Rohlen, and Steinhoff, pp. 18–20.

[7] Not surprisingly, in 1985 the prefecture receiving the largest public works expenditures was Shimane, home of longtime Finance Minister Takeshita Noboru. The second largest recipient was Niigata Prefecture, home of former Prime Minister Tanaka Kakuei, and likewise far from Tokyo. For details, see Asahi Shimbun Sha, ed. *'85 Minryoku*.

TABLE 4.1

Allocation of the Japanese General Account Budget: Prewar versus Postwar Patterns (in percentages)

	Proportion of Total Budget		
Item	1934–1936	1985	Increase (1930s to 1985)
Local government financial support	0.3	18.5	+18.2
Social welfare	0.7	18.2	+17.5
Public works	7.4	12.1	+ 4.7
Interest	16.9	19.5	+ 2.6
Food price support	—	1.3	+ 1.3
Energy	—	1.2	+ 1.2
Foreign aid	—	1.1	+ 1.1
Small business	—	0.4	+ 0.4
Cultural and scientific affairs	13.2	9.2	− 4.0
Military pensions	7.6	3.6	− 4.0
Defense	44.8	6.0	−38.8

Source: Ministry of Finance Budget Bureau Research Section (Ōkurashō Shukei Kyoku Chōsa Ka) ed., *Zaisei Tōkei (Financial Statistics)*, 1985 ed. (Tokyo: Ōkurashō Insatsu Kyoku, 1985).

share of the funds earmarked for local governments was spent this way as well.

Japanese budgetary allocation patterns in the mid-1980s actually resemble those of the United States in 1935 more than they do those of Japan at that time, or those of the United States today (see figure 4.1). Like the Roosevelt administration at the height of the New Deal, or the Scandinavian Social Democrats of the same period,[8] the Japanese government in the mid-1980s de-

[8] For details on the Scandinavian policy configurations and analysis of how they were achieved, see Esping-Andersen, *Politics against Markets*, pp. 82–88 and 203–4. For details on the specifically institutional considerations that gave rise to substantial public works spending in Sweden as the principal mode of unemploy-

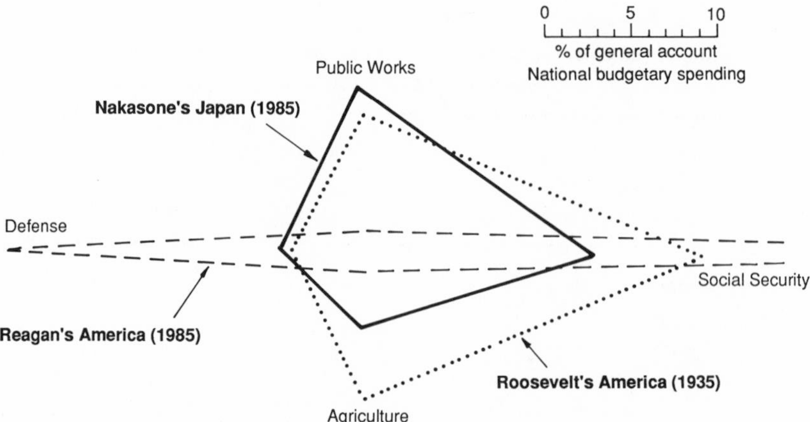

Figure 4.1. Japanese Public Policy Profiles: A New Deal Analogy?

Note: [1]U.S. social security spending in 1985 was 43.6 percent of the total federal budget.[2] Agricultural spending includes direct farm income stabilization measures and research services, but not consumer aid.

Sources: U.S. Bureau of the Budget, *The Budget of the United States Government* (Washington, D.C.: U.S. Government Printing Office, 1939), p. 8, also 1985 edition; and Ministry of Finance Budget Bureau Research Section (Ōkurashō Shukei Kyoku Chōsa Ka), ed., *Zaisei Tōkei (Financial Statistics)*, 1985 ed. (Tokyo: Ōkurashō Insatsu Kyoku, 1985).

voted a comparatively high proportion of government fiscal resources to civilian public works. Indeed, the shares of public works in the U.S. federal budget of 1935 and the Japanese general account budget of 1985 were virtually identical, as figure 4.1 suggests. Although the Japanese government devoted proportionately less to agriculture and social security than did the Roosevelt administration in 1935, the shares are remarkably similar when one adjusts for differences in overall employment structure and macroeconomic conditions. The Japanese labor force in agriculture in 1985 was less than half that of the United States in the 1930s,[9] making agricultural spending per farmer almost equal in the two cases; an army of ten million unemployed at the height

---

ment relief during the early 1930s, see Margaret Weir and Theda Skocpol, "State Structures and the Possibilities for 'Keynesian' Responses to the Great Depression in Sweden, Britain, and the United States," in *Bringing the State Back In*, eds. Peter B. Evans, Dietrich Rueschemeyer, and Theda Skocpol, pp. 123–25.

[9] In 1930, 21.8 percent of the American labor force was employed in agriculture, compared to 8.8 percent in Japan during 1985. See U.S. Department of Commerce, *Historical Statistics of the United States: Colonial Times to 1970*, p. 139; and Bank of Japan Research and Statistics Department (Nihon Ginkō Chōsa Tōkei Kyoku), *Kokusai Hikaku Tōkei* (*International Comparative Statistics*), p. 144.

of the Depression obviously accounted for America's heavier welfare spending.

Japanese government lending policies, like general-account budgetary expenditures, have a distinct welfare rather than efficiency-oriented bias. This bias has also been growing steadily stronger over the years, in the same discontinuous, crisis-related pattern characteristic of general-account budgetary expenditures themselves. Recent lending patterns, which represent one of the most important aspects of Japan's orientation toward distributive policymaking, are presented in table 4.2. Before World War II, funds heavily underwrote government bonds, whose proceeds were in turn committed heavily to military expansion.[10] During the 1950s, basic industry, trade promotion, communications, and agriculture—all essential to keeping the precarious Japanese economy viable—received relatively large shares of total government loans. During the post–oil shock period, by contrast, the bias toward urban but nevertheless grassroots-oriented projects intensified, keeping with the transformation in the LDP's underlying constituency then in process. By 1985, nearly half of all Japanese government loans went to housing and small business alone, with less than 3 percent to basic industry. Housing loans, it should be noted, have served as major incentives to the real estate development sector as well as to individual homeowners.

Aside from budgetary figures, numerous other indicators point to the distinctive, grassroots compensation-oriented character of postwar Japanese conservative policymaking. The dense, decentralized network of roads it has created across Japan suggests the ruling LDP's grassroots-oriented character. Although all of Japan is only the size of California, it has over one million *miles* of highway. Indeed, by 1977 Japan had a larger network, in absolute scale, than any other nation in the world other than the two superpowers, together with Brazil and India.[11] Road density per square mile in Japan was more than double that of Britain and France and nearly double that of West Germany.[12]

[10] During the late 1920s one also finds embryo *yokinbu* line items for educational improvement and support for agricultural villages (9.4 percent in 1925 and 0.2 percent in 1931), health insurance (.01 percent in 1927 and .08 percent in 1931), and so on. But these precursors of postwar budget patterns were miniscule beside funds directed toward the military. See Ministry of Finance Financial History of Shōwa Editorial Office (Ōkurashō Shōwa Zaisei Shi Henshū Shitsu), ed. *Shōwa Zaisei Shi* (*A Financial History of Shōwa*), vol. 12, pp. 54–55.

[11] George Thomas Kurian, *The Book of World Rankings*, p. 231.

[12] Japan had one mile of road per 0.13 square miles of territory, compared with

Table 4.2

The Shifting Distribution of Japanese Government Credit, 1955–1985 (in percentages)

	Categories with Rising Shares					
	1955	1960	1970	1980	1985	Change (1955–1985)
Housing	13.8	12.8	19.3	26.2	25.4	+11.6
Small business	8.1	12.7	12.6	18.7	18.0	+ 9.9
Roads	3.7	3.6	8.6	5.7	8.8	+ 5.1
Welfare	2.1	1.8	2.8	3.5	2.8	+ 0.7

	Categories with Declining Shares					
	1955	1960	1970	1980	1985	Change (1955–1985)
Basic industry	15.8	13.6	5.7	3.0	2.9	−12.0
Regional development	8.5	7.1	4.0	2.6	2.4	− 6.1
Disaster relief	7.7	6.5	1.6	1.7	2.3	− 5.4
Agriculture	8.9	7.1	5.0	4.9	4.3	− 4.6
Transport/ communication	12.2	14.1	13.2	9.6	8.4	− 3.8
Trade/economic cooperation	7.0	7.9	10.6	5.6	5.4	− 1.6
Education	4.5	3.5	2.2	4.4	3.6	− 0.9

Source: Ōkurashō Shukei Kyoku Chōsa Ka, *Zaisei Tōkei (Financial Statistics)*, 1985 ed. (Tokyo: Ōkurashō Insatsu Kyoku, 1985), pp. 308–9; and Ōkurashō Zaisei Shi Henshū Shitsu, ed., *Shōwa Zaisei Shi (A Financial History of Shōwa)*, Vol. 12 (Tokyo: Tōyō Keizai Shinpō Sha, 1962), pp. 144–45.

Notes: (1) Figures indicate shares of total Fiscal Investment and Loan Program expenditures. (2) Comparisons with the FILP's prewar analogue the *yokinbu* are difficult due to structural differences. In general, however, the *yokinbu* was integrated closely with the prewar general account, whose military-oriented allocation pattern was presented in table 4.1. In 1935, 41.1 percent of yokinbu funds went for government bonds, 44.7 percent to local governments (controlled by the Naimushō), and 4.9 percent to special government banks.

In sharp contrast to France's *routes nationales*, which radiate outward from Paris like the spokes of a wheel, Japan's *kōsoku dōro* (superhighways) form a much richer network, involving many small towns and byways that do not pass through Tokyo. Similarly, France's GTV high-speed train network runs only between the two largest cities of Paris and Marseilles, but Japan's Shinkansen bullet train routes, extending the length of the country, are being built in even more remote areas.

Roads and railroads are not the only types of public works one finds spread widely across the landscape of Japan. During the 1970s and 1980s, new regional airports, distributed broadly to a wide range of outlying prefectures, became a major public works item, helping to spur the development of electronics and precision-machinery production as well as passenger air traffic in these areas. In 1985 the national government appropriated over ¥500 billion (more than $2 billion) for such projects.[13]

Medical colleges have also proliferated across Japan, in a much more decentralized pattern than market forces alone would ever generate. Each of Japan's forty-seven prefectures, by LDP intervention, now has such a college. Museums, sports facilities, and cultural halls—for even the smallest hamlet—have also rapidly appeared. Due to their numbers and affluence, again largely produced by LDP intervention on their behalf, Japanese provincial museums are now able to significantly influence global art prices in certain areas of their fancy.

Although Japan's materialist conservatism showers upon potential supporters a wide range of public works benefits, some important gaps remain. For example, despite its strong tradition of road building during the past forty years, together with the proliferation of government-built sports facilities and cultural halls, the Japanese government has devoted relatively little attention to sewage systems. In 1985 only 34 percent of Japanese homes had indoor plumbing, compared to 72 percent in the United States and 97 percent in Britain.[14] Yet public road construction and repair expenditures, disbursed primarily in the countryside,

---

0.23 in West Germany, 0.26 in France, 0.40 in Italy, and 0.59 in the United States. *Ibid.*

[13] Ministry of Finance Budget Bureau Research Section (Ōkurasho Shukei Kyoku Chōsa Ka), *Zaisei Tōkei (Financial Statistics) 1985*, p. 210.

[14] Sekai no Naka no Nihon o Kangaeru Kai, ed., *Kokusai Hikaku: Nihon o Miru (Looking at Japan: International Comparisons)*. Tokyo: Chūō Hōki Shuppan Kai, 1985, p. 199.

in 1986 remained over three times as large as those for water treatment systems,[15] disbursed mainly in the densely populated urban areas of Japan. These ratios demonstrate once again the rural and regional bias of Japanese conservative policies.

Despite the heavy emphasis on public works in contemporary Japan, public works spending is by no means the only hallmark of Japanese conservative policymaking, seen in comparative perspective. Support for agriculture and nonconstruction sector small business is also striking, as future chapters will recount in more detail. The distinctive policy consequences of Japanese conservatism also show up strongly in the Japanese finance, distribution, and tax systems, through unusual patterns of regulatory policy and institutional specialization.

Historical Alternatives to Compensation

As the previous section demonstrated, it was not a foregone conclusion that Japanese public policy's postwar response to political crisis would be compensation, in the sense noted here. Some compensation had occurred in prewar Japanese politics, stressed particularly by Hara Kei and a range of *Seiyūkai* political associates intermittently for the first thirty years of the twentieth century. Generally the dominant conservative political party in Japan from its foundation in 1900 until 1940, the *Seiyūkai*, also known as the *Rikken Seiyūkai* (Friends of constitutional government) was founded by oligarch Itō Hirobumi and traditionally drew its support from landowners and regional middle-class constituencies. But much more often the conservative response to political challenge was repression. Prewar Japan could not become a fully compensation-oriented state. A restricted franchise during crucial stages of party formation, bureaucratic dominance in the policy process, and strong military counterclaims on the national budget all inhibited tendencies toward distributive politics within the prewar ruling political parties from being translated pervasively into public policy.

Distributive politics was also alien to the two most influential politicians of the early post–World War II period. Hatoyama Ichirō, the founder of the Liberal party (*Jiyūtō*) and its victorious leader in the 1946 general elections, vehemently opposed pork-

[15] Yamaichi Shōken Keizai Kenkyū Jo, *Sangyō Tōkei '85* (*Industrial Statistics '85*), p. 29.

barrel politics. One political observer of the period likened him to Gladstone in his dislike of the distributive and the expedient;[16] Hatoyama is said to have pledged his home as security for campaign loans in the early postwar period, due to lack of other funding sources. Hatoyama's immediate concern after war's end was "preservation of the national essence" (*kokutai goji*), the central theme at the first Liberal Party convention in 1946. For Hatoyama this concept implied preeminently maintenance of public order and social cohesion, with an emphasis on public security rather than economic blandishments; Hatoyama often stressed the danger of internal communist subversion and the importance of countering it through expansion of Japanese military spending to as much as 25 percent of the national budget—four times the budget share of the mid-1980s.[17] Yoshida Shigeru, the Liberal Party leader who succeeded Hatoyama after the latter's purge in the spring of 1946, did not favor a large-scale military buildup or an expansion of the police, but he took little apparent interest in distributive politics.[18] The major concerns of this former ambassador to the Court of St. James were consistently diplomatic, with the details of domestic politics secondary, apart from struggles against Communists and militant labor.

In the turbulent world of early post–World War II Japan, stable conservative political preeminence was seen as essential by both rightist politicians and the business community, but Japanese conservatives were initially hesitant at using grassroots-oriented politics as a vehicle for achieving that. As chapter 5 points out,

[16] See Kenneth E. Colton, "Pre-war Political Influences in Post-War Conservative Parties," *American Political Science Review* (October 1948), p. 942.

[17] Hatoyama justified this figure to U.S. Ambassador John Allision in late 1952 by noting that Norway and Sweden, pacific yet prudent nations after whom Japan might model its policies, were spending one-third of their respective budgets on defense. See Steeves, AMEMBASSY Tokyo to DOS, "Meeting of Mr. Ichirō Hatoyama with the Ambassador," September 18, 1952; Steeves, U.S. Embassy Tokyo to DOS, "Weekly Political Notes from Japan," May 29–June 5, 1952; and American Embassy Tokyo to DOS, "Weekly Political Notes from Japan," September 11–18, 1952.

[18] The tasks Yoshida set for himself in the immediate postwar period included: (1) preservation of the emperor and national polity, (2) repression of the revolutionary potential within Japan, (3) restoration of the traditional powers of elite rule, (4) economic reconstruction along capitalist lines, and (5) Japan's return to international stature as a partner of the Western powers. *None* related to distributive politics. Nor do Yoshida's major writings concern themselves at all with this subject. See John Dower, *Empire and Aftermath*, p. 277; and Yoshida Shigeru, *The Yoshida Memoirs*.

for example, conservatives during 1946–1947 were extremely wary of land reform and passed even a tepid bill only after considerable anguish and SCAP pressure.

The Complexity of Attempting Coercion

Force was one prospective option for maintaining conservative preeminence which found favor with many conservatives. Yet there was surprisingly little force, or even institutional coercive power, at the conservatives' disposal apart from public-employee dismissals. In contrast to the West German case, Japan's constitution did not provide a ready judicial means of curbing radical groups.[19] The national police forces, not to speak of the military, had all been disbanded, with the Self-Defense Forces not to emerge until 1951 and the National Police Agency not to be reconstituted until 1954. During the first of the three crucial crises which have shaped postwar Japanese public policy, the police of Japan were responsible to decentralized Public Safety Commissions.

The conservative lack of coercive tools for maintaining stability was by no means due to lack of interest in them. In 1951 the Ordinance Review Committee proposed establishment of a Public Security Ministry.[20] Prime Minister Yoshida announced plans to consolidate the various autonomous police forces and considered establishing a Japanese version of the U.S. House of Representatives Un-American Activities Committee to investigate domestic subversion.[21] But only the consolidation of the various police forces was ever achieved, and that only after three years of bitter struggle which in the end forced the conservatives to call police into the Diet building to clear socialist obstruction.

In late 1958 Prime Minister Kishi Nobusuke proposed a major increase in national police powers in preparation for the envis-

[19] In West Germany, as Yoshida pointed out, the Basic Law lays down the principle that political parties whose aims and acts are inimical to free and democratic social order are unconstitutional; this allowed the possibility of banning radical groups by juridical means. In Japan this had to be done through the passage of specific laws, a much more politically delicate operation, difficult to accomplish. See Yoshida Shigeru, *The Yoshida Memoirs*, p. 237.

[20] *Nippon Times*, April 27, 1951.

[21] Yoshida Shigeru, *The Yoshida Memoirs*, p. 234; and Kurt Steiner, *Local Government in Japan*, p. 255.

aged United States-Japan Security Treaty revision.[22] A storm of criticism from the Left forced him to retract his proposed police bill (*Keishoku Hōan*). This both limited the range of tools subsequently available to Japanese conservative leaders in the face of dissent and gave momentum to further protests aimed at curbing the expansion of state coercive power.

Allied forces were effectively constrained from active intervention in Japanese political affairs by strong apprehensions of the prospective political backlash within Japan that such intervention might generate.[23] In any event, from the fall of 1951 at the latest Japanese policymakers had to actively entertain the prospect of phased American withdrawal from Japan, as the Allied occupation came to a close. Forceful supression of labor unrest and political protest demonstrations had been commonplace during the prewar period, and the postwar conservatives tried to revive some of the old tactics in suitably adjusted form. But they faced sustained opposition in the Diet, which forced them to shelve most proposals. Intermittent criticism from the International Labor Organization (ILO), often coordinated with opposition party protests, also helped force the LDP to moderate efforts to curb labor, especially in the controversial area of public sector union activities.[24]

Futile Efforts to Change the Electoral System

Another mechanism which Japanese conservatives periodically considered as a tool for neutralizing political instability was revision of the national electoral system. As I pointed out in chapter 1, Japan's unusual medium-size, multiple-legislator electoral district system stimulates sharp intraparty competition within large political parties, preeminently the ruling LDP. It also affords minor parties chances at representation which they would not have under single-member district systems. This competition from both the Right and the Left has left individual Japanese conservative legislators in a position of unusual uncertainty, compared to their counterparts in the Anglo-Saxon world with its sin-

[22] For Kishi's views on the Police Bill struggle, see Kishi Nobusuke, *Kishi Kaikoroku* (*Kishi's Memoirs*), pp. 436–46.

[23] See for example, State–Army to DOS (Top Secret), "Conditions in Japan," April 7, 1949.

[24] On the transnational politics of Japanese labor union relationship with the state, see Ehud Harari, *The Politics of Labor Legislation in Japan*.

gle-member districts, particularly younger legislators with more poorly formed support networks. This intraparty competition has also intensified the dependence of Japanese politicians on grassroots pressure groups.

Postwar conservatives had clear precedent for altering the electoral system in an effort to stabilize their political position. To strengthen the dominance of the ruling Seiyūkai in the wake of the Rice Riots of 1918 Hara Kei in 1919 secured passage of a single-member electoral district system, over the determined protests of the opposition. Against the divided opposition parties, the Seiyūkai won an overwhelming victory in the general election of 1920, under the new electoral system, a development which was not lost on Hatoyama Ichirō, Kishi Nobusuke, Tanaka Kakuei, and other postwar conservative politicians intent on revising the electoral system again in similar directions.

The intense competition among conservative politicians under the prevailing medium-size district electoral system was sharply exacerbated by the conservative merger of 1955. In view of the new two-party dominated political system created by the conservative and socialist mergers during that year, many conservatives argued that Japan should have an electoral system like that of the two-party Anglo-Saxon democracies—that is, a single-member district system.[25] Faced with a Local Affairs Agency report documenting the sharp decline in the rural share of Japan's population during the early 1950s and outlining reapportionment possibilities, the Hatoyama cabinet took the offensive. It proposed "the establishment of an English-style two-party system" in an electoral system revision bill on March 19, 1956.[26] Although strongly attacked as a "Hatomander" (i.e., gerrymander Hatoyama-style) by many in the opposition, the bill passed the Lower House of the Diet on May 16, but it died in the Upper House as the legislative session ran out.[27]

[25] See, for example, Kishi Nobusuke. *Kishi Kaikoroku* (*Kishi's Memoirs*), pp. 436–46.

[26] *Asahi Shimbun*, March 21, 1956, p. 1. Miki Bukichi and Kishi Nobusuke were the principal architects of this proposal, with Kawashima Shōjirō of the Kishi faction serving as chairman of the Small-Scale Electoral District System Special Committee.

[27] Opposition strong arm tactics, rendered legitimate with the broader public by general misgivings regarding the enhanced power which electoral system changes might give the conservatives, were a major element in delaying the bill's consideration, and hence contributing to its failure to pass. See *Asahi Shimbun*, May 28, 1956; June 2, 1956; and June 4, 1956.

Although reform in the electoral system as a means of enhancing conservative political preeminence failed in 1956, the idea did not die. In October 1960, following the Security Treaty crisis, the LDP tried again to reach informal agreement with opposition parties on electoral law changes but failed.[28] Three months later the Ikeda cabinet established an Advisory Council on the Election System.[29] The idea of reform was periodically debated within the LDP, and in 1972 Prime Minister Tanaka Kakuei again formally broached the reform as the prospects of LDP defeat at the hands of the progressive opposition began building to a crisis point. After being broadly debated and stirring vigorous opposition from the Left, the Tanaka proposal for electoral reform also failed to become law. But it was seriously deliberated by the LDP throughout most of the 1971–1976 political crisis period.

Only with the waning of political crisis in the late 1970s and early 1980s was the LDP able to secure even limited electoral change, reducing the diverse internal and external pressures under which the electoral system of 1947 had placed the conservatives. In 1982 Japan introduced the list-voting system, similar to that employed in West Germany, for election of two-fifths of the 252-seat Upper House membership. This change allowed the central party leadership, dominated at the time by the large Tanaka faction, to name candidates for the one hundred at-large seats in the so-called national constituency, thus reducing the pressure group and factional influence over their selection which tended to prevail when they were directly elected through separate individual selection. In 1986 the Lower House was partially reapportioned, in accordance with a Supreme Court decision, to reflect rising urban population strength by adding seats in populous constituencies and subtracting them in a few which had lost population. But the same electoral system, strongly stimulating grassroots competition and individual uncertainty for conservative Dietmen, continued to prevail in the selection of all Lower House members.

Distributive Politics as the Alternative

Japanese conservative policymakers, it seems clear, have explored a broad range of alternatives to distributive compensation-

[28] Tōyama Shigeto, *Shiryō: Sengo Ni jyū Nen Shi* (*Twenty Years of Postwar History*), p. 182.

[29] *Ibid.*, p. 186. This was done on January 10, 1961.

oriented politics as a means of maintaining political preeminence in Japan. Both prewar precedent and the prevailing structural bias of much of the Japanese political economy in 1945, not to mention the precedent of most other strong bureaucratic nations, biased these policymakers, especially those with bureaucratic background, toward nationalist and technocratic, as well as materialist, modes of policymaking. Yet for a variety of reasons, the post-1949 Japanese conservatives persistently failed in broadening the alternatives to interest group compensation, both coercive and electoral, in their political arsenal.

Every government employs what it considers a judicious combination of "the carrot and the stick" to achieve its political and policy related objectives. Two striking aspects of the postwar Japanese case are the extents to which both the stick is missing and the pressures to provide the carrot are overwhelming. Cultural and psychological forces clearly bias Japanese politics in the direction of material compensation,[30] but differences between prewar and postwar policy patterns also show the importance of systemic aspects in shaping this outcome. The following section outlines those systemic pressures for material compensation of political demands and suggests why their salience in Japanese public policy waxes and wanes in such pronounced fashion.

Economic Growth and Public Resources

The two most salient realities of postwar Japanese political and economic life have unquestionably been Japan's extraordinary history of rapid economic growth and its heavily materialistic pattern of politics and policymaking; these are profoundly related to one another, but the connection is not simple. Economic growth both rent the fabric of Japanese society and provided budgetary resources to neutralize the political consequences of the social uncertainties it created. Yet growth provided no automatic mechanism for assuring stable political evolution, no schedule or prescriptions for policy change, and no clear assurance even that policy change to cope with the consequences of growth would in fact occur.

The general profiles of Japanese economic growth itself are well-known and require little retelling here. After a precarious

[30] See Kyōgoku Junichi, *Nihon no Seiji*, pp. 244–91.

and inflationary recovery in the early postwar years, Japan was forced into retrenchment by the Dodge Line stabilization policies of 1949. With the coming of the Korean War, however, the economy began to surge, under the stimulus of U.S. offshore procurements for the Korean conflict. Although the prospects for future growth were much more uncertain at any given time than is generally recognized today, the economy continued to grow sharply, often at double-digit rates, for more than two decades. From 1960 through 1970, the period of highest growth, real annual GNP growth averaged 11.3 percent, falling below 10 percent only in the "recession" years of 1962 (7 percent) and 1965 (5.1 percent). Between 1951 and 1973 industrial production grew over fourteen-fold, with production in steel, electronics, machinery, and other sectors of the future rising even more sharply. Despite the large scale of her economy, even at the onset of the high-growth period, Japan achieved growth at a higher rate than such major developing nations as Brazil and Iran during their most rapid stages of development.

Following the Nixon shock of 1971, and especially after the oil shock of 1973, Japanese growth slowed substantially, falling from the 9.8 percent of the 1955–1973 period to 3.7 percent over the 1974–1984 decade. But that growth remained considerably more rapid than in any other major industrialized nation (table 4.3). During the mid-1980s, Japanese growth rates were double and triple those of Western Europe and generally higher than those of either the United States or Canada.

In addition to being rapid, Japanese economic growth of the postwar period has also been somewhat cyclical. Throughout the 1950s and 1960s, as indicated in chapter 1, Japan confronted precarious balance of payments circumstances and could not manage a surplus of nonmilitary procurement exports over imports until 1965. The economy would periodically overheat and intensify balance of payments problems, forcing the Bank of Japan to tighten monetary policy to bring these expansionary booms to a halt. Thus, Japan experienced periodic "recessions," when growth would fall sharply from double digits to the 7 percent of 1962 or the 5.1 percent of 1965.

Accompanying this double-digit growth was major social transformation, as rural Japanese flocked to work in burgeoning urban factories and the service enterprises springing up around them. Within a generation, a Japanese work force which had been almost 50 percent agricultural in 1950 became more than 90 per-

TABLE 4.3
Comparative Real GNP Growth in the Industrialized World, 1971–1986 (in percentages)

Country	1971–1975	1976–1980	1981–1986
Japan	4.7	5.0	3.7
Canada	5.0	3.0	2.7
United States	2.6	3.7	2.4
United Kingdom	2.0	1.4	2.2
West Germany	2.1	3.6	1.5
France	4.0	3.3	1.3
Italy	4.1	3.8	1.2

Sources: Bank of Japan Research and Statistics Department (Nihon Ginkō Chōsa Tōkei Kyoku), *Kokusai Hikaku Tōkei (International Comparative Statistics)*, 1982 ed. (Tokyo: Nihon Ginkō, 1982), p. 26; *Kokusai Hikaku Tōkei*, 1987 ed., pp. 7–8. Real GNP for 1971–80 is in 1970 prices, and for 1981–86 in 1980 prices.

cent urban. The population of Tokyo, which had stood at 7.5 million in 1955, grew more than one-third to 10.3 million just a decade later. Along the entire Pacific coast of Japan, extending all the way from Tokyo to Ōsaka, a huge megalopolis emerged, plagued by housing, transportation, land use, and welfare problems, in addition to some of the worst air and water pollution in the world. By the mid-1960s this Tōkaidō megalopolis had a population of 50 million, roughly half the total for all of Japan.

As Mancur Olson points out, rapid economic growth can produce not only technical policy problems to be solved but also severe social and political disequilibria, flowing from the changing position of both economic gainers and losers in the social order.[31] These tensions, affecting both small business and agriculture, were superimposed in the Japanese case on a society undergoing the dislocations of traditional communal structure that often accompany urbanization. The result of converging social and economic pressures flowing from the economic growth process was increasing political disenchantment with conservative rule in the expanding Tōkaidō megalopolis of 50 million people along Honshū's Pacific coast. In 1967 Tokyo elected a progressive governor, Minobe Ryōkichi, supported by a socialist-communist co-

[31] Mancur Olson, "Rapid Growth as a Destabilizing Force," p. 541.

alition, and by 1973 all five of Japan's largest cities had progressive mayors.

While creating dislocations and strains in the social fabric which rendered unbroken conservative rule ever more problematic, rapid economic growth also forced the Japanese state and industrial society into an ever more intimate interdependence. Economic growth centering on capital intensive heavy industries such as steel, shipbuilding, and petrochemicals meant an ever-increasing weight of long-term corporate debt, owed mostly to the people of Japan since growth was in the main domestically financed. Although partially offset by the rising value of fixed assets, especially land, the rising weight of debt heightened the sense of fragility of Japanese corporations. Economic growth, in short, created and intensified institutional arrangements in the Japanese political economy that made political stability increasingly imperative for businessmen and economic bureaucrats as well as the conservative politicians who were its most immediate beneficiaries. But neither growth nor prevailing state structure necessarily decreed what form that stability might take, what steps would be taken to preserve it, or whether it would indeed persist.

Japan's rapid economic growth generated an ever-growing stream of government revenues, and in many years it also allowed the budgetary slack for both rapidly increased spending and periodic tax cuts. But patterns of growth correspond rather imperfectly to patterns of government spending in Japan (see table 4.4 and figure 4.1). General account spending grew by roughly 15 percent annually throughout the 1960s, generally at a lower rate than economic growth. However, this pattern was reversed during the 1970s; despite declining economic growth, government spending throughout the 1970s continued to rise at a double-digit pace through an expansion in government's share of aggregate expenditures. This budgetary growth has translated into a rapidly expanding pool of funds for allocation by politicians and bureaucrats to the private sector. By fiscal 1983 the general account budget amounted to ¥50.6 trillion.[32] Although

[32] In 1983 budgetary deficits and gross savings ratios for key industrialized nations were:

	Budget Deficit/GNP	*Gross Savings/GNP*
Japan	4.5%	13.3%
West Germany	1.9%	8.4%
United States	5.8%	5.9%

budgetary growth slowed in the years immediately thereafter, potential resources for budget allocation continued to increase because Japan's gross savings rate continued to be roughly triple the budgetary deficit as a share of GNP.[33]

Figure 4.2 suggests some intriguing periodic relationships between economic growth and general account spending that should not be ignored. When general account spending is lagged one to two years behind economic growth, the spending profiles for certain periods, such as the mid- and late 1960s, closely parallel economic growth patterns, as Noguchi's hypothesis that Ministry of Finance bureaucrats base their spending decisions on anticipated levels of stable future revenue would suggest.[34] But as figure 4.2 indicates, on four major occasions during the postwar period general account spending soars beyond even the lagged GNP growth figures. Three of these occasions correspond to the three periods of domestic crisis presented in this volume during the early 1950s, 1960s, and 1970s, although the fourth (1977–1979) was a period of strong international pressure on Japan to become a "locomotive" in helping reflate the global economy. Most of the years when budgetary increases have lagged behind GNP growth, such as the late 1960s and the 1980s, have been noncrisis periods, suggesting the role of politics in creating or sharply accentuating cyclical patterns in Japanese budgeting.

Although the small number of relevant data points makes precise quantitative judgments difficult, cross tabulations of the relationship between GNP increases and general account budgetary changes also suggest the effect of crisis, independent of growth, in shaping Japanese budgetary patterns. As table 4.5 suggests, in confirmation of the visual pattern indicated in figure 4.2, general account budgets between 1949 and 1986 increased more rapidly than GNP nearly twice as often during crisis periods as during noncrisis, with the converse pattern occurring during noncrisis periods. During crises, the median increase in spending was 1.4 percent more than GNP (Y = budgetary increase − GNP increase); during noncrisis periods spending rose 1.6 percent *less* than GNP.

See Bank of Japan Research and Statistics Department (Nihon Ginkō Chōsa Tōkei Kyoku), *Kokusai Hikaku Tōkei*, pp. 83–84.

[33] Ministry of Finance and Budget Bureau Research Section (Ōkurashō Shukei Kyoku Chōsa Ka), ed., *Zaisei Tōkei, 1985*, p. 8.

[34] Noguchi Yukio, "Yosan ni okeru Ishi Kettei Rūru no Bunseki, *Keizai Kenkyū* (January 1978), pp. 23–32.

TABLE 4.4

GNP Growth versus General Account Budgetary Growth in Japan, 1949–1986 (fiscal year, in percentages)

Fiscal Year	GNP Growth (Nominal)	Growth in General Account Revenue	Growth in General Account Budget	General Account Budget/ GNP
1949	26.6	49.3	51.4	20.7
1950	16.9	− 5.5	− 9.5	16.0
1951	37.9	24.9	18.4	13.8
1952	12.4	20.5	16.6	14.3
1953	15.8	11.5	16.4	14.4
1954	4.0	− 2.8	2.3	14.0
1955	13.3	− 5.0	− 2.2	11.5
1956	12.3	9.4	5.0	10.7
1957	13.0	13.6	11.1	10.6
1958	4.8	3.8	12.1	11.3
1959	15.5	9.9	12.3	11.0
1960	19.1	22.8	16.6	10.8
1961	22.5	28.3	18.4	10.4
1962	9.1	17.2	23.9	11.8
1963	18.2	9.6	19.1	11.9
1964	15.9	6.7	8.8	11.2
1965	10.6	9.6	12.4	11.3
1966	17.2	20.6	19.8	11.6
1967	17.9	16.4	14.7	11.1
1968	17.8	14.3	16.1	10.8
1969	18.0	17.3	16.5	10.7
1970	16.3	19.0	18.4	10.9
1971	11.2	17.9	16.8	11.6
1972	17.3	28.3	24.8	12.4
1973	22.0	31.0	23.9	12.7
1974	17.9	21.6	29.2	13.8
1975	10.2	5.4	9.2	13.7
1976	12.4	16.8	17.3	14.3
1977	11.0	17.4	18.8	15.3
1978	9.9	18.6	17.3	16.3
1979	8.0	14.0	13.8	17.2

TABLE 4.4 *(cont.)*

Fiscal Year	GNP Growth (Nominal)	Growth in General Account Revenue	Growth in General Account Budget	General Account Budget/ GNP
1980	8.7	10.7	11.9	17.7
1981	5.9	7.7	7.9	19.1
1982	4.9	1.2	0.9	17.3
1983	4.3	7.6	7.2	17.8
1984	6.7	1.0	1.7	17.0
1985	5.7	3.0	3.7	16.6
1986	5.1	0.7	3.0	16.1

Source: Ministry of Finance Budget Bureau Research Section (Ōkurashō Shukei Kyoku Chōsa Ka), *Zaisei Tōkei (Financial Statistics)* 1986 ed. (Tokyo: Ōkurashō Insatsu Kyoku, 1986), pp. 53–58, and pp. 186–210.

Notes: (1) General account revenue and expenditure figures are for final, certified settlement of accounts (kessangaku). (2) 1985 and 1986 figures are provisional and projected, respectively.

The independent impact of crisis on general account spending patterns appears even more clearly when individual policy sectors are considered. As table 4.5 indicates, public works, small business, agriculture, and welfare budgeting patterns all support the crisis and compensation argument, with budgetary correlations to crisis especially pronounced in the cases of small-business and welfare policy. Welfare policy achieves variation largely through sharp upward surges in spending during periods of crisis, but small business policy does so through the sharpest retrenchment during noncrisis periods of that prevailing in any policy sector examined. Agriculture follows a ratchet-like pattern similar to welfare, albeit with smaller magnitudes of increase during crisis. But in broad outline the patterns in all these policy sectors are similar.

The one policy sector examined whose budgets have not clearly risen during crisis relative to GNP and fallen during noncrisis are those for defense. Japanese defense budgets declined relative to other expenditures during both crisis and noncrisis periods until 1981, when this secular downtrend began to slowly reverse itself with both waning domestic counterpressures and rising foreign insistence on an expanded Japanese security role.

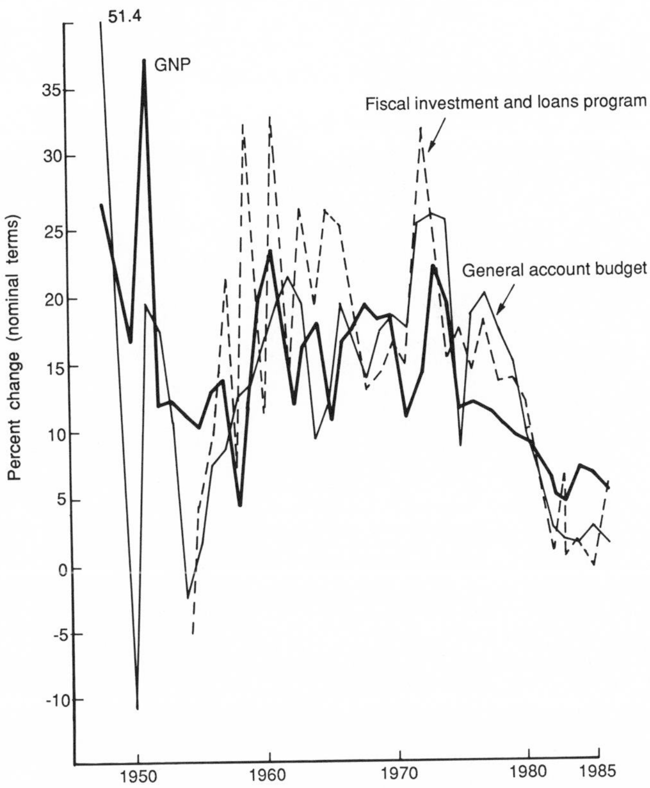

Figure 4.2. Economic Growth and Budgetary Change in Japan, 1949–1986.
Sources: Ministry of Finance Budget Bureau Research Section (Ōkurashō Shukei Kyoku Chōsa Ka), ed., *Zaisei Tōkei (Financial Statistics)*, various issues; and Bank of Japan Research and Statistics Department (Nihon Ginkō Chōsa Tōkei Kyoku), ed., *Keizai Tōkei Nenpō (Economic Statistics Annual)*, various issues.

But this seeming anomaly of persistently low Japanese defense spending is in keeping with the characterization of that defense spending as a budgetary "residual," developed in chapter 10.

Supplementing the general account budget are several other national government budgets, many of which, growing even more rapidly than the general account, are even more flexible.[35] The most important of these budgets is the Fiscal Investment

[35] These are considered only briefly in the one major English-language account of Japanese budgeting, which stresses apolitical dimensions. See John C. Campbell, *Contemporary Japanese Budget Politics*, pp. 209–11.

Table 4.5

Crisis, Economic Growth, and Budgetary Spending in Japan, 1949–1986

	General Budget Account (Total)		Public Works Spending		Small Business Spending		Agricultural Spending		Welfare Spending		Defense Spending	
	Crisis	Non-Crisis	Crisis	Non-Crisis	Crisis	Non-Crisis	Crisis	Non-Crisis	Crisis	Non-Crisis	*Crisis*	Non-Crisis
A. *Annual Budget/GNP Relationship*												
1. Budget Growth > GNP Growth	11	9	9	6	7	6	10	7	16	7	6	6
2. Budget Growth < GNP Growth	7	12	9	14	4	11	8	9	3	12	7	12
B. *Magnitudes of Budgetary Change (vs. GNP)*												
1. Crisis Periods: median spending increase minus GNP increase	+ 1.4%		+0.2%		+5.9%		+6.6%		+12.3%		−4.4%	
2. Non-Crisis Periods: median spending increase minus GNP increase	+1.6%		−3.9%		−6.8%		−0.9%		−0.8%		−0.7%	

Source: Ministry of Finance Budget Bureau Research Section (Ōkurashō Shukei Kyoku Chōsa Ka), *Zaisei Tōkei* (Financial Statistics), 1986 ed. (Tokyo: Ōkurashō Insatsu Kyoku, 1986).

Notes: (1) All budgetary calculations are percentage changes for general account (*ippan kaikei*) spending only. (2) General account, welfare, and public works figures are for 1949–1986. (3) Number of years in other categories vary according to availability of data.

TABLE 4.6

Japan's Expanding Fiscal Investment and Loan Program, 1953–1986

Year	Scale of FILP (¥ billion)	FILP/General Account (percent)	FILP/GNP (percent)
1953	337	33.4	4.5
1955	321	32.5	3.4
1960	607	38.7	3.9
1965	1620	44.3	5.4
1970	3580	45.0	5.2
1975	9310	43.7	7.1
1980	18,109	43.0	7.5
1985	20,858	39.7	6.6
1986	22,155	41.0	6.6

Sources: Ishikawa Itaru and Gyōten Toyoo, *Zaisei Tōyūshi (Fiscal Investment and Loans)* (Tokyo: Kinyū Zaisei Jōhō Kenkyū Kai, 1977), pp. 82–83; Ministry of Finance Budget Bureau Research Section, (Ōkurashō Shukei Kyoku Chōsa Ka), ed., *Zaisei Tōkei (Financial Statistics)*, 1986 ed., pp. 306–7; Yano Tsuneta Kinen Kai, ed., *Nihon Kokusei Zue (Japan National Survey Almanac)*, 1987 ed. (Tokyo: Kokusei Sha, 1987), p. 445.

Notes: (1) In fiscal 1987 the Fiscal Investment and Loan Program expanded sharply to ¥27,081 billion. This represented 50.1 percent of the general account budget and 7.7 percent of GNP—the highest levels in the history of the FILP. (2) Figures on FILP scale are net of government bond underwriting.

and Loan Program (FILP), or *zaisei tōyūshi*, which has risen from less than one third to over two fifths the scale of the general account budget since 1955, as indicated in table 4.6. While the general account budget is funded from tax revenues, FILP income derives largely from government trust funds, particularly from postal savings, postal life insurance, and various national pension programs.[36] This system of off-budget financing frees the Japanese government still further from constraints economic growth might impose on government activities and allows expanded scope for response to political pressures. As in the case of the

[36] In fiscal 1985, 24.8 percent of Fiscal Investment and Loan Program's income derived from postal savings, 10.0 percent from postal life insurance, and 15.3 percent from national pension trust funds. See Ōkurashō Shukei Kyoku Chōsa Ka, ed., *Zaisei Tōyūshi, 1985*, pp. 308–9.

general account budget, FILP spending varies rather imperfectly with patterns of economic growth. As a general proposition, FILP spending is much more volatile than that of the general-account budget, as befits its standing as a marginal source of funding for politically attractive projects not fully supported by the general account.

Rapid economic growth has without question been one of the central aspects of postwar Japanese experience, exerting profound, although often poorly understood, influence on the course of postwar Japanese politics. Understanding Japanese growth and its broader consequences for macrosocial and microeconomic structure is central to understanding why the crisis and compensation dynamic in Japanese policymaking has been both necessary and possible. But like the analysis of technocratic structure undertaken in chapter 3, an understanding of economic growth patterns tells one relatively little about the likely timing and content of public policy decisions. How imperfectly economic growth varies with budgetary aggregates in Japan is depicted in figure 4.2, as well as in tables 4.4 and 4.5. For insights into the residuals which economic growth cannot explain, it is important to look at the structural context of compensation politics.

The Structural Context of Compensation Politics

"If it is true," Scattschneider observes, "that demands largely determine public policy, it follows that policies can be explained in terms of the processes by which pressures are shaped and modified."[37] The Japanese conservatives face a political system not wholly of their liking; it both deprives them of coercive tools and generates unsettling pressures toward popular responsiveness which many of them would prefer to be without. As noted in chapter 1, the unusual middle-size district electoral system of Japan creates "institutionalized insecurity." This in turn gives Japanese conservative politicians constant incentives to seek compensation for grassroots interests in return for the support of those interests.

But this constant pressure on politicians to seek compensation for clients does not necessarily mean either consistent client or

[37] E. E. Scattschneider, *Politics, Pressures, and the Tariff*, p. 5.

politician satisfaction. The current electoral system existed between 1925 and 1945, and it has been in continuous operation since 1947, despite conservative efforts to change it. Yet there have been major changes since 1947 in both the patterns of Japanese public policy outputs and the pace of policy and institutional change, which cannot be explained by the electoral system above.

"Institutionalized insecurity" is a central reason why conservative politicians in Japan feel perennially vulnerable. But such ongoing institutional characteristics cannot by themselves account fully for these nuances in policy. Institutional features can substantiate arguments that policymakers must be sensitive to electoral interests, but they cannot identify which interests, or establish what, other than elections, causes variations in that sensitivity.

Japanese policymakers, then, are standing between an economic growth process which generates resources for political distribution and a set of political demands. Satisfaction of demands, particularly for "large, new" policies, is by no means automatic. Those demands are conveyed to political authority and processed by a distinctive transmission mechanism that plays a central role in magnifying the importance of crisis for policy change in Japan. This transmission belt intensifies the distributive policy consequences of crisis and generates cross-issue spillovers that make relatively short periods of political flux highly important in understanding the overall profiles of Japanese public policy. The transmission belt's complex, fragmented structure also prevents it from operating effectively on broad, controversial questions during noncrisis periods, thus often blocking major change when crisis does not threaten. The following pages describe that transmission mechanism between crisis and compensation and assess its consequences for Japanese public policy.

Mass Interest Groups and Compensation Politics

Japan, although not a society of explicitly political organizations, is an extraordinarily organized society at the grassroots level. Verba, Nie, and Kim found in their seven-nation study of political participation patterns, for example, that 72 percent of their entire Japanese sample belonged to some organization—by far the highest ratio of any nation in their study. In the United States, by contrast, 61 percent belonged, and in India only 16 percent.[38] Yet a strikingly low proportion of their sample for Japan, lower than for any nation except India, were members of explicitly political groups. The 59 percent share of the Japanese sample that belonged to nonpolitical organizations only was double that of the United States and far more than in any other nation sampled.

To the extent that Japanese, particularly lower-income Japanese, participate in politics, they do so through groups. Group norms and specific group instructions to members appear more important than elsewhere in determining voting and other political activity. Accordingly, Japanese political culture gives those in a position to generate group consensus (leaders in the distinctly Japanese sense of the term) the ability to powerfully influence policy output. The strategic problem for Japanese conservative leadership thus becomes more effectively coopting the leadership of formally apolitical groups, such as neighborhood associations or chambers of commerce, rather than appealing directly to the general electorate as possible in less organized societies like the United States.

Japan has an extraordinarily rich proliferation of voluntary associations, although their numbers and influence are somewhat skewed by sector. Particularly notable in comparative perspective is the intense degree of organization in relatively low-income, nonlabor sectors, a product of state incorporation strategies earlier in the century. Also important is the immense size of the organization involved and its complexity—factors making these groups both initially difficult to mobilize and powerful in a crisis once mobilized. In agriculture, for example, there is the massive National Agricultural Cooperative League (Zennō), whose constituent cooperatives had over 5.5 million members in the mid-1980s. France's analogous FNSEA (Fédération Nationale des Syndicats d'Exploitants Agricoles), by contrast, has only around 850,000 members.[39] India, despite national government intervention in food and grain pricing and a dominant yet broadly democratic party system that in many ways parallels Japan's, has no powerful national-level farm groups at all.[40]

In the small business area Japan has the Medium and Small

[38] Sidney Verba, Norman H. Nie, and Jae-on-Kim, *Participation and Political Equality: A Seven Nation Comparison*, p. 101.

[39] Vincent Wright, *The Government and Politics of France*, p. 233.

[40] Norman K. Nicholson, "Factionalism and Public Policy in India," in *Faction Politics*, Belloni and Beller, eds., p. 183.

Business Political League (around 300,000 members), the JCP-oriented Democratic Merchants and Manufacturers Association (200,000), and a range of other similar groups affiliated with specific political parties. France has had some highly successful small business movements, particularly the CID-UNATI (Comité d'Information et de Défense–Union Nationale des Travailleurs Indépendants). But these have not been as long-lived, large, or broadly distributed across the political spectrum as have their counterparts in Japan.[41]

Japan also has an extraordinarily powerful collection of regionally based civic organizations and pressure groups, many of them with strong lobbying branches in Tokyo. Each prefecture, for example, has a vigorous representative body which presses its own interests with the national government. Perhaps the strongest single political interest group of all is the Japan Chamber of Commerce and Industry (JCCI), representing small business and frequently prevailing over the big business federation Keidanren in major tests of strength between the two since the early 1970s. Local chambers are the locus of power and the principal strength of the JCCI.

As one looks across the spectrum of organizations relevant to Japanese conservatives, perhaps the most striking divergence from Western European patterns is the absence of an influential church in Japan. In France, Italy, and even to some extent Germany, the Roman Catholic Church has traditionally been the anchor of the Right. It has been especially important, at least until the 1970s, in creating a constituency for the conservatives among the working class in Europe,[42] and as an institutional center of gravity around which groups opposed to sudden, sweeping policy change might rally.

In Japan, several of the so-called New Religions,[43] such as *Rei-*

[41] On the political role of small business in France and Italy, see Suzanne Berger and Michael Piore, *Dualism and Discontinuity in Industrial Societies*, pp. 83–149.

[42] See Mattei Dogan, "Political Cleavage and Social Stratification in France and Italy," in *Party Systems and Voter Alignments*, eds. Seymour M. Lipset and Stein Rokkan.

[43] New Religions are so-called to differentiate them from the ancient, established Japanese religions—Shintōism and organized Buddhism. Most of the New Religions, many founded during the 1920s and 1930s, grew rapidly in the two decades after World War II. For further details, see H. Neill McFarland, *The Rush Hour of the Gods*; and Murakami Shigeyoshi, *Nihon Hyakunen no Shūkyō-*

yūkai and *Seichō no Ie*, have been more important than commonly recognized in providing the Japanese conservatives with a stable political base among the lower socioeconomic classes.[44] This was particularly true just after the Kōmeitō was founded in 1964, since the founding of this party escalated long-standing rivalries between the conservative New Religions and *Sōka Gakkai*, the religious sponsor of Kōmeitō, to the level of political conflict. But these groups have little influence on the overall political culture of Japan, or on lower-income groups generally, beyond their specific membership. And the active membership of the groups themselves is comparatively small, although often highly mobilized.

Paralleling the organizational fragmentation and small size of religious groups, the Japanese conservatives have found it difficult, throughout most of the postwar period, to fully utilize the strong latent potential of other traditional elements in Japanese politics and society in sustaining their preeminence. As Murakami Yasusuke points out, the Japanese conservatives have been more closely and exclusively associated with nationalism, as compared with opponents on the Left, than is true in either Italy or France.[45] But nationalism itself was in ill-repute with much of the Japanese electorate during the turbulent years of crisis when the distinctive postwar institutions and patterns of budgetary allocation were forged. Rapid social change made other traditional cultural appeals and organizational forms difficult to employ. In the absence of either strong institutional religious support or broad public acceptance of nationalism, Japan's conservatives were to that extent more politically vulnerable than their counterparts in Europe, and hence more reliant on materialist appeals to maintain their preeminence. Although the waning of crisis and the resurgence of nationalism during the 1980s has reduced this vulnerability at the margin, the institutions and resource allocation patterns forged in the heat of crisis remain, dominating the political landscape.

Japanese interest groups in general have a dual relationship with the state, flowing from their large size and relatively strong

Haibutsu Kishaku kara Sōka Gakkai made (*A Japanese Century of Religion: From the Meiji Suppression of Buddhism Movement to Sōka Gakkai*).

[44] On their political role, see Shūkyō to Seiji o Kangaeru Kai, ed., *Kami to Hotoke to Senkyosen* (*Shintō and Buddhist Deities and the Election Campaign*).

[45] Murakami Yasusuke, "The Age of New Middle Mass Politics: The Case of Japan," *Journal of Japanese Studies* 8, no. 1 (Winter 1982), pp. 54–56.

organization as well as the broad range of administrative and compensatory dealings with government in which they are engaged. They are, in normal circumstances, somewhat vulnerable to state pressure, which has successfully incorporated many of them through institutionalized compensation arrangements such as those long prevailing between agricultural cooperatives and the government. But when politics is fluid and unstable—when the state itself is in disarray—they can wield unusual influence, not least because the state and the business community feel they must reincorporate these groups without violence, so as to assure the political stability prerequisite for economic growth. Thus, Japan's mass interest groups are a strong force for redistributive compensation in times of crisis and against retrenchment when stability prevails. Their influence, in short, tends to intensify the ratchet effect that both creates new programs and expands old ones when the "window" of policy innovation is open and then sustains the status quo when it is not.

Conservative Politicians, State Structure, and Patronage

Japan is a highly organized society, with a proliferation of mass interest groups, particularly in traditionally low-income sectors other than industrial labor.[46] But it does not necessarily follow from this group orientation that Japanese public policy should have a distributive bias. To be sure, some Japanese pressure groups, such as the agricultural and small business federations, are quite large and aggressive. But these qualities alone are insufficient as an ultimate explanation. They can neither account for the fluctuating influence of these pressure groups over time within Japan, nor can they explain the relative absence of distributive politics in some nations, such as West Germany, with large and well-organized corporatist interest groups. Further, the mere existence of large, aggressive Japanese interest groups during the 1960s, 1970s, and 1980s cannot explain how interest groups themselves, or the processes which link them to the state, were first established in Japan.

Understanding the compensation orientation of much Japanese policymaking, including the cyclical aspect of that orientation,

[46] For a detailed, analytical recent survey of these groups and their relationship to policymaking, see Kōsaka Masataka, *Kōdo Sangyō Kokka no Rieki Seiji Katei to Seisaku: Nippon (Interest Group Politics and Public Policy in Industrialized States: The Case of Japan)*.

requires understanding the relationship of conservative politicians to bureaucracy, big business, and the range of pressure groups described above. These groups are the conservatives' central constituency.[47] And understanding the conservative politicians' relationship to them requires going back to the origins of conservative parties in the Meiji Period.

Although the first embryonic political parties in Meiji Japan were broadly opposed to the prevailing oligarchic governmental order, by 1900 the mainstream of the conservative party movement had become intimately related to state authority.[48] Indeed, in September of that year, what was to become the mainstream of Japanese conservative politics, the *Rikken Seiyūkai* (Constitutional Association of Political Friends, or Seiyūkai), was founded under the leadership of the most prominent establishment statesman of the time, Itō Hirobumi. Its formation was, as Fukui points out, accomplished completely on Itō's terms, and in fact it took the form of a "donation" of the party to Itō by the party's leaders, indicating their strong deference to him.[49] Five of the twelve members of the Seiyūkai's founding committee, including the chairman, were leading government officials.

The Seiyūkai was thus a quintessential "internally mobilized" party, founded by elites within the established regime in an effort to consolidate control over the party movement.[50] Throughout the prewar period it maintained relatively close ties with the career civil service. The Seiyūkai absorbed a larger portion of former bureaucrats than any of its competitors, although the relationship with officials was occasionally delicate. After World War II the Seiyūkai's successor Liberal Party,[51] in turn the central ele-

[47] In 1975, for example, farmers, small business proprietors, and their employees (including workers in the distribution sector) comprised around 57 percent of the LDP's total support across Japan. Asahi Shimbun Sha Seron Chōsa Shitsu, ed., *Nihonjin no Seiji Ishiki* (*The Political Consciousness of Japanese*), p. 78.

[48] The first embryonic political parties, frequently known as *seisha* (political company), were formed largely by discontented members of the *shi* (warrior) class and relatively well-to-do owner farmers who had traditionally dominated village politics during the so-called movement for freedom and popular rights in the mid-1870s. For details, see Haruhiro Fukui, *Party in Power*, pp. 9–16.

[49] *Ibid.*, p. 16.

[50] On the concept of an "internally mobilized" party, see Shefter, *Patronage and Its Opponents*, p. 18; Maurice Duverger, *Political Parties*, pp. xxiv–xxxvii; and Samuel P. Huntington, *Political Order in Changing Societies*, p. 415.

[51] Transwar continuities are not exact, of course, due to the occupation purge. But the postwar Liberal party was essentially the successor of the Kuhara faction of the *Seiyūkai*, of which the Liberal party's first leader, Hatoyama Ichirō, and

ment of the current Liberal Democratic Party following the conservative merger of 1955, was cut in the same state-related mold as its predecessor. This was particularly true following the great infusion of former bureaucrats into conservative politics after 1949.[52]

Japanese conservative politics does, it should be noted, have a second, less prominent political party tradition, that of the "externally mobilized" party.[53] Such parties, which emerge in confrontation with bureaucratic authority, tend to be much more issue oriented and ideological than their "internally mobilized" counterparts; conversely, they tend to be less distributively oriented. This issue-oriented, "outsider" orientation was typical of the Kenseikai and Minseitō elements of the prewar Japanese conservative tradition.[54] Its postwar successors were concentrated in the Peoples' Cooperative party, Reform party, and ultimately in the antimainstream factions of the LDP. Significantly the antimainstream's most prominent postwar representative, Miki Takeo, as prime minister authorized the arrest of the LDP's most prominent patronage-oriented politician, Tanaka Kakuei, in connection with the Lockheed scandal. But the externally mobilized tradition has been less prominent among Japanese conservative party politicians since 1900 than has the internally mobilized tradition which in turn has been so intimately linked with the bureaucracy.

Internally mobilized, establishment-oriented parties are not necessarily patronage-oriented, as the case of the German Christian Democrats makes clear.[55] Their distributive politics impulse can be either frustrated by a strongly autonomous bureaucracy or suppressed by a noncompensation-oriented national political tradition. But when an absolutist or antipatronage coalition does

---

seventeen of the twenty-eight original Dietmen in the faction with prewar legislative experience had originally been members. See Fukui, *Party in Power*, p. 35.

[52] 17.2 percent of the Liberals and 12.8 percent of the Democrats successfully returned in the 1949 election were former career officials, compared to 15.7 percent of Seiyūkai and 10.0 percent of Kenseikai Dietmen in 1919. See *Ibid.*, pp. 27, 40.

[53] Shefter, *Patronage and Its Opponents*, pp. 21–25.

[54] These parties, generally in opposition during the prewar period, had stronger Policy Affairs Research Councils than did the Seiyūkai, were more innovative policywise, included large shares of journalists, and absorbed fewer former bureaucrats than did the Seiyūkai. See Fukui, *Party in Power*.

[55] See Karl Hochswender, "The Politics of Civil Service Reform in West Germany" (Ph.D. diss., Yale University, 1962), pp. 63–65.

not become entrenched prior to the mobilization of the masses into politics, a patronage-oriented tendency generally becomes clearly visible.[56]

Faced with material demands from mass-level constituents, politicians try to secure access to state resources, if their parties are not estranged from state authority. Such a patronage-oriented pattern on the part of internally mobilized parties not confronting strongly autonomous bureaucracies has been highly pronounced among the post–World War II Italian Christian Democrats;[57] it was also salient among the French Radicals of the Third Republic[58] and common in the American state and local politics of the Northeast and Midwest for over a hundred years.[59]

Since shortly after the Seiyūkai's foundation in 1900, the internally mobilized segment of the Japanese conservative political party world has striven mightily to overcome bureaucratic resistance and entrench patronage politics. Hara Kei pursued this course vigorously as Home Minister of the Interior during 1906–08, 1911–12, and 1913–14, and as prime minister during 1918–1921. But Hara and his political party colleagues were sharply opposed by Meiji oligarchs such as Yamagata Aritomo, the big business community, and major entrenched ministries, particularly Finance.

Following World War II some important new opportunities for patronage seeking conservative politicians were opened with the abolition of the powerful Home Ministry at the end of 1947, and the almost simultaneous transition to direct election of local

[56] Martin Shefter, *Patronage and Its Opponents*, pp. 20–21.

[57] See Luigi Graziano, "Center-Periphery Relations and the Italian Crisis: The Problem of Clientelism," in Sidney Tarrow, Peter Katzenstein, and Luigi Graziano, ed., *Territorial Politics in Industrial States*; P. A. Allum, *Italy—Republic without Government?*, pp. 25–29; and Mario Caciagli, "The Mass Clientelism Party and Conservative Politics: Christian Democracy in Southern Italy," in *Conservative Politics in Western Europe*, ed., Zig Layton-Henry, pp. 264–91.

[58] See Peter J. Larmour, *The French Radical Party in the 1930s*.

[59] The best known examples of conservative patronage machines in the United States have included the Republican parties of New York and Pennsylvania, the Philadelphia Republican machine of the pre-New Deal period, and the Nassau County Republican machine in New York State. On these cases see Shefter, *Patronage and Its Opponents*, p. 6; Harry J. Carmen and Reinhard H. Luthin, *Lincoln and the Patronage*; Raymond Wolfinger, "Why Political Machines Have Not Withered Away and Other Revisionist Thoughts," *Journal of Politics* 34 (May 1972), pp. 397–98; and Robert A. Caro, *The Power Broker*, pp. 152, 204, 209, and 405.

government officials. Astute conservative politicians moved rapidly to capture the successor organizations: the ministries of Construction, Welfare, Labor, and Local Autonomy, together with the National Police Agency. They also strove to influence the newly autonomous local governments.[60] In both cases they were aided by administrative chaos and the need of officials in the fledgling successors to the Naimushō structure for political support to restore stability on terms favorable to themselves.

But in areas such as finance and industrial policy, where bureaucratic power remained strong, politicians were unable to make major inroads against the technocratic state in normal times.[61] In the face of strong cross-pressures from both bureaucrats and big businessmen intent on promoting Japanese industrial development and handicapped by a big business–oriented institutional framework evolved under the efficiency-oriented demands of war, conservative politicians and their interest group supporters could readily achieve their welfare-oriented demands in the technocratically dominated sectors only when they coincided with the strategic objectives of a bureaucracy-dominated developmental state. In such policy areas the structural context of Japanese policy formation in normal times was more similar to those of France and Germany—where internally mobilized conservative parties found themselves confronted by a powerful, autonomous bureaucratic state—than to that of Italy, with its weaker bureaucracy and stronger patronage orientation. But the breakup of the Home Ministry offered opportunities for inroads by the entrepreneurial politicians in a wide range of domestic policy sectors where national strategy and international competitiveness were not of direct concern. In those sectors Japanese policymaking often came to look more like that of Italy.

[60] Tanaka Kakuei, for example, was reputedly active in seeing the construction-related activities of the Naimushō given ministerial status rather than the agency status which the Katayama cabinet had intended for them. Tanaka argued that only with ministerial standing could road construction and housing be effectively promoted, independent of bureaucratic infighting between the agriculture and transportation ministries. Ministerial standing for construction, of course, ultimately aided Tanaka's accumulation of influence in that area. On Tanaka's lobbying activities regarding Naimushō reorganization, see Hayasaka Shigezō, "Tanaka Kakuei Mumei no Jyū Nen," pp. 381–82.

[61] Major politicians during the mid-1950s even had trouble systematically influencing the activities of the Ministry of Agriculture. See Johnson, *MITI and the Japanese Miracle*, pp. 53–54.

Intraelite Competition and Japan's Materialist Response

In the postwar Japanese policy process, as in the policy processes of many advanced industrial nations, the welfare-oriented demands of politicians have perennially collided with the efficiency concerns of technocracy.[62] To carry the day, given the technocratic bias of Japanese political structure, especially with regard to budgeting, conservative political innovators have required a broad range of allies. Intraelite competition has been crucial. Intrafactional competition within the LDP, particularly in the context of broader intraparty rivalries, has also been important; likewise, subtle differences of opinion within the business world, particularly on social policy questions, have been influential.

The road from crisis to compensation, in short, has led through pluralism and rivalry among the Japanese elite, albeit often behind closed doors, combined with a transcendent consensus on the importance of political stability. In the face of crisis, interest groups, mass media, and legislative pressures on a fragmented conservative ruling party have given strong momentum to proposals for welfare-oriented change, which both technocratic and business elites have been disposed to accept in the interest of political stability. In the absence of crisis, this intraelite pluralism and rivalry has conversely tended to block policy change, thus accentuating the cyclical, crisis-driven character of domestic policy innovation in Japan.

Conservative Factional Rivalries and the Policy Process

Factions have been endemic in Japanese politics for centuries; personalism goes to the heart of Japanese political culture. Yet since World War II—indeed, since the 1950s—political factions have taken on a formality and major influence over the conservative policymaking process in Japan which they previously had not assumed. This development, in turn, has stimulated pressures for policy innovation, especially in redistributive directions, during periods of crisis. Conversely, factionalism has con-

[62] This classic confrontation between politicians sensitive to interest group demands and pressures for patronage and bureaucrats preoccupied with planning for the nation as a whole also appears salient across Western Europe. See Aberbach, Putnam, and Rockman, *Bureaucrats and Politicians in Western Democracies*.

tributed to policy rigidity in noncrisis periods by making it difficult to centralize the authority required for policy decisions.

Until 1955 intraparty competition in conservative ranks was moderated by the relatively small size of parties. Neither the Liberal nor the Democratic party, nor any of their various permutations over the first postwar decade, was large enough to run more than one, or occasionally two, candidates in a single constituency. Hence there was relatively little pressure from the electoral system for intraparty competition.

Four major factors sharply intensified factional rivalries in conservative ranks during the 1950s and 1960s. First, and perhaps most important, a substantial number of Dietmen, led by Hatoyama Ichirō, who had been purged by the U.S. occupation forces for having collaborated with the wartime Tōjō regime, reentered politics. Many of the purgees naturally banded together against those like Yoshida who had both opposed the war more forcefully and then subsequently usurped the positions of the purgees. Second, the so-called "1955 electoral system," created by the parallel merger of major parties on the Left and the Right, intensified intraparty rivalries among the conservatives. It did so by increasing the number of members from a single conservative party running against one another in individual electoral districts. Third, conservative politicians in ministerial posts became ever more capable of shaping specific policy decisions, particularly in sectors generating substantial distributive political resources, such as construction and telecommunications; this rising capability increased the economic stakes of success for individual factions in the intraparty rivalry for cabinet posts, long a fierce psychological battle. Finally, personal rivalries among key conservative politicians became more intense and, occasionally, bitter. Following the Yoshida-Hatoyama rivalry of the 1950s, the protracted struggle between Tanaka Kakuei and Fukuda Takeo escalated during the early 1970s, sharply intensifying factional rivalries and distinctions.

Seen in comparative perspective LDP factional politics are quite distinctive, particularly in their highly institutionalized character and persistent multiple competing factions. In both these respects, LDP factional politics are sharply different from those of the American South which V. O. Key described.[63] Japan's LDP is,

[63] The southern politics which Key described was, to be sure, a one-party system which was highly factionalized. But it was distinguished by a highly transi-

as Sartori points out, a party created by "fusion," where the prior or primordial units are what are today its factions.[64] This historical reality helps explain the fundamental, highly institutionalized character of postwar Japanese conservative factions and their failure to be absorbed fully by the party structure created in 1955. The multimember district electoral system also contributes to the viability of LDP factions, as pointed out in chapter 1.

The only close contemporary parallel to the LDP among conservative parties of the West with respect to factionalism is Italy's Christian Democrats. In Italy, however, historical factors, particularly the early establishment of a unified conservative political party, have given the Christian Democratic party a preeminence vis-à-vis factions that its analogue in Japan, the Liberal Democratic party, has not enjoyed. Furthermore, the Italian electoral system does not force the intense interfactional rivalries and pressures for public works that develop in Japan.[65] Factional struggles instead tend to revolve around conflict over control of local party branches, generating less pressure for community-oriented benefits than is typical in Japan. In the aggregate, they also tend to weaken the policymaking role of the ruling conservative party;[66] in the Japanese case this has initiated important regional, small business, and agricultural policies, despite its factionalized character. Thus, one of the main engines that has created the programmatically materialist bias of Japanese conservative public policy is lacking elsewhere.

LDP factional rivalries, it should be stressed, do not *intrinsically* create a bias toward welfare-oriented policies (or toward any other specific set of policies) in the Japanese political process. But

---

tory and diffuse factional system; permanent, institutionalized factions like those of Japan did not operate except in North Carolina and Virginia. Even there, the overwhelming dominance of single factions with strong ties to upper-income groups was typical. Key's southern politics was neither issue-oriented nor responsive to the grassroots, thus contrasting in outputs as well as structure to Japanese patterns. For details, see V. O. Key, Jr., *Southern Politics*, pp. 16, 299, 306, and 309–10.

[64] Giovanni Sartori, *Parties and Party Systems*, p. 92.

[65] Bureaucratic weakness in Italy does provide the DC considerable scope for patronage. But party attempts to exploit distributive opportunities seem less related to electoral considerations than in Japan. On factionalism within Italy's Christian Democratic Party, see Frank P. Belloni, "Factionalism, the Party System, and Italian Politics," in *Faction Politics*, eds. Belloni and Beller, pp. 73–108. Also see Sartori, *Parties and Party Systems*, pp. 88–93, for a range of specific comparisons between Italian and Japanese factionalism.

[66] *Ibid.*, pp. 91–92.

they do render the ruling Japanese conservative party more vulnerable to outside pressures, and more receptive to outside policy proposals, than it would otherwise be, once those pressures have created a compelling need for policy change on the part of Japan's conservative government. Conversely, factionalism seriously impedes decisive action in the absence of strong outside pressures, thus contributing to the immobility of Japanese policymaking in noncrisis periods. Media pressure, cross-party networks, the interest group structure outlined above, and the bias of the Japanese electoral system combine, as we will see, to assure that a large *share* of the pressure confronting the faction-ridden conservatives has been for welfare-oriented policy changes, particularly during periods of major interparty political crisis for the LDP.

Cross-Party Elite Networks: The Key Policy Role of Political Marginals

Paralleling internal rivalries within the ruling LDP have been subtle differences of orientation within conservative ranks toward the opposition, which often helped generate conservative receptivity to welfare-oriented opposition proposals. Indeed, cross-party interpersonal networks, many based on prewar or early postwar relationships that developed before left-right cleavages became pronounced, supported the "politics behind politics" of extraparty political coordination, as Scattschneider would put it;[67] these networks propelled Japanese postwar policy change in sectors as diverse as agriculture, small business, welfare, and environmental policy, by shaping policy agendas.

The range of formative experiences which generated cross-party networks has been quite diverse. The Shōwa Juku, an influential young group of advisors to Prince Konoye Fumimaro during the 1930s, generated one such network. It included such people as Ryū Shintarō (longtime editor of the *Asahi Shimbun*), Ōkita Saburō (foreign minister of the Ōhira cabinet), Ogawa Heiji (of the Democratic Socialist party), Nezu Kaiichirō (Tōbu Railways), and Saeki Kiichi (Nomura Research Institute). Another cross-organizational network highly influential in economic-policy formation since the late 1940s is the early staff of the Economic Stabilization Board (*Keizai Antei Honbu*), directed by

[67] Schattschneider, *Politics, Pressures, and the Tariff*, p. 9.

Wada Hiroo (longtime head of the JSP International Bureau) and also involving Tsuru Shigeto (president of Hitotsubashi University), Ōkita Saburō, and Nagano Shigeo (chairman first of Nippon Steel and then subsequently of the Japan Chamber of Commerce and Industry).

At the heart of cross-party elite networks active in promoting policy change have been policy entrepreneurs, similar to Heclo's agents of policy change.[68] Although often outside the dominant conservative mainstream, these entrepreneurs have both an unusually diverse range of political contacts and enough access to bureaucratic expertise to develop fairly realistic policy proposals. These entrepreneurs have a stake in developing and promoting new policies precisely because they are politically marginal. Their very strength in the Japanese policy process lies in their ability to broker the complex political transactions required to initiate policy change when the stability of the prevailing political order requires such change.

Many of the major policy entrepreneurs of the postwar period, such as Miki Takeo, Ishida Hirohide, Ashida Hitoshi, Matsumura Kenzō, Kawasaki Hideji, Hayakawa Takashi, and Sonoda Sunao, were members before 1955 of the smaller, middle-of-the-road parties that merged with the Liberals in 1955 to form the LDP, but that periodically cooperated with the opposition in the pre-1955 period.[69] Some had also served together with the Socialists in the two coalition cabinets of the late 1940s.[70] Several had been among the conservatives who refused to participate in the midnight snap vote called in 1960 to ratify the United States-Japan Security Treaty, thus earning considerable esteem in the eyes of the Left.[71]

[68] See Heclo, *Modern Social Politics in Britain and Sweden*, p. 308.

[69] Miki Takeo and Ishida Hirohide, for example, had been instrumental in coordinating, with Socialists, the no-confidence vote against Finance Minister Ikeda Hayato's small business policies while Miki was secretary general of the Kaishintō. See Shioguchi Kiichi, *Kikigaki: Ikeda Hayato* (*Reminiscences: Ikeda Hayato*), p. 86.

[70] Miki Takeo himself, for example, had served as minister of communications in the Socialist-Democratic Katayama coalition cabinet of 1947–1948, together with longtime Democratic Socialist party leader Nishio Suehiro and the prominent Socialist leader of the 1970s, Wada Hiroo. For details on the Katayama cabinet, see *Asahi Shimbun*, June 18, 1947.

[71] Among this group were Ishibashi Tanzan, Miki Takeo, Matsumura Kenzō, and Kōno Ichirō, all major leaders within the LDP. Ishibashi and Matsumura were also on good terms with China, and Kōno with the USSR.

These conservatives with strong cross-party networks periodically used their networks to coordinate policy intitiatives with opposition parties on such questions as welfare, pollution, agriculture, and small business policy. In so doing they helped give Japanese policymaking a more redistributive, welfare-oriented cast than it would have had had pressure groups on the Right been the sole influences in decision making, since the opposition parties were generally closer to lower-income groups and their mainly materialist concerns than were many segments of the often business-oriented LDP.

Big Business: Pluralism in the Pursuit of Stability

Japan's big business community is famous globally for its unity and its deft internal coordination. On key issues where Japan's national economic security or internal political stability has been perceived at stake over the past forty years, the business world, or zaikai, has clearly felt constrained to stand squarely together. In the midst of early postwar recovery, as well as during the United States-Japan Security Treaty crisis of 1960, for example, the major business organizations made a special point of joint declarations and closely coordinated strategies. Yet despite their show of unity on high-profile questions, particularly issues of confrontation and cooperation with the outside world, the Japanese big business community has been extraordinarily diverse in viewpoints expressed, on many policy questions, reflecting a much broader ideological, organizational, and experiential pluralism than is often recognized. There are, for example, four major national business federations in Japan, with little overlapping membership at the key leadership levels; each has its own special character, reflecting a different set of pressures from the broader society. No major European nation has more than two such federations, and most have only one.

The largest and most important big business organization in Japan is the Federation of Economic Organizations, or Keidanren. This association has an extraordinarily broad membership—110 industry-wide groups and over 800 of Japan's largest corporations. At the heart of its formal policy making mechanism are thirty-two permanent committees and consulting organs, each of them concerned with policy definition in some subsector of the Japanese political economy and dominated by the most prominent firms in those subsectors.

Comprehensive membership[72] and complex decision-making mechanisms render Keidanren highly effective at implementing an already established consensus of the business world. It showed this ability in both helping coordinate rapid national reconstruction in the late 1940s and obtaining vital raw material supplies from developing nations such as Brazil and Mexico during the early 1970s. But for precisely the same reasons that it is effective at implementation, Keidanren has had difficulty decisively shaping policy on complex microissues such as financial liberalization, pitting one segment of its large, diverse membership against others. Policy initiation is also difficult for Keidanren, due to the time-consuming necessity of orchestrating a consensus. On most major issues of the past twenty years, Keidanren has ceded initiative in policy formation to smaller, more flexible business groups, the LDP, and the opposition parties. Only on the administrative reform question, after Japan's budget deficit had risen to crisis proportions, has it really been decisively influential on behalf of its overall antigovernment, antiredistribution bias toward policy questions. And Keidanren's success in shaping the administrative reform debate has been the product of highly unusual circumstances.[73]

Like Keidanren, Nikkeiren (the Japan Federation of Employers' Associations) is also relatively large and complex, with forty-seven regional associations and fifty-one industry associations as members. Often known as "the labor relations department of the business world," it coordinates the annual national-level *Shuntō* (Spring Struggle) wage negotiations with organized labor. As in the case of Keidanren, organizational complexity also relegates Nikkeiren to a rather formalistic role in the policy initiation process. The one major exception, of course, is labor policy, where Nikkeiren is preeminent and its tasks clearly defined. Although its relationship with the labor movement has tradition-

[72] Keidanren even numbers among its members the Japanese subsidiaries of several major foreign multinationals operating in Japan, such as IBM-Japan, Shell Sekiyu, and Mobil Sekiyu.

[73] Keidanren's vigorous former chairman Dokō Toshio has been chairman of the Council on Administrative Reform, backed strongly by Prime Minister Nakasone Yasuhiro, himself a former director of the Administrative Management Agency. Nakasone in the early 1980s staked his political future on the success of efforts to curb the size of government in Japan.

ally been rather strained, Nikkeiren has a wide range of opposition contacts through its labor negotiations. These contacts have made it sensitive to welfare-oriented demands from the Left, especially when satisfaction of those demands has helped reduce pressures for wage increases.

The Japan Chamber of Commerce and Industry (*Nisshō*) is a grassroots-oriented body, the central organ of regional chambers of commerce in 478 Japanese cities. Although many nations have chambers of commerce, Japan's seem unusually representative of small business and other relatively parochial interests. Japan's first chambers of commerce were founded in 1878, and for years they articulated the interests of big business in favor of the land tax and other industrialization policies, with disastrous implications for the countryside. But since World War II the political role of chambers of commerce has been sharply transformed.

On a wide range of questions, particularly the structure of the distribution system and tax reform, Nisshō has doggedly represented the interests of small business against larger firms, often using its strong grassroots base to mobilize assistance from LDP politicians. In both 1974 and 1983, Nisshō was the key organization forcing legislation to block the expansion of supermarkets, clashing directly with Keidanren and prevailing both times against the big business representative. Like Keidanren and Nikkeiren, Nisshō is most powerful when the interests of its membership are completely unified; given the strong localist, small business orientation of the membership, it is able to achieve that unity on a wide range of welfare-related questions and to take clear initiative with the political world where the more elite-oriented Keidanren and Nikkeiren cannot.

Nisshō's political leverage has also been immeasurably strengthened by a few key big businessmen interested in small business issues, who zealously participate in its activities. The incumbent chairman in the mid-1980s, Gotō Noboru, president of the large Tōkyū conglomerate of railway and real estate interests, had strong political connections. The previous chairman, Nagano Shigeo, a former chairman of Nippon Steel, had been one of the most powerful members of the big business mainstream;[74] through his big business contacts, Nagano mustered broad sup-

[74] Nagano had been known, during the 1950s and 1960s, as one of the "Four Emperors of Zaikai," or the big business world, who reportedly named Ikeda Hayato prime minister in the wake of the 1960 Security Treaty crisis.

port throughout the business world for government aid to small business, ostensibly to counter a perceived burgeoning communist threat.[75]

The fourth business community organization, the Japan Council for Economic Development (*Keizai Dōyūkai*), has together with the JCCI played a role in intensifying the welfare-oriented bias of Japanese public policy. JCED, in contrast to the other three zaikai organizations, is an association of individuals, rather than groups. The structure permits its members a less inhibited atmosphere for policy discussion and more flexibility in policy initiation. The roughly one thousand members of the JCED are mainly senior corporate executives at the director level or above so they are sufficiently well-connected to have substantial impact on the policy process. JCED has been primarily concerned with generating policy initiatives that express the social responsibility of business. In this connection, it has formed research teams to work on problems of urban areas, including the greening of cities, regional evolution, and the economic development of Southeast Asia. It was the first of the four major business federations to present concrete proposals for dealing with the problems of agriculture in a high-growth economy, just as the United States-Japan Security Treaty crisis was beginning to intensify.[76] In regard to these questions and others, it has advocated a broad national dialogue with the opposition parties. The JCED's ability to coordinate the development of welfare-oriented policy initiatives across party and ideological boundaries has been enhanced by the broad interpersonal networks of its senior members; many prominent labor officials and even Socialist politicians participated in activities of the JCED between its founding and the sharp polarization of labor-management relations in Japan after 1948.[77]

Looking at Japan's four major umbrella business federations in the aggregate, the one clear commonality throughout the postwar period has been their adamant desire for political stability, as evidenced by their dramatic joint declarations during periods of po-

[75] Nagano, for example, was said to have been critical in orchestrating a consensus in favor of the no-collateral loan program for small business in 1973–1974, in response to the rapid growth of the Communist-affiliated *Minshō* small-business federation during the early 1970s.

[76] *Asahi Shimbun*, April 9, 1960. Also Tōyama Shigeto, ed., *Shiryō: Sengo Ni jyū Nen Shi* (*Data: A History of the Two Postwar Decades*), vol. 6, pp. 178, 180.

[77] On these networks, see Keizai Dōyūkai, ed., *Keizai Dōyūkai San Jyū Nen Shi* (*Thirty Year History of the Council on Economic Development*).

litical uncertainty.[78] The enormous debt burdens generated in the process of capital intensive industrialization, together with the aggressive, risky international strategies pursued by many Japanese firms, have long made domestic political stability imperative for big business. Whatever ideological and practical objections business might have to economically inefficient support programs for agriculture, small business, and social welfare recipients, the prospective cost of these programs paled before the possible consequences of the unpredictability which would attend the collapse of conservative rule.

Seen in detail, the diversity of the business federations—both internally and in comparison with each other—is striking. In particular, Japan's major postwar business federations have not presented a joint front against welfare-oriented redistributive policies, in contrast to frequent patterns in Europe or in prewar Japan. To the contrary, the JCCI, closely allied with many LDP politicians, has often been a primary initiator of such welfare-oriented policies; similarly, the JCED, with its strong cross-party political ties, has initiated major policy in welfare and urban areas. The two more conservative of the business federations, Keidanren and Nikkeiren, have often been immobilized in the policy formation process by their large size and complex internal decision-making processes.

Thus, the Japanese business community is far more diverse in viewpoints and open to policy change, provided that change is consistent with broader political stability, than often supposed. As in the case of LDP factions, a process of competitive rivalry in the search for new policy options, once the need for change is clear (as in a crisis) has often led to relatively rapid and pragmatic policy shifts. This was clearly true of *zaikai* support for Prime

[78] Up to 1960, the four business federations made six joint declarations calling for political stability, most of them oriented toward ending conservative divisions prior to the Liberal and Democratic party merger of 1955. During the Security Treaty crisis of 1960 the four organizations called rather dramatically for the protection of parliamentary democracy and the reestablishment of international trust. In July 1972, once again in the midst of political crisis, six key zaikai leaders, Kikawada, Uemura, Nagano, Sakurada, Dokō, and Imazato, called on the new prime minister, Tanaka Kakuei, and presented a "request" (*yōbōsho*) calling for a political posture that would "regain the people's faith" and "create national solidarity." See Saji Toshihiko, "Zaikai wa Dō Hyōka Suru ka?" ("How Should the *Zaikai* Evaluate?"), *Chūō Kōron* (September 1972), p. 116. See also Curtis, "Big Business and Political Influence," in *Modern Japanese Organization and Decision-Making*, ed., Ezra F. Vogel, pp. 33–70, especially p. 58.

Minister Kishi in 1960, for example, which evaporated when it became clear that his continuation as prime minister after the forceful ratification of the revised United States-Japan Security Treaty was creating major popular disenchantment with the ruling LDP itself. The pluralistic nature of the big business world has also made it more willing to countenance materialist policies in times of crisis than one might initially suspect, given the technocratic bias of Japanese political structure. Organized Japanese big business tends to be efficiency-oriented in periods of stability, yet highly pragmatic and often flexible in times of crisis. This distinctive, oscillating approach to policy on the part of big business appears to be a central reason why the unusual crisis and compensation dynamic is so salient in postwar Japanese conservative policymaking.

Legislative Process: Creating Leverage for a Politically Impotent Opposition

Receptivity to redistributive policies, of course, has not reposed in only one or two of Japan's major business federations. Much more fundamentally, it has resided in the Japanese opposition parties of the Left. They, in fact, have originated most of the welfare, small business, and regional policies—distinctive in comparative context for conservative governments—which the LDP has implemented over the past three decades and claimed as its own. Therefore, exploring how and why opposition policy alternatives have ended up so frequently on the LDP's policy agenda is basic to understanding Japanese conservatism's materialist response and the peculiar redistributive bias of its policies, particularly those enacted in time of crisis. Perhaps the most basic reason for this opposition influence has been the structure of the Japanese legislative process. Both the institutions and the procedures governing lawmaking in Japan magnify the influence of even a heavily outnumbered opposition in the policy process, particularly on redistributive issues likely to concern opposition constituencies.

Japan is not, of course, the only nation in the world where legislative influences intensify the distributive or redistributive biases of policy. As Kingdon points out, Capitol Hill also often adds a geographically distributive element to public policies in the United States,[79] on issues ranging from roads and bridges to defense contracts. But the unusual structure of the Japanese legislative process does appear to magnify the specific leverage of the opposition in policymaking, particularly during crisis.

One basic reason for conservative vulnerability in the legislative process to opposition pressure has been the relatively short Japanese Diet working session. To be sure, the National Diet has been in session for an average of more than 210 days annually over the bulk of the postwar period.[80] But by tradition it has held plenary sessions only three times weekly and taken a large number of holidays, including a full four weeks in January. As a result, the Diet actually sits for an average of 80 working days annually, compared to an average of 150 days in Britain, the United States, and Italy.[81]

Time constraints operating on the ruling party in the Japanese legislative process are intensified by the Japanese system of short sessions. The Diet may indeed work for 80 to 100 days annually, but these days are divided into an average of three sessions rather than being one continuous session. Each session requires a policy address by the prime minister to the plenary meetings of both houses separately, followed by a few days of general questioning from the floor. Other key ministers may also speak. All these activities not directly related to legislation take time, which is in any case in short supply. Furthermore, all unfinished business dies at session's end, unless formally carried over by a vote; Japan is virtually alone among the advanced industrial democracies in systematically wiping the legislative slate clean several times a year.[82]

[79] Kingdon, *Agendas, Alternatives, and Public Policies*, pp. 41–42.

[80] Ordinary Diet sessions last 150 days annually, supplemented by special sessions (*tokubetsu Kokkai*) following Lower House elections and extraordinary sessions (*rinji Kokkai*) when one-quarter or more of the membership of either House demands them. Under one of these three auspices, the Diet was in session for an average of 217 days per year over the 1948–1977 period. See Mike M. Mochizuki, "Managing and Influencing the Japanese Legislative Process," Ph.D. diss., Harvard University, p. 58.

[81] Michael Ameller, *Parliaments*, pp. 129–30, cited in Mochizuki, "Managing and Influencing," p. 62.

[82] West Germany, by contrast, has a permanent assembly system which permits the Bundestag to carry on parliamentary business for an unlimited duration. In Britain outstanding bills are killed only once a year, while in the United States this occurs only at the end of each congressional session, every two years. See Mochizuki, "Managing and Influencing," p. 63.

The Diet committee system, patterned on the United States, intensifies the pressures on the Japanese ruling party toward accommodation in the legislative process still further and introduces still one more level of deliberation through which legislation must pass. Except in a highly restricted range of cases, legislation is considered in committee until the committee directors (*riji*) of both the opposition and the ruling party have decided it should be reported out to the full house. Like plenary sessions, committees by tradition only meet three days weekly so they, too, are under severe time pressure, which intensifies with the complexity and urgency of the economic and social problems before them for decision. Such pressures are strongest, of course, during periods of national political crises, especially when they coincide with factional conflict within conservative ranks.

Committee leadership traditions in the Diet provide a final form of leverage for the opposition in the Japanese legislative process. In the House of Counselors, Japan's upper house, committee chairmanships are traditionally distributed in proportion to party strength in the house; thus, there have frequently been opposition chairmen of the Judicial Affairs, Social and Labor Affairs, Communications, Transportation, Construction, Discipline, and Audit committees.[83] This practice was also followed in the Lower House between 1953 and 1958, while conservative political weakness led to opposition majorities in the Local Administration, Judicial Affairs, Education, Agriculture, Commerce and Industry, Transportation, and Budget committees between December 1976 and June 1980.[84] This presence of opposition Dietmen in strategic chairmanships in turn gave opponents of the conservatives significant influence over policy formation, especially in social policy.

[83] The construction, telecommunications, and audit committees in the Upper House, for example, were all chaired by JSP Dietmen after 1962, the judicial affairs and the pollution counter-measures committees by the JSP after 1966, and the price-counter-measures/life economics committees by the JSP after 1980. For further examples, see Satō and Matsuzaki, *Jimintō Seiken*, pp. 350–52.

[84] From 1953 to 1957 members of the Japan Socialist party actually chaired the Lower House budget committee, while JSP chairmen continued until 1958 at the local administration, audit, education, telecommunications, and education committees. From 1976 to 1980 opposition Dietmen held chairmanships at the telecommunications (JSP), audit (JSP), construction (Kōmeitō), and discipline (DSP and JSP) committees. At the audit and discipline committees, opposition chairmanships were renewed once again in 1983, with the DSP and the JSP respectively assuming these reponsibilities. For further details, see *ibid.*, pp. 346–49.

Due to the Diet's distinctive institutional traits and the rapidly increasing pressures for new legislation as the Japanese political economy grows more complex, the ruling LDP has found itself under strong pressure to coordinate views with major opposition parties in the Diet and assure timely passage of legislation. Opposition leverage, of course, is greatest in periods of crisis. At such times pressure on conservative leadership for rapid policy response is greatest, and opposition ability to legitimately obstruct the legislative process is also unusually high.

After years of actively using procedural leverage to visibly obstruct legislation, the opposition parties became more pragmatic during the 1960s and frequently accepted LDP overtures for compromise. From the late 1960s on rigid posturing became less common and the Diet Management Committee, which coordinates legislative procedures, evolved into a major forum for pragmatic policy bargaining between the LDP and the opposition.[85] The implication for policy, of course, was that the biases toward materialist and especially redistributive materialist policies were strengthened, particularly when crisis increased pressure on the conservatives for rapid action on outstanding policy issues. In such circumstances the LDP badly needed opposition cooperation and were forced to concede accordingly to minority views.

Fine Tuning the Materialist Response: Mass Media's Role

Strong intraelite competition in Japanese politics, intensified by the electoral system and factions within the LDP, tends to generate strong pressures for materialist policy outputs and for policy innovation, especially in periods of crisis. The legislative process, which strengthens the opposition, combines with subtle differences of opinion within the conservative business and political communities to strengthen the redistributive bias of policy. Pressures for policy innovation have been enhanced still further by the mass media. This was particularly true with respect to agriculture and small business during the early 1960s and social welfare and the environment during the early 1970s.

Seen in comparative context, the scale of the Japanese news-

[85] See Ellis Krauss, "Conflict in the National Diet: Toward the Institutionalization of Conflict Management in Parliamentary Politics," in *Conflict in Japan*, eds. Krauss, Rohlen, and Steinhoff.

papers and media conglomerates, together with their distinctive critical orientation toward the ruling conservative government, is striking. Not only are Japanese media many times the size of their counterparts in Europe and the United States, but their influence on policymaking is also magnified still further by the frequent unanimity of the media, the homogeneity of Japanese society, and Japan's isolation from broader international cultural forces.

All these characteristics contrast to patterns in major Western nations, where broad national cultural and social features do not reinforce the political influence of mass media nearly so strongly. The Japanese media have a deep and growing regulatory dependence on government agencies, such as the Ministry of Posts and Telecommunications, heavily influenced by the ruling LDP. Such dependence has intensified sharply since the early 1970s and creates ominous potential for future political manipulation. But despite these growing regulatory dependencies on the conservatives, Japan's mass media are nevertheless generally more critical than supportive of government in their formal coverage; this is a sharp contrast, for example, to the largely state-controlled French mass media. This complex profile of media-state relations, a phenomenon of rapidly increasing significance for Japanese policymaking since the 1950s, has been a major driving force behind emergence of the welfare, pollution, and even small business questions at the heart of Japan's policy agenda.

Japan's three leading daily newspapers are huge; they currently rank first, second, and fourth in circulation figures throughout the entire non-Communist world.[86] The largest, the *Yomiuri Shimbun*, has a morning circulation of over 8.9 million, nearly ten times that of *The New York Times*, and twenty times that of *The Times* of London or *France Soir*. The *Asahi Shimbun* is not far behind the *Yomiuri*, with over 7.5 million subscribers. Although the *Mainichi Shimbun*, originating in the Kansai area, has recently fallen into financial difficulty, it still boasts a larger following than any U.S. newspaper by a factor of four.[87] Comparative circulation figures place Japan, not surprisingly, at the top of the world. In 1977 the Japanese read 526 daily newspapers per one thousand population, with the Soviet Union second at 397

[86] Nihon Shimbun Kyōkai data.

[87] The *Mainichi Shimbun* in 1985 had over 4.2 million subscribers for its morning edition and 2.2 million for its evening edition. See Asahi Shimbun Sha, ed., *Asahi Nenkan 1985*, p. 861.

and Britain close behind; the corresponding figure for the United States was 287.

Exposure to specifically political information through the media also appears to be quite high in Japan. For example, 62 percent of the respondents in the 1976 JABISS National Election Study indicated they watched televison news programs daily, while 92 percent reported watching at least once a week. In addition, of the 95 percent who reported reading a newspaper regularly, 85 percent read at least one election-related article during the 1976 House of Representatives election campaign.[88]

The importance of the mass media in Japanese society appears to have been rising significantly during the past three decades, as suggested above. Between 1952 and 1985, for example, the circulation of daily newspapers in Japan nearly doubled, rising from 22.7 million (3.96 people per newspaper) to 48.2 million (2.49 people per newspaper). Even more important, households with television sets rose dramatically from 1,425 in 1952 to over 31.5 million in 1985;[89] surveys report the percentage of households using television as their major source of information about the world rose from 1 percent in 1956 to 90 percent by the late 1970s. Parallel use of newspapers rose from 66 percent to 78.2 percent.[90]

During this same period, the structural relationship of Japanese media to the political process clearly changed in important ways. The primary source of newspaper income shifted sharply from subscriptions and sales to advertisements, giving government and business increased leverage.[91] Newspaper companies became media conglomerates, engaged in publishing, broadcasting, and entertainment; in addition, they acquired a growing desire for land in prestigious locations in major cities to house expanding operations. These companies established or acquired television stations throughout Japan and soon required complex regulatory

[88] Bradley M. Richardson and Scott C. Flanagan, *Politics in Japan*, pp. 230–31.

[89] Yomiuri Shimbun Sha, ed., *Yomiuri Nenkan* (*Yomiuri Almanac*), 1987 ed., pp. 743, 745.

[90] Yoshimi Uchikawa, "Masukomi Jidai no Tenkai to Seiji Katei" ("The Unfolding of the Mass Media Age and the Political Process"), *Go Jyū Go Nen Taisei no Keisei to Hōkai: Nenpō Seijigaku* (*The Rise and Fall of the 1955 System: A Political Science Bulletin*), pp. 303–5.

[91] In 1960, for example, sales compromised 55.1 percent of Japanese newspaper income, compared to 44.9 percent for advertising income. By 1970 these ratios had reversed themselves, with 58.9 percent of income from advertisements and only 41.1 percent from sales. See Kido Mataichi, ed., *Gendai Jyānarizumu: Shimbun* (*Modern Journalism: Newspapers*), p. 121.

dispensations from the Ministry of Posts and Telecommunications.[92] All these developments encouraged deepening ties with conservative politicians, who in turn had grassroots-oriented priorities of their own.

The impact of the Japanese mass media on policymaking in Japan is thus twofold. On the one hand, media coverage often seems skewed to achieve a modus vivendi with powerful established interests in Japanese society, particularly during noncrisis periods. Sensitive domestic topics, such as housing policies and rigidities of land use, often are given scant attention, despite their considerable bearing on living standards and even foreign economic relations.[93] International topics are likewise often treated in rather skewed fashion, when there is a broad establishment consensus that they should be treated in a particular manner. The prospects of yen revaluation, for example, were given very little coverage during the critical summer of 1971, despite their policy salience, because the Ministry of Finance and the big business community were unified in wanting to divert public attention from that question.

In the absence of overwhelming and broad-based elite sentiment for issue suppression, however, the Japanese mass media play an unusually powerful role, comparatively speaking, in what Polsby calls "the process of systematic search."[94] They have presented, albeit selectively, the views of consumer, environmental, and feminist groups which otherwise would have had minimal

[92] The relationship between media conglomerates and the LDP deepened significantly, for example, during 1958–1959, when Tanaka Kakuei, in his first cabinet role as minister of post and telecommunications, allocated thirty-six broadcast licenses to thirty-four private broadcasters, as television broadcasting boomed just before the wedding of Crown Prince Akihiko in April 1959. The number of television stations in Japan grew from five in 1957 to nineteen in 1958 and forty-three in 1959, all of which had to be authorized by MPT. See Kido Mataichi, ed., *Gendai Jyānarizumu: Hōsō (Modern Journalism: Broadcasting)*, p. 3.

[93] A parallel example of the conservative treatment given sensitive domestic subjects was the cautious coverage by Japan's major newspapers of the explosive *Bungei Shunjū* revelations during the fall of 1974 regarding then-Prime Minister Tanaka Kakuei. An article by freelance journalist Tachibana Takashi in this relatively prestigious monthly exposed in detail Tanaka's controversial personal business dealings for the first time. Despite the considerable public importance of these revelations, they were not publicized at all in the major newspapers until a foreign journalist, Sam Jameson of the *Los Angeles Times*, raised them directly with Prime Minister Tanaka at the Tokyo Foreign Correspondents' Club.

[94] Polsby, *Political Innovation in America*, p. 173. This is the dynamic by which societies sense and respond to problems.

opportunity to seriously press their causes in the Japanese political process.[95] Recent empirical studies strongly confirm the view that Japanese decision makers see the media as extremely important in the policy process—perhaps more important than any other institution in Japanese society.[96] Indeed, comparative research suggests that Japanese decisionmakers consider the influence of mass media in their political process to be even more pervasive than do their counterparts in Western Europe and the United States.[97] But all this, it must be stressed, does not belie the existence of limits on the pluralist role of the Japanese media, particularly in sectors of real importance to big business and the ruling conservative party, such as international economic and security affairs during the late 1960s and early 1970s.

Because the closed, relatively secretive character of much technocratic Japanese decision making tends to intensify its elitist bias, the simple fact of mass media involvement tends to increase the pressures toward change in the midst of political crisis. The generally progressive orientation of the mass media has tended to compound pressures for redistributive change. They became especially intense during the early 1970s, when the proclivities of the media to support redistributive measures were reinforced by the inclinations of Prime Minister Tanaka Kakuei, to whom many broadcasters had deep ties, to redirect resource flows toward less-developed areas.[98]

Some analysts, to be sure, question how pervasive the "agenda setting" effect of the media is among the Japanese public.[99] But virtually all concede the historical importance of the media's role

[95] Kabashima Ikuo and Jeffrey Broadbent, "Referent Pluralism," *Journal of Japanese Studies*, Summer, 1986 p. 331.

[96] See Miyake Ichirō et al., *Byōdō o meguru Elīto to Taikō Elīto* (*Elites and Counter Elites who Bring about Equality*), p. 157.

[97] See *ibid.*, pp. 143–44, for comparative data on the perceptions of American and Swedish leaders.

[98] Five prominent newspaper and broadcast executives, including *Nihon Keizai Shimbun* president Enjōji Jirō, for example, were prominent members of the "Remodelling of the Archipelago Discussion Committee (*Rettō Kaizō Mondai Kondan Kai*) which popularized Tanaka's plans for development of underdeveloped regions. See Kido, ed., *Gendai Jyānarizumu*, p. 157.

[99] Kobayashi Yoshiaki, for example, finds that only 20 to 30 percent of newspaper readers, mostly of lower income and educational levels, report any "agenda setting" effect. See Kobayashi Yoshiaki, "Sōten Sentaku ni okeru Masu Media Eikyō ni kansuru Keiryō Bunseki" ("A Quantitative Analysis of Mass Media Influence in Matters of Aggregate Choice"), in Kobayashi Yoshiaki, *Keiryō Seijigaku* (*Quantitative Political Science*).

in motivating lower-income groups to pressure the sensitive policy process for redistributive measures. Mass media influence also has helped define issues, emphasize the urgency of dealing with them, and dramatize the existence of support for policy innovation. The media's policy role has been particularly strategic in times of crisis, when media pressure has intensified the sense of urgency confronting conservative policymakers and hence multiplied pressures for new policies to compensate the groups petitioning for redress. Although highly conformist and reluctant to take controversial stands during periods of political calm, the mass media's periodic activism during more turbulent times has contributed significantly to the oscillating ebb and flow of policy change, constituting the crisis and compensation dynamic.

The Profile of Japanese Policy Change: Distinctive Patterns and Processes

Japan's bifurcated partially-technocratic administrative structure interacts with a semipluralistic, highly viscous transmission mechanism for interest group pressure under conditions of relatively high growth to produce public policy. What sort of policy do these forces in concert produce? This concluding section in the overview of the crisis and compensation dynamic explores the postwar contours of Japanese public policy, the aspects that seem particularly to conform to the hypothesis presented and those that seemingly do not; the outliers will be examined to see what additional insights they produce.

Post-1949 conservative Japan's pattern of strongly distributive, rural-oriented policy outputs, it is important to stress, has not been a constant feature of the Japanese political landscape. Prewar budgetary priorities, as noted in table 4.1, were substantially different, with a much heavier emphasis on military, cultural, and scientific affairs. The Socialist-led Katayama cabinet of 1947–1948, as figure 4.3 points out, emphasized industrial price supports with much less attention to agriculture, public works, and support for local government expenditures than subsequently emerged. An early version of the characteristic grassroots-oriented budgetary emphasis of the 1960s and 1970s emerged in the turbulent years following the Dodge Line, as Yoshida's conservatives resorted to distributive politics focused on the countryside to stabilize their rule.

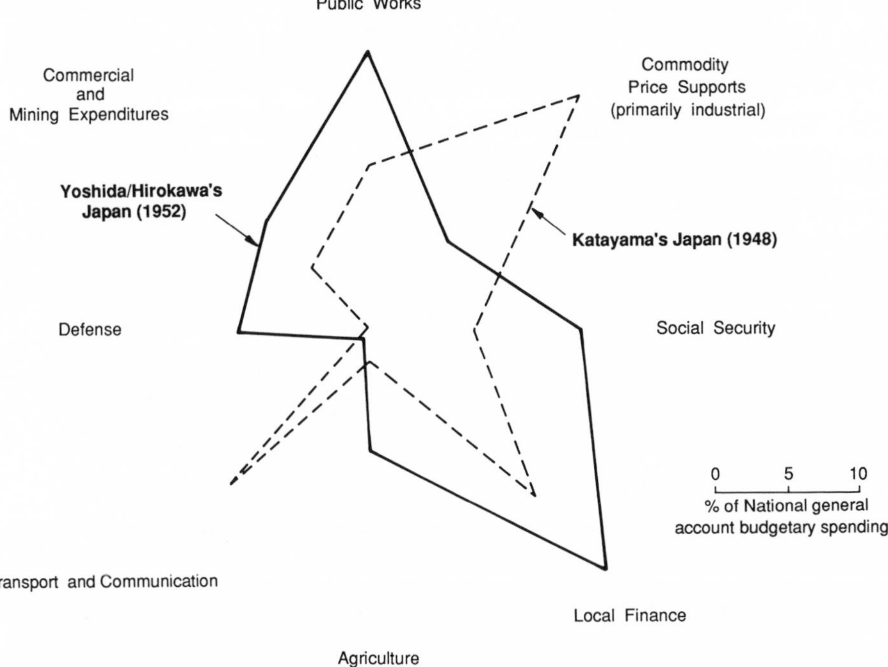

Figure 4.3. Conservative Preeminence and Budgetary Transition, 1948–1952.
Source: Ministry of Finance Financial History Office (Ōkurashō Zaisei Shi Shitsu), ed., *Shōwa Zaisei Shi (A Financial History of Shōwa)*, vol. 19, pp. 168–69.

But with the waning of political crisis in the mid-1950s and the advent of the nationalistic Hatoyama administration, Japanese government priorities shifted away from agriculture and public works, emphasizing defense, as shown in figure 4.4. Indeed, Japanese general account budgetary allocations in 1955 more closely resembled recent patterns in the major industrialized nations along these three dimensions than they have at any point since, although with the waning of political crisis Japanese budgetary priorities typically revert back toward the Hatoyama administration pattern. Budgetary shares rather than GNP shares are used here to give a sense of *relative* government priorities and their transformation, since the central analytical concern is with government policy choices and preference schedules as a political phenomenon, rather than with the implications of policies in economic terms.

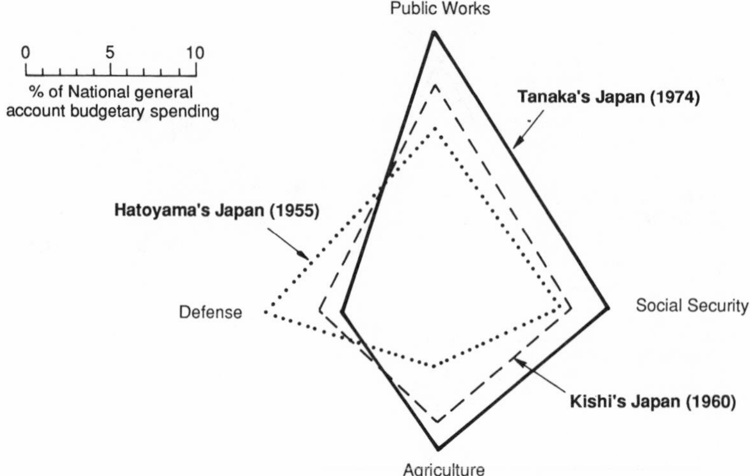

Figure 4.4. From Martial to Materialistic: Budgetary Transformation in Japan, 1955–1974.

Source: Ministry of Finance Budget Bureau Research Section (Ōkurashō Shukei Kyoku Chōsa Ka), ed., *Zaisei Tōkei (Financial Statistics)*, various issues.

Between 1955 and 1974, as figure 4.4 suggests, there was a major transformation in Japanese conservative policy priorities, albeit an oscillating, uneven one, from a martial policy profile toward a material orientation. From 1956 to 1958, defense spending comprised a higher share of the Japanese budget than it did in the West German,[100] with social welfare and even public works representing a significantly lower level of national expenditure than would later prevail. Two former participants in wartime politics and administration, Hatoyama Ichirō and Kishi Nobusuke, served as prime ministers for most of this period, striving to unify the Japanese people on the basis of nationalistic appeals. Agricultural support levels, as chapter 5 points out in some detail, were also below levels of Western Europe. Yet by the mid-1970s, in the wake of two further periods of crisis for the Japanese conservatives and the ratcheting up of compensation policies, all

[100] G. Warren Nutter, *Growth of Government in the West*, pp. 40, 42. West Germany military spending represented a higher share of GNP than did Japanese during this period, but the share of the overall West German budget allocated to defense was lower than in Japan because of heavier German social spending. The focus here is on budgetary shares due to a primary concern with intrabudget priorities, as noted above.

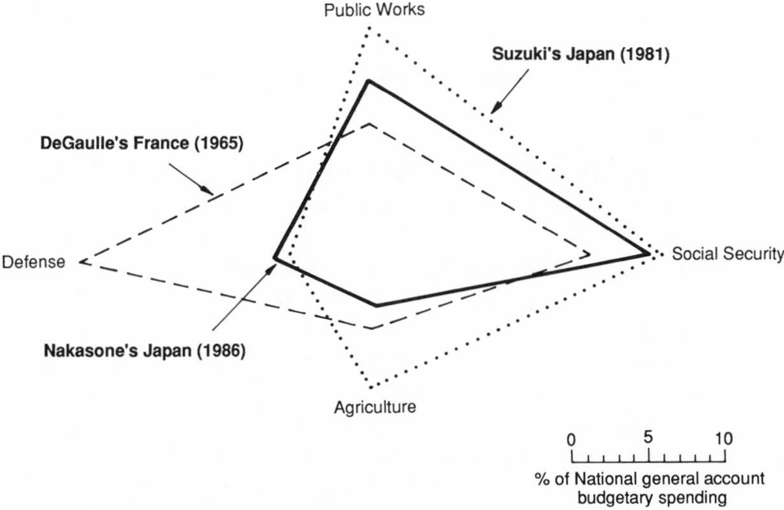

Figure 4.5. Incipient Gaullism? Japanese Budget Patterns of the 1980s in Comparative Perspective.

Sources: Ministère de l'économie des finance et du budget, *Annuiare Statistique de la France 1967*; Ministry of Finance Budget Bureau Research Section (Ōkurashō Shukei Kyoku Chōsa Ka), ed., *Zaisei Tōkei (Financial Statistics)*, 1986 ed.

of this had sharply changed. New patterns of public policy, with a strong, internationally distinctive materialist bias, had been forged.

The early 1970s, it now seems clear, proved the high-water mark of Japan's distinctive materialist-oriented policymaking; the state served primarily to generate distributive resources for consumption by political marginals, thereby maintaining political stability for its elite allies. By the early and mid-1980s, with the fading of crisis, Japanese public policy again appeared moving, albeit slowly, back toward more typical Western conservative priorities and decreased compensation, as the logic of this volume would suggest. As figure 4.5 indicates, national defense was becoming more paramount, and the material concerns of the previous two decades—public works, agriculture, and even social security—somewhat less so. Through the rhetoric of administrative reform and budgetary crisis, counterbalanced by nationalistic symbolism, the Nakasone administration was redefining the state's role in Japanese society.

Despite institutional constraints and complex counterclaims which made rapid transformation difficult, the Japan of the mid-1980s was moving toward a more Western-style balance of national security and internal distributive claims. But in its evolution toward new policy patterns, the relevant benchmarks for Japanese conservative policymakers were not so much Reagan and Thatcher, with their antiredistributive sets of priorities and radical market orientation so alien to the Japanese context. More congruent with prevailing Japanese policy patterns of the 1980s were the allocative profiles etched by Hatoyama Ichirō, Nakasone Yasuhiro's hawkish predecessor of the 1950s, adjusted as necessary to Japan's changing social structure. And internationally another possible reference point was the austere, nationalistic conservatism of Charles De Gaulle, averse to welfare spending but firmly committed to major state roles in defense and select aspects of economic life. Obviously, differences in national tradition and domestic political structure, not to mention the steady aging of Japanese society, made close correspondence between Japanese budget allocation patterns of the 1990s and those of France a quarter century previously highly unlikely. But for a Japanese conservative struggling to reconcile domestic priorities with the costs of growing international involvement, the resource allocation patterns of De Gaulle's France provided one provocative symbolic alternative to the traditional compensation politics.

The Japanese Domestic Policy Innovation Cycle

Japanese policy priorities have shifted substantially across the postwar period. One of the most striking and significant features of Japanese conservative policymaking, seen in comparative context, is the abrupt, discontinuous pattern through which transformation has occurred. One can clearly distinguish two types of policy change: primary policy innovation in the form of new programs; and secondary transformation in budgetary shares of established programs. As the following chapters demonstrate, Japanese policymaking is periodically discontinuous with respect to both types of policy change, particularly in untraded sectors of the economy where political marginals with traditional ties to both the conservatives and their opposition are numerous and well-organized. It was in sudden, sharp increments of policy change—both in programs and in patterns of funding—that Japanese conservative policies moved from martial to their distinctive materialistic pattern of the 1960s and 1970s.

The germination and development of policy proposals in Japan, as opposed to their legislation, is often a long-extended process. As John Campbell points out, ministries will characteristically request "research expenses" (*chōsahi*) to look into a problem long before they submit a substantial budget request. This process of low-level research and monitoring often continues for several years.[101] In many cases the bureaucracy, or increasingly the relevant Diet committees or subcommittees (*bukai*) of the LDP's Policy Affairs Research Council (*Seichōkai*), will send study missions abroad to examine policy solutions adopted elsewhere in the world to the problem in question; for example, this was done with respect to both the Agricultural Basic Law during the late 1950s and the pollution and welfare-related issues of the early 1970s. Extended consideration of an issue in specialized technical publications is also typical at this initial stage of policymaking.

Policymaking in sectors of the Japanese political economy, where either technocratic influences are strong or long-run national priorities are clear, tends to proceed in relatively measured fashion, largely unaffected by sudden catalytic developments. Sector-specific industrial policy, such as rationalization plans for steel, machinery, and electronics, has typically been formulated in this way. But in the nonindustrial domestic policy sectors, the process of policy innovation is substantially more episodic and volatile. A typical pattern, at least for the introduction of the major "large-new" programs at the heart of distinctive Japanese patterns in public policy, is what Polsby would call "incubated innovation," in which policies will germinate over relatively long periods.[102] When incubated ideas are translated into policy, this typically happens in broad surges involving substantial amounts of new legislation implemented in short periods of time. Thus, 1973 was not only the "first year of welfare," due to the large number of welfare programs implemented that year, but it also marked the emergence of major programs, conceived years previously, in the regional and small business policy areas, a major increase in the price of rice, and preparations for establishment of the National Land Agency in 1974. Most of these innovations

[101] Campbell, *Contemporary Japanese Budget Politics*, pp. 27–28.
[102] Polsby, *Policy Innovation in America*, p. 158.

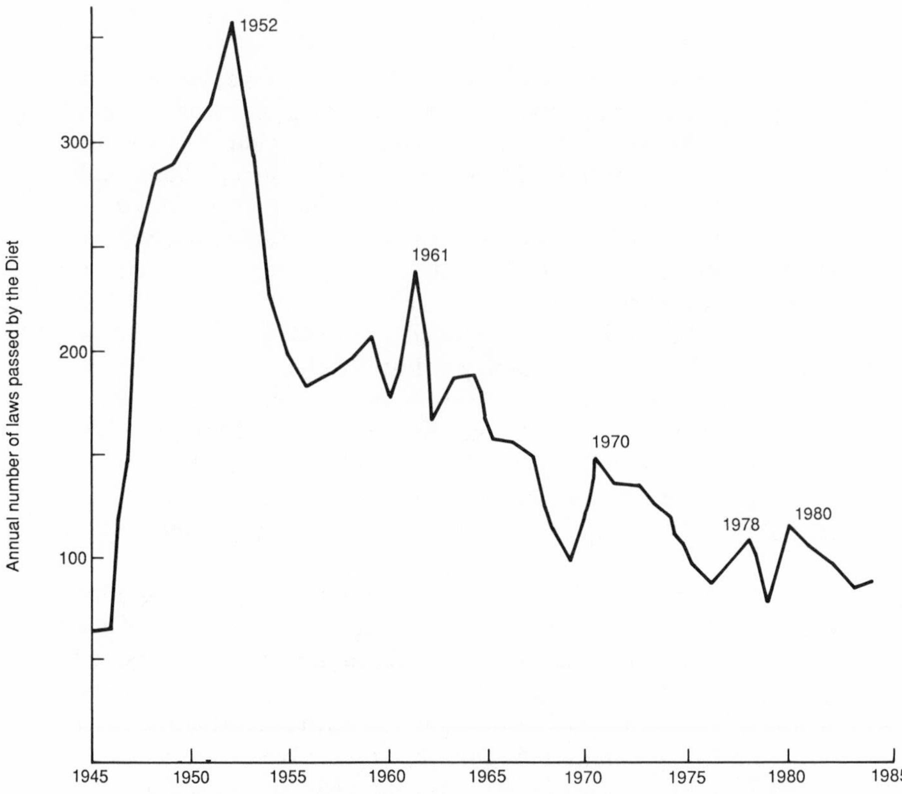

Figure 4.6. Surges of Legislative Activity in the Japanese Diet, 1945–1984.

Source: Naikaku Seido Hyaku Nen Shi Henshū Iinkai, ed., *Naikaku Seido Hyaku Nen No Ayumi (A One-Hundred Year Odyssey of Japan's Cabinet)* (Tokyo: Daikō Kabushiki Kaisha, 1985).

had been conceived during the mid- and late 1960s, often in reaction to policy developments overseas or at the local level within Japan. But they did not become national policy until the coming of crisis five to ten years later, when they were implemented in short order.

As figure 4.6 confirms, policy innovation, in the form of new legislation passed by the Diet, has historically occurred in clear-cut surges, subject to a long-term downward trend as legislative frameworks became well-established. The first and largest wave came with the restoration of conservative rule in 1949, its high point being the third Yoshida cabinet (February 1949–October

1952). During this period, an average of more than three hundred new laws were passed annually—a record distorted during 1951–52 by the legal transition from occupation to independence.

The second clear quantitative peak in innovation was 1961, when there was a sharp surge of new legislation under the Ikeda cabinet, following the Security Treaty crisis of 1960. After a near-steady decline in the amount of new legislation during the 1960s, the pace of lawmaking accelerated in 1970 and thereafter, as environmental crisis, global economic turmoil, and escalating political turbulence combined to force new issues onto the policy agenda. The "Pollution Diet" (*Kōgai Kokkai*) of 1970 and "The First Year of Welfare" (*Fukushi Gannen*) in 1973 are just two examples of the legislative surges through which the face of Japanese policy was fundamentally changed during this period.

Despite flurries of legislation in 1978 and 1980, the pace of legislative activity in Japan appears to have quieted considerably since the oil shock of 1973. Such intensification of legislative activity as occurred after the 1970s, however, also had its origins in crisis, although of an international economic rather than a domestic political variety. Innovations following the 1971, 1977–1978, and 1986–1987 yen revaluations, as well as after the 1973 and 1979 oil shocks, show this pattern clearly (see figure 4.6).

Both surges in policy innovation and major shifts in government budgetary shares tend to follow the onset of political crisis in relatively short order in Japan. Conversely, retrenchment, or at least termination of expansionary policy trends, tends to follow as crisis wanes. But there are frequently time lags before these effects are felt. During the mid-1960s, for example, rice price supports continued to increase at rates typical of the previous period of turbulence, even though crisis had waned. Some major small business policies, such as the Domain Protection Law of 1977, were translated into law some time after the threat from the Left to LDP political preeminence had begun to abate.

Lags may, as with regard to rice prices during the 1960s, be influenced by the scale of public resources available to the state for allocation. They can also be affected by tradeoffs over time within Japan's unusually "viscous" legislative process, whereby understandings on legislation or budgetary changes may in fact be implemented some time after originally conceived. But it is important to remember that delayed policy responses to the political crisis cycle remain logically related to the cycle itself, even when they are slow in materializing.

Time series data on ordinances enacted by the Japanese bureaucracy since 1945 show a similar cyclical pattern to that of legislation, although the cycles appear to lag one to two years behind legislative change itself.[103] Bureaucrats, in short, appear to alter regulatory frameworks in surges of change frequently driven by legislative innovation. Although most legislation has in Japan traditionally been drafted by bureaucrats, the officials drafting legislation have long been sensitive to turbulence in the broader political and economic environment. There is also a long tradition of member-initiated legislation in Japan being most pronounced in periods of social turmoil.[104] Such legislation was especially significant in the development of agricultural and small business policy.[105]

Behind the sharp quantitative increases in laws and ordinances during periods of crisis are major institutional innovations as well. Eight of Japan's eleven government financial institutions were established by special legislation during post-1949 periods of crisis, as indicated in table 4.7. Such institutional change through legislation in turn shapes the character of future political struggles by reorienting the structure of the state itself.

The sharply oscillating character of Japanese public policy innovation and its implications for policy content can be seen even more clearly by a cross-sectoral comparison of specific legislative changes. In consultation with Japanese government officials knowledgeable concerning a range of policy sectors, a list of major policy innovations since 1945 in six major policy sectors treated in this book was drawn up. A summary is presented in table 4.8, with a more detailed sector-by-sector version also presented in the appendices.

Moreover, a surprisingly large number of major policy innovations in Japan have occurred during relatively brief periods of time, with the early 1950s, early 1960s, and early 1970s being periods of particularly striking change (table 4.8). Perhaps even

[103] For details, see Naikaku Seido Hyaku Nen Shi Henshū Iinkai, ed., *Naikaku Hyaku Nen no Ayumi* (*A One-Hundred Year Odyssey of Japan's Cabinet*), K. Daikō, p. 207.

[104] For a graphic case study of how such legislation emerges, written by the former Private Secretary to Tanaka Kakuei, see Hayasaka Shigezō, "Tanaka Kakuei Mumei no Jyū Nen." *Chūō Kōron* (November 1986).

[105] The Agricultural and Fisheries Financial Institution (*Nōrin Gyogyō Kinyū Kōko*), for example, was authorized through member-initiated legislation in 1952, while a series of member bills were important in stimulating the Small Business Basic Law (*Chūshō Kigyō Kihon Hō*) of 1963.

TABLE 4.7

Founding Government Financial Institutions in Japan, 1945–1986

Name of Institution	Purpose	Year Established	Post-1949 Crisis Period
Era of U.S. Occupation			
Reconstruction Finance Bank	Big business finance	1946 (abolished 1949)	
Peoples Finance Corporation	Small business finance	1949	X
Housing Loan Corporation	Housing finance	1950	X
Japan Export-Import Bank	Trade finance (big business-oriented)	1950	X
Japan Development Bank	Industrial finance (big business-oriented)	1951	X
Post-Occupation Period			
Agricultural, Forestry, and Fisheries Finance Corporation	Agricultural finance	1953	X
Smaller Business Finance Corporation	Small business finance	1953	X
Hokkaidō and Tōhoku Development Corporation	Small business finance (regional)	1956	
Finance Corporation for Local Public Enterprises	Small business finance (regional)	1957	
Medical Care Facilities Finance Corporation	Small business finance (medical clinics)	1960	X
Environmental Sanitation Business Finance Corporation	Small business finance (ryokan and coffeeshop)	1967	
Okinawa Development Finance Corporation	Small business finance (regional)	1972	X

Table 4.8

The Profile of Policy Change in Postwar Japan, 1946–1986

Year	Agriculture	Regional	Small Business	Welfare	Land	Defense
1946	Land Reform Legislation					
1947	Ag. Cooperatives Law	Home Ministry Abolished				
1948			Small Business Agency			
1949	Rice Price Delib. Council		Peoples Finance Corp.	Social Security System Advisory Council		
1950	Ag. Coop. Fertilizer Sales	Local Allocation Tax		Livelihood Protection Law	National Land Comprehensive Development Law	
1951	Special Measures Law (Sekikan Hō)					U.S.-Japan Security Treaty
1952	Ag. Finance Corp. estab.					
1953						Safety Agency Defense Plan
1954						SDA formally established

1955					Housing Corp.	
1956	Producer Rice Price Declines 2.9%		Department Store Law			
1957						
1958	Producer Rice Price Declines 0.5%			Health Insurance		
1959				National Pension Law		
1960				Medical Facilities Finance Corp.		
1961	Basic Agricultural Law					
1962		New Industrial Cities Law			*Zensō* Development Plan	
1963			Small Business Basic Law	Welfare Law for Aged		
1964						
1965	Farmland Renewal Law (landlord compensation)					
1966						
1967						
1968					City Planning Law	Satō Three Nuclear Principles
1969						
1970						

Table 4.8 *(cont.)*

The Profile of Policy Change in Postwar Japan, 1946–1986

Year	Agriculture	Regional	Small Business	Welfare	Land	Defense
1971	Act for Promotion of Industry in Farm Areas					
1972		Indus. Relocation Promotion Act		Children's Allowance		
1973	Nōrin Chūkin Lends to Indiv. Starts Forex Transactions		No Collateral Loans/Large Stores Law	Free Medical Care for Aged		
1974		Regional Facilities Promotion Corp.			National Land Use Planning Law/ National Land Agency	
1975				Employment Retraining		
1976						1% defense spending limit

1977					
1978			Yen counter-measures		
1979					
1980		Technopolis Plan			
1981					
1982					
1983					
1984				Free Medical Care for Aged abolished	
1985					
1986			Yen counter-measures		1% defense spending limit abolished
1987	1st Producer. Rice Price Decline since 1958				

Note: For a more detailed account of policy innovation in Japan over the postwar period, see appendix 1.

more noteworthy, changes in several other policy sectors almost invariably accompany changes in any other single policy area. For example, the Basic Agricultural Law of 1961 was followed in short order by the New Industrial Cities Law of 1962, the National Comprehensive Development Plan (1962), the Small Business Basic Law (1963), and the Welfare Law for the Aged (1963). Policy innovation, in short, seems to occur in broad surges, across wide sectors, followed by lengthy periods of quiescence.

Cycles in Distributive Resource Allocation

Japanese public works spending has proceeded in such surges throughout the postwar period, led by politically related public works. Agricultural public works, for example, more than doubled during 1950–1954, driving the overall expansion in public works spending.[106] Similarly, allocations for road construction surged more than fivefold between 1950–1954 and 1960–1964, increasing to a full third of public works spending by the latter date.[107] From the late 1970s into the 1980s, airport construction similarly increased in relative importance, although the overall scale of public works spending began to stabilize during this period.

This policy profile of public works growth through surges contrasts sharply, it should be noted, to the more even, static growth patterns of Britain, West Germany, and especially France, at least with respect to road building.[108] It parallels more closely patterns discernible in the United States, especially during the 1960s, when the U.S. interstate highway system was being built. But the volatility of the American construction surges has generally not been as great as that in Japan. Public works construction has been related, of course, to the volatile growth patterns of the postwar Japanese economy in general. Such construction has often been used in Keynesian fashion, as a countercyclical policy tool to stimulate the economy during periods of recession.

Yet the public works construction surges do not correlate closely with growth patterns in the economy as a whole; important nuances in public works construction have varied independently of economic growth. Public works spending, for example,

[106] Sawamoto Moriyuki, *Kōkyō Tōshi Hyaku Nen no Ayumi*, p. 80.

[107] *Ibid.*

[108] See Dōro Gyōsei Kenkyū Kai, ed. *Dōro Gyōsei* (*Road Administration*), 1983 ed., pp. 671–716.

expanded rapidly during the early 1970s without a clear Keynesian rationale. These nuances in public works spending independent of the economic growth process appear to flow from the particular strength of politicians and local interest groups in Japanese policymaking. Waxing and waning patterns of competition within the dominant conservative political world seem especially important, as I will explain later in more detail.

The agricultural bias of much postwar Japanese public policy also emerged, as will be shown in chapter 5, in a series of surges followed by periods of stasis in which retrenchment occasionally but not invariably occurred. The cumulative result was a strong upward ratcheting effect on agricultural support levels. Aside from land reform, decided in the immediate aftermath of World War II and carried out in the four years thereafter, many of the major agricultural policy initiatives, combined with sharp increases in budgetary share for agriculture, came between 1949 and 1954. Once agricultural cooperatives were clearly established as intermediaries for conservative governance after 1949, agricultural subsidies surged. Rice prices also rose quite rapidly during 1949–1953 following establishment of the Rice Price Deliberation Council in 1949 and the Liberal party agricultural committee's initial intervention in rice price determination during 1950. "Land conservation and development" expenditures rose sharply during 1950–1951, receded, and then soared again in 1954. During fiscal 1956, just as the union of democratic and liberal parties to form the LDP was being consummated, combined agricultural and rural land development expenditures surpassed national defense spending for the first time in Japanese history.

After bottoming out during the late 1950s, agricultural spending began rising again in 1961–1962, with passage of the new Basic Agricultural Law and the acceleration of rice price increases in the wake of the 1960 Security Treaty crisis and the announcement of Ikeda Hayato's Income Doubling Plan. During the first half of the 1960s agricultural spending rose six times as rapidly as the overall national budget. Despite some later increases due to rice price escalation, levels of support for agriculture during the later 1960s remained within the institutional framework established rather abruptly during periods of general political turmoil and particularly intense personal political rivalry within conservative ranks, such as occurred during 1949–1954 and the early 1960s. The only other major surge of both rice prices and policy innovation in agriculture, mainly to encourage the relocation of industry to the countryside, was during the turbulent early 1970s.

Regional and local policy expenditures also began to increase in erratic steps, which appear to have been most pronounced during the early 1950s, the early 1960s, and the early 1970s. "Local finance" expenditures, or funds transferred from Tokyo to local authorities for welfare, construction, and other purposes, took an enormous leap during 1950–1952 and then leveled off. Between 1959 and 1963 they more than doubled, to ¥586 billion in the latter year. Similarly, these expenditures rose rapidly during the early 1970s but subsided thereafter.

Even Japanese defense spending patterns have at times shifted sharply. There *have* been periods in postwar Japanese history, particularly during the early and mid-1950s, when the Japanese defense budget was both relatively large (as much as 20.8 percent of total expenditures or around 2.8 percent of GNP) *and* increasing as a share of the total.[109] For more than half a decade after the creation of the Police Reserve in 1950, Japan did begin diversifying away from reconstruction expenditures toward defense, somewhat resembling Western patterns of the period. As mentioned earlier, from 1956 through 1958 defense comprised a larger share of the Japanese national budget than it did of the West German.[110] Decline in defense expenditures relative to GNP and national budget has been an erratic phenomenon, proceeding with particular force during 1959–1962 and 1966–1970. During those periods the United States-Japan Security Treaty controversy and the Vietnam War deeply polarized Japan on security questions, allowing budgetary shares previously earmarked for defense to be diverted elsewhere.

The Outliers

There are some major policy departures which do not fit neatly into the pronounced general oscillation between activism and

[109] Defense expenditures were more than 10 percent of general account expenditures, and over 1.4 percent of GNP, every year from establishment of the Police Reserve in 1950 through fiscal 1959. Defense's budget share in the general account rose in 1952, 1954, and 1956, although it failed to do so again until 1982. See Asagumo Shimbun Sha Henshū Sōkyoku, ed., *Bōei Handbook* (*Defense Handbook*), 1987 ed., 221–23.

[110] Defense comprised 9.8, 9.9, and 8.8 percent of the Japanese budget during 1956–1958, compared to 9.3, 8.0, and 8.0 percent of the West German budget. See G. Warren Nutter, *Growth of Government in the West*, pp. 40, 42.

quiescence in postwar Japanese domestic policymaking (table 4.8). The Farmland Renewal Law of 1965, advent of MITI's technopolis program (1980), and introduction of arms export controls (1967–1968) are three cases in point. These outliers, in their anomaly, provide important insights into the more general dynamics of policy change in Japan. Many of them, such as the Farmland Renewal Law, which reimbursed landlords for losses suffered in the process of land reform, are regressive, controversial measures that cannot easily clear the Diet when crisis and the media attention it engenders are pervasive. Many of the other anomalous cases involve plans initiated by the bureaucracy, particularly in the area of industrial policy. The bureaucracy clearly continues to function and often dominates the policy process during periods of domestic noncrisis. Indeed, it is during such periods, together with instances of foreign economic policymaking when bureaucratic technical expertise is needed, that the bureaucracy finds itself strongest in dealing with politicians and the private sector.

The third sort of policy change that seems to occur in periods of minimal domestic turbulence is change generated by overseas developments. Thus, Japan banned arms exports in 1968, at the height of the Vietnam War, and implemented a major yen countermeasure program in 1986, despite a lack of domestic political crisis in both cases. Since the early 1970s, foreign pressure has become increasingly central in Japanese policy innovation.

Despite a few special exceptions, however, the general pattern in Japan seems to be for policy innovation, in the sense of expanding state responsibilities, to occur in surges, during periods of domestic political crisis. And the policies and institutions emerging during those surges appear surprisingly redistributive and grassroots-oriented in character, particularly in comparison with the sorts of policies that come forth in noncrisis periods. On balance, they tend to intensify the bias toward redistributive, welfare-oriented programs by giving redistributive claims increasing institutional legitimacy.

Explaining Compensation Cycles: The Argument

Domestic policymaking in Japan since 1949, the preceding pages have suggested, has been characterized by pronounced cycles of intense policy innovation followed by extended periods of relative quiescence or retrenchment. Policy *outputs* in Japan are characterized by a salience of measures directed toward agriculture, small business, and public works. This bias grew steadily more pronounced from the 1950s through the 1970s, although in discontinuous fashion, and then receded in importance. What is the relationship between the pattern of policy outputs and the pronounced cycle of policy innovation?

The evidence presented in this chapter suggests that structural characteristics of the postwar Japanese political system deeply influence both policy outputs and the salience of the crisis and compensation cycle in policymaking, by accelerating change during crisis and blocking it during noncrisis periods. Political crisis, because of the unusual threat it poses to fundamental goals of the big business and conservative political communities in a highly leveraged, high-growth political economy, opens a "policy window" which allows bureaucracy and conservative party politicians to entertain for stability reasons the prospect of major "new-large" policy innovations and significant shifts in budgetary shares that in normal times they would not countenance.[111] The powerful, traditionally opposition-oriented mass media also heighten pressures for change during crisis, when their policy-related leverage is at its height. Cross-party networks between conservative and opposition politicians both intensify pressures for change and help to structure the form it takes.

In normal times the complex big business organizational structures and the pronounced factionalism of the LDP stand as obstacles to policy change since they make it difficult for the ruling conservatives to reach consensus, a necessary precondition for policy change. Mass media pressure is also typically less pronounced and cross-party networks less active since they enjoy less leverage in policymaking at such quiescent times. Any policy change that occurs is generally slow, incremental, and often regressive in character allowing market forces and economic efficiency to hold sway. The rice price reductions of 1956 and 1987, together with the social security cutbacks of the late 1960s and the mid-1980s, are cases in point.

In periods of crisis a common stability imperative galvanizes the conservative business and political worlds, greatly simplifying the process of consensus formation. The business world's pri-

[111] On the concept of a "policy window," see Kingdon, *Agendas, Alternatives, and Public Policies*, pp. 174–82.

mary concern is maintaining political stability, so as not to prejudice the overall environment in support of economic growth. The conservative politicians' concern is continued preeminence. With these fundamental needs threatened, Japanese conservative elites have not typically been too discriminating about the content of policy responses or their price tags during crisis periods. Whatever is necessary to defuse the crisis and sustain conservative political preeminence will receive their support. Indeed, once the political need for policy change has become evident, factionalism in the LDP has actually hastened change by stimulating rivalries among competing policy proposals. Factions compete to introduce, put their stamp on, and claim credit for the compensation measures that help bring crisis to an end. From this dynamic flows rapid surges of welfare oriented policy change once the Japanese "policy window" is opened by political crisis.

Conservative political structure and incentives typically determine the pace and timing of policy change in periods of crisis through the dynamic suggested above, but they do not determine the content. Mass interest groups representing politically marginal social constituencies, such as agriculture and small business, have more leverage than usual. Big business, by contrast, is often divided regarding specific policy measures and united only on the importance of political stability.

The net result of the "policy window" and the "redistributive policies in crisis" phenomena in combination is that Japanese public policies have assumed a surprisingly redistributive cast, given underlying social structure and the continuing preeminence of conservative party politicians throughout the postwar period. This under market pressures and big-business insistence on efficiency bias unravels only slowly and incrementally, across extended noncrisis periods. Both structural patron-client ties and the distinctive dependency psychology of Japanese politics[112] render compensation relationships difficult to reverse even after the crisis which originally provoked them has passed, as the Nakasone administration's 1986–1987 efforts to introduce a value-added tax in the face of small business opposition clearly showed. Organizational inertia and considerations of balance among competing interests also enter, rendering the compensation bestowed during crisis periods difficult to retract in less turbulent times.

The next six chapters outline the profile of Japanese conserva-

[112] See Kyōgoku Junichi, *Nihon no Seiji*, pp. 267–91.

tive policies, as they have emerged out of the crises outlined in chapters 1 and 2, and been reversed, to some extent, as crisis later waned. These chapters show how Japanese conservative policies, in their alternatively materialist and martial orientation, diverge sharply from more consistent, but typically less redistributive patterns of the Reagan, Thatcher, Giscard, and other Western conservative governments. The chapters further propose to test in detail the general hypotheses developed here and the apparent paradox of how a technocratically biased state like Japan generates redistributive policies. They also deal with deviations from the redistributive path and examine why Japan gradually lapses into retrenchment and a strong efficiency orientation when crisis does not threaten.

5

Agricultural Policy: The Wax and Wane of Rural Bias

SIXTY YEARS AGO, during the so-called Shōwa Depression of the late 1920s and the early 1930s intermittent starvation was not unknown in the smaller towns of Japan's depressed Tōhoku rice growing region. Yet government did little about this, despite the existence of universal manhood suffrage. Supported by big business interests in both the Seiyūkai and the Kenseikai, rice imports had been flooding into Japan from the colonies, particularly from large commercial operations in Korea, for more than a decade.[1]

Today, the price of rice in Japan stands at more than eight times world levels, and the peasantry of Tōhoku are prospering. Many travel to Hawaii, Europe, or Southeast Asia during their off-seasons, pondering investment strategies for the coming year as well as local sights. The Nōrin Chūkin Agricultural Cooperative Bank, swollen with cash, is among the principal underwriters of Japanese government bonds; in 1986 it was the eighth largest financial institution in the world outside the United States in terms of deposits.[2] Keidanren, representative of big business interests, has declaimed bitterly about farm support programs for more than a generation. But it had little success forestalling rice support price increases until the early 1980s, despite the huge national budgetary deficits that began after the 1973 oil shock. Even then it was able only to block further increases, achieving the rollback it had long sought only in 1987. Rice imports, of course, have been effectively blocked through restrictive administration of the Foodstuffs Control Law (*Shokuryō Kanri Hō*), although there was around $70 million of Korean rice supplied to Japan in 1984, ostensibly as repayment in kind for previous Jap-

[1] Ann Waswo, *Japanese Landlords*, pp. 117–18. The Seiyūkai and the Kenseikai were the major political parties, both relatively conservative, of the period.

[2] See *Fortune*, June 8, 1987, and August 3, 1987. The Nōrin Chūkin Bank also ranked eleventh outside the United States in terms of assets.

anese agricultural assistance.[3] Through 1986–87, the only ongoing rice imports into Japan were a special quota of Thai semipolished rice for the manufacture of Okinawan sake, averaging $4 to $5 million a year.[4]

Clearly both the public policies of Japan and the political coalitions which underlie them have shifted sharply since Taishō. Patterns of that previous period were in many respects typical for the developing world with respect to income distribution and low responsiveness to peasant interests. It is postwar Japan, especially over the past twenty years, which is divergent, both from Japan's own deeper historical traditions and from the experience of developing countries elsewhere.

Postwar Japanese patterns of agricultural policy also appear divergent in important respects from those of other industrialized nations since World War II. European nations, to be sure, have often protected inefficient agriculture. Even the United States, with its strong underlying comparative advantage, has done so in some areas, such as sugar and milk products. But both Europe and the United States reduced financial support for agriculture much more sharply during the 1960s and the 1970s than did Japan, especially with regard to grain. Grain price supports in Japan during this period, when the political position of the LDP was often insecure, increased more rapidly during periods of prosperity than was the case in Europe. Japanese price supports also appear to have fallen less precipitously during periods of economic retrenchment than in Europe. Only with the waning of political crisis and the rise of budget deficits during the late 1970s and early 1980s did Japan's conservatives begin to undertake the price support cutbacks that Europe had inaugurated five to ten years earlier. And Japan's cutbacks have been far more gradual, usually operating through freezes in nominal prices or through the operation of complex quality premiums.

Redistributive support for relatively low-income agricultural

[3] On this rice import case, see Hasegawa Hiroshi, *Kome Kokka Kokusho (The Black Book of the Rice Nation).*

[4] See United Nations, *World Commodity Statistics: Japanese Imports,* series D, annual (New York: United Nations Statistical Papers, 1984), p. 6. In 1984 Japan imported $73.4 million worth of rice—$69.3 million from South Korea as a one-time in-kind repayment of a previous crop loan and $4.1 million of semi-polished rice from Thailand, as part of the ongoing arrangement for the production of Okinawan sake. Japan also exported $34.2 million worth of rice during 1984.

groups has been a hallmark of progressive public policies for half a century and more. Social democratic governments in Sweden, Norway, and Denmark and the Roosevelt administration of the United States made such agricultural support policies a cornerstone of their broad based recovery programs during the Great Depression and persisted with these policies in later years.[5] But for conservatives, strong backing for agricultural support programs has been more unusual. The retrenchment or inaction of Hoover, Barre, and Reagan have been more common among Western conservatives than support programs like those of Yoshida, Ikeda, Tanaka, and even a reluctant Nakasone have been.

This chapter explores the political base and policy output of the Japanese conservatives' distinctive agricultural policies, contrasting those policies to analogous patterns of policymaking by conservative governments elsewhere in the industrialized world. The chapter shows in particular the process by which relatively similar Japanese and European support policies for agriculture diverged in the 1950s and 1960s, with the conservative Japanese remaining more tenacious in support of rural interests, until a growing wave of retrenchment set in after 1976. This chapter also shows the central role of the "crisis and compensation" dynamic in creating, sustaining, and then abridging a postwar Japanese agricultural policy distinctive in its strong and comprehensive support for the countryside.

Agriculture has played a key role in the political calculations of conservative governments since the early days of mass political mobilization, even though such governments have often been sparing with budgetary support. Farmers tend to be less influenced than urban blue- and white-collar employees by the anomie, the economic uncertainty, the corresponding need for a social welfare system, and the sharp sense of relative deprivation that so often accompany the industrialization and urbanization processes. When independent yeomen, they have a stability bias parallel to that of conservative elites despite differences in income level. This bias is often reinforced by the strong hold of both religion and patron-client relationships that typify the countryside. In rural and usually religiously oriented societies, preservation of elite legitimacy is often not as difficult as elsewhere.

[5] On the early politics of agricultural support programs in Scandinavia, see Gosta Esping-Anderson, *Politics Against Markets*, pp. 76–77, 81, 87.

Japanese Agricultural Policy Outputs in Comparative Perspective

In periods of political crisis, appeals to the countryside may be crucial for ruling conservative elites. The support of urban constituencies is frequently cast into doubt at such times and is difficult to systematically mobilize where, as in Japan during the late 1940s, the cities are either unorganized politically, or pervaded by militant unions. The countryside, by contrast, is often more susceptible to organization and systematic compensation politics through local rural elites or agricultural cooperatives. Conservative elites want to cement their ties to the countryside. Accordingly, crisis often induces compensation for agriculture, either in the form of new policies or expanded distributive benefits. This dynamic prevailed to a degree in the America of both the democratic and republican Roosevelts, with their innovative farm policies,[6] and in the France of De Gaulle and Pompidou following the critical days of May 1968. But nowhere has political crisis left a deeper imprint on agricultural policy, a largely redistributive imprint, than in postwar Japan. Reinforcing this redistributive influence have been structural features of the postwar Japanese political system, outlined in chapter 2, which often make public policy highly responsive to grassroots influences.

As indicated in Table 5.1, agricultural expenditures as a percentage of total government spending in Japan were substantially higher than those of any other major industrialized nation for most of the 1970s and the 1980s. Japanese agricultural spending was typically between two and four times as large a share of budgetary spending as in the United States, until U.S. expenditures rose sharply and uncharacteristically during 1982–83 to offset the deflationary effects of a strong dollar on America's farms. Postwar Japanese patterns have much closer parallels in the New Deal of Franklin D. Roosevelt than in the republican policies of the 1970s and 1980s. Both the New Deal and Japanese policies of the 1950s, 1960s, and 1970s clearly represented distributive politics in action, within a framework profoundly shaped at its origins by political crisis.

Japanese agricultural spending has been high largely due to an

[6] See, for example, Arthur M. Schlesinger, Jr., *The Coming of the New Deal*, pp. 29–84.

TABLE 5.1

Japan's Bias toward the Countryside: Agricultural Spending as a Proportion of Total Government Expenditures in Major Industrialized Nations, 1971–1984

	1971	1974	1977	1980	1983	1984
Japan	12.0	10.5	7.9	4.9	3.8	3.5
France	3.3	3.8	3.7	1.4	1.2	1.1
Britain	—	4.0	1.5	0.9	0.6	0.5
United States	2.0	0.8	1.4	2.9	4.0	3.1
West Germany	3.8	1.6	1.1	1.0	0.8	0.8

Sources: Organization for Economic Cooperation and Development, *National Policies and Agricultural Trade* (Paris: OECD, 1987), p. 129; and Ministry of Finance, unpublished data.

Notes: (1) Existence of the Common Agricultural Policy (CAP) makes precise Europe-Japan comparisons difficult. (2) European community agricultural expenditures rose by around 15 percent during 1980–1984 in constant prices, while those in Japan fell in real terms, suggesting that the gap in relative EC and Japanese commitment to agriculture was closing during the early 1980s. (3) Figures include processing, marketing, and consumer aid, 54.6 percent of the U.S. total during 1979–81, and only 1.6 percent in Japan.

unusually wide range of subsidies to agricultural groups and individual farmers, particularly to reward or discourage the production of major commodities such as rice and wheat. In fiscal 1984, for example, approximately 15.5 percent of Japan's extraordinarily high subsidy budget went to agriculture, to support nearly one-third of the 1,500 line items subsidized in the national budget as a whole.[7] Subsidies, indeed, comprise around 60 percent of the Ministry of Agriculture's annual budget. Most of these funds are intended to stimulate the structural transformation of Japanese agriculture away from rice and toward higher value-added commodities, especially livestock and poultry. But the distribution in accordance with this general strategic objective is a patchwork of specialized programs, designed primarily

[7] Zaisei Chōsa Kai, ed., *Hojokin Sōran* (*Subsidies Almanac*), fiscal 1984, pp. 4–5. Sudsidies in the early 1980s represent around 32 percent of the Japanese budget, as opposed to 4 to 6 percent in Britain and France, 8 to 10 percent in the United States, and around 18 to 20 percent in West Germany. See Hirose Michisada, *Hojokin to Seiken Tō* (*Subsidies and the Party in Power*), pp. 76, 98.

to cater to the constituent interests of Japan's large number of Dietmen from agricultural or semiagricultural districts.[8]

Among Japan's most striking policy outputs in the agricultural area, comparatively speaking, is the enormously high and, until recently, steadily rising price of rice, a commodity constituting 40 percent of Japan's agricultural output by value. As indicated in Figure 5.1, the producer rice price in Japan was actually *below* world levels until 1954, although both Japanese and global prices rose substantially, for different reasons, during the early 1950s.[9] With the end of the Korean War commodities boom, world rice prices fell somewhat, while Japanese prices remained more or less constant. But the big gap between Japanese domestic and global rice prices did not emerge decisively until after 1961, when Japanese producer prices started to escalate sharply, despite weakness in the world market. Except for a short global commodities boom in the early 1970s, world rice prices have remained relatively weak, particularly when translated into yen (Figure 5.1). But Japanese producer rice prices, pressed continually upward by political considerations, rose rapidly during 1961–1968 and then again during 1973–1975. By 1975 they had reached $1,200 per ton, or nearly four times world levels.

Not surprisingly, these high prices generated a huge rice glut, including a government stockpile of 8.7 million tons in 1980.[10] They also generated the political necessity of a consumers' subsidy to insulate consumers from the high prices offered producers. This subsidy cost the national government ¥147 billion (around $585 million) in 1984 alone.[11] During the early 1980s the Japanese government made headway in reducing its stockpile

[8] In early 1983, 195 LDP Dietman, or 68.2 percent of the ruling party members in the Diet, were members of the LDP's Agricultural Committee (*Nōrin Bukai*). This was the highest participation on any LDP committee. See Inoguchi Takashi, *Kokusai Kankei no Seiji Keizai Gaku* (The Political Economy of International Relations), p. 27. Many of these Dietmen come from districts with only a small number of full-time farmers. But Japan has an extraordinary number of *part-time* farmers, as will be seen later in more detail, and Japanese farmers generally tend to be very well organized.

[9] World prices rose due to the Korean War commodities boom. Japanese producer prices, isolated from the world market due to import controls, were driven upward by conservative political support for local rice farmers.

[10] Ministry of Agriculture, Forestry, and Fisheries Statistics and Information Section (Nōrin Suisan Sho Tōkei Jōhō Bu), *Nōrin Suisan Tōkei* (Agricultural and Fishery Statistics), 1986 ed., p. 178.

[11] Zaisei Chōsa Kai, ed., *Hojokin Sōran*, pp. 8–9.

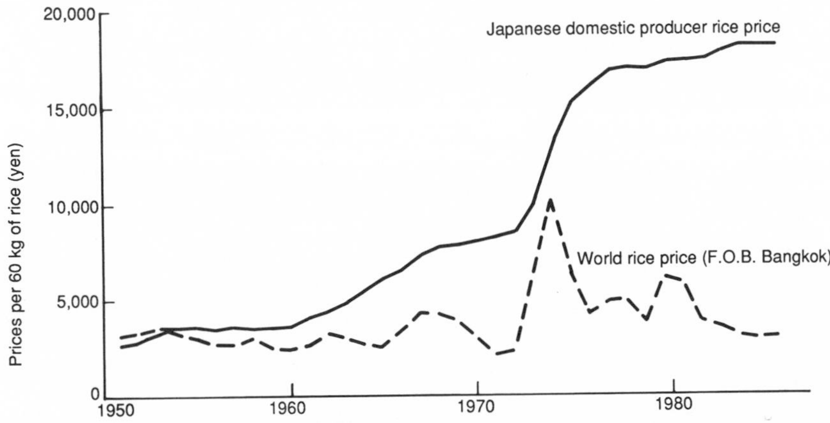

Figure 5.1. Japanese Producer Rice Prices and the World Market, 1950–1985.

Note: Prices are for 60 kg. units, in yen, with currency translations at year-end annual exchange rates.

Source: International Bank for Reconstruction and Development, *Commodity Trade and Price Trends*, 1986 ed., p. 52.

through controversial subsidized exports.[12] It also steadily reduced consumer subsidies and held the basic producer rice price constant for three consecutive years (1984–1986), with only minor adjustments in quality premiums, before reducing it for the first time in thirty-nine years during 1987. But, due to the growing strength of the yen, the gap between domestic and world rice prices continued steadily to widen. By the end of 1986 Japanese producer prices were over eight times world levels[13] in a period of massive overall Japanese trade surpluses, stimulating rising economic and political pressures abroad for rice imports into Japan.

Comparing Japanese agricultural support levels with patterns in other advanced nations, as well as with the global market, also yields important insights into Japanese agricultural policy and its

[12] Japanese rice exports reached $241 million in 1980, $371 million in 1981, $121 million in 1982, $105 million in 1983, and $33 million in 1984. Ministry of Agriculture, Forestry, and Fisheries Statistics and Information Section (Nōrin Suisan Shō Tōkei Jōhō Bu), *Nōrin Suisan Tōkei*, p. 184.

[13] By late 1986 Japan's domestic producer rice price, denominated in dollars, had reached $1,900 per ton, due to the sharp yen revaluation of 1985–1986. World prices, by contrast, were around $230 per ton. See *Japan Economic Journal*, October 18, 1986, p. 3.

TABLE 5.2

Agricultural Price Support Levels in Japan and the European Community, 1955–1980 (in percentages)

	European Community				Japan			
Item	1955	1965	1975	1980	1955	1965	1975	1980
Wheat	31.5	29.0	3.1	15.1	23.4	45.1	45.1	72.3
Rice	14.6	26.3	8.0	30.4	19.3	49.7	55.3	65.8
Beef	41.4	41.4	38.5	48.2	28.3	59.4	63.4	50.1
Eggs	13.7	18.5	7.2	5.5	−23.5	−1.9	−5.9	−1.5
Overall	23.3	28.1	20.8	26.0	15.0	40.3	42.7	45.5

Source: Hayami Yūjirō and Honma Masayoshi, *Kokusai Hikaku kara mita Nihon Nōgyō no Hogo Suijun (The Agricultural Protection Level of Japan in International Comparative Perspective)* (Tokyo: Seisaku Kōsō Forum [The Forum for Policy Innovation], November 1983), p. 20.

Notes: (1) 1955–1970 European figures are a weighted average of France, West Germany, Italy, and the Netherlands. (2) 1975 and 1980 figures also include Britain and Denmark in the averages. (3) Negative support levels indicated for eggs in Japan result from the adverse impact of feed subsidies on egg production costs, insufficiently offset by other positive support factors.

underlying political dynamics. Japanese grain price support levels have *not* been higher than those in the European community throughout all of the post–World War II period, as is often assumed (see Table 5.2). In 1955, overall European agricultural price support levels were, to the contrary, nearly 50 percent higher than those in Japan, despite a few countertrends discussed later in this chapter. For example, turbulent Fourth Republic France was strongly supporting its agriculture.[14]

By 1965, however, this situation had been dramatically reversed. The overall Japanese agricultural price support ratio had nearly tripled to 40.3 percent, while that in the European community had risen only modestly to 28.1 percent. After 1965 the changes in European and Japanese support levels were relatively small, although the gap between Europe and Japan continued to widen due to policies established earlier.

[14] On the agricultural policies of the Fourth Republic, responsive to interest-group pressure in the midst of political turbulence in a fashion broadly resembling Japan during its crisis intervals, see Gordon Wright, *Rural Revolution in France*, pp. 114–42.

Table 5.3

Quota Restrictions on Agricultural Products in Developed Countries, 1981

Country	Number	Major Items
France	23	Horses, mutton, bananas, vegetables, and fruits
Japan	22	Dairy products, beef, and oranges
Italy	6	Bananas, grapes, and citrus juice
Denmark	5	Mutton and vegetables
West Germany	4	Vegetables and potatoes
Canada	4	Milk and cream, butter, and cheese
United States	1[a]	Sugar
United Kingdom	1	Bananas

Source: JETRO (Japanese Trade Export Organization).

[a] In addition to sugar, the United States has reserved thirteen agricultural items under import restrictions (including milk, cream, butter, cheese, ice cream, peanuts, and wheat flour) through a waiver approved under the GATT agreements.

Trends in support levels for grains have been especially striking. As indicated in table 5.2, European support levels for rice were roughly those of Japan in 1955; by 1965, Japanese support levels were nearly double those of Europe. Japanese support levels for wheat were actually substantially below those of Europe in 1955; by 1965 they were 50 percent higher, with the gap continuing to widen until 1980. By 1980 Japanese wheat prices were roughly three times the world price, with support ratios more than four times those of Europe. By late 1986, they had reached eight times world levels following yen revaluation, as indicated earlier, although they had stabilized in terms of yen.

Given the sharp distortions in Japanese internal agricultural prices created by grassroots political pressure, it is not surprising that Japan also has an unusually elaborate and severe range of restrictions on agricultural imports. In fact, Japan in the early 1980s had more agricultural items under quota than any other major nation in the OECD, except France (see Table 5.3). Japanese tariffs on both processed and unprocessed agricultural goods, where quotas do not adequately bar the way to imports, are also extremely high.

This pattern of sharp, overt, and continuing protectionism in agriculture contrasts to more rapidly changing policies with respect to trade in manufactured goods, especially with regard to tariffs and quotas. The contrast is especially striking between agricultural protectionism and Japan's policies on commodity industrial products, such as cotton textiles, which are not considered strategic to Japan's industrial future and which lack powerful domestic political constituencies. Japan has been, for example, the only major industrialized nation not to invoke the safeguard provisions of the Multi-Fiber Agreement on textiles. Overall, Japan has lower aggregate tariff levels for manufactured goods than either the United States or the European community. But Japan's levels of agricultural protection remain, as has been noted, substantially higher than in the West.

Aside from generous price support programs and high levels of protection, the Japanese state has also aided Japanese farmers in numerous ways only indirectly related to agriculture. Low rates of taxation on agricultural land allow farmers in suburban areas to shelter huge amounts of potentially saleable real estate from taxation until the optimal time for sale. Many suburban farmers, often selling only small amounts of land at a time, have grown wealthy through such sales.

Much of Japan's heavy public works spending (four times the share of GNP which public works represents in the United States and twice the share in France) is concentrated in the countryside, providing part-time work for farmers.[15] The rapid expansion of local and national government administrative activities in the countryside since the 1950s has also created major and rapidly expanding new opportunities for public service employment. Regional policies have encouraged growth sectors, such as electronics and precision machinery, to locate new production facilities in the countryside, allowing expansion of both full-time and part-time employment in factories located there.

Paralleling the rapid expansion of nonagricultural job opportu-

[15] In 1985, for example the fifteen largely rural prefectures of Hokkaidō, Shikoku, and the Japan Sea coast accounted for 23 percent of Japan's public works spending but only 17.4 percent of the population. The four prefectures of the Tokyo metropolitan area, by contrast accounted for 24.8 percent of the population but received only 20.7 percent of the public works. See Asahi Shimbun Nenkan Henshū Bu, ed., *'86 Minryoku*, p. 160.

nities in the countryside, particularly during the 1950s and 1960s, was rising labor redundancy in agriculture itself. Given extensive mechanization, especially in the rice cultivation which has long constituted the bulk of Japanese farm output, the number of farmers required to sustain agricultural production was declining, leaving many looking for alternate full- or part-time employment. Regional policies promoting industrial development in the countryside, such as those that have encouraged concentration of more than 60 percent of Japan's integrated circuit production in the largely rural Tōhoku and Kyūshū regions, can be seen in substantial measure as a reaction to this grassroots predicament. In effect, the Japanese government has been responding to rural pressures by striving to wean farmers away from agriculture, without forcing them to leave the land.

Many farmers or members of farm families have eagerly taken up the new jobs created in the countryside by both government and the private sector. But they have not generally sold their farms. As a result, the share of part-time farmers deriving over half of their income outside agriculture has risen in Japan to sharply higher levels than in any of the other major industrialized nations today (Figure 5.2).[16] In 1960, by contrast, Japanese part-time farming ratios approximated those elsewhere in the industrialized world.

The welfare implications for Japanese farmers of the complex of agricultural policy measures adopted since World War II have also been striking. Farm households have dramatically reversed, in less than two decades, the 10 percent negative income gap with urban households which they suffered in 1960 (Figure 5.3). Yet they are becoming less and less reliant on farm income. Part-time farm households, given optimal advantage of the broad range of public employment and public works programs in the countryside, now enjoy per capita income levels roughly 40 percent higher than the urban average. In addition, Japanese farmers also still hold large amounts of lightly taxed land with prospects for substantial further appreciation.

The prosperity of Japanese farmers is especially dramatic when

[16] There are, it should be noted, important regional distinctions to be made. In 1984 the average farm family in Hokkaidō still derived 51.6 percent of its income from agriculture, while its counterpart on the "Silicon Island" of Kyūshū only relied on agriculture for 18.8 percent of total income. See Ministry of Agriculture, Forestry, and Fisheries Statistics and Information Section (Nōrin Suisan Shō Tōkei Jōhō Bu), *Nōrin Suisan Tōkei*, 1986 ed., p. 146.

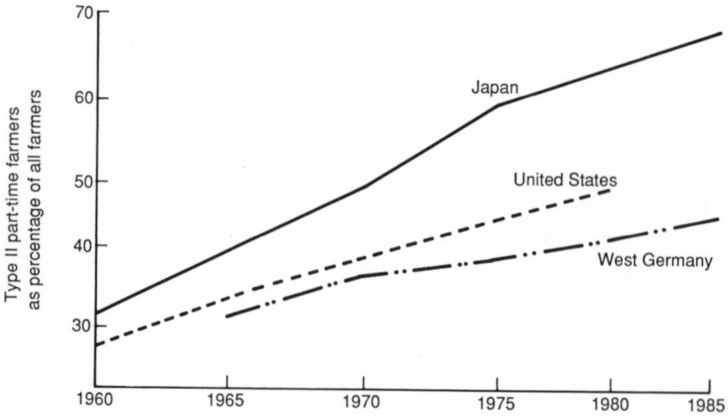

Figure 5.2. The Emergence of Marginal Part-Time Farming in Selected OECD Nations, 1960–1985.

Notes: Type II part-time farmers are those professionally engaged in farming who receive less than half their total income from farming or devote over half their working time to nonfarm employment. U.S. statistics for 1978 and 1982 are labor-based.

SOURCES: Organization for Economic Cooperation and Development, *Part-Time Farming in OECD Countries* (Paris: OECD, 1978); *Nihon Kokusei Zue*, 1986 ed.; Statistisches Bundesamt, *Statistisches Jahrbuch*, 1986 ed.; and U.S. Bureau of the Census, *Statistical Abstract of the United States*, 1986 ed.

seen in comparative context. As Tachibana Takashi points out, the labor productivity of Japanese agriculture around 1980 was less than one-tenth that of the United States, but the total income of a Japanese farm family was almost exactly that of its counterpart in the United States.[17] As depicted in figure 5.4, an average Japanese farm household in 1984 earned 19 percent more than what an average American farm family did. By the late 1980s, as a result of exchange rate shifts, the Japanese farm family's income was substantially higher. And the assets of Japan's affluent part-time farmers were further augmented beyond American levels by their holdings of more rapidly appreciating land. Tachibana attributes the extraordinary prosperity of the Japanese farm family to the high profitability of farm activities that high commodity support prices generate. Of every ¥100 in sales ¥68 represents profit for Japanese farmers—over three times the 25

[17] Tachibana Takashi, *Nōkyō: Kyodai na Chōsen* (Agricultural Cooperatives: The Massive Challenge), p. 129.

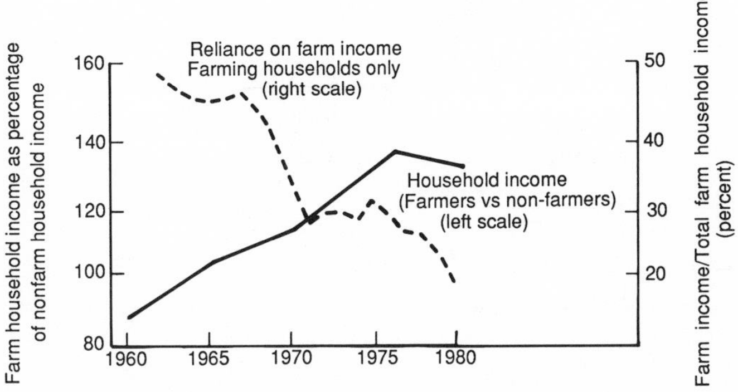

Figure 5.3. Rising Farmer Affluence and Declining Reliance on Agriculture, 1960–1980.

Notes: (1) Nonagricultural income for farm households includes money earned by family members as seasonal laborers. (2) For 1978, full-time farmers averaged 115 percent of nonfarm income; class A part-time, 143 percent; and class B part-time, 140 percent.

Sources: Ministry of Agriculture, Forestry and Fisheries (Nōrinsuisan Shō), *Nōka Keisai Chōsa (Farm Household Economy Survey)*, various issues; Prime Minister's Office Statistical Bureau (Sōrifu Tōkei Kyoku), *Toshi Kakei Chōsa (Urban Household Economy Survey)*, various issues; also, *Kokumin Seikatsu Hakusho (White Paper on the People's Livelihood)*, 1982 ed., p. 77.

percent ratio in the United States.[18] In addition, there are the substantial opportunities for nonfarm income outlined above, in both public works and rural-based private industry.

On top of the other benefits that Japan's postwar political economy has lavished on agriculture, farmers are accorded exceptionally favorable tax treatment. This allows them to shield much of the comfortable income generated through the opportunities outlined above from prying eyes at the National Tax Agency. Virtually all urban salaries are subject to withholding (Figure 5.5), yet only around 30 percent of agricultural income is subject to withholding. In fiscal 1982 only around 14.6 percent of all farmers made income tax payments at all, as opposed to 88.4 percent of all urban workers.[19] The average tax for those Japanese farmers who paid any tax at all was only ¥80,000 (slightly more than $300), or about 20 percent of the national average.[20] And yet me-

[18] *Ibid.*, p. 130.

[19] Nihon Keizai Shimbun Sha, *Za Zeimusho* (The Tax Office), p. 82.

[20] *Ibid.*

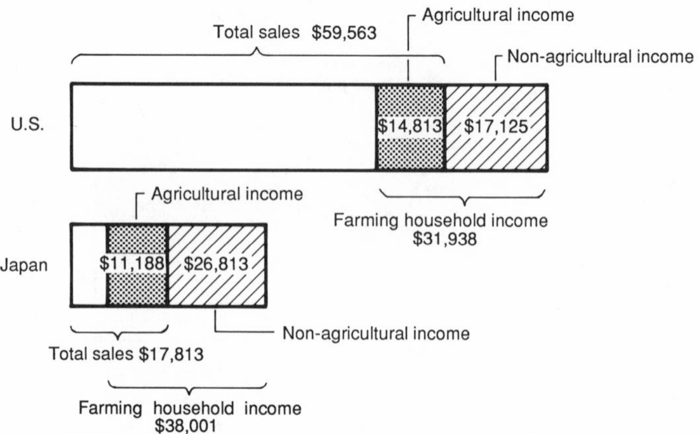

Figure 5.4. Household Income and Agricultural Sales for Farm Families: a United States–Japan comparison.

Note: White boxes represent sales, and dark and shaded areas represent income ($1 = ¥238.50).

Source: *Statistical Abstract of the United States, 1985*, and *Poketto Nōrin Suisan Tōkei* (1985 ed.), p. 130.

dian per capita farm income was more than 10 percent higher than that of the average urban worker, and farm savings were nearly twice as high. Farmers thus appear to be more affluent than city dwellers, yet they pay sharply less tax.[21]

The Early Anti-agricultural Bias of Japanese Public Policy

Farming households in Japan, as indicated above, have greatly benefitted from the operation of public policy since the 1950s. This was by no means always so. Indeed, for more than three generations after the Meiji Restoration of 1868, agriculture faced strong discrimination from a state apparatus that placed highest priority on industrialization and military security. Only with rising rural unrest in the 1920s did this begin to change and then only marginally. Even after World War II the still technocratically oriented Japanese state was initially hesitant about actively aiding the countryside, but SCAP encouragement and the exigen-

[21] *Ibid.*

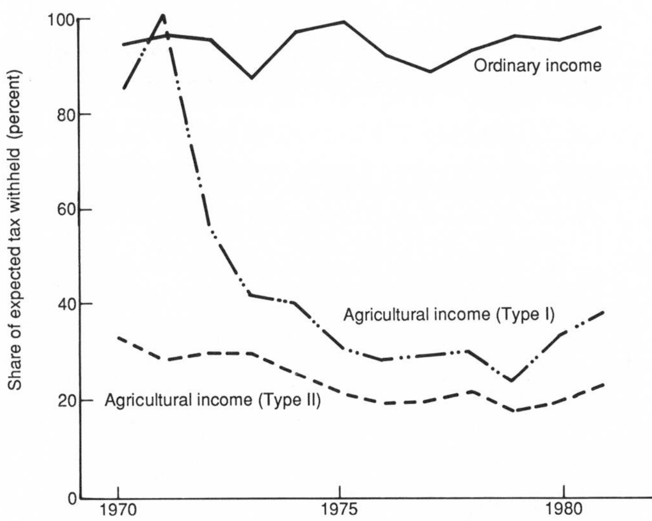

Figure 5.5 Tax Withholding for Farmers and Nonfarmers.

Notes: Type II income is income received from agriculture where the recipient also works over thirty days outside agriculture or makes over ¥70,000 annually. Type I income is agricultural income in cases where no household members make over ¥70,000 outside agriculture or work over thirty days outside agriculture.

Source: Keidanren (Federation of Economic Organizations).

cies of domestic stability within Japan made this politically expedient for the conservatives.

The discrimination faced by prewar Japanese agriculture is shown succinctly in table 5.4. Levels of taxation in relation to income produced were much higher in the agricultural sector than in other areas, due initially to the infamous Meiji land tax, enacted in 1873, and the low levels of taxation prevailing in the urban areas. The agricultural tax burden declined slowly over time, but it continued heavier than that prevailing outside agriculture throughout the prewar period.[22] One major reason for this

[22] As Nakamura points out, the Meiji system of land taxation may have introduced systematic underreporting of agricultural income, particularly for the 1870s and 1880s. See James I. Nakamura, *Agricultural Production and the Economic Development of Japan, 1873–1922*, pp. 3–21. Whatever the problems with early Meiji agricultural production data, however, evidence points to a strong consistently antiagricultural bias throughout the pre–World War II era, continuing into periods when data is considered to be relatively reliable.

TABLE 5.4
The Antiagricultural Bias of Prewar Japanese Taxation, 1883–1937

	Agriculture		Nonagriculture	
Year	Direct Tax (¥1000)	Ratio (%)	Direct Tax (¥1000)	Ratio (%)
1883–1887	63,552	22.1	9,548	3.0
1888–1892	58,479	15.5	9,779	2.3
1893–1897	65,626	12.4	13,167	2.0
1898–1902	99,050	12.1	35,378	3.2
1903–1907	113,582	11.2	79,313	5.4
1908–1912	153,441	12.5	132,196	6.4
1913–1917	167,660	12.9	145,441	4.5
1918–1922	295,672	9.2	431,081	5.4
1923–1927	304,217	10.5	506,203	5.2
1928–1932	205,450	9.7	421,311	4.3
1933–1937	197,325	7.8	559,235	4.2

Source: Ōkawa Kazushi and Henry Rosovsky, "The Role of Agriculture in Modern Japanese Economic Development," *Economic Development and Cultural Change* 9, no. 1, part 2 (October 1960), p. 62.

continuing differential, as Ōkawa and Rosovsky point out, was heavy local tax rates in Japan's rural prefectures, which were not reduced even when productive capacity lagged.[23] Bureaucratic inertia—unchallenged by strong grassroots pressures from elected local government as during the postwar period—may well have produced this pattern. Strong, centralized big business pressure may, at the same time, have prevented the more rapid rise of nonagricultural taxation, despite burgeoning government budgetary requirements.

Thus, the prewar Japanese state took heavily from the countryside, without providing much in return. In sharp contrast to postwar patterns, it provided little protection for producers in the home islands against imports. For example, foreign rice imports rose as high as 12 percent of domestic consumption in the wake

[23] Ōkawa Kazushi and Henry Rosovsky, "The Role of Agriculture in Modern Japanese Economic Development," p. 62.

of World War I, while colonial rice imports averaged over 20 percent of consumption throughout the 1920s and 1930s and severely depressed domestic rice prices during much of this period.[24] Government also failed to protect farmers against the consequences of volatility in domestic rice markets. During the mid-1880s, for example, as many as 360,000 peasants were dispossessed for failure to pay taxes due to a sharp drop in the rice price, while government did nothing.[25] During the 1920s the Japanese state was similarly slow to deal with the collapse of domestic rice prices and the social implications thereof.[26]

On the expenditure side of the prewar Japanese government budget, the neglect of agriculture was similarly striking. Virtually no subsidies were allotted to agriculture until the 1920s; agriculture was only a source of social surplus to be exploited. Although subsidies increased over the following two decades, especially as populist military cliques increased in influence, they remained low relative to the large share of the population in agriculture, and to the severity of rural distress.[27] The prevalent combination of unusually heavy taxation and denial of benefits to agriculture during the prewar period, particularly the first half century after the Meiji Restoration, may well have been a major reason that agriculture's share of national income dropped ex-

[24] As Michael Donnelly points out, the rice import issue arose in Japan as a major political question around 1900, although imports were never seriously restricted during the prewar period. Indeed, imports from the colonies were encouraged until the mid-1930s. Rice import patterns were:

	1907	1919	1925–1929	1933	1937	(unit = percent of domestic Japanese consumption)
Domestic Rice			75	72	76	
Foreign Rice	5	12	7	2	1	
Colonial Rice			18	26	23	

Source: Mochida Keizō, *Beikoku Shijō no Tenkai Katei* (*The Development of the Rice Market*) (Tokyo: Tokyo Daigaku Shuppan Kai 1970), p. 138. Cited in Michael Donnelly, "Political Management of Japan's Rice Economy" (Ph.D. diss., Columbia University, 1978), Vol. I, p. 178.

[25] See Nobutaka Ike, "Taxation and Landownership in the Westernization of Japan," *Journal of Economic History* 7 (November 1947): 175.

[26] During 1926–1931 rice prices declined 50 percent. The only state response was selective new purchases, which provided little support for smaller rice farmers. See Donnelly, "Political Management" pp. 175, 195.

[27] In 1941, for example, only 20 percent of Japanese national government subsidies went to agriculture although nearly half the population was on the land. See Ōkawa and Rosovsky, "Role of Agriculture," p. 63.

tremely rapidly during the early industrialization phase of Japanese economic development,[28] compared to the pattern of analogous stages of European industrialization.

Some aspects of the current agriculture-oriented system of Japanese public policy predate 1945. These exceptions appear to prove the general rule that grassroots pressure, combined with opposition attempts to preempt government efforts to respond to such pressure, generates "populist conservative" policy innovation in Japan.[29] As Dore and Ōuchi, Smethurst, and Kelly all point out, the degree of actual violence in the prewar Japanese countryside is often overstated.[30] Tenants often used antilandlord actions as a limited bargaining tactic, within the context of broadly shared assumptions regarding the prevailing political order.[31] But it seems clear that such turbulence helped elicit policy change favorable to agriculture in general.

Government subsidies to agriculture did begin to rise during the 1920s and 1930s. In 1921, the Rice Crop Law *did* authorize the government to partially intervene in the rice market to maintain the stability of rice prices. In 1923, the predecessor of the Nōrin Chūkin Bank was established to cater to the needs of agriculture.[32] And in 1934, a Rice Import Adjustment Law (Rinji Beikoku Inyū Chōsei Hō) did lead to active discouragement of rice imports even if imports from the colonies were allowed to continue.[33] All these developments occurred after the nationwide

[28] Ōkawa and Rosovsky point out that agriculture's share in Japanese national income dropped from 64 percent in 1878–1882 to 17 percent in 1938–1942, an unusually steep drop by international standards, particularly since the share of agriculture in the total labor force only dropped from 76 to 44 percent. See *ibid.*, p. 63.

[29] One major difference in the pre-1945 period, of course, is that "grassroots pressure" arose to a greater degree from the dissatisfaction of local notables (*meibōka*), including many landlords, than was later true.

[30] See Ronald P. Dore and Ōuchi Tsutomu, "Rural Origins of Japanese Fascism," in *Dilemmas of Growth in Prewar Japan*, ed. James William Morley, pp. 181–209, especially pp. 189–90; Richard J. Smethurst, *Agricultural Development and Tenancy Disputes in Japan, 1870–1940*, especially pp. 316–57; and William W. Kelly, *Deference and Defiance in Nineteenth-Century Japan*, pp. 290–91.

[31] Smethurst, *Agricultural Development*, pp. 349–52.

[32] The Sangyō Kumiai Chūō Kinkō, predecessor of the Nōrin Chūkin Bank, was founded in 1923. The name was formally changed to Nōrin Chūo Kinkō (or Nōrin Chūkin for short) in 1943.

[33] On agricultural policy innovation during the Taishō and early Shōwa periods, and the broader social context of that policy change, see Imamura Naraomi, *Ho-*

Rice Riots of 1918, against the backdrop of a sharp increase in tenant disputes,[34] and increasing uncertainty among landlords concerning the value of their land.

These tentative agricultural support measures were driven largely by pressure from rural-based party politicians, by populist military officers, and by often militant rural pressure groups in the background. Giving credence and legitimacy to these claims was an increasingly influential body of agrarian thought,[35] stressing the primacy of agriculture in an ideally constructed body politic. By the beginning of World War I, an extensive network of agricultural cooperatives had developed, initially encouraged and controlled by the state;[36] these groups became increasingly active in lobbying for state support to agriculture as time went by. Interest group structures were, to be sure, beginning to form during the prewar period. Levels of conflict were often high, as the "problem of the villages" deepened.[37] But the basic political reality of the countryside remained stable, dominated by the bureaucracy and conservative local political elites and based on landlordship, patron-client relations, and the corporatist nōkai. The pervasive political uncertainties of the early postwar countryside, flowing from land reform and nōkai dissolution, had not yet clearly emerged. Nor had a single dominant conservative party beset by strong internal rivalries forcing politicians into deep dependence on the grassroots. Many important administrative structures supporting compensation for farmers, such as the Rice Price Deliberation Council, were likewise absent. Neither crisis nor the mechanism for translating grassroots pressure amid crisis

---

jokin to Nōgyō Nōson (Subsidies and the Agricultural Sector and Agricultural Villages), pp. 85–127.

[34] As Dore and Ōuchi point out, until 1922 the secular tendency had been for rice-land prices to rise faster than the price of rice. After that date, however, both fell together, and rice-land prices failed to recover when rice prices did during the mid-1930s. See Dore and Ōuchi Tsutomu, "Rural Origins," pp. 190–91.

[35] For a detailed examination of pre–World War II Japanese agrarianism, or *Nōhonshugi*, against the background of Japanese economic modernization, see Thomas R. H. Havens, *Farm and Nation in Modern Japan: Agrarian Nationalism, 1870–1940.*

[36] *Ibid.* The number of agricultural cooperatives increased from 255 in 1898 to 11,160 in 1914. See Pempel and Tsunekawa, "Corporatism without Labor," p. 250.

[37] On the "problem of the villages," see Allan Cole, George Totten, and Cecil Uyehara, *Socialist Parties in Postwar Japan*, p. 371.

into grassroots compensation had yet assumed the intimate and systematic interrelationship they were to take on after 1949.

Crisis in the Early Postwar Countryside

Japan began the postwar period with sweeping changes in political structure encouraging increased grassroots independence, yet with agricultural policies and a conservative rural social structure varying initially not too sharply from the prewar and wartime patterns. Introduced fullblown during 1942, rice price controls continued, largely to prevent social chaos during the food crisis that followed war's end. The Nōrin Chūkin Bank and existing subsidy systems stayed in place, although farmers seemed to have no strong need of them. With food prices high in a Japan suddenly deprived of its traditional sources of supply in Korea and Taiwan, the countryside initially asked little of politicians other than relief from periodic food requisitions on behalf of famished urban dwellers. Landlords and other conservative groups remained in positions of precarious preeminence as the occupation commenced in late 1945.

The Japanese state's initial postwar approach to agriculture, reflecting the conservative, corporatist status quo in the countryside, was *not* strongly reformist. Indeed, the Shidehara cabinet's half-hearted land reform bill of December 1945 passed only after three cabinet meetings and intense Diet debate and was filled with loopholes beneficial to landlords;[38] it would have affected by some estimates less than one-third of tenanted land. Conservative politicians stressed vehemently in both the cabinet and the general Diet debates that even such a modest bill as Shidehara proposed could undermine the economic basis of the traditional leadership in the villages. This leadership and the conservative agricultural associations (nōkai) that reinforced its preeminence were seen as crucial supports for conservative rule in Japan as a whole.

While the Japanese conservatives during 1945–1946 were reluctant to press for rural reform, lest it compound the dangers of instability many perceived as looming, the Allied Occupation saw such reform as a central element in democratizing Japan.

[38] Dore, *Land Reform in Japan*, pp. 132–36.

General Douglas MacArthur himself was adamant in support of land reform as the first step in this process of rural democratization, both to further democratic objectives and to undercut rising rural discontent.[39] After instructing the Japanese government in December 1945 to "destroy the economic bondage which has enslaved the Japanese farmer for centuries of feudal oppression" through land reform and experiencing its tepid initial response, SCAP pressed for more radical action.[40] In October 1946, the Diet passed a much more sweeping measure, which expropriated all the land of absentee landowners and involved changes in the property rights of some six million families.[41] Because compensation was calculated in terms of prevailing 1945 land prices, the actual value of that compensation was sharply eroded by ensuing inflation.

While gradual change in the political economy of the Japanese countryside had been underway for several years, the land reform of 1946–1949 sharply accelerated this process, giving millions of farmers an autonomy from the prevailing local conservative power structure they had never previously enjoyed. The number of owner-cultivators grew by 1.7 million households, and the number of tenant households likewise sharply decreased.[42] The fluidity of social conditions in the countryside was also greatly enhanced by the abolition of the conservative agricultural associations, or nōkai, in December 1947. The nōkai had been a principal means through which the state and local rural elites had dominated the countryside since the mid-Meiji Period, following the *Dai Nihon Nōkai*'s (Great Japan Agricultural Association) establishment in 1881.

In many villages during the late 1940s, former landlords could no longer play as authoritative a role in mobilizing electoral support for the conservatives as they had previously done. Nonconservative, and even radical, rural organization threatened to take their place. The left-oriented agricultural unions (*nōmin kumiai*) in many places retained strong organization and credibility from the tenancy and food requisition struggles of the past against landlords and businessmen. Within two months of its inception in 1946, the militant Japan Farmers' Union (*Nihon Nōmin Ku-*

[39] *Ibid.*, p. 132.
[40] *Ibid.*, pp. 132–37.
[41] *Ibid.*, p. 149
[42] *Ibid.*, p. 176.

miai, or *Nichinō*) claimed over 2,000 branches and more than 250,000 members. By the end of 1948 its membership had reached 2.5 million.[43]

Politically independent agricultural cooperatives—much less strongly tied to state purposes than the traditional nōkai they succeeded—also began to proliferate rapidly, following passage of the Agricultural Cooperatives Law of 1947. From 892 at the end of March 1948, the number of cooperatives exploded to 27,819 by the end of the year.[44] U.S. occupation authorities were adamant that these cooperatives (*nōkyō*) organize and run themselves without government intervention,[45] strengthening the pluralist, democratic orientation of the countryside. But in the absence of strong public financial support, the cooperatives remained economically vulnerable, compounding uncertainty and flux in the Japanese countryside. Seventy percent of the new nōkyō were operating at a deficit during 1949, despite their monopoly on rice collections.[46]

Erosion in the traditional conservative power structure of the countryside during 1945–1948 had major political consequences. In the first postwar election of April 1946, the JSP did very well in the countryside, obtaining over 20 percent of the vote in several mainly agricultural constituencies, such as Tochigi, Gunma, Yamanashi, Shiga, Kagawa, and Shimane, in an essentially four-way electoral race.[47] During the mid-1930s Yamanashi had had the highest number of tenancy disputes in Japan per acre of tenanted land; in 1946 it gave 31.5 percent of its vote to the Socialists, a proportion exceeded only in the prewar proletarian strong-

[43] Masumi Junnosuke, *Postwar Politics,* pp. 256–57.

[44] Ministry of Agriculture (Nōrin Shō), *Nōchi Kaikaku Tenmatsu Gaiyō* (A General Survey of Land Reform), cited in Arisawa Hiromi and Inaba Shūzō, eds., *Shiryō Sengo Ni Jyū Nen Shi: Keizai,* p. 129.

[45] See GHQ's Sixteen Principles of Agricultural Organization, December 21, 1948, especially Point 8. This point stressed that the cooperatives were to be regulated by law and that no government administrative regulations should apply to their internal functioning.

[46] As late as June 1950, 215 cooperatives were even unable to return the invested savings of their members. On the travails of the cooperatives during 1949–1950, see Tanaka Toyotoshi, *Ikite iru Nōkyō Shi* (A Living History of the Agricultural Cooperatives), pp. 48–63.

[47] Cole, Totten, and Uyehara, *Socialist Parties in Postwar Japan,* p. 380. The other major parties were the Liberal Party (*Jiyūtō*), Progressive Party (*Shinpotō*), and Cooperative Party (*Kyōdōto*).

holds of Tokyo and Fukuoka. Five of the seven chief leaders of the Japan Farmers Union were elected to the Diet, including Nomizo Masaru and Kuroda Hisao of Nichinō's left wing.

In the April 1947 general elections, the first held under the middle-size multimember district electoral system, Socialists succeeded in the countryside once again. The JSP's share of the rural vote again reached 20 percent in a multiparty race, with the JSP obtaining a plurality of Diet seats in thirteen predominantly rural prefectures.[48] This success was crucial to the JSP's emergence as Japan's largest political party, and to the ascent of JSP leader Katayama Tetsu to the prime ministership. Indeed, of the 143 Socialists elected to the Lower House in 1947, thirty-one were officers of Nichinō and eight more of one of its schismatic offspring.[49] A full fifty percent of the JSP Dietmen came from Japan's sixty-nine most rural constituencies. Conversely, the conservatives did much more poorly in the countryside than many had anticipated.

The 1949 election brought a sharp rural swing away from the Socialists, driven by farmers' disillusionment with food requisitioning by the Katayama administration, which was preoccupied with food shortages in the cities. Although the election established the preeminence of Yoshida Shigeru's Liberals nationally, a sharp radicalization in some parts of the countryside also elected nine Communists.[50] This was the best JCP rural showing in Japan's electoral history before or since, against the backdrop of peasant revolution sweeping the Chinese mainland only a few hundred miles away.

Despite Yoshida's overwhelming electoral victory in January 1949, many Japanese conservatives—and U.S. occupation officials—were openly apprehensive about both the stability of conservative rule, and the rural base upon which it seemed ever

[48] Among the rural prefectures with a JSP plurality were Gunma, Niigata, and Kagawa, the homes of conservative prime ministers-to-be Nakasone, Fukuda, Tanaka, and Ōhira. The Liberal Party (*Jiyūtō*), with a plurality in seventeen rural prefectures, did slightly better in the countryside than the Socialists, but only by a small margin. See Soma Masao, ed., *Kokusei Senkyo to Seitō Seiji* (*National Elections and Party Politics*), pp. 16–17.

[49] *Ibid.*, p. 381.

[50] Communists were elected in rural areas of Niigata, Shimane, Tottori, Ishikawa, Yamaguchi, Ibaragi, Nagano, Yamanashi, and Shizuoka prefectures. See *ibid.*, pp. 430–542.

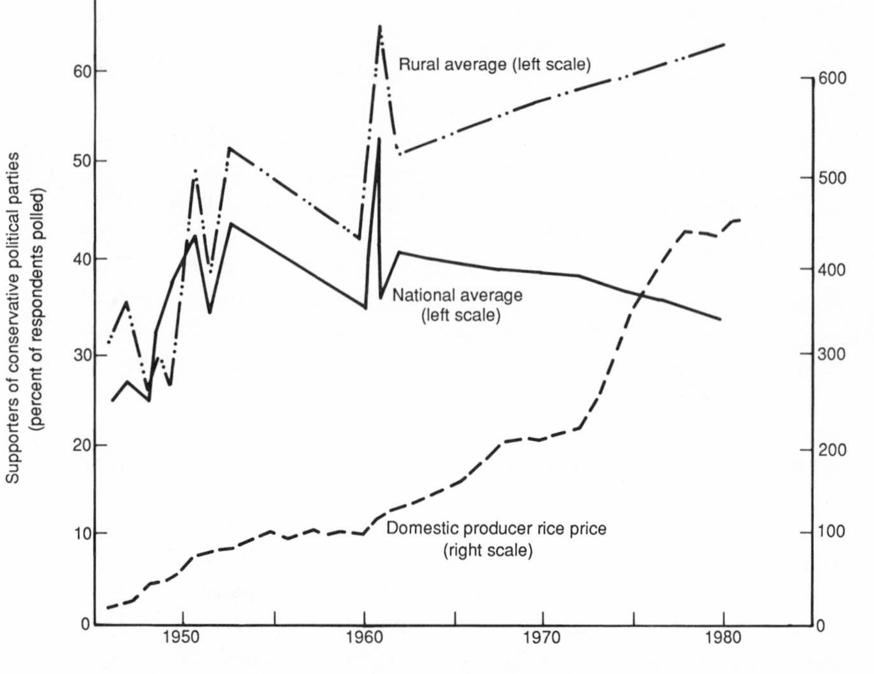

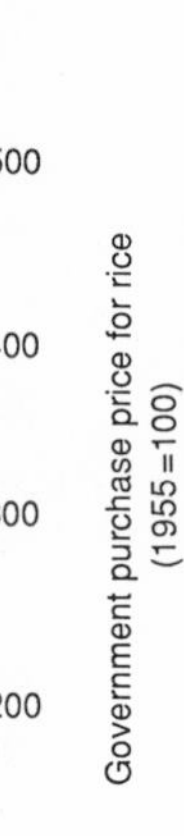

Figure 5.6. The Making of a Stable Conservative Rural Political Base, 1945–1980. *Source*: Jiji Ṯsushin national polling data and Tōyō Keizai Shinpō Sha, *Shōwa Kokusei Sōran*, vol. 1, p. 134.

more decisively to rest.[51] National opinion polls taken during October 1949 showed backing for Yoshida's Liberals among farmers and fishermen running over 10 percent behind Liberal support levels nationally.[52] As Figure 5.6 indicates, the conservatives did not begin to gain a support base in the Japanese countryside de-

[51] Recently declassified U.S. government intelligence reports from the spring of 1949, for example, stressed rural expectations of agricultural depression together with the tenuous character of conservative political organization in the countryside. See, for example, Restricted Enclosure to Dispatch No. 360 of June 6, 1949, from the United States Political Advisor for Japan, Tokyo, to the Secretary of State, on "Local Political Party Organization," pp. 1–2; together with formerly classified U.S. government agricultural surveys.

[52] National support for the Liberals, known briefly as the Democratic Liberals during this period, was 37 percent, and support among farmers and fishermen was only 25 percent. Data drawn from *Asahi Shimbun* poll, October 1–2, 1949, presented in Allan B. Cole and Nakanishi Naomichi, eds., *Japanese Opinion Polls with Socio-Political Significance*, 1947–1957, Vol. 1, p. 56.

cisively stronger than their support level nationally until well after the Security Treaty crisis of 1960. Neither the prewar Japanese tradition of rural conflict nor contemporary developments on the Asian mainland offered much assurance in 1949 regarding the stability of such rural support as Yoshida's Liberals maintained in the January 1949 election; nor did the social structure of the Japanese village, in seeming flux under the dual impact of land reform and the dissolution of the traditional, elite-dominated nōkai.

It is important to emphasize that the situation in the early postwar Japanese countryside, despite the major transformations underway, was not moving inexorably toward radicalism. Miki Takeo assessed the situation succinctly in a discussion with State Department political representatives in Tokyo: "As long as the small Japanese farmer retains the ownership of his land and a viable income from it, his political conservatism appears likely to withstand the great variety of 'propaganda' appeals which have been, and will be, addressed to the farming population by the Left."[53] But rural allegiance to the conservatives, as the story of this volume begins in 1949, was still *contingent* and *uncertain*, rather than assured. The social and institutional pillars that had buttressed it—indeed, virtually mandated it—since Meiji had been shaken by occupation reforms. Nearly ten parties, including several with a primarily agrarian emphasis, competed for rural votes.[54] At the same time, the commitment of the Japanese state to comprehensive support for agriculture, which received only 1.5 percent of the 1948 general account budget drafted by the Katayama cabinet,[55] was as yet unclear. Postwar interdependence among state, agricultural society, and the conservative political

[53] Remarks of Miki Takeo to U.S. reporting officer Charles N. Spinks, First Secretary of Mission, U.S. POLAD Tokyo to DOS, October 30, 1951. Whatever Cold War rhetoric may have been imposed in translation, the essence of the statement reflected realities of the early postreform period. The problem, however, was that although farmers after 1948 generally had land and periodic profits from agricultural sales to the famished cities, high and stable income levels, or a business framework to maintain them, were not yet well-established.

[54] In addition to the major national parties, such as the Democratic Liberal Party, the Japan Socialist Party, and the Japan Communist Party, there were also specialized agriculturally oriented parties, such as the Laborers' and Farmers' Party (*Rōdōsha Nōmin Tō*, or *Rōnō* Tō for short) on the Left and the New Farmers' Party (*Nōmin Shin Tō*) on the Right.

[55] Ministry of Finance Financial History Office (Ōkurashō Zaisei Shi Shitsu), ed. *Shōwa Zaisei Shi* (The Financial History of Shōwa), Vol. 19, pp. 168–69.

world still remained to be forged, through the crisis and compensation dynamic.

Emerging Policy Support for Agriculture

Postwar Japanese conservative politicians are distinctive in the intensity with which they have pursued distributive politics as a means of sustaining their political preeminence. Strong support for agriculture was the first element of this distributive orientation to develop after World War II, and the basic programs of support for agriculture developed during two relatively short periods—1949–1953 and 1960–1964, in addition to the great land reform of 1946–1949. These programs emerged largely under the auspices of prime ministers Yoshida Shigeru and Ikeda Hayato. Major regional programs with importance for agriculture also emerged during the early 1970s, particularly under the leadership of Tanaka Kakuei.

Although the third Yoshida cabinet (1949–1952) witnessed the birth of major agricultural programs with important distributive political implications, Yoshida himself was relatively unconcerned with the tactical details of generating and distributing political largesse.[56] Yoshida's lieutenants recognized the importance of policy innovation in agriculture as central elements of strategy against Hatoyama and stability in the political situation more generally on Yoshida's behalf. Chief among these Yoshida lieutenants was Hirokawa Kōzen, second Liberal Party secretary general after Ōno Bamboku and then Minister of Agriculture and Forestry in the Yoshida cabinet. Hirokawa, who began his career as a road construction worker, a postal deliveryman, and a labor organizer before entering conservative politics, had no background in agricultural administration,[57] but he acutely sensed the

[56] Dower, *Empire and Aftermath*, pp. 275–76.

[57] In 1926 Hirokawa organized an early labor union, the Tokyo Transportation Workers Association (*Tokyo Kōtsū Rōdō Kumiai*). Subsequently he organized strikes as president of the City Streetcar Factories League (*Shiden Kōjō Rengō Kai*), before aligning with the conservatives. Hirokawa's prewar labor ties helped give him one of the broadest personal networks in early postwar conservative politics, aiding his rise to Secretary General of the Liberal Party and then to the position of Yoshida's agriculture minister. For details on his early career, see Mainichi Shimbun Henshū Bu, ed., *Nihon Jinbutsu Jiten* (A Dictionary of Japanese Personalities), p. 302.

political potential of agricultural policies for stabilizing the Yoshida government.

Under Hirokawa's initiative, compensation for agriculture in the face of political crisis for the conservatives came in two forms—new policies strengthening the agricultural cooperative system and a sharp increase in subsidies for expanded rice production. The objective was clearly to recreate, insofar as possible, the structural dependency of farmers on the state which had prevailed during the prewar period, before being undermined by occupation reforms. These forms of compensation for agriculture were distinctive internationally in their reliance on private bodies to both fill public functions and operate in their own commercial interests with state support.

There was a major quantitative increase in support for Japanese agriculture during the 1949–1953 period of crisis for the conservatives. Agriculture's share in Japan's total general account budget nearly tripled from 3.2 percent in 1949 to 8.8 percent four years later.[58] As indicated in Figure 5.7, the producer rice price more than doubled sharply outstripping the increase of only 21 percent in the consumer price index[59] and the rate of increase in grain support prices in West Germany, as well.[60] This pattern of support for rice producers contrasted sharply with the bias of public policy in favor of the consumer during 1946–1948.[61] In addition, Japanese public works spending, most of it concentrated in rural areas, rose sharply from 8.4 percent of the budget in 1949 to 15 percent only one year later. Both the increase in producer rice prices and the expansion in public works spending established patterns in Japanese budgetary allocation, highly distinctive in comparative context and persistent for years thereafter.

It is difficult to avoid a deeply political explanation for these

[58] Ministry of Finance Financial History Office, ed., *Shōwa Zaisei Shi (A Financial History of Shōwa)*, Vol. 19, pp. 168–69.

[59] Kil Soong Hoom, "The Dodge Line," p. 164. This figure combines increases in base price and those in incentive payments.

[60] Japan rice prices rose 30 percent faster during 1949–1952 than did West Germany wheat prices, even though Japanese wheat prices rose less rapidly than did their German counterparts. See Katō Ichirō and Sakamoto Kusuhiko, eds., *Nihon Nōsei no Tenkai Katei* (The Development of Japanese Agricultural Administration), p. 41.

[61] The share of consumer price subsidies in the general account budget, for example, fell from 29.7 percent in 1949 to 10.3 percent in 1950 and to only 2.8 percent in 1953. See Ministry of Finance Financial History Office, ed., *Shōwa Zaisei Shi*, Vol. 19, pp. 168–69.

dramatic agricultural policy developments. The expenditure increases were clearly not a function of rapid economic growth since they began in 1949, a period of deep recession, more than a year before the favorable effects of the Korean War boom began to swell Japanese government coffers. Likewise, economic trends cannot explain why agriculture spending remained stagnant during the relatively prosperous mid- and late 1950s. Keynesian countercyclical policies are inadequate as explanation for agricultural spending because they cannot explain why spending increments went to the countryside rather than to cities where such stimulus could have been just as effective economically or more so. Similarly, purely economic interpretations cannot explain the shift in rice support policies during 1949 from a consumer to a producer orientation.

Some analysts view the surge of agricultural expenditures as simply representing pent-up demands from the countryside that had been artificially constrained by the Dodge Line retrenchment of 1949–1950. Clearly such political demands swelled Japanese budgets after the outbreak of the Korean War. This was especially true during 1950–1951, when international crisis provided the pretext for stability-oriented budget expansion and the recovery in public finances to allow it. But the pent-up demand theory cannot, once again, explain the substantial increases in compensation for agriculture—often *despite* opposition from SCAP economic advisor Joseph Dodge—before the Korean War began. The producer rice price, for example, rose almost 40 percent between 1949 and 1950 (Figure 5.7). Industrial wages rose only half as fast.[62] Establishment of the Rice Price Deliberation Council, dominated by officials sympathetic to producer price increases, on August 2, 1949, stimulated increases in the producer rice price, and public commitments of Finance Minister Ikeda enhanced the prospect of increases still further;[63] both developments were clearly political acts, which cannot be readily explained by contemporaneous economic developments.

The crisis and compensation argument, in contrast to other interpretations, provides a parsimonious explanation of agricul-

[62] *Ibid.*, p. 164. As Hoom points out, opposition from Dodge appears to have been finessed through such devices as statistical juggling of parity figures.

[63] On June 26, 1949, for example, Ikeda unveiled a Rice Price Plan proposing major increases in the producer rice price, in the face of the fiscal restraint proposed by Joseph Dodge just three months previously. See *Asahi Shimbun*, June 27, 1949.

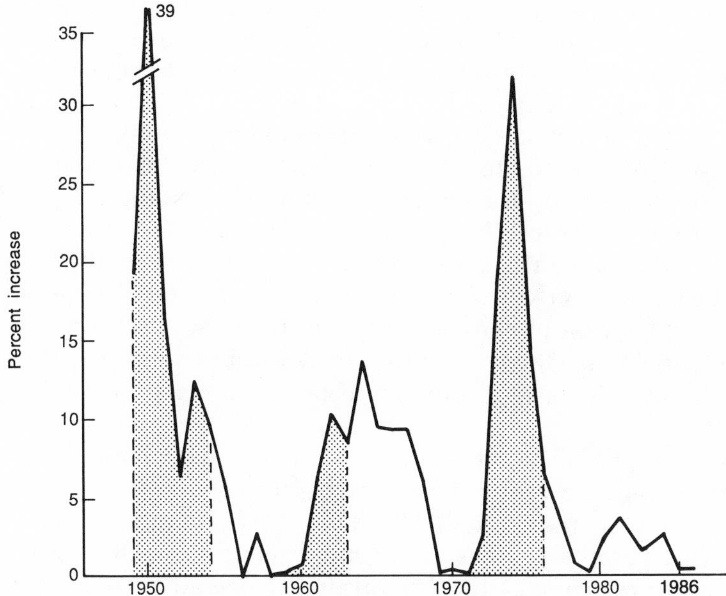

Figure 5.7. Japan's Producer Rice Price: Rates of Increase, 1949–1986.

Notes: (1) Figures are for government purchase price, average of top four classes, ¥ per 60-kg units. Incentive payments not included. (2) Shaded areas included within dotted lines are periods of domestic political crisis.

Sources: Ministry of Agriculture Forestry and Fisheries Statistical Information Division (Nōrin Suisan Shō Tōkei Jōhō Bu), *Nōrin Suisan Tōkei*, 1986 ed. (Tokyo: Nōrin Tōkei Kyoku, 1986), p. 181; IBRD, and Bank of Japan, *100 Year Statistics of the Japanese Economy*, p. 90.

tural policy developments both before and after the outbreak of the Korean War, together with those of later periods. The Yoshida government, with Hirokawa Kōzen as the major strategist, was intent on stabilizing its position both within conservative ranks and vis-à-vis the Left, by creating a stable, supportive constituency in the countryside. This countryside still remained pluralistic and politically volatile by prewar standards, in the wake of land reform and nōkai dissolution. But it had substantially more potential for organization along conservative lines than did the cities, with their more amorphous social structure.

The conservative preoccupation with stability, heightened and reinforced still further following the outbreak of the Korean War, profoundly shaped the contours of agricultural policy. It continued to drive policy innovation and subsidy growth until relative stability in both intraparty and interparty politics was achieved. Economic growth, to be sure, magnified the resources to be allocated. But largely politics, through the crisis and compensation dynamic, dictated both the distribution of those resources and the pace of policy innovation which would ultimately occur.

Corporatist agricultural associations, as noted above, were a central feature of the Japanese countryside from the 1880s through World War II. As the occupation fervor for reform abated, the conservatives naturally wanted to revive a stable, rural support base. But in the wake of land reform, universal suffrage, and the proliferation of parties catering to the common rural voter, they could not rely solely on the hierarchical ties and sentiments of the past; they had to cater more clearly to mass economic interest.

To strengthen the cooperative system and make it an effective and enthusiastic vehicle for reestablishing conservative political supremacy in the countryside, the Yoshida administration offered cooperatives extensive tax and regulatory benefits through six major revisions of the Agricultural Cooperatives Law of November 1947, passed originally under the Socialist Katayama cabinet. These revisions fundamentally altered nōkyō's economic and political functions.[64] In May 1949, for example, agricultural cooperatives were permitted to combine buying and selling functions, while in April 1951 farmers were allowed to reinvest dividends from commercial operations in the cooperative without having them taxed. In August 1950 the cooperatives took over from a government corporation the immensely lucrative sales of fertilizer to farmers; for nearly forty years since then, fertilizer sales have been a mainstay of nōkyō profitability. The same year the cooperatives also moved into the sale of agricultural feed, chemicals, and tools, as controls on private distribution in those sectors were lifted.

The Yoshida government combined compensation of the countryside with attempts at tighter control. One tactic for asserting control was centralizing the nōkyō administrative structure. In this way the conservatives who dominated nōkyō nationwide could pressure local chapters in such traditionally radical areas as Niigata, Yamanashi, and Nagano, where the prewar tradition of peasant opposition to conservative landlords was still strong.

[64] For fuller details on these revisions, see Tanaka Toyotoshi, *Ikite iru Nōkyō Shi*, pp. 37–40.

The central tool for reestablishing stability was structured compensation—recreating the subsidy system for indirect support to agriculture via loans and subsidies administered by the agricultural cooperatives and local authorities. But due to the changing structure of politics in both Tokyo and the countryside, combined with Japan's accelerating economic growth, compensation for the postwar countryside was to become far more substantial, and far more sensitive in content to grassroots demands, than had been generally true before World War II.

Since the third Yoshida cabinet of 1949–1952, subsidies have been the characteristic administrative mode of support to agriculture in Japan, in contrast to government loans, the major means of support to small business. A large share of these agricultural subsidies have been used for reclamation projects, improvements of arable land, development of better seeds, prevention of insects and diseases, and means other than price supports for increasing agricultural production.[65] The framework was established under the Land Improvement Law of 1949, while the machinery for structured compensation through subsidies to the agricultural cooperatives was formalized in April 1951 through the Law for the Reconstruction of Agricultural Finances (*Nōrin Gyogyō Kumiai Saiken Seibi Hō*). Agricultural cooperatives presented financial reconstruction plans to the Ministry of Finance, which granted incentive payments (*shōreikin*) in return. SCAP, continuing its formal preference for independent cooperatives, insisted that shōreikin in principle be returned so as not to make the cooperatives overly dependent on the state. But provision was made for exceptions in "special cases," which almost all applicants ultimately were granted by MOF.[66] In the shadow of political crisis, stability clearly superseded pluralism as the central goal of Japanese agricultural policy.

During the early 1950s demand for agricultural commodities, including rice, still substantially exceeded supply in Japan, forcing the government to control prices and engage in periodic forced rice collections in the countryside. These were enormously unpopular; many analysts viewed them as a major source of the sharply increased rural Communist vote in 1949. Since urban unrest in the wake of the Dodge Line made rice price increases through the removal of price controls difficult, the Yo-

[65] See Donnelly, "Political Management," pp. 406–7.

[66] *Ibid.*, pp. 66–67.

shida government used subsidies to allay rural disaffection, increase rural food production, and avoid the necessity of forced collections.

In 1951 the Diet passed the Special Measures Law for Cold and Snowy Rice Producing Areas, commonly known as the *Sekikan Hō*, providing subsidies to farmers from cooler areas who accelerated their rice production. In 1952 the Diet, driven by opposition pressure and deep rivalries in conservative ranks, passed parallel laws subsidizing rice production in both hot and swampy areas.[67] The three laws in concert provided subsidies for rice production in any part of Japan, thus negating the discriminatory effect of the original subsidy legislation. But while these laws had little strategic effect in encouraging rice production in any specific part of Japan as opposed to another, they were a major step in the redirection of Japanese government resources toward agriculture generally.

Subsidies were used as the vehicle for achieving these policy results because they forced dependence by recipients on central authority in Tokyo and strengthened the intermediate organizations—agricultural cooperatives and conservative local governments—through which those subsidies were administered. During the 1949–1953 period, subsidies more than tripled to ¥55.6 billion.[68] This major reason for the tripling of agriculture's share in the general account budget helped cause the share of subsidies in that budget as a whole to increase sharply from 20.6 percent of the total in 1950 to 28.1 percent in 1953.[69] This is roughly the level in both the Ministry of Agriculture and the overall national budgets where the subsidies have remained for over the past three decades.[70] Thus, both the structure of subsidy administration and the relative scale of agricultural subsidies in the Japanese budgetary constellation were established during the crucial third, fourth, and fifth Yoshida cabinets (1949–54), in response to the dual political challenge of Hatoyama and the Left, as well as to the economic opportunities created by the Korean War boom.

With the agricultural subsidy system established and with in-

[67] For details, see Hirose Michisada, *Hojokin to Seiken Tō*, pp. 105–7.

[68] Imamura Naraomi, *Hojokin to Nōgyō Nōson*, p. 76.

[69] Hirose Michisada, *Hojokin to Seiken Tō*, p. 79.

[70] In 1984 subsidies (*hojokin* plus *itakuhi*) represented 29.3 percent of the national Japanese budget. See Ministry of Finance Budget Bureau Research Section (Ōkurashō Shukei Kyoku, Chōsa Ka). *Zaisei Tōkei*, 1985 ed. (Financial Statistics, 1985 ed.), pp. 36–37.

creasingly viable and politically conservative agricultural cooperatives to implement it, the agricultural budget from the early 1950s on became an increasingly important political tool. The Yoshida administration used it to the hilt, with Agriculture Minister Hirokawa Kōzen strategically distributing subsidies and public works to head off both Socialist and right-wing conservative challenge.[71] Agriculture's share of the national general account budget soared in 1953 to the highest level in modern Japanese history.[72]

Throughout the 1950s, agriculture's budget share was quite volatile, responding flexibly to the political challenges of the moment through the crisis and compensation dynamic.[73] As political crisis waned, especially following Yoshida's resignation in late 1954 and the conservative merger (*hoshū gōdō*) of October 1955, pressures for retrenchment against the redistributive policies of the Yoshida cabinet grew. Kōno Ichirō, as agriculture minister in the Hatoyama cabinet, pressed for "low-cost agriculture" (*yasuagari nōgyō*), supported by the business world. For example, in the fiscal 1954–56 budgets, MOF cut subsidies for foodstuff production increases three years in succession after several years of steady increase.[74]

In 1955, as a significant differential in global and domestic rice prices began to emerge, both MOF and the big-business community proposed major increases in food imports.[75] The United States, with substantial unwanted food surpluses, also pressed Japan to expand imports of American wheat, barley, and rice. On May 27, 1955, the two nations concluded an agricultural trade agreement, after five months of negotiations, which included $15

[71] In mid-1950, for example, Hirokawa candidly announced that he would make the October 1950 Diet an "Enrich Farmers Diet" (*Kōnō Kokkai*), and he proceeded to do just that. See Kil Soong Hoom, "Dodge Line," p. 191.

[72] See Ministry of Finance Financial History Office (Ōkurashō Zaisei Shi Shitsu), ed., *Shōwa Zaisei Shi* (A Financial History of Shōwa), Vol. 19, pp. 168–73.

[73] These volatile budgetary shares of the 1950s contrast strongly to the more stable patterns after the mid-1960s, suggesting a possible need to qualify generalizations about "fair shares" and "budget balance" developed during the late 1970s by John Campbell. See John Campbell, *Contemporary Japanese Budget Politics*.

[74] Ministry of Finance Budget Bureau Research Section (Ōkurashō Shukei Kyoku Chōsa Ka), ed., *Zaisei Tōkei* (Financial Statistics) 1985, pp. 188–89.

[75] Masumi Junnosuke, *Gendai Seiji* (Modern Politics), Vol. 2, p. 461.

million in American rice within an overall package of $85 million in Japanese imports of U.S. surplus food.[76]

In 1956 and 1958 the Japanese government actually reduced the domestic producer rice price for the last times until 1987 and contemplated expanded rice imports from the United States, a proposal that subsequently remained dormant for many years. These proposals, emerging as conservatives became increasingly secure in their preeminence following the great political merger of 1955, stimulated agricultural interest groups to organize and prepare for the next phase of the crisis and compensation cycle.

Rural dissatisfaction was fueled by emerging tendencies in the economy. During the latter half of the 1950s, both Japanese economic growth and industrial wages began to accelerate sharply, leaving returns to agriculture far behind in their wake, despite the new support programs of the early 1950s. During the 1955–1960 period, for example, manufacturing wages rose 16.9 percent annually, while agricultural incomes rose only one-quarter as fast. Underlying this deterioration in relative agriculture income was a decline in the ratio of net product per worker. Agriculture had declined by 1960 to only 22 percent of levels in manufacturing, despite new technological prospects for agricultural mechanization which were beginning to emerge.

As rural discontent spread across Japan during the late 1950s due to the growing gap between soaring industrial wages and stagnant agricultural earnings, analysts and politicians began searching for solutions. Among the earliest and most persuasive models to appear was that of West Germany, another defeated, high-growth nation, undergoing rapid structural transformation, with whom the Japanese of the 1950s had substantial contact and for whom they had considerable respect. In 1955, when the Ministry of Finance and the big business community in Japan were both pressing for budgetary cutbacks in agriculture and an expansion of imports, West Germany enacted a Basic Agricultural Law that established the dual policy goals of agricultural modernization and productivity improvement, on the one hand, and the right of farmers to equal incomes with industrial workers on the other. This German law attracted considerable attention in Japan. Japanese agricultural interest groups began agitating

[76] *Asahi Shimbun*, May 28, 1955. Provisions included Japanese imports of $35 million in U.S. cotton, $22.5 million in wheat, $15 million in rice, $5 million in tobacco and $3.5 million in barley, together with $4 million freight charges.

strongly for a Basic Agricultural Law parallel to that of West Germany which would both declare urban-rural equality a basic goal of public policy and mandate some concrete policies for achieving it.[77] Japanese Diet delegations, as well as bureaucrats, travelled frequently to Bonn to study the German law in operation. But neither this nor other major agricultural policy changes came until Japan was again clearly rocked by political crisis.

The second period of major postwar policy change in agriculture came after the Security Treaty crisis of 1960, as both the conservatives and the Left engaged in searching assessment of their failures during the crisis period and zealously sought to outbid each other for the support of potential swing constituencies. The Socialists were much more zealous in appealing for regional and especially agricultural support than they had been in the past decade because the events of mid-1960 had shown them that the countryside was a strategic center of conservative power. This period was also, as noted in chapter 2, one of considerable turbulence within the ruling LDP, with major faction leader Kōno Ichirō threatening to leave the party and the new Prime Minister Ikeda Hayato confronting a delicate relationship with the two brothers Kishi Nobusuke and Satō Eisaku.[78] Although they headed separate factions, with subtly divergent political interests, these two had a common interest in preventing Ikeda from maintaining a stable hand on power. Throughout the conservative political world other figures, such as Miki Takeo, also vied to expand political influence by proposing policy measures divergent from those discredited in the past.

Shortly after assuming the prime ministership in the wake of the Security Treaty crisis, Ikeda Hayato announced a plan to double the incomes of Japanese by 1970. The Japan Socialist party promptly demanded that Ikeda also commit himself explicitly to doubling agricultural incomes by the same date; in early September, 1960 he unveiled a basic agricultural law proposal to achieve this end.[79] Within the LDP itself Kishi faction leaders Fukuda Takeo, chairman of the Policy Affairs Research Council, and Akagi Munenori, minister of agriculture, both with subtly diver-

[77] Masumi Junnosuke, *Gendai Seiji*, p. 462.

[78] Kishi Nobusuke and Satō Eisaku were the second and third sons respectively of Satō Hidesuke of Yamaguchi Prefecture. The former took the name Kishi when he was adopted into his uncle's family so as to continue the line of that family, which did not have a son.

[79] *Asahi Shimbun*, September 5, 1960.

gent political interests from Ikeda, also lent strong momentum to pressures for policy change. As in the case of the agricultural subsidy system of the early 1950s, agricultural policy innovation in the early 1960s thus had its roots in a perceived dual political threat to established political leadership from both the Left and within conservative ranks.

Bureaucracy, as so often true in the history of Japanese policy-making, tried to slow down the process of policy innovation and limit its budgetary implications. But in June 1961 the Basic Agricultural Law was passed. This law established the principle that government should "enable those engaged in agriculture to maintain a standard of living comparable to those engaged in other industries so that all Japanese citizens would enjoy the fruits of economic growth" and provided the broad framework within which Japanese agricultural policy has operated for the past generation.[80] While not a plan, the Basic Agricultural Law mandated that future agricultural policy goals should include:

(1) Selective expansion of agricultural production, raising productivity and increasing gross agricultural output in a manner reducing disparities in productivity between agriculture and other economic sectors.

(2) Stabilization of commodity prices, with the objective, again, of reducing intersectoral income disparities.

(3) Improvement of agriculture by enlarging farm size and creating independent farmers.

(4) Farmer education programs and measures to encourage members of farm households to seek employment in other industries.

(5) Promotion of farm welfare by improving living conditions in rural areas.

The central operational means for realizing the equality goals of the Basic Agricultural Law were assistance in agricultural mechanization and an increase in the rice price. In the wake of the law's passage, rice price deliberation procedures were changed to give LDP agricultural Dietmen (*Viet Cong Giin* as they came to be known in the mid-1960s) a more central role. All this led to a rapid escalation of rice prices, beginning in 1961, and to a related increase in government spending on agriculture.

[80] See *Nōgyō Kihon Hō* (Basic Agricultural Law), promulgated June 12, 1961, article I.

As I demonstrate in Figures 5.1 and 5.7, the post–Security Treaty crisis period was the starting point for a sharp increase in Japanese domestic producer rice prices set by the government, which ran strongly counter to both global trends and domestic patterns within Japan over the previous half decade. Between 1960 and 1964 alone, the Japanese producer rice price rose over 43 percent. This development, compounded by another sharp surge during the crisis years of 1972–1975, provided the basis for the massive stockpiles, rice account deficits, and expensive diversification programs dominating Japanese agricultural policies for more than twenty years since.

Enactment of the Basic Agricultural Law also led to substantial broadening of agricultural support policies beyond rice and introduced other nonrice related measures designed to bolster agricultural income. Before the enactment of the law, the agricultural price support policy had covered only rice, wheat, silk cocoons, raw silk, feedstuffs, and potatoes for industrial use. After the enactment of the law, however, the scope of the price policy was expanded to cover livestock products, vegetables, fruit, soybeans, rapeseed, sugar beets, and sugar cane. Support policies were ostensibly extended to new sectors to encourage structural transformation toward higher value-added sectors. The nominal objective was to increase agricultural income through improved efficiency in the use of Japan's scarce land resources. But political intervention often transformed agricultural policies into a welfare support system without major efficiency gains because they focused heavily on price support mechanisms as a policy tool and could not easily encourage consolidation of landholdings that would enable large, efficient increases in scale of production. By 1982, roughly 80 percent of Japanese agricultural production was covered by price supports, yet the rate of productivity increase was minimal.[81] The dividends were in the political rather than in the economic sphere.

Until the early 1960s, Japanese levels of support for agriculture were roughly paralleled or exceeded in many other major industrialized nations. Agricultural support levels in Japan during 1955 were actually substantially below those in major Western European nations, despite the extensive system of subsidies established during the late 1940s (table 5.5). Yet by 1965, only a few

[81] Kōnosu Kenji. *What will be the Agricultural Policies of Japan in the 1980s?* Tokyo: Japan FAO Association, 1982, p. 61.

TABLE 5.5

The 1955–1965 Decade: Japan Moves to the Top in Levels of Support for Agriculture (in percentages)

Country	1955	1965
Belgium	34.4	28.9
France	21.6	29.2
West Germany	27.4	36.8
Italy	35.3	37.9
Netherlands	12.9	18.3
United Kingdom	33.7	18.3
Japan	8.9	38.6

Source: Data prepared by the Japan Economic Planning Agency in Hemmi Kenzō, *Nōgyō* (Agriculture) (Tokyo: Chikuma Shobō, 1970), pp. 90–91.

Note: Agricultural support ratios are calculated by subtracting the value of agricultural production in international prices from the value of agricultural production in domestic prices and dividing the remainder by the value of agricultural production in domestic prices.

months after Ikeda Hayato left office as prime minister, Japan had the highest quantitative levels of support for agriculture in the industrialized world. Political crisis and resultant policy innovation, facilitated but not mandated by the process of economic growth, were directing Japan onto a path of agricultural policy which was distinctive in the industrialized world, and which contrasted particularly sharply with the laissez-faire approaches steadily gaining favor with conservatives in Britain and America.

It seems clear that policy support for agriculture, symbolized by the producer rice price but by far transcending it, intensified during and shortly after the political turmoil of the early 1960s. This was not followed by total retrenchment in the mid- and late 1960s, despite the waning of political crisis. Some retrenchment did, of course, occur. Between 1964 and 1971 virtually no new major agricultural policies were introduced other than the regressive compensation of landlords dispossessed by the Allied occupation. Rates of increase in Japanese agricultural commodity prices did not accelerate, but support prices did continue to rise at high levels through 1965 and at moderate levels for the balance of the 1960s.

Two factors explain this pattern. First, grassroots electoral pressures, sharpened by intense farm sector lobbying, put continual upward pressure on agricultural support levels, making retrenchment politically painful. Second, rapid Japanese economic growth, averaging 12.3 percent annually in real terms from 1960 to 1970, generated rapidly increasing government revenues and sharply reduced the fiscal need for retrenchment.

Farmers thus became some of the principal beneficiaries of double-digit growth in Japan: through rapidly rising agricultural producer support prices, drawn from ever fatter government coffers; through rising part–time employment outside agriculture, much of it facilitated by the state; and through sharp increases in the value of the land which they held. Government, in short, both compensated farmers directly from the proceeds of growth and helped them benefit from the prorural biases which public policy created in Japan's industrial and land use structure. Following a final sharp surge in farm prices during 1972–1975, farmers had incomes per household nearly 40 percent greater than nonfarmers and had moved even more decisively ahead of city dwellers in asset holdings, due to the value of their land.

These very real changes, it is important to reemphasize, were largely the result of policy innovation undertaken in short periods of rapid policy change, generally in the wake of political crisis. They were the dividends of economic growth, to be sure, but dividends not solely the product of economic forces. They flowed from a policy framework forged in the turbulent, insecure days of crisis and policy compensation from the late 1940s through the early 1960s. Other nations with different histories have distributed growth dividends rather differently, due in substantial measure to different but still politically determined institutional frameworks. Preeminently the policy innovations of 1949–1953 and 1961–1963 rendered Japanese agricultural policy distinctive in comparative context, even though the quantitative effects of those innovations were intensified by the emergence of growth dividends once the framework was in place.

The early 1970s also put their mark on both the institutional framework and the quantitative bias of Japanese agricultural policy. In 1970, for example, nōkyō gained the right to buy and sell land, which both enhanced their economic standing and helped fuel rising real estate speculation. In 1971 the Act for the Promotion of Industrialization in Farm Areas helped set in motion a process of rapid rural industrialization that has sharply transformed the Japanese countryside over the past two decades. In 1973 the Nōrin Chūkin Bank, repository of agricultural funds, gained the right to lend to individuals and engage in foreign exchange transactions. In 1974, creation of the Regional Promotion Facilities Corporation (*Chiiki Shinkō Seibi Kōdan*), together with new tax incentives, accelerated the relocation of Japanese high-technology industry into rural areas. During 1972–1975 producer rice prices also increased sharply, as noted earlier, continuing even after economic growth had abruptly slowed.

In Western Europe sharp cutbacks in support for agriculture followed the oil shock of 1973, but Japanese conservatives did not follow. In 1974, the government-determined producers' rice price rose by 30 percent—the sharpest increase of the postwar period. In contrast to several European nations, Japan did not cut support prices for food grains, such as rice, until the late 1980s.

But as the political turbulence of the early 1970s began to pass and economic growth began to wane, support price increases sharply decelerated, and agricultural prices gradually declined in real terms. Since 1976 the producers' real rice price has fallen every year; during 1984–1986 it failed to rise in nominal terms,[82] and in 1987 it was cut by 5.95 percent. The share of agriculture in the general account of the national budget has declined steadily since around 1974, to nearly the level at which it began its precipitous rise in 1949, under the impact of deep political crisis.

Retrenchment in support for agriculture, of course, comes at a time of large-scale budgetary deficits. But national deficits by themselves cannot provide a sufficient explanation for the changing policy patterns that have prevailed. Agricultural cutbacks, while beginning to slowly occur, did not proceed too rapidly during the period in the late 1970s when the financial pressures on the national government, as measured in terms either of deficit national savings ratios or of financial market absorptive capabilities, were most severe. They have begun to proceed with more force, particularly when agricultural public works are taken into consideration, since the mid-1980s, as the Japanese administrative reform campaign gained momentum and the scale of the Japanese deficit relative to national savings began to decline.

Some might ask how the strong momentum of agricultural

[82] *Yomiuri Shimbun*, July 12, 1985.

spending could be slowed during the late 1970s, while the agricultural cooperatives still had over six million members and before a secure conservative majority had been established in the Diet through the LDP double election victory of 1980. The most fundamental reason was that interactive crisis of the sort experienced in the early 1950s, early 1960s, and early 1970s, had passed. The opposition was still numerically strong, but it was divided, with the major inroads in LDP strength after 1976 coming from middle-of-the-road parties (Kōmeitō, the Democratic Socialist party and the New Liberal Club) who had little strength in the countryside. Within the LDP itself, concentration of power was also proceeding.

Retrenchment in agricultural spending, to be sure, was politically difficult for the LDP during this period, despite the waning of crisis. The persistent grassroots pressures outlined in chapter 1 assured that this would be so. But LDP politicians, less disturbed by opposition maneuvers than in earlier periods due to the LDP's rising relative strength, were able to engage in elaborate and often sophisticated political gamesmanship. They were able to balkanize agricultural pressure groups, as Agriculture Minister Watanabe Michio did in 1978 by making distinctions among five gradations of rice quality. Watanabe's effort effectively divided the rice lobby and allowed local politicians to direct farmers toward the issue of relative rank in the grading system and away from the magnitude of rice price increases per se.[83] Other politicians raised the issue of rice imports, which was becoming increasingly worrisome to rice farmers in Japan as Japanese domestic and world prices diverged. LDP politicians could thus direct attention once more from the rice price issue to other related questions of fundamental concern to farmers.

A final factor facilitating cutbacks in conventional agricultural support programs has been the increasing diversity of economic interests in the countryside, about which I will say more in chapter 6. Between 1975 and 1980, for example, farming income as a share of total farm household income fell from 25 to 19 percent (figure 5.4). Property income (41 percent) and nonfarm income (31 percent), largely wages from local government and industrial employment) significantly overshadowed farm income in the latter

[83] Kenzō Hemmi, "Agriculture and Politics in Japan," in *U.S.–Japan Agricultural Trade Relations*, eds. Emery N. Castle and Kenzō Hemmi, Washington, D.C.: Resources for the Future, 1982, pp. 241–42.

years.[84] By 1986 farming income as a proportion of total farm household income had fallen even further, to 14.5 percent.[85] The share of rice income in total agricultural income was similarly falling, from 38 percent in 1975 to only 30 percent of the total in 1980, although it recovered to 34 percent in 1984.[86]

Retrenchment in agricultural support programs has come, slowly but surely. Meanwhile the producers' rice price has slowly but steadily fallen in real terms; in 1987 it fell even in nominal terms, after three years at a constant level. Cutbacks have been made in rural public works. Even rice imports emerged as a serious policy question, following Keidanren's 1985 declaration of support for agricultural import liberalization, and the sharp 50 percent yen revaluation which followed shortly thereafter.[87] As political crisis wanes for Japan's conservatives, and as the political economy of the countryside diversifies, the old politics of compensation in agriculture seem to have given way to new market-oriented patterns more recognizable to American Sunbelt conservatives. At last Japan's Liberal Democrats seem to be moving slowly, in agricultural policy, at least, from welfare-oriented politics akin to the New Deal and neo-Jeffersonianism toward a pattern Ronald Reagan and Margaret Thatcher would find more congenial.

But through the support policies of the past four decades, designed to reincorporate agriculture securely back into conservative ranks following the political fluidity of the early postwar period, Japanese public policy has transformed the countryside in indelible ways. These linger even as agriculture itself begins to decline in scale and in the ability to command large subsidies, particularly when crisis wanes. Most importantly, Japanese agricultural policy, together with its correlates in the public works and regional policy domains, has created a social class, politically potent in its own right and having diverse stakes in both agricul-

[84] Bank of Japan Research and Statistics Department (Nihon Ginkō Chōsa Tōkei Kyoku), *Keizai Tōkei Nenpō* (Economic Statistics Annual), 1985 ed., pp. 337–38.

[85] *Asahi Shimbun*, August 21, 1987.

[86] *Ibid.*

[87] In early 1987 the Keidanren position was that imports of rice for use as an industrial raw material should be allowed, while "flexible responses are called for" regarding rice for home consumption. Keidanren also suggested that imports would be acceptable in the event of domestic shortages. See Mizukami Tatsuzō, "Proposals on the Rice Problem," *Keidanren Review*, No. 103, February 1987, pp. 2–6.

tural support programs and industrial development,[88] although it is not clear this was either the bureaucracy's or the political world's original intent.[89] The consequences of the emergence of this new class with multiple economic roles are profound—for agricultural policy, for industrial policy, and for the relationship of both to Japanese politics and international trade. The stake of the countryside in agricultural protection grows less intense, despite continuing breadth, and its stake in a stable world trading regime rises. The cost position of such Japanese export industries as integrated circuits and video cassette recorders, with their high concentration of rural production, is also given a flexibility, due to both the multiple income sources of their work force and direct support programs for rural industry, that allows these industries to sustain sharp international competition and exchange rate fluctuations much better than is often appreciated. Recent changes in the political economy of the Japanese countryside, set in motion years ago by the crisis and compensation dynamic, thus simultaneously reduce the utility of yen revaluation as a tool for rectifying Japanese trade surpluses and also broaden the prospective costs of foreign protectionism across increasingly industrial rural Japan.

[88] For a graphic, yet highly analytical description of this transformation at the grassroots level, see Dore, *Shinohata,* especially pp. 92–98. For a parallel ethnographic study of a fishing village turned industrial suburb, described in 1950–1951 and again in 1975, see Edward Norbeck, *Country to City: The Urbanization of a Japanese Hamlet.*

[89] Agricultural modernization (*nōgyō kindaika*), with the implication of mechanization of agriculture and the release of workers to urban industry, is the phrase used continually in the agricultural policy planning documents of the early 1960s.

6

Regional Policy: Periodic Power to the Periphery

> While the big cities suffer from the pains and irritations of overcrowding, rural areas suffer from the exodus of youth and the resultant loss of vital energy for growth. . . . Rapid urbanization has bred increasing numbers of people who have never known the joys of rural life, chasing rabbits in mountains, fishing for crucians in streams, whose only home is a tiny apartment in some huge city. With such a situation, how can we pass on to future generations the qualities and traditions of the Japanese people?
>
> TANAKA KAKUEI (1972)

TO THE ISOLATED villages of western Honshū, summer has always meant typhoon season. Unpredictably, but with unvarying seasonal logic, savage winds sweep in from the southern seas, dropping torrential rains that destroy, maim, and kill. In the aftermath, local people have traditionally banded together to pick up the pieces—alone.

Typhoons of late have not been quite what they used to be. To be sure, the natural fury of wind and sea continues unabated. But villagers no longer clean up alone. In 1983 Shimane Prefecture was hit by a typhoon and subsequent flooding that killed 103 people. Within hours, hundreds of Self-Defense Force servicemen and scores of medics, together with three cabinet ministers and the administrative leadership of every related ministry, were descending on the Shimane capital of Matsue, population 130,000 and mainly noted for its picturesque temples and nineteenth-century hospitality to Japanese-art enthusiasts Lafcadio Hearn and Ernest Fennellosa. In time, national-government compensation for typhoon damage mounted to over ¥20 billion (roughly $93 million). This equalled the entire Shimane prefectural budget for three weeks and represented more than $117,000 for every man, woman, and child in the entire prefecture.[1]

[1] In 1982 the entire Shimane Prefecture had only 790,000 inhabitants, making

It is not just government ministers and disaster relief funds that flow to Shimane from Tokyo. Shimane in 1984 was only 36th among Japan's forty-seven prefectures in terms of per capita income, with an average of ¥1,700,000 per person.[2] But it was number one in new public works construction contracts, bringing an additional ¥248,920 per person, or nearly 15 percent of prefectural income, from the national government that year.[3] Despite its poverty and relative isolation, Shimane had more museums and art galleries per capita than all but one other prefecture and more town auditoriums than all but five. It also ranked thirteenth among Japan's prefectures in number of public libraries per person.[4] Yet in national tax payments Shimane ranked forty-third per capita, even lower than its ranking in individual income.[5]

Reinforcing the power of Shimane in the policy process was its strong leverage in the conservative political world. The prefecture in the late 1980s numbered three of the most powerful members of the LDP among its five Lower House Diet representatives. All had headed major ministries and agencies,[6] while one, longstanding Finance Minister Takeshita Noboru,[7] was installed in

---

it 46th in population among Japan's 47 prefectures. Local government expenditures in 1983 were ¥322 billion, or roughly $1.5 million (at ¥215/$1.00). See Asahi Shimbun Sha, *Shin Kenbetsu Character* (New Character, by Prefecture), p. 112; and Asahi Shimbun Sha, *'84 Minryoku* (1984 Peoples' Power), pp. 100–1. See also Asahi Shimbun Sha *Asahi Nenkan 1984* (Asahi Almanac 1984), p. 224.

[2] Asahi Shimbun Sha, *'87 Minryoku*, p. 178. Figures are for the Japanese fiscal year (April through March).

[3] In fiscal 1981, for the first time, Shimane Prefecture passed Niigata Prefecture, the home of former Prime Minister Tanaka Kakuei, in value of public works construction contracts per capita. Niigata, of course, was number two. See Ibid., pp. 129 and 188. By 1984 Shimane contracts were 57 percent greater, per capita, than those for Niigata, which had fallen to fourth nationally, while Shimane remained number one.

[4] Asahi Shimbun Sha, *Shin Kenbetsu Character*, p. 113.

[5] Asahi Shimbun Sha, *'87 Minryoku*, p. 128.

[6] Sakurauchi Yoshio served as foreign minister, agriculture minister, construction minister, and secretary general of the LDP before becoming senior foreign policy advisor to Prime Minister Nakasone Yasuhiro. Hosoda Kichizō served as head of the National Defense Agency and the Administrative Management Agency, as well as chairman of the LDP Finance and Diet Management committees.

[7] Before becoming Prime Minister Takeshita served as Secretary General of the LDP (1986–87) and as Finance Minister from 1981 to 1986 in the second Suzuki and first two Nakasone cabinets. Prior to that Takeshita had been Construction Minister, chairman of the Lower House Budget Committee, and chief cabinet secretary.

November 1987 as the first Prime Minister of Japan from Shimane Prefecture since Wakatsuki Reijirō in the 1920s.[8]

Other parts of the Japanese periphery have exerted clear and dramatic power in relation to Tokyo. The clearest benefits, perhaps, have flowed to the often snowbound expanses of Niigata's Third District, near the Sea of Japan, which Tanaka Kakuei first came to represent in 1947. Symbolic of Tanaka's ability to exercise power on behalf of his own particular portion of the Japanese periphery has been the Shioya tunnel, completed in December 1983 to serve about sixty households in Tanaka's constituency at a cost of ¥1.2 billion (roughly $100,000 per household).[9] Thanks to this mountain tunnel, the children of the Shioya area were able for the first time to sleep at home during the harsh winter and commute by bus through four-foot snows rather than live in dormitories away from their families. The political power of Tanaka also brought the high-speed Jōetsu Shinkansen (bullet train), an International University, and a mechatronics-oriented technopolis to Nagaoka, a town of 180,000 at the heart of Tanaka's district. Industrial incentives attracted automakers, such as Honda, Nissan and Suzuki, who in the late 1980s produced around 40 percent of the world's speedometers in the environs of Nagaoka as well.[10]

The island of Kyūshū presents an analogous pattern to Shimane and Niigata, but with a different political dynamic. Since Texas Instruments first set up shop in Ōita Prefecture in 1968, over 190 electronics companies have established themselves in Kyūshū, giving it the title of "Silicon Island." In 1984 Kyūshū alone produced 2.8 billion chips worth $2.7 billion; that is 40 percent of Japan's entire semiconductor output and around 10 percent of the entire world's.[11] Although much about the establishment of a major global electronics complex in predominantly rural Kyūshū was market driven, the efforts of local officials such as Ōita Governor Hiramatsu Morihiko, a former director of

[8] Wakatsuki was a former Finance Ministry official who served as both finance minister and home minister before becoming prime minister during 1926–1927. He is perhaps best known for his key role in the passage of universal manhood suffrage and the Peace Preservation Law during 1925, together with his subsequent opposition to militarism and war with the United States in 1941.

[9] For details, see Fukuoka Masayuki, "Naze Tsuyoi Kakuei Seiji" ("Why Kakuei's Politics is Strong"), *Chūō Kōron*, January 1983, pp. 112–22.

[10] Sheridan Tatsuno, *The Technopolis Strategy*, p. 147.

[11] *Ibid.*, p. 176.

MITI's Electronics Policy Section, and the support of regional policies encouraging relocation of industry to the countryside also played a substantial role.

This chapter examines both the complex policies postwar conservative Japan has deployed in support of peripheral areas and the political processes engendering such support. Broad spatial distribution, it is argued, has been an unusually important element of public policy in Japan, supplementing explicitly agricultural policies and helping to distribute not only public works but also major industrial complexes, research facilities, and even high-technology sectors, such as semiconductors and telecommunications equipment, broadly across the country. As Japan's farm sector has declined in importance, public policy has helped the countryside become industrial, with major, simultaneous implications for both LDP political preeminence and Japanese international competitiveness. This support for the periphery has emerged, it is argued, in response to three factors: (1) early post–World War II changes in state structure, (2) steady grassroots pressure on Tokyo, and (3) the national-level crisis and compensation dynamic. Each period of political crisis biased public policies more strongly toward the periphery, although this bias often became less pronounced as crisis waned.

The Periphery and Public Policy: Japan in Comparative Perspective

To be sure, several major European nations have more impressive arsenals of formal tools for aiding depressed regions than does Japan. France, Italy, and Ireland, for example, all have designated state agencies whose expressed functions are restricted to regional assistance. In 1963 Charles De Gaulle established DATAR in France to prepare and implement an elaborate system of aid and restrictions aimed at promoting the decentralization of industrial and service sector activities throughout the country. DATAR has long been attached directly to the prime minister's office, from which it coordinates regional development programs both with the national plan and with the activities of other agencies.[12] Since 1950 Italy has had the Cassa per il Mezzogiorno, a

[12] Organization for Economic Cooperation and Development. *Regional Problems and Policies in OECD Countries,* Vol. 1, p. 25.

special fund financed from the national budget and accorded the status of an autonomous public agency, to promote regional development in the impoverished south.[13] Ireland has had an Industrial Development Authority, also since 1950, which has likewise aggressively sought to attract industry to depressed areas.[14]

Japan, in contrast to these three nations, has no formal state agency which broadly coordinates regional development policies. To be sure, it has several public agencies—such as the Tōhoku and Hokkaidō Development Corporation and the Okinawa Development Corporation—charged with special assistance to certain especially depressed or underdeveloped parts of the country. But these agencies do not have the overarching authority to coordinate regional development in general, powers DATAR and the Cassa formally possess. The Regional Promotion Facilities Corporation (*Chiiki Shinkō Seibi Kōdan*) promotes investment in outlying regions, especially former coal-producing areas, but it has no authority to comprehensively develop and implement regional policies, as several of its European counterparts do.

Major European national governments also have comprehensive planning frameworks for assisting local development; these appear more elaborate technically than those of Japan. Since 1954 all of France has been divided into regional action areas and subsequently into twenty-two program regions. Plans for all of these regions are coordinated with the national plan, under the direction of DATAR.[15] Italy has originated the system of *contrattazione programmata*—planned, corporatist-style agreements among government, management, and labor to undertake specific development projects.[16] And the Irish central government since 1963 has required local authorities to draft and implement specific plans for their areas.[17] In contrast to these elaborate schemes, the Japanese planning process appears far less formal and technical.

European governments also frequently have a much broader range of coercive tools at their disposal to aid regional development than does Japan. France, Britain, and Italy, for example, all impose mandatory licensing of business expansion in their capital cities, forcing firms to decentralize their operations toward

[13] *Ibid.*, p. 43.
[14] *Ibid.*, p. 62.
[15] *Ibid.*, pp. 24–25.
[16] *Ibid.*, pp. 45–46.
[17] *Ibid.*, p. 62.

regional centers.[18] In Japan there is a statutory requirement for firms to consult with government about plant location, but firms are not obliged to follow the locational recommendations made by government. Similarly, the Japanese state, unlike Italy, assigns no mandatory quotas to public agencies regarding the shares of their total investments that must be made in specific regions.[19]

Even more striking, given the Japanese reputation for compensation politics, are the differences between capital and labor subsidy patterns in Europe and those in Japan. Cross-national comparisons of this kind are extremely difficult, methodologically speaking, and can only be made in the roughest fashion. But it appears that the major European nations offer significantly larger capital and labor subsidies to new investments in depressed regions than does Japan. Throughout the 1970s, for example, capital subsidies to investment in the depressed regions of Britain funded around 15 to 20 percent of capital costs, while labor subsidies met around 5 to 7 percent of labor costs.[20] In contrast, Japan provided capital subsidies in the range of only 10 to 15 percent of capital costs and supplied only minimal labor subsidies for depressed regions. Unemployment benefits were sharply lower in Western Europe than in Japan, although Japan did have unusual programs for providing financial help during job retraining, as well as special bonuses to those who returned to work quickly.[21] Furthermore, most labor-related adjustment assistance provided in Japan, such as that for job retraining, was provided to corporations rather than to individuals.

Despite the relatively broad range of formal policy tools in their arsenals and the elaborate bureaucratic structures created to foster regional development, the major European nations have not been highly successful in their attempts to promote regional development. In neither France nor Italy, for example, was there a major reduction in the substantial interregional income gaps of these nations during the 1950s, 1960s, and 1970s.[22] In neither country did private-sector capital expenditure conform closely with area redevelopment plans.[23] Public bodies other than the re-

[18] *Ibid.*, p. 50.
[19] *Ibid.*, pp. 49–50.
[20] A. J. Brown and E. M. Burrows, *Regional Economic Problems*, p. 197.
[21] Vogel, *Comeback*, pp. 111–13.
[22] See OECD, *Regional Problems*, p. 36.
[23] *Ibid.*, p. 26.

gional development agencies themselves also proved lukewarm about relocating activities toward depressed regions. Despite the discriminatory taxes and restrictions on paper intended to force relocation to the national periphery, service industries continued to concentrate in the major metropolitan centers, even though some success was achieved before the oil shock of 1973 with the decentralization of manufacturing.

Although Japan does not have the elaborate bureaucratic apparatus for regional development promotion of several Western European nations, it appears to have been generally somewhat more successful than these nations in directing state resources toward the grassroots. It has also been relatively successful at spurring strong economic development in the national periphery. Regional income differentials between Tokyo and the poorer prefectures of Japan narrowed steadily through the oil shock of 1973 and have remained relatively stable since then. Private investment has also been moving much more aggressively into peripheral regions within Japan than into analogous parts of Western Europe. Investment in less developed regions of Japan has been spurred by heavy public expenditures for infrastructure, sharply overshadowing analogous tendencies in Europe.[24]

Japan's public works spending as a proportion of national budget expenditures in the mid-1980s was 60 percent higher than levels in France and more than double levels in all the other major industrialized nations.[25] Even more impressive in demonstrating the power of the periphery in Japan was the pattern of public works distribution. While Tokyo paid 29.6 percent of the national taxes collected throughout Japan during 1981, only 8.0 percent of the total national public works construction occurred there. The prefectures representing Japan's five largest urban centers together paid 57.6 percent of the nation's taxes, but they re-

[24] Despite cutbacks during the early 1980s, government fixed capital formation in Japan, directed disproportionately to Japan's periphery, was 5.0 percent of gross national expenditures, compared to 3.1 percent in France, 2.5 percent in West Germany, 1.9 percent in Britain, and 1.5 percent in the United States. Japanese government expenditures in this area were also roughly double the share of GNP that they were in Italy. See Ōkurashō Shukei Kyoku Chōsa Ka, ed. *Zaisei Tōkei*, 1986 ed., p. 13; and Noguchi Yukio, ed., *Zaisei* (Finance), p. 236.

[25] In 1984 Japanese government capital formation (predominantly public works) was 5 percent of GNP, compared with 1983 figures of 3.1 percent for France, 2.5 percent for West Germany, 1.9 percent for Britain, and 1.5 percent for the United States. See Ministry of Finance Budget Bureau Research Section (Ōkurashō Shukei Kyoku Chōsa Ka), ed., *Zaisei Tōkei*, 1986 ed., p. 13.

ceived less than half that proportion (24.8 percent) of the public works.[26] A disproportionate share of public works spending went to small, often poor, and agricultural prefectures like Shimane, which are far from Tokyo and contribute relatively little to national coffers.

As indicated in figure 6.1, all top eight recipients of public works per capita in 1981 lay on the periphery of Japan—four of the six on the stormy, long neglected Japan Sea coast.[27] Equally striking, three of these top eight public works recipients were also among the eight lowest contributors per capita to the nation's tax rolls. Shimane, which received 60 percent more roads, bridges, cultural halls, and so on than the national average, contributed only slightly over one-third of the tax revenue per capita. Put differently, Shimane received 52 percent more public works than Tokyo per capita, while contributing less than one eighth Tokyo's per capita share in taxes.

Also impressive was the flow of public works to Niigata Prefecture, home of former prime minister (1972–1974) and longtime national political power Tanaka Kakuei. During the early and mid-1980s, Niigata received three times as much in public works spending as it paid in taxes.[28] As of 1982, it had a direct, less than two-hour bullet train link to Tokyo, with three stops at small towns in Tanaka's relatively remote electoral district, including a huge station building and shopping arcade complex in Nagaoka, the major town of the district. In addition, two major superhighways, the Kanetsu and the Hokuriku, linked Niigata with other parts of Japan.[29] Finally, in December 1983, in that ultimate gesture of political power, a tunnel built for about sixty families in the isolated Shioya district of Tanaka's constituency

[26] These prefectures included those housing greater Tokyo, Yokohama, Nagoya, Ōsaka, and Kyoto. See Asahi Shimbun Sha, ed., *'84 Minryoku*, pp. 23–24.

[27] These four are Shimane (first, with 160 percent of the average public works, per capita per perfecture), Niigata (third with 154 percent), Tottori (fifth, with 139 percent), and Fukui (sixth, with 134 percent). See *ibid.*, pp. 26–27.

[28] See Asahi Shimbun Sha, ed., *'84 Minryoku*.

[29] For details on the government benefits garnered for Niigata Third District by Tanaka Kakuei and the political processes through which this was accomplished, see Chalmers Johnson, "Tanaka Kakuei, Structural Corruption and the Advent of Machine Politics in Japan," *The Journal of Japanese Studies*, Vol. 12, No. 1, Winter, 1986, pp. 1–28; Niigata Nippō Sha, ed., *Za Etsuzankai* (The Etsuzankai), especially pp. 54–103; and Asahi Shimbun Niigata Shikyoku, ed., *Tanaka Kakuei to Etsuzankai: Shinsō no Kōzu* (Tanaka Kakuei and the Etsuzankai: The Layout of the Depths).

Figure 6.1. Compensation for the Periphery: Top Public Works Recipients in Japan, by Prefecture, 1981

Source: Asahi Shimbun Sha, *Minryoku 1984 (People's Power 1984)* (Tokyo: Asahi Shimbun Sha, 1984).

was completed, at an approximate cost of twenty million yen per household.[30]

Among the most elaborate and costly forms of public works support for Japan's periphery has been the Japan National Railways (JNR) network. Aside from the efficient and profitable Shinkansen bullet train between Tokyo and Osaka, completed just prior to the Tokyo Olympics of 1964, the JNR also constructed a far-flung and elaborate network of local "deficit lines" (*akaji rosen*) that ran through a broad range of rural constituencies. This overextended network combined with high labor costs to generate a massive long-term JNR debt of ¥21.8 trillion (¥1.85 trillion for fiscal 1985 alone).[31] Together with rice price supports and national health insurance subsidies, the financial burden of this JNR debt was known in the mid-1980s as one of the "three K's" (*Kokutetsu, Kome, Kenkō Hoken*),[32] most clearly symbolizing LDP compensation politics. Even though the JNR was privatized effective April 1, 1987, and divided into seven independent regional firms, the importance of rail infrastructure to outlying regions, together with formal government commitments made during the privatization process that JNR employees would not be deprived of jobs,[33] made it unlikely that the Japanese state could disengage easily from past commitments to the periphery in the rail transport area, even in the absence of political crisis.

Like the major Western European nations, particularly France, Japan in the early 1960s began promoting the development of selected regional cities as industrial centers. But Japan did so even more vigorously, especially in the wake of the 1960 political crisis and the subsequent emphasis of the Left during 1961–1962 on strengthening its grassroots power. Just as France began promoting six regional cities as *Métropoles d'équilibre* to Paris, Japan in 1962 established fifteen New Industrial Cities as economic growth points to ultimately counterbalance the Tōkaidō area between Osaka and Tokyo in industrial capacity, population, and income.[34] As indicated in figure 6.2, several of these points were located well outside the traditional east-west axis of growth

[30] On the previous plight of the Shioya district and Tanaka's efforts to ameliorate it, see Fukuoka Masayuki, "Naze Tsuyoi Kakuei Seiji" ("Why Kakuei's Politics are Strong"), *Chūō Kōron*, January 1983, pp. 112–22.

[31] *Asahi Shimbun*, June 17, 1986, p. 3.

[32] In English the equivalent of "Kokutetsu, Kome and Kenkō Hoken" was "Japan National Railways, rice, and health insurance."

[33] *Asahi Shimbun*, December 12, 1986.

[34] For details on the New Industrial Cities Program, see Murata Kiyoji, *An Industrial Geography of Japan*, p. 182.

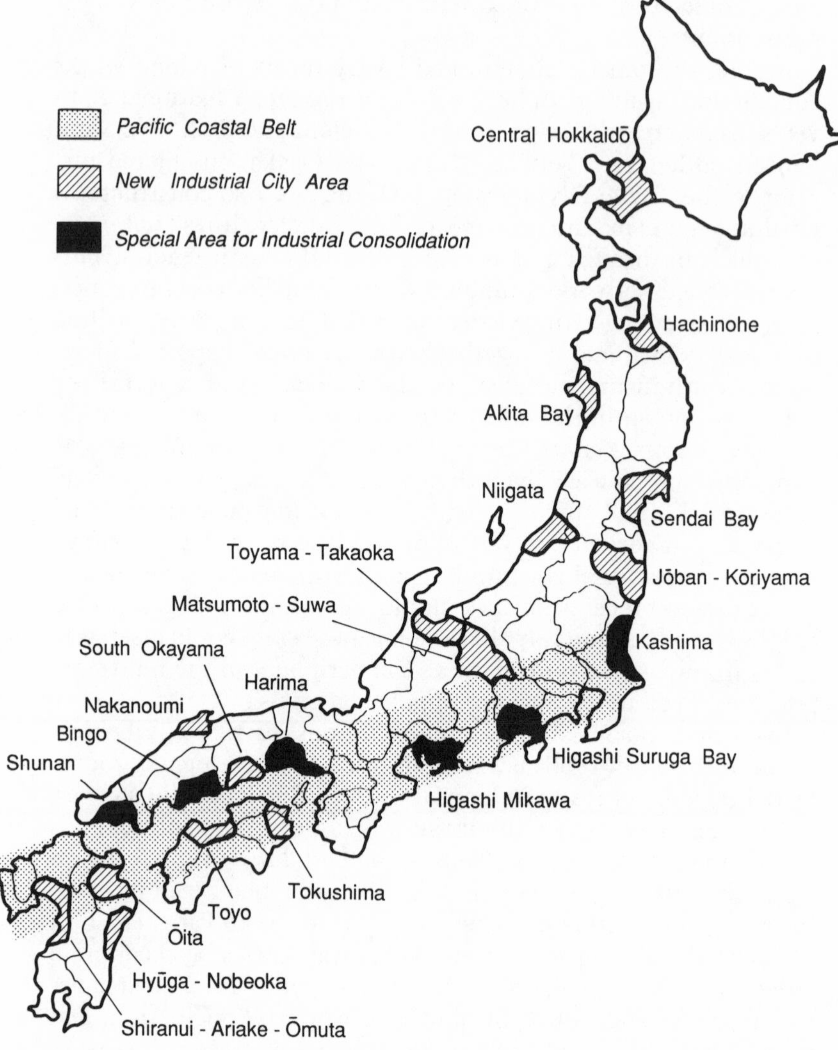

Figure 6.2. Japan's New Industrial Cities Program (1962)

along the Pacific coastal belt. However, under big business pressure, as the political turbulence of the early 1960s began to subside, the government in 1964 established six "special areas for industrial consolidation," thus compromising the regional bias of the original policy. These areas were relatively close to the traditional Tōkaidō industrial zones, indicating a temporary triumph of efficiency over equity in Japanese policymaking, in the ongoing cyclical battle between the two.

The Japanese regional programs of the 1960s, in short, appear to have been a patchwork of policies, directed sometimes toward efficiency and sometimes toward redistribution. Many of the new policies adopted, inspired by politicians, were explicitly redistribution-oriented in intent, although an efficiency-oriented cast often emerged in the implementation managed by the bureaucracy in coordination with big business. Implemented policies on the whole favored efficiency, but perhaps less decidedly so than in France. While the *Métropoles d'équilibre* are reported to have drawn resources and population from their own periphery,[35] retarding economic development in that periphery, Japanese policies attempted to minimize this tendency toward rural decline. They did so by developing local infrastructure *around* as well as in, regional centers. While striving to maximize international competitiveness, government administrators also had to keep a wary eye out for the welfare concerns of powerful grassroots interests.

The Regionalist Cast of Japanese Industrial and Scientific Policies

Much of the regionalist bias of Japanese public policies dates from the early 1950s crisis period, but that bias intensified significantly, through a ratchet effect, during the early 1960s and early 1970s, both in content and in effectiveness. During the early 1970s, particularly after the 1973 oil shock, Europe, preoccupied with the excruciating problem of winding down existing depressed industries, often lacked both the resources and the political will to simultaneously promote growth in previously underdeveloped regions. Despite a parallel, although less severe, growth slowdown, Japan became increasingly committed to the notion of "*Chihō no Jidai*" (the era of regions), as the political

[35] See Tarrow, *Between Center and Periphery*, pp. 87–88, 96–97.

strength of the conservatives in the major cities eroded and as the importance to continued LDP preeminence of smaller provincial cities with cohesive social structures and viable local economies became increasingly clear. Political crisis for the conservatives after 1971 intensified efforts to economically strengthen the traditionally conservative countryside and to limit opposition inroads there, just as it had during the early 1950s and early 1960s.

During the 1970s, Japan put a regionalist cast on its basic scientific and industrial policies to a degree unprecedented in the West. Between 1970 and 1972 three major new laws strongly increased incentives for firms to locate new manufacturing facilities in the countryside,[36] in the context of the then MITI Minister Tanaka Kakuei's Plan for the Remodelling of the Japanese Archipelago (*Nihon Rettō Kaizō Ron*).[37] A combination of economic pressures and interest group behavior elicited these changes against the backdrop of steadily rising progressive strength at the local government level, which seemed to ultimately threaten the national preeminence of the LDP. In 1974 a public corporation, the Regional Promotion Facilities Corporation (*Chiiki Shinkō Seibi Kōdan*) was at last set up to coordinate the dispersal of Japanese production facilities to new regional locations. Although similar in concept, it had more restricted planning functions than France's DATAR.

Since the early 1980s Japan has begun to develop new forms of assistance to peripheral regions largely unexplored in the West. It has been especially innovative in developing new policies which simultaneously promote high-technology industry and regional development. Three of the most fully developed Japanese policies in this regard are the technopolis, teletopia, and INS system projects, intended to disperse both research and manufacturing potential to Japan's periphery, while simultaneously linking that periphery to urban centers through sophisticated infrastructure.

The technopolis concept, first raised formally by MITI in March 1980 within the context of its Vision of the 1980s,[38] is a hybrid of two ideas: the concept of a center for the promotion of tech-

[36] These were the Under-Developed Area Development Act (1970), the Act for Promotion of Industrialization in Farm Areas (1971), and the Industrial Relocation Promotion Act (1972).

[37] This was outlined in Tanaka Kakuei, *Nihon Rettō Kaizō-Ron* (Remodeling the Japanese Archipelago).

[38] See Ministry of International Trade and Industry (Tsūsan Sangyō Shō), *Tsūshō Seisaku no Hachi Jyū Nendai Vision* (A Vision of Industrial Policy in the 1980s).

nology, and that of a community ("polis"). The proposal calls for establishing several decentralized research centers across Japan to combine three facets of the technopolis: production facilities for high-technology manufacturing, distribution centers, and other business facilities; universities and other public research and development institutions; and a housing zone for managers, teachers, engineers, scientists, and their families.[39]

MITI in 1980 originally announced a plan to build two or three technopolises. Yet forty of Japan's forty-seven prefectures immediately volunteered to host such high-technology towns. Under pressure from LDP politicians intent on generating distributive benefits for constituents, MITI in 1982 altered its initial efficiency-oriented plan and chose nineteen sites involving twenty prefectures (figure 6.3). Since 1983 construction on these new centers for the promotion of technology has been proceeding rapidly. Each specializes in a combination of sectors, ranging from mechatronics and new materials to biotechnology. And each reflects in principle the particular skills and industrial base of the region surrounding the technopolis.[40]

The Ministry of Post and Telecommunications (MPT), strongly competing with MITI for jurisdiction over Japan's expanding information processing industry, in 1984 introduced a parallel plan to establish throughout Japan a network of centers for international telecommunications and data processing, known as "teletopia." MPT proposed to link Nippon Telephone and Telegraph (NTT)'s information network system with ten model cities chosen from among forty-five candidate sites, with the system providing cable television, interactive video, and other services to both homes and offices. The teletopia centers, when completed, would serve as collecting and analysis points within their regions for digitalized information, transmitting it internationally through the communication facilities of the teletopia. As in the case of the technopolis project, local rivalries for designation have been strong, and politicians have been deeply involved in the designation process.

A third major Japanese project of the 1980s, which combines regional development and the promotion of high-technology industry in creative ways, is the so-called Information Network System (INS). The INS project coordinated by NTT is a huge com-

[39] For details of the concept and how it is being operationalized, see Ministry of International Trade and Industry, *Technopolises*.

[40] For details on the major technopolis projects, see Tatsuno, *Technopolis*, pp. 139–97.

Figure 6.3. Japan's Technopolis Program: Designated Cities (1982)

Technopolis terminology:

◦ Mother city: existing cities of 200,000 or more to provide city conveniences to the technopolis.

◦ Technopolis zone: area in which a technopolis will be built.

◦ Technopolis center: main plaza in which headquarters, conference halls, trade fair stadiums, and other civic buildings cluster.

◦ Complexes: separate districts in the technopolis zone to house similar types of buildings (e.g., an industrial complex accommodating factories, warehouses, and other business facilities).

Prefectures are given in parentheses; circles indicate the locations, not sizes, of the technopolis zones; squares indicate mother cities.

prehensive program of telecommunications infrastructure development. It also involves development of advanced data processing services and incentives to the diffusion of such services broadly across Japan. Inaugurated in 1982, the INS will provide a comprehensive digital communications network to all of Japan when completed around the year 2000, at an expected cost close to $100 billion.[41] INS will permit not only a wide range of personal computer services, like electronic shopping, but also such manufacturing functions as the control of unmanned factories in remote locations across Japan.

In early 1987 the Japanese conservative political world began an intensive drive to encourage American universities to set up branch campuses in Japan.[42] This drive involved free land, low-interest loans, student scholarships, and a range of other incentives to U.S. universities to establish operations in remote Japanese prefectures. It can be seen as yet another aspect of Japan's regionally oriented trade, industrial, and technology policies of the 1980s, shaped profoundly by the impact of politics on the Japanese policy process.

The Japanese regional policy of the 1980s, in short, has merged with communications, industrial, and science policies to produce a highly distinctive program of developing viable high-technology industries around the periphery of Japan. This program contrasts strongly both to the centralized *dirigisme* of France's *télématique,* on the one hand, and also to the more market-oriented American approach. Japan's alternative is oriented toward systematically broadening grassroots technical skills and participation in the coming information society, in ways that policies in most other major industrialized nations are not.[43]

The Periphery-Oriented Bias of Japanese Policy: Origins in Social and Political Structure

There is a strength of the periphery against the center in Japanese politics which dates far back into Japanese history, although that

[41] For details see, for example, Long Term Credit Bank of Japan, *Japan's High Technology Industries,* pp. 49–55.

[42] *New York Times,* February 19, 1987.

[43] On prospects for the development of a decentralized high technology research and production effort in Japan, see Chiiki Gijutsu Kenkyū Group, ed., *Chiiki Gijutsu no Jidai* (The Era of Regional Technology).

strength has waxed and waned with the periodic cycles of political crisis that have beset the Japanese state. As John Hall points out, "the problem of village control has always been a prominent concern of Japanese rulers, and the interaction between the large and the small communities in Japan has not been without its influences upon the lives of the elite."[44] The long period of Japanese feudalism, surviving closer to the present than in virtually any other industrialized nation, fostered the institution of the jōkamachi, or castle town. This, together with developments of the tumultuous early Meiji Period, spawned well-defined groups of local notables (meibōka) who continue to influence both local and national Japanese politics to the present day.

The Meiji Restoration imposed a strong, centralized, continental-European style national bureaucracy on a nation with lingering localist political loyalties.[45] The Meiji system of prefectural administration, for example, was (like Italy's) similar to that of Napoleonic France, with local governors appointed by the central government and firmly under its control.[46] From time to time the Home Ministry was sensitive to local demands, out of a general concern for political stability and smooth administration. The ministry undertook a few important reforms in the welfare policy area, such as the introduction of health insurance in 1922. After 1900 the political parties gradually became able to sporadically politicize the process of local administration, particularly with regard to public works,[47] but never in the systematic, large-scale fashion of the postwar period.

Broadly speaking, for nearly eighty years after the Meiji Restoration, a centralized, elitist, oligarchic, centralized system prevailed—a system in many ways strikingly parallel to antipopulist European systems of the period. Interest group pressures were inevitably mediated through this structure, which was consequently quite insensitive to pressures from below, especially the rural periphery.[48] Following the Rice Riots of 1918, the assassi-

[44] John Whitney Hall, *Government and Local Power in Japan*, pp. 10–11.

[45] For details of the prewar and wartime systems of local government, see Steiner, *Local Government in Japan*, pp. 19–63.

[46] Italy adopted the Napoleonic local government model upon unification in 1861, and Japan adopted a similarly centralized pattern after the Meiji Restoration in 1868. On Italy, see Allum, *Italy*, p. 8.

[47] See, for example, Tetsuo Najita, *Hara Kei in the Politics of Compromise, 1905–1915*.

[48] See, for example, Dower, ed., *Origins of the Modern Japanese State*, pp. 109–316.

nation of Hara Kei, and the intensification of agricultural tenant disputes during the early 1920s, a few modest reforms were introduced in support of workers and rural notables, such as health insurance (1922) and the establishment of the Nōrin Chūkin Agricultural Bank (1923).[49] But some of these reforms, particularly the relaxation of controls on rice imports after 1920, seriously harmed Japanese domestic agriculture and farming communities of the periphery.

Populist influences also seem to have had some impact on the political style of the military after 1931, leading to increased agrarian rhetoric.[50] But there was little opportunity under the rising demands of war which soon followed for any budding grassroots orientation to systematically translate itself into policy. Both pronounced distributive politics and the full-blown crisis and compensation policy dynamic had to await the post-1949 period, although some aspects were prefigured before that time. Charles Tilly has shown the important effects of war on the process of state formation, pointing, for example, to the powerful effect of the Napoleonic Wars in creating the strongly centralized French state.[51] The pressures of wartime mobilization in Japan during the 1930s and early 1940s clearly had a strong centralizing effect on state control over Japanese industrial development and its financial system.[52] Moreover, the Meiji Restoration and its aftermath had important centralizing effects on state structure, but its effects in destroying or subjugating preexisting local and regional elites was incomplete. And Japan never experienced the invasions or the catalyzing total warfare on the immediate national frontiers that had such powerful effects in centralizing domestic political structures in continental Europe. Japan remained, despite the trappings of political centralization, a nation with a far more vital and prospectively influential periphery than was generally the case in Europe.

The structural changes in center-periphery administrative re-

[49] On politics and policy innovation during the post–Rice Riot period see Masumi Junnosuke, *Nihon Seitō Shi Ron* (A Theory of Japanese Political Party History).

[50] See Richard J. Smethurst, *A Social Basis for Prewar Japanese Militarism.*

[51] Charles Tilly, ed. *The Formation of Nation States in Western Europe* (Princeton: Princeton University Press, 1975).

[52] See Johnson, *MITI and the Japanese Miracle,* pp. 116–56; Nakamura Takafusa, *Nihon no Keizai Tōsei* (Japan's Economic Controls); and Kent E. Calder, "Politics and the Market," ch. 1.

lations after 1945, allowing the relatively cohesive interests of the Japanese countryside more direct entrée to policymaking, are clearly a crucial point of departure for understanding the power of the periphery in the postwar period and the cyclical patterns of crisis and compensation through which support for it has waxed and waned since then. Most importantly, the Home Ministry, Naimushō, was abolished at the end of 1947, the primary victim of the U.S. occupation's democraticization campaign. It was succeeded by a Construction Ministry, a Labor Ministry, and a Local Autonomy Ministry,[53] together ultimately with a National Police Agency.[54] None of these entities ever recovered the awesome institutional autonomy from outside pressures the Naimushō had possessed; indeed, in their initial disorganization following the purge, the Naimushō's successors rapidly became the most politicized of ministries. As the party, factional, and kōenkai structure of the postwar period became more coherent, the groundwork was gradually laid for the emergence of politically strategic distributive politics in support of the periphery.

To understand Japanese regional policies in comparative context, particularly their relationship to grassroots pressures and the crisis–compensation dynamic, it is useful to contrast the sudden, major uncertainties and fluidity generated by Naimushō dissolution in Japan during 1947–1948 with contemporary developments in Western European nations with traditionally strong bureaucracies. In France, of course, there was no postwar interior ministry dissolution; similarly, there was little change in the social cohesion of the French administrative elite[55] and its ability to wield centralized influence versus the periphery. In West Germany, the Allies created the only federalist state among the major nations of Europe; this state allocated substantial powers to the Länder, including police powers, public administration, tax

[53] Some former functions of the Naimushō, such as the supervision of immigration formalities, also devolved upon the Justice Ministry after the end of the occupation in April 1952. See Jin Ikkō, *Jichi Kanryō* (Local Affairs Bureaucrats), p. 9.

[54] Following the dissolution of the Home Ministry, Japan underwent a radical decentralization of its police forces. Autonomous police agencies were established in all towns populated by 5,000 or more people. This decentralization was to some extent reversed by the Police Law of June 1954, which created the National Police Agency. But the ties between the police and other elements of the former Home Ministry were not, of course, resumed.

[55] On prewar–postwar continuities in the background of French administrative elites, see Suleiman, *Politics, Power, and the Bureaucracy in France*, pp. 44–63.

collection, federal law enforcement, and government fund allocation.

But to a greater degree than in Japan, German federalism was building on a viable, long-standing apparatus of autonomous local government with expertise in such matters as land use planning. In Japan such functions had traditionally been more centralized, leaving local administrators less prepared for change. Furthermore, the centralized Nazi state was destroyed simultaneously in both its political and administrative dimensions, amidst the turbulence of war which swirled across German soil in early 1945. In Japan, by contrast, a functioning conservative political party structure existed when the Naimushō was suddenly dismantled in 1947, giving the politicians more opportunity than those in Germany to influence successor ministries and thus transform administration into distributive politics.

Italy represents an important intermediate case between France and Germany that helps explain the unusual power of the periphery in Japanese policymaking, its distributive bias, and the relationship of both phenomena to Naimushō dissolution. In contrast to the German and Japanese cases, the Allied occupation did not even attempt to enforce thoroughgoing administrative decentralization; indeed, all Allied occupation forces had left Italy by January 1, 1946. The postwar purge, performed by the Italians themselves, was not extensive, and the Interior Ministry was not dismantled.[56] The Italians did introduce provisions into their postwar constitution providing for elected regional governments, but their only important jurisdictions were in the fields of public welfare and agriculture.[57] And the actual establishment of these governments was delayed until 1970 by the Christian Democrats out of fears that devolution of responsibilities to local government would increase communist influence.[58]

The traditional local government structure of Japan, like that of both Italy and France, had been adopted from the centralized Napoleonic model. But Japan's administrative structure, unlike that of Italy and France, underwent substantial decentralization at the hands of the Allied occupation. No specific regional gov-

[56] On contrasts in Allied roles in Italian and German postwar political development, see Krippendorf, *The Role of the United States in the Reconstruction of Italy and West Germany*; Wolfe, ed., *Americans as Proconsuls*.

[57] Mario Einaudi and François Goguel, *Christian Democracy in Italy and France*, pp. 47–48.

[58] Allum, *Italy*, p. 228.

ernment structure was prescribed in the postwar Japanese constitution, as had been true in Italy, but the old prefectural system was sharply transformed with the direct election of governors, which remained appointive in Italy, and with Naimushō dissolution, which also had no parallel in Italian experience. Japanese local government administrative structures, as they evolved after World War II, were ripe for grassroots political cooptation, provided that politicians had a systematic strategy and incentives for coopting them. As Muramatsu points out, prefectural governors, elected since the early postwar period, in sharp contrast to the continuing appointive status of the French prefect, have played a key role in both policy innovation, intensifying the regional cast of policy, and in garnering distributive resources for their prefectures. Their strength and activism are major contributions to the power of the periphery in postwar Japan.[59]

The conservative political predicament that fostered periphery-oriented, strongly distributive, and often economically inefficient regional policies in Japan was broadly similar to that which Tarrow argues is responsible for the populist orientation of Italian conservatism as it emerged since World War II.[60] In both cases, the conservatives were confronted simultaneously by a newly powerful urban working class movement and an uncertain rural base. As in early postwar Italy, the impulse of Japan's conservatives in the late 1940s, facing a newly liberated but highly vigorous labor movement, was to appeal to the periphery. Before the war the periphery had been a partial but by no means preeminent concern of public policy in Japan.

The differences in the nature of opposition challenge to conservative dominance in early postwar Italy and Japan were largely a matter of degree and timing. But these differences greatly affected the sort of regional policies that ultimately emerged in the two nations. In Italy, the challenge of the Left materialized earlier and somewhat more strongly than in Japan, before the administrative decentralization initially provided in the constitution could be accomplished. By 1947, the Italian Left had been expelled from the governing coalition, and Cold War battle lines were largely drawn. This early challenge encouraged the ruling Christian Democrats to retain centralized administrative struc-

[59] Muramatsu Michio, "Center-Local Political Relations in Japan," *Journal of Japanese Studies* 12 (Summer 1986): 303–27.

[60] See Sidney Tarrow, *Between Center and Periphery*, pp. 82–85.

tures dating from the Fascist period and to rely on administrative controls and a certain degree of centralized distributive allocation, especially patronage, to undercut the political inroads of the Left.

In Japan local government autonomy was much more clearly established by the time the conservatives became apprehensive about communist inroads in late 1948. With the exception of Kyoto, where Ninagawa Torazō won in April 1950 as the candidate of a socialist-communist coalition, and periodically of Fukuoka, Hokkaidō, and Hyōgo, the Left posed little challenge at the local government level in Japan. Even in the 1947 general elections, which produced the only Socialist-led cabinet at the national level in postwar Japan, only three of forty-six prefectures chose Socialist governors. Because of this early postwar weakness of the Left at the grassroots, the perenially conservative central government of Japan was more favorably disposed to local autonomy than was true in Italy. It was not until the late 1960s and early 1970s that progressive local governments became common in populous areas of Japan.[61] And by then local autonomy was so sufficiently institutionalized that it was difficult to restrain. The result of these contrasting dynamics was that local governments generally had greater autonomy in Japan than in Italy and played a greater role, especially during periods of crisis, as a stimulus to national policy innovation.

The grassroots orientation which Japan's high degree of local civic organization encouraged was intensified during 1947 by changes in the electoral system. As a compromise between conservative desires for a single-member district system and the desires of the Left for something approaching proportional representation, Japan restored the medium-size electoral district system which had prevailed between 1925 and 1945. This change forced conservative candidates increasingly to compete against one another for support, particularly in peripheral areas where conservatives were fairly popular and many ran for office. This rivalry within conservative ranks, and the ensuing grassroots leverage generated, was intensified after 1955 by the gradual strengthening of the faction system within the LDP.

[61] Before the election of Minobe Ryōkichi as Tokyo governor in 1967, Fukuoka and Hyōgo, together with Kyoto, were the only heavily urban prefectures that had experienced progressive local administration for an extended period. See Steven R. Reed, "The Changing Fortunes of Japan's Progressive Governors," *Asian Survey* 26 (April 1986): 456–57.

While the Italian conservatives also experienced factionalism, the Italian electoral system did not force factions into as intense a competition for grassroots support as was true in Japan. Furthermore, the early and rapid polarization of Italian politics brought on by the Cold War made the Italian Christian Democrats reluctant to support devolution of power to local government, since this could have required giving the communists control of some local jurisdictions.[62] As a consequence, the Italian conservatives pulled back from a commitment to regionalism and to strengthening the power of the periphery. However, this commitment proceeded somewhat further in Japan.

Aside from the bias of the Japanese electoral system, explored in more detail in chapter 1, six structural characteristics of Japanese politics have intensified the power of the periphery over the past thirty years. Perhaps most important has been the independent local government structure that has emerged since 1945. Immediately after World War II, the ability of local government to press demands against Tokyo was constrained by political culture and networks of human relations, as Steiner points out, as well as by financial constraints and lack of expertise.[63] Yet by the 1960s local governments were becoming much more sophisticated in both policy analysis and in lobbying with Tokyo,[64] and the rise of progressive local government in the late 1960s intensified the assertiveness of local governments more generally.

A second consideration strenghtening the power of the periphery is the high degree of local grassroots organization.[65] As Kyōgoku Junichi points out, chambers of commerce, junior chambers of commerce, local retailers' associations, and local small business federations are typically well-organized in the Japanese periphery, and often closely tied to local Dietmen through the kōenkai (support association) structure.[66] This strong organization allows grassroots communities to act aggressively when warranted on behalf of local interests.

[62] Einaudi and Goguel, *Christian Democracy*, pp. 47–49; and Peter Alexis Gourevitch, *Paris and the Provinces*, p. 186.

[63] See Steiner, *Local Government*, pp. 3–6, 263–99, and so on.

[64] See, for example, Ezra Vogel's account of the key role which Ōita Director of Planning Satō Taiichirō played in initiating and ultimately consummating plans for the Ōita Industrial Complex during the mid-1960s. Vogel, *Comeback*, pp. 116–17.

[65] For a striking Italian contrast to Japanese and American patterns of local organization, see Edward Banfield, *The Moral Basis of a Backward Society*.

[66] Kyōgoku Junichi, *Nihon no Seiji*, pp. 268–69.

Human networks connecting the periphery to the elite superstructure of Japanese national politics are a third structural factor intensifying the power of the periphery in Japan. All prefectures have local offices in Tokyo, and most have special meeting halls for dinners, receptions and other gatherings. Natives of local areas serving in prominent positions within the national government and business community meet periodically in groups known as *kenjin kai* (associations of people from particular prefectures of Japan) to renew contacts and occasionally mobilize support on some specific project for their home area.

Individual influence brokers, preeminently Tanaka Kakuei in the political world and Nagano Shigeo in the business world, have also been highly important in enhancing the influence of the periphery with Tokyo. For both these two and other less well-known brokers, mediating the interests of the periphery with Tokyo has been a powerful means of enhancing their influence within elite circles in Tokyo itself because it increased the ability of these brokers to deliver the support of grassroots groups on other questions.[67] For Tanaka, brokerage of grassroots interests was a key element in his successful drive for the prime ministership at the youngest age in modern Japanese history.

The political economy of land, seen so starkly in the brokerage activities of Tanaka Kakuei,[68] is a further factor that has enormously increased the salience of regionally oriented programs and public works projects in Japanese public policy. Land in the periphery of Japan is, of course, generally much cheaper than that in the core metropolitan areas, but its price can be powerfully affected by the proximity of roads and other amenities erected by the state. Through influence over the location of public works projects, therefore, Japanese politicians and bureaucrats can powerfully affect the price of land. Price differentials between totally undeveloped land and that with development potential due to the proximity of public works are particularly large in Japan, and the rates of increase in land prices have also traditionally been large. Accordingly, incentives to manipulate land prices through public works expenditures, and hence to expand the range of public works projects in remote areas, are especially strong in Japan. In-

[67] On the concept of conservative political brokerage, see Kent E. Calder, "Kanryō vs. Shomin: The Dynamics of Conservative Leadership in Postwar Japan," in *Political Leadership in Contemporary Japan*, ed. Terry E. MacDougall, pp. 1–31.

[68] For details, see Tachibana Takashi, *Tanaka Kakuei Kenkyū* (Research on Tanaka Kakuei), vol. 1.

deed, public works projects of this sort are often reportedly the source of substantial political rebates, which in turn become a major source of campaign finance.

Political overrepresentation of rural areas in the Japanese Diet has clearly reinforced the power of the periphery in Japan, although probably not as much as is often said. Estimates in the early 1980s suggested that the overrepresentation of rural districts at that time provided the ruling LDP with perhaps forty seats in the Lower House of the Diet it otherwise would not have. The system was also said to benefit the Japan Socialist Party, the largest element of the opposition, given its stronger bias toward rural, peripheral districts than the smaller opposition parties. Rural overrepresentation was significantly reduced prior to the 1986 general elections, however.

Horizontal communication and cooperation among local governments has long been neglected as a factor strengthening the periphery in its struggle with the center for political resources. But as Richard Samuels points out, such communication may have been quite important in strengthening the ability of local government to obtain desired benefits, especially in the 1970s and 1980s.[69] Horizontally organized pressure groups, such as the National Association of Governors (*Zenkoku Chiji Kai*) may be particularly important in increasing the policy role of the periphery.[70]

Postwar Politics and the Bias toward the Periphery

> The Income Doubling Plan . . . is a policy of abandoning poor villages.
>
> Sone Eki
> Democratic Socialist party representative

> We will take industry to the villages. . . . there is no need to leave.
>
> Prime Minister Ikeda Hayato
> in Diet interpellations (1960)

[69] See Samuels, *The Politics of Regional Policy in Japan.*

[70] On the national organization of local pressure groups, see Shiozawa Mutō and Murakawa Ichirō, *Chihō Roku Dantai no Soshiki to Katsudō* (The Organization and Activities of the Six Regional Associations).

DESPITE the clear importance of structural factors to understanding the power of the periphery in Japan, such factors even in their aggregate remain underpredictive. As evidenced in the epigraphs to this section, statements from the 1960 Diet, a strong undertone of bias toward the grassroots in Japanese policy on regional questions has been growing for more than four decades.[71] But this bias has been erratic in its development. It has waned as well as waxed. This oscillation is clear when one examines the Japanese public works budget, which goes mainly to Japan's periphery. As indicated in figure 6.4, the share of public works expenditures in the overall national budget soared after the conservative electoral victory of 1949 and remained high throughout the years of strong infighting within conservative ranks which preceeded the resignation of Prime Minister Yoshida Shigeru in late 1954. After a short surge and decline in 1956–1957, public works budget shares began rising again rapidly in 1959 as turmoil within conservative ranks again intensified. They remained high, moving in nuanced cycles, through the early 1970s.

To be sure, public works spending fell back, proportionate to the total budget, in 1973–1974, a period of major political crisis. But this change was only relative to other budgetary items, many of them also compensation-related, such as welfare. In absolute terms, public works budgets continued to grow sharply, despite the inflationary consequences.[72] Japanese national general account public works expenditures rose from ¥2.397 trillion in fiscal 1972 to ¥2.669 trillion in 1973 and ¥2.972 trillion in 1974, an increase of 24 percent in just two years. The share of government fixed capital formation (largely public works) in aggregate Japanese domestic expenditures rose from 5.5 percent in 1972 to 5.7 percent in 1973, before falling to an average of 5.2 percent for 1974–1976. Significantly, the comparable ratios in the United States, West Germany, Sweden, Holland, and Canada fell by much greater margins, while trends in Britain, France, and Italy

[71] See, for example, *Sangiin Kaigiroku Dai Yon Go* (Record of the Upper House Conference, Number 4), October 22, 1960, the source for the quote above.

[72] For further details, see Ministry of Finance Budget Bureau Research Section, (Ōkurashō Shukei Kyoku Chōsa Ka), ed. *Zaisei Tōkei*, 1986 ed., pp. 202–3; Economic Planning Agency Research Bureau (Keizai Kikaku Chō), Chōsa Kyoku, ed. *Kokumin Keizai Keisan Nenpō* (Accounting Yearbook of the National Peoples' Economy), 1982 edition; Organization for Economic Cooperation and Development, *National Accounts, 1971–1983, Detailed Tables*, Volume II. Paris: OECD, 1985; and Noguchi Yukio, ed. *Zaisei*, p. 236.

Figure 6.4. The Wax and Wane of Compensation Policies: Public Works Spending in Japan, 1949–1986.

Source: Ministry of Finance Budget Bureau Research Section (Okurashō Shukei Kyoku Chōsa Ka), ed., *Zaisei Tōkei (Financial Statistics)* (Tokyo: Ōkurashō Insatsu Kyoku), various issues.

were broadly comparable to Japan's, albeit from a much lower relative level of support for public works. Between 1981 and 1986, a period of noncrisis, the public works share dropped sharply to the lowest levels seen since civilian public works spending suddenly became pervasive in Japan during 1949–1950.

To complete one's explanation of the distinctive features in the Japanese policy bias toward the periphery, one must return to the importance of the crisis and compensation dynamic, in tandem with structural factors. Broadly speaking, structural factors taken in isolation appear more salient in explaining the Japanese approach to regional policy than in some other policy areas, such as welfare. Dissolution of the Home Ministry at the end of 1947 created a major power vacuum in Japanese national policymaking which local government interests and political entrepreneurs could—and did—readily fill. Direct election of provincial governors after 1947, as a result of Home Ministry dissolution, gave those officials strong incentives to seek benefits for the periphery. Well-organized regional institutions in some areas, such as Kyūshū, also enhanced grassroots power.[73] Since establishment of the middle-size electoral district system in 1947, and especially since the conservative merger of 1955, the inherent structure of political competition within the Diet has also created strong pressures for the policy process to develop distributive political resources, such as public works, and allocate them broadly across the periphery of Japan. But structural factors are clearly insufficient to explain the nuances in public works and other regionally oriented government programs over time.

The first major postwar development stimulating emphasis on regional policy was the conservative electoral victory of January 1949. Discomfitted by two years in the opposition, sensing a rising communist threat, and seeking to stabilize Japanese politics, Yoshida's Liberal party resolved to build a reliable political foundation in the countryside. Public works spending, together with the aid to the agricultural cooperatives discussed above, was the mortar. Party politicians had particular incentives to see public works programs expand since they were in a position to exercise unusual influence over their disposition, in view of the Home Ministry dissolution which had weakened potential bureaucratic rivals. With shrewd political foresight, second-term Dietman Tanaka Kakuei in 1949 set up the Local Development Subcommittee in the House of Representatives, using it to sponsor discussions of the need for expanded hydroelectric construction and other types of public works.

Despite the Dodge Line austerity program, national public works expenditures surged 69 percent in the 1950 budget.[74] Rivalry within conservative ranks, especially between Yoshida and Hatoyama Ichirō, for the prime ministership further fueled public works spending, which reached 2.94 percent of national income—well over double the 1932–1936 average—by 1953.[75] As

[73] See Vogel, *Comeback*, p. 103. Among these regional institutions active in promoting local development in Kyūshū were the *Nishi Nihon Shimbun*, the largest local paper; Kyūshū University; and the Kyūshū Economic Research Center, together with banks and electric power companies.

[74] See Kil Soong Hoom, "Dodge Line," p. 109–11, 341–42.

[75] Ministry of Finance Budget Bureau (Ōkurashō Shukei Kyoku), *Kuni no*

the conservatives strove to consolidate power following the trauma of social democratic rule and occupation reforms, roads, harbors, and dams, together with forestry, fishery, and irrigation infrastructure, began sprouting up rapidly across Japan during the early 1950s. Many of these projects were funded by local governments, severely straining their finances.[76]

One major pillar of postwar regional development was the National Land Comprehensive Development Law (*Kokudō Sōgō Kaihatsu Hō*) of 1950. This law, which Tanaka Kakuei claims originated in his Diet subcommittee, rather than with the cabinet, designated special development areas for government assistance.[77] In a pattern similar to that of later decades, nineteen areas covering virtually all of Japan were selected for support after fierce lobbying by the prefectures. The resulting program was so diluted that it provided inadequate incentives to induce firms to relocate from the Tōkaidō area, although it did generate distributive resources politicians and recipient interest groups found attractive.

The early 1950s was a period of intense political initiative in many areas of regional policy, as politicians strove to generate distributive resources of interest to constituents. Conservative politicians originated the Power Resources Development Law (1950), establishing a public enterprise to develop electric power resources through the acquisition of land and the construction of hydroelectric plants;[78] this arrangement was attractive politically because it created a framework for controlling the siting and construction of dams—an immense economic attraction to both industry and local communities during the 1950s. Dams also caught the national imagination during the 1950s and 1960s, figuring centrally in such popular films as *Kurobe no Taiyō* (The Sun of Kurobe), set around one of Japan's greatest new dam construction projects, and starring Ishihara Yūjirō. Politicians astutely used this combination of economic need and emotional

Yosan: 1954 Nendo (The 1954 National Budget) (Tokyo: Ōkurashō Insatsu Kyoku, 1954), p. 51.

[76] On details, see Ichiki Hiroshi "Chihō Zaisei no Hatan no Genin" ("The Causes of Bankruptcy of Local Finance), *Chūō Kōron* 69 (1964); and Satō Shunichi, *Sengo Ki no Chihō Jichi* (Local Administration in the Postwar Period), pp. 312–13.

[77] Tanaka Kakuei, *Building a New Japan*, p. 12.

[78] *Ibid.*, p. 12; and Samuels, *The Business of the Japanese State*, pp. 159–60.

national consensus to generate new brokerage opportunities and hence enhance their own roles in domestic policymaking.

Politicians also initiated the Road Law (1952), which provided for toll roads and a special-purpose gasoline tax earmarked for road construction. Both measures leveraged the government funds available for highway construction, a prime distributive political resource. A strategic revision of the River Law, initiated by politicians in 1951, also significantly aided the expansion of Japan's private railway network and the ability of the railways to hold down railway fares, a major departure from prewar practices, as Tanaka Kakuei points out.[79]

Two further periods, aside from the post-1949 efforts to stabilize conservative rule, have profoundly shaped the profile of Japanese regional policy and public works spending. The first was the 1958–1963 period of the Security Treaty crisis and the Income Doubling Plan. During the second, the early 1970s political crisis, LDP dominance was even more severely threatened. Politics and policymaking during 1958–1963 had several dimensions that stimulated innovations in regional policy by the Japanese conservatives. First, and perhaps most importantly, the Security Treaty crisis stimulated major tactical reassessments within both the Japan Socialist party and the Japan Communist party, orienting these groups toward greater activism outside the largest cities of Japan. The Left sensed acutely the contrast between the powerful response its antitreaty struggle stirred in Tokyo and the futility of its efforts in the countryside outside the coalfields of Kyūshū and Hokkaidō.[80] This reassessment led to an intensification of JSP grassroots organization after 1960, to the "Eda Vision" of JSP General Secretary Eda Saburō in 1962, and to Asukata Ichio's decision in 1963 to descend from the national to the local level of politics and run for mayor of Yokohama. All these developments heightened the sense of challenge felt at the grassroots level by Japan's conservatives during the early 1960s and helped to provoke innovation in regional policies during that period.

Crisis for the conservatives in 1960, as the Left became painfully aware, had been geographically concentrated almost exclu-

[79] Tanaka Kakuei, *Building a New Japan*, pp. 15–16.

[80] See Asukata Ichio, "Kakushin Jichitai no San jyū Nen" ("Thirty Years of Progressive Local Government") in *Shōwa no Sengoshi* (A Shōwa Postwar History), ed. Ozaki Hideki, pp. 12–13; and Muramatsu Michio, "The Impact of Economic Growth Policies on Local Politics in Japan," *Asian Survey* 25 (September 1975): 808.

sively in Tokyo. Only a few weeks after the massive, climactic demonstrations of June 1960, which forced cancellation of Dwight D. Eisenhower's Tokyo visit, the LDP, for example, overwhelmingly won a major gubernatorial election in Gunma Prefecture, practically on Tokyo's doorstep. But there was one major exception to the placidity outside Tokyo—the bitter Miike strike in the coal mines of Kyūshū.[81] This strike helped direct increased conservative political attention to the coal mining areas' economic plight and transition problems, which had been intensifying during the 1950s. It led to new legislation targeted at the difficulties of coal mining areas, even though the workers most affected were traditionally beyond the conservative circle of compensation. As in welfare, agricultural, and small business policymaking, a tacit coalition of antimainstream conservatives and opposition politicians seems to have led the way to policy change. Socialist backing for the miners was reinforced by the sympathy of Labor Minister Ishida Hirohide[82] and the calls of influential LDP maverick Kōno Ichirō for nationalization of the coal industry.[83] During 1961 it was further amplified by large-scale coal union demonstrations before the Diet and the major ministries, culminating in a meeting between union representatives and Prime Minister Ikeda.[84]

On September 1, 1960, only six weeks after the height of the Security Treaty crisis, and while the Miike strike was still in progress, the Coal Mining Facilities Corporation was reorganized into the Rationalization of the Coal Industry Corporation (*Sekitan Kōgyō Gōrika Jigyōdan*), with enhanced price subsidies and government funds for reemploying dismissed miners and for buying up mining rights.[85] The following year the corporation began to subsidize the Ministry of Labor's Employment Promotion Projects Corporation (*Koyō Sokushin Jigyōdan*), also set up in 1961 to find new jobs for coal miners and other workers who had

[81] In the background of this strike was an extraordinarily rapid decline in employment in the Japanese coal industry, due particularly to headlong rationalization. Between 1953 and 1963, employment in the Japanese coal industry dropped by 7.8 percent, nearly double the rates of decline in Britain (4.6) and France (3.9), even though output in Japan was still increasing, which it generally speaking was not in Europe. See Brown and Burrows, *Regional Economic Problems*, p. 96.

[82] See Ishida Hirohide, *Watakushi no Shōwa Seiji Shi*, p. 110.

[83] Johnson, *Japan's Public Policy Companies*, p. 129.

[84] Imai Kōzō, *Sekitan (Coal)*, new ed. (Tokyo: Yūhikaku, 1966), pp. 38–40, cited in Samuels, *The Business of the Japanese State*, p. 114.

[85] Johnson, *Japan's Public Policy Companies*, p. 129.

been laid off in corporate rationalization efforts.[86] In response to union protests, a coal industry task force was set up, ultimately generating a program to subsidize production at an annual level of 55 million tons by guaranteeing long-term, large-scale consumption by heavy industry.[87]

In 1962 MITI set up the Coal Mine Area Rehabilitation Corporation (*Santan Chiiki Shinkō Jigyōdan*) to build industrial parks in old coal mining areas and to encourage nonmining industries to move there. Between 1962 and 1982 this corporation and its successors built 113 industrial parks across Japan's coal mining districts, 76 of them in Kyūshū where the labor unrest of 1959–1960 had been concentrated.[88] By the 1980s the long-depressed island of Kyūshū had become the center of Japanese integrated circuit production.

A third dimension of crisis in the late 1950s and early 1960s was the intensification of internal rivalries within conservative ranks. The rivalry between Prime Minister Kishi and recently resigned MOF Minister Ikeda Hayato during the spring of 1959, for example, seems to have intensified public consideration of a grassroots-oriented Income Doubling Plan.[89] Conservative rivalries also seem to have helped elicit supplements oriented toward compensating traditional LDP grassroots constituencies and prospective supporters, such as small businessmen and farmers.

Throughout 1959 and early 1960, no clear consensus existed on the short-run advisability of greatly expanded aid for Japan's periphery within the context of longterm planning.[90] In August 1960, just after the Security Treaty crisis, the Ministry of Local Autonomy (*Jichishō*) announced a detailed program for regional industrialization; MITI came out with an alternative that October. The major opposition parties joined the controversy, which was also taken up by the powerful, antigovernment mass media. As so frequently in Japan's postwar political history, intraelite competition for support in a period of crisis, fanned by the media,

[86] *Ibid.*

[87] Samuels, *The Business of the Japanese State*, p. 114.

[88] Vogel, *Comeback*, p. 109.

[89] See Walter Arnold, The Politics of Economic Planning in Postwar Japan: A Study in Political Economy (Ph.D. diss., University of California Berkeley, 1984), p. 256.

[90] MOF's Satō favored "go-slow" policies, while the Economic Planning Agency, the LDP Economic Research Council, and the advisors of MITI Minister Ikeda could not agree on the relative priority of assistance to industry and to regional and agricultural groups. See *ibid.*, pp. 184–99, 211–12.

strongly pressured a basically reluctant Ministry of Finance to support policy innovation and gave MOF a rationale for departing from its usual stern insistence on fiscal discipline.

The pressure for a more decisive regional policy gained particular force when that policy assumed simultaneously what Lowi would call "distributive" and "constituent" characteristics.[91] The distributive traits allowed LDP politicians to determine how benefits would be allocated geographically, while the constituent dimensions permitted bureaucrats to define the terms on which industries were invited to locate in designated areas. Thus was born the concept of the new industrial city as a means of achieving balanced regional development, addressing both the strategic objectives of bureaucracy and the political needs of the LDP. Keidanren, and the national business community more generally, wanted only two or three growth poles, located within the Inland Sea area close to the Pacific Belt. The LDP, in contrast, presented a plan in January 1961 calling for the establishment of twenty new industrial cities scattered among the twenty-two prefectures and twenty-two other municipalities that had applied for regional assistance from the government.

Ultimately the New Industrial Cities Promotion Law was enacted in August 1962, with fifteen sites to be designated. This was the first concrete legislation enacted under the provisions of the so-called National Comprehensive Development Plan (1962), the modified version of Ikeda's Income Doubling Plan which emerged during the politically delicate period after 1960. Like France's concept of the *Métropoles d'équilibre*, operationalized at almost exactly the same time, the New Industrial Cities Promotion Law provided financial assistance for infrastructure construction at selected "growth points" across Japan, many of them in peripheral areas; however, the Japanese legislation provided a much broader geographical area of emphasis than did that of France.

In 1964, with the waning of crisis, Japan created six additional "Special Industrial Consolidation Areas," relatively close to urban centers, also signalled for preferential treatment.[92] This program, undertaken at the insistence of a big business community

[91] Lowi, "Four Systems," *Public Administration Review* (July/August 1972): 300.

[92] This latter program, undertaken at the insistence of the big business community, illustrates the dynamic of "post-crisis compensation politics," often not as redistributive as that during a period of crisis.

reluctant to relocate heavily toward remote rural areas even with government support, undercut the purposes of the 1962 New Industrial Cities Promotion Law. But in a period of relative stability, such as the mid-1960s, big business had more leverage in the policy process, compared to local governments of remote areas, than was true in more turbulent times.

In the end Japanese business invested substantially more heavily in the "Special Industrial Consolidation Areas" established in 1964, which were all in the Pacific Coastal Belt area close to major urban centers, than it did in the more remote "new industrial cities" that had been designated in 1962. Ten years after the new industrial cities legislation was enacted the average industrial output of the special areas was around ¥925 billion ($4.63 billion at ¥200/$1.00), compared to ¥450 billion ($2.25 billion) for the new industrial areas. But despite the relatively slow growth of these areas, due partially to dilution after 1962 of the regional-policy incentives supporting them, the government infrastructural commitment to them nevertheless appears to have been quite substantial, compared to patterns in Western Europe and the United States.

For nearly a decade from the early 1960s, the redistributive bias of regional policy innovation in Japan weakened, as did the sense of political crisis for the conservatives. To be sure, as during the 1950s, there were new regional programs for the Kinki Region (1963) and the Chūbu Region (1966). And public works expenditures for the periphery continued, even accelerated, with the quickening pace of national economic growth. But the pendulum of policy emphasis shifted away from the equity bias of the Ikeda administration to a more pronounced efficiency orientation.

The early 1970s prompted another surge of regional policy innovation in Japan, driven by rapid economic growth, rising urban land prices, pollution, and an increasingly precarious political situation for the Liberal Democrats, requiring vigorous countermeasures. As Gary Allinson pointed out during this period, farmers who had been the traditional bulwark of the LDP electorally were rapidly declining in number, but the LDP could still preserve its political power by relying on the *areas* in which its former constituency resided.[93] There the social fabric remained more cohesive and basic political inclinations more conservative than in

[93] Gary Dean Allinson, "The Moderation of Organized Labor in Japan," *Journal of Japanese Studies* (Spring 1975): 435.

the polluted, overcrowded, and increasingly frustrated metropolitan areas of the Tōkaidō.

Active regional policies, epitomized in the 1972 "Plan for the Remodeling of the Japanese Archipelago" of MITI Minister Tanaka Kakuei, were one important means of aiding these urbanizing former rural areas, providing windfall real estate profits to politicians, farmers, and local entrepreneurs, and supplying employment to a broad range of swing constituencies prospectively, but not categorically, loyal to the LDP.[94] As in the early 1960s, regional policies of the early 1970s thus had dual, mutually reinforcing industrial and political objectives.

Following the Under-Developed Area Development Act (1970) and the Act for Promotion of Industrialization in Farm Areas (1971), the Diet enacted the major Industrial Relocation Promotion Act (1972) and set up the Public Regional Development Corporation (1974). Under the new legislation, all of Japan was classified into either Departure Promotion Areas, for regions already overcrowded and overenlarged, or Relocation Reception Areas, for regions which should attract new industries. Relocation Areas by the 1980s covered 86.5 percent of Japan.[95] Inducements such as loans, subsidies, and tax incentives are provided for industries moving to Relocation Reception Areas, and since 1974 industrial parks have been established across Japan by the Regional Development Corporation.

During the political crisis of the 1970s, with the rapid proliferation of citizen action groups, Japanese regional policymaking came to include an increasingly complex set of state–society consultations, long typical in Western Europe. Unlike the earlier Japanese national plans, developed more exclusively by LDP leaders and responsible bureaucrats in Tokyo, the Third Comprehensive Development National Plan, announced in 1977, involved regional advisory councils much more heavily in its formulation. The Third Plan also called for broader participation by local communities in developing local blueprints for implementing the national plan itself.[96]

[94] 1967 Japanese election study data, for example, showed that nonmetropolitan workers in large enterprises voted 42 percent for the LDP, as opposed to 19 percent for such workers in metropolitan areas. Small business support for the LDP was also higher (70 vs. 59 percent) in nonmetropolitan areas. See Scott C. Flanagan and Bradley M. Richardson, *Japanese Electoral Behavior*, p. 73.

[95] Murata, *Industrial Geography of Japan*, p. 184.

[96] National Land Agency of Japan, *Sanzensō* (The Third Comprehensive National Development Plan), p. 10.

Some analysts might try to explain the regionalist bias of Japanese public policy solely in terms of heavy preexisting concentrations of industry in particular areas of Japan, especially the Tōkaidō belt between Tokyo and Ōsaka and a consequent technocratic desire by industrial planners to diversify plant locations. Such an argument is partially correct for capital-intensive, pollution-intensive heavy industries such as petrochemicals, where a desire to minimize negative externalities clearly appears to have affected siting decisions during the 1960s and the 1970s. But it does not fully explain the special *timing* of regional policy innovations, such as the new industrial cities program.

Even more importantly, the industrial concentration argument cannot account for Japanese policies toward the spatial distribution of relatively new sectors, such as electronics and precision machinery, where industrial concentration appears lower than in some other major industrial nations and where negative externalities, such as pollution, are in any case relatively small.[97] For example, there is no clear economic reason for locating a major mechatronics research center, Japan's International University, and several new high-technology ventures in Nagaoka, a small town two hundred miles from Tokyo in the electoral district of former Prime Minister Tanaka Kakuei. For all sectors, particularly the newer, more technology-intensive ones, a major political supplement to economic and technocratic explanations for Japanese regional policy decisions is clearly necessary.

The distinctive regional policy departures of the early 1980s have their origins more in emerging international challenge to Japanese industry than in domestic political crisis. In the wake of the 1973 oil shock, the importance of accelerating the transition of Japan's industrial structure away from energy-intensive basic industry and toward "knowledge-intensive" high-technology sectors of the future become manifest. Yet whether major Western nations, increasingly conscious of Japan's rapid economic advance and finding their own economies jeopardized in a low-growth era, would continue providing a continuous flow of

[97] Cross-national comparisons with respect to spatial distributions of industry are by their very nature imprecise, but some useful rough orders of magnitude can be established. It seems clear, for example, that France's electronics industry in the early 1980s was significantly more concentrated geographically than that of Japan despite the relative unimportance of negative externalities to siting decisions in that industry. See Philippe Aydalot et al., *Atlas Economique des Régions Françaises*, pp. 53, 57; and Asahi Shimbun Sha, ed., *Minryoku '82*, pp. 82–83.

patents to fuel a Japanese transition to high-technology was unclear. Thus, in February 1975, Keidanren outlined the concept of a "technology sufficient society" (Gijutsu Rikkoku) and urged the government to take measures to realize it. In the hands of the LDP and the bureaucracy, this notion became by March 1980 the notion of a "technopolis," first announced as government policy in MITI's Vision for the 1980s.[98]

During the early 1980s, public works expenditures, largely distributed to the periphery of Japan, began to fall significantly (figure 6.4). From 1984 to 1987 the absolute level of public works spending in the national general account budget fell for four consecutive years. The privatization and breakup of the Japan National Railways, finally implemented in April 1987, further inhibited welfare rather than efficiency-oriented public works construction at Japan's periphery. Yet, as suggested in figure 6.1, public works continued during the mid-1980s to maintain broad geographical distribution. Japan continued, for example, to build airports, art museums, and medical colleges in far-flung areas, although not as rapidly as in earlier years. Other regionally oriented programs also remained in place.

Japan thus advances toward the 1990s with a distinct regionalist bias to its industrial and technology policies—indeed, to its entire economic structure. Big business, to be sure, often benefits from such policies, but it does so by locating new facilities in outlying areas, especially the countryside. Reflecting this regionalist bias, Japan is developing high-technology industries spread broadly across the national periphery and a national data communications network to match. Rural Nagano Prefecture, with only 1.8 percent of Japan's population, in 1985 produced over seven times that share of Japan's precision machinery, while remote Kumamoto Prefecture in Kyūshū with an even smaller population generated 12 percent of Japan's and 5 percent of the entire world's integrated circuits.[99]

Given the increasing political stability of conservative rule in Japan, the crisis-driven political pressures that have often intensified this regionalist orientation to policy may begin to abate.

[98] For details on the evolution of the technopolis concept in the Japanese political process, see Ōsono Tomokazu, *Hasshin: Technopolis Kōsō* (Starting Point: Technopolis Structure). On the relationship of the technopolis concept to Japanese industrial policy, see Tatsuno, *Technopolis Strategy.*

[99] Asahi Shimbun Sha, ed., *Minryoku '86*, pp. 110, 145; and Tatsuno, *Technopolis Strategy*, p. 180. Kumamoto figures are for 1983.

But the structural features of Japanese politics that impel a grassroots orientation—preeminently the electoral system in the Lower House and the rivalries in conservative ranks which flow from it—will most likely remain. Occupation reforms and the institutional residue of previous crises, reinforced by the growing policy role of the LDP, have cast the Japanese policy process in a regionally oriented mode that is highly distinctive in comparative context and will be difficult to alter no matter how fundamentally the political dynamic of the past three decades may change. Peripheral Japan may no longer be very rural. But the power of the periphery remains—reincarnated in the alliance of localist and big business, often high-technology, interests which increasingly dominates the political economy of the Japanese countryside.

7

Small Business Policy: The Confluence of Industrial Policy and Welfare

> Small employers . . . the noncommissioned officers of civil society.
>
> MARUYAMA MASAO (1952)

ONE OF the most striking features of recent Japanese public policy, viewed both in comparative context and against the backdrop of Japanese history, has been the fluctuating but generally pronounced bias shown toward the small, across a range of industrial, trade, and credit-policy sectors, often at the expense of the large.

Historically small businessmen have often been a major constituency of several Western conservative parties, including the Christian Democrats (DC) of Italy, the Radicals of France, and the Republicans of the United States. At critical junctures in Western political modernization, small business and related groups have been relatively large.[1] Although largely inert and often disunified in economically and politically stable times, in moments of crisis, as in Germany and America during the early 1930s, small business has become a critical swing group determining the course of national politics, as Arno J. Mayer points out.[2]

But only rarely have the public policies of major nations been systematically designed to serve the interests of small firms, despite their periodically strategic role in political life. While the Reagan administration in the mid-1980s was attempting to disband the U.S. Small Business Administration and end its meager

[1] Germany in 1914, for example, had two million lower- and middle-level civil servants, 1.5 million traditional craftsmen and artisans, and 700,000 retailers compared to about 13 million industrial workers. See Arno J. Mayer, "The Lower Class as Historical Problem," *Journal of Modern History* (September 1975), pp. 409–36.

[2] *Ibid.*, p. 419.

and declining volume of subsidized loans,[3] the small business–oriented People's Finance Corporation in Japan disbursed nearly the volume of subsidized loans annually of the vaunted Japan Export-Import Bank, an amount which by 1983 had reached almost four times the scale of 1973.[4] Japanese tax policies, export policies, competition policies, and policies toward the rationalization of the distribution sector, to name only a few, were likewise sharply biased in favor of the small. This pattern contrasted sharply with not only major conservative administrations, such as those of Reagan and Thatcher, but also with socialist governments, such as those of Mitterand in France or Palme in Sweden. Even in Italy, with a political and social configuration more similar to Japan than most other Western industrial nations, state support for small business has not been nearly as active, pronounced, and systematic as in Japan.

To establish the dimensions of contrast between Japanese and Western policies toward small business, it is important to look in detail at specific policies in some major sectors of concern. While suggesting concretely how Japanese policies appear biased in favor of the small, this chapter will also consider how the pronounced grassroots sensitivity of Japanese conservative policymaking, especially in periods of political crisis, first helped to produce this result and then helped defend it against pressures for retrenchment.

Small Business in Japanese Society

Throughout the postwar period Japan has had an unusually large number of both small businesses and small business employees, a reality that has inevitably made small business issues a concern of policymakers. In 1953, as pressure for a comprehensive small business policy began to gather force, 73.5 percent of Japan's entire work force in manufacturing was employed in firms with

[3] Japanese government agencies for small business finance in 1982 disbursed 17.5 times the volume of loans and undertook 13.3 times the volume of loan guarantees of the American Small Business Administration, according to Japanese government unpublished data.

[4] Bank of Japan Research and Statistics Department (Nihon Ginkō Chōsa Tōkei Kyoku), ed., *Keizai Tōkei Nenpō* (*Economic Statistic Annual*), 1984 ed. (Tokyo: Nihon Ginkō Chōsa Tokei Kyoku, 1985), pp. 101–2.

TABLE 7.1

The Heavy Concentration of the Japanese Work Force in Small Business (in percentages)

Country	Share of Work Force Employed in Small Businesses Manufacturing	Distribution (wholesale/retail)	Services
Japan (1981)	74.3	87.4	69.2
West Germany (1970)	50.0	62.4	77.3
United States (1982)	46.9	71.4	59.6
United Kingdom (1982)	51.6	46.5	N.A.

Source: Small and Medium Enterprise Agency Chūshō Kigyō Chō, ed., *Chūshō Kigyō Hakusho* (*Small Business White Paper*) 1986 ed. (Tokyo: Ōkurashō Insatsu Kyoku, 1986), appendix display 41.

Note: Definitions of small business vary marginally, as follows:

(1) Manufacturing: Fewer than 500 employees in West Germany and the United Kingdom; 300 in Japan, and 250 in the United States.

(2) Wholesale trade: Less than 50 employees in West Germany, and 100 elsewhere.

(3) Retail trade: Less than 50 employees in all countries.

fewer than three hundred employees.[5] By 1981, despite strong concentration tendencies accompanying the transition to lower economic growth after the 1973 oil shock, this ratio had increased to 74.3 percent.[6] Meanwhile, the share of small businesses in the total nonagricultural labor force, including distribution, had risen to 81.4 percent. Indeed, more than 50 percent of the total Japanese labor force in 1981 worked in enterprises employing less than *thirty* workers. In the manufacturing, distribution, and service sectors respectively, the share of the Japanese labor force working for small businesses is much larger than in the major Western industrial nations (table 7.1)

Much of small business, particularly in the distribution sector,

[5] Small and Medium Enterprise Agency Promotion Department Research and Public Affairs Section (Chūshō Kigyō Chō Shinkō Bu Chōsa Kōhō Ka), *Chūshō Kigyō Kankei Shiryō Shū* (Compilation of Small Business Related Data), Vol. 31, No. 3, Table 2, p. 2.

[6] Small and Medium Enterprise Agency (Chūshō Kigyō Chō), ed., *Chūshō Kigyō Hakusho* (White Paper on Small Business), 1986 ed. (Tokyo: Ōkurashō Insatsu Kyoku, 1986), Appendix III.

TABLE 7.2

The Employment Importance of Small Business in the Japanese Political Economy

Small Business	Employment Change, 1972–81 (Small Firms Only)
Wholesale/Retail Distribution	+2.922 million
Services	+1.540 million
Construction	+1.120 million
Large Business	**Employment Change, 1972–81 (Large Firms Only)**
Manufacturing	−0.777 million
Construction	−0.152 million
Transport	−0.066 million

Source: Small and Medium Enterprise Agency Chūshō Kigyō Chō, ed., *Chūshō Kigyō Hakusho* (*Small Business White Paper*) 1986 ed. (Tokyo: Ōkurashō Insatsu Kyoku, 1986), appendix 3, page 3.

Note: Definitions of small businesses follow table 7.1.

serves as a labor reservoir. Its inefficiencies help absorb surplus workers who would be unemployed if distribution, services, and traditional manufacturing were uniformly as efficient as the highly competitive and modernized export sectors. With rising affluence among Japanese consumers, specialty shops and the demand for specialty services have been proliferating in Japan over the past two decades. The combination of rising demand and legal constraints on the expansion of large-scale distribution has supported a steady work force expansion in such untraded sectors (table 7.2). The existence of new jobs in these increasingly inefficient, nontraded "labor-sponge" sectors has allowed the work force to expand and unemployment to remain relatively low, despite widespread automation.[7] Redundant workers, mainly sub-

[7] Between 1980 and 1985 employment declined in the general machinery, manufacturing materials, and consumer-related manufacturing sectors, while output rose 15 to 60 percent in each case. In electrical machinery, output rose over 100 percent, with virtually no change in employment. See Ministry of Labor (Rōdō

contract employees, can thus be redeployed from manufacturing with only minimal impact on the unemployment rate; this rate remained a low 2.8 percent in Japan during 1986, compared to 6.9 percent in the United States and 11.7 percent in the European community.[8]

As noted in table 7.2, all three sectors where employment increased most rapidly during the 1972–1981 period were in the small business area. These included a massive increase of nearly three million workers (over 6 percent of the 1981 labor force) in the grossly "inefficient" distribution sector, so remarkably effective in absorbing redundant workers. Overall, small business nonagricultural employment in Japan rose by 6.8 million over the 1972–1981 period, compared with an increase of only 121,000—less than *one fiftieth* as much—in large firms.[9] Small business, and the policy assistance it has received through strong political support, has allowed Japan to preserve its low unemployment rate into the turbulent 1980s, despite extensive automation in many industrial sectors.

Small business thus serves major social security as well as employment-related functions in Japan today. Because welfare payments have traditionally been low and retirement early, especially in large firms, the elderly have found themselves needing work opportunities after retirement.[10] Managing small shops, which often distribute products of the proprietor's former company, frequently provides the answer.

Central Pillars of Current Small Business Policy

According to a recent survey by the Organization for Economic Cooperation and Development, Japan has the most extensive range of policy tools for assisting small business in the industrial-

---

Shō), ed., *Rōdō Hakusho* (Labor White Paper), 1985 ed. (Tokyo: Nihon Rōdō Kyōkai, 1985), p. 138.

[8] Japan Institute for Social and Economic Affairs, *Japan 1985: An International Comparison*, p. 72.

[9] Small and Medium Enterprise Agency (Chūshō Kigyō Chō), ed., *1986 Chūshō Kigyō Hakusho*, appendix 3, p. 3.

[10] A disproportionate share of the unemployed in Japan are elderly for precisely these reasons. In 1985, 42.9 percent of Japan's unemployed were older than 45, compared to 16.4 percent in the United States and 30.3 percent in Britain. See Japan Institute for Social and Economic Affairs, *Japan 1986*, p. 76.

TABLE 7.3

The Arsenal of Small Business Policies: An International Comparison of Policies Designed to Increase Efficiency and Facilitate Adaptation of Small Business

Form of Assistance	Germany	Italy	Great Britain	Japan
Access to capital	*	*	*	*
Introduction of new processes and techniques	*	*	*	*
Product marketing on the home and international markets	*		*	*
Industrial organization	*	*		*
Assistance to technology-based enterprises		*		*
Personnel training in management techniques	*	*	*	*
Employment of highly qualified manpower		*	*	*
Government procurement	*		*	*
Compliance with administrative regulatory requirements	*		*	*
Assistance vis-à-vis bigger enterprises			*	*
Others	*	*	*	*

Source: Organization for Economic Cooperation and Development, *Industrial Adjustment Policies* (Paris: OECD, 1978), p. 17.

ized world. As shown in Table 7.3, Japan uses all major means of support for small business surveyed by the OECD, a record equaled by no other nation. This pattern of Japanese comprehensiveness in small business policy tools is, interestingly, uncharacteristic of Japanese industrial structure policy in general. Japan fails, for example, to employ several types of manpower-oriented adjustment measures, such as policies to facilitate geographical and occupational mobility, which are common elements of industrial policy in Europe.[11]

Credit Policies

As indicated in table 7.3, one of the most common types of small business support policy is preferential access to capital, employed in thirteen of the fifteen advanced industrial nations surveyed. It was perhaps the single most important tool of Japanese small business policy over the two decades of double-digit economic growth, and is still important, particularly in political terms. Due to the decidedly big business orientation of the financial system when high growth began, a development of the efficiency orientation of wartime mobilization, small businesses in Japan have historically tended toward high rates of bankruptcy and relatively low asset bases. Japanese commercial banks, with broad opportunities for lending to large, rapidly growing firms in capital-intensive industry, have traditionally been rather reluctant to lend to small firms. Government credit has hence been especially crucial to the survival and growth of small companies—a form of compensation for both their political support and their acquiescence in an overall economic structure exposing them to profound uncertainties.

Japanese national fiscal and monetary policy coordination throughout the high-growth period further compounded the problems of small firms, intensifying the tendency toward political pressures for compensation. As Hugh Patrick points out, credit restraint was the primary tool employed by the financial authorities in dealing with balance of payments deficits and inflationary pressures during the high-growth period; this restraint fell disproportionately on small firms lacking close ties with the commercial banks.[12] Government was forced by small business interest group pressure into the gap, both to provide government credit and also to jawbone private banks into improving the terms on which they offered funds to small firms.

Currently three general purpose government financial institutions essentially lend to only small business. Among these three,

[11] See Organization for Economic Cooperation and Development, *Selected Industrial Policy Instruments* (Paris: OECD, 1978), p. 14–15.

[12] See Hugh T. Patrick, "Cyclical Instability and Fiscal-Monetary Policy in Postwar Japan," in *The State and Economic Enterprise in Japan*, William W. Lockwood, ed.

the Peoples' Finance Corporation (PFC), founded in June 1949, supplies funds primarily to extremely small enterprises virtually devoid of international competitiveness. The PFC achieved special prominence with the creation of the so-called no-collateral loan program in 1973, which supplies funds mainly to factories of less than twenty workers and to service businesses of less than five employees. By 1986 the PFC's annual loan volume was nearly that of the Export Import Bank of Japan, with no-collateral loans its major financial product.

More than two million small businessmen now have close ties to both the PFC through this no-collateral loan system and the JCC which administers it.[13] This system, without an analogue elsewhere in the industrialized world, enabled the PFC and its counterparts to grow explosively from the early 1970s until 1980 (table 7.4). Growth of government small business credit slowed somewhat during the early 1980s relative to both the Japanese financial system as a whole and government credit for larger firms. But it accelerated once again during 1986–1987, under the impact of sharp yen revaluation and insistent small business political pressures.

The second of the major small business financial institutions, the Small Business Finance Corporation (*Chūshō Kigyō Kinyū Kōko*), founded in 1953, provides loans as investment funds and long-term working capital necessary for modernization and rationalization. More closely linked to the industrial policy process than its counterpart PFC, the SBFC concentrates on lending for purposes which relate specifically to government policy objectives, such as pollution control, energy conservation, and productivity enhancement. For example, SBFC played a major role in the rationalization of the Japanese auto parts industry during the late 1960s, a major step in the automobile industry's overall path to global competitiveness.[14] The third government-affiliated small business bank, the older Central Cooperative Bank for Commerce and Industry (*Shōkō Chūkin Bank*) was founded in 1936; it provides finance mainly to business cooperatives and their members, especially in geographically concentrated (*sanchi sangyō*) industries, such as pottery, silk weaving, small-scale shipbuilding, and flatware.

In addition to the three major small business finance institu-

[13] Hirose Michisada, *Hojokin to Seiken Tō*, p. 49.

[14] For details, see Kent E. Calder, "Politics and the Market," appendix 1.

TABLE 7.4

The Volatile Growth of Government Loans to Japanese Small Business, 1970–1986

(*Unit* = Billion yen in loans outstanding)

Major Government Lenders to Big Business	1970	1975	1980	1986
Japan Development Bank	1,905	3,341	5,018	7,530
Export Import Bank of Japan	1,521	3,217	5,077	5,444
Subtotal	3,226	6,558	10,095	12,974
Major Government Lenders to Small Business	**1970**	**1975**	**1980**	**1986**
Central Cooperative Bank for Commerce and Industry[a]	1,204	3,431	5,372	8,599
Small Business Finance Corporation	895	2,357	4,350	5,152
Peoples Finance Corporation	708	2,036	4,023	5,284
Subtotal	2,807	7,824	13,745	19,035

Source: Bank of Japan Research and Statistics Department (Nihon Ginkō Chōsa Tōkei Kyoku) *Keizai Tōkei Nenpō (Economic Statistics Annual)* (Tokyo: The Bank of Japan, various issues).

[a] Semigovernmental body.

tions, four other specialized bodies, most without analogues outside Japan, also provide significant assistance to small firms. These are the Environmental Sanitation Business Finance Corporation (*Kankyō Eisei Kinyū Kōko*), the Medical Care Facilities Corporation (*Iryō Kinyū Kōko*), and two regional finance institutions, the Hokkaidō-Tōhoku Development Corporation and the Okinawa Development Finance Corporation. Together they provide around $8 billion annually in specialized government loans at preferential interest rates.[15]

[15] See Bank of Japan Research and Statistics Department (Nihon Ginkō Chōsa Tōkei Kyoku), *Keizai Tōkei Nenpō*, appropriate issues.

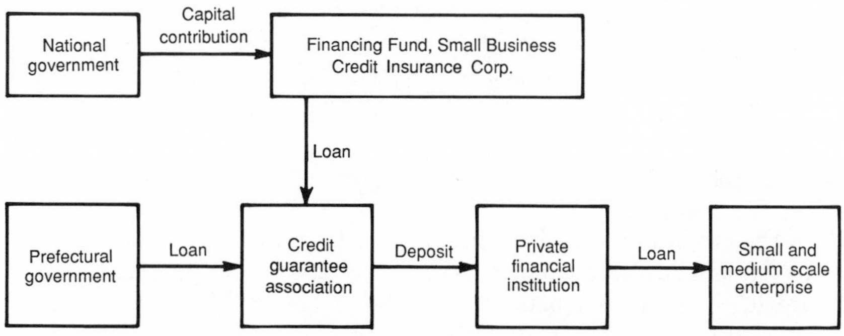

Figure 7.1. Organization of Credit Insurance for Small Businesses.
Source: Japan Small Business Corporation, *Small Business Policies* (Tokyo: Small Business Corporation, 1983), p. 71.

Beyond directly supplying credit, the Japanese government also facilitates extensive credit guarantees to small businesses that borrow from private banks. As indicated in figure 7.1, these involve a government capital contribution, together with loans from prefectural government, rather than direct guarantees. But the amount of the capital contribution itself has been substantial, and the guarantees generated thereby are huge. In 1981 the Small Business Credit Insurance Corporation had ¥5.155 trillion in insurance outstanding, including special insurance to encourage technology commercialization, equipment modernization, and introduction of the latest pollution control equipment into small firms.[16]

As noted earlier, the system of private lending in Japan has long been skewed in favor of large firms with close ties to commercial banks. During periods of tight credit, with loan volume down, banks have often been prone to demand that marginal borrowers provide large "compensating balances," or mandatory savings deposits at low interest, in return for the opportunity to borrow. Small businesses in particular have suffered from this practice. During the 1950s, bank demands for compensating balances, which effectively raised interest rates for small business borrowers, rarely met government intervention. But during former Prime Minister Tanaka Kakuei's tenure as minister of finance (1962–1965), the MOF began a sporadic but often aggressive inter-

[16] Japan Small Business Corporation, *Outline of Small and Medium-Sale Enterprise Policies of the Japanese Government*, p. 70.

vention with respect to private banks, pressuring them to either eliminate compensating balances or at least modify their terms.[17] This pattern has continued with intensity roughly proportionate to the fluctuating political influence of small business.

Tax Policies

In the credit area, Japanese public policies may be more favorable to small business than anywhere else in the industrialized world;[18] likewise, Japanese tax policies appear highly favorable toward small firms. Although rates of effective taxation against corporations in general are relatively high in Japan, there is a pattern of sharp and growing pro–small business and pro-agriculture discrimination in tax policy, unusual elsewhere in the industrialized world, both in its tendency and its intensity. In the United States, early tax policies of the conservative Reagan administration, such as the Tax Reform Act and the Accelerated Cost Recovery System of 1981, together with the Tax Equity and Fiscal Responsibility Act of 1982, granted disproportionately large benefits to large firms and correspondingly meager advantages to small ones.[19] Yet in Japan national tax policies were significantly and increasingly more favorable to the small firm.

Both small firms[20] and cooperative business associations, almost exclusively composed of small firms cooperating for some specific policy-related purpose, pay sharply lower rates of taxation than do large corporations; this gap has widened significantly over the past fifteen years (table 7.5). The seven and twelve point differential between standard corporate (i.e., big business) tax rates on the one hand and those assessed small firms and business cooperatives on the other rose more than a third between 1968 and 1984, to 10 and 17 percent respectively.

[17] For details, see Nihon Ginkō Kyōkai Ni Jyū Nen Henshū Shitsu, ed., *Ginkō Kyōkai Ni Jyū Nen Shi* (Bankers Association Twenty Year History).

[18] Belgium is generally regarded as having the most extensive small business credit policies in the Western industrialized world, and Japan's small business credit facilities are far more extensive than those of Belgium. See OECD, *Selected Industrial Policy Instruments*, p. 146 for details. (Belgium's 1975 loans were $81 million in an economy of around $80 billion, while Japan's were $43.5 billion in an economy of $1 trillion.)

[19] U.S. House of Representatives, *A Report of the Committee on Small Business*: U.S. House of Representatives *Ninety-Eighth Congress*, pp. 119–20.

[20] Small firms were in 1985 defined for purposes of tax legislation as those with under ¥100 million capitalization and under ¥8 million in gross income.

TABLE 7.5

The Growing Small Business Bias of Japanese Corporate Tax Policy, 1968–1986 (in percentages)

	Basic Tax Rate			
	Large Corporations[a]		Small Firms	
Year	Undistributed Profits	Dividends	Undistributed Profits	Dividends
1968	35	26	28	22
1970	36.75	26	28	22
1974	40	28	28	22
1975	40	30	28	22
1981	42	32	30	24
1984	43.3	33.3	31	25
1986	43.3	33.3	31	25

Sources: Nihon Sozei Kenkyū Kyōkai, *Zeisei Sankō Shiryō Shū (Collected Reference Material regarding the Tax System)* (Tokyo: Nihon Sozei Kenkyū Kai, May 1984), pp. 104–5; and Ministry of Finance internal data.

Notes: (1) The definition of firms eligible for the preferential rates offered to small business has broadened from "income of under ¥3 million annually and capitalization under ¥ 100 million," as defined in 1968, to "annual income under ¥8 million and capitalization under ¥100 million" in 1985. (2) Effective April 1, 1987, the undistributed profits tax rate for large and small firms declined to 42 and 30 percent respectively, while that for dividends declined to 32 and 24 percent, accompanied by some minor, technical changes in rate applicability. (3) Tax rates for so-called *kyōdō kumiai*, or cooperative associations, were even lower than for small business throughout the 1968–1986 period.

[a] This refers to the tax rate for "futsū hōjin."

Japanese policies regarding deductions and depreciation have become less and less favorable to large firms. This is especially clear in contrast to the increasingly liberal deductions and depreciation for large firms afforded under the tax codes of many Western industrialized nations during the early 1980s, especially those with conservative, ostensibly probusiness governments. The special provisions of the tax code most beneficial to large firms in Japan, such as the nontaxable severance payment allowance and currency fluctuation reserve systems, have become increasingly less useful as a means of sheltering income from taxation. The government is placing increasingly stringent limits on the amount of income that businesses shelter under these systems.[21] Yet at the same time the Japanese government has been differentially raising base rates of corporate taxation for large firms.

Aside from formal provisions of tax law, the owners of small firms in Japan are said to benefit, like farmers and medical doctors, through the tax law administration. Compared to the employees or even the senior executives of major firms, small businessmen have far more flexibility in pricing and accounting for their services. They have particularly good prospects for avoiding detection of any tax evasion, due to their small size and frequently strong political contacts. According to the *Nihon Keizai Shimbun*, 60 percent of Japanese small businesses were not paying any corporate taxes during the early 1980s, due to paper losses in their business operations.[22] It is safe to assume that a substantial proportion of these losses may have been contrived for tax reasons.

The implicit power of small business influence over Japanese government tax policy has been shown twice over the past decade in the dramatic defeats of major Ministry of Finance tax legislation designed to deal with the huge national government deficits. In 1979 the late Prime Minister Ōhira Masayoshi candidly proposed introduction of a value-added tax (VAT) strongly opposed by small business on the eve of a Lower House election campaign, but strong interest group pressure forced him to retract the proposal. The LDP suffered major reverses, despite Ōhira's retraction, and did not raise the value-added tax issue again until after a resounding electoral victory in 1986.[23] When the Nakasone administration once again proposed a VAT in late 1986, it was careful to limit controls over very small stores.

[21] The permissible nontaxable severance reserve has been reduced from 100 percent of severance payment liabilities in 1955 to 40 percent since 1980. See Keidanren, Problems in the Current Taxation System and Proposals for Future Direction of Policy, p. 3.

[22] Nihon Keizai Shimbun Sha, *Za Zeimusho*, p. 82.

[23] The contrasts to France in this regard are striking. The French government in the mid-1950s also proposed introduction of a value-added tax, received by vehement small business opposition. This the bureaucracy and the political world largely ignored, passing the tax measure over small business opposition. This was said to be, together with nationalistic backlash to the Indochina and Algerian wars, a major factor in the sudden surge of Poujadisme, which culminated with the Poujadistes gaining fifty seats in the 1956 National Assembly elections. See René Rémond, *The Right Wing in France*, pp. 333–36.

Even then the LDP faced a long and bitter Diet struggle during 1986–1988, arguably the bitterest of the 1980s, in an attempt to implement just a five percent VAT. Similarly, the Finance Ministry in 1981 proposed introduction of the so-called "greencard" system, which would consolidate reporting of dividend and interest income around a single identification number, similar to the social security number in the United States. This proposal likewise triggered massive opposition, much of it from small businessmen, who together with farmers and doctors have much wider opportunities in Japan to conceal assets than do white-collar employees. Coordinated opposition by these groups to the greencard proposal reportedly led to its retraction in 1985.

Trade Policies

Japanese trade policy exhibits the same bias toward small business characteristic of the credit and tax policy sectors. Most special fiscal and monetary incentives for the promotion of small business exports have disappeared in the face of strong foreign pressure for reduction of Japanese trade surpluses, but these incentives were dismantled much later than equivalent measures supportive of big business.[24] In the midst of sharp yen revaluation during 1985–1986, multibillion dollar small business countermeasures moved rapidly into place. And small business promotion remains the special priority objective of the government's Japan Export Trade Organization (JETRO), despite the ambivalence of Japan's large general trading companies (*sōgō shōsha*) toward such a policy. Indeed, even five of the seven telephone listings of the Japan Trade Center in New York City during the mid-1980s referred to small business related functions.

On the import side, Japanese trade policy once again offers special supports to small business and agriculture. All twenty-seven formal quota restrictions still remaining in 1985 protected products of these two sectors, including twenty-two shielding agriculture. Aside from agriculture, the sectors of most vigorous Japanese protectionism—even greater than that afforded strategic high-technology infant industries—are those involving processing by small Japanese businesses of imported raw materials, such as plywood, other processed lumber products, and silk textiles.

[24] See Japan Export Trade Organization, *Japanese Trade Incentives*, on this point.

Public Policy and the Distribution Sector

In sector specific as well as credit, tax, and trade policies, the bias of Japanese politics and administration toward the small clearly shows itself. The most dramatic case in point, no doubt, is distribution. Japan has a strikingly more complex and inefficient distribution system than any other industrialized nation, contrasting sharply to Japan's celebrated efficiencies in other areas. There are, for example, about 65,000 retail outlets for electric appliances in Japan, three times the number in West Germany and even more than in the United States, although Japan has only half the U.S. population. Japan has three times as many retail outlets for clothing as either Britain or France and twice as many as the United States.[25] Japan has triple the number of retailers per capita of Britain and West Germany, double that of the United States, and one third more per capita than even France, with its long tradition of Poujadiste and other protest against distribution sector rationalization.[26] Even the scale of the largest Japanese retailers does not approach that of their Western counterparts. For example, Daiei, the largest Japanese retailer, has only one seventh the sales and only one fifth the number of outlets of Sears, its American counterpart.[27] This is the precise opposite of patterns in manufacturing. For example, Japan's ten largest steel mills had nearly double the production capacity of their American competitors.[28]

Public policy is a primary cause of the inefficiencies in Japanese distribution. Like most major European nations and even the United States, Japan entered the industrial era with a cumbersome traditional network of small family stores. Some nations, notably the United States, allowed market forces to rationalize this network in the late nineteenth and early twentieth centuries.[29] Some, like Britain, countenanced rationalization dur-

[25] Hugh Sandeman, ed., *Japan*, p. 30.

[26] See Thomas K. McCraw and Patricia A. O'Brien, "Production and Distribution: Competition Policy and Industry Structure," in *America versus Japan*, ed. Thomas K. McCraw, p. 101.

[27] Sears annual sales for 1983 were $35.9 billion compared to $5.1 billion for Daiei. The top ten U.S. retailers averaged $14.1 billion in annual sales, compared to $2.65 billion for their Japanese counterparts. See *ibid.*, p. 103.

[28] Japan's ten largest steel mills had a crude steel production capacity during 1977–1978 of 106.5 million tons, compared with 58.9 million for the ten largest American plants. See *ibid.*, p. 87.

[29] On the rationalization of distribution in the United States, see Louis Bucklin,

ing the high-growth era of the 1950s and 1960s, while others allowed some concentration of distribution as a rationalization measure following the oil shock of 1973.[30] But Japan moved, albeit erratically, in the opposite direction, sharply tightening political barriers to rationalization during the early 1970s, after gradually dismantling those barriers during the previous decade.

As a result of the tight controls over market-oriented changes in Japan's distribution system, which became formalized in the early 1970s, the predominance of small stores is being preserved. Of Japan's retail outlets 60 percent still employ only one or two people, and 45 percent of wholesalers employ four or fewer people. The distribution sector, sheltered by public policy from structural change, serves as a massive "labor sponge" absorbing a substantial fraction of workers rendered redundant by rapidly progressing automation. Between 1965 and 1984, employment in distribution increased in every year but 1973, the year the Large-Scale Retail Store Law was passed.[31] Manufacturing employment, by contrast, declined in eight of those years, including seven of eleven years between 1973 and 1984.[32]

As indicated earlier in the chapter, employment in the distribution sector rose by nearly three million over the 1972–1981 decade, a figure equivalent to about 5 percent of the entire Japanese labor force in 1981. Had distribution-sector unemployment remained constant, unemployment in Japan would have been more than triple the 2 to 3 percent it has consistently averaged over the past decade and close to European and American levels. Conservative policies have, by forestalling rationalization of the distribution sector, deprived the Left of a political issue which might otherwise seriously threaten continued political preeminence of the Right in Japan. They have also indirectly served the ends of industrial policy, by making aggressive automation in export sectors politically palatable through defusing its employment consequences.

Competition and Evolution in the Distributive Trade, and Joseph Cornwall Palamountain, Jr., *The Politics of Distribution.*

[30] For details concerning policies toward rationalization of the distribution sector in major European nations, see for example, Commission of the European Community, *Preliminary Study on Competition in the Retail Trade*; Commission of the European Communities, *Changes in the Structure of the Retail Trade in Europe*; and Ross L. Davies, ed., *Retail Planning in the European Community.*

[31] Ministry of Labor (Rōdō Shō), *Rōdō Hakusho* (Labor Handbook), 1985, appendix 8.

[32] *Ibid.*

Other Sectoral Policies

Distribution is by no means the only area where the sector-specific policies of the Japanese government have significantly aided small business. Targeted government assistance to the auto parts industry was strategic in fueling international competitiveness in that sector.[33] Indeed, a crucial competitive difference between the Japanese auto industry and many of its East Asian competitors such as the Korean industry, for years lay precisely in the early, successful rationalization of the components sector of the Japanese auto industry. This was carried out through small-business policy mechanisms, such as low interest loans from the Small Business Finance Corporation.

Small business policies have also been important in the rationalization of depressed industries, both those of the 1960s, such as coal and cotton textiles,[34] and the much larger problems of structural adjustment after the oil shock of 1973. Energy shock and yen revaluation, together with the need to preserve traditional industries, values, and skills as well as to reinvigorate depressed regions, were used as rationales for policy measures with pronounced small business orientation. In a rare confluence of domestic political crisis (1971–1976) and international economic crisis (1971–1972, 1973–1974, 1977–1978, and 1979–1980), a blizzard of small business–related legislation ensued, including the Law Concerning the Promotion of Traditional Craft Industries (1974), the Domain Protection Law (1977), the so-called yen revaluation countermeasures legislation (1978), and the Law on Extraordinary Measures for Small and Medium Enterprises Located Together in Specific Areas (the so-called *sanchi taisaku*, enacted in 1979).

Significantly, all these measures were enacted during periods of either domestic political or international economic crisis, as defined in chapter 1. During the domestic crises (1949–1954, 1958–1963, and 1971–1976) the need to preempt opposition overtures to crucial swing constituencies, like small business, was especially acute. Even after JSP and JCP strength waned with the 1976 election, yen revaluation, oil shock, and periodic trade conflicts threatened small business from outside and continued to

[33] See Kent E. Calder, "Politics and the Market," pp. 427–41.

[34] The 1976 Law on Extraordinary Measures for the Structural Improvement of Textile Industries, which encouraged the move from cotton to synthetic fibers, was a typical example.

provoke some degree of innovation in small business policy. During the 1975–1982 period, small firms in thirty-eight industries were designated under the Small and Medium Enterprise Promotion Law as eligible for special modernization plans.[35] Among these were printed circuit boards and industrial tools, two sectors thought to have considerable future potential, although most were traditional, noncompetitive sectors ranging from Japanese screens to scrap iron. Among the best known cases of government assistance to small business in Japan has been that of machine tools, a sector where the Japanese political economy's pervasive bias toward the small has had clear implications for international competitiveness.

Machine Tools: Competitiveness Through Aid to the Small

Japan's machine tools sector, like machine tool industries everywhere in the world, is dominated by small business. In the mid-1980s there were around six hundred machine tool firms in Japan,[36] with more than 90 percent of the nearly two thousand Japanese plants manufacturing machine tools employing less than fifty workers. Many of the smaller machine tool plants were located in outlying towns near the Japan Sea coast, with one major center being Nagaoka, Niigata Prefecture, in the center of former Prime Minister Tanaka Kakuei's electoral district.

In addition to the small firms, there are also several relatively large and rapidly growing affiliates of major Japanese electronics makers. For example, Fanuc, an affiliate of Fujitsu, currently produces around 50 percent of Japan's numerical control machine tools. These large firms are not as well-connected politically as many of the smaller firms, but they have indirectly benefited substantially from government policies in machine tools that are oriented to aid the small, particularly through the assistance given their subcontractors.

The economic success of the Japanese machine tool industry over the past two decades has been dramatic. In 1958 Japan imported 40 percent of its meager consumption of ¥34.4 billion in machine tools; the import share fell steadily to 31 percent in

[35] Small and Medium Enterprise Agency, *Outline of Small and Medium Enterprise Politics of the Japanese Government*, p. 10.

[36] Yamaichi Shōken Keizai Kenkyū Jo, ed., *Sangyō Tōkei 1984*, p. 155.

1960, 18.5 percent in 1965, and only 7.3 percent by 1973.[37] Domestic production by 1973 was nine times the figure of only fifteen years before; in fact, 11.5 percent of this production was now exported. Less than a decade later in 1982, domestic production had doubled again to ¥578.8 billion, of which 31.6 percent was exported.[38]

The impact of this Japanese success in machine tools has been especially strong in the United States. Between 1965 and 1981, Japanese producers' share of the U.S. market in numerical control machining centers, one of the most rapidly growing segments of the industry, rocketed from 3.7 percent to 50.1 percent.[39] Exports in this segment represented 55.8 percent of Japanese production, and over half of the exports (25.7 percent of total Japanese production) went to the United States.[40] This ratio of U.S.-bound exports to total production prevails across nearly the full range of Japanese machine tool exports.

In many industrialized nations, such as France and the United States, the machine tools sector has been hurt by government administrators' bias against the small or by an indifference to the escalating perils many small firms have experienced in an era of low growth, high interest rates, and intermittent, highly deflationary oil shocks. Yet in Japan public policy seems to have had the reverse effect; sensitive to the particular problems of small firms, it has provided them with the information, insulation from capricious risk, capital, and assistance in market development they need to survive and prosper in a volatile global economic environment.

Machine tools is an area where the structural bias of the Japanese political economy toward the small has coincided with the requisites of sectoral development. This coincidence has had strong positive implications for global Japanese competitiveness, in an area of rising importance for industrial structure through-

[37] Chokki Toshiaki, *Kōsaku Kikai Gyōkai* (Machine Tools Industry), Tokyo: Kyōiku Sha, 1978, p. 92; and Yamaichi Shōken Keizai Kenkyū Jo, ed., *Sangyō-Tokei 1984*, p. 156.

[38] Yamaichi Shōken Keizai Kenkyū Jo, ed., *Sangyō Tōkei 1984*, p. 157.

[39] Houdaille Industries, Inc., Petition to the President of the United States through the Office of the United States Special Trade Representative for the Exercise of Presidential Discretion. Authorized by Section 103 of the Revenue Act of 1971, p. 2.

[40] *Ibid.*, p. 127.

out the trilateral world.[41] The sensitivity of Japanese public policy toward the small started to emerge long before the machine tool industry began its spectacular growth with the emergence of numerical controls during the 1970s, but it provided a context in which politicians and bureaucrats were conditioned to be alert to opportunities missed by public policy elsewhere in the world.

One striking feature of Japanese industrial policy toward machine tools, seen in comparative perspective, has been the reality of any coordinated policy at all. In France, the state sporadically intervened during the 1945–1947 period in machine tool development. But it then gave up systematic attempts to coordinate development of the sector until the late 1970s, seeing the needs of the industry as too difficult to evaluate and its products too highly diversified.[42] Behind this indifference was a general administrative disdain for small business and a frustration at dealing with small firms, often family businesses, which were continually opposing government attempts at rationalization.

In Japan, by contrast to France, the supervising ministry (MITI) encouraged creation of the Japan Machine Tool Producers Association in 1953 and then introduced the first of three basic laws for the electronic and machinery industries in 1956. From February 1954, machine tools benefited through a so-called "link system," by which the proceeds from sugar quotas sold in Japan were applied to support the industry's development. Although this system was abolished in the 1960s, it had been supplemented long before then by a range of financial and tax incentives. Japan Development Bank special loans extended to the designated machinery industries, of which machine tools was a central member, rose from ¥3.4 billion in 1956 to around ¥12.9 billion in 1973 before falling back to around ¥2.5 billion in 1980.[43] Machinery related special loans from the Small Business Financial Corporation, of which a very large share went to machine tools, averaged over ¥3 billion annually throughout the

[41] As Piore and Sabel point out, industrial society in the 1980s is witnessing the rapid emergence of production through systems of flexible specialization, in which numerically controlled machine tools play a central role. See Michael J. Piore and Charles F. Sabel, *The Second Industrial Divide*.

[42] See Jean Michel Saussois, "Industrial Policy at Sector Level: The Case of the Machine Tool Industry in France" (Paper presented at the 4th EGOS Conference, Firenze, November 3–5, 1983), p. 6.

[43] Houdaille Petition, p. D185.

1960s and around ¥1 billion annually ever since.[44] Research and development grants from the Japanese government to its machine tool industry averaged ¥8 to 10 billion annually from 1965 to 1975.[45] Among the most important actions of the Japanese government in relation to machine tools was its coordination of small firms, which might otherwise have had trouble coming together, through rationalization cartels. MITI has also sponsored joint arrangements for parts and materials purchase, production quotas, and restrictions on kinds of products manufactured, most recently under Article 2 of the 1971 Law for Special Measures to Promote Machinery and Electronics Industries.

Specialization, though difficult for small businesses, is also critical to competitiveness because there are major economies of scale in the machine tool industry. In particular, MITI has forced specialization in sophisticated components and systems which use state-of-the-art machinery, under the Elevation Plans authorized by the Third Extraordinary Measures Law of July 1978. The French state, as Jean Michel Saussois points out, has only attempted enforcing such specialization half-heartedly and with little success.[46]

Perhaps the most striking success of Japanese industrial policy in relation to machine tools has been to link that sector to electronics through the development of numerical control machinery. The actual perception of these linkages and the development of numerical control machinery itself are achievements of Japanese industrial policy in general, beyond the scope of this chapter. But machining centers, numerical controlled punching machines, and other such equipment have achieved market success for reasons profoundly linked to Japan's bias toward the small. In particular, the accelerated depreciation programs for machines and equipment used by small businesses, the accelerated depreciation program for high-efficiency machine tools, government leasing programs, government information programs, and other new industrial policy measures of the 1970s, oriented heavily toward small business, created and expanded the market for numerically controlled machinery. Aggressive, persistent entrepreneurship clearly had a major role, and government support was relatively minor in financial terms. But the government was in-

[44] *Ibid.*, p. D187

[45] Julian Gresser, *Partners in Prosperity*, p. 170.

[46] Saussois, "Industrial Policy," p. 8.

dispensable at a number of key strategic points, as in providing information and assistance during the 1960s for export marketing.[47]

The share of numerical control machinery in total Japanese machine tool production rose from 7.8 percent in 1970 to 67.9 percent in 1986. This in turn created economies of scale in numerical control machinery, giving Japan tremendous competitiveness in foreign markets.[48] These developments have no analogue in either France or the United States, just as the early Japanese appreciation of commercial applications for synergisms between machinery and electronics likewise do not.[49]

Ezra Vogel correctly points to Japanese machine tool industry development as a clear case of efficient state nurturing of industrial competitiveness,[50] but it is important not to ignore the broader political context of this effort. The Japanese government has not always assisted sectors dominated by small but potentially promising firms. Indeed, there are important cases as late as the mid-1950s when it specifically refused to do so.[51] But during certain key periods, such as the early 1960s and early 1970s, it has assisted them vigorously. To understand when and how the Japanese government, or any government, energetically supports small businesses with long-run economic potential, and what tools it uses to do so, one must look at the political as well as the industrial strategic context of state actions.

Crisis and the Making of Small Business Policy

Throughout its modern history Japan has had one of the most pronounced dual economic structures in the industrialized

[47] Vogel, *Comeback*, p. 79.

[48] Yamaichi Shōken Keizai Kenkyū Jo, ed., *Sangyō no Subete '87*, p. 130.

[49] The U.S. military, U.S. military contractors, and U.S. universities, of course, recognized even earlier than the Japanese that electronics and precision machinery could be linked. Indeed, discoveries at the Servo-mechanics Laboratory at MIT in 1952 stimulated the original Japanese commercial applications work in numerical controls; see Vogel, *Comeback*, p. 80. But while Japanese firms seized avidly on prospective commercial applications and pursued them, Western firms generally did not.

[50] *Ibid.*, pp. 58–95.

[51] Amagasaki Steel, for example, had some of the most advanced blast furnace technology in Japan, but it was allowed to go bankrupt in 1954, with the Bank of Japan refusing to intervene. For details of the Amagasaki bankruptcy case, see Calder, "Politics and the Market," appendix 4.

world—that is, characterized by both a large, highly developed big business sector and an analogous small business segment. Big business has been well-organized and politically as well as economically powerful; small firms have often borne the brunt of cyclical adjustment, either through interest rate increases or through exchange rate realignment.[52] Time and time again Japanese small businesses have been exposed to sharp, painful shocks which have, particularly during the prewar period and the 1950s, sent many firms into bankruptcy. Even during the late 1970s, the rate of bankruptcy in Japan was twice that in the United States, and the average liabilities per bankruptcy were also twice as great.[53]

With the overall structure of the Japanese political economy dominated by a bureaucracy and big business world strongly oriented toward stability, a major driving force behind the evolution of small business policy has inevitably been crisis, specifically political crisis perceived by conservative politicians as threatening the continuity of both ruling party preeminence and the predictable macroeconomic management accompanying it. To be sure, the substance of policy has usually been drafted by technocrats. But it has been legislators who largely determine when the "policy window" is open and what sort of policy passes through it. Policy developments during crisis, especially conservative concessions to swing constituencies courted also by the Left, have given Japanese small business policy a distinctive populist flavor and helped preserve unbroken the continuity of conservative rule.

The first major crisis to shape Japanese small business policy was the Great Depression of the 1930s and the political turmoil surrounding it. During this period small business suffered greatly, especially during the two years that Inoue Junnosuke so resolutely deflated the Japanese economy by insisting Japan remain on the gold standard. As Nakamura Takafusa points out, the profound economic pressure of that period largely created Japan's distinctive dual industrial structure, which persists today.[54]

[52] See Hugh T. Patrick, "Cyclical Instability and Fiscal-Monetary Policy in Postwar Japan," in *The State and Economic Enterprise in Japan*, ed. William Lockwood.

[53] Gary Saxonhouse "Industrial Restructuring in Japan," *Journal of Japanese Studies* (Summer 1979): 273–320.

[54] On the emergence of Japan's dual-industrial structure in the midst of eco-

Crisis led to radicalism and ultimately to policy innovation by conservative governments preoccupied with stability. Unemployment steadily mounted, and in 1931 restless small businessmen, many newly thrown into bankruptcy by the double punch of depression and the rapid expansion of large department stores, founded the radical *Zen Nihon Shōkō Tō* (All Japan Commercial and Industrial party). Its dissatisfaction was influential in creating Japan's first small business finance institution, the Shōkō Chūkin Bank, founded in 1936.[55] This party, together with more moderate small business groups, such as the Retailers Association (*Kouri Shōten Renmei*), was also instrumental in the enactment of the Department Stores Law of 1937. This law restricted the expansion of large retailing, which had so severely threatened Japanese small business from the late 1920s.[56] A pattern of strategic political intervention to forestall concentration tendencies in distribution, together with the political unrest concentration threatened to entail, was established; this pattern of intervention was to be repeated again and again, well into the 1980s.

Following World War II, the same pattern of militant, seemingly radical opposition leading to conservative cooptation continued to prevail, indeed, in even more pronounced fashion than before the war. The Dodge Line of 1948–1949 led to severe hardship for small business, which bore the brunt of deflationary adjustment then just as it had in the 1930s. In 1948 an average of seven to eight people a day were dying of hunger in Tokyo alone.[57] In the midst of this economic chaos and suffering, the Living Standards Improvement Association (*Seikatsu Yōgo Dōmei*) was born. Changing its name to the National Commercial Association Cooperative Movement (*Zenkoku Shōkō Dantai Rengō Kai* or *Minshō*) in June 1952, this radical group was closely affiliated with, although independent from, the Communist party. Through insistent pressure on the conservatives by the media, on opposition parties in the Diet, and on progressive local

nomic crisis, see Nakamura Takafusa, *Economic Growth in Prewar Japan*, pp. 213–31.

[55] Shōkō Chūō Kinko, *Shōkō Chūkin Yon Jyū Nen Shi* (A Forty-Year History of the Shōkō Chūkin Bank).

[56] For details, see, for example, Shindō Jinshirō, *Minshō:Zenshōren no Ayumi* (The Path of the All Japan Commercial Federation); and Zenshōren Shi Henshū Iinkai, *Minshō: Zenshōren no San Jyū Nen* (Thirty Years of the All-Japan Commercial Federation).

[57] Shindō Jinshirō, *Minshō: Zenshōren no Ayumi*, vol. 1, p. 45.

government and through direct lobbying of its own, Minshō has in fact strongly influenced much of the agenda for Japanese small business policy over the past three decades, despite its defiant outsider status.

To an even greater degree than in the prewar period, political and economic crisis has driven not only interest group formation but also the evolution of small business policy. The first such postwar crisis arose in 1946–1947, when the government decided to allocate industrial funds quite narrowly to big business dominated sectors, like coal, steel, and electricity, thought fundamental to national economic recovery. Many small businesses went bankrupt, and opposition groups grew restive. Faced with impending national elections, the first Yoshida cabinet in February 1947 decided on a three-point small business program and established the basic framework for policy since that time. It included provisions for:

(1) Management instruction, provided by both civilian groups and public organizations;
(2) Promotion of small business organizations by small commercial cooperatives (*Shōkō Kyōdō Kumiai*); and
(3) Expanded government financial support for small business.[58]

The socialist Katayama cabinet that came to power the next month also supported this policy, setting a pattern of nonpartisan consensus within the Diet on small business policy, largely continuing to the present day.[59] In November 1947, the Katayama cabinet proposed the establishment of a "Small Business General Bureau" (*Chūshō Kigyō Sōkyoku*). Eight months later, in August 1948, the Small Business Agency was established. Former Kyoto University dean of economics, Ninagawa Torazō, became its first director, recruited by Mizutani Chōzaburō, then minister of Commerce and Industry in the Ashida cabinet and a Socialist supporter of small business from the Kyoto First District since entering the Diet in 1928.

The momentum of policy innovation continued and even in-

[58] Small and Medium Enterprise Agency (Chūshō Kigyō Chō), ed., *Chūshō Kigyō Chō Ni Jyū Go Nen Shi* (A Twenty-Five Year History of the Small Business Agency), 1973, p. 7.

[59] Mochizuki notes that by the 1965–1979 period small business issues were the one and only complex of issues upon which all of the three major non-Communist opposition parties agreed unanimously with the LDP in the Diet. See Mike Mochizuki, "Managing and Influencing the Japanese Legislative Process," p. 303.

tensified under the combined impact of the deflationary Dodge Line, the vigorous advocacy of Ninagawa, and the still precarious political circumstances of Japan's conservative parties, despite the Liberal election triumph of January 1949. The 3.1 million small businessmen of Japan made up a substantial fraction of the 10 million kōenkai (support association) members who sustained conservative politicans; these small businessmen were also a critical swing constituency.[60] In May 1949 the Small and Medium Enterprises Cooperative Associations Law, designed to facilitate small business mergers and protect small firms from big business encroachment was passed. In June 1949 the People's Finance Corporation (*Kokumin Kinyū Kōko*) was founded to provide funds to distributors and other extremely small firms. During the 1970s it came to play a most important role in sustaining LDP political preeminence with the advent of the no-collateral loan system.

Deep resistance to small business policy within the bureaucracy and big business remained, despite some steps forward under the impact of economic crisis and the vulnerable political circumstances of the two conservative parties. Finance Minister Ikeda Hayato was skeptical of suggestions that the Japanese government devote major resources to small business, and the occupation forces also remained skeptical about the need for small business policy, since the dual structure of the Japanese economy had no close analogue in the United States or Britain and could readily be justified only by analogy to defeated Germany. In the absence of domestic party political pressures, policies largely ignoring small business could well have prevailed in Japan. The catalytic role of perceived econopolitical crisis in engendering small business policy innovation was thus crucial.

The role of Ninagawa Torazō in creating and sustaining pressures for small business policy innovation, both during the 1949–1950 period that he served as the Small Business Agency's first director and subsequently, cannot be exaggerated. While SBA director, Ninagawa fought vigorously with both SCAP and the Yoshida government for small business.[61] He openly criticized Finance Minister Ikeda Hayato's proposed policies toward small business in a MITI Bulletin and was finally dismissed as director-general of the SBA for predicting a "March crisis" in the Japanese

[60] Soong Hoom Kil, "Dodge Line," pp. 336–37.

[61] Johnson, *MITI and the Japanese Miracle*, p. 222.

economy of 1950, centering on small business, which the Yoshida administration could not solve.[62]

On February 10, 1950, the dismissed Ninagawa returned to a hero's welcome in Kyoto's large small business community. Ninagawa was immediately drafted as a JSP, JCP, and Labor-Farmer party coalition gubernatorial candidate; a month later he defeated a conservative to become governor of Kyoto. Within months, several of Ninagawa's staff followed him from the Small Business Agency in Tokyo, providing the intellectual basis for innovative small business policies at Japan's periphery.

For the following *twenty-eight years* of his career as progressive governor of Kyoto, Ninagawa was a major force for small business policy innovation nationally, combining personal and staff expertise with the strong motivation of a progressive politician to offer alternatives to the status quo. His leverage in the national policy process was strengthened both by ties with the left-oriented national media and by cross-party interpersonal network ties with conservative mavericks. Ninagawa was reputed, for example, to have coordinated policy proposals privately with future LDP Prime Minister Miki Takeo, a member of the JSP-led Katayama cabinet of 1947–48.

Ninagawa's long and powerful role in small business policy innovation was complemented over the years by a host of other policy entrepreneurs with credibility across party lines in periods of political crisis. The Socialist Mizutani Chōzaburō, MCI minister during 1947–1948, retained old bureaucratic contacts into the late 1950s; Democratic Socialist Party leader Kasuga Ikkō, himself a small businessman, had strong conservative political ties during the 1970s and 1980s. On the Right, Ayukawa Gisuke, wartime head of the Nissan *konzerne* in Manchuria, worked vigorously for small business causes during the 1950s through a network of longstanding personal ties stretching from Prime Minister Kishi Nobusuke, a wartime acquaintance in Manchuria, to JSP leaders Asanuma Inejirō and Katsumata Seiichi. During the 1970s Nagano Shigeo, chairman of Nippon Steel who became chairman of the small-business-oriented Japan Chamber of Commerce and Industry, played a similar, albeit less flamboyant, advocacy role on behalf of small firms.

[62] Gotōda Teruo, "Politics, Power, and Personalities in the Prefectural Government of Kyoto: A Study of Japanese Local Politics," Ph.D. diss., University of California 1983, pp. 132–33.

The second wave of postwar innovation in Japanese small business policy, following the rush of developments in 1949–1950, came during 1952–1954, the latter part of the first major postwar crisis period. The Korean War boom which had immensely benefited small business was coming to an abrupt end, triggering a rash of bankruptcies, provoking industrial concentration, and raising unemployment. Sharp recession coincided with a period of unusual political uncertainty for conservatives, aggravated by incessant criticism from progressives like Kyoto Governor Ninagawa. The supportive Allied political presence was receding, following the occupation's end in April 1952, yet conservatives could not unite on whom they wanted to rule Japan. These deep splits within conservative ranks, described more fully in chapters 1 and 2, rendered conservative politicians especially sensitive to grassroots pressures, such as those from the well-organized small business groups.

Small business pressure groups were beginning to form rapidly during this period, in response to economic crisis and accompanying concentration tendencies in both manufacturing and distribution. In 1950 the Small Business Organizations League (*Chūshō Kigyō Dantai Renmei,* or *Nichūren*), was formed. 1952 saw the birth of the communist-affiliate *Zenshōren.* In April 1956, *Chūseiren* was founded by Ayukawa Gisuke, who invested over ¥500 million in organizing small businesses politically after he was purged by the occupation forces. By late 1956 an average of one hundred small business labor union groups per month formed to engage in some sort of political activity.[63] The Japanese political process could hardly be called monistic or unified in this policy area.

The outcome of this situation was a period of major policy innovation favoring small business, together with strategic vetoes of anti–small business legislation. In August 1952 a law was passed to permit "adjustment associations" (in effect legalized cartels) to control small business over-production, through selective exemptions from the Anti-Monopoly Law. In September 1953 the Small Business Finance Corporation was founded at Diet initiative in response to interest group pressure, despite opposition from bureaucrats who favored other institutional forms.[64] Small

[63] *Asahi Shimbun,* December 12, 1956.

[64] See Small and Medium Enterprise Finance Corporation (Chūshō Kigyō Kinyū Kōko), *Chūshō Kigyō Kinyū Kōko Ni Jyū Go Nen Shi* (Twenty-Five Year History of the Small Business Finance Corporation), pp. 65–88 for details.

business groups had been struggling six years to realize this goal,[65] and their struggle produced results. Associations to insure small business against certain kinds of risk were authorized.[66] A textile consumer tax revision bill was also shelved due to demonstrations, strikes by such groups as the Nishijin silk weavers of Kyoto,[67] and determined small-business lobbying. During 1954 administrative controls were reintroduced to restrain the growth of large retailers who had expanded following repeal of the Department Store Law at occupation insistence during 1947.

By 1956 the Japanese small business movement had determined leadership, broad elite contacts, and enhanced funding, with the involvement of figures such as Ayukawa Gisuke. The movement had rising organizational strength, with four major federations of small businessmen recently organized.[68] As the Poujadiste movement in France was surging to its zenith, Japanese small business protest also had internationally induced momentum. But two critical elements of the political and economic situation had changed since the period of great institutional innovation in the early 1950s. First, economic crisis had passed. Even more important, the conservatives were now politically unified, following the crucial resignation of Prime Minister Yoshida Shigeru in December 1954, the unification of the Liberal and Democratic parties in November 1955, and the sudden death of the influential Ogata Taketora in January 1956.

In the stable new political and economic environment of the mid-1950s, small business groups, for all their new fervor and organization, found it difficult to attain their policy goals. The Small Business Organization Law (*Chūshō Kigyō Dantai Hō*) initially died in a House of Counselors committee, sidetracked by a potent big business–big labor coalition.[69] Only in November 1957, nearly eighteen months after the inception of the bill, did

[65] On this struggle, see Nakajima Hidenobu, "Sengo Chūshō Kigyō Undō no Rekishi to Kyōka" ("Postwar Small and Medium-size Enterprises: Their History and Consolidation"), *Chūshō Kigyō Jyānaru* (Aug. 1968), pp. 1–13.

[66] Small and Medium Enterprise Agency (Chūshō Kigyō Chō), ed., *Chūshō Kigyō Chō Ni Jyū Go Nen Shi*, p. 21.

[67] Allan B. Cole, *Political Tendencies of Japanese in Small Enterprises* (New York: Institute of Pacific Relations, 1959), p. 142.

[68] *Ibid.*, pp. 70–91.

[69] For details, see *ibid.*, pp. 56–59, and Kobayashi Naoki, "The Small and Medium Sized Enterprises Organization Law," in Itō Hiroshi, ed., *Japanese Politics: An Inside View*, p. 60.

it finally become law. Similarly, small business was unable, despite years of effort, to secure legal penalties against companies delaying payments to subcontractors; the LDP in 1956 only accepted weakened legislation providing for investigations by an ineffectual Fair Trade Commission.[70] The day of pervasive small-business influence in Japanese politics had not yet dawned, although the Japanese bureaucracy lacked the dominance of policymaking displayed by the French bureaucrats of the same period, when they introduced and passed a value-added tax through the National Assembly (1956) over strong Poujadiste protests.[71]

Crisis next rocked Japanese conservatism in 1958–1960. Following the Security Treaty crisis, the new Prime Minister Ikeda Hayato moved quickly to palliate the basic potential constituencies of the opposition. Beginning with decisive intervention to peacefully terminate the extended Mitsui Miike coal mine strike, Ikeda moved on to propose a new Basic Agricultural Law. Then the man who ten years before had told the Diet in opposing small business aid that "The poor should eat barley" initiated Japan's most sweeping reform of small business policy.[72] Policy innovation in this area was thus influenced by two crisis-related factors: (1) direct pressures from the opposition and influential small business groups, and (2) desires by conservative leaders to defuse political tensions by preempting the opposition.

As a first response to the turbulence around 1960 in the small business policy area, Japanese conservatives attempted a fuller incorporation of small firms within the structure of conservative administrative and political power. In May 1960 the Organization of Commerce and Industry Law was enacted, authorizing subsidies for conservative civic bodies in their advisory work with small firms; Chambers of Commerce (*Shōkō Kaigi Sho*) and Prefectural Commerce and Industry Committees were the major

[70] Cole, *Political Tendencies of Japanese in Small Enterprises*, p. 91.

[71] This movement presents a fruitful basis for comparison with the contemporary Japanese small business movements. On Poujadisme, see Stanley Hoffmann, *Le Mouvement Poujade*; also, Dominique Bourne, *Petits bourgeois en revolte? Le Mouvement Poujade.*

[72] Finance Minister Ikeda, queried by the press about the early 1950 economic crisis following Diet interpellations also said "it could not be helped" that numerous small business bankruptcies would occur. See *Asahi Shimbun*, March 3, 1950.

targets of this legislation.[73] In July 1961, the ruling Liberal Democratic Party also established its own small business affiliate, the Small Business General League (*Chūshō Kigyō Sō Rengō*), in the face of strong opposition from established small business pressure groups, such as Ayukawa Gisuke's Chūseiren. The LDP's move led to a rapid alignment of the small business pressure groups with individual political parties. By 1965 each of the major parties had a small business pressure group affiliate, thus seriously eroding the influence of the independent, nonparty pressure groups and transforming Japanese small business policymaking from a pluralist to a more clientelistic mode.

The second pillar of the Ikeda administration's crisis-response strategy was policy innovation, drawing heavily on ideas proposed earlier by the opposition parties and the independent small business pressure groups. The urge to innovate gained a particular edge by the way economic circumstances converged with political crisis: between 1959 and 1961, the number of independent and family businesses in Japan dropped by 620,000, due to inability to compete with larger firms for labor supplies.[74] Small firms, with a strong need for government assistance, were lobbying all the major political parties in an effort to get it. The concept of a Small Business Basic Law to systematize monetary, tax, and other measures of support for small business had been pressed strongly during the late 1950s by Ayukawa Gisuke and other small business leaders without full success. In the wake of the Security Treaty Crisis and the ascension of Ikeda Hayato to the prime ministership in July 1960, this concept gathered greater momentum.

Early in 1962, the Japan Socialist Party strongly criticized the Ikeda cabinet's "Rapid Economic Growth Measures" for their supposed bias toward big business and failure to consider the plight of small business, agriculture, and the working class.[75] Both the JSP and the Democratic Socialist Party announced an intention to submit to the Diet a Small Business Basic Law to correct these inequities. With an Upper House election immi-

[73] Particular emphasis was placed on developing policies of private sector assistance for small manufacturing firms with fewer than twenty employees and small distributors with less than five employees. for details, see Small and Medium Enterprise Agency (Chūshō Kigyō Chō), *Chūshō Kigyō Chō San Jyū Nen Shi* (*A Thirty-Year History of the Small Business Agency*), p. 23.

[74] Zenshōren Shi Henshū Iinkai, ed., *Minshō*, p. 131.

[75] *Asahi Shimbun*, January 24, 1962.

nent, LDP Diet members strongly pressed the Ministry of International Trade and Industry to immediately draft a cabinet bill to address the issues the opposition was proposing to raise. When MITI refused to produce one abruptly, citing various technical complications, the LDP introduced its own Members' Bill. After a year of political skirmishing, the Small Business Basic Law was passed in 1963 as an Ikeda administration cabinet bill, but it was profoundly influenced in both timing and substance by the opposition.

In late fall 1964, just as the Tokyo Olympics were ending, the Japanese economy began spiraling downward into its worst postwar recession. Many thought that the days of rapid growth were over. Bankruptcies soared, with small business taking the brunt of the downturn. Yet no major new small business support programs were forthcoming. For despite the economic crisis, the political world was stable. As the rigidity of small business policy during 1964–1965 shows clearly, political rather than economic crisis often elicits policy compensation for small business in Japan.

While the economic crisis of 1964–1965 did not generate much new small business policy or greatly expanded support expenditures, it clearly gave birth to protest, which evolved into policy when broad-based national political crisis emerged to support that protest. The dynamics of this sort of incubated policy change are clear in the birth of the no-collateral loan system—one of the largest government credit programs in Japan by the late 1970s. This system clearly and unambiguously originated in radical grassroots demands and initiatives, rather than in the designs of the bureaucracy. During the recession of 1965, Minshō, the Left-oriented small business federation, began stridently demanding no-collateral loans for small business, citing two major precedents: It argued that small, distressed firms deserved equal treatment with both the large but unstable Yamaichi Securities, one of Japan's "Big Four" securities firms, which was granted an extraordinary no-collateral Bank of Japan loan during 1965 through the intervention of MOF Minister Tanaka Kakuei, and the dictatorial Park Chung Hee regime in South Korea, which was granted ¥180 billion in unconditional yen credits the same year. The conservative Satō administration initially demurred, but the sympathetic left-wing prefectural government of Ninagawa Torazō in Kyoto acceded to Minshō's request in 1966.

In the absence of political crisis, the Satō administration and the responsible bureaucrats adopted a generally technocratic, unresponsive stance on small business issues during the late 1960s. Like the French, whose industrial policy was highly influential in Tokyo at the time,[76] Japanese industrial strategists admired industrial concentration and gave small firms rather low priority. Political pressures did not force the bureaucrats to restrain the impulses these principles of industrial strategy generated. National authorities failed to adopt the no-collateral loan system, ignoring Kyoto's example.

Even more important were changes in the distribution sector. MITI permitted existing department stores, such as Seibu, to open many new branches and allowed major new chains like Daiei to expand. MITI also encouraged small independent operators to cooperate in forming voluntary chains,[77] amidst predictions of a "distribution revolution" involving the emergence of mass retailing and the decline of small stores,[78] as in fact occurred in several of the major European nations.

Despite reluctance by conservative national authorities in Tokyo throughout the late 1960s, more and more of the progressive local governments of Japan's major urban areas introduced the no-collateral system, using it to attract small business support from the LDP at both the local and national levels. As indicated in figure 7.2, Minshō's national membership rose spectacularly, from less than 80,000 when Kyoto introduced the no-collateral loan system in 1966, to more than 200,000 by 1972.[79] In the general elections of 1972, national small business support for the Left brought the combined Socialist-Communist vote to well over 30 percent in many of Japan's largest metropolitan areas.[80]

Like most innovations in small business policy, establishment of the no-collateral loan program at the national level was provoked by crisis—in this case political crisis for the ruling LDP. The December 1972 Lower House elections saw both a sharp loss of seventeen seats for the LDP and a dramatic gain from fourteen

[76] For details, see Johnson, *MITI and the Japanese Miracle*, pp. 267–68, 275–304.

[77] Thomas McCraw, ed., *America versus Japan*, p. 109.

[78] See, for example, Hayashi Shūji. *Ryūtsū Kakumei* (Distribution Revolution) (Tokyo: Chūō Kōron Sha, 1962).

[79] Minshō internal data.

[80] In Kyoto, for example, the Communists polled 24.6 percent of the total vote in 1972, while the Socialists polled 19 percent, for a joint total of 43.6 percent. In Ōsaka the joint total was 38.8 percent and in Tokyo 39.5 percent. See Soma Masao, ed. *Kokusei Senkyō to Seitō Seiji*, pp. 570–71.

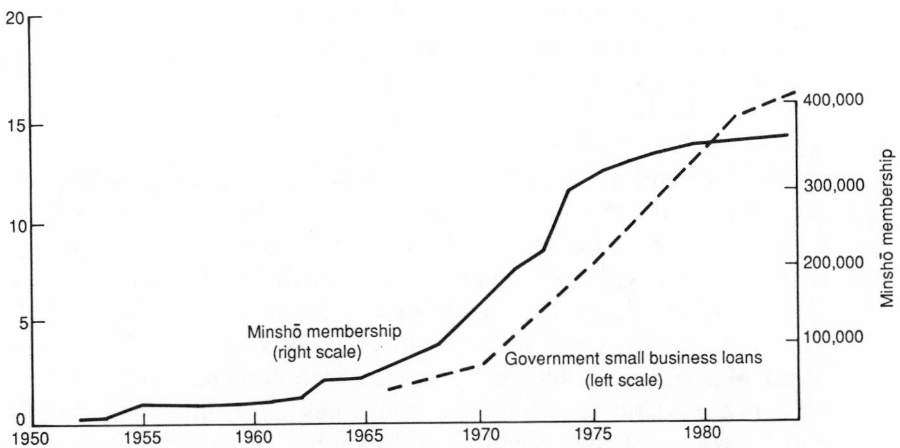

Figure 7.2. Crisis and Compensation: Government Small Business Loans and the Rise of Minshō (loans outstanding by the three major small business specialist government financial institutions).

Sources: Bank of Japan Research and Statistics Department (Nihon Ginkō Chosa Tōkei Kyoku), *Keizai Tōkei Nenpō (Economics Statistics Annual)* (Tokyo: Bank of Japan, various issues). Figures on Minshō membership are from unpublished Minshō internal data.

to thirty-eight total seats in the Lower House for the Communists. In many of Japan's major urban centers, Communist candidates drew over 20 percent of the vote, their highest levels in history. LDP margins nationwide were correspondingly thin. The election was traumatizing for both LDP politicians and the big business community, who saw it opening the prospect of political and economic chaos in the not-too-distant future.

Small business voters were highly organized, given the strength of corporatist relationships within Japan's tiny firms, and had specific material interests to which the LDP could appeal through financial and tax benefits. They had much more potential for LDP organizers desperately intent on broadening the party's political base than the disillusioned young "floating voters" of the cities, with their strong antiestablishment orientation. Progressive Kyoto Governor Ninagawa Torazō had been cultivating small business effectively,[81] as had progressive Tokyo Governor Minobe Ryōkichi, among others.

[81] On Ninagawa administration policies in the 1960s and 1970s, see Ellis Krauss, "Opposition in Power," pp. 383–424.

As conservative strategists plotted a response to the new challenge from the Left, they noted the Ninagawa-Minobe compensation strategy and resolved to counter it. In 1971, then secretary general of the LDP Nakasone Yasuhiro had presciently noted that left-oriented small business groups like Minshō were "taking away small and medium business people who are the political backbone of the LDP."[82] Both Nakasone and Japan Chamber of Commerce Chairman Nagano Shigeo were subsequently major advocates of an aggressive plan to court small business as a key element in the desperate LDP attempt to retain a Diet majority. The eight million small-scale employers of Japan were, as Maruyama Masao had so succinctly put it, "the non-commissioned officers of civil society"[83] on the front lines, as Japanese conservatives saw it, of the crucial struggle against resurgent communism.

Following the LDP's 1972 general election debacle, the conservative response was prompt, across a broad range of small business as well as other policy sectors. The no-collateral loan program, which the Left had pioneered in Kyoto, Tokyo, and elsewhere, was finally implemented by the conservatives at the national level, with loans approved through the conservative local Japan Chamber of Commerce branches, and then rapidly expanded. At the direction of Prime Minister Tanaka, MITI began investigating creation of a special Small Business Ministry.[84] In one year alone (1973–1974) central government small business expenditures rose 29 percent, largely due to subsidies charged to the general account budget in support of the new no-collateral loan program. By 1979, small business policy expenditures had reached ¥28.6 billion, or more than seven times the level of 1972.[85] Perhaps even more importantly, the conservative government gave a wide range of new tax dispensations to small business in an attempt to combat Minshō's tax-oriented strategy. As these aggressive new conservative compensation strategies for

[82] Zenshōren Shi Henshū Iinkai, ed., *Minshō*, p. 251.

[83] See Maruyama Masao, "The Ideology and Movement of Japanese Fascism," *The Japan Annual of Law and Politics*, No. 1 (1952), pp. 95–128, especially section 5, "Social Exponents of the Fascist Movements."

[84] Small and Medium Enterprise Agency (Chūshō Kigyō Chō), *Chūshō Kigyō Chō Ni Jyū Go Nen Shi*, pp. 10–13

[85] Ministry of Finance Budget Bureau Research Section, *Zaisei Tokei*, 1986 ed., p. 224 and p. 231.

small business began to take hold, the meteoric membership growth rates for Minshō fell sharply (figure 7.3).

Among the most important small business policy innovations of the early 1970s crisis period, from an international perspective, was the Large Scale Retail Store Law, passed in early fall 1973 to control the expansion of the chain stores threatening smaller firms. Under this legislation any firm wanting to establish a retail outlet with floor space over 1,500 square meters had to obtain the prior permission of MITI before opening a new store. In making authorization decisions, MITI was to be advised by a local Council for Regulating Commercial Activities, consisting of community merchants, consumers, and scholars—most of them typically unsympathetic to chain store expansion. Similar licensing procedures were extended in 1978 to all retail outlets over 500 square meters, virtually halting chain store expansion.[86]

During late 1973, the first oil shock rudely hit Japan. Structural adjustment policies, together with restraints on the expansion of supermarkets, soon followed. Included among the adjustment policies was a system of long-term, low-interest overseas investment and "foreign trade preparation finance" schemes, channelled through the Small Business Finance Corporation.

Even as the political strength of the Left and the sense of domestic crisis for the conservatives began to wane in the late 1970s, international economic crisis continued periodically to threaten small business and stimulate policy innovation. Following the sharp revaluation of the yen during 1978, additional small business measures were introduced, both for specific industries and for particular producing regions (*sanchi*) that were affected. Then during 1985–1986 import competing firms, together with Japanese small businesses engaged in international trade, were hit with the traumatic shock of massive, abrupt yen revaluation. Within six months, the yen rose over 40 percent against the dollar. Almost immediately, the government responded with a program of loans and subsidies valued at well over $1 billion. International crisis, it seemed, was capable of generating compensation just as had domestic crisis before it.

The 1980s have shown some important nuances in the treatment of small business which affirm the operation of the crisis

[86] During the 1981–1984 period, for example, applications to MITI for new stores of 500- to 1500-meter floor space averaged around 300 per year—only one for every 400,000 Japanese consumers. Internal MITI documents, cited in McCraw, ed., *America versus Japan*, p. 111.

and compensation dynamic. Support measures for small business in the wake of the 1985–1986 yen revaluation were less extensive and less readily tendered than had been the case in similar circumstances during the 1970s. Government small business support programs in the domestic area, such as no-collateral loans, were also less extensive, as a share of both the general account budget and off-budget credit programs, than they had previously been. But Japanese public policy's small business bias, created and reinforced in previous crisis periods, remained much stronger than anywhere in the industrialized West.

Conservative rule has weathered successfully the wide range of crises and threats which it has faced. But the imprint of those past crises remains deep on today's small business policy in Japan and on the institutional structures created to administer it. Small business has historically composed a large portion of employment in Japan. But small firms and their representatives have never had entree to the technocratic circles of the powerful bureaucracy or of big business. The strategic position of small businessmen as an organized swing constituency—the "non-commissioned officers of civil society"—has made them vital to the conservatives. At no time has this been more true than in those periods of crisis that have so profoundly shaped the institutional structure and policy orientations of modern Japan, even after crisis has passed.

8

Welfare Policy: Strategic Benevolence

The rulers feed the people and in return the people have a great debt of gratitude toward them. Ruler and people are one body.

YOSHIDA SHŌIN (1858)

JAPAN is conventionally considered to have one of the poorest social security systems in the industrial world. As many Americans and especially Europeans see it, this has been the inevitable price Japan has paid for its extraordinary economic growth. Conventional wisdom argues that by channelling such heavy shares of resources into industrial plants and equipment, especially for strategic sectors of the future, Japan leaves little for the elderly, the infirm, and the indigent.

For many years, there was much truth to these Western observations. Even by the late 1960s, the Japanese government's welfare expenditures were only one-half the share of GNP of those in the United States and one-third of levels in France and West Germany. Only in the area of health insurance were its efforts comparable to those in other major industrialized nations. And since the inception of national health insurance in 1922 Japan's welfare efforts had been focused on maintaining a healthy workforce rather than providing for the nonworking needy. Only in late 1958, amidst a sustained challenge from the Left to the ruling Liberal Democrats, were health care benefits legally extended to all citizens, with implementation achieved in early 1961. Despite rising affluence, pensions, child allowances, and other welfare benefits, Japan lagged sharply behind the West throughout most of the ensuing decade.

During the early and mid-1980s, Japan did continue to devote a smaller share of national income to social security *benefits* actually received by its citizens than major Western industrial nations (figure 8.1). But as figure 8.1 also indicates, Japan had a significantly smaller proportion of elderly. Since the early 1970s, Japanese welfare *entitlements*, claims for future benefits under existing legislation, have in many areas risen sharply to approach

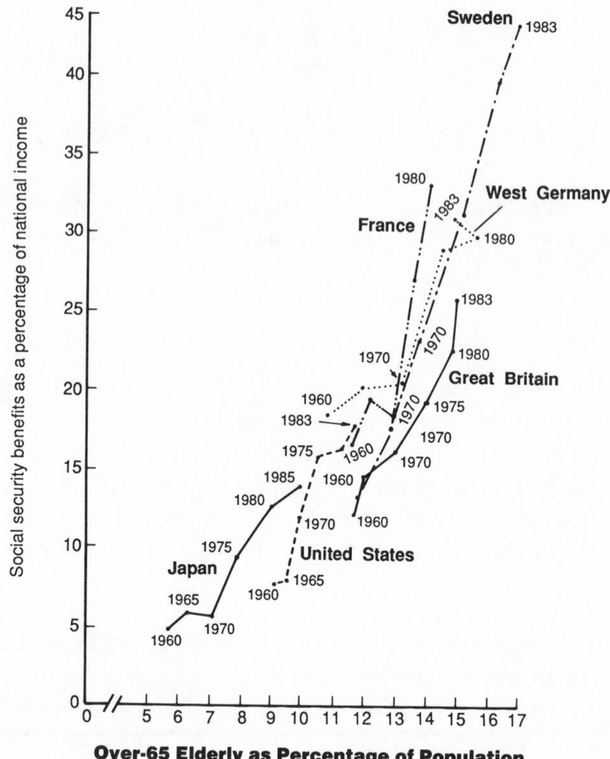

Figure 8.1. The Historical Evolution of Welfare Costs, 1960–85.

Source: International Labour Organization (ILO), *The Cost of Social Security, Basic Tables*; United Nations (UN), *Demographic Yearbook*; OECD, *National Accounts of OECD Countries*; Ministry of Health and Welfare (Kōseishō), *Kōsei Hakusho (White Paper on Welfare)*, various issues.

or even exceed analogous levels in the West. As indicated in figure 8.1, Japan in the early 1980s devoted nearly double the proportion of GNP to welfare that the United States did in 1965, when it had a comparable proportion of elderly.

Welfare policy patterns, like their counterparts in the agricultural, small business, and regional policy areas, show the sensitivity of the Japanese state to grassroots pressures, especially once a critical threshold of public pressure is achieved. They also indicate the contrasting tendency toward inaction or retrenchment during periods of relative political stability. Expansion in welfare's share of the Japanese national budget has come in sudden surges during major periods of flux in national politics (figure

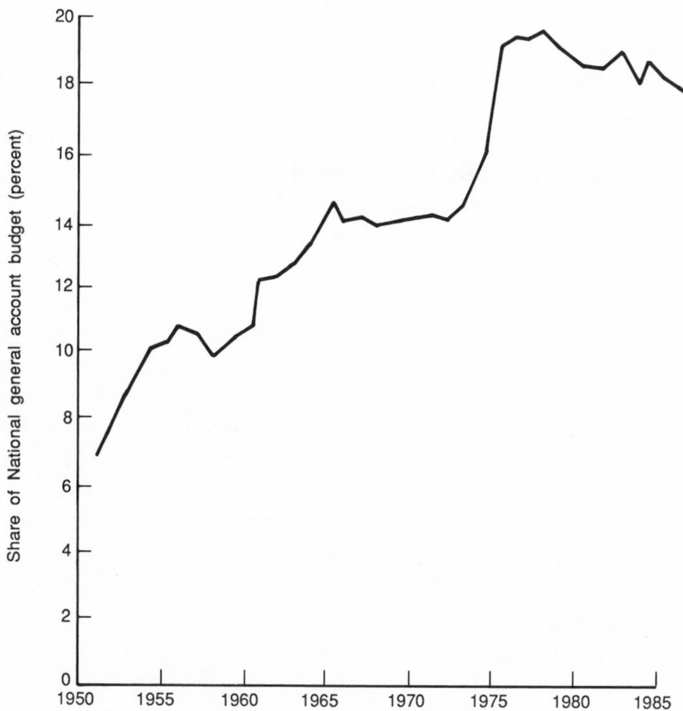

Figure 8.2. The Fitful Emergence of the Japanese Welfare State, 1949–1986: Welfare's Share in the General Account Budget.

Source: Ministry of Finance Research and Statistics Section (Ōkurashō Shukei Kyoku Chōsa Ka), ed., *Zaisei Tōkei (Financial Statistics)* (Tokyo: Ōkurashō Insatsu Kyoku), various issues.

8.2). Indeed, 95 percent of the increase in welfare's budget share since the late 1940s came in six crucial years. In well over half the noncrisis years since 1949, welfare's share in the general account budget has actually declined, although the magnitude of retrenchment has not been sufficient to prevent a gradual ratcheting up of welfare budget shares due to the large increases during crisis years. Declines in welfare shares of the national budget occurred in seven of the ten years from 1976 to 1986, despite the steady aging of Japanese society during that period.

Like developments in older policy areas, welfare spending represents another strategic broadening of the LDP's circle of compensation in response to periodic crises of confidence in the conservative political order which wracked Japan during the 1950s,

1960s, and 1970s. This broadening occurred even though Japan has lacked the strong, institutionalized labor union role in policymaking that helped accelerate welfare spending across Western Europe from the 1930s on. But the distinctive Japanese conservative preemption of opposition demands in times of political crisis produced a parallel complex of welfare policies in Japan as well, before budgetary stringency and the waning of crises combined to stimulate their modification.

The Distinctive Profile of Japanese Welfare Policy in the 1980s

In keeping with the general practice of conservative governments throughout the industrialized world, the Japanese LDP has not nationalized the health care delivery system. Medical care is provided by private physicians, as in the United States, France, and West Germany. The Japanese system contrasts to those of Sweden and Britain, where Socialist governments have made doctors employees of a National Health Service.

In common with conservative patterns in Germany and France, Japanese welfare policy has given early precedence to accident and health insurance, which enhances the prospect of a healthy work force. Although more than a generation behind Bismarck, Japanese conservative leaders of the early twentieth century were influenced by his example in giving precedence to programs which both reinforced industrial potential and indicated state concern for the rising working class.[1] Early policy in conservative Third Republic France, like that in Japan, also broadly followed German priorities but failed to move significantly beyond the area of health policy.[2]

Heavy Support for Medical Care

Japanese policies in the medical area currently diverge from Western patterns, especially those of nations traditionally dominated by conservative governments, in several major respects.

[1] On the early origins of these programs, see Sheldon M. Garon, "Parties, Bureaucrats, and Labor Policy in Prewar Japan, 1918–1931" (Ph.D. diss., Yale University, 1981).

[2] On the early evolution of French welfare policy, see Ashford, *Policy and Politics in France*, pp. 228–65.

TABLE 8.1

Japan's Government Support for Health Care in Comparative Context, 1983 (in average annual percentage of medical services/products paid by a public fund)

	Hospital Bills	Ambulatory Med. Services	Medicines/Med. Appliances
Sweden	99	91	70
Britain	99	88	93
Japan	89	90	89
France	92	58	75
Germany	79	84	70
United States	54	56	90

Source: Organization for Economic Cooperation and Development, *Measuring Health Care, 1960–1983: Expenditure, Costs, and Performance* (Paris: OECD Social Policy Series no. 2, 1985), pp. 71–73.

Note: Figures are for 1982.

Among the most distinctive is the unusually high share of national medical expenses covered by public funds.

As indicated in Table 8.1, the Japanese state engages in particularly vigorous support of ambulatory (i.e., walk-in) medical care, undertaken largely by Japan's proliferation of small clinics. The share of ambulatory medical care paid by public funds in Japan was in 1983 nearly as high as in Sweden and higher than in any other major industrialized nation in the world. The share of patient expenses paid by government for medicines and medical appliances was also very high by international standards (see table 8.1).

Of the share of medical expenses covered by public funds, in each nation employer contributions to national insurance programs routinely provide a proportion. But the burden actually carried by national and local government budgets was by the 1980s quite high in Japan and sharply higher than a generation before. As evident from figure 8.3, the government share in Japanese national medical expenditures for 1985, including both national and local government contributions, was almost 30 percent. Although significantly lower than the comparable figure for 1980, due to recent fiscal retrenchment discussed later in this

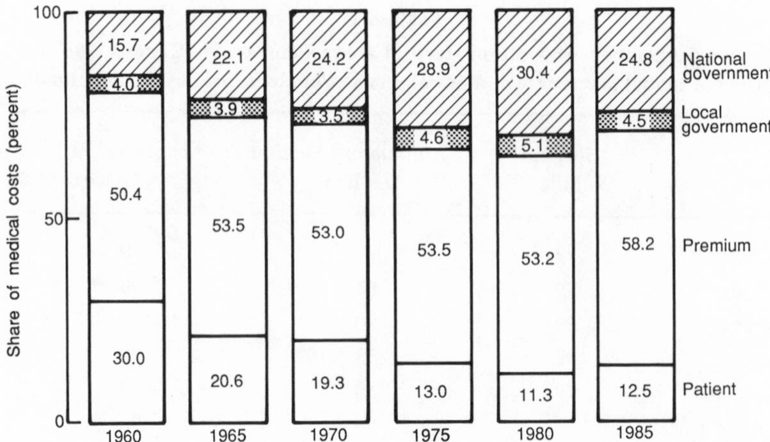

Figure 8.3. The Fluctuating Role of the Japanese Government in Support of Medical Costs, 1960–1985.

Source: Ministry of Health and Welfare (Kōsei Shō), *Kōsei Hakusho (White Paper on Health and Welfare)*, 1986 ed. (Tokyo: Ōkurashō Insatsu Kyoku).

chapter, this governmental share was half again as high as the analogous governmental share in 1960.

Pharmaceuticals and the State

Among the most distinctive aspects of the Japanese medical structure is the unusually large role which drug-related expenditures play in overall medical costs. With $13 billion total sales in 1984, Japan is the second largest pharmaceutical market in the world and the largest per capita consumer of pharmaceuticals. Expenditures for drugs in 1981 made up 38.7 percent of total Japanese medical costs, compared to 19.9 percent in France, 17.3 percent in West Germany, 10.5 percent in Britain, and 8.8 percent in the United States.[3] Politics and public policy have much to do with the dramatic share of overall Japanese national health expenditures spent on drugs. First of all, pricing policies by the Ministry of Health and Welfare's Pharmaceutical Affairs Bureau, which sets the prices on all drugs, have been oriented toward widespread use of drugs. Especially since 1980–1981, the MHW has been putting strong downward pressure on drug prices, in an

[3] Iryō Hoken Seido Kenkyū Kai (Medical Insurance System Research Council), ed., *Me de Miru Iryō Hoken Hakusho* (The Medical Insurance White Paper, Graphic edition). Tokyo: Gyōsei Publishing, 1985, p. 4.

effort to force pharmaceutical firms toward greater efficiency through mass production and to reduce government budget deficits under the administrative reform drive. While previous reductions had been less than 6 percent, in 1981 the MHW reduced standard drug prices by an average of 18.6 percent, followed by another sharp 16.6 percent cut in March 1984 and a further 6 percent reduction in March 1985.[4]

A second major factor increasing demand for drugs in Japan is the national dispensing system: physicians and hospitals not only prescribe but also sell drugs to their patients. This sharply contrasts to patterns in the United States and most other industrial nations.[5] The doctor receives a fee (set by the MHW) for prescribing and also earns a profit on the sale of the same drugs. While MHW reimbursement to doctors is based on manufacturers' list prices, physicians usually earn a significantly higher margin on drug sales to their patients than the reimbursement schedule provides, due to discounting by the manufacturers. Because doctors are paid less well for other services, drug dispensing becomes an important source of income for them.

There have been several bureaucratic efforts since World War II to alter the current Japanese dispensing system; none of then have been successful. General Crawford F. Sams, chief of the SCAP Public Health and Welfare Section, who first tried to change the system, was supported in July 1949 by the official report of an American pharmaceutical survey mission.[6] In June 1951 a bill separating prescription and pharmacy in fact passed the Diet, to be implemented in 1955. Following the occupation, however, the new legislation was emasculated. Thirty years later, in October 1984 the Drug Industry Policy Research Council, an advisory body to the Pharmaceutical Affairs Bureau of the MHW, again proposed a separation.[7] But LDP sensitivity to Japan Medical Associ-

[4] *Scrip*, no. 963, January 9, 1985, p. 16.

[5] This system allowing doctors to both prescribe and sell drugs has been politically controversial in Japan since shortly after the Meiji Restoration. Concern for its preservation in the face of U.S. occupation-inspired efforts to substitute American-style separation of prescription and dispensing functions was the major factor behind emergence of the Japan Medical Association as a powerful pressure group during the early 1950s. See William E. Steslicke, *Doctors in Politics*, pp. 46–49.

[6] *Ibid.*, p. 47.

[7] *Pharma Japan*, no. 934, December 3, 1984, pp. 10–14; *Scrip*, no. 943, October 24, 1984, p. 17.

ation (JMA) pressure seems likely to make change impossible once again.

In comparative perspective, Japanese health policies permit both high incomes for medical doctors and low insurance fees for their patients, demonstrating again the unusual sensitivity of Japanese policymaking to non–big business interest group pressure. Pricing of medical services, which generates large government deficits, strikingly parallels in this respect the pricing of rice and increasingly exceeds it in fiscal consequences, as the aging of Japanese society proceeds apace and as the farming population decreases.[8] The unification of prescription and dispensing functions, together with the accompanying large-scale use of prescription drugs, shows the power of the Japan Medical Association, just as high rice prices show the power of the agricultural cooperatives (nōkyō).

The power of the JMA in this instance contrasts strongly to the relative political weakness of the pharmaceutical firms, forced to absorb the bulk of drug price reductions due to a pricing and distribution structure giving greater leverage to physicians. Medical costs to patients continue at extremely low levels, even in the face of massive national health insurance budget deficits. Despite increasingly persistent bureaucratic and big business efforts since 1980 to raise fees and rationalize the national health insurance system, this phenomenon shows the veto power of consumers, especially rural consumers, of medical service suppliers, and the politicians who support them. Rural dwellers, often poorer and older than urban dwellers, spend a generally larger proportion of their income on health;[9] traditionally they have been more active in pressing for high government subsidies of medical care.

In addition to its low fee national health insurance system, Japan was also distinguished for a decade from 1973 by free medical care for senior citizens over seventy years of age. Of the major

[8] In fiscal 1986 the general account appropriation of ¥5.964 trillion for social insurance, mostly to cover deficits in the national health insurance account, the ¥596 billion to cover deficits in the Foodstuff Administration Special Account, and the large deficit appropriations for the Japan National Railways were three of the largest items in the national budget. See Ministry of Finance Budget Bureau Research Section (Ōkurashō Shukei Kyoku Chōsa Ka) ed., *Zaisei Tōkei* (Financial Statistics) *1986*, pp. 239–40, 278–79. The Foodstuff Account's deficit fell 40 percent during 1982–1986, while the social insurance appropriation rose by 8 percent during that period.

[9] For details, see Iryō Hoken Seido Kenkyū Kai, ed., *Me de Miru Iryō Hoken Hakusho*, pp. 110, 112.

Western industrialized nations, only those with socialized medicine, such as Britain and Sweden, featured such a system. But free medical care for the aged was abolished in 1983, when a patient copayment system under the Insurance for the Aged Law (*Rōjin Hoken Hō*) was introduced. This legislation passed only after a bitter political battle that demonstrated the weakening leverage of mass interests over the ruling conservatives in a noncrisis period. In 1984 additional modification in Japan's medical insurance program introduced a new system for retirees under seventy that shifted some of their costs from the deficit-ridden national health insurance system to more affluent employer related systems, mainly in the private sector. Thus, by the mid-1980s, the elderly were paying nominal but rising fixed fees for individual doctor visits, and a growing share of medical costs was being shifted back to the private sector.

Due to the combination of huge subsidies to national health insurance and special medical programs for the aged, many of them distinctive internationally, the Japanese government in 1980 devoted 43.3 percent of its welfare related expenditures to medical care. Relatively low pension expenditures were another cause of this imbalance. Medical care programs were more than half again as large a share of total welfare spending in Japan as anywhere else in the Western industrial world.[10] Despite important steps toward retrenchment during the early 1980s, including abolition of free medical care for the aged, this basic pattern continued.

Nonmedical Programs

With the exception of medical care, the Japanese welfare system seems less impressive in comparative perspective. Japan does have a children's allowance system, available to those with three or more children under eighteen years of age.[11] Such a system does not exist in the United States, although it is common else-

[10] Medical expenditures as a share of total welfare costs were around 43.3 percent in Japan during 1980, compared to 27.0 percent in the United Kingdom, 26.8 percent in the United States, 25.4 percent in West Germany, 23.8 percent in Sweden, and 22.2 percent in France. See Iryō Hoken Kenkyū Kai, ed., *Me de Miru Iryō Hoken Hakusho*, p. 94.

[11] For details, see, for example, Ministry of Health and Welfare, *Health and Welfare Services in Japan*, pp. 47–48.

where in the world.[12] Japan's childrens' allowance was established in January 1972, during the same wave of welfare policy innovation that produced free medical care for the aged a year later. Japan also has a system of employment insurance, significantly reformed in April 1975, providing financial support to corporations for training and other related purposes and thus reducing the economic pressures on firms to lay off workers.[13] The government also offers subsidies to companies employing workers over sixty years of age. But in its programs for the elderly, especially in such areas as support for construction of old age homes, Japan continues to lag behind other nations of the industrialized world.[14] Welfare budget cuts in the early 1980s, with the waning of political crisis, exacerbated the gaps between Japan and other parts of the industrialized world in this respect.[15]

Explaining Postwar Japan's Profile of Welfare Policy Innovation

The importance of preexisting social structures, particularly state structures and the transmission belts that link them to the broader society, cannot be ignored in the analysis of policy outputs.[16] In the case of postwar Japanese welfare policy, transwar institutional continuities were greater than in most areas of policymaking outside industrial policy. For example, the Japanese

[12] By the late 1960s, sixty-two countries, including Canada, Australia, New Zealand, and most Western European nations, provided childrens' allowances. See Jidō Teate Kondan Kai, "Jidō Teate Seido ni kansuru Hōkoku," December 20, 1968, pp. 28–29, cited in MacDougall, *Political Opposition and Local Government in Japan*, p. 372.

[13] For details, see Japanese Government Social Services Agency, *Outline of Social Insurance in Japan 1984*, pp. 47–48.

[14] On the nursing home as an institution in Japan, see Ruth Campbell, "Nursing Homes and Long-Term Care in Japan," *Pacific Affairs* (Spring 1984): 78–89.

[15] Welfare budget cuts included a 10 percent reduction in national subsidies toward local governments for aiding the poor as well as a reduction in the level of national subsidies toward the self-employed workers pension system (*Kōsei Nenkin*). For details, see *Nihon Keizai Shimbun*, July 29, 1985.

[16] On this point see, for example, Evans, Rueschemeyer, and Skocpol, eds., *Bringing the State Back In*. For a specific application of this approach to the politics of welfare-policy formation, see Ann Shola Orloff and Theda Skocpol, "Why Not Equal Protection? Explaining the Politics of Public Social Spending in Britain, 1900–1911, and the United States, 1880s–1920." *American Sociological Review* 49 (December 1984): 726–50.

Ministry of Health and Welfare was established in 1938, while much of the public health insurance structure dates from the 1920s. Early post-World War II changes in state administrative structure were less abrupt in the welfare area than in policies for agriculture, public works, or small business.

But transwar structures and precedents provide only a sketchy and highly inadequate guide to postwar welfare policy formation. As in so many other areas of Japanese policymaking, the dominant theme of postwar policy innovation in the welfare area seems to be one of crisis and compensation during the postwar period itself.[17] In other words, welfare issues have arisen on the Japanese policy agenda as major topics for consideration when political crisis (or conservative perceptions that crisis is imminent) have threatened the continued preeminence of the ruling Liberal Democratic Party or the dominant coalition within the party. Crisis has then prompted consideration of new compensation measures for prospective supporters of the conservatives in response, directed especially toward politically organized swing constituencies. Just as crisis forced broadening the conservative circle of compensation to agriculture in the late 1940s and to small business fifteen years thereafter, it also encouraged the slow evolution of welfare policy over the 1950s and 1960s in the health care area, followed by the explosion of innovative new programs during the early 1970s.

Structural Dimensions

If anything, crisis has been a more important engine of change in the welfare policy area than in most sectors, as evidenced by the sharp and sudden shifts in welfare budget patterns noted in figure 8.2. Political crisis has been especially important in inducing Japanese welfare policy change because actors who serve as agents of welfare innovation in other nations have been relatively weak in Japan. Civil servants, whom Heclo found central in driving Swedish and British social policy innovation,[18] have been instra-

[17] In discussing policy innovation here, I am referring primarily to what John Campbell calls "new-large" decisions since these are the major decisions with sufficient import to create significant cross-national contrasts in policy output over relatively short periods of time. For Campbell's useful typology of decision-making types, see Campbell, "The Old People Boom and Japanese Policy Making," *Journal of Japanese Studies* (Summer 1979): 329–50.

[18] Heclo, *Modern Social Politics in Britain and Sweden*, p. 301.

mental in policy definition and agenda formation in Japan, but the MHW has not had the political strength to secure enactment of major legislation on its own initiative. Organized labor, a traditional backer of expanded welfare benefits elsewhere, has also been weak.

When, as during the early 1980s, crisis has not pressed heavily on the conservatives, tendencies toward retrenchment in the welfare area have been strong. This has been true, despite the emergence of new pro-welfare pressure groups and the advent of new media-oriented lobbying techniques.[19] Welfare pressure groups have generally not been active in the kōenkai, or support associations, of LDP politicians. They have hence been relatively ineffective in the Japanese policy process, except in crisis situations where the LDP has been forced to appeal to groups beyond its established constituencies. The only welfare related pressure group with major influence in conservative ranks has been the JMA, and doctors have historically forged political ties with a broad range of groups besides the conservatives.

Prewar Precedent

Postwar Japanese welfare policy had its origins in the crises of the prewar period. Labor unrest in the wake of World War I provoked Home Ministry bureaucrats into the Health Insurance Law (*Kenkō Hoken Hō*) of 1922, patterned in part after private sector precedents, such as the Kanebō Mutual Aid Association (*Kanebō Kyōsai Kumiai*) of 1905. This law provided health insurance for many factory workers, especially in large firms, although it left many farmers and small business employees outside its purview. The turbulence of the 1930s and the need for social solidarity in preparation for war were major factors behind the establishment of the Ministry of Health and Welfare (1938) and the passage of National Health Insurance (1938), Seamens' Insurance (1939), and Workers' Pension Insurance (1941). In 1944 Workers' Pension Insurance was extended to cover white-collar workers as well. By the latter stages of World War II, 56 percent of all Japanese were covered by national health insurance, a ratio which fell in the confused aftermath of World War II.[20]

[19] On recent changes in interest group structure and in pressure group tactics, see Stephen J. Anderson, "Nihon Shakai Fukushi no Seisaku Keisei Katei" ("Japan's Welfare Policy Process"), Juristo Sōgō Tokushū No. 41, 1985, pp. 174–75.

[20] Tokyo Daigaku Shakai Kagaku Kenkyū Jo, ed., *Fukushi Kokka* (The Welfare State), vol. 5, p. 16.

After 1945 the political context of welfare policy formation shifted sharply, although many programs and means for administering them remained temporarily constant, the period was one of massive need and meager resources. Most political parties initially stressed reconstruction. But the Japan Communist Party from a very early period stressed welfare, increasing pressure for Japanese welfare policies from the late 1940s.[21] The Laborers' Accident Insurance Law was passed in April 1948, in the midst of early postwar labor turbulence.[22] There was also a flurry of legislation, without substantial price tags, under the Socialist-Democratic cabinets of Katayama and Ashida; the measures included the Unemployment Insurance Law (1947), the Government Employees Relief Association Law (1948), and the Medical Practitioners' Law (1948).

Postwar Crises and Policy Change

The deep economic crisis of 1949, which saw a doubling of Japanese unemployment within a year,[23] drew sharp criticism from the Left, coupled with demands for new welfare measures.[24] This period also witnessed significant policy innovations by the conservatives, including the Emergency Unemployment Countermeasures Law (1949) and the Livelihood Protection Law (*Seikatsu Hogo Hō*) of 1950. Under pressure from the Reform Party (Kaishintō), which described itself as the "nationalist opposition" (*kokkateki yatō*) and exercised surprising influence on policy during its short two-year life (1952–1954), a system of military pensions (*gunjin onkyū*) was also revived.

The second period of postwar political crisis (1958–1963) led to even more extensive policy change. Universal health insurance and national pensions, the cornerstones of postwar Japanese welfare policy, were passed within a relatively short period in 1958–

[21] On the JCP's early postwar welfare policy efforts, including establishment of the annual *White Papers on Japanese Children*, see Nihon Kodomo o Mamoru Kai, ed., *Kodomo Hakusho* (White Paper on Japanese Children), annual; and Nihon Kyōsantō Chūō Iinkai, *Nihon Kyōsantō Roku Jyū Nen 1922–1982* (Sixty Years of the Japan Communist Party, 1922–1982), pp. 120–24. The White Paper has been published annually since 1949.

[22] Tokyo Daigaku Shakai Kagaku Kenkyū Jo, ed., *Fukushi Kokka*, p. 8.

[23] The number of totally unemployed rose from 190,000 in 1948 to 380,000 in 1949. See *ibid.*, p. 7.

[24] See, for example, the Japan Socialist Party Basic Line of 1949. Shakai Bunko, ed., *Nihon Shakaitō Shi Shiryō* (Materials on Japan Socialist Party History), pp. 178–79.

1959. But they, like the Basic Agricultural and Small Business Laws, the no-collateral loan system, and so many other Japanese policy innovations, originated as systematic proposals during periods of stability; they were debated for years before translation into policy amidst political crisis. Both national health insurance and national pensions had important prewar and wartime antecedents disrupted by the confusion and other economic priorities of the early postwar period. Both were revived after World War II, largely at the initiative of local rather than national government, and both were also spurred by the profound and rapid social transformation which the forces of rapid economic growth were stimulating across the face of Japan during the 1950s. But politics clearly provided the catalyst for the legislative realization of both policies.

Throughout the history of Japanese welfare policy since 1949 one finds a strong dualism between the origination of concepts and plans for action on the one hand and actual implementation on the other. The intellectual evolution of the concept of welfare and the welfare state in Japan has been extended and relatively gradual, influenced heavily by overseas developments. Notions such as national health insurance, the children's allowance, and free medical care for the aged would enter and permeate Japan, often without impact on policy for years. The process of translation into policy, however, has been a much more sudden and volatile one, shaped profoundly by the advent of crisis. At the heart of the political, as opposed to intellectual, processes that stimulated such volatile welfare policy innovation in Japan between 1949 and the late 1970s were sharp divisions within Japanese politics over how welfare reform should proceed. T. J. Pempel aptly characterizes these divisions as a split among "redistributors, refiners, and reluctants."[25]

In essence, the Left and a few supporters elsewhere in Japanese society saw social welfare as a form of income redistribution, and they advanced proposals with high price tags that would achieve that objective. The Ministry of Finance and much of the Japanese business and political world was "reluctant" to move toward change, emphasizing the need for devoting resources to national economic development or keeping them in the private domain. In the middle were "refiners," preeminently government bureaucrats with the ministries of Labor and Health and Welfare, who

[25] Pempel, *Policy and Politics in Japan*, pp. 140–41.

formulated actual policy proposals to meet much more general political demands.

To this formulation should be added the volatile pressures of the crisis and compensation dynamic, which periodically broke the impasse between redistributors and reluctants, thus allowing actual policy to emerge. The political turbulence of the first crisis period (1949–1954) helped generate worker-oriented policy changes relating to unemployment and accident insurance, together with corporatist structural mechanisms for debating new welfare policy proposals.[26] But this turbulence failed to generate a national pension system, although it was recommended in October 1950 by the Social Security System Advisory Council as one of its first acts. The Council repeated its recommendation for a national pension system in 1952, when a special pension measure for government and military officials (*kōmuin/gunjin onkyū*) was passed by the Diet; once again its proposal was not realized.

These developments reaffirm that while political crisis in Japan tends to generate a significant range of new legislation, it generates these measures *selectively*, through the prevailing interest group structure and budgetary constraints.[27] In the early 1950s nationalist pressures from Kaishintō Dietmen such as Hayakawa Takashi, a classmate of prime minister-to-be Nakasone Yasuhiro in the wartime Home Ministry, helped secure a system of government pensions, while European precedents for a welfare state cited by these Dietmen served as an intellectual catalyst. In the early 1950s fiscal constraints impelled the Ministry of Finance to resist generalized pension and health insurance measures more strongly than it later did. And the LDP circle of compensation had not extended to the elderly, the primary potential beneficiaries of such a measure.

Pressure for a national pension system also began building

[26] The Social Security System Advisory Council (*Shakai Hoshō Seido Shingikai*) was established by the conservative Yoshida cabinet in May 1949.

[27] The Japanese political system has historically generated less resistance to selective, distributively oriented welfare measures than has that of the United States. As Orloff and Skocpol point out, the distributive, politically oriented character of the Civil War pension system was a major reason that the United States abolished, rather than expanded, its public pension system during the early twentieth century. See Orloff and Skocpol, "Why Not Equal Protection." Structural factors can also be cited to account for a persistent distributive orientation of such policies on the Japanese side, although a pervasive cultural acceptance of hierarchy and the legitimacy of case-specific distinctions among individuals can also not be ignored.

from the example of local governments, just as was to be true of free medical care for the aged during the early 1970s. From 1951 local governments across Japan began introducing noncontributory "pensions for the respected elderly" (*keirō nenkin*). Initially these pensions were nominal and mainly symbolic, but gradually they became more substantial financially. By the latter half of the 1950s, most Japanese municipalities had such systems.[28]

Spurring the needs for a comprehensive pension system and even more immediately a comprehensive national health insurance system were rapid changes in the Japanese economy of the 1950s. Huge numbers of Japanese were leaving not only the farms of Tōhoku and Kyūshū for the factories of the Tōkaidō industrial belt, but also the protective cocoon of rural society for high-risk urban life. Between 1954 and 1957 alone, as the *Keizai Hakusho* (Economic White Paper) of 1958 gravely pointed out, predominantly urban wage employment increased by three million workers; two million of these new workers were in small business.[29] While large firms had relatively comprehensive internal social welfare systems, small businesses did not; neither did the old people who were increasingly left at home alone on the farms as their sons and daughters flocked to the urban factories of high-growth Japan.

In 1955, 68.1 percent of all Japanese were covered by some sort of medical insurance, either corporate or public,[30] but most employees in small firms lacked coverage. Furthermore, costs were rising in existing programs due to the rapid surge of new workers to the cities. The Ministry of Finance responded by trying to introduce a 10 percent user fee (the so-called *ichi-bu futan kin*). Doctors and labor unions combined to oppose this. Disruption by their parliamentary backers created the chaotic *Rantō Kokkai* (free-for-all Diet) of 1956, in which the MOF's proposed user fee was blocked, intensifying the financial difficulties of existing health insurance funds.

The incoming Ishibashi cabinet first broached 100 percent national health insurance coverage as a priority of Japanese public policy in the fateful budget of 1957, which also rejected major requests from both the Self-Defense Forces and the United States for a defense buildup. Prime Minister Ishibashi Tanzan, in a ma-

[28] Tokyo Daigaku Shakai Kagaku Kenkyū Jo, ed., *Fukushi Kokka*, p. 27.

[29] Economic Planning Agency (Keizai Kikaku Chō) *Keizai Hakusho* (Economic Yearbook), 1958 ed., Tokyo: Ōkurashō Insatsu Kyoku, 1958, pp. 378–79.

[30] Tokyo Daigaku Shakai Kagaku Kenkyū Jo, ed., *Fukushi Kokka*, p. 19.

jor New Year's 1957 address at the Hibiya Kōkaidō in Tokyo, declared the construction of a Japanese welfare state involving national health insurance, housing construction, and tax reduction, one of his five central policy priorities.[31] Ishibashi's successor, Kishi Nobusuke, concurred in a call for Health Insurance for the Whole Nation (*Kokumin Kai Hoken*) during 1957. But the proposal was not enacted immediately.

Economic developments intensified the pressures for action. In mid-1957, Japan entered the "bottom of the pan recession" (*nabezoko fukyō*), which continued until mid-1958. This intensified the gap between the haves and the have nots in Japan, and it was particularly hard on urban small business; after May 1957 sharp credit restraint by the Bank of Japan accompanied it. These economic realities made parts of the bureaucracy, such as the Economic Planning Agency, more supportive of redistributive policies. As the 1958 *Keizai Hakusho*, published by the EPA, pointed out, "For well-balanced development, it is necessary to increase the income shares of less-developed sectors, and to redistribute it through the financial system and through social welfare. The nation must also deal with its balance of payments. If these problems are neglected, there is a danger that social tensions could rise."[32]

Political developments, against the backdrop of widening income differentials and small business distress, provided the catalyst for change, as post-1949 Japan moved toward its second period of domestic crisis. The Socialists, as indicated, topped the so-called "one-third barrier" in the 1956 Upper House elections. In 1958 the LDP promised a system of national pensions in the general election campaign, but the JSP continued to gain. Interest group pressure from farmers, small businessmen, and veterans was also mounting.[33] In late 1958 internal tensions within the

[31] Ishibashi's other four priorities were normalization of Diet management, improvement of bureaucratic political relations, expansion of employment and production, and contribution to world peace through the United Nations. See *Asahi Shimbun*, January 9, 1957; Tsutsui Kiyotada, *Ishibashi Tanzan*, pp. 388–89; and Jiyū Minshutō, *Ishibashi Naikaku no Shisei Dai Issei* (The Inaugural Address of the Ishibashi Cabinet) (Tokyo: Jiyū Minshutō, 1958).

[32] Economic Planning Agency (Keizai Kikaku Chō) *Keizai Hakusho*, 1958 ed., p. 378.

[33] In 1958 the activist Chūseiren small business federation, headed by former Manchurian business magnate Ayukawa Gisuke, made a major small business retirement allowance proposal, while veterans pressed for an increase in *onkyū* pensions adopted in 1952, and the agricultural cooperatives pressed for an agri-

LDP and the protracted confrontation between Right and Left over police and national security issues also began to intensify, as indicated in chapter 2.

In the face of all these pressures, the Japanese conservatives enacted four major welfare measures within a few months of one another while Kishi Nobusuke was prime minister: the New National Health Law (*Shin Kokumin Kenkō Hō*) of 1958, the National Pension Law (*Kokumin Nenkin Hō*), the Welfare Pensions for the Aged, Mothers and Children, and Disabled Persons Law (*Rōrei Boshi Shōgai Fukushi Nenkin Hō*), and the Minimum Wage Law (*Saitei Chingin Hō*) of 1959. In contrast to Ikeda Hayato, Tanaka Kakuei, Miki Takeo, or most other major Japanese conservative leaders of the postwar period, who were domestically oriented, Kishi's basic policy interests appear to have been primarily international.[34] But in one of the great ironies of modern Japanese politics the events of the times led Kishi into major welfare policy reforms and frustrated his deep desire for a smooth ratification of the revised United States-Japan Security Treaty. The momentum given proposals by previous economic and political developments, the LDP's desire to undercut appeals from the Left, and a personal desire to increase foreign confidence in Japanese willingness to forego low wage–oriented trade competition helped shape Kishi's welfare policies.[35]

The shock of the Security Treaty crisis in 1960 also intensified pressures toward both welfare policy reform and increased funding of already existing welfare programs. In the political uncertainty following the resignation of Kishi Nobusuke and the decision to hold general elections, the new Prime Minister Ikeda Hayato moved rapidly to preempt politically popular opposition programs. Ikeda aggressively borrowed especially heavily from the Socialists, who had placed considerable emphasis on welfare reform. One of the nine central elements of his 13,000-word "new policy" statement of September 5, 1960, was the need for drastic improvement of the social security system. Indeed, Ike-

---

cultural pensions system. See Tokyo Daigaku Shakai Kagaku Kenkyū Jo, ed., *Fukushi Kokka*, p. 25.

[34] Kishi's memoirs, for example, focus heavily on his international dealings, particularly regarding United States-Japan Security Treaty revision and relations with Southeast Asia. See Kishi Nobusuke, *Kishi Nobusuke Kaikoroku* (The Memoirs of Kishi Nobusuke).

[35] Kishi argued, for example, that a minimum wage law was useful in "increasing foreign confidence in Japanese export industry." See *ibid.*, p. 466.

da's statement proclaimed that one of the "three pillars of the new policy" was the social security program:[36]

> The expansion of social security is an important pillar of the new policy. With the aim of building a welfare state (*fukushi kokka*), our party has provided health insurance for the whole nation as well as national pensions. But as part of the new policy, an epoch-making expansion of social security will be carried out so as to guarantee that there will not be a single hungry or poverty-stricken person in the nation.[37]

Ikeda's statement, sounding decidedly nonconservative outside the turbulent context of the times, promised a planned annual expansion of the social security system, promotion of welfare pensions and public assistance programs, and improvement in the national environment generally through the construction of adequate housing and better sewage facilities. Most importantly, Ikeda made an explicit commitment to the goal of creating a "welfare state" in Japan, involving government responsibility for the expansion of public welfare. This commitment virtually duplicated longstanding appeals of the Socialists and the Communists, which had been given additional force by the political crisis that had raged only a few months previously. It also reaffirmed and expanded the commitments of conservative prime ministers Ishibashi Tanzan and Kishi Nobusuke, made during the 1957–1958 period.

Ikeda's wholesale cooptation of progressive policy proposals during the fall of 1960 helped win him one of the great conservative electoral victories of the entire postwar period. Following the election, the Ministry of Finance sharply cut back the initial enthusiastic efforts of the LDP Social Security Research Council to increase social security program appropriations by ¥100 billion, in the 1960 MOF budget draft. But much of this funding was restored in the year-end "revival negotiations" between the LDP and interest groups, when party concern for the delicate political situation first had an opportunity to override bureaucratic prudence.[38] In fiscal 1961 social security expenditures ultimately

[36] For the full text of the Ikeda "new policy" statement ("The Meaning of the General Election and an Outline of the New Policy"), see Jiyū Minshutō, "Sōsenkyo no Igi to Shin Seisaku no Gaiyō," in *Kokkai Nenkan, 1961*, pp. 657–61.

[37] *Ibid.*, p. 658. Quoted in Steslicke, *Doctors in Politics*, p. 105.

[38] For the details of the 1961 social security budget negotiations, focusing on the health insurance payments to doctors controversy, see *ibid.*, pp. 131–40.

soared 35 percent over those in 1960, although part of this increase was due to implementation of the Kishi proposals for full national health insurance legislated during 1958.[39] The final amount allocated to Welfare Ministry programs represented an all-time high, roughly 11 percent of total government expenditures, and welfare spending continued to increase relative to other categories throughout the early 1960s.[40] With the memories of Kishi's dictatorial handling of the United States-Japan Security Treaty fresh, the leverage of the opposition in the Diet was unusually strong. And welfare expansion was one policy area in which the opposition had a relatively strong interest. To elicit acceptance of Ikeda's ambitious Income Doubling Plan oriented toward industry and to achieve smooth Diet management the LDP was under strong pressure to expand support for welfare.

Welfare's budget share kept growing until 1965, due largely to expanded funding for the new programs developed during the late 1950s. An increase in national-government subvention of medical care for the aged to 70 percent of total costs and the enactment of a new Welfare Law for the Aged, both developments in 1963, also contributed to the expansion of welfare spending. Welfare's budget share would have grown even faster during the early 1960s if more elderly people had been enrolled long enough to be eligible for pensions. The Kishi period legislation, undeniably broad in its prospective coverage, was quite conservative in the number of years needed for eligibility, although these constraints were later softened by allowing relatively low "five-year" and "ten-year" pensions. This conservatism regarding eligibility requirements meant that it took several years to feel the full budgetary impact of the welfare policy innovations decided in the heat of political crisis.

Once political crisis had passed, the initial momentum of preemptive conservative reform in the welfare area dissipated, although the budgetary effects of new entitlements continued to unfold. The reluctant elements of the conservative political coalition, such as big business groups and the Ministry of Finance, no longer had the overriding, stability-related reasons for backing welfare expansion that they had had in the early 1960s. Organ-

[39] The National Health Insurance Law of 1958 established health insurance for all, but it could not be implemented until 1961 because insurance pools had to be established in each locality under a four-year plan set up in 1958. I am indebted for this information to John Campbell.

[40] Steslicke, *Doctors in Politics*, p. 137.

ized grassroots pressure groups, especially in medicine and agriculture, sustained the rising support for medical insurance programs. But in the face of strong counterpressures from agriculture, small business, and regional groups presenting claims on government resources to which the Japanese political system was strongly sensitive, support for broader welfare reform gradually stagnated during the mid- and late 1960s.

Various technical details of legislation, and bureaucratic interpretation thereof, sharply limited the financial benefits provided under the broad eligibility welfare progams established during the late 1950s and early 1960s. The basis for determining public pensions was lifetime earnings; the high growth and rapid inflation of the 1960s meant pensions were rarely close to a workers' wages at retirement.[41] In addition, bonuses and fringe benefits, a basic part of most workers' annual salaries, were excluded in computing base salaries for retirement benefit purposes. Furthermore, retirement benefits contained no cost-of-living adjustments, in contrast to frequent American and European patterns; their real purchasing power rapidly declined in the highly inflationary environment of the 1960s.

The LDP periodically adopted explicit pension payment targets before general elections, such as the ¥10,000 pension before the 1965 Upper House election, the ¥20,000 pension before the Lower House elections of 1969, and the ¥50,000 pension before the elections of 1972.[42] But the relative overall level of nonmedical support for retirees, compared to the rising income levels of workers themselves, continued to decline. Around 1970 the level of benefits provided to retirees under the national pension system amounted to only 10 to 15 percent of the average annual wage of those employed in manufacturing, compared to an average ratio of 50 to 60 percent in Western Europe.[43] In the absence of broad national political crisis, policymaking fell largely into the hands of fiscally conservative bureaucrats insensitive to gradually intensifying popular demands for welfare-state expansion.

To some extent the pension issue during the 1960s was a relatively abstract question for the bulk of the Japanese people. Ja-

[41] Significantly, the pensions of government employees (*onkyū* pensions, as they are known in Japanese) have long been calculated on the basis of earnings at the time of retirement, obviating this problem for one of the few organized segments of the retiree community.

[42] Pempel, *Policy and Politics in Japan*, p. 141.

[43] *Ibid.*, p. 143.

pan's age structure was still relatively young, with a smaller share of the population approaching or experiencing retirement than was true in major Western nations. Due to the slow maturity of the general Japanese pension system, a substantial fraction of the retired population (larger than the share on general public pensions) was receiving either government employee (*onkyū*) or noncontributory welfare pensions. But public pensions were inevitably a major issue for the future, especially for small business and agriculture, lacking the comprehensive support network corporate paternalism provided in large firms. Improved public pensions were also a major topic of debate and policy action during the 1960s in the major Western industrial nations to whom Japanese policymakers looked so often for precedents in other policy fields. The United States, for example, was legislating The Great Society of Lyndon Johnson, while the Social Democrats in West Germany and Labour in Britain were generating even more substantial expansions of the welfare state than was the United States.

New proposals for welfare policy innovation, to be sure, emerged with increasing frequency in Japan during the years of political quietism from late 1963 through the end of the 1960s. In 1964, for example, the Central Child Welfare Committee presented a series of possible approaches to a childhood allowance system to the national government.[44] In December 1968 a Childhood Allowance Conference Group, with membership drawn from government, business, labor, and the academic world, presented a detailed proposal on the same subject to the Health and Welfare Ministry.[45] In 1969 the Japan Socialist party introduced its own bill for a national childhood allowance system. But none of these measures was immediately enacted.

As it was being broadly discussed at the national level and recommended by several government advisory committees, the childhood allowance system was also being steadily introduced at the local level—particularly by progressive local governments in major urban areas where policy innovation was a major competitive weapon against conservative national government. In April 1967, Musashino City in the suburbs of Tokyo became the first local government to set up a childhood allowance program;

[44] MacDougall, *Political Opposition and Local Government in Japan*, pp. 373–74.

[45] *Ibid.*, p. 374.

the emergence of a progressive assembly majority and the support of Socialist mayor Gotō Kihachirō facilitated this program.[46] By the end of 1969, 171 local governments had adopted similar programs, with Tokyo itself introducing one in December 1969.[47] During fiscal 1971, Tokyo metropolis alone provided over $10 million to more than 116,000 children, with extensive media coverage of the program.[48] Yet Ministry of Finance officials, together with big business leaders, continued to resist implementation of childrens' allowances at the national level, pointing to the high prospective budgetary costs.

A similar process of policy invention and preparation for more sweeping change was also continuing with respect to free medical care for both the aged and children with cancer. Once again, local government was the crucial early innovator. The small town of Sawauchi, Iwate Prefecture, for example, began paying all health costs of its elderly in 1960. The issue was taken up by the opposition nationally during the mid-1960s, with the Japan Communist party beginning its call for free medical care for the aged in 1964.[49] But the conservative Satō administration did not act.

Several local governments gave the issue major momentum during the late 1960s, as they began to embrace free medical care for the aged in response to grassroots pressure. Akita and Kanagawa prefectures began to subsidize health care costs for the elderly in April 1969, and by the fall thirty to forty cities across Japan had established similar programs. The vast majority of them established a minimum age of eighty and had reimbursement systems.[50]

In October 1969, the progressive Minobe administration in Tokyo took the major step of providing free medical care for all over the age of seventy, substantially improving upon the benefit levels provided by other local government programs.[51] Both the ac-

[46] "Chihō Jichitai ni okeru Jidō Teate Seido no Jisshi Jōkyō" ("Circumstances for Bringing a Childrens' Allowance System into Operation in Local Governments"), pp. 1–6. Cited in *ibid.*, p. 375.

[47] *Ibid.*

[48] Tokyo Metropolitan Government, *Tokyo Steps Up Social Welfare*, p. 61.

[49] Campbell, "The Old People Boom and Japanese Policymaking," p. 331.

[50] MacDougall, *Political Opposition and Local Government in Japan*, p. 368.

[51] In October 1969, Tokyo also announced that it would introduce a system of free medical care for children with cancer, a program suggested to the national government in December 1967 by the Japanese Pediatrics Association but never implemented. On December 3, 1969, Tokyo Governor Minobe announced a fiscal

celerating media interest in the question and a rising consensus on free medical care at the prefectural level intensified pressure on the LDP for action. By April 1972, forty-four of forty-seven prefectures had adopted free medical care programs, increasing pressure on the conservatives at the national level still further.

Once again, crisis for the conservatives inspired major policy change at the national level. The central crisis, described more fully in chapter 2, was the specter of progressive challenge to LDP political dominance that the long string of leftist local government victories from the late 1960s created, and it was sharply amplified by the heavy Communist gains in the Lower House election of December 1972. The battlegrounds were the largest urban centers of Japan, where many conservative strategists came to regard the welfare issue, like small-business support programs, as critical.

While innovations of the late 1950s provided much of the formal outline for a Japanese welfare state, the early 1970s provided the financial substance, in the form of both broad and relatively generous entitlements. The major welfare policy innovations of this period came in a sudden surge, just as environmental policy had come forth only two years previously.[52] Many of the policy decisions, such as that regarding free medical care for the aged, were made in late 1971 and early 1972 in response to previous moves by progressive local governments[53] and in anticipation of upcoming national elections where LDP success was problematic. Further decisions to expand welfare programs were taken the following year, as the LDP's political plight and the strength of the Left became dramatically clear. New welfare policies emerging

---

1971 budgetary appropriation for this item; just two weeks later the national government committed itself to a similar plan, using Tokyo as its model. For details, see *ibid.*, pp. 380–86. It is important to note that while this national level policy innovation occurred before the political crisis for the conservatives of the early 1970s reached its high point, tension had already begun to build with the Minobe progressive victory in 1967 and the approaching gubernatorial campaign of 1971. Furthermore, the amount of compensation involved—¥200 million for the 1971 national budget—was minimal, so the costs to the national government of responding flexibly were small.

[52] On innovation in Japanese environmental policymaking, see Margaret A. McKean, "Pollution and Policymaking," in T. J. Pempel, ed., *Policymaking in Contemporary Japan*, pp. 201–38; also see Susan J. Pharr and Joseph L. Badaracco, Jr., "Coping with Crises: Environmental Regulation," in McCraw, ed., *America Versus Japan*, pp. 229–60.

[53] See Kawashima Masahide, "Kakushin Jichitai to Shakai Fukushi" ("Progressive Local Governments and Social Welfare"), *Sekai* (1972), pp. 113–26.

during this period included the Childrens' Allowance (implemented during January 1972–April 1974), free medical care for the elderly (January 1973); indexation of welfare pensions to the inflation rate (1973), sharp increases in both Employees' Pension and the National Pension (1973), major increases in reimbursement provisions under National Health Insurance (October 1973), and provision of intracorporate retraining subsidies to reduce economic pressures to lay off employees (December 1974). Together these measures brought per capita entitlement standards for many Japanese welfare programs close to Western European levels and introduced several programs, such as the childrens' allowance, which did not exist in the United States.[54] The combination of new programs, rising numbers of eligible under old programs, and increasing per capita benefits generated a massive quantitative increase in Japanese public outlays for welfare; during the six years from 1969 to 1975 outlays for the two major public pension programs outlined above (equivalent in the aggregate to American social security) rose from ¥177 billion to ¥2331 billion, a more than thirteenfold increase.[55] Welfare's share in the national general account budget, as noted in figure 8.2, soared from 13.4 percent in 1972 to 19 percent only two years later.

As John Campbell points out, the political dynamics of welfare policy innovation in the early 1970s varied sharply by type of issue, or "decisional arena."[56] In some cases, especially the development of small, new programs, the distinctive responsiveness of the Japanese political system to grassroots interests does not appear to have driven policy innovation.[57] Indeed, most welfare policy issues of the early 1970s were entitlement programs, where the transformation of individual grassroots interests into policy was complicated by the involvement of much broader social groups. Yet the combination of generalized sensitivity to lo-

[54] Monthly old wage pensions in Japan during 1983, for example (based on the Employees' Pension Insurance program), averaged 43.5 percent of average wages in manufacturing industry, compared to 42.9 percent in West Germany, 45.7 percent in Sweden, 45.9 percent in the United States, and 48.0 percent in Britain. See Japanese Government Social Insurance Agency, *Outline of Social Insurance in Japan*, 1984 ed., p. 15.

[55] John Campbell, "The Old People Boom and Japanese Policymaking," p. 321.

[56] *Ibid.*, p. 329.

[57] Campbell finds that in such cases bureaucrats, who tended to dominate policymaking in such instances, were reacting only to a very generalized sense of public interest. See *ibid.*, pp. 339–46.

cal interests created by the Japanese electoral system, compounded by intra-LDP rivalry and by the power of the mass media, created a situation highly conducive to policy change under the crisis conditions the LDP confronted during the early 1970s.

This pressure from the periphery for new welfare programs, magnified by media attention, increased the potential returns to policy innovation for "policy entrepreneurs" within the LDP, such as those described in chapter 4. As in the case of small business and agricultural policy, the principal entrepreneurs in the case of free medical care for the aged appear to have been antimainstream LDP politicians with relatively precarious standing in conservative ranks. These people, with little to lose and much to gain from embracing novel policy proposals, often acted in concert with local opposition politicians in analogous positions within the ranks of the Left. In 1968–1969, for example, Minister of Welfare Sonoda Sunao gave considerable momentum to the medical care for the aged movement initiated by the Left supporting it in the face of opposition from Minister of Finance Fukuda Takeo.

Further momentum was given to the free medical care issue when Tokyo Governor Minobe Ryōkichi decided to introduce at the local level the proposal Sonoda had supported but had been manifestly unable to achieve nationally. As media coverage of internal differences within the LDP focused attention nationally on the welfare issue, other LDP politicians found it in their interest to climb on the bandwagon. Ultimately Minobe's proposal for free medical care to those over seventy was forced on a reluctant finance ministry during the 1972 budget negotiations, effective in January 1973.[58]

As the LDP began to feel more secure following its Upper House electoral victory of 1974, the engine of welfare policy innovation by Japan's conservatives once more ground to a halt. To be sure, proposals for expansions of the Japanese welfare state have continued to germinate, such as Miki Takeo's Life Cycle Plan, a comprehensive social-welfare package first presented in 1975.[59] Despite some marginal increases in benefit levels, however, there have been few major new departures in Japanese welfare policy since 1974.

[58] *Ibid.*, pp. 334–35.

[59] Realization of Miki's plan was blocked by strong Ministry of Finance opposition. See Pempel, *Policy and Politics in Japan*, pp. 141, 163–64.

As noted earlier, there has also been significant retrenchment in areas such as free medical care for the aged, with the waning of crisis. The 1985 pension reform unified the various pension systems and cut back sharply on future, although not current, benefits. Yet major cutbacks in welfare programs have been slow and difficult for government to achieve. Years of intense pressure by the Ministry of Finance against free medical care for the aged, for example, were required to produce a 1983 Health Care for the Aged Law stipulating only that people over seventy pay ¥400 a month for outpatient care and ¥300 a day for hospitalization.[60]

In its near veto power over change in entitlement programs, grassroots pressure group influence continues to make itself felt in the formation of Japanese welfare policy. But without deep political crisis for the ruling Japanese conservatives, supporters of expanded welfare commitments find it difficult to take the political initiative. Without crisis, the logic of technocracy asserts itself, increasingly conscious of the rising costs that a full-scale welfare state in a rapidly aging society would inevitably bring to Japan as it approaches the twenty-first century.

[60] This 1983 law provides that people aged 70 or more pay ¥300 a day in the hospital for a maximum of two months as well as ¥400 at their first visit to the doctor each month. For details on the legislation and the political process which achieved it, see John Creighton Campbell "Problems, Solutions, Non-Solutions and Free Medical Care for the Elderly in Japan," *Pacific Affairs* (Spring 1984): 53–64.

9

Land Use Policy: Exclusive Circles of Compensation

CONSERVATIVE POLICIES redound to the welfare of many Japanese in ways ranging from income distribution to regional and small business policy. But as suggested earlier, those policies are a mixed blessing. Although responsive to areas far from the nation's capital in ways perhaps unequalled in any other industrialized nation with respect to provision of roads, bridges, and incentives for industrial relocation, Japanese conservative policymaking does not respond equally to all the citizenry. It operates through circles of compensation which distinguish sharply between haves and have-nots, as indicated in chapter 4. Policy solutions often involve, as in the case of welfare policy during the early 1970s, expanding the circle to include more participants, but usually someone is still left on the outside.

Nowhere is the paradoxically responsive yet inegalitarian face of Japanese conservative policymaking more clear-cut than in the case of land use policy, especially for planning the use of urban land. There the LDP's conventional approach to conflict—of resolution through expanding either the circle of recipients or the pie itself—cannot readily work, since Japan has severely limited supplies of land. More resources cannot readily be created, and those who want to enjoy unimpeded the fruits of ownership must compete directly with one another for the privilege. Major supporters of the ruling conservatives in industry, banking, and agriculture have a stake in rising prices for land, which in turn provides much of the collateral for the massive debts contracted in the process of high-speed, capital-intensive industrialization. In the face of strong, conflicting interests, policymakers from institutionally weak bureaucratic successors of the Home Ministry and from political parties highly sensitive to interest group pressure find it virtually impossible to plan coherent land use. Despite periodic symbolic gestures in times of crisis, the constraints on substantive creativity in land policy are strong. Citizens, especially those of urban areas, bear the cost of this inaction.

All this is not to say that change is impossible. During 1986 the price of an average commercial land site in Tokyo rose 34.4 percent, and that of a residential site 18.8 percent—some of the sharpest increases in the postwar period.[1] The land assets of metropolitan Tokyo (Tokyo-to) were valued at close to ¥400 trillion—eight times those of the northern island of Hokkaidō, and two-fifths those of the entire United States.[2] Huge distortions in the distribution of national assets—between the owners and the nonowners of urban land—were stirring both domestic resistance and rising foreign appreciation of how land-use rigidities impeded Japan's ability to change its global economic role. But the obstacles to basic reform in Japanese land-use policy lie deep in the prevailing structure of the domestic Japanese political economy, making fundamental change controversial and sharply resisted by vested interests.

This chapter explores the Japanese approach to land use planning in comparative context, with particular attention to how postwar Japan has ordered its urban areas. As in other domestic policy sectors examined in this volume, I argue that postwar Japanese public policy has to some degree responded to citizen pressures for land use policy change during periods of political crisis. But the intensity of response and the degree of implementation as crisis wanes have been sharply less than in the other sectors considered, with fateful implications for Japan's ability to meaningfully expand domestic housing-related investment and to absorb at home the huge capital surpluses that would otherwise surge with fateful consequences throughout the world economy.

The chapter begins with factual analysis of Japan's land situation. It then moves to Japan's relatively successful tradition of prewar land use planning and to the successes of postwar West Germany in this area before returning to the origins of postwar Japanese policy profiles in Home Ministry dissolution, economic growth, and the crisis and compensation dynamic. This sequence of presentation is important because it enables the reader to see clearly the dimensions of the analytical problem: postwar Japan's rather chaotic land use profiles are not simply the inevitable static consequence of population density but rather form a paradoxical situation that could have developed differently than it in

[1] Takeuchi Hiroshi, "Japan's Soaring Land Prices," *Journal of Japanese Trade and Industry*, no. 4 (1987), pp. 44–47.

[2] Calculations for Japanese domestic land values are by the Research Institute of Construction and Economy in Tokyo. See *The Economist*, October 3, 1987, p. 25.

fact has. Once the counterintuitive aspects of Japan's land use profiles are identified, by showing both nuances in current Japanese land use profiles and alternatives in other heavily populated nations, an effort is made to explain those anomalies and their relationship to the crisis and compensation dynamic of Japanese policymaking.

Again, Japan's high population to land ratio cannot adequately explain the failures of Japanese land use policy. Other advanced, heavily populated nations, such as the Netherlands and West Germany, have developed much more systematic approaches to land use, as Japan itself did prior to World War II and indeed began to do once again during the late 1940s. Ironically, the same process of democratization followed by rapid economic growth which so stimulated the pronounced crisis and compensation dynamic of policy change in other domestic sectors within Japan produced the reverse effects with respect to land use policy. This sequence first dismantled the Home Ministry (*Naimushō*), the only domestic sector ministry with experience at systematic planning. It also increased the sensitivity of policymaking to political party influence and then sharply intensified the incentives of particularistic interest groups to resist and circumvent the half-hearted attempts at land-use planning the Japanese state did manage to undertake.

Japan's approach to land use planning, in short, can by no means be categorized simply as "creative conservativism," as postwar Japanese public policy in general has been seen.[3] Typically policy has cosmetically changed during periods of crisis when land use issues have been salient, also true in other policy areas under examination in this volume. For example, in the single year 1974, Japan imposed a heavy general tax on profits from land sales and a special tax directed at holders of unused land suitable for housing in urban areas, while also establishing a National Land Agency. But land use policy has also been characterized by an especially pronounced contrast between policymaking and objectives expressed in either the midst of crisis or subsequent policy implementation. In fact, land use policy measures have quite frequently been compromised at the implementation stage, to a more substantial degree than typical in the other policy areas under examination.

Three major factors help account for the somewhat unusual

[3] Pempel, *Policy and Politics in Japan.*

manner in which the crisis and compensation dynamic operates with respect to land use policy. Perhaps the most important is the nonfungible character of land itself. In the growing Japanese economy of the postwar period, most demands against the Japanese state have been made and satisfied in terms of money, but monetary satisfaction has not been possible with respect to land. A second major influence on the progress of land use policy issues has been the salient importance of land in the strategic planning of both Japanese businessmen and Japanese conservative politicians. Throughout the postwar period, land has been the major form of collateral for the massive loans which highly leveraged Japanese industry has contracted. Major land use policy changes with negative implications for land prices could have threatened the borrowing capacity, or even the solvency, of major corporations. Land related transactions have also been important in generating political funds for conservative politicians. Third, since 1948 no bureaucratic agency in the land use policy area has been strong enough to formulate and impose coherent policy. Primary responsibility until 1974 rested with the politically ineffectual Economic Planning Agency, and the National Land Agency created then is also weak.

In combination these three factors have made the costs of fundamental change in land use policies for principal conservative support constituencies substantially higher than in other policy areas, thus encouraging Japanese conservative policymakers to attempt unusually evasive strategies when the waves of political crisis sweep around them. Typically they have tried either to redefine land use issues into tractable housing, finance, or regional policy questions on the one hand, or, on the other, they have introduced cosmetic policy changes, such as the housing-land tax (*takuchi nami kazei*) of 1973, which have been heavily compromised with the waning of crisis. But to fully understand the actual role which crisis and compensation has played in Japanese land use policy formation, one must first understand Japanese policy profiles and their structural context.

Conventional Wisdom and Land Use Realities

Japanese conservative commentators often tend to present the urban problems of present-day Japan in deterministic fashion: Housing plots are small, streets are narrow, and public infrastructure is poor because Japan is a crowded country. Even those, such as former Prime Minister Tanaka Kakuei, who have disputed the inevitability of existing patterns of population distribution have not seen much potential for improved utilization of land within existing urban areas.[4]

Comparative analysis, sensitive to Japanese realities as they have evolved over time, is especially useful in evaluating these deterministic notions. Such analysis suggests, contrary to the conventional wisdom in Japan, that Japan is decidedly *not* the most heavily populated nation in the world, relative to area, even though it may be much more densely settled than large continental powers such as the United States. As indicated in table 9.1, both the Netherlands and Belgium have considerably more people than Japan per unit of area. Yet their cities also have both far more park space than those of Japan and a much more spacious sense. Furthermore, the Netherlands spent four times the share of its national budget on housing in 1981 that Japan did,[5] while Amsterdam had nearly fifteen times the park space per capita of Tokyo (table 9.1). Likewise, Singapore is much more heavily populated than Japan, nearly as heavily as Ōsaka Prefecture.[6] Yet it also has an atmosphere of spaciousness, rare in the Japanese context, in part due to a vigorous public housing program which supplies residences to over eighty percent of the population, as opposed to 6 percent in Japan.[7] Significantly, eighty percent of the people of crowded Singapore, in a 1980 international opinion survey, were satisfied with their housing conditions, as opposed to 76 percent in West Germany, 71 percent in the United States, 56 percent in India, and only 44 percent in Japan.[8]

It is indeed true that Japan is somewhat more mountainous than many of the most populated industrial nations. Only 21 per-

[4] For Tanaka's views on reorienting Japanese land use patterns, see Tanaka Kakuei, *Nihon Rettō Kaizō-Ron*. Also available in English translation, as *Building a New Japan: A Plan for Remodelling the Japanese Archipelago*.

[5] Housing expenditures in 1986 comprised 8 percent of the national budget in the Netherlands, and 1.8 percent in Japan. See OECD, *National Accounts, 1971–1983*, vol. 2; and Ministry of Finance Budget Bureau Research Section (Ōkurashō Shukei Kyoku Chōsa Ka), ed., *Zaisei Tōkei*, 1986 ed., p. 233.

[6] The population density of Ōsaka Prefecture (*Ōsaka Fu*) in October 1985 was 4,641 people per square kilometer, while that of Singapore was 4,353. See Yano Tsuneta Kinen Kai, ed., *Nihon Kokusei Zue (Japan in Graphics)*, 1987 ed., pp. 31, 67.

[7] Roy Hofheinz, Jr., and Kent E. Calder, *The Eastasia Edge*, p. 105.

[8] Kokumin Seikatsu Center, ed., *Zusetsu: Kurashi no Kokusai Hikaku (An Illustrated International Comparison of Living Standards)*, p. 41.

TABLE 9.1
Japanese Population Densities in Comparative Context

Nation	Population/Square Kilometer	Park Space/ Per Capita (Square Meters per Person)
Singapore	4,353	
Malta	1,203	
Bangladesh	672	
Barbados	585	
Taiwan	522	
South Korea	412	4.5 (Pusan)
Netherlands	353	29.4 (Amsterdam)
Belgium	324	9.2 (Brussels)
Japan	**318**	**2.2 (Tokyo)**
West Germany	246	37.4 (Bonn)
United Kingdom	228	30.6 (London)
Switzerland	156	15.1 (Geneva)
France	100	12.2 (Paris)
United States	25	45.7 (Washington, D.C.)

Sources: Yano Tsuneta Kinen Kai, ed., *Nihon Kokusei Zue (Japan in Graphics)*, 1987 ed. (Tokyo: Kokusei Sha, 1987), pp. 31–35; also Kokumin Seikatsu Center, ed., *Zusetsu: Kurashi no Kokusai Hikaku (An Illustrated International Comparison of Living Standards)* (Tokyo: Kokumin Seikatsu Center, 1985), p. 44; Sekai no Naka no Nihon o Kangaeru Kai, ed., *Kokusai Hikaku: Nihon o Miru (International Comparison: Looking at Japan)* (Tokyo: Chūō Hōki Shuppan Kabushiki Kaisha, 1985), p. 204; and National Land Agency (Kokudo Chō), ed., *Kokudo Tōkei Yōran (National Land Statistics Almanac)*, 1987 ed. (Tokyo: Taisei Shuppan Sha, 1987), p. 48.

Note: Park space figures are for the following dates: Japan, 1985; United States, South Korea, Britain, and Belgium, 1976; and West Germany, the Netherlands, Switzerland, and France, 1984.

cent of Japan's area is topographically suitable for housing, compared to 49 percent in the United States, 62 percent in France, and 64 percent in both Britain and West Germany.[9] Yet this reality alone can explain neither the unusual lack of urban planning

[9] National Land Agency (Kokudo Chō) *Kokudo Hakusho (National Land Yearbook)*, 1983 ed.

nor the failure to provide for social amenities in Japan's cities. For example, Switzerland, densely populated and even more mountainous than Japan, has nevertheless been able to achieve esthetically pleasing urban development, with Geneva devoting seven times more land area per capita to parks than Tokyo does.

In the final analysis the allocation of scarce land among competing purposes has in any nation an important political-economic dimension which is *not* predetermined by geographical realities. Japan in 1984 devoted 14.3 percent of its total land area to agriculture, 2.8 percent to roads, and only 2.4 percent to housing.[10] Over the previous decade the share devoted to roads had been rising more rapidly than that for housing.[11] Within the Tokyo metropolitan area, there still remained, in 1983, 426 square kilometers of arable farmland, or 12.6 percent of the entire metropolitan area, despite major housing shortages. None of these realities was predetermined by Japan's geographical situation; less roads or less farmland were a clear alternative to less residential land, should Japan have decided to make that choice. The tradeoffs actually chosen were profoundly shaped by the interplay of politics and public policy, as will be seen.

Although neither Japanese urban land, nor land in Japan more generally, is as scarce in absolute terms as often argued, that land *is* enormously expensive. According to recent Economic Planning Agency estimates, one can buy the whole United States more than twice over for the total price of all the land in Japan; the Japanese archipelago, only *one twenty-fifth* the physical size of the U.S., at the end of 1985 was valued at ¥1,051 trillion, or over $5.2 trillion at then current exchange rates.[12] Its hypothetical market value had risen 133 percent over the preceding decade.

The price of much urban land in Japan has risen even more sharply, to levels much higher than elsewhere in the industrialized world. As indicated in figure 9.1, average land prices in the suburbs of Tokyo during the early 1980s were running well above $1,000 per square meter, or around ten times levels in comparable parts of Vancouver or Seoul. Japanese urban land prices also

[10] Yano Tsuneta Kinen Kai, ed., *Nihon Kokusei Zue*, 1987 ed., p. 54.

[11] *Ibid.* Between 1972 and 1974 the share of Japan's total land area devoted to roads grew from 2.2 to 2.8 percent, but that devoted to housing grew only from 1.9 to 2.4 percent.

[12] Takeuchi Hiroshi, "Japan's Soaring Land Prices," *Journal of Japanese Trade and Industry*, no. 4 (1987), p. 44.

appear to be substantially higher than equivalent levels in various parts of West Germany.[13]

Another graphic indicator of the high price of Japanese urban land is the ratio of land prices to worker income. In 1970 the Japanese Economic Planning Agency showed that a Japanese worker would have to work six years and 149 days to acquire 150 square meters of land in a location within forty minutes commuting distance from the center of Tokyo. To acquire land under similar conditions in other countries, an American worker would have to work 45 days, a West German worker 174 days, and a French worker two years and 290 days.[14]

As in so many areas of the Japanese political economy, the sharp divergence of Japanese rates of land price increases from patterns elsewhere in the industrialized world has largely been the product of the past four decades. Rapid Japanese economic growth has been only one reason. Administrative and political considerations, including collateral requirements making land ownership effectively a condition for bank borrowing, agricultural price supports which increase demand for farm land, agricultural land taxation policies, and restrictions on high-rise buildings, have all significantly influenced the price of urban land. Japanese urban land prices rose at rates consistently exceeding 20 percent annually throughout the high growth period of 1955–1973 (table 9.2). This was sharply higher than land price increases in densely populated and relatively rapidly growing West Germany, even adjusting for the substantial inflation differential between the two countries.[15] After leveling off in the late 1970s and early 1980s, Japanese land prices began accelerating again in 1986–1987, with prices for residential land within twenty kilometers of the Tokyo city center doubling in a single year.

By the mid-1980s, an average newly-built home in the suburbs of Tokyo cost around eight times the annual income of the aver-

[13] In 1976, for example, housing land prices in Kobe were 57 percent higher than in Munich, roughly equivalent in size, while those in Sendai were 134 percent higher than in Hanover, and in Kanazawa 47 percent higher than in Mannheim. See Kurokawa Nobuyuki, "Skyrocketing Prices of Land Hit the Social Structure," *Japan Quarterly* (April–June 1981), p. 209.

[14] *Ibid.*, p. 208.

[15] In Japan, home building land prices rose 184 percent between 1962 and 1973 compared to 88 percent in West Germany. See Prime Minister's Office Statistical Bureau, *Japan Statistical Yearbook*, various years; and Statistisches Bundesamt *Deutsches Statistiches Jahrbuch*, selected years.

TABLE 9.2
Japan's Urban Infrastructure Crisis

	Percentage of households connected to sewage	Park space per capita (m²)	Average width of streets (meters)
U.K.	97 (1976)	30.4 (London)	16.6 (London)
W. Germany	91 (1983)	26.1 (West Berlin)	20.1 (W. Berlin)
U.S.	72 (1979)	45.7 (Washington)	23.2 (New York)
Japan	34 (1984)	2.0 (Tokyo 1985)	13.6 (Tokyo 1985)

Sources: Ministry of Construction (Kensetsu Shō) *Kensetsu Tōkei Yōran (Construction Statistics Almanac)* (Tokyo: Ōkurashō Insatsu Kyoku, 1984); Ministry of Construction (Kensetsu Shō), *Kensetsu Hakusho (White Paper on Construction)* 1986 ed. (Tokyo: Ōkurashō Insatsu Kyoku, 1986); Kokumin Seikatsu Center, *Kurashi no Kokusai Hikaku (An Illustrated International Comparison of Living Standards)* (Tokyo: Kokumin Seikatsu Center, 1985), p. 44.

Note: Figures for 1976 unless otherwise noted.

age Japanese worker. Such a worker in 1985 could expect to pay around 15 percent of his entire anticipated lifetime income for such a home, even before the sharp land price appreciation of 1986–1987 began.[16] It was also significantly higher than prevailing inflation rates in Japan (see figure 9.1). Thus, the ability of the average Japanese to purchase a new home had sharply deteriorated over the previous two decades. This was precisely the reverse of the situation in West Germany, where the price of building and land in relation to personal income was actually less than it had been during the early 1960s.[17]

Since land prices are high, for a range of political as well as economic reasons, urban Japanese tend to live on extremely small parcels of land, even though land itself is not physically in short supply to nearly the degree normally assumed. During 1978, 52 percent of all houses built in Tokyo and 67 percent of those built in Ōsaka were erected on sites smaller than 100

[16] This calculation was by Yoshimoto Kiyoshi, Mitsui Bank economist. See *The Economist*, October 3, 1987, p. 25.

[17] In 1976 the average price of West German building land, in relation to personal disposable income, was 5 percent lower than in 1962. See Graham Hallett, *Housing and Land Policies in West Germany and Britain*, p. 92.

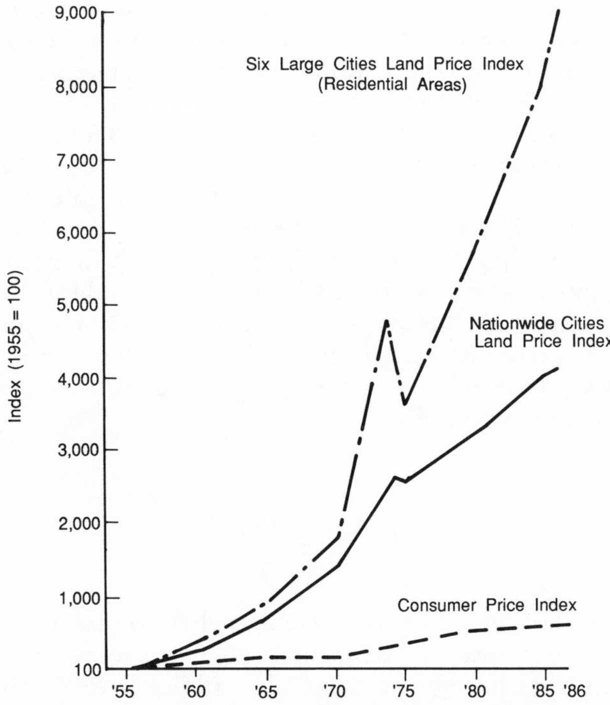

Figure 9.1. The Sharp Rise of Japanese Land Prices, 1955–1986.
Source: Japan Real Estate Institute data, as reported in Prime Minister's Office Statistical Bureau (Sōrifu Tōkei Kyoku), ed. *Nihon Tōkei Nenkan (Japan Statistical Yearbook)*, 1955–1986 ed. (Tokyo: Mainichi Shimbun Sha, annual).

square meters. Yet only one-third of house sites nationwide were built on such tiny pieces of land. In the countryside particularly, such sites tend to be much more spacious.

Seen in comparative context, the urban infrastructure of Japan's major cities is also deplorable, despite the extraordinarily high levels of Japanese public investment more generally. Japanese have roads and bullet railway trains in great profusion, but they sorely lack conventional sewage systems. Only 30 percent of Japanese homes were connected to sewage systems in 1982, compared to 72 percent in the United States and over 90 percent in Western Europe (table 9.2). Park space was also strikingly scarce, and streets narrow. In contrast to European patterns, few suburban Japanese streets had sidewalks, despite the safety hazard thereby implied.

The failures of Japanese land use policy become especially paradoxical against the backdrop of what is generally regarded as Japanese success through systematic planning in so many other areas. From the late 1920s, Japan developed elaborate systems for allocating credit, controlling physical allocation of scarce resources such as coal and oil, and building national telecommunications and electric power grids.[18] Since 1948 it has had a comprehensive system of macro- and sectoral economic planning under the auspices of the Economic Planning Agency.[19] And Japan's industrial policies are broadly regarded as the most systematic, comprehensive, and sophisticated in the world. Given the intensity of planning in the Japanese financial and industrial sectors, the hesitancy of planning for land use and the country's failure to attack issues of such central social importance stand in sharp and glaring contrast.

Japan's Long Tradition of Land Use Planning

The recent failures of Japanese public policy to plan effectively in the land use area—the frequent failure even to recognize any possibility of planning—are especially striking in view of Japan's long tradition of concern for urban planning, dating to the mid-Meiji period. The initial focus of planning efforts was Tokyo, and the initial stimulus nationalism. Meiji leaders wanted to remake Tokyo, one of the largest cities in the world since the eighteenth century, into a world-class capital from a visual standpoint. In 1877 construction of Ginza Dōri, one of the main thoroughfares of modern Tokyo, was begun. Prior to his appointment as the eighth governor of Tokyo in 1884, Yoshikawa Akimasa accompanied Prime Minister-to-be Itō Hirobumi to Europe and the United States on an inspection tour, looking for further ideas on how to modernize Tokyo.[20] Yoshikawa's reactions were later incorporated into the Tokyo Municipal Area Reform Regulations (1888), Japan's first written city planning law. The same year a

[18] See Johnson, *MITI and the Japanese Miracle*, pp. 85–156; and Nakamura Takafusa, *Nihon no Keizai Tōsei*.

[19] See Haruhiro Fukui, "Economic Planning in Postwar Japan," *Asian Survey* (April 1972), pp. 327–48.

[20] For details on the Yoshikawa inspection tour and its ultimate policy implications, see Hanayama Yuzuru, *Gendai no Tochi Shinwa (The Modern Land Myth)*.

city planning commission was also established for Tokyo, predating by nearly forty years even the early origins of systematic Japanese industrial policy.[21]

Early in the twentieth century, the movement toward systematic land use planning intensified, spurred by deepening interest at the Home Ministry (Naimushō). In 1909 the Cultivated Land Consolidation Law (*Kōchi Seiri Hō*), an early step toward regional land use planning, was passed. In 1918 an Urban Planning Section (*Toshi Keikaku Ka*) was established in the minister's secretariat of the Home Ministry. In 1919 Japan enacted a new National City Planning Law which superseded Yoshikawa's 1888 Tokyo municipal measure. Based on Germany's so-called Adickes Law of 1902, this new Japanese legislation provided designated zoning across the major urban centers of Japan at the option of individual municipalities. By 1930, ninety-seven cities were covered by the provisions of the law, although only twenty-seven cities had actually introduced zoning.[22] Thus, the 1919 National City Planning Law gradually introduced the concepts of segregated zoning and land use control, based on German precedent.

The Great Kantō Earthquake of 1923 gave bureaucrats the opportunity to utilize the new National City Planning Law to operationalize their planning aspirations. This massive disaster leveled much of Tokyo, leaving nearly 250,000 people dead, severely injured, or missing and around 500,000 homes destroyed. Its trauma provided strong incentives to reconstruct the national capital in more systematic fashion. To the Earthquake Recovery Commission (*Shinsai Fukkō-in*), headed by Gotō Shimpei,[23] as well as to the general public, the major reason for the huge number of casualties was clear. Vast stretches of Tokyo simply lacked the parks, broad avenues, and other open space where citizens might assemble to escape the raging fires which would inevitably accompany major earthquakes in a Japan of predominantly

[21] See Johnson, *MITI and the Japanese Miracle*, pp. 83–115.

[22] See Ishida Yorifusa, *Nihon Kindai Toshi Keikaku no Hyaku Nen (One Hundred Years of Modern Japanese Urban Planning)*, p. 135.

[23] Gotō (1857–1929) was serving his second term as Home Minister at the time of the earthquake, after having previously served as Governor of Tokyo (1920–1923), Minister of Communications in two cabinets, president of the Southern Manchurian Railway, and civilian governor of Taiwan. He was one of Japan's most renowned administrators.

wooden structures. Substantial changes had to be made in land use patterns within Tokyo.

In response to the earthquake, the government created the Post-Quake Reconstruction Scheme. This plan, carried out over a period of seven years, involved large-scale rezoning and readjustment over as much as 3,100 hectares in Tokyo alone (about 70 percent of the devastated area), including such central parts of Tokyo as Kyōbashi, Nihonbashi, Kanda, and Kōjimachi. The plan was particularly successful in appropriating land for roads. Virtually all landowners within the Reconstruction Enforced Area were compelled to give up 10 percent of their land without compensation, producing a total acreage which comprises nearly one half of the total land devoted to roads in midtown Tokyo today. In addition, large numbers of landowners were forced to give up substantially more land to the state for nominal payments, adding more than 50 percent to the amount of land amassed through the original compulsory contribution. With the forced land contributions, the Japanese state built the four-lane Shōwa Dōri from Shimbashi to Ueno.[24] It also forced many temples, shrines, and factories out of Tokyo. The population of such areas as Asakusa, Honjo, and Nihonbashi decreased by 20 to 30 percent, substantially reducing the prospective safety hazards in the event of another earthquake.

Perhaps the most successful efforts in Japanese history at land use planning were those undertaken in Manchuria under Japanese occupation (1931–1945). In Harbin, for example, 24,500 hectares were appropriated for parks and other purposes, under a 1936 city plan which paralleled those of many German and Northern European cities of the period.[25] The Manchukuo government was far more aggressive in appropriating land from farmers for public facilities than even in prewar Japan because the farmers of Manchukuo were either local Chinese or immigrants from Japan and Korea (*kaitaku nōmin*), who did not have the established rights of counterparts in the home Japanese islands.[26] The authoritarian powers of the Manchukuo government also weakened the prospects for grassroots resistance.

As the mobilization for war began, the Japanese state appropriated increasing amounts of land for military-related facilities, as

[24] See Sugai Shirō, *Kokudo Keikaku no Keiji to Kadai (Revelations and Topics regarding National Land Use Planning)*, p. 128.

[25] *Ibid.*, p. 203.

[26] See Ishida Yorifusa, *Nihon Kindai Toshi Keikaku no Hyaku Nen*, pp. 158–64.

in Germany. During the early days of World War II, Japan launched its first major nationwide efforts at land use planning. On September 24, 1940, the National Land Planning Ordinance (*Kokudo Keikaku Settei Yōkō*) was decreed by cabinet order; its major purpose was to anticipate and prepare for overcrowding and food shortages resulting from rapid war-related population shifts. These might otherwise have seriously undermined social stability and hence the Imperial war effort.[27] Its major concern was thus national and political stability rather than the quality of urban life. The ordinance, actively applied in Manchuria, had potential for more general application.

In May 1943 the Cabinet Planning Board, heart of the wartime planning apparatus, launched an even more ambitious scheme—the National Capital Transformation Proposal. This ambitious scheme, motivated both by air defense considerations and long-range desires for a more efficient, more imposing Tokyo, proposed comprehensive planning for the entire area within a forty to fifty kilometer radius of Tokyo Station.[28] In line with its political objective of transforming Tokyo into a majestic capital city on the order of Berlin, London, and Paris, the plan envisaged a radical reduction in land devoted to industrial and commercial usage within Tokyo, from 219 to only 70 square kilometers, through a system of rigorous zoning, including building height and land use restrictions.[29] It also proposed devoting 40 percent of Tokyo's entire area to public facilities, including a new airport, and to extensive green belts, especially surrounding major arteries in and out of Tokyo.

In November 1943, the *Kikaku-in* (Cabinet Planning Board) was dissolved, and its land use planning functions were absorbed by the Home Ministry (*Naimushō*). That powerful ministry was also actively interested in land use planning, including the Capital Transformation Plan. During 1943 it had begun to develop postwar regional land use plans of its own for both Tokyo and Ōsaka. Toward war's end the Naimushō also began devising land use plans to accelerate food production in a starving Japan. Had the Home Ministry's central role in the Japanese political economy remained unchanged, patterns of postwar land use policy would likely have been much different. But the Naimushō had

[27] See Sugai Shirō, *Shiryō: Kokudo Keikaku (Data on National Land Planning)*, p. 225.

[28] For details, see *ibid.*, pp. 86–219.

[29] *Ibid.*, p. 247.

little opportunity to exert a decisive role in land use planning. The confusion at war's end, the purge, and finally the dissolution of the ministry itself in late December 1947 all assured this was not to be.

With the introduction of a sharply different political system after 1945, and particularly after the dissolution of the Naimushō at the end of 1947, postwar Japanese land use policies began to diverge from an emerging prewar and wartime tradition of systematic planning by a politically influential, often social welfare-oriented national bureaucracy. They also began to diverge ever more sharply from policy patterns in other heavily populated industrial democracies, including those with conservative governments. By contrasting postwar policy evolution to both the earlier Japanese heritage and also contemporary trends in heavily populated democracies with conservative governments, such as Adenauer and Erhard's West Germany, one begins to uncover the political dynamic that has driven postwar Japanese land policy in directions it was by no means fated by geographical or economic forces to evolve.

Successful Land Use Planning in a Densely Peopled Democracy: the West German Case

West German land policies provide an especially useful contrast to those of Japan because the two nations have confronted similar historical, political, and demographic circumstances, especially during the crucial early postwar period, which sharply influenced future land use patterns. Both West Germany and Japan have, as noted earlier, roughly similar overall population densities. Both nations were dominated for over a decade from the early 1930s by totalitarian regimes that appropriated large amounts of land for military purposes, leaving their successors in 1945 with substantial public land potentially useful in satisfying social needs. Both nations were bombed heavily during World War II and faced massive reconstruction challenges. Both confronted confused land use and ownership patterns at war's end, which offered scope for rational land use planning and gave the state broad options concerning its proceedings. Both Japan and Germany confronted Allied occupiers intent on promoting democratic land ownership patterns through land reform and other means. Finally, following war's end both were governed almost exclusively by conservative parties for virtually a full generation; Germany until the Kiessinger-Brandt Grand Coalition of 1966–1969, and Japan to the present day, excepting only the 1947–1948 Katayama-Ashida coalitions.

If anything, one might anticipate that early postwar Japanese land use planning would be more systematic and land price increases more moderate than in West Germany. Dislocations created by refugee inflow and postwar administrative confusion were substantial in both nations, but if anything greater in Germany, across which savage fighting had swirled for several months in early 1945. Even after the initial influx of repatriates at war's end, refugees continued to flow in a steady, often volatile stream from the East, until erection of the Berlin Wall in 1961. Postwar Japan, after the initial inflow from China and the former colonies, had no counterpart to this massive refugee flow into West Germany, with all the pressures on land use and housing stock it generated. Economic growth and urban transformation, with their attendant pressures on land use, were also more rapid in Germany than in Japan for most of the pre-1960 period.

Yet West Germany, contrary to what demographic and economic pressures of the first two postwar decades might appear to dictate, developed a much more systematic land use policy than did Japan; the German policy allowed systematic planning and prevented volatile fluctuations in land prices.[30] First, German policies discouraged land price speculation during the recovery period by retaining until 1961 the land price freeze imposed by the Nazi government in 1936. Since then, detailed figures on land transactions throughout the country have been published by the Federal Statistical Office, making real estate markets as transparent as possible and thus discouraging speculation.

Perhaps the most striking feature of early postwar West German land use policy was the prominence of land use development planning, especially that undertaken by local government. Before 1960, substantial initiative was taken in this regard by the

[30] Land prices in Germany rose moderately during the 1960s, but this was only a correction of distortions introduced by the 1936–1961 price controls. Over the 1914–1971 period, real West German land prices rose less than half as fast as incomes. Since 1969 German land prices relative to personal income have been essentially flat, except for a short surge during the late 1970s and early 1980s. See Hallett, *Housing and Land Policies*, p. 96; and *Deutsches Statistiches Jahrbuch*, various issues.

Länder, which had played a major role in housing and land use planning since the 1920s.[31] A strong Federal Building Act was passed by the Bundestag in 1950, but it was held up for ten years in the Constitutional Court.[32] Thus, there was a substantial period when the strong planning capabilities of the Länder, and their political ability to neutralize interest group pressure, were central to the success of German land use planning.

After a modified Federal Building Act was passed in 1960, federal authorities took on substantial responsibility for land use planning, with particular emphasis on systematic creation of greenfield suburbs around major cities. They also were relatively successful in promoting coherent land use planning by local authorities. German planning successes at both the federal and Länder levels contrast sharply to much more haphazard Japanese development of expanding urban centers.

Substantial government land was left by prewar governments to their successors in Germany, a major resource for postwar land use planning, maintaining the coherence of the planning process. During the 1970s, about 25 percent of total sales of land for housing in Germany were sales of public land by local authorities.[33] Much is also owned by nonprofit housing enterprises, churches, or other charities. In cities over 500,000 in West Germany, shares of undeveloped land owned by the city range from 23 to 50 percent, with much of the land acquired by public authorities since the war. In contrast to Japanese authorities, those in Germany have actively bought as well as sold land, helping the state to play a more active role in housing development.

Tax policies have not been as important in Germany as in some other parts of Europe (Britain, for example) in influencing land prices and land use. Germany introduced a tax on realized

[31] Both municipalities and the Länder had been marginally involved in the housing and land use area since the late nineteenth century through granting low cost loans and providing building lots on an occasional basis. The role of the Länder increased sharply after 1923, when they were authorized to levy a special tax on owners of existing housing stock to subsidize new construction. Their role in planning and funding new housing construction led to establishment of an elaborate local government housing bureaucracy, which persisted even after World War II. They took an active interest in land use planning, especially for housing construction, at that time. See Hellmut Wollman, "Housing Policy: Between State Intervention and the Market" in *Policy and Politics in the Federal Republic of Germany*, eds. Klaus von Beyme and Manfred G. Schmidt, pp. 130–38.

[32] *Ibid.*, p. 142.

[33] *Ibid.*

gains in land site value during 1911, shortly after Britain's liberal government did so, but the Germans abolished it in 1936. The 1972 Act to Promote Town Planning (*Stadtbauforderungsgesetz*) introduced a "betterment levy" (*Ausgleichsbetrag*) to appropriate windfall profits from urban renewal projects to private contractors. But this is applicable only in small, clearly defined areas where there is substantial local expenditure. The Social Democratic party has been trying to introduce a more general tax on increases in site value, but this has been strongly opposed by the conservative Christian Democrats. Generally, the differences between Right and Left over development taxes in Germany are sharp, as in Britain, and parallel those in Japan, although the European Left is much more vocal in pressing such issues than is that of Japan. But there is generally no special tax rate for urban agricultural land in Europe, such as profoundly influences land use patterns in Japan.

German housing policies, interestingly, have been more oriented toward landlords than those of Japan. In contrast to Britain and many areas of the United States, West Germany in the postwar period has not had rent controls, which were imposed during the Weimar Period and found to be disastrous in constricting the supply of housing. Housing subsidies are also available to any landlord willing to let "at cost rents." The bottom line of German housing policy, in short, has been creating as much housing as efficiently and systematically as possible, through an eclectic approach employing both state participation and market-oriented elements.

The Travails of Postwar Planning: Japanese Politics and Land Use

Postwar Japanese land use policies, as suggested above, have been strikingly divergent both from major patterns in Japan's own past and also from patterns in other densely populated nations of the industrialized world. There has been substantially less development planning, and the plans developed have been more thoroughly emasculated by interest group pressure.[34] Zoning policies

[34] Local government land use planning in such urban centers as Sapporo, Nagoya, and Kōbe is a partial exception to this general pattern. But much of this planning, especially in Sapporo, has prewar origins; hence it confirms the general argument here.

have been ineffective, and the state has not been as able to compel the private sector to make compulsory land contributions for public purposes as it was in the prewar period. Politics has severely circumscribed the power of eminent domain.

Tax policies have operated both to accelerate the rate of land price increase and to discourage investment in housing stock. There is, for example, preferential taxation on agricultural land in urban areas, which encourages both land hoarding and inefficient low density land use. High taxes on the sale of land, Japan's distinctive response to the huge land price increases of the early 1970s, in fact help to encourage such price increases by also discouraging the orderly sale of land even when substantial demand exists. Rent controls and other constraints on landlord use of rental property create strong disincentives to develop high-quality rental housing. In contrast to the United States and most other industrialized nations, interest expenses on primary residences are not tax deductible in Japan; this, in turn, discourages Japanese from investing in improvements to their own homes.[35]

Japan began the postwar period with a seemingly serious attempt at land planning, in the tradition of recovery from the Great Kantō Earthquake of 1923. In September 1945, the Home Ministry proposed the National Land Development Plan (*Kokudo Kaihatsu Keikaku An*). Its imperatives for postwar development were: (1) rebuilding destroyed areas; (2) coping with natural disasters; (3) increasing agricultural land acreage; and (4) expanding industry. Industrial development, in short, only rated fourth place.

As is so often the case of Japanese conservative policymaking, political crisis provided the crucial catalyst for major policy innovation. As World War II drew to a close, the Naimushō was deeply concerned about the possibility of social chaos flowing from the sharp transformations of Japanese society which demobilization and disarmament seemed likely to cause. To reduce the prospective uncertainty, it formulated the National Reconstruction Land Policy (*Fukkō Kokudo Keikaku*) of 1946 and proposed the Special Urban Planning Law, also passed in 1946. Both

[35] According to the Japanese Ministry of Construction, tax expenditures for housing in Japan under the 1984 budget were only ¥82 billion, compared to 3.4 times this amount in Britain, 7.6 times in West Germany, 20.3 times in France, and 40.4 times this in the United States. See Naitō Tetsu, "Jitsugen Dekiru ka? Shotokuzei Genzei, Jūtaku Genzei?" ("Can a Reduction in Income and Housing Taxes be Realized?"), p. 76.

were intended to be comprehensive efforts at land use planning, including provisions for housing construction.

In contrast to European patterns, however, these plans were mainly realized only in their big business related dimensions. The National Reconstruction Land Policy led to the creation of industrial combinants at Ōita and Chiba, with local governors given responsibility for determining and implementing specific land use plans. The Special Urban Planning Law was employed to sequester land for expanding railway terminals and the plazas fronting them in Shinjuku, Shibuya, and Gotanda, as well as for broadening major Tokyo traffic arteries.[36] But early postwar plans failed either to lay out well-arranged housing zones or even to rationalize transportation patterns to nearly the degree achieved in 1923–1924. Indeed, they, and Japanese land policy generally, descended into the special interest politics and state incapability that represent the least attractive face of Japanese conservative policymaking. In Tokyo, landowners successfully resisted the 15 percent compulsory uncompensated contribution of land which the government tried to force upon them, reportedly mobilizing conservative political forces to do so.[37] In 1949 they forced a revision in the law to provide for compensation.

Allied occupation forces failed to intervene on any of these issues, considering them beyond their general mandate to promote democratization while discouraging radical tendencies. One of SCAP's few impacts in the land use area apparently was encouraging abolition in 1950 of the Tokyo city planning tax, one of the city's few means of raising funds for land purchases.[38] Attempts to procure land for public purposes beyond the compulsory contributions also largely failed, with Tokyo municipal authorities securing only 6.8 percent of the 20,000 hectares they had planned to acquire in Tokyo; local authorities outside Tokyo secured 61.2 percent of their planned total.[39] Although insufficient public funds were cited as the reason for failure, it is striking to note the huge sums being dispensed at the same time by the Reconstruc-

[36] For details, see Hanayama Yuzuru, "The Housing Land Shortage," *Japan Economic Studies*, 1983, pp. 29–31.

[37] On the fate of the 1946 Special Urban Planning Law, see Ministry of Construction (Kensetsushō), *Sensai Fukkō Shi (Chronicle of the Reconstruction of War-Damaged Areas)*, vol. 1.

[38] Yamada Masao, *Toki no Nagare: Toshi no Nagare (The Current of the Times: The Current of the City)*, p. 410.

[39] Ishida Yorifusa, *Nihon Kindai Toshi Keikaku no Hyaku Nen*, p. 231.

tion Finance Bank to aid rehabilitation of the coal, steel, shipping, and fertilizer sectors.[40] The central government rarely intervened to aid local authorities in their urban development programs and it failed to develop a coherent approach of its own. Urban land use clearly had a lower rank in both the national and local government scale of priorities than did industrial recovery; it did not merit either aggressive state regulatory intervention or substantial use of scarce public funds to prevent public programs from being emasculated by interest groups.[41]

Industrial recovery was also the primary concern of national government in Germany over the first postwar decade. But in Germany the Länder vigorously planned urban land use, often using government land as the catalyst for developments centering on public housing projects. In a few cases, such as Nagoya, Kōbe, and Sapporo, Japanese local governments in the early postwar period developed rather far-sighted land use planning programs that helped minimize problems of overcrowding and urban sprawl, together with poor social amenities, emerging elsewhere as high economic growth began. Some other local governments, such as Yokohama, later achieved a partial semblance of planning through their strategic utilization of new land made available by U.S. military withdrawals and reclamation.[42] But these cases of successful local planning were pronounced exceptions, generally undertaken by left-oriented local governments relatively insulated from the grassroots agricultural, construction, and real estate interests so commonly central to the local conservative circles of compensation.

The general failure of Japanese local governments to come up with comprehensive land use policies, despite their new powers in this area, is one of the most striking realities of the early postwar period in Japan and lies at the root of the current land use crisis facing Japan. Grassroots pressures from farmers and developers, many of them affiliated with conservative politicians, ap-

[40] See, for example, Jerome B. Cohen, *Japan's Economy in War and Reconstruction*.

[41] Tokyo seems to have been especially disfavored. Although the war-damaged area of Tokyo constituted 26.6 percent of Japan's total, its share of total government subsidies for rebuilding was only 10.9 percent in 1949. See Ishida Yorifusa, *Nihon Kindai Toshi Keikaku no Hyaku Nen*, p. 230.

[42] On the history of city planning in Yokohama, particularly after the funding of the Planning Adjustment Office (Kikaku Chōsei Shitsu) in 1968 by the Asukata administration, see Tamura Akira, *Toshi Yokohama o Tsukuru (Building the City of Yokohama)*.

pear to have been a major element in this policy failure, especially in areas such as Tokyo, where the Right consistently dominated local government during the late 1940s. Another major factor, ironically, was counterpressure from organized grass-roots interests on the Left, particularly local public employee unions. In Tokyo during the late 1940s, for example, municipal allocations for planning-related land purchases were continually preempted by public employee union demands for increased wages in a period of incessant inflation.[43]

The Crucial Role of Naimushō Dissolution

After the reforms of 1946, one of the most crucial gaps in Japanese land use policy for nearly half a decade was a failure of conception. Although Japan had pressing land use problems, especially in urban areas, few analysts made systematic attempts to solve them, in sharp contrast to patterns in Germany. No national level administrative authority in Japan had the ability to enforce even such solutions as those proposed earlier. This strange failure of conception, contrasting so strongly to prewar and wartime patterns of self-conscious planning, was largely due to the abolition in 1947 of the Home Ministry (Naimushō). This abolition, as noted in chapter 4, stands in strong contrast to continuities of local administration in France, Britain, and even to some degree in Italy. Although West Germany sharply weakened the power of central authority after 1945, it also had a stronger prewar tradition of autonomous local government than did Japan, providing local authorities experienced in urban planning when the responsible national agencies were reorganized at war's end.

During the prewar period, and even in its initial planning after war's end, Japan's Naimushō had indicated a sensitive, urban welfare-oriented approach to land planning, similar to patterns evolving in Europe. The abolition of the ministry, a key element of Japan's democratization in the eyes of the Allied occupation, removed this crucial actor from the scene. Although the occupation intervened little in the day-to-day details of land use policy formation, its decision to dismantle the one government entity with both the inclination and expertise in the late 1940s to sys-

[43] Interview with former *Naimushō* official and Tokyo city planning director, Tokyo, July, 1985.

tematically plan land use had a decisive impact on policy development in that area. As a result, Japanese land use policymaking became more "democratic" than it had previously been; it was more responsive to grassroots pressure. But whether policies developed were more capable of serving the public welfare, broadly conceived, was another question.

In early postwar West Germany, local government was the driving force behind cohesive urban land use planning. In theory this could have happened in Japan as well, to a much greater degree than it actually did. Local governments throughout Japan were not directly affected by the dissolution of the Home Ministry, and they had gained substantial new formal powers shortly after war's end. Preexisting land use plans developed by the Home Ministry could have provided a guide to rational city planning; land prices did not begin to climb sharply until the Korean War, so budgetary constraints did not present an insurmountable obstacle to obtaining the necessary land.

Yet most local government did not seriously attempt to plan local land use during the five-year window before the Korean War, and the ensuing rush of industry and workers to the large cities of Japan vastly complicated the planning process. Cross pressures from grassroots interest groups of the Left and the Right, against a Japanese state unable to resist, lie at the heart of government's fateful inaction. Tokyo city officials of the period recall civic demonstrations against proposed thoroughfares and other public construction projects, in which landholders could have had vested interests. Municipal funds for land purchases were also continually a problem in the face of union pressures for wage hikes and the welfare concerns of the needy, while landholders were wary of any financial compensation offered, in view of the continuing virulent inflation of the period. As the Shoup and Kambe reports undertaken during the occupation pointed out, Japanese local governments found themselves at war's end with a mass of new responsibilities and severely restricted revenue powers. At the same time grassroots pressure groups were becoming increasingly insistent. One major casualty was funding to support coherent land use planning.

For a crucial seventeen-month period during 1947–1948, the unstable coalition cabinets of Katayama and Ashida, preoccupied with burning ideological and economic issues such as nationalization of the coal mines, had little time for the controversial affairs of local municipalities such as community land use. This preoccupation intensified the overall failure of conception regarding land use policy. Those who cared about land use planning were whipsawed by crosspressures from labor activists striving to divert municipal funds to wages, landlords resisting application of eminent domain against their property, and citizens simply distrustful of government authority after long years of mobilization.

Into the vacuum left by the demise of the Home Ministry and the incapacity of local government stepped SCAP, interest groups, and politics. The politicians, for example, succeeded in having the Public Works Bureau (*Doboku Kyoku*) of the Naimushō upgraded from its scheduled agency status to ministerial rank.[44] But no similar action was taken to augment or emphasize land use planning functions previously exercised by the Naimushō.

Formal responsibility for national land use planning ultimately devolved until 1974 on the Economic Planning Agency. But the EPA, an ideological stepchild after the fall of the Katayama-Ashida coalition cabinets and Japan's clear rejection of socialism, with limited budget, staff, and span of clearcut responsibility, had little political leverage to systematically engage in land use planning even should it have wanted to do so. It was politically incapable of the definitive nationwide policy coordination in which the Home Ministry had routinely engaged. In this power vacuum, the power of fissiparous grassroots political influences increased.

Land Policy Minus Effective Urban Planning

The result of Naimushō dissolution, coupled with political crisis for the conservatives requiring them to cultivate grassroots political interests, was a sharp shift in land use policy toward preoccupation with regional development, construction, resource exploitation, and industrial progress, coupled with a neglect of city planning. First evidence of this new orientation was the National Land Comprehensive Development Law *(Kokudo Sōgō Kaihatsu Hō)* of May 26, 1950. This legislation, which former Prime Minister Tanaka Kakuei claims originated in his Local Development

[44] Hayasaka Shigezō, "Tanaka Kakuei Mumei no Jyū Nen," *Chūō Kōron* (November 1986), pp. 381–82.

Sub-Committee, only two years after he joined the Diet,[45] came at a crucial time in the history of Japanese land policy development, less than a month before the outbreak of the Korean War. Japanese land prices were still stable, and the supply of urban land for public purposes was still relatively plentiful, unconstrained by the fierce speculative fevers which were to rise and continue with the onset of rapid economic growth, beginning only a few weeks hence. Japan could still have succeeded in systematic urban land use planning on the postwar European pattern, if both the political will to plan and the administrative structures to support planning had existed. But they did not. Article Seven of the new law authorized local governments to proceed with local land use plans, but it provided no incentives, other than authorizing a partial central government subsidy of survey costs. The major programs pursued immediately under provisions of the law focused on hydroelectric power development, using the U.S. TVA program as a model.

Regional competition and strong political involvement made it impossible to designate two to three sites for TVA-style projects, as originally anticipated. Ultimately twenty-two special development areas were authorized over the five-year life of the plan (1953-1958), each being designated by cabinet order rather than bureaucratic fiat.[46] This program represented the first major land policy decision determined by politicians, rather than by the formerly all powerful Home Ministry. Yet in contrast to West German patterns of the period, such as Germany's Federal Building Act of 1950, it had nothing to do with housing or other use of land by individual citizens.[47]

The bias of Japanese land use planning across the 1960s was similar. In 1962 the Ikeda administration inaugurated Japan's first countrywide land use plan, the National Comprehensive Development Plan (*Zensō*), which specified the ideal location of industrial complexes and the necessary infrastructure to service them. But neither this plan nor its successor, the *Shin Zensō* of

[45] Tanaka Kakuei, *Building a New Japan*, p. 12.

[46] *Ibid.*, p. 42.

[47] Several minor regional land use plans evolved during the 1950s, including plans for the development of Tōhoku (1957), the Tokyo area (1958), Kyūshū (1959), Hokuriku (1960), and Chūgoku-Shikoku (1960). But none of these were pieces of an overall national land use plan, nor were they systematically related. And none but the Tokyo plan had an urban development content. See Sugai Shirō, *Shiryō*, p. 85.

1964, addressed quality of life issues relating to urban land use, including pollution, green space, and overall deterioration of the visual environment. Advocates of urban policies were not yet a part of the conservative coalition, which in the absence of crisis had few incentives to broaden its circle of compensation. For the industrial planning bureaucracy, such issues were secondary; and the ministry most concerned with domestic life quality questions, the Naimushō, had been abolished at the end of 1947.

As the large cities of Japan expanded rapidly during the 1960s, one of the principal obstacles to rational urban land use planning was increasingly the system of preferential taxation for agricultural land. Under the Local Taxes Law of 1949, farmland was given special tax treatment to encourage agricultural production and compensate for the prevailing system of compulsory sale of farm products to the government at low prices. In 1964 a revision of this law applied the rule of *ad valorum* or market-value appraisal to farmland and standardized the diverse criteria among municipalities for the assessment of land. This change, which would have sharply increased taxes on farmland, was bitterly opposed by farmers' organizations and opposition parties and sharply modified to permit continued preferential tax treatment for farmland.[48] Thus began a running battle between urban planners and rural interest groups over land taxation, which continued into the late 1980s without decisive resolution.

The late 1960s and early 1970s brought modest formal policy change, largely emasculated in practice, which illustrated the political difficulties in Japan of systematic land use planning. In 1968 the New City Planning Law (*Shin Toshi Keikaku Hō*) was passed in the wake of pressure from progressive local governments, dividing cities into urban areas and urban adjustment areas. At the same time, a development permission system was established to give government considerable formal power to partition areas for housing, commerce, and industry. Farms within the urban area were again to be imposed a fixed asset tax as heavy as that on the surrounding housing area, to encourage conversion of farms into housing sites. But government had the power to grant exemptions and changes in classification, while new legislation narrowed the incentives under the law to convert farmland

[48] See Hanayama Yuzuru, *Land Policy and Land Markets in a Metropolitan Area*, pp. 45–46.

to housing.[49] Furthermore, the development permission system did not apply to areas less than 1,000 square meters, prompting the construction of tiny houses (*mini kaihatsu*), which rapidly became known as "rabbit hutches" in the West.

In March 1971 the Supplementary Provisions of the Local Taxes Law were again revised to provide for a gradual increase in urban farmland tax rates to market levels within three to five years. This measure passed the Diet fairly smoothly in 1971. But it was never implemented, for complex political reasons deeply related to the coming of political crisis, which are discussed in detail in the next section.

At the same time that explicit policy during the late 1960s and early 1970s failed to practically address urban land use issues, implicit policy was compounding the problems the failure of planning in the late 1940s had begun to generate. In particular, government policies began to accelerate demand for land, without solving problems of planning and land supply, thus seriously exacerbating the rise in land prices just beginning to gain momentum during the 1950s. Government policies encouraging collateral requirements for the extension of business loans, for example, accelerated business acquisitions of land, thus driving up land prices and providing the basis for further business borrowing. Government infrastructure construction had the same effect, as did government agricultural support programs encouraging the production of rice and other such commodities in substantially greater quantities than market forces would otherwise dictate.

In 1955 the Hatoyama cabinet inaugurated Japan's first systematic postwar housing policy, although previous ad hoc programs had existed to care for the homeless. Rising pressures for policy change during the turbulent early 1950s, followed by campaign promises by all four of the largest political parties in the spring 1955 general election campaign to introduce major new housing policies, provided the catalyst. The Japan Housing Corporation was established in July, 1955 and began building in suburban areas. The Housing Loan Corporation, founded in the midst of crisis in 1950 with a meager budget, also inaugurated an expanded loan system to finance housing construction. But these measures simply added to demand for housing land, without af-

[49] This 1969 legislation was the law regarding adjustment of Agricultural Promotion Areas (*Nōgyō Shinkō no Seibi ni kansuru Hōritsu*), which followed closely on the New City Planning Law (*Shin Toshi Keikaku Hō*).

fecting land supply or infrastructure. By 1965, due to the negative externalities generated, the Housing Corporation was facing active resistance from residents of suburban areas when it attempted to locate new housing facilities there.

One of the few major instances of systematic urban planning across the two decades from 1946 to the late 1960s was the National Capital Region Development Act of 1956. Significantly, this plan emerged as policy during a period of unusual political stability, only a year after the great Liberal and Democratic party merger of 1955. While stability has not generally been conducive to redistributive policy innovation, it has occasionally facilitated bureaucratic planning initiatives controversial with interest groups. Modeled after the Greater London Redevelopment Plan, the act stressed the creation of new towns, such as those to which one-third of London's population ultimately moved after World War II. The Japanese version ultimately proposed to locate twelve million people on 90,000 hectares centering on mid-Tokyo, with sharp distinctions between town areas and farmland to eliminate sprawl.

Needless to say, interest group pressure and the dislocations of rapid economic development ultimately frustrated realization of this plan. In 1965 it was modified to provide for systematic development of suburban land through Suburban Development Zones. It provided the conceptual basis for distinctions among areas in terms of their appropriate developmental patterns. These distinctions later dominated Japanese land use planning as it became, in theory at least, more systematic; for example, they were basic to the Land Use Conversion Plan of 1977. But they did not in practice prove effective in encouraging systematic land use.

As noted earlier, public land sales in West Germany since World War II have often been used as a strategic element in comprehensive urban housing and land use programs, reinforcing the effectiveness of planning. But in Japan such sales have had a very different function; they have commonly been used as a strategic political resource, distributed among the backers of LDP politicians to generate political funds or to repay old political debts. Political pressure, in short, has undermined the coherence of the planning process, aided by the structural sensitivity of the Japanese political system to such pressure.

This pattern was especially pronounced under former Prime Minister Tanaka Kakuei. As Tachibana Takashi points out, for example, the average amount of public land disbursed to the private sector annually during the years 1962–1965, when Tanaka was minister of Finance, was three times the annual average for the postwar period from 1957 to 1971.[50] Much of the land disbursed by Tanaka was prime real estate in central Tokyo near the Imperial Palace, which had been in government hands since before the Meiji Restoration.

As a result of Tanaka's intervention, pieces of government land were reportedly disbursed to several of the major mass media, including the *Asahi Shimbun, Yomiuri Shimbun, Nihon Keizai Shimbun,* Kyōdō Press, and Jiji Press, as well as to major corporations, including Mitsui Corporation and the Sanwa Bank, as sites for their headquarters. Much of the public land generated by the withdrawal of American forces in Japan over the 1950s and 1960s was also distributed to firms and interest groups as political compensation. Remarkably little was devoted to public purposes or to housing as is common in Europe.[51] Beginning under the Nakasone administration, the national government since 1983 has once again proposed major sales of public land, including that of public corporations to be privatized, together with loosening of urban building restrictions in an effort to spur domestic demand.[52] Japan's pattern of public land dispersal over the past three decades may show the responsiveness of the state to outside interests, just as small business, agricultural, and regional policy does, but whether it promotes general public welfare is much more problematic.

Political Crisis and Land Use Policy Formation

The general pattern of postwar Japanese conservative policymaking, as outlined in this volume, is flexibility in times of political crisis, strategically preempting the demands of the opposition. When applied in the land use policy area, however, this strategy presents the LDP with some serious dilemmas. Case-by-case land

[50] Tachibana Takashi, *Tanaka Kakuei Kenkyū,* vol. 1, p. 75.

[51] When the U.S. Navy withdrew from Yokohama in the early 1970s, for example, some of the land returned by the Americans went to provide public parks and housing. But this use of former military land for general public purposes was relatively unusual for Japan.

[52] For details, see Ishida Yorifusa, *Nihon Kindai Toshi Keikaku no Hyaku Nen,* pp. 325–32.

transactions, together with related regulatory dispensations, are basic to conservative politics. Their distributive character makes them ideal resources for compensation politics, since they can spread among political supporters without generating the more potentially severe conflicts of interest among them which broad, categorical regulatory decisions or redistributive legislation would create. Most LDP politicians do not want systematic land use planning; case-by-case decision making is politically advantageous, and they cannot easily make concessions via planning to defuse political dissent. Many in the business world, although not specifically opposed to planning, are averse to major policy change that might adversely affect land values. Land, after all, has traditionally served as indispensable collateral for Japan's huge mountain of corporate debt. Yet both the conservative business and political worlds also feel the need in time of crisis to accommodate opposition demands, which periodically emerge in the land policy area.

For years the LDP was able to keep a relatively low profile on land use issues, as it desired to do, even during periods of political crisis. In 1961, during a period of LDP political vulnerability due to the Security Treaty crisis and rising opposition militancy in local politics, the Socialists and the Kōmeitō raised the land issue briefly, enough to provoke a joint LDP-JSP-Kōmeitō declaration that land use planning was gravely needed. But little else was done.

During November 1965, in response to opposition and media pressure, the Land Price Countermeasures Council (*Chika Taisaku Kakuryō Kyōgikai*) suggested an increase in the land tax to encourage more rural landholders to sell and thus increase the overall supply of housing land. But no substantive steps were taken immediately.

In 1968 the City Planning Law of 1919 underwent its most sweeping revisions in four decades, in the wake of strong pressure from rapidly strengthening progressive local governments. For example, in 1967 Minobe Ryōkichi had been elected governor of Tokyo, and soon after he, together with other colleagues in the opposition, began to strongly criticize the LDP's lack of urban policies.[53] Just before the July 1968 Upper House elections, the LDP announced an Urban Policy Outline (*Toshi Seisaku Taikō*) to appeal to city voters and passed a new City Planning Law. This law

[53] *Ibid.*, p. 305.

provided Japan's first ever formal mechanism for restricting the disorderly development of housing land.

After the election the parties apparently lost interest in land use planning once again,[54] and the issue fell back into the hands of the Ministry of Construction and concerned interest groups. The boundaries among the various types of land use areas—Town Areas, Urbanization Promotion Areas (UPAS), and Urbanization Control Areas—were not well-defined, and developers were continually asking, usually successfully, for expansion of the UPA's to a much greater degree than city planners desired.[55] In addition, the newly intensified planning effort stimulated formation of interest groups designed to skew land policy outputs in the direction of their own interests.[56] Land use in Japan's urban areas became more and more distorted, with only sporadic outcry from either opposition parties or mass media.[57] The LDP and to a certain extent other political actors as well were responding to local interest group pressure, especially from developers and construction firms, rather than to planning imperatives. But they were also striving to obscure this de facto policy stance.

It was during 1972–1974, a period of deep, pervasive political crisis for the conservatives, that land issues first came sharply to the center of Japanese politics, although they had been considered more peripherally during previous periods of turbulence as well. The political vulnerabilities of the conservatives made them supersensitive to outside political demands, as in the other policy areas examined in this volume. But in the land use area, powerful political cross-currents, rooted in strong and deeply divergent economic interests, generated a hodge-podge of contradictory policy measures, compensating conflicting interests and preserving political stability at the cost of policy coherence.

First to be compensated were the farmers with urban and sub-

[54] *Asahi Shimbun*, August 12, 1968, p. 12.

[55] Between 1970 and 1980, for example, the area designated urban in Japan expanded to more than twice the area actually needed for urban purposes. See Kurokawa Nobuyuki, "Skyrocketing Prices," p. 213.

[56] One of these, for example, the National Land Readjustment Counter-measures League (*Kukaku Seiri Taisaku Zenkoku Renraku Kaigi*) founded in 1968, lobbied for higher payments for dispossessed landowners. See Ishida Yorifusa, *Nihon Kindai Toshi Keikaku no Hyaku Nen*, pp. 229–30.

[57] The 1968 revisions of the City Planning Law created the so-called "productive greenbelt system" (*seisan ryokuchi seido*). In accordance with this system, a farmer in an urban area is exempted from regular taxation at housing tax rates if he declares his intent to farm the land for at least five years. There is no requirement that he actually farm for this period of time.

urban land holdings. In early 1971, as indicated above, changes in the Local Taxes Law and related administrative rules provided for an increase over three to five years in urban farmland taxation to market levels. But with the rising political turbulence of late 1971 and early 1972, rural opposition to implementation of these changes began surging as well.[58] In February 1972 the agricultural cooperatives sponsored a large conference to oppose the proposed tax changes, with participation from *all* political parties, and provoked establishment of a Diet Members' League for Farmland in Urban Promotion Areas, with 150 LDP rural Dietmen at its core. Ultimately the four opposition parties—including even the Communists—joined with the LDP in proposing postponement of market-value taxation of farmland "that can be recognized as plots used for farming" where the owner declares intent to continue farming for at least ten years, subject to periodic verification by local authorities. This measure was approved on March 30, 1973, and it became a major obstacle to the expansion of housing land, critical to the suppression of the rapid urban land price spiral which was just beginning to accelerate.

Ironically it was also during the early 1970s that discontent with prevailing LDP land use policies also began to swell among the urban dwellers, the indirect victims of policies such as preferential taxation for farmland. During 1972, the price of land suitable for housing rose across Japan an average of 29 percent (table 9.2). The following year, in the wake of the ominous rise of Communist strength in the December 1972 elections, housing land prices rose another 26 percent. In eighteen months major Upper House elections were pending in which many expected the LDP to lose its Diet majority; urban as well as rural support was crucial to the conservatives.

The Liberal Democratic party introduced three new measures that on their face seemed to go far in suppressing rising land prices and creating an equitable supply of land for common citizens in the major cities of Japan. First, the government imposed a heavy tax on land sales, ostensibly to appropriate windfall profits. Second, it introduced a standard housing-land tax (*takuchi nami kazei*), imposed on land suitable for housing in urban areas, to force agricultural land hoarders (i.e., those who were not bona fide farmers under the meaning of the 1971 legislation discussed above) to sell. Third, in 1974 the National Land Agency (*Kokudo Chō*) was established both to consolidate land planning functions

[58] Hanayama Yuzuru, *Land Markets and Land Policy*, p. 47.

from agencies across Japan and to devise more coherent land use policies.[59] While compensating farmers on important tax issues, the LDP also extended symbolic benefits to urban dwellers, in a bid for their support.

With the narrow LDP Upper House election victory in mid-1974, the crisis of LDP political survival gradually abated. Japanese conservative policymaking moved away from its welfare-oriented patterns of crisis concessions once again and toward more routine, less egalitarian patterns. In 1977 under the Land Use Conversion Plan (*Tochi Riyō Tenkan Keikaku Sakutei Jigyō*), towns and villages were charged with encouraging conversion of agricultural land into housing. But they were not given any strong tools or incentives for doing so.[60] In November 1977, the ten-year Sanzensō comprehensive development plan was announced, with the objective of suppressing both pollution and the continuing, although more subdued, rise in land prices. But this new plan presented no concrete measures to increase urban land supply. Due to the combined effects of stagnant selling prices for land, and the preferential taxation for farmland, the annual supply of private land for housing purposes fell by around 50 percent between 1973 and 1980.[61]

In November 1980, another law was passed to aid farmers in selling their land by forming cooperatives to do so. But there were neither compulsory measures nor any tax incentives to encourage conversion to housing use. Indeed, by the mid-1980s, market incentives ran sharply the other way, with large prospective land price increases on the horizon and taxation on agricultural land often only 0.5 percent of that on housing land.[62] The 1974 law imposing punitive taxes on agricultural land capable of

[59] Establishment of a "General Development Agency" (*Sōgō Kaihatsu Chō*) with essentially the functions the National Land Agency finally assumed was proposed by the Temporary Administrative Research Committee (*Rinji Gyōsei Chōsa Kai*) in September 1964. But in the typical Japanese conservative pattern of incubated innovation, this idea was only translated into policy ten years later, in the midst of political crisis. For details on evolution of the National Land Agency concept, see Kyōiku Sha, ed., *Kokudo Chō (The National Land Agency)*, pp. 34–36.

[60] National government controls over prefectural land use policies in Japan appear much less extensive than in Britain. On the problems of coordinating local and national level land policies, comparing the Japanese experience with that of Britain, see Andrew H. Dawson, ed., *The Land Problem in the Developed Economy*, pp. 108–15.

[61] *Mainichi Shimbun*, April 16, 1985.

[62] *Asahi Shimbun*, July 20, 1987.

conversion to housing was so riddled with exceptions that it too had minimal effect, since it exempted land "that can be recognized as plots used for farming," in accordance with the previous 1973 legislation.

Despite housing shortages, Tokyo in the early 1980s continued to have 30,000 farm families, who produced 70 percent of the metropolitan area's consumption of cauliflower, 50 percent of its cabbage,[63] and a similarly large share of its onions. While many of these families were serious farmers, committed to a way of life pursued by their forebearers for generations, nearly half had no agricultural sales whatsoever,[64] and appeared to be planting nominal amounts of vegetables as a cover for land speculation. More than a decade after punitive agricultural land tax legislation was enacted, 85 percent of all urban farmland was still administratively exempted from its provisions.[65] Low-level pressure from farmers and real estate interests, particularly against local governments responsible for exemptions from punitive taxation, sharply curtailed the effectiveness of these measures. If converted to housing, urban farmland in Tokyo alone could provide residential space for a million people equal to the average space occupied by Tokyo dwellers in 1986–1987.[66]

This picture of state incapacity, of course, contrasts sharply to the patterns of Japanese industrial policy. There a combination of cohesive state bureaucracy, largely untouched by postwar reforms, and the relative moderation of political attempts at intervention made systematic, although market-oriented, attempts at planning possible. Land use decisions, with the immense possibilities for gain and loss they presented to domestic actors, were much more deeply involved in the turbulence of the domestic political scene, particularly after the technocratic possibility in the land use area was compromised by occupation reforms.

By the early 1980s the precariousness of Japanese conservative preeminence had passed and so had, at least momentarily, seri-

[63] Tachibana Takashi, *Nōkyō (The Agricultural Cooperatives)*, pp. 34–35.

[64] Forty-six percent of Tokyo's 30,000 farm households had no agricultural sales, while 14 percent had annual agricultural incomes under ¥200,000 (around $1000) per year. See *Ibid.*, p. 34.

[65] In 1985, 85 percent of the urban farmland in the Tokyo metropolitan area in principle subject to provisions of punitive early 1970s legislation was in fact exempt from its application. See *Yomiuri Shimbun*, May 26, 1987.

[66] The population of the 23 *ku* of Tokyo in 1986 was slightly over 8.3 million, and the conversion of urban farmland to housing was expected to increase the supply of residential land by around 10 percent. See *The Economist*, October 3, 1987, p. 28.

ous conservative gestures toward systematic planning in the land use area. The measures of the 1980s, such as sales of public land for private development and deregulation of land use restrictions, were designed to dismantle systematic planning efforts rather than to enhance them. Even the implementation of such egalitarian measures as had been passed in time of crisis was now being compromised by special interest groups and the lack of strong, autonomous regulators who could fashion a coherent consumer-oriented policy. A host of administratively granted exceptions, for example, blunted the pressures on farmers located in Urbanization Promotion Areas to convert only nominally farmed agricultural land to housing. The distinctive sensitivity of the conservative political world to organized pressure, together with their structural difficulties in providing public goods for society at large, were once again manifest,[67] although there were signs by the mid-1980s of strong underlying pressures from the mass media and government deliberative councils for change. In April 1985, for example, the Japanese Economy Research Deliberative Council, (*Nihon Keizai Chōsa Kyōgi Kai*), chaired by the respected former Tokyo University Professor Arisawa Hiromi, called for housing interest tax changes and "liberation" of agricultural land in cities for housing purposes. In late 1986 the second Maekawa Report and several business groups demanded full application of existing agricultural land taxation laws, and Construction Minister Amano Kōsei agreed in Diet interpellations to "study" this possibility.[68]

But in the absence of full-scale political crisis actual land use policy change was very slow in coming, despite the strong pressure from intellectuals, citizens' groups, and the business world. The contrast to the longtime decisiveness of the technocracy in the industrial policy area was striking. Whatever the genius of Japanese conservative policymaking in maintaining political stability, its weaknesses as a method of systematic policymaking were strikingly clear in the land use area.

[67] Schattschneider seemed right—the people were indeed only semisovereign due to the power in the policy process of organized groups. See Schattschneider, *The Semi-Sovereign People*.

[68] On these developments, see *Mainichi Shimbun*, April 16, 1985; *Nihon Keizai Shimbun*, March 20 and 21, 1987; and *Asahi Shimbun*, July 20, 1987.

10

The Residual: Defense

> Aspiring sincerely to an international peace based on justice and order, the Japanese people forever renounce war as a sovereign right of the nation and the threat or use of force as means of settling international disputes.
>
> Chapter II, Article 9
> of the Japanese Constitution (1947)

FOR MANY Western conservatives in the 1980s, including the administrations of Ronald Reagan and Margaret Thatcher, military security has been, together with the exercise of domestic police power, among the few legitimate ends of government. Even for conservatives with more ambitious conceptions of government, more organic notions of society, and stronger emphasis on the coherence of social fabric, national security has traditionally been key. Proponents of a materialist response to the challenge of conservative governance in an age of mass politics may have seen tactical utility in public works or welfare spending, as the pragmatic Bismarck and Disraeli once did. But for virtually all of even these materialists, national defense was infinitely more fundamental.

Western conservatives only infrequently give thought to dimensions of national security beyond military aspects, and indeed often equate the two. But in reality they are distinct because national security must incorporate an economic element. Even traditional military security stands upon an economic base.

Japanese conservatives, of course, have definitions of security, stressing economic dimensions, that allow them to reconcile the general conservative emphasis on preserving national coherence and stability with the particular policy approaches they adopt. Yet few aspects of Japanese public policy are more striking to the foreign observer than its approach to defense, particularly in view of the martial bias of conservative policy generally dominant elsewhere in the world. During fiscal 1984, Japan budgeted slightly less than 1 percent of GNP for defense spending, compared to the average for NATO's six major powers of around 4.2

TABLE 10.1
Japan's Low Defense Spending in Comparative Perspective

Nation	Defense Expenditures per Capita (¥1000)	Share of National Budgetary Expenditures (in percentage)	Defense Expenditures/ GNP (in percentage)
United States	234	29.2	7.2
West Germany	115	27.9	4.3
United Kingdom	108	11.9	5.1
France	102	17.5	4.1
Italy	39	5.6	2.6
Japan	22	5.2	0.99

Source: Japan Defense Agency, *Defense of Japan 1984* (Tokyo: The Japan Times, 1984), p. 147.

percent each,[1] as indicated in table 10.1. Only in 1987 did Japan's defense budget exceed, just barely, 1 percent of GNP. Defense spending per capita in Reagan's America was ten times the level of Nakasone's Japan. Although the huge overall scale of the Japanese economy rendered Japanese defense spending eighth in the world or higher during the 1980s, this amount was only equal to the gross turnover of the Japanese ice cream[2] or pinball machine industries.[3]

The steady revaluation of the yen after the Plaza accord of September 1985 led to some upward adjustment of the absolute magnitude of Japanese defense commitments, calculated in dollars. But this exchange rate realignment had little direct effect on actual Japanese defense capabilities since virtually all military costs were denominated in yen. In contrast to the United States and several European nations, Japan had no forces stationed overseas. Japan also manufactured virtually all military equipment at home, albeit much of it under license from foreign firms.[4]

[1] Differences in accounting practices regarding military pensions render Japanese defense spending about 1.5 percent of GNP by NATO standards. But a substantial gap between Japanese and NATO spending patterns remains, no matter what accounting standards are used.

[2] *Asahi Shimbun*, July 24, 1980.

[3] *International Herald Tribune*, December 7, 1981.

[4] In the case of the F-15 fighter, for example, Japan imported six from the

This chapter explores the origins of Japan's low current defense spending and unusual constraints on defense operations, with special attention to the crisis and compensation dynamic's interaction with salient institutional features of Japanese state structure. It argues that Japanese defense budgets are low first and foremost because counterpressures from agriculture, public works, and other grassroots-oriented sectors of the Japanese political economy have been strong, due to the ratchet effects of the crisis and compensation dynamic. Furthermore, the subordinate status of the Self-Defense Agency, the conflicting objectives of defense related interest groups, and the lack of clear-cut, generally accepted military security objectives have made it difficult to resist these counterpressures when they occur. Finally, opposition pressures in periods of global and domestic tension have generated policy constraints, such as the longstanding 1 percent of GNP limit on military spending, that have intensified the status of defense as residual. Thus, defense policy bears important relation to the crisis and compensation process dynamic, although structural factors are also unusually important in shaping policy. These arguments are explored via an analysis of defense budget time series data since the early 1950s, together with detailed historical examination of discontinuities regarding budget shares and nonbudget restrictions on military activity.

Current Defense Spending Against the Backdrop of the Past

Japan's low post-1956 defense spending is remarkable against the backdrop of Japanese history. During the period from the Meiji Restoration of 1868 until the end of World War II, defense spending reached a high at 68 percent of GNP in 1944. But it never dropped below 2 percent of GNP, even during peacetime, except for the three placid years 1891–1893, before the Sino-Japanese War dramatically involved Japan as a central actor on East Asian regional security questions.[5]

United States directly and planned to manufacture the remaining sixty-nine of its proposed seventy-five in Japan under license from McDonnell Douglas. See Kent E. Calder, "The Rise of Japan's Military-Industrial Base," *Asia-Pacific Community* (Summer 1982). In 1984 the Self-Defense Agency spent over 90 percent of its total budget for defense procurements domestically. See JEI *Report*, January 9, 1987, p. 6.

[5] Bank of Japan Research and Statistics Department, *Hundred-Year Statistics of the Japanese Economy*, pp. 34–35, 130–31.

Nearly as striking in comparative perspective as the low level of Japanese defense spending itself has been its rigidity in the face both of strong American pressure and rising Soviet capabilities in the Far East. The U.S. pressure on Japan to expand its defense commitments apparently began before the outbreak of the Korean War, when John Foster Dulles in mid-June 1950 first met Prime Minister Yoshida Shigeru.[6] During the autumn of 1953 State Department Assistant Secretary of State for Far Eastern Affairs Walter S. Robinson, together with Detroit banker Joseph M. Dodge, originator of the so-called Dodge Line, tried to secure a commitment that Japan would significantly expand her defense force over the succeeding few years.[7] John Foster Dulles reiterated these demands in congressional testimony during July 1953, proposing that Japan should increase her troop strength from 120,000 to 350,000.[8] Four months later, before the Japan America Society in Tokyo, Vice President Richard Nixon called Japan's "no-war" Article 9 a mistake and urged a Japanese military force of at least 320,000.

The response of the Yoshida administration to American pressure was equivocal in each case, as the stance of its successors was to remain for more than a generation. When pressed, Japan generally pledged marginally expanded defense cooperation with the United States, especially favoring the idea of a hardware buildup financed by the United States itself.[9] But after an intriguing increase during the mid-1950s, discussed later in this chapter, Japanese spending on defense, measured in relation to GNP or even share of the national budget, consistently declined. Yoshida and his successors continually stressed the vulnerability to communist influence which a weak Japanese economy would face and the consequent strategic importance to the free world of Japanese industrial, rather than military, spending. In this way Japanese policymakers both deflected U.S. pressures for a military buildup and also freed domestic resources for alternate uses.

The high point of Japanese defense spending during the entire post-occupation period, proportional to both GNP and the Japanese national budget, was achieved in 1954, two years after the

[6] John Dower, "The Eye of the Beholder," *Bulletin of Concerned Asian Scholars* 2 (October 1969): 22.

[7] See Dower, *Empire and Aftermath*, pp. 449–63.

[8] See *Asahi Shimbun*, September 7, 1953, on Japanese defense planning of this period and its relation to American pressure.

[9] Dower, *Empire and Aftermath*, p. 444.

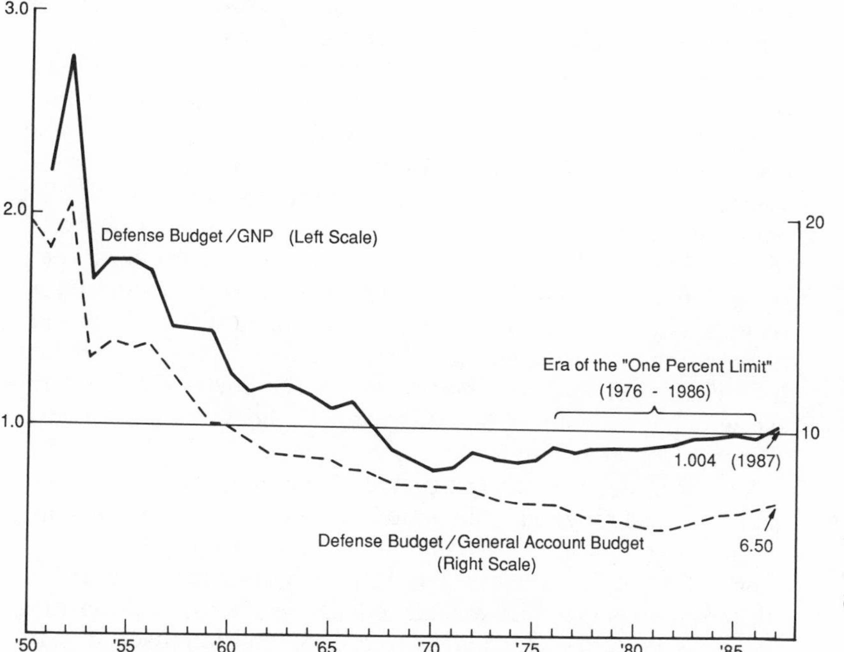

Figure 10.1. The Decline and Rise of Japanese Defense Spending: Ratio of Defense Spending to GNP and the General Account Budget

Source: Asagumo Shimbun Sha Henshū Sō kyoku, ed., *Bōei Handbook (Defense Handbook)*, 1987 ed. (Tokyo: Asagumo Shimbun Sha, 1987), pp. 221–23.

end of the Allied occupation. Defense spending reached almost 14 percent of the general account budget compared to roughly 11 percent for public works and 9 percent for welfare. From 1956 until 1981, as indicated in figure 10.1, the defense share of the total budget was consistently down.[10] Only in fiscal 1987 did Japanese defense spending regain the one percent of GNP level below which it receded precisely two decades before. And it did so amidst intense protracted political resistance to breaking a sup-

[10] The defense budget relative to GNP hit its low point in 1970, at 0.79 percent of GNP, while the defense share of the total general account budget reached its nadir in 1981. See Asagumo Shimbun Sha Henshū Sō Kyoku, ed., *Bōei Handbook* (Defense Handbook), 1987 ed., pp. 222–23. The low point relative to GNP came earlier than that relative to budget because the size of budget relative to GNP was expanding steadily during the 1970s. Primary emphasis is placed on budget *shares*, because this research is primarily concerned with acts of political choice, of which budget shares represent the more direct manifestation.

posedly inviolable 1 percent of GNP limit on defense spending that, in fact, had been introduced only ten years earlier.[11]

Since the high-water mark of Japanese defense spending relative to GNP in the mid-1950s, Soviet air and naval forces deployed in the Far East have increased manyfold. American troops and even naval strength in the region has sharply declined.[12] The Soviets have deployed over 135 SS-20 missiles and about 80 TU-22M Backfire bombers in eastern Siberia within range of Tokyo.[13] Since 1978–1979 the Russians have strongly reinforced their troops on the four islands of the Japanese-claimed Northern Territories as well. Moreover, they have stationed three aircraft carriers in the Sea of Japan and Pacific waters. These include the Kiev-class aircraft carrier *Minsk*, one of the Soviet Union's largest, which was deployed to Vladivostok in the midst of the Tokyo Summit Conference of 1979.

American defense officials pressed Japan to expand its defense capabilities throughout this period, through two major wars and numerous crises in the Pacific area. They have stressed the urgency of expanded commitments through dramatic shifts in the United States-Japan bilateral trade balances, from a U.S. surplus as late as 1975 to a U.S. deficit of over $50 billion just ten years later. Key U.S. congressmen have angrily threatened protectionist measures or withdrawal of security guarantees should Japan not substantially accelerate her defense buildup.[14]

U.S.-Japan logistical cooperation intensified during the early 1980s, and a defense technology transfer agreement was signed. With the waning of crisis and the rise of a new generation that had not experienced World War II, popular attitudes toward defense were slowly changing. Prime Minister Nakasone Yasuhiro (1982–1987) was also a supporter of defense, and with strong sup-

[11] The Miki cabinet introduced this 1 percent of GNP "ceiling" on defense expenditures in 1976.

[12] In 1954, for example, there were 210,000 U.S. troops in Japan. By 1984, there were only 24,000. At the height of the Vietnam War the United States had 200 ships in the Far East; by 1981 this had fallen to 51. See Martin E. Weinstein, *Japan's Postwar Defense Policy, 1947–1968*, p. 111; Japan Defense Agency, *Defense of Japan 1984*, p. 29; and T. Tsurutani, "Japan's Security, Defense Responsibilities and Capabilities," *ORBIS* (Spring 1981).

[13] Japan Defense Agency, *Defense of Japan 1984*, pp. 30–31.

[14] During the summer of 1985, for example, both the Senate and the House of Representatives overwhelmingly passed resolutions criticizing Japanese defense spending levels, especially in relation to maritime self-defense. See *JEI Reports*, June 21, 1985, and July 19, 1985.

port from the United States he secured a continuing exception for defense from the annual zero ceilings on budgetary growth imposed on most budget categories under the administrative reform program. Yet Japanese defense spending remained low, in comparative international context, and rose only from 5.2 to 6.5 percent of the general account across the five years of Nakasone's prime ministership—lower than its share in 1973.[15] Authorized Japanese ground forces in 1987 remained at the 180,000 man level agreed in the Ikeda-Robertson communique of 1953, while the Self-Defense Forces as a whole have never achieved their maximum authorized strength of 270,000 men. Next-door South Korea, with one-fifteenth the GNP and one-third the population, kept 600,000 men under arms during the late 1980s.[16]

There was a period, during and even after the Korean War, when the acceleration of Japanese defense spending and the emergence of substantial Japanese defense capability appeared quite possible. Several Japanese business organizations, especially the defense committee within Keidanren, backed by MITI, sensed that arms production and export could help sustain the economic momentum of the Korean War special procurements boom. In the economic downturn at the end of the Korean War, alternate civilian prospects looked bleak.

Many purged politicians, including Hatoyama Ichirō and Kishi Nobusuke, also saw rearmament as a way of asserting Japan's national identity in the face both of Communism and a potentially over-obtrusive American embrace. Recently declassified U.S. government documents indicate that Hatoyama in 1952 indicated to U.S. Ambassador John Allison that Japan needed to spend possibly 25 percent of the national budget on defense, roughly double the share committed at that time and more than four times the prevailing budgetary share for defense during the late 1980s.[17] During the 1952 election campaign Reform party (*Kaishintō*) spokesmen set 3.5 percent of GNP as the appropriate level for Japanese defense spending, only to see their rather

[15] Asagumo Shimbun Sha Henshū Sō Kyoku, ed., *Bōei Handbook* (Defense Handbook), p. 223.

[16] *Yomiuri Shimbun*, July 25, 1987, and Far Eastern Economic Review. *Asia 1987 Yearbook* (Hong Kong: Far Eastern Economic Review, 1987), p. 6.

[17] Hatoyama reportedly cited the cases of Norway and Sweden, nations which he said were devoting one-third of their budgets to defense. See Steeves, American Embassy to DOS, "Meeting of Mr. Ichirō Hatoyama with the Ambassador," September 18, 1952.

hawkish suggestions eclipsed by Hatoyama, and by Liberal Party calls for 4 percent of GNP defense spending[18]—quadruple the levels of the 1980s. Only Yoshida and his backers, among the three major conservative groups, were relatively reluctant to increase military spending.

In the face of combined U.S. and right-wing conservative pressure within Japan, from both Hatoyama and the Kaishintō, the Yoshida cabinet was forced to propose some major rearmament. This it did as compensation particularly to the right-wing groups within Japan who were threatening the continuance of Yoshida's rule. On August 28, 1953, Vice Prime Minister Ogata Taketora announced that an increase in ground forces of between 20,000 and 40,000 men was being contemplated for 1954. Nine days later, the Safety Agency (*Hoanchō*) released a draft of its own tentative five-year defense plan, which proposed 210,000 men for the ground forces, a navy of 170 ships, and 1,400 aircraft, by 1958.[19]

The Safety Agency defense plan showed strikingly the Japanese conservative tendency, in times of political crisis, to adopt the policy demands of the opposition. In this case the Yoshida administration preempted the Hatoyama and Ashida right wing in an attempt to stabilize its increasingly precarious position.[20] These efforts were a classic case of crisis and compensation, that dynamic pervasive across many sectors of Japanese policymaking, as has been noted throughout this volume. Yet Japan never came close to fulfilling this plan, for the combination of progressive and grassroots conservative pressures against it proved too strong. Other crises arose, demanding compensation for other groups, and the defense lobby was too weak to hold its own against these counterpressures. It had little powerful bureaucratic or political support, and the major defense producers of the early 1950s, such as Komatsu Limited and Daidō Steel, found that they could prosper in high-growth civilian markets. Even in 1985, after five consecutive years of defense budget increases, Japan had only 155,000 troops in its ground forces, 167 war ships

[18] American Embassy to DOS, "Weekly Political Notes from Japan," September 11–18, 1952.

[19] See *Asahi Shimbun*, September 7, 1953; and Yoshida Naikaku Kankōkai, *Yoshida Naikaku* (The Yoshida Cabinet), p. 605.

[20] As Shindo Eiji points out, the Yoshida cabinet defense plan of 1953 quite clearly adopts the Kaishintō's previously established position on rearmament. See Ashida Hitoshi, *Ashida Nikki*, vol. 4, p. 5.

in its navy, and 350 military aircraft.[21] This was substantially lower military strength than both the Yoshida government and its conservative opponents Hatoyama, Ashida, and Shidehara Kijūrō had proposed more than thirty years previously, despite the growing Soviet military presence in the Far East.[22] In addition, Japan retained a wide range of policy restrictions on arms exports, nuclear weapons production and basing, and military spending relative to GNP that neither existed nor were even serious policy options during the 1950s.[23]

Why has Japanese defense spending relative to GNP and the national budget not accelerated more rapidly since the mid-1950s to levels of other middle-range powers? One argument often cited is a so-called "defense allergy" of the Japanese general public. To be sure, the Japanese people throughout the postwar period have been somewhat less defense-conscious than Americans, French, or Germans, but there was a promilitary surge in the 1950s among conservatives. Major political figures, such as Hatoyama Ichirō, were quite forthright in demanding rearmament, and a major fraction of the Japanese people supported their views.[24] In 1955, 23 percent of the Japanese public even favored the acquisition of nuclear weapons—more than double the ratio of the early 1980s.[25] Although support for accelerated military spending was not strong at the mass level in Japan during the 1980s, both the big business community and rather popular leaders like Naka-

[21] Japan Defense Agency, *Defense of Japan 1984*, p. 29.

[22] Ashida in 1951 proposed defense forces of 200,000 and defense expenditures at 8.5 percent of the national budget. See Ashida Hitoshi, *Ashida Hitoshi Nikki*, vol. 4, p. 3.

[23] Since 1968, for example, Japan has observed a ban on the production, use, basing on Japanese soil, and transit through Japanese waters of nuclear weapons. Since 1968 it has observed a full ban on the export of arms, initiated in partial form the previous year, although since 1983 it has exported dual use technology, even to military consumers. Between 1976 and fiscal 1987 it limited military spending to less than 1 percent of GNP, although this limit was in fact breached in 1987.

[24] A September 1952 Kyōdō public opinion poll, for example, indicated that 54 percent of those polled favored rearmament with 35 percent opposed and 11 percent with no opinion. This was during the Korean War, but after the military situation on the peninsula had largely stabilized. See U.S. Embassy Tokyo to DOS, "Weekly Political Notes from Japan," September 4–11, 1952.

[25] Support for nuclear weapons acquisition in 1981 was 11 percent, with 82 percent, opposed, according to NHK News. See NHK Hōsō Seron Chōsa Jo., ed., *Zusetsu: Sengo Seron Shi* (A Postwar History of Public Opinion in Graphs), Vol. 2 (Tokyo: Nihon Hōsō Shuppan Kyōkai, 1982), p. 171.

sone Yasuhiro favored it. Pacifist sentiment is relatively low and waning in Japan, especially in the rising generation that did not experience World War II, although there are small groups with strong media ties who are highly vocal on such matters.[26]

Constitutional prohibitions, similarly, cannot provide a sufficient explanation for the low levels of military commitment over the past generation. Article Nine of the Japanese "no war" constitution is quite vague on the question of appropriate self-defense forces, stipulating only that "land, sea, and air forces, as well as other war potential will never be maintained." This article has generally been given broad interpretations by both Japanese leaders since Yoshida Shigeru and the courts. The constitution provides no clear constraints on *levels* of military spending, and extremely high levels could conceivably be achieved within the established restrictions on offensive deployments. This would be especially true should complex forms of missile defense systems begin to evolve, as suggested by the Strategic Defense Initiative (SDI) of the Reagan administration. Antiballistic missile (ABM) systems could be one such constitutionally ambiguous area for Japan.

The Structural Context of Low Defense Spending

To make sense of the low overall levels of Japanese defense spending in the face of escalating Soviet buildups and U.S. pressure for response, one must first consider precisely the two varieties of structural biases in the Japanese political system that help render defense spending a residual. First, the electoral system and the grassroots-oriented kōenkai structure generate civilian counterpressures to defense. Second, the structural weaknesses of prodefense forces themselves make it difficult for them to resist these civilian counterpressures for such distributive benefits as roads and bridges.

Japanese conservative politicians, as mentioned, must frequently compete against one another for election to the Diet, due to existence of the multimember district system. To prevail in

[26] Support for abolishing the Self-Defense Forces, or reducing them sharply in scale, for example, ranged constantly between 8 and 17 percent throughout the 1958–1981 period, rising higher only during the heart of the Vietnam War (1969–1972). See *ibid.*, p. 173.

such competition, since World War II the successful among them have developed so-called kōenkai, or support organizations. These bodies often have many small businessmen, especially public works contractors, among their members. They continually demand pork-barrel benefits as a quid pro quo for continued cooperation, thus forcing Dietmen to press the Ministry of Finance for national budgets oriented heavily toward such distributive allocations.

Many nations, of course, have strong interest group lobbies clamoring for compensation, although their politicians are not generally as sensitive as those of Japan to such pressures, due to differences in electoral system, party structure, and political culture discussed in chapter 4. But these nations also usually number the uniformed military, together with the defense industry, among the powerful national interest groups.

Contemporary Japan is crucially different. Because its military forces were dismantled after World War II and remain relatively small in terms of personnel despite their gradual re-creation, the armed services vote itself is not too significant. Japan's entire Self-Defense Forces in 1986 only had 242,000 men under arms, compared to around 2.2 million in the U.S. military.[27] Similarly, few Japanese corporations rely heavily on defense procurements for sales or profitability, although there were many more during and shortly after the Korean War, when defense contractors exercised substantially greater political influence. In the United States of the mid-1980s, the top ten defense contractors supplied around half of their total production to the Pentagon;[28] in Japan the largest defense contractor, Mitsubishi Heavy Industries, relied on defense procurements for only between 10 and 20 percent of sales. Most other defense contractors were much less dependent.[29]

[27] In addition, the Self-Defense reserves included about 43,600 men in 1986—43,000 land and 600 marine self-defense personnel. But the reserves situation did not substantially change the overall picture of a relatively small force under arms. For details, see Far Eastern Economic Review, *Asia 1987 Yearbook*, p. 18.

[28] This ratio ranges from the 80 percent dependence of Grumann on defense contracts as a share of total sales to the relatively low 31 percent dependence of Boeing. See Sheila Tobias, Peter Goudinoff, Stefan Leader, and Shelah Leader, *The People's Guide to National Defense*, p. 247. Japan Defense Agency, *Defense of Japan 1984*, p. 29; and *Report of the Secretary of Defense to the Congress, Fiscal 1985 Defense Budget*, p. 74.

[29] In fiscal 1985 Mitsubishi Heavy Industries (MHI) relied on defense procurements for 13.7 percent of its total sales. Only two of the other top ten defense

Japan does have some interest groups which stress emphatically the importance of expanded military spending. Most important is probably the Japan Defense Industry Committee (*Nihon Heiki Kōgyō Kai*), an affiliate of Keidanren founded in the early 1950s. Keidanren as a whole supports increased defense spending generally. But as a huge federation of roughly 800 member firms and 110 industry associations, it is too unwieldy to lobby in a highly specific fashion on any issue, especially on questions as controversial as defense. Keidanren is also handicapped in lobbying by its reluctance to fund individual LDP politicians in their struggles with one another, its declining overall importance as a funding source for the LDP, and the clear economic interest of its defense industry members in an expanded military budget, which undercuts the broader political legitimacy of their appeals.

At the mass level, the strongest supporters of defense spending in Japan have traditionally been veterans' groups. Several of these with as many as 700,000 members have been quite active in the policy process; this was especially true during the 1950s, when veterans' groups were still numerically strong and had been freed from occupation restrictions on their activities. But the numerical strength of veterans' groups has been steadily waning since then through natural attrition. And their interests with respect to defense have been primarily in expanded veterans' pensions and only secondarily in expansion of the defense budget as a whole. In contrast to NATO accounting patterns, veterans benefits are not formally calculated as part of the defense budget in Japan. However, in years when the Ministry of Finance has established a unified joint ceiling for both defense spending and veterans' pensions, as it did in 1981, veterans have backed away from support for current defense expenditures and have pushed their own suddenly conflicting interests.[30] This has seriously undermined the position of the defense lobby more generally, as has the diffusion of nationalist sentiments toward a range of symbolic concerns, such as the status of the Yasukuni Shrine to the war dead and the government's relationship to it.

Defense in the mid-1980s had a hard core of perhaps twenty-five key Diet supporters who consistently backed proposals for

---

contractors obtained more than 10 percent of their sales from defense. See Yamaichi Shōken Keizai Kenkyū Jo, ed. *Sangyō no Subete* (Everything about Industry), 1987 ed., p. 300.

[30] See Ōtake Hideo, *The Politics of Defense Spending in Conservative Japan*, p. 24.

defense spending no matter what the counterpressures might be.[31] Only one or two of these men were well-placed in the LDP as a whole. Both in numbers and terms of members' political influence, the "national defense tribe" of Diet supporters was dwarfed by its analogues in the areas of commerce, agriculture, construction, telecommunications, transportation, and even welfare.

Virtually all major supporters of defense with intraparty prominence had dual allegiances to groups elsewhere in the political economy. When budgetary political issues increasingly became zero-sum games in the latter stages of the budgetary process, these politically prominent supporters frequently defected from support of defense spending to their primary allegiances. The foreign office spent its political capital on fighting for foreign aid within its specific sphere of jurisdiction; prominent Dietmen likewise fought for their primary constituencies. For example, Kanemaru Shin, a key member of the *kensetsu zoku* (construction lobby), defected to the support of public works, and Sakata Michita, a member of the *bunkyō zoku* (educational lobby), defected to expanded support for schools.[32]

Defense was left an orphan, to the extent that the political resources it generated did not coincide with the demands of dominant Japanese interest groups. Resources committed to defense provide material compensation to 242,000 regular Self-Defense Force members, 43,600 reservists, and a handful of large defense contractors. These constituencies pale in political magnitude next to the twenty-eight million small business employees and ten million farmers of Japan.

The structure of Japanese budgeting itself helps perpetuate defense spending's status as a residual rather than a strategic priority in Japan, a situation created by more fundamental factors. As in most areas of Japanese decisionmaking, the early phases of defense budgeting are crucial in determining the final overall shape and scale of policy output.[33] And at these stages interest group pressure for accelerated military spending is relatively weak.

[31] Inoguchi Takashi and Iwai Tomoaki identified twenty-one members of the "national defense tribe" in the Diet following the 1986 double election—seventeen in the Lower House and four in the Upper House. See Inoguchi Takashi and Iwai Tomoaki, *Zoku Giin no Kenkyū* (Research on "Tribe" Dietmen), p. 304.

[32] *Ibid.*, pp. 295–304.

[33] See Ōtake Hideo, "Bōei Hi Zōgaku o meguru Jimintō no Tōnai Rikigaku"

The annual Japanese budgeting process begins with a lengthy, crucial stage of intra-agency formulation roughly from April until the end of August.[34] For most agencies, this is a period to coordinate positions internally, so as to present the most persuasive and unified front possible in later budgetary struggles with other agencies and with the political world. But hawks within the Japan Defense Agency are critically handicapped at this intra-agency stage, in comparison with their counterparts in other agencies. For the most crucial JDA post in the sensitive early stages of defense budget formation, the directorship of the JDA accounting bureau, is held by an official on loan from the Ministry of Finance (MOF).

The Ministry of Finance has a reputation for fiscal conservativism, which for sixty years and more is said to have worked against expanded defense spending.[35] MOF also has far more alumni in the Diet than any other ministry, and these alumni are often pushed by constituents to support expanded public works and welfare expenditures that conflict with defense. These institutional and political biases, both of which act to suppress defense spending, operate not only on budget examiners and higher level MOF officials at the latter stages of budgeting but also on the JDA Accounting Bureau chief at the early stages. They thus act to preempt the natural bureaucratic dynamic within the JDA toward agency expansion, which could otherwise lead to increasing defense budgets.

The JDA strategic planning process, in contrast to budgeting, involves far less input from the accounting bureau chief. It also is not subjected to the intensely political, grasssroots-oriented annual budgeting process. Accordingly, Japan is able to make rational, strategic defense plans, such as the "56 Chūgyō,"[36] but it has much more difficulty implementing them.

(Inside Story of the Power Balance within the LDP with Regard to the Strengthening of Armaments), *Asahi Journal* 23 (January 30, 1981).

[34] For an excellent introduction to the Japanese general account budget process, especially insightful regarding patterns during the 1970s, see Campbell, *Contemporary Japanese Budget Politics.*

[35] MOF Minister Takahashi Korekiyo, for example, is said to have stood strongly against military budget expansion during the early 1930s, a principal reason for his subsequent assassination.

[36] The "56 Chūgyō" is Japanese for the Fiscal 1981 Mid-Term Estimate—a medium-range, five-year planning document announced in the early 1980s to supplement the ten-year National Defense Program Outline of October 1976. "Chūgyō" are intradepartment, multiyear estimates of both projects to be carried out by the

The low defense spending bias of Japanese budgeting continues at the latter stage of the budgetary process, often becoming even more intense there. The low cabinet standing of the defense agency in Japan, the only major industrial nation whose defense establishment lacks full ministerial status, is one major problem. In cabinet deliberations, the JDA generally has a less influential institutional advocate than do other agencies. Even more importantly, the JDA budget must, in the interministerial phase of budgeting, once again confront the scrutiny of the Ministry of Finance with its generally antidefense bias. MOF almost single-handedly formulates the defense budget. Once the JDA has made its initial proposal, MOF generally relies on the principle of balance in mediating interagency demands; this practice has worked against recent JDA efforts to achieve a defense buildup by creating a bias against change in the status quo distribution among agencies.[37] Only the explicit exemption of defense spending, together with foreign aid, from general MOF zero ceilings on budget increases during the early 1980s allowed defense spending to escape from this pressure for balance.

Finally, in the so-called "revival negotiations" (*Fukkatsu Sesshō*)[38] after the Ministry of Finance draft budget is released in mid-December, LDP politicians press for inclusion of additional grassroots-oriented projects. Expanded public works spending has traditionally been central among these; this pressure for new pork-barrel projects has often tended to reduce the relative share of defense in the total national budget even further.

At the final stages of defense budget formation, the role of the prime minister is often crucial. He has often rejected foreign pressures and confirmed the structural bias of the postwar Japanese political system toward welfare type spending. The result has then often been defense budget stagnation, even in the face of substantial external political pressure. In fiscal 1981, for example, Japan managed only a 7.61 percent defense spending increase, despite the Soviet invasion of Afghanistan and a Japanese pledge to U.S. Defense Secretary Harold Brown of substantially

---

Ground, Maritime, and Air Self-Defense Forces and of estimated costs to realize these projects. For further details, see Japanese Self Defense Agency, *Defense of Japan 1984*, pp. 134–35.

[37] "Balance" could be and was invoked as a defensive strategy by the SDF to forestall budget share erosion, however.

[38] In these negotiations, LDP politicians marginally revise the MOF budget proposal, to include their own pet projects. For details, see Campbell, pp. 172–99.

expanded defense commitments. A central reason for this failure, as Ōtake Hideo clearly points out, was the unwillingness of Prime Minister Suzuki Zenkō to place strong priority on defense over welfare.[39] The prime minister, in short, is one of the few actors in the Japanese policy process capable of offsetting the structural bias toward low defense spending. When he does not act aggressively in support of defense, as was the case in 1981, defense budget increases will almost invariably be low in relation to strategic threat and the demands of the outside world. Conversely, when prime ministerial intervention is resolutely on the side of defense, moderate increases may occur.

This latter pattern prevailed under the Nakasone administration, which exempted defense from a general zero ceiling on budget expenditures, imposed to cut the large budget deficit. During each of Nakasone's five years in office, the military budget went up by at least 5.2 percent annually, while overall expenditures rose only 1.7 percent a year. But the lingering power of the antidefense spending bias in Japan, the power of forces rendering it a residual, was clearly demonstrated by the difficulty Prime Minister Nakasone had in his efforts to revise a 1 percent limit on defense spending as a share of GNP. This "limit," only in effect since 1976, had no basis in either law or long-standing tradition. But the 1 percent barrier was only breached in the fiscal 1987 budget, after more than two years of persistent effort by Nakasone and pressure from the United States and following a general election in which the conservative LDP won what was arguably its greatest victory in postwar political history.[40]

Crisis, Compensation, and Defense Policy Outputs

Political structure and culture are clearly central to understanding Japan's distinctive patterns of defense policy output, but in themselves these variables are underpredictive. They cannot account for the nuances of Japanese defense policymaking, especially for the symbolic elements such as the 1 percent limit on defense spending, the three nuclear principles, and the ban on arms exports. They cannot explain the origins of institutions

[39] See Ōtake Hideo, *Politics of Defense Spending*, pp. 25–28.

[40] See *Asahi Shimbun*, December 30, 1986.

themselves. Nor can they explain the timing of policy innovation. For a full explanation of defense policy profiles one must ultimately return, as in so many policy sectors in Japan, to the importance of crisis and compensation in shaping both institutions and resource allocation patterns.

Some important differences between the functioning of the crisis and compensation dynamic with respect to defense policy and that in Japanese domestic policy sectors should be noted from the outset, although they do not affect the overall empirical relevance or parsimony of the argument itself. Although the three major domestic convulsions which so profoundly influenced postwar agricultural, regional, small business, welfare, and to some degree land use policy also had major impacts in defense as well, the impact was more indirect, in view of defense policy's role as residual of the policy process. Defense supporters, who generally lacked full cabinet representation or complete national legitimacy, could not claim equal treatment with the other interests that were liberally compensated in times of political crisis. Broader national political crises, in short, put sharp, sudden pressure on defense budgets through the counterpressures in other, more politically influential sectors which they generated. The unusually extended, complex process of defense budget formation, American support, and the involved long-term understandings which it generated,[41] could only in part isolate defense spending from the broader political storms periodically pulsing through the Japanese political economy. Only during the 1980s, a period of unusual political calm, were defense budgets specifically exempted from the allocative ceilings pertaining in other policy sectors. And this special exemption for defense provoked resentments that made its continuation in more domestically troubled times uncertain.

Defense policy is also affected *directly* by political pressures, as are policies in other sectors. But since defense policy is at once domestic and foreign policy, it is influenced by a somewhat dif-

[41] As Campbell points out, multiyear Defense Buildup Plans, upon which annual defense budgets are normally based, are the subject of long negotiations among the Defense Agency, the Economic Planning Agency, the Foreign Ministry, and the Ministry of Finance before they are actually decided. Since the consensus building process is so complex, MOF budgeters are wary of upsetting a consensus so laboriously reached and create a greater rigidity in the face of short-run pressures for change than may be present in many budget sectors. See Campbell, *Contemporary Japanese Budget Politics*, pp. 215–26.

ferent set of actors than are the other policies discussed in this volume, actors who apply somewhat different criteria to the functioning of policy. As a consequence, Japanese defense policy is to some extent affected both by the major domestic crisis periods and also by periods of international tension related to defense. The Quemoy-Matsu tensions between the United States and China in 1958, the United States-Soviet Union tensions following the U-2 incident of 1960, and especially the protracted international tensions flowing from the Vietnam War, for example, all left some mark on the course of Japanese defense policy, although they did not trigger the spending increases which external crisis has so often stimulated in the Western industrialized world.

Defense issues have long been central in the symbolic dealings—camp conflict, as T. J. Pempel has termed it[42]—between the ruling Liberal Democratic party and its opposition. Opposition demands have been strong and high profile, making peace-oriented LDP policy overtures a central means of restoring harmony in the overall national political process. Given the structural constraints on rapid lawmaking and the rising range of policy matters requiring legislative treatment, such harmony has been especially important in the Diet. Relatively dovish LDP pronouncements on defense have been one means of achieving it.

The major crises in Japanese postwar conservative political history have all had a profound impact on defense policy formation, both direct and indirect. The crisis within conservative ranks during the early 1950s—Yoshida versus the Hatoyama Liberals and the Reform party (*Kaishintō*) of Shidehara Kijūrō and Ashida Hitoshi—encouraged a temporarily hawkish cast in Japanese defense policy during the early and mid-1950s, as noted, which cannot be explained by prevailing political structure.[43] The Korean War and the sense of alarm this induced in Japanese conservative political and business circles certainly intensified this hawkish cast but cannot fully explain it either, since relatively high defense spending and plans for an accelerated buildup persisted after the war was over and fears had subsided. Rising nationalism

[42] See Pempel, *Patterns of Japanese Policymaking.*

[43] For details on the defense orientation of the *Kaishintō* in the early 1950s, and the reasoning behind it, see Ashida Hitoshi, *Ashida Hitoshi Nikki*, vol. 4, pp. 3–6, 104. Ashida played a particularly active role in the *Kaishintō's* agitation for rearmament, founding the New Military Promotion League (*Shin Gunbi Sokushin Renmei*) in February 1952.

after seven long years of occupation was also no doubt a factor, but nationalism too faces difficulties in precisely explaining the wax and wane of prodefense policies.[44]

One major, though often forgotten, aspect of Japanese conservative support for a strong military during the early and mid-1950s was the Right's strong fear of internal subversion. In the immediate aftermath of the Allied occupation, as American troops were being steadily withdrawn and a major war was raging only miles from Japanese shores, conservatives sensed keenly a potential "security void," intensified by the dissolution of the prewar national police force by the occupation. For example, Hatoyama Ichirō used his first public address since being purged in 1946, a speech delivered at the Hibiya Kōkaidō in Tokyo to launch the 1952 general election campaign, to stress that indirect communist aggression against Japan, spearheaded by the Japan Communist party, was a distinct possibility, and that Japan should "stand up again" to counter such threats.[45] Hatoyama also stressed, on another occasion, his contention that the JCP had a "formidable plan" for violent revolution and that a Japanese army was consequently needed for internal security purposes.[46] Even the more moderate Yoshida Shigeru favored creation of a Japanese equivalent to the House Un-American Activities Committee to help investigate and deter domestic unrest.[47]

The hawkishness of much conservative opinion in the early 1950s was further encouraged by the positions of some right-wing Japanese socialists, which appear highly incongruous in the light of subsequent policy stances taken by the JSP and even the DSP. One Socialist politician, Kamekawa Tetsuya of the JSP, reportedly went so far as to tell State Department officials attached to the occupation forces that "The Socialist Party believes that the stability of conditions in the Far East could be enhanced by the acceptance of voluntary Japanese enlistments in the Armed Forces of the United States of America. [This act] would improve

[44] The increasing legitimacy of the Japanese military after John Foster Dulles formally asked the Japanese government in February, 1951 to rearm also led to increasingly overt political and paramilitary activity by former veterans groups. For details, see Guillain, "The Resurgence of Military Elements in Japan," *Pacific Affairs* (September 1952): 211–25.

[45] See *Asahi Shimbun*, September 12, 1952, evening edition; and U.S. Embassy to DOS, "Weekly Political Notes from Japan," September 11–18, 1952.

[46] U.S. Embassy to DOS, "Weekly Political Notes from Japan," May 29–June 5, 1952.

[47] Yoshida Shigeru, *Yoshida Memoirs*, p. 234.

the morale of the young people of Japan," improve United States-Japan relations, "and the question of the retention of military and/or naval bases in Japan would evaporate. . . ."[48] This statement, of course, made in the shadow of the sudden North Korean invasion of South Korea, is presented as remembered by U.S. officials and drawn from recently declassified documents; there is no suggestion that it represents an official position of the Japan Socialist Party. But it remains startling in the sharp contrast it presents to subsequent Japanese opposition pronouncements on defense from the 1950s until after the Vietnam War in 1975. Its remarkably non-ideological character was echoed in the relatively pragmatic dialogue concerning Keidanren's 1952 rearmament proposals, which was conducted in the pages of the later strongly antimilitarist *Asahi Shimbun*.[49] *Chūō Kōron* also published pragmatic nonjudgmental analyses of the post-Korea prospects for Japanese arms exports to the United States.[50]

Following the end of the Korean War a strong core of promilitary opposition to Yoshida's preference for a largely unarmed Japan continued to persist and even strengthen. As Arisawa Hiromi pointed out in 1953, World War II had given the Japanese economy a portfolio of heavy and chemical industries that provided a basis for military production, even though the specifically arms related sectors had been dismantled.[51] The Korean conflict had reinforced military industrial capabilities, while export prospects in civilian sectors remained low. Many major Japanese defense contractors of the Korean War period, such as Komatsu Limited and Kobe Steel, saw the prospect of substantial arms exports to the developing world as an alternative to their activities of the previous three years.[52] The big business community more generally was eager to obtain Mutual Security Assistance (MSA) aid from the United States,[53] which required as a quid pro quo a steady expansion of Japanese military capabilities. Politically,

[48] U.S. POLAD, Tokyo, "Memorandum of Conversation" with Mr. Kamekawa Tetsuya of the Japan Socialist party, August 7, 1950.

[49] See, for example, *Asahi Shimbun*, December 25, 1952.

[50] See, for example, Takemura Tadao, "Nihon Gunju Sangyō no Senzairyoku to Genjitsusei" ("Potential and Reality of Japanese Defense Industry"), *Chūō Kōron* 67 (November 1952): 112–18.

[51] Arisawa Hiromi, "Heiki Seisan to Nihon Keizai" ("Arms Production and the Japanese Economy"), *Chūō Kōron* 68 (1953): 14–22.

[52] See Ōtake Hideo, ed., *Nihon Seiji no Sōten* (Points of Contention in Japanese Politics), p. 18.

[53] Masumi Junnosuke, *Postwar Politics in Japan, 1945–1955*, p. 296.

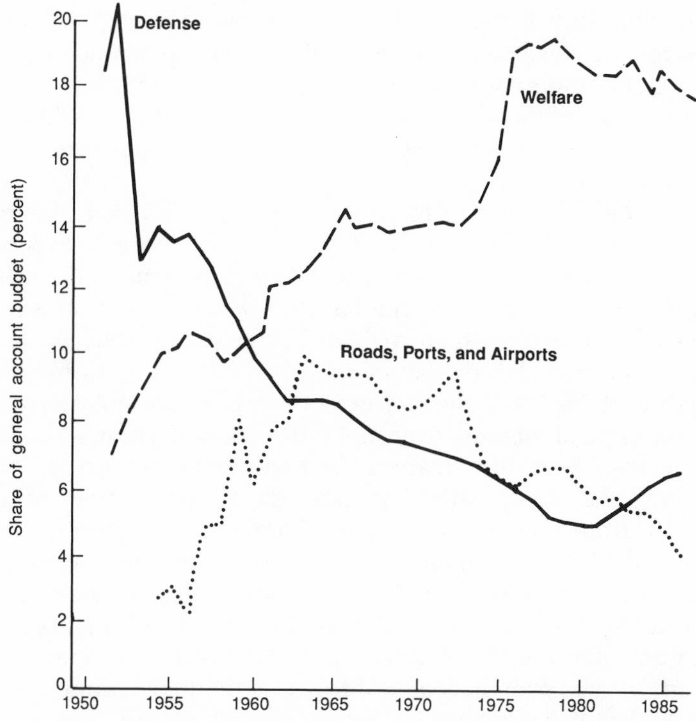

Figure 10.2. Japanese Defense Spending and Budgetary Counterclaims, 1951–1986.

Source: Ministry of Finance Budget Bureau Research Section (Ōkurashō Shukei Kyoku Chōsa Ka), *Zaisei Tōkei (Financial Statistics)* (Tokyo: Ōkurashō Insatsu Kyoku), various issues.

both of Yoshida's major conservative rivals supported a substantial military buildup. In the face of all these pressures defense spending rose from 13.01 percent in 1953 to nearly 14 percent of the national budget in 1954 even in the face of the cease-fire in Korea (figure 10.2). Challenge from the Right also helped provoke the hawkish Safety Agency defense plan of September 1953, an explicit compromise with the Kaishintō.

The era of high military spending, under pressure from the Right, was gradually coming to a close by 1956. The Kaishintō had merged with Yoshida's Liberals to form the LDP, and no independent powerful rightist challenge existed. As figure 10.2 suggests, between 1956 and 1960 the sharpest shift in the relative share of defense in overall Japanese budgetary expenditures took place. This shift in four years produced almost half of the entire variation in the budgetary share of defense spending from its post-occupation high point in 1954 to its nadir in 1981. Understanding that shift is thus of utmost importance to grasping the position of defense in Japan's overall profile of postwar public policies.

The rapid shift from a Japanese defense commitment broadly comparable, as a share of total national government expenditures, with those of Japan's defeated Axis counterparts in Europe during the mid-1950s,[54] to the familiar recent pattern of a low-defense Japan was intimately related to broader uncertainties in Japanese politics. For the period of Kishi Nobusuke's prime ministership (1957–1960), the relationship was quite straightforward: Kishi wanted at all costs to secure ratification of a revised United States-Japan Security Treaty and faced strong opposition both within the LDP and, particularly after the Police Bill controversy of 1958, from an invigorated Left. The building political crisis encouraged him to restrain defense and to raise welfare spending, thus pacifying his opposition and achieving his primary objectives in the diplomatic area. Despite Kishi's hawkish image, the Japanese defense budget actually declined from 12.6 to under 10 percent of the general account during his tenure as prime minister, and declined a further 1.2 percent during his earlier tenure as deputy prime minister (1956–1957). Both public works and welfare spending—primary forms of compensation for the constituencies to whom Kishi appealed—rose conversely to the relative decline in defense appropriations. As noted in Chapter 8, Kishi as prime minister was responsible for introducing major innovations regarding pensions and health insurance proposed by his dovish predecessor Ishibashi Tanzan, in his bid to marshall broad-based support for his controversial initiatives regarding the security treaty and constitutional reform.

But the policy transition to a low-defense posture begins even earlier than Kishi, in a period when the crisis and compensation hypothesis alone cannot fully explain policy change. Especially

[54] Defense as a proportion of "total government expenditures" (a broader category than the share of the general account budget used for intra-Japanese budgetary calculations here, but the only comparative standard available) in 1956 was 9.9 percent in Italy, 9.7 percent in Japan, and 9.3 percent in West Germany. The ratios for 1960 were 10.2 percent for West Germany, 8.4 percent for Italy, and 5.7 percent for Japan. See G. Warren Nutter, *Growth of Government in the West*, pp. 64–66.

fateful was the budget of 1957, when defense spending was virtually static in absolute terms, and fell as a proportion of the overall national budget from 13.8 to 12.6 percent,[55] despite strong requests from the United States for more aggressive expansion.

Two factors help explain the anomaly of declining relative defense commitments during 1956–1957. One was the advent of the Ishibashi cabinet, among the most "dovish" in Japanese postwar history.[56] Ishibashi defeated Kishi Nobusuke in a very close race for LDP president in late 1956, and he resigned only three months later after formulating the fateful fiscal 1957 budget. Ishibashi followed one of the postwar period's most hawkish prime ministers, Hatoyama Ichirō, which helps explain the shift to a more restrained defense posture. Second, heavy political counterpressures to help correct local government deficits were weighing on the Ishibashi government. These flowed in large measure from the considerable local public works spending of the turbulent early 1950s and could be considered a delayed response to the political crisis of that period.

Initial pressure on defense spending as a share of the overall general account budget appears to have come in fiscal 1957 from public works (see figure 10.2). The roads, ports, and airports segment of the general account jumped in that year from 2.4 percent to 5 percent of the general account. This pressure came from within the recently unified LDP, where grassroots political competition and distributive demands against Tokyo were sharply enhanced by the conservative merger of October 1955 and by the rapidly worsening fiscal deficits of Japanese local governments, which had assumed the major share of public works construction in the early 1950s.[57] Thus, counterpressures on the defense budget in the late 1950s were in part a reaction to the political turbulence of the early 1950s at the local level. This turbulence had generated distributive demands against the local governments which they alone could not sustain.

With rising patronage demands from a larger number of Dietmen to support, conservative political demands against the Min-

[55] Asagumo Shimbun Henshū Sō Kyoku, *Bōei Handbook*, 1987 ed., p. 221.

[56] During the Ishibashi cabinet Ishida Hirohide served as chief cabinet secretary, Miki Takeo as LDP secretary general, and Ishibashi himself for a period as head of the Self-Defense Agency. All were leading "doves" who refused to vote on the United States-Japan Security Treaty in 1960.

[57] Annual aggregate local government deficits in Japan rose from nothing in fiscal 1949 to ¥6 billion in 1953 and ¥50.4 billion in fiscal 1955.

TABLE 10.2

Transition from Guns to Butter: Shifts in General Account Budgetary Shares, 1956–1963 (in percentage of general account budget)

Category	1956	1958	1963	Change, 1956–1963	Change, 1958–1963
Defense	13.8	11.3	8.5	−5.3	−2.8
Welfare	10.7	9.9	12.6	+1.9	+2.7
Public Works	2.4	5.1	10.0	+7.6	+4.9

Source: Ministry of Finance Budget Bureau Research Section (Ōkurashō Shukei Kyoku Chōsa Ka), *Zaisei Tōkei (Financial Statistics)* (Tokyo: Ōkurashō Insatsu Kyoku, various issues).

istry of Finance increased, with consequent pressures against segments of the national budget lacking strong domestic political supporters. Defense lacked powerful bureaucratic or interest group constituencies as big business interests shifted to commercial areas. Defense was, in fact, a prime candidate for a residual budget category, to be cut back as more politically potent categories expanded their respective shares.

The severe pressure upon Japan's defense budget by public works and welfare expansion, both significantly linked to deeper competitive patterns in the Japanese politics of the late 1950s, can be seen in relative shifts in budgetary shares (table 10.2). Between 1958 and 1963, the heart of the second major crisis period examined in this volume, welfare spending's budgetary share increased by 2.7 percent and that of public works spending by 4.9 percent. Over the longer 1956–1963 period, including two years of internal struggle within conservative ranks before broader political crisis erupted, the welfare share rose by 1.9 percent and that of public works by 7.6 percent.

The sharp decline in defense budgetary shares during the late 1950s must also be seen against the backdrop of hardening opposition attitudes regarding defense, with which Kishi was forced to deal. In the early 1950s many industrial unions saw Japan's high unemployment and uncertain export prospects and imagined arms production as economically necessary, even after the end of the Korean War. However, this attitude had dissipated by the late 1950s. Deepening Socialist ties with China, antagonistic to Japanese rearmament, also had an effect, dramatized by the March 1959 declaration in Beijing by JSP Secretary General Asanuma Inejirō that "American imperialism is the common enemy of the peoples of Japan and China." The advent of Kishi, former minister of munitions in the wartime Tōjō government, as prime minister during 1957, also strongly provoked the Socialists and encouraged them to oppose defense spending with increasing vigor. The emerging arguments against defense spending can be seen clearly in the pages of *Sekai* and *Chūō Kōron*, two of Japan's most prominent, opposition journals of elite opinion.

In 1953 Tokyo University economist Arisawa Hiromi warned against the economic logic of expanded military production in Japan, as indicated above, and suggested that unless "democratic" counterpressures were exerted such production would most likely increase in the coming few years.[58] A barrage of antimilitary articles followed the end of the Korean War.[59] Throughout the 1950s the refrain continued: all military capability was wrong and unnecessary; it should be scrapped; and this was possible only through a policy of unarmed neutrality.[60] Articles also strongly stressed the opportunity costs of defense spending, particularly the pressure it put on welfare and public works spending by local government.[61]

Reflecting strong counterpressures against defense spending, to which the conservatives were particularly sensitive during periods of political crisis, both quantitative and qualitative expansion of Japanese military capabilities began to slow sharply. Although the authorized strength of the Self-Defense Forces increased quite rapidly during the mid- and late 1950s—from 152,110 in 1954 to 230,935 in 1959—it halted there rather abruptly. Between 1960 and 1967, authorized SDF strength increased by under 20,000 men, or less than the reduction in U.S. forces in Japan,[62] despite the rising regional security threat posed by the deepening conflict in Vietnam. Defense budgets, consis-

[58] Arisawa Hiromi, "Heiki Seisan to Nihon Keizai." *Chūō Kōron* 1953, Volume 68, Number 1.

[59] See, for example, Nakamura Takeshi, "Heiki Seisan" (The Production of Arms), *Chūō Kōron* 9 (1954): 108–13.

[60] See, for example, Maeshiba Kakuzō, Hayashi Saburō, Rōyama Yoshio, and Ōbata Misao, "Gunshuku wa Yume Ka?" ("Is Arms Reduction a Dream?"), *Sekai* 8 (1957).

[61] See Kimura Kihachirō, "Watakushitachi no Seikatsu to Yosan" ("Our Life and the Budget"), *Sekai* 3 (1960).

[62] Weinstein, *Japan's Postwar Defense Policy*, p. 111.

tently more than 10 percent of the national general account budget through fiscal 1959, dropped steadily thereafter, relative to the budget as a whole, as indicated in figure 10.2. A "defense allergy" interpretation of Japanese budgeting cannot explain why defense spending relative to both GNP and national budget was relatively high and stable during the 1950s, yet declining sharply thereafter.

Continuing criticism from the Left, intra-LDP dissension on security issues, and counterpressures from budget categories inflated by programs either created or expanded during crisis put downward pressure on the defense budget long after the Security Treaty crisis itself had ended. First came the Vietnam War, and the LDP needed to coopt opposition and media criticism of Japan's partial support for the U.S. war effort. This protracted foreign affairs crisis for the LDP merged, in turn, with the serious domestic political crisis of the early 1970s. The cumulative result was a decade and more of opposition-inhibited security policy in Japan, reinforced by the structural bias of Japanese politics and policymaking toward agriculture, small business, and ultimately welfare. When the *budgetary* share of public works ceased to rise, welfare took its place in exerting downward pressure on defense (figure 10.2). There was a sharp, continuous decline in defense spending as a share of the national budget—from 10 percent of the general account in 1960 to 8.2 percent in 1965, 7.2 percent in 1970, and finally to a low of 5.1 percent in 1981. The profile of allocative choices in Japanese public policy, in short, shifted steadily from martial to materialistic.

Political crisis for Japan's conservatives since the early 1960s has generated compensation for antagonists of a strong defense policy in symbolic as well as material forms. Indeed, the crisis-compensation framework appears crucial in explaining Japan's unusual patchwork of symbolic restrictions and taboos in the defense area. As noted earlier, during the 1950s both the defense debate and defense policy formation were relatively free of the distinctive limits and taboos which now so constrain Japanese security policy formation and implementation. Virtually all of these emerged in the heat of political controversy during the 1960s and 1970s as concessions from a vulnerable and internally divided Liberal Democratic party to its intransigent progressive opposition. Some of the new constraints, such as the 1976 1 percent barrier, emerged during the three pervasive, general spending political crises discussed in chapter 2. Others were more limited responses to political conflict in the foreign policy field, particularly stemming from the Vietnam War.

Aside from Article Nine of Japan's no-war constitution, the first major constraint to emerge was the arms export ban. The ban, originating in the fervent protests of the late 1960s against Japanese involvement in the Vietnam War, was linked to revelations that miniature SONY cameras and other Japanese components were being used in the U.S. air war against North Vietnam. Both the arms export ban and the three nonnuclear principles[63] were propounded in 1968, at the height of the Vietnam War, and were among the surprisingly few major policy innovations by Prime Minister Satō Eisaku. Before pressures from the Left against security policies of the conservatives became severe around 1960, neither of these proposals had even been broached. Indeed, these restrictive proposals stood in sharp contrast to the hopeful expectations of many Japanese businessmen, and even some government officials during the mid-1950s, that Japan could become an "Arsenal of Democracy," exporting weapons on America's behalf throughout the non-Communist world.

The 1 percent limit on military spending has similar origins in crisis and compensation, related to even broader, more pervasive political dynamics in Japan. In 1976 the Miki administration, for whom strategic ties to the opposition parties were a major source of leverage within the ruling LDP, was caught in the midst of a sharp struggle for political existence. Antimilitary elements in Japanese politics were much stronger in the mid-1970s than they became during the 1980s, or even, for that matter, following the December 1976 general election, when the JCP and the JSP taken together lost sixteen seats.[64] In an attempt to secure smooth acceptance of the National Defense Program Outline for the years after fiscal 1977 without deeply estranging elements in its complex, wide-ranging support coalition, the Miki government announced a 1 percent limit on military spending. Japan also ratified the nuclear nonproliferation treaty in the same year. As in the case of the arms export ban and the three nuclear principles, Japan's 1 percent limit on military spending was unknown during the 1950s and can hardly be considered a traditional, culturally

[63] The Anti-Nuclear Three Principles stipulate that Japan will not make or deploy nuclear weapons, nor will it allow them to pass through its territory.

[64] Although the JSP gained five seats in 1976, the more militant JCP lost twenty-one seats, and their combined vote declined from 31.1 to 27.4 percent of the national total.

ordained aspect of the Japanese approach to national security. Significantly, it was first declared policy by Self-Defense Agency chief Sakata Michita, in the midst of Diet interpellations defending the Miki administration's defense program outline against opposition criticism, only six weeks before the crucial 1976 elections.[65]

As I have argued throughout this volume, political crisis tends to generate new programs in Japan, and the balance of interest group pressures tends to determine their funding (i.e., the level of compensation for affected groups). This dynamic has profound implications for the size of the budget's residual—that is, national defense spending. To the extent that the sense of political crisis that has beleaguered Japan's conservative politicians for two generations and more abates and to the extent that interest group pressures competitive with defense begin to ease, the likelihood of a significant rise in Japanese military spending increases, provided there are domestic and international forces pressing for such a change.

The slight recent growth in the share of defense spending within overall national budgetary expenditures—from 5.1 percent in 1981 to 6.2 percent in 1986—appears partially the result of this phenomenon. U.S. pressure and Prime Minister Nakasone Yasuhiro's forthright personal support for defense spending increases, supported by gradually resurgent Japanese nationalism, were leading to steady, if slow, defense budget growth. Abrogation with the fiscal 1987 budget of the 1 percent of GNP limit on military spending as crisis-related counterpressures in other areas decline should make further defense budget increases easier. But it is important not to forget the broader institutional context, much of it generated by previous crises, which continues to render defense a residual.

The Japanese political system tends to be structurally sensitive to organized pressure, especially for compensation in distributive terms. Thus, to the extent that interest groups with a particular stake in military expansion begin to grow, prospects for military budget increases in Japan are intensified. Since the early 1980s, for example, heavy industrial firms with a major stake in a defense buildup have been joined by electronics and telecommunications manufacturers, for whom military procurements are in-

[65] For details, see *Asahi Shimbun*, October 20, 1976, evening edition.

creasing in importance.[66] Resurgent nationalism might help legitimate such a buildup. Over time, Japanese military spending could thus become much more than a residual, beginning to acquire momentum of its own. But its progress would no doubt continue to be influenced by the dual pressures which have so deeply shaped postwar Japanese conservative policymaking in general—the urge for political stability in the face of crisis and the search for distributive benefits with which to compensate key groups and defuse crisis when it emerges.

[66] Nippon Electric's defense procurements for the Self-Defense Agency rose, for example, from ¥16.4 billion in 1981 to ¥26.1 billion in 1982 and ¥124.5 billion in 1983, as defense early warning systems and electronic countermeasures rose increasingly in importance. See Yamaichi Shōken Keizai Kenkyū Jo, ed., *Sangyō Tōkei*, 1985 ed., p. 296.

11

Explaining Patterns in Japanese Public Policy

THE CENTRAL CONCERN of this book, as emphasized in the introduction, has been understanding the relationship between Japanese politics and public policy between 1949 and 1986. Despite an underlying political structure and political culture that one might expect to bias the public policies of the Japanese conservatives in a technocratic direction, domestic, non-industrial policies have at times been remarkably sensitive to grassroots pressure and strongly oriented toward material compensation. Yet this propensity toward materialism has waxed and waned in intensity. While the early 1950s, 1960s, and 1970s were periods of rapid budgetary expansion, policy innovation, and increased benefits for the less fortunate, the mid-1950s, the mid-1980s, and in many respects the late 1960s were periods of relatively little expansion, even retrenchment.

The conventional wisdom about Japanese politics and public policy has stressed stability, continuity, and consensus. This volume, by contrast, emphasizes insecurity, change, and conflict, together with the powerful incentives of Japanese government and business to neutralize these uncertainties through the policy process. Conservative political dominance may have continued in Japan for four decades unbroken, but public policies in most sectors have shifted sharply over that period, even in areas such as agriculture and defense where often thought immutable. Punctuating periods of equilibrium and calm have been crucially important moments of political crisis, decisively important in shaping these policy transformations.

It is important to keep the scope and econopolitical significance of political crisis for Japan's political leadership of the first two postwar generations in clear perspective. Time series analysis presented in this volume of both Japanese budgetary data and new legislative initiatives has confirmed a pattern of sharp, discontinuous policy change in postwar Japan, particularly regarding the introduction of new welfare-oriented domestic policies. This pattern contrasts sharply with both the political continuity prevalent in Japan throughout most of the postwar period and also with the frequent emphasis in existing literature on balance and stability in Japanese policymaking. In the case of welfare policy, for example, entitlement levels nearly doubled in a single year—the "first year of welfare" (*Fukushi Gannen*)—1973, when numerous new social security programs were introduced. In agriculture, small business, and regional policy, the patterns were similar.

This volume has not argued that Japanese society itself has been chronically unstable throughout the postwar period. There has clearly been an evolution over time. During the late 1940s there were major disruptions in the social fabric; over six million Japanese streamed home from former colonies, and many established social relationships were thrown into disorder by occupation reforms.[1] During the 1950s and 1960s, the Japanese economy also underwent major structural transformation in the course of rapid growth, generating inevitable social tensions among groups either benefiting or suffering from this change. But in many ways Japanese society, with its relative lack of class conflict and its broad coalition supporting the economic growth process, has been remarkably stable, particularly since the mid-1970s. By 1986 national opinion polls indicated, for example, that almost 88 percent of all Japanese thought of themselves as "middle class," with more than half feeling that they were in the "middle of the middle class."[2]

THE DOMESTIC AGENTS OF POLICY CHANGE

Regardless of Japanese society's stability in general, the political institutions and policy patterns that characterized Japan even in the 1980s were forged in an earlier more uncertain age, when the major elements of the ruling conservative coalition both faced

[1] 5,096,323 repatriates (military and civilian combined) streamed back to Japan in 1946; 743,757 in 1947; 303,624 in 1948; and 17,844 in 1949. See Ministry of Welfare Support Bureau (Kōseishō Engo Kyoku), *Hikiage nado Engo San Jyū Nen no Ayumi* (*The Thirty Year Course of Evacuation and other Support*).

[2] In a May 1986 stratified poll by the prime minister's office, only 0.2 percent of the 7,857 respondents characterized themselves as upper class, 8.6 percent as lower class, and 87.6 percent as middle class. 51.8 percent thought they were in the "middle of the middle class." See Prime Minister's Office Public Relations Office (Naikaku Sōri Daijin Kōhō Shitsu), *Kokumin Seikaku ni kansuru Yoron Chōsa* (*Public Opinion Polls regarding the People's Life*), May 1986 ed.

very real political uncertainties and had an uncommonly low tolerance for political risk. Faced with unwelcome uncertainty and flux, policymakers created new institutions and programs to enhance stability, which in turn profoundly shaped politics and policymaking, even as the original rationale for their creation receded from the general consciousness. The roots of the uncertainty that forged post-1949 institutions and allocative patterns—many created in reaction against early occupation reforms—were to some extent social. In the wake of the massive labor dismissals of the Dodge Line and the Red Purge period, as well as the huge dislocations generated by the purge and the return of six million repatriates, Japanese society was undeniably in flux. But more fundamentally the uncertainties were political and economic. They had their origins in Japan's unusual juxtaposition of major occupation political reforms during 1945–1948, followed by volatile and unorthodox, but sustained economic growth for two decades and more. They made maintaining political stability the developmental problem of the post-1949 Japanese state.[3]

Across the long decades of growth, an increasingly stable and affluent Japanese society confronted a fractious political system, the unsettling pluralistic heritage of occupation, and an economy with little tolerance for political instability, due to its ambitious, risky, highly leveraged economic growth strategies. The politically dominant conservative mainstream of former bureaucrats, to be sure, fixed its eyes firmly on economic efficiency and growth, with little interest in redistributive diversions. But the ability of this technocratically oriented mainstream to dominate the Japanese policy process—and its own judgments as to how much economic rationality was politically prudent—clearly waxed and waned. Although it fixed the conventional lines of post-1949 development on industrial, trade, and even noneconomic policy issues in stable periods, an alternate policy agenda prevailed in periods of political crisis.

During the period of high growth, oriented strongly toward capital intensive heavy industries such as steel, shipbuilding, and petrochemicals, Japanese industry contracted higher and higher debt-equity ratios, which welded state and industrial society into ever more intimate interdependence. Highly leveraged corporate

[3] On the concept of developmental problem and application to the American experience, see Stephen Skowronek, *Building a New American State*, pp. 3–18.

strategies, especially those dependent on long-run prospects in uncertain global markets, naturally increased big business adversity to major political change. The logic of those strategies also strengthened business willingness to pragmatically accept small policy changes desired by nonelite groups in the interest of equity, thus forestalling a shift in ruling parties, with the major attendant uncertainties for business and inefficiency that would entail.

At the same time, high growth also accelerated the process of urbanization within Japan. It widened income differentials between farm and country as well as between large and small business, with the attendant escalation of social tensions such widening differentials evoked. Finally, high growth generated resources to enable both public and private sectors to actively address the disruptions caused by growth.

But economic growth alone cannot explain the profiles of postwar Japanese public policy, especially outside the industrial and trade policy areas. Indeed, the programmatic basis for Japan's distinctive domestic policy profiles in all sectors examined began well before growth started to accelerate with the onset of the Korean War. And policy profiles fluctuated significantly over the high-growth period, in ways poorly correlated with economic performance.

The evidence presented in this volume suggests the central political force driving domestic policy transformation in Japan between 1949 and 1986 was the crisis and compensation dynamic, mediated with big business acquiescence, primarily by conservative party politicians. Many of these politicians were former bureaucrats, and they relied heavily on major government ministries to draw up the details of policy and provide strategic information. In this sense the policy role of bureaucracy was crucial. But ultimately political decisions, often made in periods of simultaneous Left-Right confrontation and intraparty turmoil within the ruling LDP, crucially broadened the ruling party's circle of compensation, determined the timing of policy innovations expanding government functions, and gave postwar Japanese conservative policies their unusual intermittently redistributive cast.

This finding of salient political influence at decisive moments in the evolution of Japanese public policy is consistent with both Heclo's conclusions regarding the type of circumstances in which politicians and bureaucrats have been most influential in the formulation of British and Swedish social policy[4] and also Hall's findings regarding the role of politicians in British and French economic policy formation.[5] It parallels LaPalombara's emphasis on the virtuosity of Italian politicians in achieving policy innovation and effective political management in turbulent political circumstances.[6] Intriguing cross-national similarities in the strategic role of middle-of-the-road politicians serving as policy entrepreneurs (for example, liberals in Britain and Sweden, or antimainstream conservatives such as Miki Takeo in Japan) also appear in the policy innovation process.[7]

The long preeminence of a single dominant conservative party is one of the truisms of Japanese politics, and the dominance of the LDP-bureaucratic-big business coalition has been assumed to characterize Japanese policymaking as well. One of the most surprising empirical findings of this research was the frequent importance of cross-party alliances, often but not always tacit, to the process of major policy innovation in Japan. Cross-party interactions figured importantly, for example, in the institution of small business, welfare, pollution, and city planning legislation during the 1960s and 1970s. They were especially important during periods of simultaneous crisis between government and opposition on the one hand and within conservative ranks on the other, when the hand of policy entrepreneurs with extensive cross-party networks was strongest. During such periods, party political cleavages grew less salient, and competing cross-party alliances often, although not universally, emerged. Much remains to be learned about cross-party networks and the ways in which they influence policymaking in Japan.

During noncrisis periods such as the early 1980s, the mid-1950s, and the late 1960s, there has, of course, been some degree of domestic policy change in Japan. But policy change during such periods has typically been significantly less extensive and less abrupt than during crisis periods. Furthermore, the policy change that has transpired during noncrisis periods has involved primarily retrenchment and withdrawal from previous state commitments, as in the case of administrative reform during the 1980s, rather than the initiation of new programs expanding state responsibility. Among the few exceptions to this pattern have

[4] Heclo, *Modern Social Politics*, p. 293.

[5] Hall, *Governing the Economy*, pp. 273–76.

[6] Joseph LaPalombara, *Democracy Italian Style*, pp. 285–86.

[7] Heclo, *Modern Social Politics*, p. 296.

been new policies generated by outside foreign pressure, amidst escalating international economic crisis.

Considerable attention has been given in recent scholarly literature to the relative preeminence of bureaucrats and politicians in Japanese policymaking. The evidence examined here suggests the dangers of overgeneralization, either over time or across sector. The French pattern of broad, persistent dominance of policymaking by a cohesive administrative elite[8] has not been fully sustained in Japan, but important areas of bureaucratic preeminence nevertheless continue to persist.

As chapters 6 through 9 made clear, entrepreneurial conservative politicians such as Hirokawa Kōzen and Tanaka Kakuei were important in restructuring Japanese agricultural, regional, and public works policies as early as the period of flux following the dissolution of the agricultural associations (1947) and the Home Ministry (1948). Political initiative was also important in the postwar establishment of veterans' and civil servants' pensions (1952), the Small Business Finance Corporation (1953), and the Self-Defense Agency (1954). It likewise figured significantly in shaping the great surge of legislation during the second crisis period (1958–1963), including measures such as the Agricultural and Small Business Basic Laws (1961 and 1963). Clearly political influence in Japanese policymaking was salient long before the 1970s, when many analyses characterize it as first coming to the fore.

Although politicians appear to have been important in Japanese policymaking more frequently and from an earlier period than often thought, evidence also suggests that bureaucrats retain even into the late 1980s more influence in policymaking than some partisans of political preeminence would concede. In some important areas, such as industrial policy, the bureaucracy even in the late 1980s remained preeminent in the formulation of overall policy agendas, even where politics had some impact on the choice of tools for achieving those goals—for example, orienting the bureaucracy toward regional dispersal of high-technology industrial plants and research facilities. The emergence of depressed industries following the oil shocks of 1973 and 1979, together with the proliferation of orderly marketing agreements in such sectors as steel (1969), color televisions (1977), and auto-

[8] On the persistent preeminence of the French administrative elite, see Ezra Suleiman, *Elites in French Society*.

mobiles (1981) have also helped expand bureaucratic influence at the expense of the market. Political influence in these sectors has generally remained peripheral, where bureaucratic jurisdiction has been clear. As suggested briefly in chapter 10, partial relaxation of bans on exports of dual military and civilian-use components and technology since the early 1980s has also generated regulatory opportunities for the bureaucracy in the defense sector. Periodically, but quite infrequently, the bureaucracy has also taken planning-related initiatives in non-industrial domestic policy, as with regard to the National Capital Region Development Plan of 1956. These bureaucratic planning initiatives have been, aside from policy retrenchment through administrative reform, among the relatively few policy innovations of non-crisis periods. But they have often been compromised by interest-group pressure during subsequent periods of turbulence.

Both political and bureaucratic influences on Japanese policymaking thus appear prominent throughout the 1949–1986 period examined in this book; sometimes the salience of fused interpersonal decisionmaking networks makes it impossible to distinguish between the two. Simple categorical analyses stressing either political or bureaucratic preeminence thus fail to capture the complex reality of this period. Although a comprehensive examination of the forces determining the relationship of these two sets of actors in Japanese policymaking is beyond the scope of this book, the evidence presented here provides three possible contributions to a more nuanced theory.

First, there are important, persisting cross-sectoral variations in the relationship between Japanese politicians and bureaucrats, with early postwar changes in state structure being the key to understanding them. The relatively great influence of politicians in regional, public works, and land use policy throughout the post 1949 period, for example, is a function in large part of the disorganization of the bureaucracy in that sector following the dissolution of the Home Ministry at the end of 1947, at precisely when both international and domestic pressures made policy innovations directed toward assuring domestic political stability important. Conversely, the continuing institutional coherence of MITI and the Ministry of Finance, relatively unaffected by the purge or occupation reforms, helped industrial and financial bureaucrats to retain fairly consistent preeminence over politicians in those areas, much as their counterparts in the cohesive French civil service were able to do.

Second, subject to the constraints established by preexisting state structure, there has been a long-run trend in Japan since at least the late 1960s toward increased party political influence in policymaking, in both crisis and noncrisis periods, as politicians have increased both personal policy expertise and their ability to mobilize technocratic know-how. More than thirty years of continuous LDP political dominance and strengthening alignments of some ministries with specific LDP factions have increased political influence over the professional future of individual bureaucrats and the consequent willingness of such officials to provide strategic information to politicians. No precise extrainstitutional equivalent to France's Grand Corps has existed to provide bureaucratic cohesion and systematic resistance to political pressures. Although the overall importance of LDP internal organs in the Japanese policymaking process remains a point of some controversy on which further evidence is needed,[9] the long experience and broad expertise of LDP staff, coupled with the convening power of the party, is also steadily enhancing party political influence in such areas as tax policy.[10] Jurisdictional conflicts in the bureaucratic world are having a parallel effect in sectors such as telecommunications, biotechnology, and finance where such conflicts are salient.[11] With the waning of political crisis in the early 1980s, big business and bureaucrats intent on economizing regained important new opportunities to exert political leverage, as evident in the progress of administrative reform. But this leverage, and consistent bureaucratic influence in agenda setting across many policy areas, did not prevent some expanded party political influence in such sectors as tax policy.

Third, beyond the details of state structure and its transformation, although profoundly related to both, lies the crisis and compensation dynamic, which itself influences the respective policy roles of politicians and bureaucrats in cyclical ways as yet virtually unexplored. Aberbach, Putnam, and Rockman, speaking of American and Western European government officials, argue that "the 'sensors' of politicians key in on signals from the grass-

[9] For a view emphasizing the importance of these organs, and the institutionalization of LDP influence in policymaking more generally, see Satō Seizaburō and Matsuzaki Tetsuhisa, *Jimintō Seiken (The LDP Administration)*.

[10] See Kishiro Yasusuke, *Jimintō Zeisei Chōsa Kai (The LDP Tax System Research Committee)*.

[11] See Johnson, *MITI, MPT, and the Telecom Wars*; and T. J. Pempel, "The Unbundling of Japan, Inc.," *Journal of Japanese Studies* 13, no. 2 (1987), pp. 302–3.

roots and are more likely to detect sociopolitical problems [than those of bureaucrats]."[12] The evidence presented in this book suggests that the same proclivities are observable in Japan; this helps explain why, in times of political turbulence and flux, politicians take unusual initiative in policymaking and stability-oriented bureaucrats and big businessmen defer to and even encourage such political initiative and preeminence. In noncrisis periods, by contrast, politicians sense no need to take such initiative; the systematic, efficiency-oriented bureaucracy prevails, and redistributive, welfare-oriented policies adopted during crisis periods are curtailed. Pronounced, if intermittent, bureaucratic weakness in some sectors would seem to force reformulation of theories of "bureaucratic led mass inclusionary pluralism," perhaps through recognition of cyclical variations in its relevance, although the specifics of such reformulation are beyond the scope of this research.[13]

It has been argued that the basic distributional system of grants and other policy favors between center and periphery in Japan is essentially bureaucratic.[14] Although this volume does not examine distribution channels for political resources in detail, a finding of frequent bureaucratic involvement in apportioning grants and other favors to local authority, even in domestic sectors dominated by successors to the Naimushō, does not contradict the general crisis and compensation argument developed here, particularly if made with respect to relatively stable periods such as the late 1970s and early 1980s. Compensation, flowing through any one of a number of formal channels, can involve complex, often fused bureaucratic and political relationships behind the scenes. The crucial point for an understanding of Japan's distinctive public policy outputs is not the nature of the formal channels of compensation but their patterns of oscillation over time and how the institutional parameters within which compensation takes place were originally formed. Even when bureaucrats in postwar Japan decisively dominate allocative processes,

[12] Aberbach, Putnam, and Rockman, *Bureaucrats and Politicians in Western Democracies*, p. 254.

[13] Inoguchi Takashi, *Nihon Seiji Keizai no Kōzu* (*The Composition of the Japanese Political Economy*).

[14] Reed, *Japanese Prefectures and Policymaking*, p. 38. The field research on which this assertion was based was undertaken in the pollution, housing, and high school education areas during 1976–1977.

they operate within a broader context, much more than the product of routine administrative decision.

The Link between Foreign and Japanese Policy Innovation

Hugh Heclo has suggested the importance of international precedent in determining both the intellectual context of policy debate and the specific policies adopted in individual national settings.[15] There is strong evidence in the preceding pages of this dynamic operating in Japan. Although Japanese policymakers have not uncritically adopted what they have seen abroad, often reacting only belatedly to policy ideas developed elsewhere, American, West German, British, French, and even occasionally Eastern European policy ideas have often deeply influenced the details of Japanese policy change since 1949.

Policy innovation outside Japan is typically inventoried by the Japanese bureaucracy on a fairly systematic, ongoing basis. Throughout the 1960s, for example, the Japanese Ministry of Health and Welfare monitored carefully the Great Society of Lyndon Johnson, together with parallel social innovation in Sweden, West Germany, and Britain. But monitoring led to major policy changes within Japan only after the coming of domestic political crisis in the early 1970s. It significantly influenced Japan's policy agenda, but with much less impact on the timing of policy change.

The situation was similar in the agricultural policy area. Japan kept particularly close watch, as noted in chapter 5, over the drafting and implementation of West Germany's Basic Agricultural Law of 1955 and ultimately patterned its own legislation after the German model. But policy innovation in Japan did not occur until six years after that in Germany, stimulated by the crisis and compensation dynamic inside Japan following the Security Treaty crisis of 1960.

The salience of foreign borrowing in the Japanese policy process has clearly varied widely by sector; it appears most pronounced in the welfare area, where Japan has traditionally thought of the Western nations as highly advanced and itself as somewhat backward. In regional policy the form of foreign pro-

[15] Heclo, *Modern Social Politics in Britain and Sweden*, pp. 310–12.

grams, such as the American TVA program, was often borrowed but converted through different Japanese political realities into a more explicitly distributive political program than originally true in the United States. Foreign urban planning policies, particularly those of Germany, were adopted often by Japanese policymakers in the prewar period. But they had much less currency in postwar Japan, particularly at the national level, despite Japan's chronic and escalating problems in land use.

The cross-sectoral variation in the speed and the propensity with which Japan has adopted Western policy paradigms suggests once again the importance of preexisting institutional structure, in tandem with the crisis and compensation dynamic, in determining policy outcomes. It also casts doubt on straightforward convergence interpretations of political economy in the advanced industrial world. The force of imported ideas is not overpowering in Japan, just as *gaiatsu*, or foreign pressure, is not omnipotent. But these ideas often add a crucial seed of ferment and some potential intellectual structure to diffuse preexisting frustrations and to the search for alternatives to discredited existing policy. Foreign precedents are elements important in shaping policy change of historical context that cannot be forgotten.

Policy Context: The Importance of the Early Postwar Period

With respect to future historical research, this volume suggests a particular need for added attention to the Japanese policy process of the 1950s and the early 1960s. Recent scholarship has stressed the importance of a "trans-war" perspective to understanding phenomena ranging from industrial policy and labor relations to foreign affairs.[16] But in most of the sectors examined here—particularly defense, regional, and land use policy—the *discontinuities* across the wartime divide were most striking. The purge, the disbanding of the military, the dissolution of the Naimushō, land reform, and the abolition of the nōkai were all acts of the occupation taken within three years of McArthur's arrival at Atsugi in late August 1945. These acts not only created a profound unease and indeterminacy in Japanese conservative ranks that

[16] See, for example, Johnson, *MITI and the Japanese Miracle*; Dower, *Empire and Aftermath*; Gordon, *Evolution of Labor Relations in Japan*; and Samuels, *The Business of the Japanese State*.

shaped attitudes and institutions for years thereafter, but they also created a sharp divide in many domestic policy sectors that suggests the importance of attention to the early postwar period.

The 1950s and the early 1960s are especially critical to understanding subsequent Japanese policymaking because they were periods of considerable flux during which the distinctive institutions and patterns of postwar Japanese domestic policymaking were formed. Those years present the story of a conservative struggle to recreate order in the face of new forces and values that simultaneously made restoration of the past impossible and political stability imperative. The early 1970s also left a strong imprint on policy outputs, as indicated throughout this volume, but they are comparatively better known.

This research has suggested the clear importance of the 1950s as a critical divide with respect to defense policy. Japanese defense spending relative to GNP was quite high through the mid-1950s, as indicated in chapter 10, but thereafter its share began to drop. The 1950s were also the period during which agricultural cooperatives assumed their current character, universal national health insurance was introduced, and government financial institutions were set up to assist both small business and agriculture, as well as basic industry.

Particularly important is deeper analysis of conservative politics in the 1945–1955 decade before formation of the Liberal Democratic party and of the long-run implications of early post–World War II developments for both political institutions and policy processes. The LDP after all was only Japan's fifty-first postwar political party;[17] its development since 1955 has not taken place in a void abstracted from the deeper past. Chapter 4 suggested that Japan's early postwar experience was surprisingly turbulent in comparative perspective, with the Liberal party of "One Man" Yoshida Shigeru enjoying stable majorities less often than its counterparts in postwar Germany or even Alcide de Gasperi's Italy. Yoshida's dominance was compromised not only by perennial conflict within conservative ranks but also by the fateful Democratic-Socialist coalition of 1947–1948. This coalition preceded by nearly a decade the ultimate conservative coalition merger of 1955 that formed the LDP and generated political rela-

[17] Satō Seizaburō and Matsuzaki Tetsuhisa, *Jimintō Seiken* (*The LDP Administration*), p. 178.

tionships that continued to disrupt conservative solidarity for a generation thereafter.

One unexplored aspect of early postwar conservative politics that bears particular consideration is the tangled history of the antimainstream conservative political parties perpetually rivalling Yoshida Shigeru and Ikeda Hayato's mainstream Liberal party for a share of political power. Although this volume has not examined these parties in detail, fragmentary evidence suggests an influence on policymaking highly disproportionate to their numerical Diet strength. The Kaishintō (Reform party), for example, gave strong momentum to national health insurance (*kokumin kai hoken*), expanded veterans' pensions (*onkyū*), increased defense spending, and established the National Defense Agency, even though the party only existed for two years (1952–1954). These antimainstream conservative groups, it should be stressed, were most influential in times of crisis, when they helped give public policies devised during crisis their distinctive, often redistributive cast.

The evidence presented in this volume suggests two possible implications of the 1945–1955 Japanese conservative political experience that might be examined in greater detail. First, that experience may have contributed to the strong initial salience of factionalism, as opposed to party organization, in postwar Japanese policymaking. As Sartori points out, the LDP is a party created by "fusion," in contrast to the Italian DC's experience, where prevailing party factional structure was created by "fission," after an experience of initial postwar unity.[18]

The policy chapters of this volume suggest that the "fused" character of the LDP may well have intensified pressures within Japan for policy change during periods of crisis. It may also have strengthened a preoccupation within the LDP toward community-oriented distributive policy concerns such as road and bridge building, rather than the patronage-based struggles for party control Italy experienced. Evidence from the policy chapters also highlights the cross-party networks flowing from the fluid, inchoate character of the 1945–1955 Japanese party system. These networks significantly influenced crisis policymaking by the Japanese conservatives on such questions as small business and welfare policy as late as the early 1970s, giving conservative policies their unusual eclectic and often redistributive flavor. More evi-

[18] Sartori, *Parties and Party Systems*, p. 92.

dence from a broader range of cases is clearly needed. And the comparative implications of different patterns of party evolution and cross-party contact for policy outputs could also be assessed in greater detail than has been possible here.

Many other perspectives on the process of policy innovation during the early postwar years that transcend the analysis of party and factional structures could also be fruitful in deepening understanding of policymaking during the important early postwar period. One might look more carefully at the relationship of local governments to the national policy process. This volume has suggested that local activity may have been surprisingly important in a range of policy areas from land use planning and public works to welfare, generating local financial crises which in turn indirectly pressured defense spending by the mid-1950s.

Another area for further research would be an examination of the American influence on the Japanese public policies that emerged following the end of the occupation in April 1952. Clearly much in this profile of policies displeased Washington, including low defense spending and persistently protectionist Japanese approaches to trade. Given Japanese reliance on the United States for supplies of capital and export markets, American leverage against Japan was presumably substantial during the 1950s. Yet the United States did not evoke a shift in Japanese policies in many areas of seeming American concern. Despite a Treaty of Commerce and Navigation formally providing the United States reciprocal access to Japanese markets equivalent to that enjoyed by Japanese in the United States, little attempt was made to enforce its provisions. Why the United States did not press Japan harder on economic issues and how the United States influenced the process of Japanese policy formation more generally in the years before emergence of major trade conflict between the United States and Japan after 1969 are important, yet largely unexplored subjects for future research.

Broad Waves of Policy Change

Japanese conservative politicians have never been happy with conflict and have tried continually to coopt, defuse, and suppress it. But political conflict has nevertheless been pervasive in Japan—both between government and opposition, and within ruling conservative political ranks as well. Even Japanese rural society—the part of Japan generally considered to be most consensus oriented—has experienced significant conflict at some critical historical junctures with major implications for the sort of agricultural policy that has emerged.

The bulk of the major Japanese policy innovations and the large budgetary increases in each of the domestic policy sectors examined here (i.e., agricultural, regional, small business, land use, and welfare policy) occurred during one of three major periods of domestic political turbulence: 1949–1954, 1958–1963, and 1971–1976. Furthermore, there were major quantitative or qualitative changes in policy outputs in each sector during each of these periods. These facts suggest a general pattern of Japanese domestic policy innovation proceeding in broadly pervasive spasms of creativity, each extending across a wide range of policy sectors.

Broad waves of policy creativity seem to occur in Japan during crisis periods, as noted earlier, due to a complex interaction of interparty and intraparty politics. This interaction is stimulated and intensified by pluralism in big business ranks, a viscous legislative process that requires continual interparty coordination, and the enormous power of the Japanese media. Once consensus on the need for innovation in one individual sector has been achieved, pressures for broader change often build rapidly. Initially uncompensated interest groups typically use the preceding instances of policy change as a pretext for making their own demands. John Campbell's concept of "balance," suggesting a bias in Japanese fiscal allocation toward established "fair shares" among recognized claimants,[19] is thus useful in explaining why broad spasms of policy change occur across many sectors once the need for some change is initially recognized. But the "balance" concept cannot, of course, explain that critical first decision to admit the possibility of change.

There appear few close analogues in current Western political systems to most of these Japanese structural characteristics. And the structural differences may well be intensifying, particularly with regard to the respective policymaking roles of ruling political parties and administrative elites in Japan as compared to Western Europe and the United States. As Richard Rose points out, arguably the most important influences of political parties in policymaking is to "de-routinize" issues, calling into question

[19] See Campbell, *Contemporary Japanese Budget Politics*, pp. 93–95.

existing approaches and thus unleashing the forces of policy innovation.[20] Under circumstances of political crisis, Japan's ruling Liberal Democratic party has done this par excellence, whatever its manifest rigidities in more placid times. This flexibility in times of crisis is crucial to understanding why the LDP in Japan has prospered since its foundation in 1955, while so many other elite groups, both in Japan and elsewhere, have fallen from preeminence.

A dominant Democratic party, closely in touch with the American grassroots, was similarly innovative across a broad range of policy areas during Franklin D. Roosevelt's Hundred Days in the United States. So were the Swedish Social Democrats of the 1930s, who flexibly combined agricultural protectionism with major assistance programs for industrial workers. As late as 1957–1958 the United States responded flexibly to the Sputnik challenge, with programs ranging from interstate highways to support for foreign language education. But atrophy in both the organizational capabilities and the grassroots contacts of many European and American parties, in a period of declining public resources for allocation, seems recently to have eroded both the incentives and the ability of these parties to engage in broad-based policy innovation other than tax reform or retrenchment in the nondefense functions of the state. The structural conditions under which waves of policy innovation can occur and the international pervasiveness of the broad, cross-sectoral spasms of policy change that postwar Japan has experienced remain a subject for further research.

Intersectoral Nuances

Japanese policy in each sector examined was decisively altered during each crisis period. In addition, intersectoral nuances over time in the scope and character of policy change should not be ignored. Change in agricultural policy, for example, was somewhat more extensive during the first and second crises (1949–1954 and 1958–1963) than during the third (1971–1976). Conversely, small business and regional policy innovation was somewhat more vigorous in the latter two periods than during the first. Retrenchment has also often proceeded at a subtly different

[20] Rose, *Do Parties Make a Difference?* p. 152.

pace from sector to sector as crisis has waned. Small business spending, for example, typically fell more rapidly with the waning of crisis than that for agriculture and welfare, as chapter 2 pointed out. These nuances simply reflect the changing political constituency of the Liberal Democratic party and cross-sectoral differences in the structure of responsible government agencies, together with the changing structure and growth patterns of the Japanese economy, and the shifting lines of competition with opposition groups. The fundamental dynamic of broad-based waves of policy response to long-pending problems in time of political crisis—mediated by a factionally divided ruling conservative party—was not basically altered.

Japanese defense commitments, contrary to the popular wisdom, changed significantly over the course of the 1960s and 1970s. Under the impact of domestic foreign policy controversies and rising claims for financial support from nondefense interest groups, defense budgets that were fairly large proportionate to the overall Japanese national budget in the 1950s fell to by far the lowest budgetary shares in the industrialized world. A range of limitations on the defense related activities of Japanese government, such as the arms export ban (1968), the nonnuclear three principles (1968), and the 1 percent of GNP limit on defense spending (1976) also emerged. None of these restrictions had ever been seriously considered until the extended defense related controversies within Japan intensified after 1958. With the waning of controversy regarding defense in the late 1960s, some such constraints began to disappear. For example, the arms export ban was compromised by the export of dual military-civilian use components and technology from Japan to the United States for use by defense contractors in the early 1980s; and the "1 percent barrier" on defense spending was abrogated in the 1987 budget.

Due to its distinctive dual character as both domestic and foreign policy, Japanese defense policy has been shaped by a somewhat different range of influences than the other policy sectors considered in the volume. Thus, there have been secondary defense-specific waves of crisis and compensation superimposed on the political cycles shaping policy more generally. In particular, there was some major defense policy change during the Vietnam War, such as the arms export ban, despite the general conservatism of policy in most sectors during that period.

Only land use policy, alone among the major sectors examined here, changed little in reality over most of the 1949–1986 period.

There was markedly less legislation relating to land use than in any of the other policy sectors considered; only 70 laws passed during the entire 1949–1986 period compared to 405 in the social welfare area, for example.[21] But even in land use policy some substantial formal policy changes were undertaken rather abruptly during the periods of general political crisis, despite problems in their implementation; the National Land Comprehensive Development Law of 1950, the National Comprehensive Development Plan (*Zensō*) of 1962, and the National Land Use Planning Law of 1974 are three major cases in point.

One reason for the unusual lack of actual innovation in land use policy was no doubt the structure of the issue as posed to government. The question was not preeminently budgetary, and the issue could not be easily resolved in distributive terms; rather, it was a question of interposing state power to systematically plan in an area where, after 1947, the bureaucratic structures required to undertake such planning were woefully weak.

A second reason for relative policy inaction in the land use area, even in times of broader political crisis, involved the emerging conservative circle of compensation and the concerns of nascent interest groups within it. As Scattschneider stresses, "new policies create new politics,"[22] and the implicit policy of inaction in Japanese land use planning clearly shows this. Real estate development and speculation became immensely profitable in Japan for contractors, builders, and even farmers. All were early participants in the conservative political coalition. For them land use was a distributive issue—how public land and public works contracts could be divided—rather than a regulatory one. Only when the conservatives felt pressed to include individual white-collar workers in their circle of compensation during the political crisis of the early 1970s did the periodic formal regulatory innovations in land use policy begin to increase in actual significance. Even then conflicts of interest within the conservative coalition continued to make actual implementation of land use planning measures difficult. By 1986, for example, only 15 percent of the agricultural land suitable for housing in urban areas was actually

[21] Unpublished tabulation by the Diet Legislative Office. Land use figures are for bills passed through the Lower House Construction Committee, while those counted as welfare were measures passed by the Committee on Social and Labor Affairs.

[22] Schattschneider, *Politics, Pressures, and the Tariff.*

being charged the high taxes assessed under legislation passed ten years before, as indicated in chapter 9.

The intersectoral nuances presented in the case studies of this volume jointly reaffirm the importance of preexisting state structure. State structure clearly is an important intermediate variable, influencing the way interest group pressures, including those arising during political crises, are translated into policy outputs in Japan. The dissolution of the Home Ministry (Naimushō) at the end of 1947, for example, helps account for the apparently paradoxical differences between the general coherence of industrial policy, even in many of its small business related dimensions, and the incoherence of land use policy. The strong grassroots political orientation of many regional policies, including public works programs, also appears intensified by Naimushō dissolution, which weakened the responsible bureaucratic institutions when assertive entrepreneurial party politicians such as Tanaka Kakuei were gaining power. In similar fashion, the defense budget's status as a residual in overall budgetary planning has been intensified by the Self Defense Agency's lack of ministerial status and its related subordination to MOF and MITI.

In each case an ebb and flow of policy innovation, corresponding to the macropolitical tensions in the broader Japanese polity, transcend state structure alone. But the way in which these tensions are translated into policy is clearly influenced by the distinctive institutional configurations of the Japanese state. Structural change, especially in the early postwar period, disarmed the Japanese technocratic state in many domestic policy dimensions, rendering it vulnerable to the cyclical pressures of crisis and compensation.

Some of the institutional context for postwar Japanese public policymaking, particularly in the industrial, financial, labor, and health policy areas, was certainly established before World War II; indeed, much of it emerged out of the economic and political turbulence of the 1930s. But a major theme of the policy case studies in this volume was the large share of institutional context shaping the parameters of postwar policymaking that was a product of postwar developments themselves. Aside from Naimushō and armed forces dissolution, which profoundly affected the course of regional, land use, and defense policy, most of the structural framework for agricultural and small business policy was also a postwar creation. Although the post-1947 agricultural cooperatives superficially resembled the nōkai of the Meiji and

Taishō periods, both their economic functions and their internal political structure were profoundly different. In the small business area, the Shōkō Chūkin Bank of the prewar period was supplemented by an autonomous Small Business Agency, founded in 1948, and a much broader range of small business support infrastructure than had existed before World War II.

The post-1948 operation of the crisis and compensation dynamic recast the structural reforms of the early occupation, such as land reform and Naimushō dissolution, thus making the institutional context of postwar Japanese public policymaking ever more distinct from that of prewar Japan. Aside from the agricultural cooperatives and the Rice Price Deliberation Council, post-1948 crises gave birth to the Peoples' Finance Corporation (*Kokumin Kinyū Kōko*), new industrial cities legislation, and the machinery for issuing no-collateral loans to small firms. Similarly, postwar crisis brought universalized national health and pension systems, even though more of the framework for these programs had been developed before World War II than was typical in most policy areas considered here. Beginning with the Korean War, rapid economic growth also generated the resources for many policy initiatives simply not financially possible during the prewar period. Recent recognition of the important watersheds of the 1920s and 1930s, in short, must be clearly complemented with a revived acceptance of the early Allied occupation (1945–48) as a great divide in Japanese political history, together with a deepened appreciation of the important policy restructuring in reaction to it during the 1950s.

Crisis, Compensation, and Japanese Policy Profiles

The crisis and compensation framework is important to understanding the distinctive, comparative features of Japanese policy output because it provides a parsimonious explanation for both domestic policy change and policy rigidities over a broad range of individual cases from the early postwar period to the present. It also explores the cyclical aspect of Japanese domestic policymaking, too long neglected. Crisis and compensation explains in a single theory the underlying anomalies of post-1948 Japanese policymaking: its oscillation between innovation and quietism, and its unusual approaches to equity and efficiency. Programmatic domestic policy change involving expansion of governmental programs, I argue here, occurs predominantly because conservative leadership perceives political threats to its preeminence, either from the opposition or from within conservative ranks, and strives to neutralize these threats. When the perception of political threat (crisis) wanes, government begins to qualify the programmatic changes it has made and to reduce incrementally its level of compensation to prospective supporters.

Thus, welfare's share of national general account budgets was scaled back not only in the 1980s but also in the mid-1950s and the late 1960s, following earlier crisis-related surges. Incremental retrenchment in noncrisis periods also reduced agricultural budget shares (mid-1950s and 1980s), lowered rice prices (1956 and 1987), eroded the decentralizing impact of the New Industrial Cities Law during the mid-1960s, and blunted pressures from the National Land Use Planning Law for conversion of agricultural land to housing during the 1980s. Crisis may indeed generate remarkably redistributive patterns of compensation to lower-income groups in Japan.

Many of these patterns have been given a degree of permanence through redistributive institutional forms that crisis has created, often in the distant past. In this sense past crises, such as those preceding the conservative merger of 1955, can continue to exert deep influence on policy patterns long after those crises have dissipated. But the perennial tendency toward retrenchment rather than expansion in noncrisis times cannot be ignored. Indeed, this sharp oscillation in Japan between "the drift toward conservatism and the urge for innovation," as Mosca puts it,[23] gives real force to the crisis and compensation dynamic itself.

Trends in economic growth are certainly related to this dynamic. High growth increases the resources available for distribution, while low growth conversely reduces them. Budgetary allocations to would-be conservative supporters have generally proved higher in high-growth crisis periods than when growth was lower. Yet superimposed on relationships between growth and compensation has consistently been the crisis and compensation dynamic. Across the 1960s, for example, growth was quite consistently high, aside from the 1965 recession, averaging 12.3 percent annually in real terms from 1966 through 1970. Yet both the most rapid budgetary growth and the most intense innova-

[23] See Mosca, *The Ruling Class.*

tion in public policies was concentrated during the first three years of the decade—by far the most turbulent politically. Thereafter the rate of policy innovation fell, even though growth remained high. Similarly, economic growth was relatively robust during the 1981–1985 period, compared to that during the last phase of the third crisis period (1974–1976) and to that elsewhere in the world during the early 1980s. But little new Japanese public policy actually materialized during the first half of the 1980s, aside from retrenchment-oriented administrative reform, even though the illusion of activism was created through the many new initiatives proposed by a proliferation of government advisory committees such as the Maekawa Commission. Budgetary growth was stagnant, despite a substantial excess of savings over investment in the Japanese economy as a whole. Following the decline of the progressive local governments in the late 1970s and the LDP landslide victory of 1980, the conservatives could afford to retrench, and they did.

In assessing the relevance of the crisis and compensation argument to Japanese policymaking, it is important not to forget the complex *feedback effects* operative in the process. Crisis, as the case studies have shown, generates both new institutions and shifts in budgetary shares; these products of crisis in turn generate their own constituencies. Although the Japanese policy process is less sensitive to elite interest group pressure, relatively speaking, during crisis periods than otherwise, it is a highly viscous process with multiple pressure points, even in noncrisis times. This viscosity of Japanese policy formation makes it quite easy for groups opposing change to protect their interests. Japanese policymaking also shows a rather high regard for precedent. As a consequence, retrenchment in noncrisis periods often fails to fully reverse the policy innovations and budgetary expansions of crisis intervals. This dynamic produces a ratchet-like process of gradual increase in the budgetary shares of key groups in the conservative circle of compensation, rather than a perfect cyclical pattern of compensation and full retrenchment. Japanese welfare, small business, regional, and agricultural spending from the 1950s through the late 1970s all showed this ratchet-like pattern, as the case studies indicate.

Paralleling the unfolding of the crisis and compensation dynamic have been important one-way secular changes in the Japanese political economy that have added nuances to its operation. Japan has changed from being a primarily rural society in

1949, with nearly half of total employment in agriculture, into a nation with a far stronger industrial and service-sector orientation. An unusual share of both industrial employment and production remains in the countryside, but only 7 percent of Japan's work force was in agriculture in 1986—roughly one-seventh of the 1949 level.[24] The decline of full-time and even part-time farmers has obviously affected their political ability to sustain agricultural support programs, particularly in the absence of political crisis, as chapter 5 made clear.

The role of organized labor has also clearly changed in Japanese society and politics, particularly since the mid-1970s. The unionization ratio of 50 percent in 1949 had declined to a 28.2 percent ratio by 1986, with the number of days lost to labor disputes in the mid-1980s falling to less than one-tenth of 1949 levels.[25] Private-sector labor, under the pressure of technological change and the growing export reliance of Japanese industry after the 1973 oil shock, forged closer ties with both management and the ruling Liberal Democratic party to protect its economic position; more militant public-sector labor was destroyed as a political force by the mid-1980s through extensive privatization.

These structural changes in the economic and political role of organized labor in Japan clearly weakened the ability of existing opposition parties to generate the sort of interactive political crises that had formerly generated major policy change. Their influence was further weakened by the steady rise of nationalism in Japan, with bitter memories of World War II beginning to fade. As Murakami points out, the increasing salience of nationalism and tradition in Japan tends to consolidate the conservative political position there in ways not equally true in western Europe because the Japanese conservatives are uniquely and exclusively identified with indigenous nationalist symbols to a greater degree than in much of Europe.[26]

Across the two generations examined in this volume, a clear secular trend in Japan toward the "nationalization of politics" cut across, but ultimately gave momentum to, the crisis and

[24] 45.2 percent of total employment was in agriculture during 1950. See Bank of Japan Statistics Department, *Hondo Shuyō Keizai Tōkei* (*Hundred Year Statistics of the Japanese Economy*), p. 53.

[25] Japan Institute for Social and Economic Affairs, *Japan 1988: An International Comparison*, p. 73.

[26] Murakami Yasusuke, "The Age of New Middle Mass Politics: The Case of Japan," *Journal of Japanese Studies* (Winter 1982), p. 55.

compensation dynamic. During the early postwar period, both policy problems and policy solutions were often local in character. But as the resources available to Tokyo for distribution grew and as party factions and support association structure became more institutionalized, a national mechanism for interest articulation through conservative politics was born. This has made the mobilization of national resources to solve local problems somewhat easier in the 1970s and 1980s than in the late 1940s; it has stirred greater national interest group involvement in policymaking than was previously the case. Thus, the emergence of policy "tribes" is a long-run secular trend cutting across the crisis and compensation dynamic, although influenced by it. Indeed, many of the "tribes," such as the *Nōrinzoku* (agricultural tribe) both achieved and then fortified their positions of political strength through the crisis and compensation dynamic.

Apart from long-term changes in the role of LDP politicians in policymaking, both through "policy tribes" and through party political institutions and networks described earlier, some long-range structural changes in the Japanese economy have also had important bearing on conservative politics and policymaking. Rising trade dependence, the increasing industrialization of the Japanese countryside, and Japan's increasing investments overseas have intensified and broadened the stakes of Japanese in a stable world economy, while also rendering those stakes more diverse. Excess liquidity and foreign pressures for liberalization impair the control capabilities of the bureaucracy, making coherent strategic responses to pressing national problems increasingly difficult.

Increasing turbulence in the international economy since 1971, coupled with rising protectionist pressures outside Japan, have made external influences increasingly salient in Japanese domestic policymaking. This has been particularly true as Japan's global creditor status has intensified sharply since 1985. The importance of foreign pressure in stimulating domestic policy change within Japan was also multiplied from the late 1970s on by the declining vitality of purely domestic forces for policy change within Japan, as indicated in chapter 2. Transnational policy coalitions have also become increasingly important in Japanese policy formation.

Despite important ongoing secular changes in Japanese politics and society, there is little evidence that the crisis and compensation dynamic is at an end, however, much international and domestic forces may be propelling its transformation. As a resource-poor, politically isolated nation subject to intensifying international criticism, Japan still perceives itself as vulnerable, and its conservative political and business leadership retains its low tolerance for domestic political risk. The decline of bureaucratic control and coordination capabilities, the fragmentation of the Japanese political economy into multiple pockets of highly specific power, and the increasing salience of transnational policy coalitions[27] all increase compensation demands on the Japanese political system, at the same time that they make political outcomes more volatile and uncertain. Despite the waning in traditional labor-based opposition party political strength, the catch-all Liberal Democratic party also confronts prospectively major internal tension, as domestic cleavages between consumers and inefficient producers, both of them backing the LDP, continue to deepen over trade and housing issues.[28]

Political uncertainty could also ultimately be furthered by the emergence over the past decade of a new middle mass in Japanese society that, while fundamentally conservative, has been only intermittently willing to support the LDP at the ballot box, as the sharp fluctuations in voting rates and support levels for the LDP by middle-class voters over the four 1979–1986 general elections have indicated.[29] International developments could also interact with domestic forces in complex, catalytic fashion to spur a resurgence of political crisis and compensation for domestic interests, as they did following the Nixon shocks, the Tanaka-Fukuda po-

[27] See Pempel, "The Unbundling of Japan, Inc.," pp. 281–306; Inoguchi Takashi and Iwai Tomoaki, *Zoku no Kenkyū* (*Research on "Policy Tribes"*); and Ellis Krauss and Muramatsu Michio, "The Conservative Policy Line and the Development of Patterned Pluralism," in Yamamura and Yasuba, eds., *The Political Economy of Japan*, vol. 1, pp. 516–54.

[28] On intensifying divergences of interest and policy orientation within the LDP during the late 1980s, see Hirose Michisada, "Jiyū Ha to Minshu Ha to Jimintō Seiji ni ima Kiretsu ga Hashiru" ("In LDP Politics there is now a Crack Running between the Liberal Faction and the Democratic Faction"), in Ishii Shinji, ed., *Jimintō to iu Chie* (*The Wisdom Called the LDP*), pp. 239–52.

[29] Voter turnout, in particular, has been volatile, with major impact on final configuration of the Diet, due to peculiarities of the multi-member district electoral system. In 1979 voter turnout for the Lower House elections was 67.9 percent, in 1980 74.5 percent, in 1983 67.9 percent, and in 1986 71.4 percent. In the major metropolitan areas turnout fluctuated even more sharply. See Murakami Yasusuke, "The Japanese Model of Political Economy," in Yamamura and Yasuba, eds., *The Political Economy of Japan*, vol. 1, pp. 81–82.

litical conflict, and the United States-Japan textile trade settlement of late 1971, which provided heavy compensation of domestic textile producers. Secular changes neither provide an alternate explanation for phenomena subsumed under crisis and compensation, nor do they seem likely to bring the dynamic itself to an end, however much the policy sectors in which it operates may shift. Crisis and compensation appear integral to the separate but reinforcing uncertainties of Japan's domestic political and international economic circumstances.

The Efficiency-Stability Trade Off

Few of the policies described in this volume can be called economically efficient in their direct contribution to industrial productivity or economic growth. To the contrary, the story of Japanese agricultural, regional, small business, and land use policies for the first two postwar generations is a tale of conspicuous waste by a purely economic calculus. It is a chronicle of rice prices at eight times world levels, of distribution systems with one-tenth the sales per employee of the United States, of small towns clogged with every sort of cultural center, and of uncontrolled urban sprawl, interspersed with minute, inefficient vegetable gardens. After reviewing the manifest inefficiency of Japan's domestic policy sectors, one begins to wonder both where the economic juggernaut so clearly visible to foreign competition could possibly have come from and why domestic policy patterns so differ from the common generalizations about Japanese policymaking in internationally traded sectors.

Some have presented Japan's domestic inefficiencies as part of a broader strategic plan, intended to systematically create a stable environment for economic growth by establishing labor reservoirs that can absorb redundant workers. Certainly big business in Japan, as noted in chapter 1, has had a deep interest in political continuity, given the huge debt burden and delicate cash flow conditions typically prevalent in Japanese industry by the mid-1950s. Similarly, the industrial policy bureaucracy had a complementary interest in strategic industrial development. But it was not clear operationally in many cases how these general goals of big business and the bureaucracy could or should be translated into concrete policy. Other political actors in Japan had different sets of priorities. A detailed analysis of Japanese domestic policy innovation and implementation over the past two generations does *not,* in short, support an interpretation of domestic policy formation primarily in *long-run* strategic terms.

At a very broad level of generality, one can perhaps characterize postwar Japanese industrial and domestic policies as "a delicate political settlement."[30] But from the perspective of political analysis, such an interpretation begs many central issues. It does not, for example, explain *why* such a settlement might be achieved or who might conclude it. Empirically, the notion is difficult to operationalize, especially given the structural complexity of both the business world with its four major peak federations and the ruling conservative party with its pronounced factionalism. The five case study chapters of this volume have yielded no evidence of a social compact or even a clear, coherent understanding among politicians, bureaucrats, big business, and other interest groups as to how tradeoffs across policy sectors should proceed. Such understandings appear to be far less explicit and concrete than is common in Western Europe, particularly Scandinavia. To the contrary, the dominant picture for Japan is of a stream of discrete, ad hoc decisions among an often changing cast of political actors, producing frequently contradictory results from sector to sector and from period to period. The one continuity was a persistent willingness of conservative elites in Japan to compensate potential backers for their stability-maintaining support in times of political crisis, and to do so in a fashion that balanced the demands of major groups within the conservative circle of compensation.

In the final analysis the verdict on Japanese domestic policies of the 1949–1986 period must be that of E. E. Schattschneider contemplating the history of the American protective tariff: "a dubious economic policy turned into a great political success."[31] As in the case of American tariff policy until the mid-1930s, politicians systematically converted Japanese domestic policies into distributive political resources to be divided among prospective backers in compensation for their support. Through a variety of materially oriented policies, pragmatically introduced in rather *ad hoc* fashion, conservative politicians were able to maintain a predictable political environment generally favorable to business. In this environment Japanese firms had the confidence to assume the aggressive, highly leveraged growth-oriented strategies that

[30] McCraw, ed., *America versus Japan,* p. 376.

[31] Schattschneider, *Politics, Pressures, and the Tariff,* p. 283.

ultimately led them to such striking long-run success on the international scene. In other words, short-run economic inefficiency had a political efficacy and, as it turned out, even a long-run economic efficiency of its own.

Rapid Economic Growth and Political Processes: Implications of the Postwar Japanese Case

The postwar Japanese crisis and compensation dynamic described in these pages has a broader economic context—one dominated by an extraordinary pattern of economic growth. Real economic growth in Japan averaged 9.8 percent from 1955 to 1973, including virtually continuous double-digit growth across the decade of the 1960s. Even during the first post oil shock decade (1974–1984), Japanese growth averaged 3.7 percent, in real terms, the highest in the industrialized world.

The central objective of this research has been to understand the processes of Japanese public policy formation rather than to comprehend the Japanese growth process or its implications for their own sake. The two issues are not synonymous, as has been emphasized repeatedly. Political structure and process exert independent effects on policy outcomes that cannot be explained by growth alone. Indeed, they powerfully shape the institutional context within which growth occurs.

But growth clearly conditioned to some degree both the demands of interest groups and the range of prospective responses open to policymakers interacting with one another in the crisis and compensation dynamic. Growth also had independent effects transcending the scope of this volume in shaping the evolution of the Japanese political economy. An added benefit of analyzing in detail the politics of Japanese policy formation during both periods of double-digit growth and lower growth rates is insight into the relationship between growth and politics, with a theoretical import going beyond the politics of policy innovation per se.

Since Japan's economy began its long surge of rapid growth during the Korean War, several other nations, such as South Korea, Taiwan, Singapore, Brazil, and more recently China, have grown at close to double-digit rates for extended periods of time. Several have succeeded in doing so under "developmental state" institutional arrangements broadly similar to those of early postwar Japan, in which state and private industry cooperated closely with one another. But the implications of high economic growth for the way that nations make public policy remain remarkably unexplored.

There is, to be sure, a substantial and growing body of literature exploring state capabilities in interaction with social institutions and the implications of state capability for public policy.[32] A common theme has been the importance of state structure as a determinant of policy profiles. Yet this literature rarely considers these issues within the context of high-growth societies, despite the unusual pressures on and opportunities for the state that high growth generates. Such existing literature focuses particularly on industrial development strategies rather than on how rapid growth affects the political context of public policy formation.

Evidence presented in this volume clearly affirms the importance of preexisting state structure in shaping the policy profiles of high-growth developmental states. The sharp contrasts evident in Japan between a technocratic orientation in industrial policy and a sharp materialist orientation in many nontraded sectors of the Japanese political economy, for example, seem to have been profoundly shaped by the contrasting institutional fates of the prosperous postwar Ministry of Commerce and Industry (Shōkōshō) and a dismantled Home Ministry (Naimushō). But the experience of the high-growth Japanese political economy recounted here also suggests the particular importance in the case of high-growth political systems of going beyond state structure for an explanation of policy.

Rapid economic growth seems to have had five distinctive consequences for the state-society relationship in postwar Japan which bear examination in a broader comparative context:

(1) High growth stimulated shifts in distribution of wealth and provoked societal transformations, such as accelerated urbanization, that greatly intensified political demands against the Japanese state. Growth thus appeared to intensify disposition toward political crisis, although it did not precipitate crisis itself. It helped create a combustible mixture but did not light the match.

(2) High growth, in an economy oriented toward debt-based heavy industrialization, gave the Japanese private sector a lower

[32] See, for example, Skocpol, *States and Social Revolutions*; and Evans, Rueschemeyer, and Skocpol, eds., *Bringing the State Back In*.

threshold of tolerance for political uncertainty than would otherwise have been the case.

(3) High growth generated a rapidly expanding pool of resources available for public allocation. These resources provided the wherewithal for interest group compensation, although neither a plan for compensation nor the direct impulse to engage in it.

(4) High growth intensified private-sector dependencies on the state for credit, infrastructure, and regulatory dispensations, spawning intense distributive political interactions between the state and industrial society.

(5) As a consequence of the foregoing, high growth forced a range of issues onto the policy agenda that were not primary strategic concerns of the Japanese state. Although intermittently matters of high priority, they had little direct relation to industrial competitiveness or national economic security. But growth did not create a political process for dealing with these issues. That was the province of the political system and its response through the crisis and compensation dynamic.

For further comparative research on the politics of policymaking in high-growth societies, Japan's experience with high growth poses a number of issues:

(1) Conversion mechanism. How do high-growth polities convert the perception of threats to political stability into a complex of policies for dealing with such instability? How do politicians and bureaucrats, in particular, relate to one another in this process?

(2) Responsiveness to citizen demands. Are other high-growth polities responsive to grassroots distributive demands evident in postwar Japan? Why or why not? What position do these other polities take regarding entitlement demands, especially for improvements in welfare programs?

(3) Insurance premium. What political insurance premium must business groups pay to the state in return for vigorous, stability-oriented policy measures, especially during periods of political crisis? How are such premiums arrived at? What form do they take?

(4) Clientelism. What are the long-run consequences for state-society relations of the intimate interdependence between business and government fostered by the stability requirements of a high-leverage political economy? How autonomous does the state remain? What leverage does the private sector obtain? What are the long-run implications for international competitiveness, especially in market-driven sectors?

(5) Crisis period policy responses. Do other high-growth, high-leverage polities exhibit the crisis and compensation pattern of broad waves of often redistributive policy change that postwar Japanese policymaking appears to have manifested? Or is policy change more piecemeal and halting and more regressive in character than in Japan? How do cross-sectoral response patterns compare to those in Japan?

(6) Government-opposition party relationships. How common in high-growth polities is the Japanese pattern of one party dominance and persistent cooptation of opposition proposals as opposed to alternation of government and opposition parties with contrasting policy programs? How is Japan's periodically flexible dominant-party democracy pattern related to rapid economic growth?

(7) The state as central, determining actor in the policy process. Given the unusually strong pressures exerted on the state by broader society in the high-growth polity and the unusually protean, often turbulent character of civil society itself in such systems, how valid for such polities are state-centric models of political behavior? How do the relative salience of state and societal actors vary between high-growth and lower-growth political systems or as growth waxes and wanes in the same nation? What sorts of actors do high-growth systems bring to the fore in a nation's political process? What sort of actors do they discourage?

This focus on the relationship between politics and policymaking in the postwar Japanese developmental state has provoked many of these questions, and they should be relevant for research on a broad range of high-growth polities. But the clearest applications are most likely with respect to high-leverage developmental states in East Asia. For South Korea, in particular, the political experience of the Japanese developmental state should be relevant, especially as Korea moves toward greater political pluralism and its conservatives increasingly need specifically political strategies to promote the political continuity requisite to sustained rapid, high-leverage economic growth.

Japanese Conservative Policymaking and Democracy

Throughout Japan's modern history, as E. H. Norman, T. J. Pempel, and others have stressed, there has been a deeply rooted antipluralist bias to much of Japanese political structure and culture. This has been most conspicuous in labor-management relations, where the weakness of organized labor has deprived Japan of a major pluralistic element common in Western democracies. The hierarchical bias of traditional Japanese political culture, with its special regard for imperial authority and by extension the national bureaucracy, has likewise discouraged the assertion of citizen rights against the state; so has the Japanese tradition of administrative law, derived from German jurisprudence. Perhaps most important, a pervasive national siege consciousness due to perennial confrontations with the industrialized West, both in the military and the economic spheres, has prevailed. This consciousness has led dissenting groups within Japan to mute their differences with the state in the face of transcendent national challenge from abroad.

Despite the deep antipluralist structural and cultural bias of Japanese society, it does not follow that Japanese conservative policymakers have consistently dominated either the definition of issues or the ultimate shape of policy outputs in Japan.[33] To the contrary, several of the most distinctive policies of the Japanese conservatives in fact originated with the opposition, as the preceding case studies have made clear. No-collateral loans for small business, childrens' allowances, free medical care for the aged, and clear limits on defense spending, to cite only a few instances, all originated first with the Left, at either the national or the local level. Before the conservative merger of 1955 conservative opposition parties like the *Kaishintō* also significantly influenced policy.

Many policy proposals examined here were adopted by the party in power from the Left, and others from the conservative opposition. Virtually all such borrowed measures were translated into public policy during periods of simultaneous political crisis between government and opposition, on the one hand, and within conservative ranks, on the other. During such crisis periods, in other words, government was highly responsive to a broad range of popular views, often implementing in great surges of policy innovation measures broached futilely for years. Yet during periods of greater stability government responsiveness to opposition views was much less pronounced.

The empirical findings of this volume indicate three major

[33] For a somewhat contrasting view, see Pempel, *Policy and Politics in Japan*, p. 306.

conclusions about Japanese democracy counter to conventional wisdom, and they suggest avenues for possible future research. First, there has at times been a highly creative and realistic opposition, generating ideas that now have the force of law in Japan. It is historically shortsighted to brand the Japan Socialist party, in particular, as being categorically "unimaginative," "ideological," and "devoid of popular support." Whatever their characteristics of the 1980s, the Socialists of the late 1960s and early 1970s at the local level were setting the national agenda for small business, regional, and ultimately welfare policy; during the early 1960s they were highly creative and pragmatic at the national level as well. Eda Saburō's 1962 vision for Japan—American standard of living, Soviet levels of social welfare, British parliamentary government, and a Japanese peace constitution—was among the most creative and farsighted political pronouncements of its time. The "Eda Vision," as it was known, presented long-run standards to the ruling Liberal Democrats that they emulated to an uncanny degree over the succeeding generation. In the early 1960s the Japanese Socialists were every bit as pragmatic as West German Socialists, who rode their realism to a slice of national political power in the Grand Coalition of 1966. Indeed, it was precisely the streak of realism which the Japanese Left periodically showed during the 1950s, 1960s, and 1970s which posed to the conservatives some of their gravest challenges.

But clear, creative alternatives have not been consistently presented to the Japanese conservative government by its opposition, rendering the quality of democratic dialogue in Japan uneven. During the early 1980s, for example, the Japan Socialist party failed to actively take issue with LDP housing and land use policies, despite the manifest costs of those policies to the people of Japan. Neither did the JSP offer creative alternatives to deepening trade frictions or to problems of Japanese national defense. Only with land prices in major metropolitan areas rising explosively did the JSP begin to actively question the welfare costs of prevailing policies. Even then, the transition was hesitant; the JSP, for example, continued to support producer rice-price increases, despite consumer criticism. Clearly more research is needed on why the Japanese Left has so varied in the realism with which it approaches issues of public policy.

In times of crisis, a second major finding suggests, Japanese government can be highly responsive to popular desires for distributive policy changes—indeed, perhaps more so than commonly true in the West. Japanese politics can also severely penalize those perceived to be contravening democratic procedures in time of crisis, as the strong mass reaction against Kishi Nobusuke's arbitrary tactics in forcing ratification of the 1960 United States-Japan Security Treaty indicated.

Yet the Japan of noncrisis periods appears, the third finding indicates, much less democratic than when crisis pertains. To be sure, the Japanese policy process is continuously sensitive to grassroots pressures for routine distributive benefits, transmitted to the central government by individual Dietmen from their support organizations or kōenkai. The distinctive Japanese electoral system and the elaborate legislative support organizations it generates assure that this will be so, at least for the conservative Dietmen. Since the 1950s a steady trend toward pluralism in the Japanese economy has helped decentralize the structure of political funding and broaden the base of involvement in conservative politics. But in noncrisis periods there often remains a troublingly monistic character to Japanese politics and a lack of sensitivity to those beyond the conservative circle of compensation. The basic conditions of the pluralist model of democracy seem not to be clearly met.

Never did a lack of pluralism in postwar Japanese politics, at once loosening barriers to economic rationalization and complicating efforts to expand the state's welfare role, seem clearer than in the aftermath of the LDP's massive election victory of July 1986. The Japanese economy had been growing steadily more diversified, and in many sectors market oriented, since the internationalization and the economic slowdown of the early 1970s. However, in the political sphere the power of the opposition had fallen to its lowest levels since the early 1960s. Yet despite the overwhelming Diet strength of the LDP, opposition forces in coalition with small business were able during 1986–1987 rather dramatically to forestall Nakasone administration attempts to introduce a value-added tax. They also placed their stamp on income tax policies and stimulated incremental change in the land policy area. With media support they seemed to retain the ability to delay retrenchment in existing welfare-oriented policies, although their ability to shape new policies remained problematic.

And the numerical strength of the two central mainstream factions within the LDP had risen to unprecedented heights. Perhaps more importantly, the locus of policymaking was moving steadily away from the viscous Diet legislative process and a bureaucracy largely neutral in political terms toward the internal committees (bukai) of the Liberal Democratic party. There the threats of noncooperation in the legislative process, which had traditionally strengthened the Opposition even in time of nominal political weakness, could no longer pertain. Private corporatist bargains between conservative politicians and the business world were becoming easier to strike and enforce, with the waning of crisis and the seeming advent of more stable Japanese politics.

So is Japan democratic? The answer to this question, posed in the introduction, is tied profoundly to the distinctive cyclical character of conflict and crisis, together with the profound importance of such crisis in triggering policy change. The structure of postwar Japanese politics does not conform closely either to classic majoritarian nor even to consensus models of democracy.[34] Japanese political processes do not consistently provide that "all who are affected by a decision should have a chance to participate in making that decision."[35] To the contrary, in routine periods Japanese politics is generally dominated by insiders at the expense of the general public—a highly undemocratic trait, as Schattschneider points out.[36]

But as Schattschneider also observes, "The power of the people in a democracy depends on the *importance* of the decisions made by the electorate, not by the *number* of decisions they make."[37] Nowhere do Japanese voters decide in referendum fashion; their influence is consistently mediated through interest groups and elite policy entrepreneurs. Yet at major points of political crisis, Japanese politics meets the requirement of popular responsiveness, stressed as fundamental by democratic theorists, remarkably well, due to the unusual concern of Japanese conservative politicians and businessmen for political stability. Amidst the throes of political discord in 1960, the conservative Ikeda Hayato's first act as Prime Minister was to solve the violent Miike coal strike in Kyūshū, followed soon after by concessions to the small business and agricultural groups he had castigated ten years before; Yoshida Shigeru and Tanaka Kakuei were similarly flexible where stability demanded. Due to the peculiar difficulties of orchestrating policy innovation in less troubled times,

34 For details on these models, see Lijphart, *Democracies*, pp. 1–36.

35 See Lewis, *Politics in West Africa*, pp. 64–65.

36 Schattschneider, *Politics, Pressures, and the Tariff*, p. 90.

37 Schattschneider, *Semi-Sovereign People*, p. 140.

these crisis-induced changes, bearing the clear stamp of popular demands during crisis periods, came to dominate Japanese domestic policy profiles as they have evolved since 1949. The crisis and compensation cycle within the context of viscous decision-making processes that force concessions to the Opposition explains the seeming contradiction of policies supportive of low-income groups in a generally elite-dominated political system.

Implications for International Affairs

Looming larger and larger on the global scene, Japan's economic and security role in the world of the late 1980s is characterized by four distinctive traits—massive trade surpluses, low military spending relative to both GNP and other budgetary categories, conservative fiscal policies overall, and massive capital outflows. By 1986, these traits in their interaction with high domestic savings rates and unprecedented corporate liquidity had made Japan decisively the largest creditor in the world. All four distinctive aspects of Japan's international role are profoundly related to the political dynamics described in the foregoing pages.

The policy steps discussed in previous chapters were taken preeminently to assure conservative political supremacy and serve the interests of the conservative circle of compensation within Japan. But the political stability they engendered has had profoundly important, unintended international consequences, particularly in complicating demand stimulation efforts within Japan and thus helping accelerate Japan's outflow of capital. Japanese capital ouflows, combined with rapid expansion of American fiscal deficits after 1981, have helped make Japan the principal financial underwriter of American global hegemony. They have sharply stimulated the American economy in the short run; at the same time that they have intensified United States-Japan frictions in the trade area through the depreciatory effect of Japanese capital flows into dollars on the value of the yen.

The political dynamics described in this volume have had substantial, relatively unexplored implications for Japanese import and export potential and thus for the persistent trade surpluses that perennially complicate Japan's relations with the outside world. Programs oriented toward small business and outlying regions of Japan have since the early 1970s become a central part of industrial policy. Many of these, such as the regional policies supporting the establishment of integrated circuit production in Kyūshū during the 1970s or the small business policies promoting rationalization in auto parts during the late 1960s, have directly supported export industry. Indeed, such policies have helped transform the Japanese countryside into a manufacturing base that by the mid-1980s was nearly as industrial as the major metropolitan centers of Japan, with only a minor fraction of the work force in the countryside primarily reliant on agriculture. As more export industries have relocated to the countryside since the 1960s, the elaborate complex of rural support policies, including rice price subsidies, public works employment, and local government work have created safety nets to support export industries and their workforces. As agricultural Japan becomes progressively less rural and more industrial, the process and terms of its transition have increasingly important implications for international trade, yet to be systematically explored.

Just as the thrust of the public policies described in this volume has helped sustain Japan's traditional export orientation, so has that thrust complicated import expansion. Japan's agricultural protection particularly through quotas and other nontariff barriers, in such areas as beef, oranges, and rice, is well known, although under pressure in the late 1980s from the combined effects of political stability, urban middle-class disaffection, rural industrialization, and market forces. Also important in forestalling import expansion is the complex and inefficient distribution system, with 30 percent more employees than the six major Japanese export manufacturing sectors combined.[38] The Large Scale Retail Store Law of 1973, the Department Store Law of 1956, and other such pro-small business legislation prevent the rapid emergence of national chains that could efficiently expand imports, as such chains typically do in the United States.

Structural factors, in concert with political dynamics outlined above, have discouraged both defense spending and rapid conversion of agricultural land to residential purposes. Until the mid-1970s the flow of funds within the Japanese political economy was directed traditionally toward industrial investment. Public works and other nonmilitary domestic budgetary items were

[38] Distribution sector employment in 1982 was 6.42 million. Employment for electrical machinery, transportation equipment, machinery, chemicals, iron/steel, and precision machinery *combined* was 4.55 million. See Ministry of Labor Secretariat Statistical Information Department (Rōdō Shō Daijin Kanbō Tōkei Jōhō Bu), *Rōdō Tōkei Nenpō* (*Labor Statistics Annual*), 1984 ed., table 10.

sharply higher relative to GNP than in the United States, due to the political dynamic in Japan of crisis and compensation, combined with more routine grassroots pressures.[39]

With the waning of crisis and as general concern over the possible fiscal consequences of Japan's rapid aging began to intensify, pressures for budgetary expansion in Japan fell sharply during the early 1980s. As a consequence, the fiscal deficit also declined—from 5.6 percent of GNP in 1980 to only 3.4 percent in 1986. Capital investment was simultaneously contracting in Japan, while savings remained high.[40] The one possible major source of new civilian domestic demand—urban real estate development—was largely foreclosed by the land use rigidities described in chapter 9. Meanwhile, the U.S. fiscal deficit expanded sharply, from 2.5 percent of GNP in 1980 to 4.8 percent in 1986.[41] The result, in view of diminished Third World investment opportunities due to the global debt crisis and the conservatism of Japanese investors, was a massive capital outflow to the United States. This outflow began to reshape the very structure of the global political economy in the few short years of the Reagan administration, by accelerating the pace of U.S.-Japan economic integration. These flows also thrust Japan into a crucial and unprecedented role in both supporting U.S. economic and security objectives and forcing the United States to give increasing weight to Pacific as opposed to Atlantic commitments.

In the face of these tumultuous capital flows and the exchange rate realignments and trade frictions they engendered, the Japanese domestic political economy of the late 1980s found itself largely without an active engine of domestic policy change, apart from market pressures. As this research has shown, a primary

[39] Bank of Japan Research and Statistics Department (Nihon Ginkō Chōsa Tōkei Kyoku), *Kokusai Hikaku Tōkei* (*International Comparative Statistics*), 1986 ed.; and U.S. Office of Management and Budget, *Budget of the United States*, fiscal year 1986. The 1985 Japanese and American national budget deficits were 3.9 and 5.2 percent of GNP respectively. But with defense spending deducted, the Japanese deficit would remain 2.9 percent, while the U.S. would enjoy a 0.6 percent surplus.

[40] Japanese household propensity to save was 16 percent in 1980. 1985 savings propensities in other nations were: West Germany 11.4 percent; France 8.8 percent; Britain 7.0 percent; and U.S. 5.2 percent. In all but West Germany the 1980–1985 decline in savings ratios was greater than in Japan. See Bank of Japan, *Kokusai Hikaku Tōkei* (*International Comparative Statistics*), 1987 ed., pp. 43–46.

[41] U.S. Department of Commerce Bureau of the Census, *Statistical Abstract of the United States*, 1987 ed. Figures for 1986 are provisional.

mechanism of large-scale domestic policy change and fiscal expansion in Japan from World War II through the early 1970s was an interactive combination of Left-Right confrontation and internal conflict within conservative ranks. Yet by the 1980s opposition influence had waned, while steady expansion of the major factions supporting the prime minister in power left antimainstream elements in the LDP with much less intraparty leverage than they had enjoyed a decade before. Domestic policy became increasingly a matter of retrenchment through the administrative reform program, with government rescinding many of the favors to agriculture, local governments, and welfare recipients which it had earlier extended in the heat of crisis.

Throughout the first three decades following the Allied occupation, as noted in chapter 10, national defense in the conventional sense of a strengthened military establishment was in Japanese conservative policy processes a residual—a peripheral, low priority concern to be addressed after the more pressing imperatives of national economic survival and distributing material benefits to the conservative circle of compensation had been satisfied. The waning of crisis and the declining political salience of civilian counterpressures in the late 1970s and the early 1980s raised the prospect that this residual might be redefined into something more vital. The underlying conservatism of the emerging Japanese new middle mass also provided support for such a redefinition, should a clear, credible impetus for expansion of military capabilities emerge.

Since the early 1970s, as chapter 2 pointed out, the engine of change in Japanese public policy, to the extent that such change occurs, has increasingly come to be international crisis. Two oil shocks and three sharp yen revaluations between 1971 and 1986 led to major innovations in small business policy. This was the only policy sector of those considered here where state compensation of LDP client groups, particularly in the form of government loans and tax incentives, continued to expand after the last of the three domestic postwar crises ended. Foreign political pressures, especially threats of protectionism and retaliation, and market forces became the main vehicles for achieving changes desired not only by foreigners but also by many Japanese. This combination of foreign and market pressures was, for example, crucial in accelerating the liberalization of both financial and telecommunications markets in Japan during the mid-1980s.

This is not, of course, to say that Japan responded or would prospectively respond indiscriminately to foreign pressures, either in the civilian or the military sphere, without regard to their substance, scope, or mode of presentation. As pointed out in chapter 2, the best prospects of Japanese policy change through foreign pressure existed where established consumer interests, transnational corporate interests within Japan, and market forces combined to reinforce such foreign pressure. This combination of propitious circumstances appeared to prevail in finance, telecommunications, and a small number of related high-growth sectors, where foreign pressure was playing a positive role in integrating the Japanese economy steadily with the broader world.

Japan in the late 1980s confronted what were arguably the most severe external pressures it had faced in the entire postwar period, combining a 52 percent yen revaluation during 1985–1987 with the first formal United States sanctions applied bilaterally against Japan since 1945. But while focused foreign pressure clearly produced incremental change in traditionally traded sectors of the Japanese economy dominated by large firms, it was still unclear how rapidly and thoroughly such pressure could transform the Japanese political economy as a whole. Standing as formidable barriers against major change were Japan's employment structure, with a heavy share of the labor force in inefficient distribution or import substitution sectors, a broadly shared sense of national vulnerability due to natural resource shortages, nationalism, and the pervasive psychology of community and support for the vulnerable among one's own.[42] Prevailing psychology and interest group structures stirred the impulse within Japan to meet crisis with compensation of one's own for the losses that external turbulence imposed on them, rather than by shifting to new patterns of interdependence that threatened greater vulnerability. This bifurcated structure of the Japanese political economy suggested the wisdom of a foreign approach to Japan in the short run, concentrating pressures strategically on advanced traded sectors to minimize a nationalist backlash likely to gain greatest momentum in more vulnerable, backward sectors overstaffed with workers.

For the longer run, the logic of crisis and compensation, as explored in these pages, suggests the importance of a strong domestic constituency within Japan for greater openness in the Japanese political economy as a crucial precondition for major actual

[42] Kyōgoku Junichi, *Nihon no Seiji*, pp. 244–91.

change in that direction. At least partial acceptance of economic liberalization within the ranks of the ruling conservatives—a process set gingerly in motion by the Nakasone cabinet during 1986–1987—must necessarily combine with mass media support and strong pressure from a resurgent opposition to generate fundamental transformation. When this configuration exists and care is taken to neutralize nationalist backlash, foreign pressure might well be a powerful catalyst for fundamental, rapid policy change on foreign economic issues, subject to the employment and resource constraints discussed above. With the compensation-oriented Takeshita Noboru, deeply tied to small-scale manufacturers, public works contractors, and other domestic groups, as prime minister from October 1987 and with the international economic environment increasingly volatile, a clear consensus on transition toward a liberal, fully market-oriented integration with the broader world economy had still not emerged. But market forces flowing from the strength of the yen were exerting steady economic pressure for wide-ranging transformation within Japan.

Japanese public policy is neither an immutable cultural artifact nor a mechanical response to salient characteristics of state structure. Subtly influenced by culture, with parameters profoundly shaped by the configurations of the state itself, policy evolves in response to social forces, especially crisis. Crisis, in both its government versus opposition and in its intraparty dimensions, has been the driving force behind the policy responsiveness of Japanese conservative policymakers across the long, often uncertain years of confrontation with the political consequences of both early postwar Allied reforms and subsequent economic growth. Should that sense of crisis disappear, Japan's policy process could confront serious rigidity and ultimately even instability, in view of the nation's technocratic, often rigid, and increasingly fragmented sociopolitical structure. Complacency would surely in the long run bring dangerous pressures from the outside world as well as from within Japan. Without the perception of crisis, in short, Japanese conservative political leadership could well confront the real crisis it has feared but successfully finessed for so long.

APPENDIX I:

Major Innovations in Six Key Japanese Public Policy Sectors, 1945–1986[a]

A. Agricultural Policy

R	12/18/45 —	First Agricultural Land Reform Law
R	10/11/46 —	Second Agricultural Land Reform Law
R	11/19/47 —	Agricultural Cooperatives Law (Nōgyō Kyōdō Kumiai Hō)
X	8/2/49 —	Rice Price Deliberation Council established (Beika Shingikai)
X	6/6/49 —	Land Improvement Law (Tochi Kairyō Hō)
X	6/20/50 —	Fertilizer Control Law (*Hiryō Torishimari Hō*) revised. Agricultural cooperatives take over lucrative sales of fertilizer from government corporation
X	3/30/51 —	Special Measures Law for Cold and Snowy Rice Producing Areas (*Sekisetsu Kanrei Tansaku Chitai Shinkō Rinji Sochi Hō*)
X	4/7/51 —	Farmers allowed to reinvest dividends from commercial operations in agricultural cooperatives without being taxed on those dividends
X	4/9/51 —	Law for the Reconstruction of Agricultural Finances (*Nōrin Gyogyō Kumiai Saiken Seibi Hō*)

[a] Policy innovations selected through both discussion with Japanese specialists in each policy area and detailed examination of *Roppō Zensho.* Dates indicated are dates of promulgation, rather than date of passage or effective date of validity, unless otherwise noted.

Notations are as follows:

X Policy innovations by conservative government in crisis periods after 1948
R Policy innovations during occupation reforms preceding the primary period of analysis
I Policy innovations by conservatives in response to international economic crisis after 1948

X 7/15/52 — Agricultural Land Law passed
X 12/29/52 — Agriculture, Forestry, and Fishery Finance Corporation (*Nōrin Gyogyō Kinyū Kōko*) established
X 6/2/60 — New mode of calculating rice prices established
X 6/12/61 — Basic Agricultural Law (*Nōgyō Kihon Hō*)
6/3/65 — Farmland Renewal Law compensating landlords (*Nōchi Hoshō Hō*)
7/13/68 — Promotion of noncontrolled rice transactions
5/16/69 — Establishment of independent distribution of rice by farmers (optional)
5/15/70 — Agricultural cooperatives gain right to buy and sell land
X 6/21/71 — Act for Promotion of Industrialization in Farm Areas (*Nōson Chiiki Kōgyō Dōnyū Sokushin Hō*)
X 1973 — Nōrin Chūkin Bank gains right to lend to individuals and to engage in foreign-exchange transactions
6/11/81 — New Foodstuffs Regulation Law
1984 — Agricultural loan subsidies at the Agriculture, Forestry, and Fishery Finance Corporation curtailed, and interest rates raised
1987 — Producer rice price reduced for first time since 1958

B. Regional Policy

R 5/3/46 — Regional Administration Law (*Chihō Jichi Hō*)
R 12/31/47 — Home Ministry abolished
R 7/7/48 — Regional Finance Law (*Chihō Zaisei Hō*)
X 6/1/49 — Local Autonomy Agency (*Jichi Chō*) established
X 5/11/50 — Hokkaidō Development Law (*Hokkaidō Kaihatsu Hō*)
X 5/26/50 — National Land Comprehensive Development Law (*Kokudo Sōgō Kaihatsu Hō*)
X 5/30/50 — Law Establishing Subventions for Equilibrium in Local Finance (*Chihō Zaisei Heikō Kōfukin Hō*)

X 7/31/50 — New Regional Tax Law (*Shin Chihō Zei Hō*)

X 5/15/54 — Regional Equalization Tax Law (*Chihō Kōfuzei Hō*)

5/17/57 — Tōhoku Development Promotion Law (*Tōhoku Kaihatsu Sokushin Hō*)

X 3/30/59 — Kyūshū Regional Development Promotion Law (*Kyūshū Chihō Kaihatsu Sokushin Hō*)

X 7/1/60 — Local Autonomy Ministry (Jichishō) established

X 8/60 — Local Autonomy Ministry announced detailed program for regional industrialization

X 10/60 — MITI announces plan for regional industrialization

X 12/27/60 — Hokuriku Regional Development Promotion Law (*Hokuriku Chihō Kaihatsu Sokushin Hō*)

X 1/61 — Liberal Democratic party announces plan for twenty industrial cities

X 11/13/61 — Underdeveloped Regions Industrial Development Promotion Law (*Tei Kaihatsu Chiiki Kōgyō Kaihatsu Sokushin Hō*)

X 5/10/62 — New Industrial Cities Promotion Law

X 10/5/62 — Comprehensive National Development Plan (*Zensō*)

7/3/64 — Industrial Consolidation Special Areas Promotion Law (*Kōgyō Seibi Tokubetsu Chiiki Seibi Sokushin Hō*) Six special areas for industrial consolidation established relatively close to Tōkaidō industrial zones

X 6/21/71 — Act for Promotion of Industrialization in Farm Areas (*Nōson Chiiki Kōgyō Dōnyū Sokushin Hō*)

X 6/16/72 — Industrial Relocation Promotion Act (*Kōgyō Saihaichi Sokushin Hō*)

X 6/20/74 — Regional Promotion Facilities Corporation (*Chiiki Shinkō Seibi Kōdan*)

1980 — MITI announces plan to build two to three technopolises; forty prefectures volunteer

1982 — MITI alters initial plan; chooses nineteen sites in twenty prefectures

1982 — Work commences on the Information Network System (*INS*)

C. Small Business Policy

R	2/15/47 —	Yoshida's Three Point Small Business Program
R	11/47 —	Establishment of Small Business General Bureau
R	8/1/48 —	Establishment of Small Business Agency
X	6/1/49 —	Peoples Finance Corporation (*Kokumin Kinyū Kōko*) founded
X	6/1/49 —	Small Business and Joint Cooperatives Law (*Chūshō Kigyō tō Kyōdō Kumiai Hō*)
X	8/52 —	Law concerning Temporary Disposition for the Stabilization of Designated Small Enterprises permits "adjustment associations" to control production through exemptions from the Anti-Monopoly Law
X	9/11/53 —	Small Business Finance Corporation (*Chūshō Kigyō Kinyū Kōko*) founded
X	1954 —	Administrative controls over large store expansion reintroduced
	1956 —	Small Business Organization Law (*Chūshō Kigyō Dantai Hō*) dies in Upper House. Finally passed in 1957, in weakened form
	5/22/56 —	Law for the Furtherance of Small Business Promotion Finance (*Chūshō Kigyō Shinkō Shikin Josei Hō*)
	5/23/56 —	Department Store Law (*Hyakkaten Hō*)
X	5/20/60 —	Organization of Commerce and Industry Law
X	11/4/60 —	Cabinet decision to extend ¥20 billion in loans to small business by March, 1961
X	3/31/63 —	Small Business Modernization Promotion Law (*Chūshō Kigyō Kindaika Sokushin Hō*)
X	7/20/63 —	Small Business Basic Law (*Chūshō Kigyō Kihon Hō*)
	6/3/67 —	Environmental Sanitation Facilities Financial Corporation (*Kankyō Eisei Kinyū Kōko*) established
I/X	9/23/71 —	Cabinet announces emergency support policy for small firms affected by the "Dollar Shock" of August 1971
X	10/73 —	No-collateral loan system (*mutampo yūshi seido*) established (*JCP* began demanding in

1965, and Ninagawa introduced in Kyoto during 1966)

X 10/1/73 — Large Scale Retail Store Law (*Daikibo Kouri Tenpo Hō*). Came into effect 4/1/74

X 1974 — Law concerning Promotion of Traditional Craft Industries

X 3/4/74 — Emergency small business finance package, in wake of oil shock

X 11/15/76 — Special Law for the Promotion of Small Business Diversification (*Chūshō Kigyō Jigyō Tenkan Taisaku Rinji Sochi Hō*)

I 9/3/77 — MITI announces small business emergency

9/24/77 — Small and Medium Enterprise Domain Protection Law (*Chūshō Kigyō Bunya Chōsei Hō*)

I 4/1/78 — Small Business Bankruptcy Prevention System (*Chūshō Kigyō Tōsan Bōshi Kyōsai Seido*) established

I 10/20/78 — Temporary Small Business Countermeasures Law for Designated Depressed Regions (*Tokutei Fukyō Chiiki Taisaku Rinji Sochi Hō*)

1979 — Prime Minister Ohira Masayoshi proposes value-added tax (subsequently shelved)

1981 — Ministry of Finance greencard proposal (retracted in 1985)

I 1986 — Yen revaluation countermeasures plan

D. Welfare Policy

R 12/1/47 — Unemployment Insurance Law (*Shitsugyō Hoken Hō*) and Unemployment Allowance Law (*Shitsugyō Teate Hō*)

X 5/19/49 — Social Security System Advisory Council (Shakai Hoshō Seido Shingikai) established

X 5/4/50 — Livelihood Protection Law (*Seikatsu Hogo Hō*)

X 6/20/51 — Law relating to the Separation of the Medical and Pharmaceutical Professions (*Iyaku Bungyō Hō*). Separation to be implemented in 1955, later postponed until 1956

X 8/1/53 — Major revision of the Health Insurance Law

		(*Kenkō Hoken Hō*) extends the period of benefits
X	5/19/54 —	Welfare Pensions Insurance Law (*Kōsei Nenkin Hoken Hō*), retroactive to 5/1/54
	2/10/57 —	Prime Minister Kishi Nobusuke announces plan for Health Insurance for the Whole Nation (*Kokumin Kai Hoken*)
X	12/27/58 —	New National Health Law (*Shin Kokumin Kenkō Hō*)
X	4/15/59 —	Minimum Wage Law (*Saitei Chingin Hō*)
X	4/16/59 —	National Pension Law (*Kokumin Nenkin Hō*)
X	11/1/59 —	Welfare Pensions for the Aged, Mothers and Children, and Handicapped and Disabled Persons (*Rōrei Boshi Shōgai Fukushi Nenkin*). Noncontributory welfare pension system established for the aged, the handicapped, and mothers and children
X	9/5/60 —	Ikeda makes social security one of the "three pillars" of his new policy platform
X	4/1/61 —	Health care benefits extended to all citizens by introduction of universal national health insurance (*Kokumin Kai Hoken*)
X	7/1/62 —	Social Insurance Agency established
X	4/1/63 —	Revision of the National Insurance Law (*Kokumin Hoken Hō*); provides 70 percent subvention of medical care for the aged
X	7/11/63 —	Welfare Law for the Aged (*Rōjin Fukushi Hō*)
	1969 —	Childrens' allowance (*jidō teate*) (proposed by JSP; introduced by Musashino City in 4/67 and the city of Tokyo in 12/69)
	5/27/71 —	Childrens' Allowance Law (*Jidō Teate Hō*)
X	1/73 —	Free medical care for the aged (proposed by the JCP; in 1964); introduced by Sawauchi City (Iwate Prefecture) in 1960; introduced for citizens over 70 by Tokyo from 10/69
X	4/1/75 —	Employment insurance reform (revision of Health Insurance Law) provides substantial expansion of retraining; bill passed in 12/74
	2/1/83 —	Health Care for the Aged Law (*Rōjin Hoken Hō*). People over 70 pay nominal fee for medical care

1984 — Free medical care for the aged actually abolished through revision of the Health Insurance Law

9/84 — Government decides to reexamine children's allowance (*jidō teate*) ultimately limiting eligibility to reduce fiscal burden

E. Land Use Policy

R 9/45 — National Land Development Plan (*Kokudo Kaihatsu Keikaku An*)

R 5/29/46 — Emergency Housing Ordinance (Jūtaku Kinkyū Sochi Rei)

R 9/1/46 — National Reconstruction Land Policy (*Fukkō Kokudo Keikaku Yōkō*)

R 6/19/46 — Special Urban Planning Law (*Tokubetsu Toshi Keikaku Hō*) proposed

X 5/27/50 — National Land Comprehensive Development Law (*Kokudo Sōgō Kaihatsu Hō*)

X 6/6/50 — Housing Finance Corporation (*Jūtaku Kinyū Kōko*) established

7/8/55 — Japan Housing Corporation Law (*Nihon Jūtaku Kōdan Hō*)

4/26/56 — National Capital Region Development Act

X 10/5/62 — National Comprehensive Development Plan (*Zensō*)

6/15/68 — City Planning Law (*Toshi Keikaku Hō*)

5/30/69 — New National Comprehensive Development Plan (Shin Zensō)

X 4/25/73 — Tax on land suitable for housing in urban areas (*takuchi nami kazei*) introduced

X 6/25/74 — National Land Use Planning Law (*Kokudo Riyō Keikaku Hō*)

X 6/26/74 — National Land Agency (*Kokudo Chō*) established

11/4/77 — Third National Comprehensive Development Plan (*San Zensō*) announced

11/78 — Land Use Conversion Plan for encouraging conversion of agricultural land into housing

11/14/80 — Agricultural Housing Association Law (*Nōjū*

Kumiai Hō) passed to aid farmers in selling land through cooperatives

F. Defense Policy

X 7/8/50 — MacArthur decrees formation of the National Police Reserve

X 9/8/51 — U.S.-Japan Security Treaty signed in San Francisco

X 10/15/52 — Security Law enacted authorizing 110,000 ground troops and 8,000 marine troops

X 8/1/53 — Weapons Production Law (*Buki tō Seizō Hō*)

X 9/6/53 — Safety Agency (Hoanchō) Defense Plan announced, providing for 210,000 men in the ground forces, 170 ships, and 1,400 aircraft. (In 1986 Japan had 156,000 men in the ground forces, 165 ships, and 350 aircraft)

X 1954 — Post-Occupation highpoint in defense spending/GNP

X 3/8/54 — Mutual Security Agreement (MSA) signed

X 6/2/54 — Self-Defense Forces and Self-Defense Agency Law (*Bōeitai-Bōeichō Setchi Hō*)

X 7/1/54 — Self-Defense Agency (*Bōeichō*) established

4/20/56 — Revision of the two major defense laws (*Bōeitai Hō* and *Bōeichō Setchi Hō*)

X 8/28/58 — Plan for the expansion of the Self-Defense Forces (*Jieitai Zōkyō Keikaku*)

X 12/31/58 — Special reduction of ¥3 billion in Japanese compensating payments to support U.S. forces in Japan

X 6/19/60 — U.S.-Japan Security Treaty renewal ratified, amidst broad political turbulence. In October 1960

X 10/12/60 — JSP chairman Asanuma Inejirō assassinated by son of a SDA officer

X 6/2/61 — Further revision of the two major defense laws

X 11/1/62 — Defense Facilities Agency (*Bōei Shisetsu Chō*) established

4/21/67 — Partial arms export ban under the three principles on arms exports

1968 — Total arms export ban and three Satō nuclear principles introduced

4/27/71 — Self-Defense Agency announces fourth defense capacity preparation plan

X 6/8/76 — Japan ratifies Nuclear Non-Proliferation Treaty, signed in 1970

X 11/5/76 — One percent/GNP limit established for defense spending

10/23/79 — Japan decides to participate for first time in RIMPAC Pacific regional military exercises (actual participation was from 2/26/80)

1981 — Defense spending hits its post-Occupation low point relative to the general account of the national budget

7/23/82 — 1983-1987 Defense Capacity Preparation Plan (*Bōeiryoku Seibi Keikaku*) announced by the National Defense Council; provides for expenditures of ¥16 trillion; if realized, would make breach of the one-percent/GNP barrier likely

1/14/83 — Revision of the arms export ban to permit export of defense-related components

11/8/83 — U.S.-Japan agreement on military technology transfer

11/84 — U.S.-Japan Joint Military Technology Commission inaugurated

12/86 — One-percent/GNP limit on military spending, established in 1976, is formally abolished

APPENDIX II

Japanese House of Representatives General Election Results, 1946–1986[a]

	Seats	% of Seats	% of Votes
1. **April 10, 1946**	464*		
Liberal (Jiyūtō)	140	30.2	24.4
Progressive (Shimpotō)	94	20.3	18.7
Cooperative Democratic (Kyōdō Minshuto)	14	3.0	3.2
Socialist (Shakaitō)	92	19.8	17.8
Communist (Kyōsantō)	5	1.1	3.8
Minor parties	38	8.2	11.7
Independents	81	17.4	20.4
*Two seats unoccupied			
2. **April 25, 1947**	466		
Liberal	131	28.1	26.9
Democratic (Minshutō)	126	27.0	25.0
Citizens' Cooperative (Kokumin Kyōdōtō)	29	6.2	7.0
Socialist	143	30.7	26.2
Communist	4	0.8	3.7
Minor parties	25	5.4	5.4
Independents	13	2.8	5.8
3. **January 23, 1949**	466		
Democratic	69	14.8	15.7
Citizens' Cooperative	14	3.0	3.4
Democratic Liberal (Minshu Jiyūtō)	264	56.7	43.9
Socialist	48	10.3	13.5
Labor-Farmer (Rōnōtō)	7	1.5	2.0
Communist	35	7.5	9.7

[a] *Notes*: (1) The size of the House of Representatives was progressively expanded from its original 466 to 467 (for 2/55 election), 486 (for 1/67 election), 491 (12/72 election), 511 (12/76 election), and 512 (7/86 election). This was done to help offset representational discrepancies as population shifted from rural to urban areas. (2) Totals do not always add perfectly, due to rounding.

Source: Miyakawa Takayoshi ed., *Seiji Handbook*. Tokyo: Seiji Kōhō Center, 1979–1986; and *Asahi Shimbun* data.

	Seats	% of Seats	% of Votes
Minor parties	17	3.6	5.2
Independents	12	2.6	6.6
4. **October 1, 1952**	466		
Liberal	240	51.5	47.9
Reform (Kaishintō)	85	18.2	18.2
Right-wing Socialist	57	12.2	11.6
Left-wing Socialist	54	11.6	9.6
Labor-Farmer	4	0.9	0.7
Communist	—	—	2.6
Minor parties	7	1.5	2.7
Independents	19	4.1	6.7
5. **April 19, 1953**	466		
Reform	76	16.3	17.9
Hatoyama Liberal	35	7.5	8.8
Yoshida Liberal	199	42.7	39.0
Right-wing Socialist	66	14.2	13.5
Left-wing Socialist	72	15.4	13.1
Labor-Farmer	5	1.1	1.0
Communist	1	0.2	1.9
Minor parties	1	0.2	0.4
Independents	11	2.4	4.4
6. **February 27, 1955**	467		
Liberal	112	24.0	26.6
Democratic	185	39.6	36.6
Right-wing Socialist	67	14.3	13.9
Left-wing Socialist	89	19.1	15.3
Labor-Farmer	4	0.9	1.0
Communist	2	0.4	2.0
Minor parties	2	0.4	1.3
Independents	6	1.3	3.3
7. **May 22, 1958**	467		
Liberal Democratic (Jiyū Minshutō)	287	61.5	57.8
Socialist	166	35.5	32.9
Communist	1	0.2	2.6
Minor parties	1	0.2	0.7
Independents	12	2.6	6.0
8. **November 20, 1960**	467		
Liberal Democratic	296	63.3	57.5
Democratic Socialist (Minshu Shakaitō)	17	3.6	8.7
Socialist	145	31.0	27.5

	Seats	% of Seats	% of Votes
Communist	3	0.6	2.9
Minor parties	1	0.2	0.3
Independents	5	1.0	2.8
9. **November 21, 1963**	467		
Liberal Democratic	283	60.6	54.7
Democratic Socialist	23	4.9	7.4
Socialist	144	30.8	29.0
Communist	5	1.1	4.0
Minor parties	0	0.0	0.2
Independents	12	2.6	4.8
10. **January 29, 1967**	486		
Liberal Democratic	277	57.0	48.8
Democratic Socialist	30	6.2	7.4
Kōmeitō	25	5.1	5.4
Socialist	140	28.8	27.9
Communist	5	1.0	4.8
Minor parties	0	0.0	0.2
Independents	9	1.9	5.6
11. **December 27, 1969**	486		
Liberal Democratic	288	59.2	47.6
Democratic Socialist	31	6.4	7.7
Kōmeitō	47	9.7	10.9
Socialist	90	18.5	21.4
Communist	14	2.9	6.8
Minor parties	0	0.0	0.2
Independents	16	3.3	5.3
12. **December 10, 1972**	491		
Liberal Democratic	271	55.4	46.9
Democratic Socialist	19	3.5	7.0
Kōmeitō	29	6.6	8.5
Socialist	118	24.1	21.9
Communist	38	7.1	10.5
Minor parties	2	0.4	0.3
Independents	14	2.9	4.9
13. **December 5, 1976**	511		
Liberal Democratic	249	48.7	41.8
New Liberal Club	17	3.3	4.2
Democratic Socialist	29	5.7	6.3
Kōmeitō	55	10.8	10.9
Socialist	123	24.1	20.7
Communist	17	3.3	10.4
Minor parties	0	0.0	0.1
Independents	21	4.1	5.7

	Seats	% of Seats	% of Votes
14. **October 7, 1979**	511		
Liberal Democratic	248	48.5	44.6
New Liberal Club	4	0.8	3.0
Democratic Socialist	35	6.9	6.8
Kōmeitō	57	11.2	9.8
Socialist	107	20.9	19.7
Communist	39	7.6	10.4
Social Democratic League	2	0.4	4.9
Independents	19	3.7	
15. **June 22, 1980**	511		
Liberal Democratic	286	56.0	47.9
New Liberal Club	12	2.4	3.0
Democratic Socialist	32	6.3	6.6
Kōmeitō	33	6.5	9.0
Socialist	107	20.9	19.3
Communist	29	5.7	9.8
Social Democratic League	3	0.6	0.7
Minor parties	0	0	0.2
Independents	11	2.2	3.5
16. **December 18, 1983**	511		
Liberal Democratic	250	48.9	45.8
New Liberal Club	8	1.6	2.4
Democratic Socialist	38	7.4	7.3
Kōmeitō	58	11.4	10.1
Socialist	112	21.9	19.5
Communist	26	5.1	9.3
Social Democratic League	3	0.6	0.7
Minor parties	0	0	0.1
Independents	16	3.13	4.9
17. **July 6, 1986**	512		
Liberal Democratic	300	58.6	49.4
New Liberal Club	6	1.2	1.8
Democratic Socialist	26	5.1	8.8
Kōmeitō	56	10.9	9.4
Socialist	85	16.6	17.2
Communist	26	5.1	6.4
Social Democratic League	4	0.8	0.8
Minor parties	0	0	0.2
Independents	9	1.8	5.8

Bibliography

Aberbach, Joel D., Robert D. Putnam, and Bert A. Rockman. *Bureaucrats and Politicians in Western Democracies*. Cambridge, Mass.: Harvard University Press, 1981.

Adachi Toshiaki. *Jimintō Jinbutsu Fūun Roku (Bibliography of LDP Personalities)*. Tokyo: Shinsedai System Center, 1983.

———. *Za Jimintō (The LDP)*. Tokyo: Tsubasa Shoin, 1984.

Adelman, Paul. *Gladstone, Disraeli, and Later Victorian Politics*. London: Longman, 1970.

Allen, G. C. *A Short Economic History of Japan, 1867–1937*. 2d ed. London: Allen and Unwin, 1962.

Allinson, Gary Dean. "The Moderation of Organized Labor in Japan." *Journal of Japanese Studies* 1, no. 2 (Spring 1975), pp. 409–36.

Allum, P. A. *Italy—Republic Without Government?*. New York: W. W. Norton, 1973.

Almond, Gabriel A., and Scott C. Flanagan, eds. *Crisis, Choice, and Change: Historical Studies of Development*. Boston: Little, Brown, 1973.

Anderson, Malcolm. *Conservative Politics in France*. London: Allen and Unwin, 1974.

Anderson, Stephen J. "Nihon Shakai Fukushi no Seisaku Keisei Katei" ("Japan's Welfare Policy Process"). *Juristo Sōgō Tokushū: Tenkan Ki no Fukushi Mondai (Juristo Special Issue: Welfare Problems in a Period of Transition)* No. 41 (1985), pp. 172–76.

Andrain, Charles F. *Politics and Economic Policy in Western Democracies*. North Scituate, Mass.: Duxbury Press, 1980.

Arai Shunzō and Morita Hajime. *Bunjin Saishō: Ōhira Masayoshi (Prime Minister as a Man of Letters: Ōhira Masayoshi)*. Tokyo: Bunsho Dō, 1982.

Arisawa Hiromi. "Heiki Seisan to Nihon Keizai" ("Arms Production and the Japanese Economy"). *Chūō Kōron* no. 1 (1953), pp. 13–22.

———. *Shōwa Keizai Shi (An Economic History of the Shōwa Era)*. Tokyo: Nihon Keizai Shimbun Sha, 1976.

Arisawa Hiromi, and Inaba Shūzō, eds. *Shiryō Sengo Ni Jyū Nen Shi: Keizai (Data on the Twenty Postwar Years: Economics)*. Tokyo: Nihon Hyōron Sha, 1966.

Arnold, Walter. "The Politics of Economic Planning in Postwar Japan: A Study in Political Economy." Ph.D. diss., University of California Berkeley, 1984.

Asagumo Shimbun Sha Sō Kyoku, ed. *Bōei Handbook* (*Defense Handbook*). 1987 ed. Tokyo: Asagumo Shimbun Sha, 1987.

Asahi Shimbun Nenkan Henshū Bu, ed. *Minryoku (People's Power).* 1984–1987 eds. Tokyo: Asahi Shimbun Sha, 1984–1987.

Asahi Shimbun Niigata Shi Kyoku, ed. *Tanaka Kakuei to Etsuzan Kai: Shinsō no Kōzu (Tanaka Kakuei and The Etsuzankai: The Layout of the Depths).* Tokyo: Yamate Shobō, 1982.

Asahi Shimbun Seiji Bu, ed. *Seitō to Habatsu (Party and Faction).* Tokyo: Asahi Shimbun Sha, 1968.

Asahi Shimbun Sha. *Asahi Nenkan (Asahi Almanac).* Tokyo: Asahi Shimbun Sha, various issues.

Asahi Shimbun Sha Seron Chōsa Shitsu, ed. *Nihonjin no Seiji Ishiki (The Political Consciousness of Japanese).* Tokyo: Asahi Shimbun Sha, 1976

Asahi Shimbun Sha. *Shin Kenbetsu Character (New Character, by Prefecture).* Tokyo: Asahi Shimbun Sha, 1983.

Ashford, Douglas. *Policy and Politics in France.* Philadelphia: Temple University Press, 1982.

Ashida Hitoshi. *Ashida Hitoshi Nikki (The Ashida Diaries).* Vols. I–IV. Tokyo: Iwanami Shoten, 1986.

Asukata Ichio. "Kuni no Seiji kara Chihō no Seiji e" ("From National Politics to Regional Politics"). *Sekai* 7, no. 223 (July 1964), pp. 143–54.

———. "Shakaitō e no Teigen" ("A Proposal to the Socialist Party"). *Sekai* 16, no. 263 (January 1967), pp. 55–59.

———. "Kakushin Jichitai no Sanjyū Nen." ("Thirty Years of Progressive Local Government"). In *Shōwa no Sengoshi (A Shōwa Postwar History),* edited by Ōsaki Hideki. Tokyo: Tambun Sha, 1976.

Aydalot, Philippe, et al. *Atlas Economique des Regions Françaises.* Paris: Economica, 1982.

Baerwald, Hans H. "Lockheed and Japanese Politics." *Asian Survey* 26, no. 9 (September 1976), pp. 817–29.

———. *Party Politics in Japan.* Boston: Allen and Unwin, 1986.

———. *The Purge of Japanese Leaders under the Occupation.* Berkeley and Los Angeles: University of California Press, 1959.

Banfield, Edward. *The Moral Basis of a Backward Society.* Glencoe, Ill.: The Free Press, 1958.

Bank of Japan Research and Statistics Department (Nihon Ginkō Chōsa Tōkei Kyoku). *Meiji Ikō Hondo Shuyō Keizai Tōkei (Fundamental Statistics for Japan since Meiji).* Tokyo: Nihon Ginkō Tōkei Kyoku, 1966.

———. *Keizai Tōkei Nenpō (Economic Statistics Annual).* 1985 and 1986 eds. Tokyo: Nihon Ginkō Tōkei Kyokū, 1986 and 1987.

———. *Kokusai Hikaku Tōkei (International Comparative Statistics).* 1980, 1984, 1986 eds. Tokyo: Nihon Ginkō, 1980, 1984, 1986.

———. *Waga Kuni no Kinyū Seido (Our Nation's Financial System).* Tokyo: Nihon Ginkō, 1976.

Barker, Ernest, ed. *The Politics of Aristotle.* Book 5. Oxford: Clarendon Press, 1946.

Beer, Samuel. *Modern British Politics.* New York: W. W. Norton, 1982.

Belloni, Frank P., and Dennis C. Beller, eds. *Faction Politics: Political Parties and Factionalism in Comparative Perspective.* Santa Barbara, Calif.: ABC-Clio, Inc., 1978.

Berger, Gordon. *Parties out of Power in Japan, 1931–1941.* Princeton: Princeton University Press, 1977.

Berger, Suzanne D., ed. *Organizing Interests in Western Europe.* Cambridge: Cambridge University Press, 1981.

Berger, Suzanne, and Michael Piore. *Dualism and Discontinuity in Industrial Societies.* Cambridge: Cambridge University Press, 1980.

Beyme, Klaus von, and Manfred J. Schmidt, eds. *Policy and Politics in the Federal Republic of Germany.* Aldershot, England: Gower, 1985.

Billings, Robert S. "A Model of Crisis Perception: A Theoretical and Empirical Analysis." *Administrative Science Quarterly* 25, no. 2 (June 1980), pp. 300–16.

Binder, Leonard, James S. Coleman, Joseph LaPalombara, Lucian W. Pye, Sidney Verba, and Myron Weiner. *Crises and Sequences in Political Development.* Princeton: Princeton University Press, 1971.

Bisson, T. A. *Prospects for Democracy in Japan.* New York: Macmillan, 1949.

Black, Cyril, Marius B. Jansen, Herbert S. Levine, Marion J. Levy, Jr., Henry Rosovsky, Gilbert Rozman, Henry D. Smith II, and S. Frederick Starr. *The Modernization of Japan and Russia.* New York: Free Press, 1975.

Blake, Robert. *Disraeli.* New York: St. Martin's, 1966.

Blaker, M. K., ed. *Japan at the Polls.* Washington, D.C.: American Enterprise Institute, 1976.

———. "The Conservatives in Crisis." In *A Season of Voting,* edited by H. Passin. Washington, D. C.: American Enterprise Institute, 1979.

Bogdanor, Vernon, and David Butler, eds. *Democracy and Elections: Electoral Systems and Their Political Consequences.* Cambridge: Cambridge University Press, 1983.

Bourne, Dominique. *Petits bourgeois en revolte? Le Mouvement Poujade.* Paris: Flammarion, 1977.

Brecher, Michael, ed. *Studies in Crisis Behavior.* New Brunswick, N.J.: Transaction Books, 1978.

Broadridge, Seymour. *Industrial Dualism in Japan.* Chicago: Aldine Publishing Company, 1966.

Brown, A. J., and E. M. Burrows. *Regional Economic Problems: Comparative Experiences of Some Market Economies.* London: Allen and Unwin, 1977.

Bucklin, Louis. *Competition and Evolution in the Distributive Trade.* Englewood Cliffs, N.J.: Prentice Hall, 1972.

Burke, Edmund. *Reflections on the Revolution in France.* Edited by Conor Cruise O'Brien. London: Penguin Books, 1968.

Butler, David, Howard R. Penniman, and Austin Ranney, eds. *Democracy at the Polls: A Comparative Study of Competitive National Elections.* Washington, D.C.: American Enterprise Institute, 1981.

Calder, Kent E. "Kanryō vs. Shomin: The Dynamics of Conservative Leadership in Postwar Japan." In *Political Leadership in Contemporary Japan,* edited by Terry E. MacDougall. Ann Arbor: University of Michigan Occasional Papers in Japanese Studies no. 1, 1982, pp. 1–31.

———. "Politics and the Market: The Dynamics of Japanese Credit *Allocation,* 1946–1978." Ph.D. diss., Harvard University, 1979.

———. "The Emerging Politics of the Trans-Pacific Economy." *World Policy Journal* 2, no. 4 (Fall 1985), pp. 593–623.

———. "The Rise of Japan's Military-Industrial Base." *Asia-Pacific Community* no. 17 (Summer 1982), pp. 26–41.

Calhoun, Craig. *The Question of Class Struggle.* Chicago: University of Chicago Press, 1982.

Callon, Scott. "Politics, Technology, and the State: The Pentagon Role in Laissez-faire America." B.A. thesis, Princeton University, 1986.

Campbell, John C. *Contemporary Japanese Budget Politics.* Berkeley: University of California Press, 1979.

———. "The Old People Boom and Japanese Policy Making." *Journal of Japanese Studies* 5, no. 2 (Summer 1979), pp. 329–50.

———. "Problems, Solutions, Non-Solutions, and Free Medical Care for the Elderly in Japan." *Pacific Affairs* 57, no. 1 (Spring 1984), pp. 53–64.

Campbell, Ruth. "Nursing Homes and Long-Term Care in Japan." *Pacific Affairs* 57, no. 1 (Spring 1984), pp. 78–89.

Carmen, Harry J., and Reinhard H. Luthin. *Lincoln and the Patronage.* New York: Columbia University Press, 1943.

Caro, Robert A. *The Power Broker.* New York: Alfred A. Knopf, 1964.

Castle, Emery N., and Hemmi Kenzō. *U.S.-Japan Agricultural Trade Relations.* Washington, D.C.: Resources for the Future, 1982.

Castles, Francis G., ed. *The Impact of Parties: Politics and Policies in Democratic Capitalist States.* Beverly Hills: Sage Publications, 1982.

Cawson, Alan, ed. *Organized Interests and the State: Studies in Meso-Corporatism.* Beverly Hills: Sage Publications, 1985.

Cerny, Philip G., and Martin A. Schain. *French Politics and Public Policy.* New York: St. Martin's, 1980.

Chandler, Lester V. *America's Greatest Depression.* New York: Harper and Row, 1970.

Chiiki Gijutsu Kenkyū Group, ed. *Chiiki Gijutsu no Jidai (The Era of Regional Technology).* Tokyo: Tsūshō Sangyō Chōsa Kai, 1982.

Chō Yukio. "Exposing the Incompetence of the Bourgeoisie: The Financial Panic of 1927." *Japan Interpreter* 8, no. 4 (Winter 1974), pp. 492–501.

Chokki Toshiaki. *Kōsaku Kikai Gyōkai (The Numerical Control Machinery Industry)*. Tokyo: Kyōiku Sha, 1978.

Chubb, Judith. *Patronage, Power, and Poverty in Southern Italy: A Tale of Two Cities*. Cambridge: Cambridge University Press, 1982.

Cohen, Jerome B. *Economic Problems of Free Japan*. Princeton: Princeton University Center of International Studies, 1952.

———. *Japan's Economy in War and Reconstruction*. Reprint. Westport, Conn.: Greenwood Press, 1973.

Cole, Allan B. *Japanese Society and Politics: The Impact of Social Stratification and Mobility on Politics*. Boston University Studies in Political Science, no. 1. Boston: Boston University, 1956.

———. *Political Tendencies of Japanese in Small Enterprises*. New York: Institute of Pacific Relations, 1959.

Cole, Allan B., and Nakanishi Naomichi, eds. *Japanese Opinion Polls with Socio-Political Significance, 1947–1957*. Vol. 1. Published under the auspices of The Fletcher School of Law and Diplomacy, Tufts University, and The Roper Public Opinion Poll Research Center, Williams College.

Cole, Allan, George Totten, and Cecil Uyehara. *Socialist Parties in Postwar Japan*. New Haven: Yale University Press, 1966.

Colton, Kenneth E. "Pre-war Political Influences in Postwar Conservative Politics." *American Political Science Review* 142, no. 5 (October 1948), pp. 940–69.

Colton, Kenneth E., Hattie Kawahara Colton, and George O. Totten, eds. *Japan since Recovery of Independence*. Philadelphia: Annals of the American Academy of Political and Social Science, 1956.

Commission of the European Community. *Changes in the Structure of the Retail Trade in Europe*. Luxembourg: Office for Official Publications of the European Community, 1982.

———. Preliminary Study on Competition in the Retail Trade. Luxembourg: Office for Official Publications of the European Communities, 1978.

"Consider Japan," *The Economist*, September 1, 1962, pp. 787–823 (Part One); and September 8, 1962, pp. 907–36 (Part Two).

Cornford, James. "The Transformation of Conservatism in the Late Nineteenth Century." *Victorian Studies* 7, no. 1 (September 1963), pp. 35–66.

Curtis, Gerald L. *Election Campaigning Japanese Style*. New York: Columbia University Press, 1971.

———. "Big Business and Political Influence." In *Modern Organization and Decision Making*, edited by Ezra F. Vogel. Tokyo: Charles E. Tuttle Company, 1975, pp. 33–70.

Dahl, Robert A., ed. *Political Oppositions in Western Democracies.* New Haven: Yale University Press, 1966.

Davies, Ross L. *Retail Planning in the European Community.* Westmead, England: Saxon House, 1979.

Dawson, Andrew H., ed. *The Land Problem in the Developed Economy.* London: Croom Helm, 1984.

Destler, I. M. *Making Foreign Economic Policy.* Washington, D.C.: The Brookings Institution, 1980.

Destler, I. M., and Hideo Satō, eds. *Coping with U.S.-Japan Economic Conflict.* Lexington, Mass.: Lexington Books, 1982.

Destler, I. M., Haruhiro Fukui, and Hideo Satō. *The Textile Wrangle.* Ithaca: Cornell University Press, 1979.

Dodge, Joseph. "Japan—Its Problems, Progress, and Possibilities." Address delivered at the 48th Annual Banquet of the American Institute of Banking, New York: February 2, 1952.

Donnelly, Michael. "Political Management of Japan's Rice Economy." 2 vols. Ph.D. diss., Columbia University, 1978.

Dore, Ronald P. *Land Reform in Japan.* New York: Schocken Books, 1985.

———. *Shinohata: A Portrait of a Japanese Village.* New York: Pantheon Books, 1978.

———. "Japanese Election Candidates in 1955." *Pacific Affairs* 29, no. 2 (June 1956), pp. 174–81.

———. *British Factory-Japanese Factory.* Berkeley: University of California Press, 1973.

Dore, Ronald P., and Ōuchi Tsutomu. "Rural Origins of Japanese Fascism." In *Dilemmas of Growth in Prewar Japan,* edited by James William Morley. Princeton: Princeton University Press, 1971.

Dōro Gyōsei Kenkyū Kai, ed. *Dōro Gyōsei (Road Administration),* 1983 ed. Tokyo: Zenkoku Dōro Riyōsha Kaigi, 1983.

"Doru Chōtatsu no Kanōsei to Genkai" ("The Prospects for and Limitations on Raising Dollar Funds"). *Ekonomisuto,* May 31, 1960, pp. 6–18.

Dower, John W., ed. *Origins of the Modern Japanese State: Selected Writings of E. H. Norman.* New York: Random House, 1975.

———. *Empire and Aftermath: Yoshida Shigeru and the Japanese Experience, 1878–1954.* Cambridge, Mass.: Harvard University Council on East Asian Studies, 1979.

———. "The Eye of the Beholder." *Bulletin of Concerned Asian Scholars* 2 (October 1, 1969) pp. 16–25.

Downs, Anthony. *Inside Bureaucracy.* Boston: Little, Brown, 1967.

Duverger, Maurice. *Political Parties.* London: Methuen, 1959.

Economic Planning Agency (Keizai Kikaku Chō), ed. *Keizai Hakusho (Economic White Paper).* 1958–1960 eds. Tokyo: Ōkurashō Insatsu Kyoku, 1958–1960.

———. *Kokumin Shotoku Hakusho (White Paper on National Income)*. 1960 and 1961 eds. Tokyo: Ōkurashō Insatsu Kyoku, 1960, 1961.

———. (Keizai Kikaku Chō Chōsa Kyoku), ed. *Kokumin Keizai Keisan Nenpō (Accounting Yearbook of the National People's Economy)*. 1982 ed. Tokyo: Ōkurashō Insatsu Kyoku, 1982.

———. (Keizai Kikaku Chō Chōsa Kyoku), ed. *Chiiki Keizai Kōzō no Shin Tenkai (The New Development of Regional Economic Structure)*. Tokyo: Ōkurashō Insatsu Kyoku, 1984.

Eda Saburō. *Nihon no Shakaishugi (Japanese Socialism)*. Tokyo: Nihon Hyōron Sha, 1967.

———. "Shakai Shugi no Atarashii Vision" ("A New Vision of Socialism"). *Economisuto* 40, no. 41 (October 9, 1962), pp. 32–40.

Eda Saburō and Shinohara Hajime. "Kakushin Seitō to shite no Hansei" (Reflections of a Progressive Party"). *Sekai* 10, no. 178 (October 1960), pp. 79–86.

Einaudi, Mario, and François Goguel. *Christian Democracy in Italy and France*. Notre Dame: University of Notre Dame Press, 1952.

Esping-Anderson, Gosta. *Politics Against Markets: The Social Democratic Road to Power*. Princeton: Princeton University Press, 1985.

Evans, Peter B., Dietrich Rueschemeyer, and Theda Skocpol, eds. *Bringing the State Back In*. Cambridge: Cambridge University Press, 1985.

Far Eastern Economic Review. *Asia 1987 Yearbook*. Hong Kong: Far Eastern Economic Review, 1987.

Fenno, Richard F., Jr. *Home Style: House Members in Their Districts*. Boston: Little, Brown, 1978.

Fisher, Larry Warren. "The Lockheed Affair: A Phenomenon of Japanese Politics." Ph.D. diss., University of Colorado, Boulder, 1980.

Flanagan, Scott C., and Bradley M. Richardson. *Japanese Electoral Behavior: Social Cleavage, Social Networks, and Partisanship*. London: Sage Professional Papers, 1977.

Flora, Peter, and A. J. Heidenheimer, eds. *The Development of Welfare States in Europe and America*. New Brunswick, N.J.: Transaction Books, 1981.

Fodella, Gianni, ed. *Japan's Economy in a Comparative Perspective*. Tenterden, Kent: Paul Norbury Publications, 1983.

Fogarty, Michael P. *Christian Democracy in Western Europe, 1820–1953*. London: Routledge and Kegan Paul, 1957.

Fujimoto Atsushi. *Ōsaka Fu no Rekishi (The History of Osaka)*. Tokyo: Yamakawa Shuppan Sha, 1980.

Fujita Hiroaki. *Nihon no Senkyokusei (Japan's Electoral District System)*. Tokyo: Tōyō Keizai Shinpō Sha, 1978.

Fujiyama Aiichirō. *Seiji, Waga Michi: Fujiyama Aiichirō Kaikoroku (Politics, My Life: The Memoirs of Fujiyama Aiichirō)*. Tokyo: Asahi Shimbun Sha, 1976.

Fukui, Haruhiro. "Economic Planning in Postwar Japan." *Asian Survey* 12, no. 4 (April 1972), pp. 327–48.

———. *Party in Power: The Japanese Liberal Democrats and Policy-making*. Berkeley and Los Angeles: University of California Press, 1970.

Fukuoka Masayuki. "Naze tsuyoi Kakuei Seiji" ("Why Kakuei's Politics is Strong"). *Chūō Kōron* 98, no. 1 (January 1983), pp. 112–22.

———. *Gendai Nihon no Seitō Seiji (Party Politics in Modern Japan)*. Tokyo: Tōyō Keizai Shinpō Sha, 1986.

———. *Nihon Seiji no Fūdo (The Topography of Japanese Politics)*. Tokyo: Gakuyō Shobō, 1985.

Furber, Holden, ed. *The Correspondence of Edmund Burke*, Vol. 5. London: Cambridge University Press, 1965.

Garon, Sheldon. "Parties, Bureaucrats, and Labor Policy in Prewar Japan, 1918–1931." Ph.D. diss., Yale University, 1981.

Gekkan Shakaitō Henshū Bu, ed. *Nihon Shakaitō no San Jyū Nen. (Thirty Years of the Japan Socialist Party)*. Tokyo: Nihon Shakaitō Chūō Honbu Kikanshi Kyoku, 1978.

Gerschenkron, Alexander. *Bread and Democracy in Germany*. Berkeley: University of California Press, 1943.

———. *Economic Backwardness in Historical Perspective*. Cambridge, Mass.: Harvard University Press, 1960.

Gluck, Carol. *Japan's Modern Myths: Ideology in the Late Meiji Period*. Princeton: Princeton University Press, 1985.

Goldthorpe, John H., ed. *Order and Conflict in Contemporary Capitalism*. Oxford: Clarendon Press, 1984.

Gordon, Andrew. *The Evolution of Labor Relations in Japan: Heavy Industry, 1853–1955*. Cambridge: Harvard University Council on East Asian Studies, 1985.

Gotō Mitsuyuki. *Nihon Shakaitō (Japan's Socialist Party)*. Tokyo: Rōdō Daigaku, 1973.

Gotō Motō, Uchida Kenzō, and Ishikawa Masumi. *Sengo Hoshu Seiji no Kiseki (The Course of Postwar Conservative Politics)*. Tokyo: Iwanami Shoten, 1982.

Gotō Teruo. "Politics, Power, and Personalities in the Prefectural Government of Kyoto: A Study of Japanese Local Politics." Ph.D. diss., University of California 1983.

Gourevitch, Peter. "International Trade, Domestic Coalitions, and Liberty: Comparative Responses to the Crisis of 1873–1895." *Journal of Interdisciplinary History* 8 (1977), pp. 281–313.

———. *Paris and the Provinces: The Politics of Local Government Reform in France*. Berkeley: University of California Press, 1980.

———. *Politics in Hard Times: Comparative Responses to International Economic Crises*. Ithaca: Cornell University Press, 1986.

Government Section, GHQ, SCAP. *The Political Reorientation of Japan*. 2 vols. Washington, D.C.: Government Printing Office, 1949.

Green, W., and D. Clough. *Regional Problems and Policies*. London: Holt, Rinehart, and Winston, 1982.

Gresser, Julian. *Partners in Prosperity: Strategic Industries for the U.S. and Japan*. New York: McGraw Hill, 1984.

Grew, Raymond, ed. *Crises of Political Development in Europe and the United States*. Princeton: Princeton University Press, 1978.

Groth, A., and L. L. Wade, eds. *Comparative Resource Allocation*. Beverley Hills and Longdon: Sage Publications, 1984.

Guillain, Robert. "The Resurgence of Military Elements in Japan," *Pacific Affairs* (September 1952), pp. 211–25.

Hadley, Eleanor M. *Antitrust in Japan*. Princeton: Princeton University Press, 1970.

Hall, John Whitney. *Government and Local Power in Japan, 500 to 1700: A Study Based on Bizen Province*. Princeton: Princeton University Press, 1966.

Hall, Peter. *Governing the Economy: The Politics of State Intervention in Britain and France*. Oxford: Oxford University Pess, 1986.

Hallett, Graham. *Housing and Land Policies in West Germany and Britain*. London: Macmillan, 1977.

Hanayama Yuzuru. *Gendai no Tochi Shinwa (The Modern Land Myth)*. Tokyo: Asahi Shimbun Sha, 1981.

———. *Land Markets and Land Policy in a Metropolitan Area*. Boston: Oelgeschlager, Gunn, & Hain, 1986.

Harari, Ehud. *The Politics of Labor Legislation in Japan*. Berkeley: University of California Press, 1973.

Hasegawa Hiroshi. *Kome Kokka Kokusho (The Black Book of the Rice Nation)*. Tokyo: Asahi Shimbun Sha, 1984.

Hatakeyama Takeshi. *Habatsu no Uchimaku (The Inside Story of Factions)*. Tokyo: Rippū Shobō, 1976.

———. "Ikeda Sengokko Naikaku ga unda Datsu Ideologii" ("The Counter Ideology which Ikeda's Cabinet of Children Born After the War Created"). *Asahi Journal* (October 1981), pp. 84–88.

Hatoyama Ichirō. *Gaiyū Nikki, Sekai no Kao (A Diary of Traveling Abroad: The Face of the World)*. Tokyo: Chūō Kōron Sha, 1938.

———. *Hatoyama Ichirō Kaikoroku (The Memoirs of Hatoyama Ichirō)* Tokyo: Bungei Shunjū, 1957.

Havens, Thomas R. H. *Farm and Nation in Modern Japan: Agrarian Nationalism, 1870–1940*. Princeton: Princeton University Press, 1974.

———. *Fire Across The Sea*. Princeton: Princeton University Press, 1987.

Hayakawa Kazuo. *Tochi Mondai no Seiji Keizai Gaku (The Political Economy of Land Problems)*. Tokyo: Tōyō Keizai Shinpō Sha, 1977.

Hayami Yūjirō and Honma Masayoshi. *Kokusai Hikaku kara mita Ni-*

hon Nōgyō no Hogo Suijun (The Agricultural Protection Level of Japan in International Comparative Perspective). Tokyo: Seisaku Kōsō Forum, November 1983.

Hayasaka Shigezō. "Tanaka Kakuei Mumei no Jyū Nen" ("Tanaka Kakuei's Ten Years Without a Name"). *Chūō Kōron* (November 1986).

———. *Hayasaka Shigezō no Tanaka Kakuei Kaisōroku* (Hayasaka Shigezō's Memoirs of Tanaka Kakuei). Tokyo: Shogakkan, 1987.

Hayashi Katsuya. *Nihon Gunji Gijutsu Shi (The History of Japanese Militaristic Technology).* Tokyo: Aoki Shoten, 1957.

Hayashi Shigeru and Tsuji Kiyoaki. *Nihon Naikaku Shiroku (The Historical Record of Japanese Cabinet).* Tokyo: Daiichi Hōki Shuppan, 1981.

Hayashi Shūji. *Ryūtsū Kakumei (Distribution Revolution).* Tokyo: Chūō Kōron Sha, 1962.

Heclo, Hugh. *Modern Social Politics in Britain and Sweden: From Relief to Income Maintenance.* New Haven: Yale University Press, 1974.

Hellman, Donald. *Japanese Domestic Politics and Foreign Policy.* Berkeley: University of California Press, 1969.

Hemmi Kenzō. *Nōgyō (Agriculture).* Tokyo: Chikuma Shobō, 1970.

Hermann, Charles F., ed. *International Crisis: Insights from Behavioral Research.* New York: The Free Press, 1972.

Hewes, Laurence I., Jr. *Japan—Land and Men: An Account of the Japanese Land Reform Program, 1945–1951.*. Ames, Iowa: Iowa State College Press, 1955.

Hibbs, Douglas A., Jr. "Political Parties and Macroeconomic Policy." *American Political Science Review* 71 (1975), pp. 1467–87.

Hiramatsu Morihiko. *Technopolis e no Chōsen (The Challenge toward Technopolis).* Tokyo: Nihon Keizai Shimbun Sha, 1983.

Hirasawa Masao. *Nihon Kanryō Chizu (A Map of Japan's Bureaucrats.)* 2 vols. Tokyo: Kokusai Shōgyō Shuppan Kabushiki Kaisha, 1976.

Hironaka Toshio. "Keisatsu Minshuka wa Zenmenteki ni Hōkai suru" ("Police Democratization will be completely destroyed"). *Chūō Kōron* (December 1958), pp. 64–74.

Hirose Michisada. *Hojokin to Seikentō, (Subsidies and the Party in Power).* Tokyo: Asahi Shimbun Sha, 1981.

———. "Rieki Haibun System wa Henka shita ka?" ("Has the Resource Allocation System Changed?"). *Sekai,* no. 448 (March 1983), pp. 105–13.

Hiroshima Shi Shichō Shitsu, ed. *Nichibei no Chihō Jichi Toshi Mondai (Urban and Regional Problems of the United States and Japan).* Tokyo: Gyōsei, 1983.

Hochswender, Karl. "The Politics of Civil Service Reform in West Germany." Ph.D. diss., Yale University, 1962.

Hoffman, Stanley. *Le Mouvement Poujade.* Paris: Colin, Cahiers de la Fondation Nationale des Sciences Politiques, no. 81, 1956.

Hofheinz, Roy, Jr., and Kent E. Calder. *The Eastasia Edge.* New York: Basic Books, 1982.

Honda Yasuharu. "Hanabanashiki Ichizoku: Miki Takeo Ikka" ("The Magnificent Family: The Miki Takeo Household"). *Bungei Shunjū* 53, no. 2 (January 1975), pp. 296–310.

Horie Masanori. "Miike Sōgi no Kyōkun" ("Lesson of the Miike Dispute"). *Chūō Kōron* 75, no. 6 (1960), pp. 140–52.

Horikoshi Teizō, ed. *Keizai Dantai Jyū Nen Shi (Ten Year History of the Federation of Economic Organizations).* Vol. 2. Tokyo: Keizai Dantai Rengōkai, 1963.

Hoston, Germaine A. *Marxism and the Crisis of Development in Prewar Japan.* Princeton: Princeton University Press, 1986.

Houdaille Industries, Inc. Petition to the President of the United States through the Office of the United States Special Trade Representative for the Exercise of Presidential Discretion, unpublished.

Hrebenar, Ronald J., ed. *The Japanese Party System: From One Party Rule to Coalition Government.* Boulder, Colo.: Westview, 1986.

Huntington, Samuel P. *American Politics: The Promise of Disharmony.* Cambridge, Mass.: Harvard University Press, 1981.

———. *Political Order in Changing Societies.* New Haven: Yale University Press, 1968.

Huntington, Samuel P., and Joan M. Nelson. *No Easy Choice: Political Participation in Developing Countries.* Cambridge, Mass.: Harvard University Press, 1976.

Ichikawa Fusae and Miki Takeo. "Kinken Seiji kara no Dasshutsu" ("Escape from Money Politics"). *Asahi Journal* 16, no. 3 (August 9, 1974), pp. 4–11.

Ichiki Hiroshi. "Chihō Zaisei no Hatan no Genin" ("The Causes of Bankruptcy of Local Finance"). *Chūō Kōron* 69, no. 11 (November 1954), pp. 72–78.

Ike, Nobutaka. "Taxation and Landownership in the Westernization of Japan." *Journal of Economic History* 7 (November 1947).

———. *A Theory of Japanese Democracy.* Boulder, Colo.: Westview, 1980.

Ikeda Hayato. "Sekkyoku Zaisei wa Infure Zaisei de wa nai" ("Positive Finance is not Inflationary Finance"). *Chūō Kōron* 72, no. 3 (March 1957), pp. 101–5.

Ikematsu Fumio and Miki Takeo. "Shin Hoshushugi no Seishin" ("The Spirit of New Conservatism"). *Economisuto* (February 1960), pp. 50–54.

Imamura Naraomi. *Hojokin to Nōgyō Nōson (Subsidies and the Agricultural Sector and Agricultural Villages).* Tokyo: Ie no Hikari Kyōkai, 1978.

Inoguchi Takashi. *Nihon Seiji Keizai no Kōzu (Contemporary Japanese Political Economy).* Tokyo: Tōyō Keizai Shinpō Sha, 1983.

Inoguchi Takashi. *Kokusai Kankei no Seiji Keizai Gaku (The Political Economy of International Relations)*. Tokyo: Tokyo Daigaku Shuppan Kai, 1985.

Inoguchi Takashi and Iwai Tomoaki. *Zoku Giin no Kenkyū (Research on "Tribe" Dietmen)*. Tokyo: Nihon Keizai Shimbun Sha, 1987.

Inoki Masamichi. *Hyōden: Yoshida Shigeru (A Critical Biography: Yoshida Shigeru)*. 2 vols. Tokyo: Yomiuri Shimbun Sha, 1978, 1980.

———. *Gendai Nihon no Seiji (Contemporary Japanese Politics)*. Tokyo: Ushio Shuppan, 1969.

Institut national de la statistique et des études de l' économie, des finances, et de la privatisation, *Annuaire Statistique de la France*, various issues.

International Bank for Reconstruction and Development, *Commodity Trade and Price Trends*. Baltimore: Johns Hopkins University Press, 1986.

International Monetary Fund. *Government Financial Yearbook*, 1973–1987 eds. Washington, D.C.: International Monetary Fund, 1973–1987.

Irving, R. E. M. *The Christian Democratic Parties of Western Europe*. London: Allen and Unwin, 1979.

Iryō Hoken Seido Kenkyū Kai (Medical Insurance System Research Council), ed. *Me de Miru Iryō Hoken Hakusho (The Medical Insurance White Paper, graphic ed)*. Tokyo: Kyōkei Publishing, 1985.

Ishi Hiromitsu. "An Overview of Postwar Tax Policies in Japan." *Hitotsubashi Journal of Economics* 23, no. 2 (February 1983), pp. 27–30.

Ishida Hirohide, Ota Kaoru, and Hayakawa Masaru. "Miike no Rōdō Mondai" *(The Miike Labour Problem)*. *Chūo Kōron* 75, no. 9 (September 1960), pp. 110–21.

Ishida Hirohide. "Hoshu Seitō no Vision" ("Vision of a Conservative Party"). *Chūō Kōron* 78, no. 1 (January 1963), pp. 88–97.

———. *Watakushi no Seikai Shōwa Shi (My History of the Shōwa Political World)*. Tokyo: Tōyō Keizai Shinpō Sha, 1986.

Ishida Yorifusa. *Nihon Kindai Toshi Keikaku no Hyaku Nen (One Hundred Years of Modern Japanese City Planning)*. Tokyo: Jichitai Kenkyū Sha, 1987.

Ishikawa Hideo. "Nōkyō Mittsu no Kao" ("The Three Faces of the Agricultural Cooperatives"). *Chūō Kōron* 88, no. 5 (May 1973).

Ishikawa Masumi. *Data Sengo Seiji Shi (A Data History of Postwar Politics)*. Tokyo: Iwanami Shoten, 1984.

———. *Sengo Seiji Kōzō Shi (A History of Postwar Political Structure)*. Tokyo: Hyōron Sha, 1978.

Itō Hiroshi. *Japanese Politics: An Inside View*. Ithaca: Cornell University Press, 1983.

Itō Masataka. "Minobe Ryōkichi o meguru Yatō no Jijō." ("The Circumstances of the Opposition Party Surrounding Minobe Ryōkichi"). *Chūō Kōron* 90, no. 4 (April 1975), pp. 236–41.

Itō Masaya. *Ikeda Hayato to Sono Jidai (Ikeda Hayato and His Era).* Tokyo: Asahi Shimbun Sha, 1985.

———. *Jimintō Sengoku Shi (The Civil War in the LDP).* 2 vols. Tokyo: Asahi Sonorama, 1982, 1983.

———. *Shin Jimintō Sengoku Shi (The New Civil War History of the Liberal Democratic Party).* Tokyo: Asahi Sonorama, 1983.

Itō Mitsuharu. *Hoshu to Kakushin no Nihonteki Kōzō (The Japanese-Style Structure of Conservatives and Progressives).* Tokyo: Chikuma Shobō, 1970.

Jain, Shail. *Size Distribution of Income.* Washington, D.C.: World Bank, 1975.

Jansen, Marius B. "From Hatoyama to Hatoyama," *Far Eastern Review* 14, no. 1 (November 1954), pp. 65–79.

———. *Sakamoto Ryōma and the Meiji Restoration.* Princeton: Princeton University Press, 1961.

Jansen, Marius B., and Gilbert Rozman, eds. *Japan in Transition: From Tokugawa to Meiji.* Princeton: Princeton University Press, 1986.

Japan Defense Agency. *The Defense of Japan 1984.* Tokyo: Japan Times, 1984.

Japan Export Trade Organization. *Japanese Trade Incentives.* No date.

Japanese Government Social Services Agency. *Outline of Social Insurance in Japan 1984.* Tokyo: Japan International Corporation of Welfare Services, 1985.

Japan Institute for Social and Economic Affairs. *Japan: An International Comparison,* 1982–1986 eds. Tokyo: Japan Institute for Social and Economic Affairs, 1983–1987.

Japan Labor Bulletin, various issues.

Japan Small Business Corporation. *Outline of Small and Medium-Scale Enterprise Policies of the Japanese Government.* Tokyo: Small and Medium Enterprise Agency, 1983.

Jiji Tsūshin Sha, ed. *Sengo Nihon no Seitō to Naikaku: Jiji Seron Chōsa ni yoru Bunseki (Postwar Japanese Parties and Cabinets: Analysis from Jiji News Agency Public Opinion Polls).* Tokyo: Jiji Tsūshin Sha, 1981.

Jin Ikkō. *Jichi Kanryō (Local Affairs Bureaucrats).* Tokyo: Kōdansha, 1986.

———. *Ōkura Kanryō.* Tokyo: Kōdansha, 1982.

Johnson, Chalmers. "Japan: Who Governs? An Essay on Official Bureaucracy." *The Journal of Japanese Studies* 2, no. 1 (Autumn 1975), pp. 1–28.

———. *Conspiracy at Matsukawa.* Berkeley: University of California Press, 1972.

Johnson, Chalmers. *Japan's Public Policy Companies*. Washington, D.C.: American Enterprise Institute for Public Policy Research, 1978.

———. *MITI and the Japanese Miracle*. Stanford: Stanford University Press, 1982.

———. *MITI, MPT, and the Telecom Wars: How Japan Makes Policy for High Technology*. Berkeley: BRIE Working Paper no. 21, September 1986.

———. "Reflections on the Dilemma of Japanese Defense," *Asian Survey* 26, no. 5 (May 1986), pp. 557–72.

———. "Tanaka Kakuei, Structural Corruption, and the Advent of Machine Politics in Japan," *The Journal of Japanese Studies* 12, no. 1 (Winter 1986), pp. 1–28.

Johnson, R. W. *The Long March of the French Left*. New York: St. Martin's, 1981.

Juristo (Jurist). *Nihon no Rippō (Japan's Legislation)*, no. 805 (Winter 1984).

———. *Nihon no Seitō (Japan's Political Parties)*, no. 35 (Summer 1984).

———. *Senkyo (Elections)*, no. 38 (Spring 1985).

———. *Tenkanki no Tochi Mondai (Urban Problems in a Period of Transition)*, no. 34 (Spring 1984).

Kabashima Ikuo. "Supportive Participation with Economic Growth: The Case of Japan," *World Politics* 36, no. 3 (April 1984), pp. 309–38.

Kabashima Ikuo and Jeffrey Broadbent. "Referent Pluralism: Mass Media and Politics in Japan." *Journal of Japanese Studies* 12, no. 2 (Summer 1986), pp. 329–62.

Kamata Satoshi. *Nihon no Heiki Kōjō* (Defense Factories in Japan). Tokyo: Ushio Shobō, 1979.

Kaminogō Toshiaki. "Kakushin Jichitai no Eikō to Hisan" ("The Triumph and the Tragedy of Progressive Local Government"). *Bungei Shunjū* 53, no. 3 (March 1975), pp. 92–124.

Kanbayashi Teijirō and Mure Sanae. *Nihon Sangyō no Hatten to Chūshō Kigyō Mondai (The Development of Japanese Industry and Problems of Small Business)*. Tokyo: Tokoro Shoten, 1984.

Katayama Naikaku Kiroku Kankōkai, ed. *Katayama Naikaku: Katayama Tetsu to Sengo no Seiji (The Katayama Cabinet: Katayama Tetsu and Postwar Politics)*. Tokyo: Katayama Naikaku Kankōkai, 1980.

Katō Ichirō and Sakamoto Kusuhiko, eds. *Nihon Nōsei no Tenkai Katei (The Development of Japanese Agricultural Administration)*. Tokyo: Tokyo Daigaku Shuppan Kai, 1967.

Katsumata Seiichi, ed. *Nihon Shakaitō Kōryō Bunken Shū (Collected Materials concerning Resolutions of the Japanese Socialist Party)*. Tokyo: Nihon Shakaitō Chūō Honbu Kikan Shi Kyoku, 1981.

Katznelson, Ira, and Aristide R. Zolberg. *Working Class Formation:*

Nineteenth-Century Patterns in Western Europe and the United States. Princeton: Princeton University Press, 1986.

Kawai Etsuzō. *Nihon no Nōgyō to Nōmin (Japan's Agriculture and Farmers)*. Tokyo: Iwanami Shoten, 1956.

Kawano Kōnosuke. *Fukuda Takeo*. Tokyo: Nihon Jihō Sha, 1966.

Kawashima Masahide, "Kakushin Jichitai to Shakai Fukushi" ("Progressive Local Governments and Social Welfare"). *Sekai* 10, no. 323 (1972), pp. 113–26.

Keizai Dantai Rengōkai, *Keidanren Geppō* (Keidanren Monthly).

———, ed. *Keizai Dantai Rengōkai San Jyū Nen Shi (A Thirty-Year History of the Federation of Economic Organizations)*. Tokyo: Nihon Keieishi Kenkyū Jo, 1978.

———. Problems in the Current Taxation System and Proposals for Future Direction of Policy. Tokyo: Keidanren, September 25, 1984. Mimeo.

Keizai Dōyūkai, ed. *Keizai Dōyūkai San Jyū Nen Shi (Thirty Year History of the Council on Economic Development)*. Tokyo: Keizai Dōyūkai, 1976.

Kelly, William W. *Deference and Defiance in Nineteenth-Century Japan*. Princeton: Princeton University Press, 1985.

Kennan, George F. *Memoirs, 1925–1950*. Boston: Little, Brown, 1967.

Keohane, Robert O., and Joseph S. Nye. *Power and Interdependence: World Politics in Transition*. Boston: Little, Brown, 1977.

Key, V. O., Jr. *Southern Politics*. New York: Vintage Books, 1949.

Kido Mataichi, ed. *Gendai Jyānarizumu: Hōsō (Modern Journalism: Broadcasting)*. Tokyo: Jiji Tsūshin Sha, 1973.

———, ed. *Gendai Jyānarizumu: Shimbun (Modern Journalism: Newspapers)*. Tokyo: Jiji Tsūshin Sha, 1973.

Kikuiri Ryūsuke. "Jimintō ga Yatō ni naru Hi" ("The Day the LDP Becomes an Opposition Party"), *Bungei Shunjū* 51, no. 6 (April 1973), pp. 162–74.

Kil Soong Hoom. "The Dodge Line and the Japanese Conservative Party." Ph.D. diss., University of Michigan, 1977.

Kimura Kihachirō. "Watakushitachi no Seikatsu to Yosan" ("Our Life and the Budget") *Sekai* 3, no. 111 (March 1960), pp. 78–91.

Kimura Toshio. *Nihon Sangyō Ron (A Theory of Japanese Industry)*. Kyoto: Hōritsu Bunka Sha, 1984.

Kingdon, John W. *Agendas, Alternatives, and Public Policies*. Boston: Little, Brown, 1984.

Kinoshita Takeshi. *Katayama Naikaku Shi Ron (A Historical Essay on the Katayama Cabinet)*. Tokyo: Hōritsu Bunka Sha, 1982.

Kirk, Russell, ed. *The Conservative Reader*. New York: Penguin Books, 1982.

Kishi Nobusuke. *Kishi Nobusuke Kaikoroku: Hoshu Gōdō to Ampo*

Kaitei (The Memoirs of Kishi Nobusuke: The Conservative Merger and the Security Treaty Revision). Tokyo: Kōsaidō, 1983.

———. *Waga Seishun: Oitachi no Ki, Omoide no Ki (My Youth: the Diary of My Childhood and My Time of Memories)*. Tokyo: Kōsaidō, 1983.

Kishi Nobusuke, Itō Takashi, and Yazawa Kazuo. *Kishi Nobusuke no Kaisō (The Memoirs of Kishi Nobusuke)*. Tokyo: Bungei Shunjū, 1981.

"Kishi Rosen no Fukkatsu" ("Reappearance of the Kishi Line"). *Sekai*, no. 237 (August 1965), pp. 157–62.

Kishimoto Kōichi. *Nihon no Gikai Seiji (Japan's Legislative Politics)*. Tokyo: Gyōsei Mondai Kenkyū Jo Shuppan Kyoku, 1983.

Kishiro Yasuyuki. *Jimintō Zeisei Chōsa Kai (The* LDP Tax Policy Research Committee). Tokyo: Tōyō Keizai Shinpō Sha, 1985.

Kissinger, Henry. *White House Years*. Boston: Little Brown, 1979.

Kiuchi Nobutane. "A Japanese Viewpoint on 'Reconsider Japan.' " *The Oriental Economist* 33, no. 655 (May 1965), pp. 257–61.

Kiuchi Takao. *Hoshu Honryū no Hatan (The Ruin of the Conservative Mainstream)*. Tokyo: Fumin Kyōkai, 1985.

Kobayashi Naoki, Shinohara Hajime, and Soma Masao. *Senkyo (Elections)*. Tokyo: Iwanami Shoten, 1960.

Kobayashi Yoshiaki. *Keiryō Seijigaku (Quantitative Political Science)*. Tokyo: Seibundō, 1985.

Koblik, Steven, ed. *Sweden's Development from Poverty to Affluence, 1750–1970*. Minneapolis: University of Minnesota Press, 1975.

Kokkai Binran (Diet Handbook). Tokyo: Nihon Seikei Shinbunsha, annually or semiannually.

Kokkai Nenkan Hakkō Kai, ed. *Kokkai Nenkan*, 1961 ed. Tokyo: Kokkai Nenkan Hakkō Kai, 1961.

"Kokkai ni miru Fukyō Ronsō" ("Conflict and Harmony Seen in the Diet"). *Sekai*, no. 239 (October 1965), pp. 107–10.

Kokumin Seikatsu Center, ed. *Zusetsu: Kurashi no Kokusai Hikaku. (An Illustrated International Comparison of Living Standards)*. Tokyo: Kokumin Seikatsu Center, 1985.

Kōmei Senkyo Renmei, ed. *Shūgiin Senkyo no Jisseki: Dai Ikkai—Dai Sanjyū Kai (Results of House of Representatives Elections: From the First Election to the Thirtieth Election)*. Tokyo: Kōmei Senkyo Renmei, 1967.

Komiya Ryūtarō, Okuno Masahiro, and Suzumura Kōtarō, eds. *Nihon no Sangyō Seisaku (Japanese Industrial Policy)*. Tokyo: Tokyo Daigaku Shuppan Kai, 1985.

Kon Hidemi. *Yoshida Shigeru*. Tokyo: Kōdansha, 1967.

"Konmei Tsuzukeru Ni Dai Seitō." ("Two Large Parties, Thrown into Confusion"). *Ekonomisuto* (February 1962), pp. 4–15.

Kōnosu Kenji. *What will be the Agricultural Policies of Japan in the 1980s?* Tokyo: Japan FAO Association, 1982.

Kōsaka Masataka, ed. *Kōdo Sangyō Kokka no Rieki Seiji Katei to Seisaku: Nippon. (Interest Group Politics and Public Policy in Industrialized States: The Case of Japan).* Tokyo: Toyota Zaidan Jōsei Kenkyū Hōkoku Sho, April 1981.

Kosugi Takashi. "Minobe Ryōkichi no Shippai" ("The Fail of Monobe Ryōkichi"). *Bungei Shunjū* 56, no. 10 (October 1978), pp. 122–45.

Koyama Hirotake. *Nihon Gunji Kōgyō no Shiteki Bunseki (A Historical Analysis of Japan's Defense Industries).* Tokyo: Ochanomizu Shobō, 1972.

Koyama Ken and Shimizu Shinzō. *Nihon Shakaitō Shi (History of Japan's Socialist Party).* Tokyo: Haga Shoten, 1965.

Krasner, Stephen D. "Approaches to the State: Alternative Conceptions and Historical Dynamics." *Comparative Politics* 16, no. 2 (January 1984), 223–46.

Krauss, Ellis S. "Opposition in Power: The Development and Maintenance of Leftist Government in Kyoto Prefecture." In *Political Opposition and Local Politics in Japan,* edited by Kurt Steiner, Ellis S. Krauss, and Scott C. Flanagan. Princeton: Princeton University Press, 1980.

———"The Urban Strategy and Policy of the Japanese Communist Party: *Kyoto," Studies in Comparative Communism* 12, no. 4 (Winter 1979), pp. 322–50.

Krauss, Ellis S., Thomas P. Rohlen, and Patricia G. Steinhoff, eds. *Conflict in Japan.* Honolulu: University of Hawaii Press, 1984.

Krippendorf, Ekkhart. *The Role of the United States in the Reconstruction of Italy and West Germany.* Berlin: Zentrale Universitaetsdruckerei der FU, 1981.

Kurian, George Thomas. *The Book of World Rankings.* New York: New American Library, 1979.

Kurokawa Nobuyuki. "Skyrocketing Prices of Land Hit the Social Structure," *Japan Quarterly* 28, no. 2 (April–June 1981), pp. 206–216.

Kurumada Chiharu. *Gunji Kōgyō Ron (The Theory of Defense Industry).* Tokyo: Nihon Hyōron Sha, 1934.

Kusano Atsushi. *Nichibei Orange Kōshō (The U.S.-Japan Orange Negotiations).* Tokyo: Nihon Keizai Shimbun Sha, 1982.

Kusayanagi Daizō. *Nihon Kaitai (The Dissolution of Japan).* Tokyo: Gyōsei, 1985.

Kusuda Minoru. *Shushō Hisho Kan: Satō Sōri to no Jyū Nenkan (The Prime Minister's Private Secretary: Ten Years with Prime Minister Satō).* Tokyo: Bungei Shunjū, 1975.

Kyōgoku Junichi. *Nihon no Seiji (Japanese Politics).* Tokyo: Tokyo Daigaku Shuppan Kai, 1983.

Kyōgoku Junichi. *Nihonjin to Seiji (The Japanese and Politics)*. Tokyo: Tokyo Daigaku Shuppan Kai, 1986.

———. *Seiji Ishiki no Bunseki (The Analysis of Political Consciousness)*. Tokyo: Tokyo University Shuppan, 1969.

Kyōiku Sha, ed. *Kokudo Chō (The National Land Agency)*. Tokyo: Kyōiku Sha, 1981.

LaPalombara, Joseph. *Democracy Italian Style*. New Haven: Yale University Press, 1987.

———. *Interest Groups in Italian Politics*. Princeton: Princeton University Press, 1964.

Larmour, Peter J. *The French Radical Party in the 1930s*. Stanford: Stanford University Press, 1964.

Layton-Henry, Zig, ed. *Conservative Politics in Western Europe*. New York: St. Martin's, 1982.

Leichter, Howard M. *A Comparative Approach to Policy Analysis: Health Care Policy in Four Nations*. Cambridge: Cambridge University Press, 1979.

Lewis, W. Arthur. *Politics in West Africa*. London: Allen and Unwin, 1965.

Liberal Democratic Party (Jiyū Minshutō), ed. "Sōsenkyo no Igi to Shin Seisaku no Gaiyō." ("The Significance of the General Election and an Outline of the New Policy.") In *Kokkai Nenkan*, pp. 657–61. Tokyo: Kokkai Nenkan Hakkō Kai, 1961.

———, ed. *Waga Tō no Kihon Hōshin (The Basic Resolutions of Our Party)*. Tokyo: Jiyū Minshutō Kōhō Iinkai, 1975.

———. *Ishibashi Naikaku no Shisei Dai Ichigoe (The First Words of the Ishibashi Cabinet)*. Tokyo: Jiyū Minshutō, 1957.

———, ed. *Jiyū Minshutō: Ni Jyū Nen no Ayumi (The Liberal Democratic Party: A Twenty Year Course)*. Tokyo: Jiyū Minshutō, 1975.

———. *Seisaku Geppō* (Policy Monthly), various issues.

Lijphart, Arend. "Comparative Politics and the Comparative Method." *American Political Science Review* 65, no. 3 (Sept. 1971), pp. 682–93.

———. *Democracies*. New Haven: Yale University Press, 1984.

Lipset, Seymour M., and Stein Rokkan, eds. *Party Systems and Voter Alignments: Cross-National Perspectives*. New York: Free Press, 1967.

Lockwood, William W., ed. *The State and Economic Enterprise in Japan*. Princeton: Princeton University Press, 1965.

Long Term Credit Bank of Japan. *Japan's High Technology Industries*. Tokyo: The Long-Term Credit Bank of Japan, May 1983.

Lowi, Theodore J. "American Business, Public Policy, Case Studies, and Political Theory." *World Politics* 16, no. 4 (July 1964).

———. *The End of Liberalism: The Second Republic of the United States*. 2d ed. New York: W. W. Norton, 1979.

———. "Four Systems of Policy, Politics, and Choice." *Public Administration Review* 32, no. 4 (July–August 1972), pp. 298–310.

Lynch, John. *Toward an Orderly Market.* Tokyo: Sophia University Press, 1968.

MacDougall, Terry E., ed. *Political Leadership in Contemporary Japan.* Ann Arbor: University of Michigan Center for Japanese Studies, 1982.

———. "Political Opposition and Local Government in Japan: The Significance of Emerging Progressive Local Leadership." Ph.D. diss., Yale University, 1975.

Machin, Howard, and Vincent Wright. "Why Mitterand Won: The French Presidential Elections of April–May, 1981." *West European Politics* 5, no. 1 (January 1982).

Macmillan, Harold. *The Middle Way.* London: St. Martin's, 1966.

Maeshiba Kakuzō, Hayashi Saburō, Royama Yoshio, and Obata Misao. "Gunshuku wa Yume ka?" ("Is Arms Reduction a Dream?"). *Sekai* 8, no. 140 (1957), pp. 66–85.

Mayhew, David. *The Electoral Connection.* New Haven: Yale University Press, 1974.

Maier, Charles S. *Recasting Bourgeois Europe: Stabilization in France, Germany, and Italy in the Decade after World War I.* Princeton: Princeton University Press, 1975.

Mainichi Shimbun Henshū Bu, ed. *Nihon Jinbutsu Jiten (A Dictionary of Japanese Personalities).* Tokyo: Mainichi Shimbun Sha, 1952.

Mainichi Shimbun Sha, ed. *Seihen (The Political Incident).* Tokyo: Mainichi Shimbun Sha, 1975.

Maruyama Masao. The Ideology and Movement of Japanese Fascism. *The Japan Annual of Law and Politics,* no. 1 (1952), pp. 95–128.

Masaki Hisashi. *Nihon no Kabushiki Kaisha Kinyū (Japanese Corporate Finance).* Kyoto: Minerva Shobō, 1973.

Masujima Hiroshi. *Gendai Nihon no Seitō to Seijo (Party and Politics of Contemporary Japan).* Tokyo: Ōtsuki Shoten, 1966.

———. *Gendai Seiji to Taishū Undō (Contemporary Politics and Mass Movements).* Tokyo: Aoki Shoten, 1966.

Masumi Junnosuke. *Gendai Nihon no Seiji Taisei (The Modern Japanese Political System).* Tokyo: Iwanami Shoten, 1969.

———. *Gendai Seiji* (Contemporary Politics). 2 vols. Tokyo: Tokyo Daigaku Shuppan Kai, 1985.

———. *Nihon Seitō Shi Ron (A History of Japanese Political Parties).* 7 vols. Tokyo: Tokyo Daigaku Shuppan Kai, 1965, 1966, 1967, 1968, 1979, and 1980.

———. *Postwar Politics in Japan, 1945–1955.* Berkeley: University of California Center for Japanese Studies Japan Research Monograph no. 6, 1985.

Masumi Junnosuke. *Sengo Seiji (Postwar Politics)*. 2 vols. Tokyo: Tokyo Daigaku Shuppan Kai, 1983.

Matsumoto Takamasa. *Jika to Takuchi (Land Prices and Housing Land)*. Tokyo: Kyōiku Sha, 1978.

Matsushita Keiichi. "Chiiki Minshushugi no Kadai to Tenbō" ("Prospects for Regional Democracy"). *Shisō* 5, no. 443 (1961).

———. "Kakushin no Kakushin wa Ikani Kanō ka?" ("What Possibility Exists for the Reform of Progressivism"). *Asahi Journal* 10, no. 23 (June 1968), pp. 35–41.

———. *Sengo Minshushugi no Tenbō (The Future Perspectives of Postwar Democracy)*. Tokyo: Nihon Hyōron Sha, 1965.

Mayer, Arno J. *Dynamics of Counterrevolution in Europe, 1870–1956*. New York: Harper Torchbooks, 1971.

———. "The Lower Class as Historical Problem." *Journal of Modern History* 47, no. 3 (September 1975), pp. 409–36.

Mayhew, David. *The Electoral Connection*. New Haven: Yale University Press, 1974.

McArthur to DOS. Classified Memo, No. 4229, June 15, 1960.

McCraw, Thomas K., ed. *America Versus Japan*. Boston: Harvard Business School Press, 1986.

McFarland, H. Neill. *The Rush Hour of the Gods: A Study of the New Religious Movements in Japan*. New York: Macmillan, 1967.

McIntosh, Malcolm. *Japan Re-armed*. London: Francis Pinter Publishers, 1986.

Mendel, Douglas H., Jr. "Behind the 1960 Japanese Diet Election." *Asian Survey* 1, no. 1 (March 1961), pp. 3–12.

Merritt, Richard L., and Anna J. Merritt, eds. *Innovation in the Public Sector*. Beverly Hills: Sage Publications, 1985.

Meyer, Armin H. *Assignment Tokyo*. Indianapolis: Bobbs-Merrill, 1974.

Mikuni Ichirō. *Shōwa Shi Tanbō (Reporting on Shōwa History)*. Tokyo: Banchō Shobō, 1975.

Minichiello, Sharon. *Retreat from Reform: Patterns of Political Behavior in Interwar Japan*. Honolulu: University of Hawaii Press, 1984.

Ministry of Agriculture, Forestry, and Fisheries (Nōrin Suisan Shō). *Nōchi Kaikaku Yōran (Land Reform Handbook)*. Assorted issues.

———. *Nōrin Suisan Tōkei (Agricultural and Fishing Statistics)*. 1986 ed. Tokyo: Nōrin Tōkei Kyōkai, 1986.

———. *Nōchi Kaikaku Yōran (Land Reform Handbook)*, assorted issues. Ministry of Construction (Kensetsu Shō). *Kensetsu Hakusho (White Paper on Construction)*. Tokyo: Ōkurashō Insatsu Kyoku, 1986.

———. *Sensai Fukkō Shi (Chronicle of the Reconstruction of War-Damaged Areas)*. Vol. 1. Tokyo: Toshi Keikaku Kyōkai, 1959.

Ministry of Finance Budget Bureau (Ōkurashō Shukei Kyoku). *Kuni no*

Yosan (The National Budget), 1949–1986 eds. Tokyo: Ōkurashō Insatsu Kyoku, 1949–1986.

Ministry of Finance Budget Bureau and Financial Bureau (Ōkurashō Shukei Kyoku/Rizai Kyoku). *Yosan oyobi Zaisei Tōyūshi Keikaku no Setsumei (Explanation of the Budget and Fiscal Investment and Loans Program)*, 1983–1986 eds. Tokyo: Ōkurashō Insatsu Kyoku, 1983–1986.

Ministry of Finance Budget Bureau Research Section (Ōkurashō Shukei Kyoku Chōsa Ka). *Zaisei Tōkei (Financial Statistics)*, 1984–1986 eds. Tokyo: Ōkurashō Insatsu Kyoku, 1984–1986.

Ministry of Finance Financial History of Shōwa Editorial Office (Ōkurashō Shōwa Zaisei Shi Henshū Shitsu), ed. *Shōwa Zaisei Shi (A Financial History of Shōwa)*. Vol. 12. Tokyo: Tōyō Keizai Shinpōsha, 1976.

Ministry of Health and Welfare (Kōsei Shō). *Kōsei Hakusho (White Paper on Health and Welfare)*, 1961 and 1986 eds. Tokyo: Ōkurashō Insatsu Kyoku, 1961, 1986.

———. *Health and Welfare Services in Japan*. Tokyo: Japan International Corporation of Welfare Services, 1984.

Ministry of Health and Welfare Support Bureau (Kōseishō Engo Kyoku). *Hikiage nado Engo San Jyū Nen no Ayumi (The Thirty Year Course of Evacuation and Other Support)*. Tokyo: Kōseishō, 1977.

Ministry of International Trade and Industry (Tsūsan Sangyō Shō). *Technopolises*. Tokyo: Japan External Trade Organization, 1983.

———. *Tsūshō Seisaku no Hachi Jyū Nendai Vision (A Vision of Industrial Policy in the 1980s)*.

———, ed. *Tsūshō Hakusho (White Paper on International Trade)*, 1969 and 1986 eds. Tokyo: Ōkurashō Insatsu Kyoku, 1969, 1986.

Ministry of Labor Secretariat Statistical Information Division (Rōdō Shō Daijin Kanbō Tōkei Jōhō Bu). *Rōdō Tōkei Nenpō (Labor Statistics Annual)*. Tokyo: Rōdō Hōrei Kyōkai, 1984.

———, ed. *Rōdō Hakusho (Labor White Paper)*. Tokyo: Nihon Rōdō Kyōkai, 1985.

Ministry of Local Affairs (Jichishō), ed. *Chihō Zaisei Hakusho (White Paper on Regional Finance)*. Tokyo: Ōkurashō Insatsu Kyoku, 1986.

Mitsui Kōzan Kabushiki Kaisha, ed. *Miike Sōgi (The Miike Dispute)*. Tokyo: Nihon Keieisha Dantai Renmei, 1963.

Miyakawa Takayoshi, ed. *Seiji Handbook (Politics Handbook)*. 1979–1986 eds. Tokyo: Seiji Kōhō Center, 1979–1986.

Miyake Ichirō, Watanuki Jōji, Shima Kiyoshi, and Kabashima Ikuo. *Byōdō o Meguru Eriito to Taikō Eriito (Elites and Counter Elites who Bring about Equality)*. Tokyo: Sōbunsha, 1985.

Miyamoto Kenichi. "Kokudo Kaihatsu to Toshi Seisaku" ("National Land Development and Urban Policies"). *Sekai* no. 280 (March 1969), pp. 243–57.

Miyamoto Kenichi. "Ōgata Project to Shigen: Kokudo Kaihatsu ni Kakerumono" ("Large Projects and Nature: Some Elements Lacking in Urban Development Policy"). *Asahi Journal* (July 1968), pp. 84–85.

Miyazaki Yoshimasa. *Saishō: Satō Eisaku (Prime Minister: Satō Eisaku).* Tokyo: Shin Sangyō Keizai Kenkyūkai, 1980.

Miyazawa Kiichi. "Seiji no Genba kara no Shiron: Kisoteki Juyō no Settei ni Tsuite" ("A Sketch from the Real World of Politics: About Establishing the Fundamentally Important). *Chūō Kōron* 89, no. 7 (July 1974), pp. 72–89.

———. "Shakai Seigi no tame ni" ("Toward Social Justice"). *Jiyū Shinpo* (July 1973).

Mizoguchi Toshiyuki. "Sengo Nihon no Shotoku Bunpu to Shisan Bunpu." ("The Distribution of Income and Wealth in Postwar Japan"). *Keizai Kenkyū* 25, no. 3 (October 1974).

Mizukami Tatsuzō. "Proposals on the Rice Problem." *Keidanren Review,* no. 103 (February 1987), pp. 2–6.

Mochizuki, Mike. Managing and Influencing the Japanese Legislative Process: The Role of Parties and the National Diet. Ph.D. diss., Harvard University, 1982.

Moore, Joe. *Japanese Workers and the Struggle for Power, 1945–1947.* Madison: University of Wisconsin Press, 1983.

———. "Production Control: Workers' Control in Early Postwar Japan." *Bulletin of Concerned Asian Scholars* 17, no. 4 (October–December 1985), pp. 2–26.

Morley, James William, ed. *Dilemmas of Growth in Prewar Japan.* Princeton: Princeton University Press, 1971.

Morris, I. I. *Nationalism and the Right Wing in Japan.* Oxford: Oxford University Press, 1960.

Mosca, Gaetano. *The Ruling Class.* Edited by Arthur Livingston. Translated by Hanna D. Kahn. New York: McGraw-Hill, 1939.

Murakami Shigeyoshi. *Nihon Hyakunen no Shūkyō Haibutsu Kishaku kara Sōka Gakkai made (A Japanese Century of Religion: From the Meiji Suppression of Buddhism Movement to Sōka Gakkai).* Tokyo: Kōdansha, 1968.

Murakami Yasusuke. "Shin Chūkan Taishū Seiji no Jidai." ("The Age of New Middle Mass Politics.") *Chūō Kōron* 95, no. 15 (December 1980), pp. 202–29.

———. "The Age of New Middle Mass Politics: The Case of Japan." *Journal of Japanese Studies* 8, no. 1 (Winter 1982), pp. 29–72.

Murakawa Ichirō. *Nihon Hoshutō Shōshi (A Brief History of the Japanese Conservative Party).* Tokyo: Kyōiku Sha, 1979.

———. *Nihon no Seisaku Kettei Katei (Japan's Policymaking Process).* Tokyo: Gyōsei, 1985.

———. *Seisaku Kettei Katei (The Process of Policy Decisionmaking).* Tokyo: Kyōiku Sha, 1979.

Muramatsu Michio. "Center-Local Political Relations in Japan: A Lateral Competition Model." *Journal of Japanese Studies* 12, no. 2 (Summer 1986), pp. 303–27.

———. "The Impact of Economic Growth Policies on Local Politics in Japan." *Asian Survey* 15, no. 9 (September 1975), pp. 799–816.

———. *Sengo Nihon no Kanryōsei (The Bureaucratic System of Postwar Japan).* Tokyo: Tōyō Keizai Shinpō Sha, 1981.

Muramatsu Michio and Ellis Krauss. "Bureaucrats and Politicians in Policymaking: The Case of Japan." *American Political Science Review* 78, no. 1 (March 1984), pp. 126–46.

Murata Kiyoji. *An Industrial Geography of Japan.* London: Bell and Hyman, 1980.

NHK Hōsō Seron Chōsa Jo, ed. *Zusetsu: Sengo Seron Shi (A Postwar History of Public Opinion in Graphs).* Tokyo: Nihon Hōsō Shuppan Kyōkai, 1982.

Nagano Shigeo. *Waga Zaikai Jinsei (My Life in Zaikai).* Tokyo: Diamond Sha, 1982.

Nagasaki Yukio. "Nōmin no Rieki o wasureta Nōkyō" ("Agricultural Associations which Forgot the Concerns of Farmers"). *Economisuto* (March 1967), pp. 46–50.

Nagasu Katsuji, Narita Tomomi, and Shimizu Shinzō. "Nihon no Kōzō Kaikaku" ("Japan's Structural Reform"). *Sekai* 3, no. 183 (1961), pp. 98–114.

Naikaku Seido Hyaku Nen Shi Henshū Iinkai, ed. *Naikaku Seido Hyaku Nen Shi (A One-Hundred Year History of Japanese Cabinets System, Two Volumes).* Tokyo: Naikaku Kanbō, 1985.

———. *Naikaku Hyaku Nen no Ayumi (A One-Hundred Year Odyssey of Japan's Cabinet).* Tokyo: Daikō Kabushiki Kaisha, 1985.

Naitō Kunio. *Minobe Tosei no Sugao (The Real Face of the Minobe Administration).* Tokyo: Kōdansha, 1975.

Naitō Naritada. *Shimane Ken no Rekishi (The History of Shimane Prefecture).* Tokyo: Yamakawa Shuppan Sha, 1983.

Naito Tetsu. "Jitsugen Dekiru ka? Shotokuzei Genzei, Jūtaku Genzei?" ("Can a Reduction in Income and Housing Taxes be Realized?"), *Shūkan Tōyō Keizai,* June 15, 1985, pp. 73–77.

Najita, Tetsuo. *Hara Kei in the Politics of Compromise, 1905–1915.* Cambridge: Harvard University Press, 1967.

Najita, Tetsuo, and J. Victor Koschmann, eds. *Conflict in Modern Japanese History: The Neglected Tradition.* Princeton: Princeton University Press, 1982.

Nakajima Hidenobu. "Sengo ni okeru Chūshō Kigyō, Undō no Rekishi to Kyōka" ("Postwar Small and Medium-size Enterprises: Their History and Consolidation") *Chūshō Kigyō Jyānaru* (August 1968), pp. 1–13.

Nakamura, James I. *Agricultural Production and the Economic Devel-*

opment of Japan, 1873–1922. Princeton: Princeton University Press, 1966.

Nakamura Keiichirō. *Miki Seiken, 747 Nichi (The Miki Administration: 747 Days)*. Tokyo: Gyōsei Mondai Kenkyū Jo, 1981.

Nakamura Kikuo. *Shōwa Seiji Shi (History of Shōwa Politics)*. Tokyo: Keiō Tsūshin, 1962.

Nakamura Kikuo and Kamijō Sueo. *Sengo Nihon Seiji Shi (History of Postwar Japanese Politics)*. Tokyo: Yūshodo, 1973.

Nakamura Takafusa. *Economic Growth in Prewar Japan*. New Haven: Yale University Press, 1983.

———. *Nihon Keizai: Sono Seichō to Kōzō (The Japanese Economy: Its Growth and Structure)*. Tokyo: Tokyo Daigaku Shuppan Kai, 1980.

———. *Nihon no Keizai Tōsei: Senji Sengo no Keiken to Kyōkun (Japan's Economic Controls: Experiences and Lessons from the Wartime and Postwar Period)*. Tokyo: Nihon Keizai Shimbun Sha, 1974.

Nakamura Takeshi. "Heiki Seisan" ("The Production of Arms"). *Chūō Kōron* 9, no. 9 (September 1954), pp. 108–113.

Nakamura Yūichirō. *Chōsen suru Chūshō Kigyō (Entrepreneurial Small Business)*. Tokyo: Iwanami Shoten, 1985.

Nakano Minoru, ed. *Nihongata Seisaku Kettei no Henyō (The Japanese-Style Policy Process)*. Tokyo: Tōyō Keizai Shinpō Sha, 1986.

Nakano Yoshihiko, Hirokoshi Hisasuke, and Hidaka Rokurō. "Nōson o Dō Kaeruka?" ("How do We Change the Agricultural Village?"). *Sekai* 7, no. 179 (1960), pp. 64–68.

Nakasone Yasuhiro. *Atarashii Hoshu no Ronri (A New Theory of Conservatism)*. Tokyo: Kōdansha, 1978.

———."Dai-Seijika wa Minna Kazamidori da" ("All Great Politicians are Weathervanes") *Bungei Shunjū* 61, no. 1 (January 1983), pp. 136–48.

Nakayama Ichirō. "Hoshu Seiken no Shin Kadai" (New Topics of the Conservative Administration). *Bungei Shunjū* 63, no. 3 (March 1985).

Naruto Masayasu. *Sengo Jichitai Kaikaku Shi (A History of Postwar Local Government Reform)*. Tokyo: Nihon Hyōron Sha, 1982.

Nash, George H. *The Conservative Intellectual Movement in America since 1945*. New York: Basic Books, 1976.

National Land Agency (Kokudo Chō). *Kokudo Riyō Hakusho (White Paper on the Use of National Land)*. Tokyo: Ōkurashō Insatsu Kyoku, 1985.

———. *Sanzensō (The Third Comprehensive National Development Plan)*. Tokyo: Government Printing Office, 1977.

Nihon Ginkō Kyōkai Ni Jyū Nen Henshū Shitsu, ed. *Ginkō Kyōkai Ni Jyū Nen Shi (Bankers Association Twenty-Year History)*. Tokyo: Zenkoku Ginkō Kyōkai Rengō Kai, 1965.

Nihon Keizai Shimbun Sha, ed. *Za Zeimusho (The Tax Office)*. Tokyo: Nihon Keizai Shimbun Sha, 1984.

———, ed. *Jimintō Seichō Kai (The LDP Policy Affairs Research Council)*. Tokyo: Nihon Keizai Shimbun Sha, 1983.

Nihon Kodomo o Mamoru Kai, ed. *Kodomo Hakusho (White Paper on Children)*. 1985 ed. Tokyo: Kusadō Bunka, 1985.

Nihon Kokuyū Tetsudō, ed. *Nihon Kokuyū Tetsudō Hyaku Nen Shi (The Hundred-Year History of the Japan National Railways)*. Vols. 13 and 14. Tokyo: Nihon Kokuyū Tetsudō, 1963, 1964.

Nihon Kyōsantō Chūō Iinkai. *Nihon Kyōsantō Roku Jyū Nen 1922–1982 (Sixty Years of the Japan Communist Party, 1922–1982)*. Tokyo: Nihon Kyōsantō Chūō Iinkai Shuppan Kyoku, 1982.

Nihon Nōsei Shi Henshū Iinkai, ed. *Sengo Nihon Nōsei Shi (History of Japanese Postwar Agricultural Administration)*. Tokyo: Sengo Nihon Nōsei Shi Kankō Kai, 1967.

Nihon Rōdō Kumiai Sōhyō Kai. *Sōhyō Ni Jyū Nen Shi* (A Twenty-Year History of Sōhyō), Vol. 1. Tokyo: Rōdō Junpō Sha, 1974.

Nihon Seiji Keizai Kenkyū Jo. *Nikkyō no Tebiki (An Introduction to the Japan Communist Party)*. Tokyo: Nihon Seiji Keizai Kenkyū Jo, various issues.

Nihon Seikei Shimbun Shuppan Bu, ed. *Bessatsu Kokkai Binran (Annex to the National Diet Handbook)*. 3 vols. Tokyo: Nihon Seikei Shimbun Sha, 1980.

Nihon Shakaitō Hensan Kai. *Nihon Shakaitō Shi*. Tokyo: Nihon Shakaitō Hensan Kai, 1963.

Nihon Shōkō Kaigi Sho, ed. *Kokusai Hikaku Tōkei Yōran (Japan and the World in Statistics)*. 1986 ed. Tokyo: Nihon Shōkō Kaigi Sho, 1986.

Nihon Sozei Kenkyū Kyōkai. *Zeisei Sankō Shiryō Shū (Collected Reference Material Regarding the Tax System)*. Tokyo: Nihon Sozei Kenkyū Kai, 1984.

Nihon Rōdō Kyōkai Zasshi (Journal of the Japan Labor Association). May 1987.

Nihon Shihon-shūgi Hattatsu Shi Kōza (Symposium on the History of the Development of Japanese Capitalism). 7 vols. and supplement. Tokyo: Iwanami Shoten, 1932–1933, reissued, 1982.

Niigata Nippō Sha, ed. *Za Etsuzankai (The Etsuzankai)*. Niigata: Niigata Nippō Jigyō Sha Shuppan Bu, 1983.

Nishibe Susumu, "Tanaka Kakuei no Shakai-teki Hiyō" ("The Social Cost of Tanaka Kakuei"). *Chūō Kōron* 98, no. 3 (March 1983), pp. 72–83.

Nishikawa Seiji, ed. *Gendai Nippon no Toshi Mondai: Gendai Shihon Shugi to Toshi Mondai (The Problems of City in the Contemporary Japan: Contemporary Capitalism and Urban Problems*). Vol. 1. Tokyo: Tanbun Sha, 1973.

Nishiyama Yūzō, ed. *Gendai Nippon no Toshi Mondai: Toshi Keikaku to Machizukuri (Urban Problems in the Contemporary Japan: The City Plannings and the Establishment of Town).* Vol. 2. Tokyo: Tanbun Sha, 1971.

Noguchi Yukio. *Gyō Zaisei Kaikaku (Reform of Administration and Finance).* Tokyo: PHP Kenkyū Jo, 1981.

———, ed. *Zaisei (Finance).* Tokyo: Kyōiku Sha, 1984.

———. "Decision Rules in the Japanese Budgetary Process." *Japanese Economic Studies* 7, no. 4 (Summer 1979), pp. 51–75.

———. "Yosan ni okeru Ishi Kettei Rūru no Bunseki" ("Decision Rules in the Japanese Budgetary Process"). *Keizai Kenkyū* 29, no. 1 (January 1978), pp. 23–32.

Norbeck, Edward. *Country to City: The Urbanization of a Japanese Hamlet.* Salt Lake City: University of Utah Press, 1978.

Nukishima Masamichi. "Jibun Jishin ni toute mita koto" ("The Things I saw through Self Reflection"). *Sekai* no. 292 (March 1970), pp. 137–41.

Nutter, G. Warren. *Growth of Government in the West.* Washington, D. C.: American Enterprise Institute, 1978.

Ochi Michio. *Chichi: Fukuda Takeo-Sono Ningen, Sono Zaisei (Father: Fukuda Takeo—His Personality and His Financial Policy).* Tokyo: Sankei Shimbun Sha, 1963.

Ōhira Masayoshi Kaikoroku Kankō Kai, ed. *Ōhira Masayoshi Kaikoroku: Shiryō Hen (The Memoirs of Ōhira Masayoshi: Documents).* Tokyo: Ōhira Masayoshi Kaikoroku Kankō Kai, 1982.

Okamoto Fumio. *Satō Seiken: Heiwa to Hanei no naka no Chōki Hoshu Seiken no Kiroku (Satō Eisaku: The Record of Long Term Conservative Policy Amidst Peace and Prosperity).* Tokyo: Hakubu Shuppan, 1974.

Ōkawa Kazushi, and Henry Rosovsky. "The Role of Agriculture in Modern Japanese Economic Development." *Economic Development and Cultural Change* 9, no. 1, part 2 (October 1960), pp. 43–68.

Okimoto, Daniel, ed. *Competitive Edge.* Stanford: Stanford University Press, 1984.

Olson, Mancur Jr. "Rapid Growth as a Destabilizing Force." *Journal of Economic History* 23, no. 4 (December 1963), pp. 529–52.

Ōmakari Tadashi. *Asanuma Inejirō: Sono Hito, Sono Jinsei (Asanuma Inejirō: Himself and His Life).* Tokyo: Shiseidō, 1961.

Ono Michihiro et al. *Sōhyō Rōdō Undō San Jyū Nen no Kiseki (Tracing Thirty Years of the Sōhyō Labour Movement).* Tokyo: Rōdō Kyōiku Center, 1980.

Organization for Economic Cooperation and Development. *Agricultural Policy in Japan.* Paris: OECD, 1974.

———. *Industrial Adjustment Policies.* Paris: OECD, 1978.

———. *Measuring Health Care, 1960–1983: Expenditure, Costs, and Performance.* Paris: OECD, 1985.

———. *National Accounts, 1971–1983, Detailed Tables*. Vol. 2. Paris: OECD, 1985.

———. *National Politics and Agricultural Trade*. Paris: OECD, 1987.

———. OECD *Economic Surveys, Japan. (1969 Annual Report)*. Paris: OECD, 1969.

———. *Part-Time Farming in* OECD *Countries*. Paris: OECD, 1978.

———. *Public Expenditure Trends*, no. 5. Paris: OECD Studies in Resource Allocation, 1978.

———. *Regional Problems and Policies in* OECD *Countries*. Vol. 1. Paris: OECD, 1976.

———. *The Role of Industrial Incentives in Regional Development*. Paris: OECD, 1979.

———. *Selected Industrial Policy Instruments*. Paris: OECD, 1978.

———. *Social Expenditure, 1960–1990: Problems of Growth and Control*. Paris: OECD, 1985.

Orloff, Ann Shola, and Theda Skocpol. "Why Not Equal Protection? Explaining the Politics of Public Social Spending in Britain, 1900–1911, and the United States, 1880s–1920." *American Sociological Review* 49 (December 1984), pp. 726–50.

Ōsono Tomokazu. *Hasshin: Technopolis Kōsō (Starting Point: Technopolis Structure)*. Tokyo: NCB Shuppan, 1983.

Ōta Kaoru. "Minobe Tosei o Hihan Suru" ("I Criticize the Minobe Administration"). *Bungei Shunjū* (January 1971), pp. 120–34.

———. "Shakaitō no Kōzō Kaikaku Ron ni taisuru Nanatsu no Gimon" ("Seven Questions about the Theory of Structurally Transforming the Socialist Party"). *Chūō Kōron* 3, no. 76 (March 1961), pp. 136–45.

Ōta Takehide. "Jimintō: Post Satō Seiken e no Tenbō ("The Liberal Democratic Party: Prospects for the Post Satō Administration"). *Chūō Kōron* (August 1971), pp. 106–31.

Ōtake Hideo. "Bōeihi Zōgaku o meguru Jimintō no Tōnai Rikigaku." ("Inside Story of the Power Balance within the LDP with the Strengthening of Armaments.") *Asahi Journal* 23, no. 4 (January 30, 1981), pp. 10–17.

———. *Gendai Nihon no Seiji Kenryoku Keizai Kenryoku (Political Power and Economic Power in Modern Japan)*. Tokyo: Sanichi Shobō, 1979.

———. *The Politics of Defense Spending in Conservative Japan*. Ithaca: Cornell University Peace Studies Program Occasional Paper no. 15, February 1982.

———. *Nihon no Bōei to Kokunai Seiji (Japan's Defense and Domestic Politics)*. Tokyo: Sanichi Shobō, 1983.

Ōtake Hideo, ed. *Nihon Seiji no Sōten (Points of Contention in Japanese Politics)*. Tokyo: Sanichi Shobō, 1984.

Ōyama Yoshikazu. "Kokusaika Jidai Nōkyō Kaikaku o Teigen suru"

("Suggestions for Agricultural Reform in the Era of Internationalization"). *Economisuto* (January 1987), pp. 34–39.

Ozaki Hideki, ed. *Shōwa no Sengo Shi (The Postwar History of Shōwa).*

Packard, George R., III. *Protest in Tokyo.* Princeton: Princeton University Press, 1966.

Palamountain, Joseph Cornwall, Jr. *The Politics of Distribution.* Cambridge, Mass.: Harvard University Press, 1955.

Passin, Herbert. "The Sources of Protest in Japan." *American Political Science Review* 56, no. 2 (June, 1962), pp. 391–403.

Pempel, T. J. *Patterns of Japanese Policymaking.* Boulder, Colo.: Westview, 1978.

———. *Policy and Politics in Japan.* Philadelphia: Temple University Press, 1982.

———, ed. *Policymaking in Contemporary Japan.* Ithaca: Cornell University Press, 1976.

———. "The Unbundling of 'Japan, Inc.': The Changing Dynamics of Japanese Policy Formation." *Journal of Japanese Studies,* 13, no. 2 (1987), pp. 271–306.

Pempel, T. J., and Keiichi Tsunekawa, "Corporatism without Labor? The Japanese Anomaly." In *Trends toward Corporatist Intermediation,* edited by Philippe Schmitter and Gerhard Lehmbruch. Beverly Hills: Sage Publications, 1979.

Piore, Michael J., and Charles F. Sabel. *The Second Industrial Divide.* New York: Basic Books, 1984.

Polsby, Nelson W. *Political Innovation in America: The Politics of Policy Initiation.* New Haven: Yale University Press, 1984.

Powell, G. Bingham, Jr. *Contemporary Democracies: Participation, Stability, and Violence.* Cambridge, Mass.: Harvard University Press, 1982.

Premchand, A., and Jesse Burkhead, eds. *Comparative International Budgeting and Finance.* London: Transaction Books, 1984.

Pridham, Geoffrey. *Christian Democracy in West Germany: The CDU/CSU in Government and Opposition, 1945–1976.* London: Croom Helm, 1977.

Prime Minister's Office Statistical Bureau (Sōrifu Tōkei Kyoku), ed. *Nihon Tōkei Nenkan (Japan Statistical Yearbook),* 1954–1984 eds. Tokyo: Nihon Tōkei Kyōkai, 1954–1984.

Prime Minister's Secretariat (Naikaku Sōridaijin Kanbō), ed. *Satō Naikaku Kokkai Enzetsu Shū (The Satō Cabinet's Speeches).* Tokyo: Naikaku Sōridaijin Kanbō, 1972.

Quigley, Harold S., and John E. Turner. *The New Japan: Government and Politics.* Minneapolis: University of Minnesota Press, 1956.

Reed, Steven R. "The Changing Fortunes of Japan's Progressive Governors." *Asian Survey* 26, no. 4 (April 1986), pp. 452–65.

———. *Japanese Prefectures and Policymaking*. Pittsburgh: University of Pittsburgh Press, 1986.

Reischauer, Edwin O. "The Broken Dialogue with Japan." *Foreign Affairs* 39, no. 1 (October 1960), pp. 11–26.

———. "Some Thoughts on Japanese Democracy." *Japan Quarterly* 8, no. 1 (January 1961), pp. 98–103.

Rémond, René. *The Right Wing in France: From 1815 to de Gaulle*. Philadelphia: University of Pennsylvania Press, 1969.

"Returns for Governor, Senate, and House." *Congressional Quarterly* 42, no. 45, November 10, 1984, pp. 2923–30.

Richardson, Bradley M. "Urbanization and Political Participation," *American Political Science Review* 67 (1973), pp. 433–52.

Richardson, Bradley M., and Scott C. Flanagan. *Politics in Japan*. Boston: Little, Brown, 1984.

Riron Henshū Bu, ed. *Tokuda Kyūichi Den (The Autobiography of Tokuda Kyūichi)*. Tokyo: Riron Sha, 1952.

Roberts, John G. *Mitsui: Three Centuries of Japanese Business*. New York: John Weatherhill, 1973.

Robinson, E. A. G., ed. *Backward Areas in Advanced Countries*. London: Macmillan, 1969.

Rokkan, Stein, and Derek W. Urwin. *Economy, Territory, Identity: Politics of West European Peripheries*. Beverly Hills: Sage Publications, 1983.

Romanesco, Albert U. *The Politics of Recovery: Roosevelt's New Deal*. New York: Oxford University Press, 1983.

Rose, Richard. *Comparative Policy Analysis: The Programme Approach*. Glasgow: University of Strathclyde Studies in Public Policy no. 138, 1985.

———. *Do Parties Make a Difference?* Chatham, N. J.: Chatham House Publishers, 1980.

———. *How Exceptional is American Government?* Glasgow: University of Strathclyde Centre for the Study of Public Policy, Studies in Public Policy 150, 1985.

———. "The Programme Approach to the Growth of Government." *British Journal of Political Science* 15, no. 1 (1984).

———, ed. *Public Employment in Western Nations*. Cambridge: Cambridge University Press, 1985.

———. *Understanding Big Government: The Programme Approach*. Beverley Hills and London: Sage Publications, 1984.

Rosovsky, Henry. *Capital Formation in Japan, 1868–1940*. Glencoe, Ill.: Free Press, 1961.

Rossiter, Clinton. *Conservatism in America*. Cambridge, Mass.: Harvard University Press, 1960.

Ryū Shintarō. "Some Doubts about Economic Growth." *Japan Quarterly* 9, no. 2 (July–September 1962), pp. 275–84.

Saji Toshihiko. "Zaikai wa Dō Hyōka Suru ka?" ("How Should the Zaikai Evaluate?"). *Chūō Kōron* 9, no. 9 (September 1972), pp. 116–29.

Sakamoto Mamoru. *Shōwa Shi no naka no Rōdō Undō (The Labor Movement in the Context of Shōwa History)*. Tokyo: Nihon Rōdō Kyōkai, 1982.

Sakamoto Mamoru, Sakisaka Itsurō and Ōuchi Hyōe. "Miike no Tatakai o Mitsumete" ("Looking Hard at the Miike Struggle"). *Sekai*, no. 174 (June 1960), pp. 11–27.

Samuels, Richard J. *The Business of the Japanese State: Energy Markets in Comparative and Historical Perspective*. Ithaca: Cornell University Press, 1987.

———. *The Politics of Regional Policy in Japan: Localities Incorporated?* Princeton: Princeton University Press, 1983.

Samuelsson, Kurt. *Sweden: From Great Power to Welfare State*. London: Allen and Unwin, 1968.

Sandeman, Hugh, ed. *Japan*. London: The Economist, 1983.

Sangiin Kaigi Roku. Dai Sanjyū Rokkai Kokkai (Record of Upper House Proceedings, 36th Diet). October 21–23, 1960.

Sartori, Giovanni. *Parties and Party Systems*. Cambridge: Cambridge University Press, 1976.

Satō Atsushi. "Kakushin Tosei Ichi Ken no Yūkō Shatei" ("Sizing Up One Year's Progressive Party Administration in Tokyo"). *Asahi Journal* 10, no. 18 (May 5, 1968), pp. 44–48.

Satō Kiroko. *Satō Hiroko no Saishō Fujin Hiroku (The Secret Record of the Wife of a Prime Minister)*. Tokyo: Asahi Shimbun Sha, 1974.

"Satō Seiken o Torimaku Kinchō" ("Tension Surrounds the Satō Administration"). *Sekai*, no. 229 (January 1965), pp. 180–93.

Satō Seizaburō and Matsuzaki Tetsuhisa, "Jimintō Chō Chōki Seiken no Kaibō" ("Autopsy on the Super-long-term Reign of the LDP"). *Chūō Kōron* 99, no. 11 (November 1984), pp. 66–100.

———. "Jimintō Kokkai Unei no Tettei Kenkyū" ("A Complete Study of the LDP's Diet Management"). *Chūō Kōron* 7, no. 7 (1985), pp. 394–415.

———. *Jimintō Seiken (The LDP Administration)*. Tokyo: Chūō Kōron Sha, 1986.

Satō Shunichi. *Sengoki no Chihō Jichi (Local Administration in the Postwar Period)*. Tokyo: Ryokufū Shuppan, 1985.

Saussois, Jean Michel. "Industrial Policy at Sector Level: The Case of the Machine Tool Industry in France." Paper presented at the 4th *EGOS* Conference, Firenze, November 3–5, 1983.

Sawamoto Moriyuki. *Kōkyō Toshi Hyaku Nen no Ayumi (A Hundred Year History of Public Works Investment)*. Tokyo: Taisei Shuppan Kai, 1981.

Saxonhouse, Gary. "Industrial Restructuring in Japan." *Journal of Japanese Studies* 5, no. 2 (Summer 1979), pp. 273–320.

Scalapino, Robert A. "Japan and the General Elections." *Far Eastern Survey* 21, no. 15 (October 29, 1952), pp. 149–54.

———. *The Japanese Communist Movement, 1920–1966*. Berkeley: University of California Press, 1967.

Schattschneider, E. E. *Politics, Pressure Groups, and the Tariff*. New York: Prentice-Hall, 1935.

———. *The Semi-Sovereign People*. Hillsdale, Ill.: Dryden Press, 1975.

Schlesinger, Arthur M., Jr. *The Coming of the New Deal*. Boston: Houghton Mifflin, 1958.

———. *The Cycles of American History*. Boston: Houghton Mifflin, 1986.

Schmitter, Philippe C., and Gerhard Lehmbruch, eds. *Trends toward Corporatist Intermediation*. Beverly Hills: Sage Publications, 1979.

Schnitzer, Martin. *Income Distribution: A Comparative Study of the United States, West Germany, East Germany, the United Kingdom, and Japan*. New York: Praeger, 1974.

Seers, Dudley, and Kjell Ostrom. *The Crisis of the European Regions*. New York: St. Martin's, 1983.

Sekai no naka no Nihon o Kangaeru Kai, ed. *Kokusai Hikaku: Nihon o Miru (Looking at Japan: International Comparisons)*. Tokyo: Chūō Hōki Shuppan Kai, 1985.

Shakai Bunko, ed. *Nihon Shakaitō Shi Shiryō (Materials on Japan Socialist Party History)*. Tokyo: Kashiwa Shobō, 1965.

Shefter, Martin. *Patronage and its Opponents: A Theory and Some European Cases*. Ithaca: Cornell University Western Studies Program Occasional Papers, May 1977.

Shimazaki Yuzuru. "Miike Sōgi Sōkatsu no tame no Hōkoku" ("A Report Summarizing the Miike Dispute"). *Chūō Kōron* 76, no. 6 (June 1961), pp. 122–36.

Shimizu Seihachirō. "Genkō Senkyo Seido no Mujun o Tsuku" ("Pointing Out the Contradiction of the Contemporary Electoral System"). *Chūō Kōron* 74, no. 4 (March 1959), pp. 158–70.

Shimizu Shinzō. *Sengo Kakushin Seiryoku. (The Power of Postwar Progressivism)*. Tokyo: Aoki Shoten, 1969.

Shindō Jinshirō. *Minshō: Zenshōren no Ayumi (The Course of the All Japan Commercial Federation)*. 3 vols. Tokyo: Higashi Ginza Insatsu Shuppan, 1976.

Shinobu Seizaburō. *Sengo Nihon Seiji Shi. (Postwar Japanese Political History)*. Vol. 1. Tokyo: Keisō Shobō, 1965.

Shinohara Hajime, "Sangiin Sen wa Mini o Hanei shita ka?" ("Did the Upper House Elections Reflect the People's Will?"). *Asahi Journal* 10, no. 30 (July 21, 1968), pp. 8–17.

Shinohara Miyohei. *Growth and Cycles in the Japanese Economy*. Tokyo: Hitotsubashi University and Institute of Economic Research, Economic Research Series no. 5, 1962.

Shioda Maruo, *Sumai no Sengo Shi (A Postwar History of Housing)*. Tokyo: Simul Shuppan Kai, 1975.

Shioguchi Kiichi. *Kikigaki: Ikeda Hayato (Reminiscences: Ikeda Hayato)*. Tokyo: Asahi Shimbun Sha, 1975.

Shiota Ushio. *Hyaku Chō En no Haishin (The Betrayal of One Hundred Trillion Yen)*. Tokyo: Kōdansha, 1985.

Shiozawa Motō and Murakawa Ichirō. *Chihō Roku Dantai no Soshiki to Katsudō (The Organization and Activities of the Six Regional Associations)*. Tokyo: Kyōiku Sha, 1979.

Shiratori Rei. *Nihon ni okeru Hoshu to Kakushin (Conservatism and Progressivism in Japan)*. Tokyo: Nihon Keizai Shimbun Sha, 1973.

Shiratori Rei. *Nihon no Naikaku (Japan's Cabinet)*. 3 vols. Tokyo: Shin Hyōron, 1981.

Shōkō Chūō Kinko. *Shōkō Chūkin Yon Jyū Nen Shi. (A Forty Year History of the Shōkō Chūkin Bank)*. Tokyo: Shōkō Chūō Kinko, 1977.

"Shōryo no naka no Satō Taisei" ("The Satō Administration in the Midst of Turbulence"). *Sekai*, no. 307 (June 1971), pp. 182–86.

Shūgiin Kaigi Roku, Dai San Jyū Rokkai Kokkai (Record of Lower House Proceedings, 36th Diet), October 17–23, 1960.

Shūkyō to Seiji o Kangaeru Kai, ed. *Kami to Hotoke to Senkyosen (Shintō and Buddhist Deities and the Election Campaign)*. Tokyo: Tokuma Shobō, 1980.

Silberman, Bernard, and Harry D. Harootunian, eds. *Japan in Crisis*. Princeton: Princeton University Press, 1974.

Skocpol, Theda. *States and Social Revolutions*. Cambridge: Cambridge University Press, 1979.

Skowronek, Stephen. *Building a New American State: The Expansion of National Administrative Capacities, 1877–1920*. Cambridge: Cambridge University Press, 1982.

Small and Medium Enterprise Agency (Chūshō Kigyō Chō), ed. *Chūshō Kigyō Chō Ni Jyū Go Nen Shi (A Twenty-Five Year History of the Small Business Agency)*. Tokyo: Chūshō Kigyō Chō, 1973.

———. *Chūshō Kigyō Chō San Jyū Nen Shi (A Thirty-Year History of the Small Business Agency)*. Tokyo: Chūshō Kigyō Chō, 1979.

———. *Outline of Small and Medium Enterprise Policies of the Japanese Government*. Tokyo: Ministry of International Trade and Industry, January 1983.

———. *Chūshō Kigyō Hakusho (White Paper on Small Business)*, 1978–1986 eds. Tokyo: Ōkurashō Insatsu Kyoku, 1978–1986.

Small and Medium Enterprise Agency Guidance Division Distribution Transactions Section (Chūshō Kigyō Chō Shidō Bu Torihiki Ryūtsū Ka), ed. *Bunya Chōsei Hō (The Sectoral Adjustment Law)*. Tokyo: Gyōsei, 1984.

Small and Medium Enterprise Agency Promotion Department Research and Public Affairs Section (Chūshō Kigyō Chō Shinkō Bu Chōsa

Kōhō Ka). *Chūshō Kigyō Kankei Shiryō Shū (Compilation of Small Business Related Data)*, vol. 31, no. 3.

Small and Medium Enterprise Finance Corporation (Chūshō Kigyō Kinyū Kōko), ed. *Chūshō Kigyō Kōko Ni Jyū Nen Shi (Twenty-Year History of the Small Business Finance Corporation)*. Tokyo: Dainippon Insatsu, 1974.

Smethurst, Richard J. *Agricultural Development and Tenancy Disputes in Japan, 1890–1940*. Princeton: Princeton University Press, 1986.

———. *A Social Basis for Prewar Japanese Militarism: The Army and the Rural Community*. Berkeley: University of California Press, 1974.

Smith, Paul. *Disraelian Conservatism and Social Reform*. London: Routledge and Kegan Paul, 1967.

Smith, Thomas C. *Political Change and Industrial Development in Japan: Government Enterprise, 1868–1880*. Stanford: Stanford University Press, 1955.

Snyder, Louis. *The Blood and Iron Chancellor*. New York: Van Nostrand, 1967.

Soma Masao, ed. *Kokusei Senkyo to Seitō Seiji (National Election and Party Politics)*. Tokyo: Seiji Kōhō Center, 1977.

Statistisches Bundesant. *Statistisches Jahrbuch 1986 fur die Bundesrepublik Deutschland*. Stuttgart: W. Kohlhammer Gmbh, 1986.

Stein, Herbert. *The Fiscal Revolution in America*. Chicago: University of Chicago Press, 1969.

Steiner, Kurt. *Local Government in Japan*. Stanford: Stanford University Press, 1965.

Steiner, Kurt, Ellis S. Krauss, and Scott C. Flanagan, eds. *Political Opposition and Local Politics in Japan*. Princeton: Princeton University Press, 1980.

Stepan, Alfred. *The State and Society: Peru in Comparative Perspective*. Princeton: Princeton University Press, 1978.

Steslicke, William E. *Doctors in Politics*. New York: Praeger, 1973.

Stockwin, Arthur. *Divided Politics in a Growth Economy* (London: W. W. Norton, 1975.

Storey, D. J., ed. *The Small Firm: An International Survey*. London: Croom Helm, 1983.

Sugai Shirō. *Kokudo Keikaku no Keiji to Kadai (Revelations and Topics regarding National Land Use Planning)*. Tokyo: Daimeidō, 1975.

———. *Shiryō: Kokudo Keikaku (Data on National Land Planning)*. Tokyo: Daimeidō, 1975.

Sugaya Akira. *Nihon Iryō Seisaku Shi (A History of Japanese Medical Policy)*. Tokyo: Nihon Hyōron Sha, 1981.

Suleiman, Ezra N., ed. *Bureaucrats and Policymaking*. New York: Holmes and Meier, 1984.

Suleiman, Ezra N. *Elites in French Society: The Politics of Survival.* Princeton: Princeton University Press, 1978.

———, ed. *Parliaments and Parliamentarians in Democratic Politics.* New York: Holmes and Meier, 1986.

———. *Politics, Power, and Bureaucracy in France: The Administrative Elite.* Princeton: Princeton University Press, 1974.

Sumiya Mikio and Taira Koji, eds. *An Outline of Japanese Economic History, 1603–1940.* Tokyo: University of Tokyo Press, 1979.

Sweet, Morris L. *Industrial Location Policy for Economic Revitalization: National and International Perspectives.* New York: Praeger Special Studies, 1981.

Szajkowski, Bogdan, ed. *Marxist Local Governments in Western Europe and Japan.* London: Frances Pinter, 1986.

Tachibana Takashi. *Nōkyō: Kyodai na Chōsen (Agricultural Cooperatives: The Massive Challenge).* Tokyo: Asahi Shimbun Sha, 1980.

———. "Tanaka Kakuei Kenkyū: Sono Kinmyaku to Jinmyaku" ("Research on Tanaka Kakuei: His Money Connections and Personal Contacts"). *Bungei Shunjū* 52, no. 11 (November 1974), pp. 92–131.

———. *Tanaka Kakuei Kenkyū: Zenkiroku (Research on Tanaka Kakuei: The Complete Report).* Vol. 2. Tokyo: Kōdansha, 1982.

Tagawa Kazuo. *Sengo Nihon Kakumei Undō Shi (History of Postwar Japan's Reform Movements).* Vol. 1. Tokyo: Gendai Shinchō Sha, 1970.

Taguchi Fukuji. *Nihon no Kakushin Seiryoku (The Power of Japanese Progressivism).* Tokyo: Kōbundō, 1961.

———. "Nihon Shakaitō Ron" ("A Theory of the Japan Socialist Party"). *Chūō Kōron* 1, no. 76 (1961), pp. 26–49.

Tahara Sōichirō. *Sengo Zaikai Sengoku Shi (A Civil War History of the Postwar Business World).* Tokyo: Kōdansha, 1986.

Tait, Alan A., and Peter S. Heller. *International Comparisons of Government Expenditure.* Washington, D.C.: International Monetary Fund, April 1982.

Takagi Sanae, Enoki Akira, and Seki Masahiko. "Satō Naikaku Chōmei no Uchimaku" ("The Inside Story of the Satō Cabinet's Long Life"). *Chūō Kōron* 85, no. 1 (1973), pp. 112–23.

Takemura Tadao."Nihon Gunju Sangyō no Senzairyoku to Genjitsusei" ("The Potential and Reality of Japanese Defense Industry"). *Chūō Kōron* 67, no. 11 (November 1952), pp. 112–18.

Takenaka Heizō. *Kenkyū Kaihatsu to Setsubi Tōshi (Research, Development, and Capital Investment).* Tokyo: Tōyō Keizai Shinpō Sha, 1984.

Tamura Akira. *Toshi Yokohama o Tsukuru (Building the City of Yokohama).* Tokyo: Chūō Kōron Sha, 1983.

Tanaka Kakuei. *Building a New Japan: A Plan for Remodeling the Japanese Archipelago.* Tokyo: Simul International, 1972.

———. *Daijin Nikki (The Diary of a Minister).* Niigata: Niigata Shinpō Jigyō Sha, 1972.

———. *Nihon Rettō Kaizō Ron (Remodeling the Japanese Archipelago).* Tokyo: Nikkan Kōgyō Shimbun, 1972.

———. *Watakushi no Rirekisho (My Autobiography).* Tokyo: Nihon Keizai Shinpō Sha, 1966.

Tanaka Shūsei. "Hoshu Shintō Kessei no Susume" ("Suggestions for the Foundation of a New Conservative Party"). *Jiyū* (December 1973), pp. 76–83.

Tanaka Toyotoshi. *Ikite iru Nōkyō Shi (A Living History of the Agricultural Cooperatives).* Tokyo: Ie no Hikari Kyōkai, 1976.

Tanaka Zenichirō. *Jimintō no Doramatsurugii (The Dramaturgy of the LDP).* Tokyo: Tokyo Daigaku Shuppan Kai, 1986.

Tarrow, Sidney. *Between Center and Periphery: Grassroots Politicians in Italy and France.* New Haven: Yale University Press, 1977.

Tarrow, Sidney, Peter J. Katzenstein, and Luigi Graziano, eds. *Territorial Politics in Industrial Nations.* New York: Praeger, 1978.

Tatamiya Eitarō. *Shōwa no Seijikatachi (The Politicians of Shōwa).* Tokyo: Kōbundō, 1963.

Tateyama Manabu. "Kokutetsu Shisan Hyaku Chō En o Kanshi Seyo!" ("Let's Keep Watch on the JNR's 100 Trillion Yen Assets"). *Bungei Shunjū* 64, no. 10 (October 1986), pp. 176–200.

Takeuchi Hiroshi. "Japan's Soaring Land Prices." *Journal of Japanese Trade and Industry,* no. 4 (1987), pp. 44–47.

Tatsuno, Sheridan. *The Technopolis Strategy: Japan, High Technology, and the Control of the Twenty-first Century.* New York: Prentice-Hall, 1986.

Taylor, A. J. P. *Bismarck.* New York: Alfred Knopf, 1955.

Taylor, C. L., ed. *Why Governments Grow.* Beverly Hills and London: Sage Publications, 1983.

Thayer, Nathaniel B. *How the Conservatives Rule Japan.* Princeton: Princeton University Press, 1969.

Thompson, E. P. *The Making of the English Working Class.* Rev. ed. Harmondsworth: Penguin, 1968.

Tilly, Charles, ed. *The Formation of Nation States in Western Europe.* Princeton: Princeton University Press, 1975.

———. *From Mobilization to Revolution.* Reading, Mass.: Addison-Wesley, 1978.

Tobias, Sheila, Peter Goudinoff, Stefan Leader, and Selhah Leader. *The People's Guide to National Defense.* New York: William Morrow, 1982.

Tochi Jūtaku Gyōsei Kenkyū Kai, ed. *Tochi Taisaku to Jūtaku Taisaku (Land Policy and Housing Policy).* Tokyo: Ōkurashō Insatsu Kyoku, 1982.

Togawa Osamu. *Kishi Nobusuke to Hoshu Antō (Kishi Nobusuke and the Dark Struggle of the Conservatives)*. Vol. 5. Tokyo: Kōdansha, 1982.

———. *Nihon Seiji no Tenbō (The Prospects for Japanese Politics)*. Tokyo: Nihon Bungei Sha, 1975.

———. *Tanaka Kakuei to Seiken Kōsō (Tanaka Kakuei and the Struggle for Political Power)*. Tokyo: Kōdansha, 1982.

———. *Yoshida Shigeru to Fukkō no Sentaku (Yoshida Shigeru and the Choice for Recovery)*. Vol. 6. Tokyo: Kōdansha, 1982.

Tōhata Shirō. "Amerika Nōgyō ga Nihon ni motsu Imi" ("The Meaning of American Agriculture for Japan"). *Chūō Kōron* 72, no. 1 (January 1957), pp. 68–75.

Tōhata Shirō and Matsuura Tatsuo. *Shōwa Nōseidan (A Discussion of Shōwa Agricultural Politics)*. Tokyo: Ie no Hikari Kyōkai, 1980.

Tokyo Daigaku Shakai Kagaku Kenkyū Jo, ed. *Fukushi Kokka (The Welfare State)*. Vols. 5 and 6. Tokyo: Tokyo Daigaku Shuppan Kai, 1985.

Tokyo Metropolitan Government. *Tokyo Steps Up Social Welfare*. Tokyo: Tokyo Metropolitan Government, 1974.

Tokyo Shimbun Tokushu Hōjin Shuzai Han. *Tokushu Hōjin o Kiru (Carve Up the Special Corporations)*. Tokyo: Sanshūsha, 1980.

Tomioka Takeo. *Chūshō Kigyō Chō (The Small Business Agency)*. Tokyo: Kyōiku Sha, 1975.

Tōyō Keizai Shinpō Sha. *Shōwa Kokusei Sōran (Shōwa National Affairs Almanac)*. Vol. 2. Tokyo: Tōyō Keizai Shinpō Sha, 1980.

Tōyama Shigeki. *Shiryō: Sengo Ni Jyū Nen Shi (Data: A History of the Twenty Postwar* Years). Vol. 6. Tokyo: Nihon Hyōron Sha, 1967.

Trimberger, Ellen Kay. *Revolution from Above: Military Bureaucrats and Development in Japan, Turkey, Egypt, and Peru*. New Brunswick, N.J.: Transaction Books, 1978.

Tsuchiya Kiyoshi. "Zaikai Interview: Nagano Shigeo." *Chūō Kōron* 70, no. 10 (October 1955), pp. 214–21.

Tsuchiya Takao. *Nihon Keizai Shi (An Economic History of Japan)*. Tokyo: Kōbundō, 1955.

———. *Nihon Shihon-shugi Shi Ronshū. (Collected Essays on the History of Japanese Capitalism)*. Tokyo: Ikusei Sha, 1937.

Tsuji Kiyoaki, ed. *Shiryō: Sengo Nijyū Nen Shi (Documents: A History of the Twenty Years after the War)*. Vol. 2. Tokyo: Nihon Hyōron Sha, 1966.

Tsurutani, T. "Japan's Security, Defense Responsibilities and Capabilities." *ORBIS* 25, no. 1 (Spring 1981), 89–106.

Tsutsui Kiyotada. *Ishibashi Tanzan: Jiyūshugi Seijika no Kiseki (Ishibashi Tanzan: The Course of a Democratic Politician)*. Tokyo: Chūō Kōron Sha, 1986.

Uchida Kenzō. *Habatsu (Factions)*. Tokyo: Kōdansha, 1983.

———. *Sengo Nihon no Hoshu Seiji (Conservative Politics of Postwar Japan)*. Tokyo: Iwanami Shoten, 1970.

Uchida Kenzō, Matsuo Fumio, and Yamamoto Susumu. "Sengo Hoshu Taisei no Zasetsu to Tenkan" ("Breakdown and Conversion of the Postwar Conservative Order"). *Sekai,* no. 318 (May 1972), pp. 96–116.

Uchihashi Katsuo. "Akajisen Haishi wa Kokutetsu o Sukuwanai" ("The Abolition of Deficit Lines will not Help the JNR"). *Bungei Shunjū* 59, no. 10 (September 1981), pp. 130–48.

Uchikawa Yoshimi. "Masukomi Jidai no Tenkai to Seiji Katei." ("The Unfolding of the Mass Media Age and the Political Process"). *Gojyu Go Nen Taisei no Keisei to Hokai: Nenpō Seijigaku (The Rise and Fall of the 1955 System: A Political Science Bulletin).* Tokyo: Iwanami Shoten, 1977.

Uchino Tatsurō. *Japan's Postwar Economy: An Insider's View of its History and its Future.* Translated by Mark A. Harbison, from *Sengo Nihon Keizai Shi.* Tokyo: Kōdansha International, 1983.

United Nations, *World Commodity Statistics 1984: Japanese Imports,* 1984 ed. New York: United Nations Statistical Papers, Series D. Vol. 34, nos. 1–11, 1985.

U.S. Bureau of the Budget. *The Budget of the United States Government.* Washington, D.C.: Government Printing Office, 1939.

U.S. Department of Commerce. *Historical Statistics of the United States: Colonial Times to 1970.* Washington D.C.: Government Printing Office, 1975.

U.S. Department of Defense. *Report of the Secretary of Defense to the Congress, Fiscal 1985 Defense Budget.* Washington D.C.: Government Printing Office, 1984.

U.S. Embassy Steeves to DOS. "Meeting of Mr. Ichirō Hatoyama with the Ambassador." September 18, 1952.

U.S. Embassy to DOS. "Weekly Political Notes from Japan." 1952, various issues.

U.S. House of Representatives. *Report of the Committee on Small Business: Ninety-Eight Congress.* Washington, D.C.: Government Printing Office, 1985.

U.S. Office of Management and Budget. *Budget of the United States,* fiscal year 1986. Washington, D.C.: U.S. Government Printing Office, 1986.

U.S. POLAD Tokyo to DOS. "Japanese General Elections of January 23, 1949."

U.S. POLAD Tokyo to DOS. "Memorandum of Conversation with Mr. Tetsuya Kamekawa of the Japan Socialist Party." August 7, 1950.

U.S. POLAD Tokyo to DOS. "Remarks of Takeo Miki to U.S. reporting officer Charles N. Spinks, First Secretary of Mission, U.S. POLAD." October 30, 1951.

Utsunomiya Tokuma. "Seifu wa Minobe Tose o Ijimeruna!" ("The

Government Should Not Ridicule the Minobe Administration!"). *Chūō Kōron* 89, no. 9 (September 1973), pp. 118–27.

Verba, Sidney. *The Civic Culture*. Boston: Little, Brown, 1965.

———. "Sequences and Development." In *Crises and Sequences in Political Development*, ed. by Leonard Binder. Princeton: Princeton University Press, 1971.

Verba, Sidney, Norman H. Nie, and Jae-on-Kim. *Participation and Political Equality: A Seven-Nation Comparison*. Cambridge: Cambridge University Press, 1978.

Vogel, Ezra. *Comeback*. New York: Simon and Schuster, 1985.

———, ed. *Modern Japanese Organization and Decision Making*. Tokyo: Charles E. Tuttle, 1975.

Von Laue, Theodore H. *Sergei Witte and the Industrialization of Russia*. New York: Columbia University Press, 1963.

Wada Hiroo Ikō Shū Kankō Kai, ed. *Wada Hiroo Ikō Shū (Collected Works of Wada Hiroo)*. Tokyo: Nōrin Tōkei Kyōkai, 1981.

Wakata Kyōji. *Gendai Nihon no Seiji to Fūdo (Contemporary Japanese Politics and Its Topography)*. Kyoto: Minerva Shobō, 1981.

Ward, Robert E., and Sakamoto Yoshikazu, eds. *Democratizing Japan*. Honolulu: University of Hawaii Press, 1987.

Waswo, Ann. *Japanese Landlords: The Decline of a Rural Elite*. Berkeley: University of California Press, 1977.

Watanabe Tsuneo. *Habatsu: Nihon Hoshutō no Bunseki (Factions: An Analysis of Japan's Conservative Party)*. Tokyo: Kōbundō, 1964.

———. "Jimintō Kuzureru no Hi" ("The Day the LDP Collapses"). *Chūō Kōron* 88, no. 9 (September 1973), pp. 312–24.

Watanuki Jōji. "Kakushin Kyōtō no Kageri" ("Stalemate in the Collaboration among Liberal Parties"), *Asahi Journal* 17, no. 17 (April 25, 1975), pp. 4–10.

———. *Nihon no Seiji Shakai (Japan's Political Society)*. Tokyo: Tokyo Daigaku Shuppan Kai, 1967.

———. *Politics in Postwar Japanese Society*. Tokyo: University of Tokyo Press, 1977.

Watanuki Jōji, Miyake Ichirō, Inoguchi Takashi, and Kabashima Ikuo. *Electoral Behavior in the 1983 Japanese Elections*. Tokyo: Sophia University Institute of International Relations, 1986.

Weinstein, Martin E. *Japan's Postwar Defense Policy, 1947–1968*. New York: Columbia University Press, 1971.

Weiss, John. *Conservatism in Europe, 1770–1945: Traditionalism, Reaction, and Counter-Revolution*. London: Thames and Hudson, 1977.

Wilensky, Harold L. *The Welfare State and Equality: Structural and Ideological Roots of Public Expenditures*. Berkeley: University of California Press, 1975.

Wolfe, Robert, ed. *Americans as Proconsuls*. Carbondale: Southern Illinois Press, 1984.

Wolferen, Karel van. "The Japan Problem." *Foreign Affairs* 65, no. 4 (Winter 1986–1987), pp. 288–303.

Wolfinger, Raymond. "Why Political Machines Have Not Withered Away and Other Revisionist Thoughts." *Journal of Politics* 34 (May 1972).

Wray, William. *NYK*. Cambridge: Harvard University Council on East Asian Studies, 1984.

Wright, Gordon. *Rural Revolution in France: The Peasantry in the Twentieth Century*. Stanford: Stanford University Press, 1964.

Wright, Vincent. *The Government and Politics of France*. 2d ed. New York: Holmes and Meier, 1983.

Yamada Masao. *Toki no Nagare: Toshi no Nagare (The Current of the Times: The Current of the City)*. Tokyo: Toshi Kenkyū Jo, 1973.

Yamada Takao. *Sengo Nihon Shi (Postwar Japanese History)*. Tokyo: Gakushū no Tomo Sha, 1980.

Yamaichi Shōken Keizai Kenkyū Jo, ed. *Sangyō Tōkei (Industrial Statistics)*, 1982–86 eds. Tokyo: Yamaichi Shōken Keizai Kenkyū Jo, 1982–1986.

———. *Sangyō no Subete (Everything about Industry)*. 1987 ed. Tokyo: Yamaichi Shōken Keizai Kenkyū Jo, 1987.

Yamakawa Kikue and Sakisaka Itsurō. *Yamakawa Hitoshi Jiden (The Autobiography of Yamakawa Hitoshi)*. Tokyo: Iwanami Shoten, 1982.

Yamamoto Fumio. *Nihon Mass Communication Shi (History of Japanese Mass Communication)*. Tokyo: Tōkai Daigaku Shuppan Kai, 1981.

Yamamoto Yōsuke. "Tokushū: Nihon no Kome, Nihon Nōgyō Saisei e no Karte" ("Special Issue: Japanese Rice, A Blueprint for the Reconstruction of Japanese Agriculture"). *Chūō Kōron* (February 1987), pp. 80–115.

Yamamura, Kōzō and Yasuba Yasukichi, eds. *The Political Economy of Japan (The Domestic Transformation)*. Vol. 1. Stanford: Stanford University Press, 1987.

Yanaga Chitoshi. *Big Business in Japanese Politics*. New Haven: Yale University Press, 1968.

Yano Tsuneta Kinen Kai, ed. *Nihon Kokusei Zue (Japan in Graphics)*. Tokyo: Kokusei Sha, 1987.

Yasuhara Kazuo. *Keidanren Kaichō no Sengoshi (The Postwar History of Keidanren Chairmen)*. Tokyo: Business Sha, 1985.

Yomiuri Shimbun Seiji Bu, ed. *Jimintō no San Jyū Nen (The LDP's Thirty Years)*. Tokyo: Yomiuri Shimbun Sha, 1985.

Yomiuri Shimbun Sha, ed. *Yomiuri Nenkan (Yomiuri Almanac)*. Tokyo: Yomiuri Shimbun Sha, 1987.

Yoshida Shigeru. *Japan's Decisive Century, 1867–1967*. New York: Praeger, 1967.

———. *Kaisō Jyū Nen (The Memoirs of Ten Years)*. Tokyo: Shinchō Sha, 1963.

———. *Nihon o Kettei shita Hyaku Nen (The Hundred Years which Determined Japan)*. Tokyo: Nihon Keizai Shimbun Sha, 1967.

———. *Ōiso Zuisō (The Ōiso Essays)*. Tokyo: Sekka Sha, 1962.

———. *Sekai to Nippon (The World and Japan)*. Tokyo: Baneho Shobō, 1963.

———. *The Yoshida Memoirs: The Story of Japan in Crisis*. Translated by Yoshida Kenichi. London: William Heinemann, 1961.

Yoshikawa Kenji, ed. *Gendai Nippon no Toshi Mondai: Toshi Mondai to Jichitai Gyō—Zaisei (Urban Problems in Contemporary Japan: Urban Problems, Local Administration, and Finance)*. Vol. 7. Tokyo: Tambun Sha, 1970.

Yoshimura Tadashi. *Nihon Seiji no Shindan (The Examination of Japanese Politics)*. Tokyo: Tōkai Daigaku Shuppan, 1973.

Yoshino, Michael Y. *The Japanese Marketing System: Adaptations and Innovations*. Cambridge, Mass.: MIT Press, 1971.

Zaisei Chōsa Kai, ed. *Hojokin Sōran (Subsidies Almanac)*. Fiscal 1984. Tokyo: Nihon Densan Kabushiki Kaisha, 1984.

Zenkoku Nōgyō Kyōdō Kumiai Chūō Kai, ed. *Kongo no Nōgyō Seisaku to Nōgyō Yosan (Future Agricultural Policy and the Agricultural Budget)*. Tokyo: Nōson Gyoson Bunka Kyōkai, 1986.

Zenshōren Shi Henshū Iinkai. *Minshō: Zenshōren no San Jyū Nen. (Thirty Years of the All-Japan Commercial Federation)*. Tokyo: Tokyo Insatu Shuppan, 1976.

Zuckerman, Alan S. *The Politics of Faction: Christian Democratic Rule in Italy*. New Haven: Yale University Press, 1979.

Zysman, John. *Governments, Markets, and Growth*. Ithaca: Cornell University Press, 1983.

Index